# The Hallmark Features

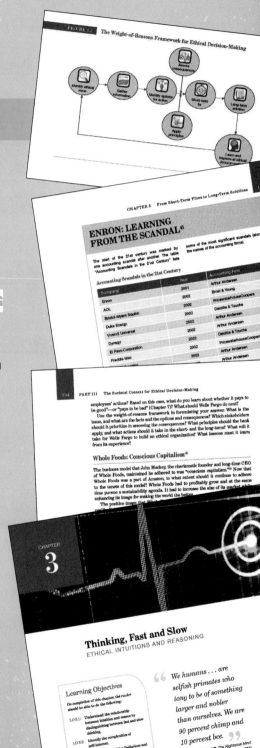

**Managing Business Ethics: Making Ethical Decisions** teaches students how to navigate ethical issues they will encounter, using an ethical decision-making framework applied throughout the book.

- A weight-of-reasons ETHICAL DECISION-MAKING FRAMEWORK helps students understand the steps for making the right decisions and the importance of thinking through both short-term and long-term effects.

- CASE APPLICATIONS give students an opportunity to apply the weight-of-reasons framework to ethical dilemmas.

- Twenty REAL-WORLD CASES on timely topics are included, such as sexual harassment at Google, pharmaceutical companies and the opioid epidemic, and Whole Foods's conscious capitalism.

- Unique chapter on THINKING, FAST AND SLOW explores behavioral findings on how people make ethical decisions.

# SAGE Publishing:
# **Our Story**

At SAGE, we mean business. We believe in creating evidence-based, cutting-edge content that helps prepare students to succeed in today's ever-changing business world. We strive to provide you with the tools you need to develop the next generation of leaders, managers, and entrepreneurs.

- We invest in the right **AUTHORS** who distill research findings and industry ideas into practical applications.

- We keep our prices **AFFORDABLE** and provide multiple **FORMAT OPTIONS** for students.

- We remain permanently independent and fiercely committed to **QUALITY CONTENT** and **INNOVATIVE RESOURCES**.

# Managing
# BUSINESS ETHICS

*To my family, my amazing wife, Judy, my son, David, and his wife, Laura, both editors of note, my other son, Ariel, who brings us fantastic music from Spotify, his employer, and to all the wonderful students at the Carlson School like Tim Hargrave, with whom I have had the opportunity to interact.*

— Alfred A. Marcus

*I dedicate this book first and foremost to my family, who give meaning, sorrow, and joy to my life. And to all the ethical and unethical people I have come across. They have made the lessons of this book real to me.*

— Timothy J. Hargrave

Sara Miller McCune founded SAGE Publishing in 1965 to support the dissemination of usable knowledge and educate a global community. SAGE publishes more than 1000 journals and over 600 new books each year, spanning a wide range of subject areas. Our growing selection of library products includes archives, data, case studies and video. SAGE remains majority owned by our founder and after her lifetime will become owned by a charitable trust that secures the company's continued independence.

Los Angeles | London | New Delhi | Singapore | Washington DC | Melbourne

# *Managing* BUSINESS ETHICS

## Making Ethical Decisions

Alfred A. Marcus

*University of Minnesota*

Timothy J. Hargrave

*Central Washington University*

Los Angeles | London | New Delhi
Singapore | Washington DC | Melbourne

FOR INFORMATION:

SAGE Publications, Inc.
2455 Teller Road
Thousand Oaks, California 91320
E-mail: order@sagepub.com

SAGE Publications Ltd.
1 Oliver's Yard
55 City Road
London EC1Y 1SP
United Kingdom

SAGE Publications India Pvt. Ltd.
B 1/I 1 Mohan Cooperative Industrial Area
Mathura Road, New Delhi 110 044
India

SAGE Publications Asia-Pacific Pte. Ltd.
18 Cross Street #10-10/11/12
China Square Central
Singapore 048423

Acquisitions Editor: Maggie Stanley
Editorial Assistant: Janeane Calderon
Content Development Editor: Darcy Scelsi
Production Editor: Rebecca Lee
Copy Editor: QuADS Prepress (P) Ltd.
Typesetter: C&M Digitals (P) Ltd.
Proofreader: Sally Jaskold
Indexer: Sheila Hill
Cover Designer: Gail Buschman
Marketing Manager: Sarah Panella

*Library of Congress Cataloging-in-Publication Data*

Names: Marcus, Alfred A. (Alfred Allen), 1950- author. | Hargrave, Timothy J., author.

Title: Managing Business Ethics: Making Ethical Decisions / Alfred A. Marcus, University of Minnesota, Timothy J. Hargrave, Central Washington University.

Description: Los Angeles: SAGE [2021] | Includes bibliographical references and index.

Identifiers: LCCN 2019034547 | ISBN 978-1-5063-8859-5 (paperback) | ISBN 978-1-5063-8857-1 (epub) | ISBN 978-1-5063-8858-8 (epub) | ISBN 978-1-5063-8860-1 (pdf) | ISBN 978-1-5063-8861-8 (pdf)

Subjects: LCSH: Business ethics.

Classification: LCC HF5387 .M3455 2021 | DDC 174/.4—dc23

LC record available at https://lccn.loc.gov/2019034547

This book is printed on acid-free paper.

20 21 22 23 24 10 9 8 7 6 5 4 3 2 1

# Brief Contents

# Detailed Contents

## 5    From Short-Term Fixes to Long-Term Solutions    130

## 6    Building Ethical Organizations    164

# PART III: THE SOCIETAL CONTEXT FOR ETHICAL DECISION-MAKING    199

## 7    Legal Compliance and Beyond    200

## 8    The Role of Stakeholders in Ethical Decision-Making    242

## 9    Ethics, Strategy, and Grand Challenges      276

## PART IV: CASES      313

## 10    Cases      315

# Preface

Are business school ethics courses and the textbooks they use effective? Do they help prepare business school students to make tough ethical decisions? While most business schools today have a commitment to ethics across all levels of the curriculum, many commentators have their doubts about business ethics courses. Business schools have been assigned some of the blame for the wave of ethics scandals that took place in the early 2000s, the dubious activities of financial firms that contributed to the Great Recession several years later, and more recent instances of corporate wrongdoing, many of which are documented in this book.[1]

While it has not been our experience that business schools are guilty of teaching a profit-first and perhaps even amoral and avaricious "win at all costs" mentality, as they have been accused of doing,[2] we do believe that business schools as a whole are not adequately preparing students to address the complex ethical challenges they face. Too many business ethics courses and the textbooks they use tend to focus on moral philosophy; they acquaint students with philosophical frameworks for thinking about ethics and present them with ethical dilemmas similar to those they can expect to encounter in the business world. Unfortunately, though, they tend to fall short when it comes to preparing students to deeply understand and creatively respond to these dilemmas. For one, they underestimate or disregard impediments to ethical decision-making such as our mental limitations and biases, and the impact of social influences on our decisions. They tend not to account for the human predilection to obey our bosses, conform with group norms, and make fast, intuitive decisions rather than carefully apply rational decision-making frameworks. Just as they overlook the impediments to good decision-making, so too they do not give enough attention to the tools that help decision-makers to overcome these impediments. Jonathan Haidt, business ethics chair at New York University's Stern School, summarizes the current situation when he writes,

> I have yet to find any evidence that a single ethics class, on its own, can improve ethical behavior after the course has ended. . . . You can teach a student all you want about utilitarianism, Immanuel Kant or stakeholder theory, but five years later, when her colleagues are competing to sell worthless securities to unsuspecting retirees, her conscious reasoning is unlikely to be strong enough to stop her from running with the herd.[3]

The purpose of this textbook is to address these limitations of business ethics teaching head-on. Our goal has been to develop a textbook that takes seriously the individual, group, and organizational barriers to ethical decisions and also provides students with the means to overcome these barriers. The book has five distinctive features that will give students a richer understanding of business ethics and the tools they need to effectively address the ethical dilemmas they do and will face as managers.

*The weight-of-reasons framework:* The centerpiece of this textbook is the weight-of-reasons framework. While most, if not all, ethical decision-making textbooks present decision-making frameworks, we believe that the weight of reasons is uncommonly practical and accessible. (After all, the original idea for the framework, which we have extended and enriched significantly, came from Benjamin Franklin—one of America's first and greatest practical problem solvers). The framework incorporates the two best-known ethical frameworks, teleology and deontology. In addition, it recognizes that in the short term, because of uncertainty, time pressures, politics, and other factors, managers often cannot always develop ideal solutions that get at the roots of the problems they face. For this reason, it includes a step for building from short-term fixes to long-term solutions. Furthermore, to underscore the point that managers should strive to develop and continuously improve their habit of systematic, imaginative ethical decision-making, we include assessment and learning as the final step of the framework. The goal of the weight-of-reasons framework is not to faithfully apply particular philosophical perspectives on what is right; it is to manage dilemmas and solve ethical problems.

*Deeper understanding of the barriers to good ethical decisions:* The intellectual core of this book is the idea that to effectively address ethical dilemmas, you have to understand what makes ethical decision-making so difficult. The insights of great philosophers about what we should do and how we should live can end up being useless to students if these students do not also understand how they think and make decisions, and how their surroundings influence those decisions. For this reason, in Chapter 3, we provide an in-depth discussion of the limits of human reasoning; explain "fast thinking," that is, our reliance on intuition rather than careful analysis to make decisions; and explore the surprisingly complex concept of self-interest, which provides the lens through which we perceive and address ethical dilemmas. Similarly, in Chapter 4, we extensively cover how the psychological need to belong and the tendencies toward group conformity and obedience to authority often result in unethical decisions. Throughout Chapters 3 and 4, we present the results of the fascinating research that has shaped understanding of human decisions. These include Milgram's infamous Obedience experiments, which explored why seemingly ethical people engage in cruel behavior.

*Extensive toolkit for addressing ethical dilemmas:* Of course, our book would not be very useful if we explained the impediments to ethical decision-making but did not provide the solutions to these. The primary tool we provide is the weight-of-reasons framework. Using it enables one to avoid the pitfalls of fast thinking so that one can instead slow down and make better choices.

We then load many other decision-making tools onto the platform that the weight-of-reasons provides. We have drawn from the literatures on decision-making, political science, organization theory, paradox management, stakeholder management, and other fields to provide students with a full toolbox for addressing ethical dilemmas. In Chapter 4, we teach students about the importance and limitations of "speaking truth to power," and we present political tools that students can employ to "close the circle"—take ownership of ethical issues to see that they are successfully addressed. Then in Chapter 5, we present a full range of decision-making techniques that students can employ to establish ongoing learning processes that help them build from short-term fixes to long-term solutions. Specific learning tools and approaches we discuss include systems thinking to uncover the roots and complexity of ethical dilemmas, "both/and" thinking to reframe seemingly irreconcilable tensions, and moral imagination to explore novel approaches to solving ethical problems. We also discuss the fundamental importance of team decision-making to solving ethical problems. When individuals work together and engage in processes of constructive conflict, they can challenge one another's assumptions and create practical paths forward that none could have imagined individually.

Chapters 6 through 8 provide more tools for addressing ethical dilemmas. In Chapter 6, we discuss how to build an organization that supports and promotes ethical decision-making, and then in Chapter 7, we present an overview of many of the laws that students will have to take account of as they make ethical decisions. In the latter chapter, we stress that following the law is often not sufficient from an ethical standpoint, and we describe approaches such as corporate social responsibility and sustainable business that companies take to going beyond the law.

In Chapter 8, we provide students with different views on how they should prioritize the stakeholders that are affected by their ethical decisions, and how to include these stakeholders in decision-making processes. In this chapter, we also discuss whether "it pays to be good"—that is, whether acting ethically can lead to higher profits. This is important because the pressure to earn profits is a reality for most managers. We discuss how managers can use decision-making tools such as those presented in Chapter 5 to find "win–win" solutions that are both ethical and profitable. We don't pretend that there are always easy answers, however.

*Deeper coverage of ethical frameworks:* Like most ethical decision-making textbooks, this book covers utilitarian (teleological), Kantian (deontological), and virtue ethics. We believe, however, that our coverage of these frameworks is more thorough and thought provoking than that found in other textbooks. For example, for each of the frameworks, we present different formulations, provide critiques, and offer examples. In the section on teleology, we compare the utilitarian perspectives of Bentham and Mill, discuss the problem that utilitarianism permits violating some people's basic human rights, and present the Ford Pinto case as an example of a "teleological error."

In addition, this textbook covers two approaches to ethics not typically covered in ethics textbooks. Specifically, we offer extended discussions of both Rawls's theory of justice and Gilligan's ethic of care.

*Fresh and new cases, including the most recent and significant ones from companies like Amazon, Google, Facebook, VW, Wells Fargo, and others:* We present dozens of cases that give students the opportunity to confront the biggest ethical challenges facing today's business decision-makers. These cases are found within the chapters, at the ends of the chapters, and at the end of the book. We present cases on, among other topics, working conditions at Amazon, sexual harassment at Google, Facebook's impact on political discourse, the "Dieselgate" scandal at Volkswagen (VW), pharmaceutical companies' role in promoting the opioid crisis, unethical sales practices at VW and Wells Fargo, and BP's massive oil spill in the Gulf of Mexico.

Unlike other ethics textbooks, we also devote an entire chapter to addressing the unprecedented grand ethical challenges that humanity now faces. These include global climate change and ending global poverty and inequality. We encourage students to use the weight-of-reasons framework and other decision-making tools presented in the book to address these challenges, and we present relevant cases. These include cases on sustainability at Walmart and ExxonMobil's efforts to suppress information about global climate change. In Chapter 9, we present a case on Tesla's goal of bringing about an electric car revolution, and compare the company's efforts to Better Place's failed attempt to do the same thing. We also present the case of Theranos and Elizabeth Holmes in that chapter.

We believe this textbook will prepare students to deal with the hard ethical questions they actually will face in their jobs and their careers. We have strived to write a book that brings to light just how difficult ethical decision-making can be, because the world—and our own brains—often leads us away from doing the right thing. At the same time, this book provides students with the tools and techniques for overcoming these barriers. We do not suggest that there are easy answers. Rather, we help students recognize the difficulties of decision-making and the complexities of the problems they face and then ask them to use their imaginations, work with others, and take practical steps to solve these problems. The decision-making framework and related tools we set out in this book will help them to get at the roots of the dilemmas they encounter and work from short-term fixes to long-term solutions.

## Cases Found in the Book

| Title | Industry | Event/Issue |
| --- | --- | --- |
| Bayer: The Acquisition of Monsanto | Agriculture, chemicals, pharmaceuticals | Genetically modified foods |
| BP: The Big Oil Spill: What Went Wrong | Oil | Industrial accident |
| Dow-DuPont: The Bhopal Disaster | Chemicals | Industrial accident |
| Facebook: Privacy and the Public Interest | Social media | Consumer privacy, misinformation |
| Ford: Safety Recalls | Automobiles | Vehicle safety recalls |
| General Mills: Nutrition | Food products | Nutrition |
| Google: Doing No Harm? | Information and technology | Social issues, climate change, sustainability, anticompetitive practices |
| Google: Problems With Sexual Harassment | Information and technology | Sexual harassment |
| Intel: Mobileye | Technology | Issues related to autonomous vehicles |

| Title | Industry | Event/Issue |
|---|---|---|
| Malinckrodt: The Opioid Crisis | Pharmaceuticals | Opioid crisis |
| Microsoft: Addressing Bribery | Technology | Bribery |
| Merck and Johnson & Johnson: Problems With Consumer Safety | Pharmaceuticals, medical products | Consumer safety |
| VW: Dieselgate | Automobiles | Defrauding government, consumers |
| Wells Fargo: Can It Come Back? | Banking | Defrauding consumers |
| Walmart: Sustainability | Retail | Environmental sustainability |
| Whole Foods: "Conscious Capitalism" | Groceries | Corporate social responsibility |

## Digital Resources

# $SAGE edge™

edge.sagepub.com/marcusethics

**SAGE Edge for instructors** supports your teaching by making it easy to integrate quality content and create a rich learning environment for students with the following:

- A **password-protected site** for complete and protected access to all text-specific instructor resources

- **Test banks** that provide a diverse range of ready-to-use options that save you time. You can also easily edit any question and/or insert your own personalized questions

- **Multimedia content** that meets the learning needs of today's media-savvy students and brings concepts to life

- **Sample course syllabi** for semester and quarter courses that provide suggested models for structuring your courses

- **Editable, chapter-specific PowerPoint® slides** that offer complete flexibility for creating a multimedia presentation for your course

- **Lecture notes** that summarize key concepts by chapter to help you prepare for lectures and class discussions

**SAGE Edge for students** enhances learning, it's easy to use, and offers the following:

- An **open-access site** that makes it easy for students to maximize their study time, anywhere, anytime

- **Multimedia resources** that bring concepts to life, are tied to learning objectives, and are curated exclusively for this text, featuring

- **eFlashcards** that strengthen understanding of key terms and concepts

- **eQuizzes** that allow students to practice and assess how much they've learned and where they need to focus their attention

- **Chapter summaries** with **learning objectives** that reinforce the most important material

## NOTES

1. Kamerick, M. (2017, December 15). Can business schools make companies ethical? *Fast Company.* Retrieved from https://www.fastcompany.com/4050 8606/can-business-schools-make-companies-ethical

2. Queen, L. E. (2015, September 28). Business schools breed unethical businessmen. *New Republic.* Retrieved from https://newrepublic.com/article/122940/business -schools-breed-unethical-businessmen

3. Haidt, J. (2014, January 13). Can you teach businessmen to be ethical? *The Washington Post.* Retrieved from https://www.washingtonpost.com/news/on-leadership/ wp/2014/01/13/can-you-teach-businessmen-to-be -ethical/?utm_term=.2c6393d77981

# Acknowledgments

SAGE wishes to thank the following reviewers for their valuable feedback during the development of this book:

J. B. Arbaugh, University of Wisconsin Oshkosh

Christal Blalock, Chattahoochee Technical College

Wade M. Chumney, California State University, Northridge

Ericka N. Covington, Coppin State University

Anthony J. Horky, Esq., Florida Atlantic University

James L. Hunt, Mercer University

Amy Conlan Jordan, Loyola University Chicago

David M. Kopp, Barry University

Barbara J. Limbach, Chadron State College

Iraj Mahdavi, National University, School of Business and Management

Mike Mutschelknaus, Saint Mary's University of Minnesota

Ron Pardee, Riverside City College

Karen Rush, Campbellsville University

Tracy Wallach, University of Massachusetts, Boston

Sandi Zeljko, Lake-Sumter State College

# About the Authors

Alfred A. Marcus is the Edson Spencer Endowed Professor in strategy and technological leadership in the Strategic Management and Entrepreneurship Department at the Carlson School of Management, the University of Minnesota, and the Technological Leadership Institute in the University of Minnesota's Institute of Technology. He is the author of *Innovations in Sustainability: Fuel and Food*, published by Cambridge University Press in 2015 and the author of *Strategies for Managing Uncertainty: Booms and Busts in the Energy Industry*, published by Cambridge University Press in 2019. *Innovations in Sustainability* won the "Outstanding Book" award in 2016 for the ONE division at the Academy of Management. He was coeditor of a special 2011 fall issue of the *California Management Review* on regulatory uncertainty and the natural environment. From 1995 to 2001, he was chair of the Strategic Management and Organization Department at the Carlson School. He has consulted with numerous major corporations and has received grants from government agencies. Since 2006, he also has taught in the MBA program of the Technion Israel Institute of Technology. He received his bachelor's and master's degrees from the University of Chicago and his PhD from Harvard University. In 2005 and 2015, he won the outstanding teacher of the year award in the Carlson School MBA programs, and he has won a similar award at the Technion.

Timothy J. Hargrave is a professor at Central Washington University. He teaches courses on organizational management, strategic management, managing change, business and society, sustainable business, and business ethics. His specific research interests include moral imagination, the management of contradictions, and the emergence and growth of green industries. His research has been published in *Business Ethics Quarterly, Academy of Management Review, Academy of Management Journal, Organization Science*, and many other outlets. Prior to coming to academe, Dr. Hargrave worked in Washington, D.C., on global climate change policy. He earned his PhD in strategic management and organization from the University of Minnesota's Carlson School of Management, where Alfred Marcus sat on his dissertation committee. Dr. Hargrave also holds an MBA and a master's degree in energy and resources from the University of California at Berkeley.

# Introduction to Ethical Decision-Making

## THE INDIVIDUAL

©iStockphoto.com/onurdongel

Ethics shines light on the decisions and actions we take, enabling us to lead better lives.

# A Commonsense Approach to Business Ethics

## Learning Objectives

On completion of this chapter, the reader should be able to do the following:

LO 1.1: Explain why it is difficult to make ethical choices.

LO 1.2: Describe what an ethical decision is.

LO 1.3: Recognize the tragic nature of ethical decision-making: Someone may be hurt.

LO 1.4: State why intuition must be supplemented by reason in making ethical choices.

LO 1.5: Explain how the weight-of-reasons framework leads to addressing root causes and not just implementing quick fixes.

LO 1.6: Apply the weight-of-reasons framework for ethical decision-making.

" *When difficult cases occur, they are difficult chiefly because . . . all the reasons pro and con are not present. . . . To get over this, my way is to divide . . . a sheet of paper . . . into two columns, writing over the one pro and the other con. . . . I endeavor to estimate their respective weights . . . and . . . find . . . where the balance lies. . . . And though the weight of reasons cannot be taken with the precision of algebraic quantities . . . when each is thus considered separately and comparatively, and the whole lies before me . . . I think I can judge better, and am less able to take a rash step.* "

—**Benjamin Franklin**,
18th-century U.S. author, politician, and scientist

## Introduction: Ethics Is Tough!

**LO 1.1:** Explain why it is difficult to make ethical choices.

The Greek philosopher Socrates (ca. 400 BCE) famously said, "The unexamined life is not worth living." He and other ancient Greeks proposed that a human being should not blindly follow laws, nor be driven simply by self-interest, desire, and emotion alone. In other words, you should not simply follow orders and give into popular taste, nor simply act based on habit, with the decisions you make being a response to society's expectations or what an authority commands. Rather, as human beings, we must reflect on and scrutinize our actions. We have a duty to ask the following:

- Why am I acting as I do?

- What implications do my actions have for others?

- Are they consistent with principles I want to uphold and want others to accept?

Asking these questions means living "the examined life." Ethics is about the ability to examine your life, to regulate narrow self-interest, and to "do the right thing" for a larger group, whether it be your family, community, society, or the world. We human beings have survived because of our ability to consider ends beyond our narrow self-interest and to cooperate.

©iStockphoto.com/marekuliasz

Ethical problems are complex and difficult to understand, and they confront us with tough choices.

**Decision**
A specific commitment to action

**Decision process**
A set of actions that begins with the identification of a stimulus for action and ends with the specific commitment to action

**Ethical decision**
A decision that the decision-maker perceives as involving questions of good and bad, right and wrong

**Unstructured decision**
A decision for which there is no predetermined and explicit set of steps within the organization

## What Ethics Is About

Unfortunately, figuring out the "right thing to do" often turns out to be a tall order. One reason is that *ethical problems themselves are complex and difficult to understand, and they confront us with tough choices.* Business ethics is not about solving easy problems that have neat and clean solutions; rather, it is about deciding what to do when you face decisions that lie in a gray area where no easy answers exist. Although good ethical decision-makers seek to identify win–win scenarios and minimize harm, as we discuss in Chapter 5, sometimes ethical decisions involve trade-offs between competing goals and obligations in which not every party can be wholly satisfied. Some person or some group may be harmed—perhaps yourself. The harm may be temporary or permanent. It may be accepted voluntarily with full knowledge or imposed arbitrarily without you or the group understanding how or why they have been hurt. For example, what should you do when you are torn between staying loyal to a friend and calling attention to that friend's misdeed? Or what should you do when you realize that what is best for your company is unfair to a particular individual? Mustn't the rights of each individual be put ahead of what is good for the company?

## Ethical Decisions and Ethical Dilemmas

**LO 1.2:** Describe what an ethical decision is.

Ethical decisions are hard to address not only because they are complex and pose uncomfortable trade-offs but also because they involve *uncertainty.* Chances are you do not have complete information about the situation you are addressing, nor do you know how others will respond to your actions. You cannot be sure of the consequences of your actions for yourself, your organization, or the society. You do not have perfect knowledge of who will benefit and who will lose. Yet you have to act, and the decisions you have to make are fraught with risk to yourself and others.

Ethical decisions also can be tough simply because *people tend to have great difficulty in making complex decisions.* Researchers have long studied how people make decisions. A **decision** is "a specific commitment to action," and a **decision process** is "a set of actions . . . that begins with the identification of a stimulus for action and ends with the specific commitment to action." An **ethical decision** is one that decision-makers perceive as involving questions of good and bad, right and wrong. Tough ethical decisions often get made through what are known as **unstructured decision** processes, where people in organizations have no predetermined set of steps it takes to address the problem at hand since the problem is so complex and has not been encountered before.[1] An ethical dilemma is a type of unstructured decision in which people may have a clear understanding of the problem, but they cannot decide between alternative courses of action, since all the alternatives appear to have undesirable properties.

Decision scientists have long advocated that businesspeople making unstructured business decisions apply a reasoning process that encompasses identifying a problem ("I am hungry"), identifying and weighing decision criteria (price, type of food, location), identifying alternatives (places you

©iStockphoto.com/izustun

We all have a limited view of the world.

could eat), evaluating these alternatives vis-à-vis the criteria you wish to achieve, and then making a decision (what you will do to quench your hunger).[2] It turns out, however, that people often do not use this type of reasoning process or are stymied when they try to. There are many reasons for this, which we will examine in Chapters 3 and 4. One of the main ones that deserves attention upfront is the concept of bounded rationality, or in other words limitations on our cognitive ability that inhibit us from formulating problems well and gathering and processing information to solve them.[3] Your senses are constantly bringing in more information than your brain can handle, so it very selectively pays attention to some information, while screening out other information. On entering a room, you may see a table but not the faces of some of the people in the room; then you very quickly categorize and interpret the information that you do perceive so that you can act ("That is a table; I will sit at it."). Although we tend not to recognize it, we are all like the person in the photo who has a very limited view of the reality around him. We encourage you to watch the "Count the Passes" video[4] to see how limited our cognition actually can be (access the link on the student companion site at edge .sagepub.com/marcusethics)

## Someone May Be Hurt

LO 1.3: Recognize the tragic nature of ethical decision-making: Someone may be hurt.

The fact that problems are hard to understand and the fact that we have a limited ability to understand them means that we have difficulty in effectively addressing ethical dilemmas. This problem is often one of judgment rather than moral weakness; quite often, we want to do the "right thing" but have a hard time figuring out what the "right thing" to do is. Very few instances exist where we have perfect

**Dilemma**
A particular type of unstructured decision in which one has a clear understanding of the problem but cannot decide between alternative courses of action, because all have undesirable aspects

**Bounded rationality**
Limited cognitive capacity. Due to bounded rationality humans perceive and interpret some of the information available to their senses while filtering out other information

information about a situation or can fully predict the consequences of our actions. In addition, there are some instances where we do not have good options. A good option would benefit everyone equally, but this is not always possible. We all wish that with enough imagination, we could achieve win–win outcomes, but we should not be naive. Making ethical decisions sometimes involves hard choices in which we apportion costs and benefits to different groups and individuals. Thus, ethical decisions can have a tragic dimension. We may have to decide whom we expect to hurt and whom we will benefit and in what proportions.

Knowing that tough ethical decisions cause us pain and anguish, we may try to avoid them. However, for our mental health, it is not good to pretend that dilemmas do not exist. We are better off recognizing them for what they are and dealing with them as best we can. That is the purpose of this book—to highlight these dilemmas and provide you with some tools to deal with them as best you can.

## Intuition Versus Reasoning

LO 1.4: State why intuition must be supplemented by reason in making ethical choices.

When we confront ethical dilemmas, we may cut off the rational parts of our brain and rely on the intuitions that we have about what is right and what is wrong. Indeed, psychologist Jonathan Haidt, who has written extensively about ethics, argues that intuitions are the main factor driving our ethical decision-making, and we use our reason only to create *self-serving rationalizations* after the fact to justify choices we have made.[5] According to Haidt, we follow our desires and emotion and are not very reflective about ethics. Brain scans show that people's ethical choices tend to be made in rapid-fire, semiautomatic, and nonconscious ways.

We discuss fast ethical thinking in Chapter 3 of this book. Much of our thinking about ethics is fast and intuitive, but not all of it. When we face a troubling ethical dilemma, we tend to think carefully and deeply, and from our reflection comes better choices than would arise if we depended on intuitions alone. This book offers a tool for you to think more slowly about ethics.

Your intuitions may be a source of positive ethical feelings, but they do not tell you what to do. Experienced managers, who have honed their moral inclinations over time, make some decisions based on intuitions alone, but this type of fast ethical thinking is likely to work well only when they address *familiar questions and problems* they repeatedly confront. In novel and complex situations, intuitions are not a reliable guide to action. They can send conflicting signals that leave us paralyzed. Therefore, we need to reflect. Reflection gives us a better sense about what we should do. Without reflection, our intuitions can take us down harmful and destructive paths.

Therefore, supplement your intuitions with reason. Step back and *think deliberately* about the ethical dilemmas you face. Since reasoning can have a positive bearing on the choices you make, make ethical decisions in business based on reason. The purpose of this book is to provide a commonsense way of applying reason to ethical choices.

## A Commonsense Method of Making Ethical Choices: The Weight-of-Reasons Framework

**LO 1.5:** Explain how the weight-of-reasons framework leads to addressing root causes and not just implementing quick fixes.

In this book, we provide a commonsense method to make ethical decisions in a more reasoned manner. It is the "weight-of-reasons" framework laid out in Figure 1.1. Benjamin Franklin, a doer and thinker who achieved much of value, first proposed the weight-of-reasons framework in 1772 in a letter to Joseph Priestley. The gist of the approach, captured in the quotation from Franklin at the beginning of the chapter, is to carefully consider the pros and cons of the actions we take based on an understanding of the issue and facts.

Franklin opposed impulsive decision-making. He referred to his approach as a moral or prudential algebra.[6] As you make an ethical decision, you may come to the realization that you have seen an issue before and it fits into a pattern, in which case, your thinking requires less deliberation. However, in situations where you feel your intuitions are pulling you in contradictory directions, you need to apply the framework to identify options, generate new solutions, eliminate core factors that brought the problem to the forefront in the first place, and build a higher level of aptitude within yourself and your organization for making ethical choices.[7]

**FIGURE 1.1**    The Weight-of-Reasons Framework for Ethical Decision-Making

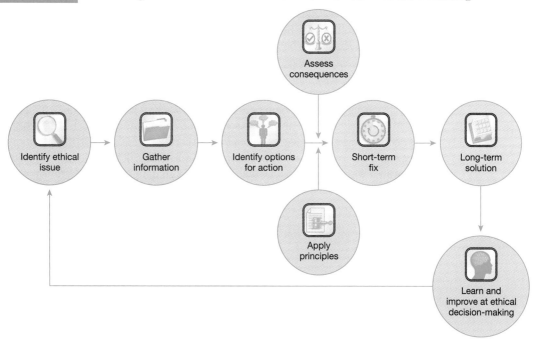

In using the weight-of-reasons framework, we reflect on our behavior by addressing the following questions:

1. What is the key ethical issue we face?

2. What are the major facts that have bearing on this issue?

3. What are the main options to address it?

4. What are the likely consequences—the *pros and cons* of following through on these options?

5. What key principles must we uphold regardless of the consequences?

6. What should we do *now*?

7. What must be done *over time* to address the issue's root causes?

8. What can be learned that is of lasting value to ourselves and our organizations from engaging in this process?

## Understanding the Framework

The weight-of-reasons approach is a "commonsense" approach to ethical decision-making.[8] Common sense means being realistic about the constraints on our reasoning (Figure 1.2). We do not have unlimited facts. We must do the best we can with what we have. Our rationality is bounded, we are under time pressure, and face uncertainty. We can gather more information to try to make better decisions, but these decisions are likely to be satisfactory ones and not perfect ones.[9] However, a less-than-perfect choice can be a platform for feedback, enabling us to carry out further inquiry and analysis, search for causes, and come closer to correcting a problem.

In using the weight-of-reasons framework, we need to recognize that ethical dilemmas are symptoms. Our initial ways of dealing with them puts us on the road to discovery wherein we can understand better a dilemma's root cause and create a plan to address it. The weight-of-reasons framework should help us arrive at such an approach. Rarely does it provide a perfect solution. When there are limits on our time, thinking capacity, and other resources, we should use the framework, but accept that no matter how far we go with it, the outcome will have some limitations. Since there is always

FIGURE 1.2    Commonsense Ethical Decision-Making

**Commonsense ethics means the following:**

- Knowing when to trust your intuitions and when to engage in reasoning

- Doing the best you can with the resources you have

- Coming up with quick fixes and also over time developing long-term solutions that address underlying root causes

room for improvement, we should apply the framework in an iterative fashion. Using the framework in this way means that we are doing more than "putting out fires"—developing short-term fixes to recurring immediate problems, while ignoring their underlying causes. We may have to start with a quick fix, but over time, if the dilemma is repeated, then we can work from an initial solution toward a longer-term answer that addresses the root causes and helps prevent the dilemma from arising again.

That is the ultimate goal—admittedly a lofty one. Seek to address the dilemma in the short-term but consider why it arose and try to put arrangements in place that will preclude, to the degree that this is possible, its recurrence. As we discuss in Chapter 5, addressing underlying problems means being ready to establish learning processes that progressively uncover different aspects of issues and generate alternative courses of action.

A significant advantage of the weight-of-reasons framework is that it enables you to lessen regret and minimize the remorse you might otherwise feel if you only acted based on intuition. As Franklin suggested, the aim of relying on the weight of reasons is to ensure that you do not make *rash decisions for which you feel remorse later*. If you sincerely adhere to the framework, you will have better assurance that you and your organization have engaged in a process of due diligence before you take action. Applying the framework is not simple, however, and it requires creativity. Adhering to it should not be viewed as a bureaucratic routine, an exercise in "checking boxes." Like any tool, it can be applied insincerely. You must open yourself to it. Otherwise it will not lead to better choices.

The commonsense weight-of-reasons approach is consistent with the perspective of America's greatest contribution to philosophy: the tradition of pragmatism. Unlike other Western philosophers, pragmatists, including Charles Sanders Peirce, William James, George Herbert Mead, and John Dewey, believed that the purpose of thinking was not to develop a more accurate picture of reality—which is probably unknowable—but rather simply to solve the practical problems that we come up against. In the process, we make improvements in society without any pretense that these improvements will be utopian in nature and usher in perfection.[10] The pragmatic nature of the weight-of-reasons approach, however, should not be taken to mean that the framework does not involve principles. In fact, it incorporates the two major philosophical approaches to ethics in that it focuses on consequences and duty. We discuss these approaches further in the next chapter.

Though we often refer to the framework as a tool that you can use *as an individual*, it would be best to carry it out by interacting with people in your organization and outside it. We need external checks on both our intuitions and reasoning. When time and resources permit, decision-making processes involve teams of cognitively diverse members who share common goals. Being an ethical agent entails refining our intuitions and reasoning as members of a community. The community in all likelihood possesses practical wisdom and experience that we may lack, and thus, reliance on it can improve the decisions we make. The role of groups in ethical decision-making, however, is complicated, and the culture and climate of an organization can influence managers to make bad decisions as well as good ones. Chapter 4 discusses how teams and organizations influence ethical decision-making, Chapter 5 deals with the question of how to curb the potential abuses of group decision-making, and Chapter 6 addresses the question of how to build an entire organization that supports using frameworks such as the weight of reasons.

## Medical Products: The Complicated Business of Addressing Risks

**LO 1.6:** Apply the weight-of-reasons framework for ethical decision-making.

The best way to begin to understand the weight-of-reasons framework is to use it to address a sample ethical dilemma.

# MEDICAL SALES CALL

This case requires you, as a salesperson for a medical products company, to have a sensitive discussion with a prominent surgeon about a particularly difficult operation she might be called on to do for a patient. This patient has a serious, but not necessarily life-threatening, problem, which causes her a considerable amount of discomfort and makes everyday activity difficult. The surgeon asks you as the salesperson, "What is the 'best procedure for my patient?'" She is not looking for just any procedure, but the best one. Your company has a long-standing relationship with the surgeon who, like others in her field, takes the views of salespeople very seriously since they bring to the surgeon's attention information about new developments that might assist her in providing the best care for patients.

Your company supports two approaches to addressing the patient's problem. One relies on abdominal incisions and the other on vaginal ones. Based on your experience, you believe both these approaches *probably are adequate* for dealing with the problem the patient has. However, you just saw a demonstration of a new procedure that is carried out laparoscopically, or in a minimally invasive way. This procedure was developed by your competitor, who claims that it can produce *better clinical results*. In a study your competitor sponsored, the overall complication rate was just 3.6% as opposed to 10.3% for the abdominal incision and 4.9% for the vaginal incision (see Table 1.1). What should you say to the physician when she asks you what she should do?

**TABLE 1.1    Complication Rates With Abdominal and Vaginal Incisions and Laparoscopy**

| Complication Rates | Abdominal Incision | Vaginal Incision | Laparoscopy |
|---|---|---|---|
| Hemorrhage | 3.4 | 2.4 | 1.8 |
| Acute myocardial infection | 0.2 | 0.3 | 0.0 |
| Postoperative fever or infection | 4.0 | 0.0 | 0.9 |
| Intestinal obstruction | 0.4 | 0.0 | 0.0 |
| Urinary complication | 0.6 | 0.3 | 0.0 |
| Bladder injury | 0.2 | 0.3 | 0.0 |
| Accidental perforation of blood vessel, nerve, or organ | 1.5 | 1.6 | 0.9 |
| All complications combined | 10.3 | 4.9 | 3.6 |

Your company makes $17,800 in profit per physician use of the incision-based procedures it supports, plus you earn $6,250 in commission. By age 80, 18% of all women will have some type of procedure like this performed, or else their lives will be seriously impaired. Nonsurgical solutions can be used for a limited period. Ultimately, a patient is likely to need a surgical procedure to correct the problem, but there can be long-term complications associated with the surgery no matter how it is carried out. The after-surgery complication rate for the incision-based procedures your company supports has been high—a large percentage of women must have the procedure done again or they require a repair after the original surgery is carried out, which has risks of its own.

With the new noninvasive procedure, the precise after-surgery complication rate is not known, though the company that sells the procedure claims it is almost certain to be lower. On the other hand, a disadvantage of the new procedure is that 3 hours are needed to perform a laparoscopic operation, as opposed to only 1 hour via abdominal or vaginal incision. In addition, the patient must have a general anesthesia as opposed to a local one. However, an advantage of the laparoscopic procedure is that it is likely the patient can resume normal life and go back to work in two weeks as opposed to six weeks with an abdominal or vaginal incision.

You take seriously that under Section 5 of the Federal Trade Commission Act you are not allowed to deceive or mislead a customer when the customer asks a question like the doctor posed. Your company drilled the awareness into you that you should never lie or deceive a customer. The laws of the U.S. government mandate that you cannot make a fraudulent claim, including one of omission where you leave out relevant information. Any claim you make must be substantiated, which means it must be backed by tangible and quantifiable proof.

U.S. law also makes it illegal to slam the competition. A competitor that believes you have made unfair or inaccurate statements can register a complaint against your company and sue. Any suggestion that your product performs better than a competitor's must be supported by solid evidence. These rules apply to companies selling a product, advertising agencies, web masters, and salespeople.

Although the laws that prevent fraudulent claims reflect ethical principles, they are not easy to enforce. The problem is that the government must bring a case against each business that may violate the law, an expensive and time-consuming process that puts a large burden of proof on aggrieved parties and on government attorneys. Very few cases are pursued relative to the large amount of fraud that takes place. Federal Trade Commission laws cannot prevent all the fraud that takes place and all the misleading advertising claims companies make.

Your company has trained you to be practical, think for yourself, exercise good judgment, and show moral self-restraint. So how are you going to respond in this instance? And how would you explain your decision to the supervisor to whom you report?

You do not have much time to work through what you will do, and at the moment, you are feeling very conflicted. Your inclination is to favor the product you have been selling and to tell the physician to use the vaginal or abdominal incision since it is the product you have been hired to sell. It is the product you know the best, and it is a proven procedure. You have sold it to many surgeons and earned monetary rewards for your company from it many times in the past. The surgeon asking the question has successfully carried out past surgeries. You ask yourself, why make a change? You note that the surgeon herself is not a disinterested party and she earns a considerable sum when she carries out the procedure.

The procedure you are selling does have some advantages. It takes less time than laparoscopy. The patient would not have to undergo general anesthesia. The hospital therefore would save money. The doctor has experience with your product. It is unlikely she could do the surgery with the competitor's product, for which she has not been trained, so she would have to withdraw from the case and hand off the patient to another physician. She would not earn a fee. The patient would lose her tie to the doctor who has cared for her until this point and would have to establish a trusting relationship with another physician. Would the patient appreciate this change?

*(Continued)*

(Continued)

Your sense is not to tell the physician what you know about a competitor's procedure because it is her job to understand the options for her patient. However, you are concerned that the physician already knows about the laparoscopic alternative, though she may not be fully informed about the recent tests that showed its superiority. She may be testing you to see how up-to-date you are. She may ask you to compare the two procedures. She may be seeking a recommendation from you to use a procedure that she herself knows may not be the best option for the patient; then she could avoid criticism and responsibility if something went awry. She could blame it on the company and the salesperson who recommended the procedure without informing her about the alternatives. You want to treat the situation as just another business transaction and avoid answering the physician's question. The situation is making you very uncomfortable. Your anxiety grows and you do not know what to do.

## Applying the Framework

The weight-of-reasons framework can help you engage in further reflection and systematically address this dilemma by comparing options, assessing consequences, applying principles, and arriving at short- and long-term plans for dealing with the problem.

### Identify the Ethical Issue

The *issue* is how you can provide the patient with a procedure that minimizes her risk and results in as fast a recovery time as possible with the least likelihood of permanent damage, while at the same time fulfilling your obligations as a salesperson to your company.

### Gather Information

The *facts* are all of those above. They include that you saw a competitor's less invasive product demonstrated with the claim of fewer complications and quicker recovery times. The less invasive procedure involves less chance of doctor error. However, it is also true that your product has been on the market for a long time, the procedure it supports takes less time to do, the doctor is more practiced in using it, and it relies on local rather than general anesthesia, all of which benefit the patient.

### Identify Options

For now, the *options* are that the surgeon could (a) use one of the procedures your company supports because she has experience in using them, and is likely to get good patient results. The odds are in her favor, and there is no need to break with the status quo. However, you also could (b) suggest that the surgeon refer the patient to a doctor who has been trained in using the new procedure, if you believe the results for the patient would be better, in accordance with what the surgeon asked, inasmuch as she was seeking the "best" procedure for the patient. Or you could (c) suggest that the surgeon and the patient delay taking any action until more information is available, so they can make a more informed comparison of the probable outcomes of new and old procedures as they become available. After all, the ailment from which the patient suffers is not immediately life threatening.

## Assess Consequences

The *consequences* of pursuing these options are as follows:

- Option 1 would mean increased revenue for your company, a commission for you, a fee for the surgeon, and, for the patient, a surgery that has high odds of success but is more invasive and therefore more risky, though it takes less time than the new alternative you have seen demonstrated.

- Option 2 would mean no revenue for your company and the surgeon, no commission for you, and, for the patient, a procedure that is less invasive and risky but is more time-consuming, has been used less frequently, and requires general anesthesia.

- Option 3 would result in foregone income for you, your company, and the surgeon, and no treatment for the patient for now. Delaying may mean the patient continues to be uncomfortable, but her life would not be threatened and she may be able to get by for the time being with a temporary nonsurgical fix that partially reduced her discomfort.

## Apply Principles

Your *principles* are to maintain the trust of the surgeon and patients. They are your customers, and you must serve them by providing them with the information they need to make decisions that protect and benefit their health.

## Take Short-Term Action

The *short-term actions* you decide to take are as follows:

- Remind the surgeon that you represent your company.

- Tell her she should feel free to consult with experts besides you, as you have a vested interest and better knowledge of your company's procedure than those of other companies.

- Explain to her what you found out about the laparoscopic procedure, adding that you do not represent the competitor's product and that your knowledge is incomplete.

- Suggest to her that if she wanted to know, more she could go elsewhere, such as to the competitor, other doctors, or the hospital.

- Advise the surgeon that the decision about which procedure to use ultimately rests with the patient, and tell her it probably would be best to confer with the patient and obtain her informed consent.

- Indicate that the patient could get a second opinion from a physician who does the laparoscopic procedure.

- End by restating that the patient needs to be well-informed, and to the extent possible, must control this decision that affects her life.

In providing this response to the physician's question, you accept that it may mean that neither your company nor the surgeon ends up carrying out the procedure and earning money from it.

## Arrive at a Long-Term Solution

The *long-term action* you decide on after your discussion with the surgeon is to go back to your company and your supervisor to address the underlying cause of the dilemma. You wish to convey the following to your supervisor:

- The issue is not likely to be a one-time problem.

- The introduction of the competitor's product is likely to have long-lasting impacts on your company's strategy, so the company needs to reconsider its strategy.

- Your company's job is not just to sell this product; its role is to be a trusted source of information for doctors and patients.

- Your aim is to cultivate long-term relationships based on a reputation for honesty and reliability.

- Your desire is to ensure the good name of your company and maintain its reputation.

- The company therefore needs to undertake a systematic comparison of when, under what conditions, and *if* its products remain safe and viable for patients.

- If the product does not have a future, the company should consider *not* offering it for sale.

- If the product still is viable, the circumstances under which this is the case should be clearly spelled out.

You tell your supervisor that you want to work with the company to gather additional data on patient recovery, risk, and other product attributes like cost, track record, and ease of carrying out the procedure and what steps the company should take next.

## Learn Lessons From the Situation

Your company needs to be on top of situations such as this. That means working with doctors, insurance companies, and hospitals that administer the procedure to understand when and if a procedure is still valid to use, under what circumstances, and for what type of patient. If a product is not competitive, or just weakly so, and it poses avoidable risks and can cause unnecessary harm, your company should explore options such as ramping up R&D to catch up with the competitor or phasing out or even abandoning the product. If the product ultimately is inferior and has other negative attributes, and the risk to the patient in using the product cannot be reduced, sales might have to be halted. Legally, the company might be subject to lawsuits for continuing to sell the product and its reputation could be seriously impaired. On the other hand, if the product still has some valid uses in particular circumstances, then the company should have a policy of selling it *only* under these conditions.

The company, moreover, must be aware that it is likely to face situations like the one this dilemma presented again when a product it sells is surpassed by a competitor's product on some product attributes. It needs to have policies and routines in place for how to deal with this type of issue, for in the fast-paced world of medical innovation companies' products are regularly leapfrogging each other.

## Beyond Your Intuitions

By addressing this dilemma using the weight-of-reasons framework, you gain an *understanding that goes beyond your intuitions* about the situation and what you and your company should do. You broaden your perspective to understand the larger implications, not only for your company but also for the physicians, hospitals, and patients you serve. As a medical products salesperson, next time you face a question about which treatment would be right for a patient, you can draw on the lessons learned from this case.

## Some Pointers in Using the Framework

This process of using the weight-of-reasons framework is one of performing due ethical diligence. By applying the framework, the medical product salesperson in the case sees that the right thing to do is to put patients' needs first and provide them with the knowledge they require to make better choices. The case also should help you understand that applying the weight-of-reasons framework correctly is not easy. The framework provides a check on one's intuitions rather than a means of reinforcing or rationalizing them. The following are some pointers to apply the framework effectively.

 ### Step 1: Identifying the Issue

The process of applying the weight-of-reasons framework begins with the recognition that an ethical issue exists. Social psychologists refer to this first moment as **sensebreaking**, in which we recognize that something unusual has happened and that

**Sensebreaking**
The disruption of sensemaking by an unusual event or contradictory evidence

**Cognitive dissonance**
The mental discomfort that one feels when evidence contradicts one's beliefs or expectations

**Sensemaking**
The process of identifying, interpreting, and acting on information from the external environment

**Framing**
The process of perceiving particular information from the environment and attaching specific meanings to it

something may be amiss. In these moments we experience cognitive dissonance.[11] When we recognize that what we have perceived does not match our expectations, we feel discomfort, are aroused from mindless decision-making based on habit, and start to pay attention.[12] At this point, however, we tend to suppress and resist these feelings rather than taking them as an invitation to make changes. We display what social psychologists have called moral muteness and hope that the dilemma just goes away. But if we can get beyond this feeling, we move to sensemaking, or trying to identify, interpret, and act on the information we have.

When an ethical problem arises, a common reaction is to ignore it. Although the dilemma is troubling, and at an emotional level ties us up in knots and makes us anxious, afraid, and annoyed, our tendency may be to downplay it rather than deal with it. In fact, it is because it makes us anxious, afraid, and annoyed that we want to downplay it. In addition to ignoring and suppressing the problem, and dismissing it, our tendency is to frame the problem as something recognizable so that we can address it without thinking.[13] In doing so, we tend to choose categories that enable us to relieve our concerns and anxieties rather than forcing us to confront them. ("Oh, that's an engineering problem, so it's not my problem.") Framing helps us understand our environments but often leads us to have false or incomplete understandings.

Framing can lead us to avoid calling a dilemma "ethical." If, for example, you frame a dilemma as being solely a "practical" matter, judgment call, or strategic issue, then you may confine your thinking about it to economic and technical considerations—and ignore ethical ones. In the role of the medical products salesperson in the case above, it would have been easy for you to just continue to recommend your product even if you had a nagging feeling that this course of action was not the right one to take.

Even when we frame a dilemma as an ethical one, we may frame it in a particular way that captures some of its ethical aspects but misses others. Framing a dilemma as being about "honesty" may trigger different thinking than framing it as being about "fairness." While both may be valid, seeing it in one way means not seeing it in the other. In the Medical Products case above, if you had just framed the problem as addressing the needs of the patient *by offering a less invasive product*, then you would not have made much headway. Framing the dilemma more broadly as how best to serve the "needs of the patient" made it possible to make progress. Framing it in this way was better for your company as well.

Therefore, we have a number of recommendations for how to better frame ethical dilemmas.

- *First, do not ignore intuitions that are ethical—pay serious attention to those feelings inside you that tell you that someone, maybe yourself and others, might be hurt by what you choose to do or not do.* When you have suppressed or dismissed a dilemma but still have discomfort that something is amiss, take that as an opportunity to use approaches to reasoning such as the weight-of-reasons framework to identify and move toward a solution. You may realize that what may seem like a purely economic matter is legitimately an ethical matter that involves potential harm to you or others.

- *Next, when listening to this intuition, do not assume that the first instinct you have is the best or final way to take action.* Consider alternative framings. You may be highlighting consequences for just a single stakeholder. What you deem a matter of focusing on the interests of this stakeholder probably also involves consequences for other stakeholders. Also, invite people other than yourself to participate in the decision-making process, especially people with backgrounds and experiences different from yours. This can be very helpful in broadening the way in which you frame an ethical dilemma.

- *To effectively frame a dilemma, start by asking some of the questions presented in the framework.* This is especially important when you face an immediate problem, and there is little time and few resources. Even if you do not ask all of them, at least ask some of them before you act. Consider the facts, for example. Consider what you know and do not know. Ruminate a bit about your options. You can then initiate a process of going deeper, refining what you can do and what you need to know, and exploring alternatives to arrive at better short- and long-term plans of actions.

 ## Step 2: Getting the Facts

Once you identify the issue, the next step is to gather information. This may sound obvious, but in fact, humans have a tendency to skip this step. They tend to "fill in" the facts they expect to see. Managers may say things like, "Let me handle this; I've seen this kind of thing before." They end up substituting their preconceived notions for the facts. A related problem to avoid is confirmation bias.[14] In gathering facts to address ethical problems, people often find the facts that they are looking for while ignoring, suppressing, or failing to see facts that contradict their preconceived beliefs. If you think the problem may be that "Joe cut corners again," you will go looking for evidence that Joe did so, fail to see evidence of other explanations, and maybe even discount information that Joe did his job well.

People in organizations also tend to focus on individuals but ignore more systemic drivers. This is known as fundamental attribution error.[15] We tend to put blame on individuals rather than trying to understand problems from a broader perspective. Did Joe actually cut corners again, or is everyone in the company cutting corners because of the perverse incentives management put in place? Consider the recent Wells Fargo fraud case as an example. In this case, employees throughout the organization were cheating customers, taking actions such as signing customers up for new products and services they had not requested, and then charging them fees on their accounts. This fraud was not carried out by a few dishonest employees who cut corners but rather resulted from top-down pressure from corporate leaders, who made it essentially impossible for any employee to succeed in the company without cutting corners. To date, Wells Fargo has paid $185 million in fines over the case, and the company still faces many ongoing lawsuits. This case led to Wells Fargo's Chief Executive Officer John Stumpf's resignation. A case at the end of the book gives you the opportunity to consider the Wells Fargo scandal more carefully.

Finally, in gathering information about an ethical dilemma, *make sure the facts are major ones that have a bearing on the issue*. It can be easy to jump in and start fishing for information without really considering what information you need, or where you are most likely to find it. Distinguish between relevant and irrelevant facts. Realize that in some instances there are too many facts and they are hard to interpret. In other instances, recognize that critical information is missing. Make inferences from what you know but do not go too far afield. When there are important uncertainties, admit to them and seek to reduce them.

Ideally, you will apply the weight-of-reasons method more than once as more information comes to light. The underlying dilemma is not going to vanish immediately, and you must be patient that each stab your organization makes at resolving it will bring it closer to a better solution. In the Medical Products case above, the salesperson's answer to the physician is just a start in the company reexamining its long-term strategy.

 ## Step 3: Identifying the Options for Action

As with identifying the issue and gathering information, identifying alternative courses of action involves going beyond your first intuitions. In identifying courses of action, it is important that you do more than consider courses of action your organization has taken in the past. While you certainly want to draw on the past and think about what has worked before, this will not be enough because each dilemma is likely to be unique. Therefore, it is important to consider how actions you have taken in the past need to be modified, combined, or discarded altogether to address the issue you now face.

You must be creative and imaginative in identifying options your organization has not taken previously. Because past experiences have such a strong bearing on how we approach problems, generating a new or creative alternative may be difficult to do by yourself. Therefore, you are likely to benefit by working with others to assess options—especially people who are trusted for their judgment but have the boldness to take a different perspective.

While it is important to be imaginative, it is also important to *list real options your organization actually would carry out*. You can brainstorm and create many options and then compress them. In theory, the number of options might be infinite, but only three or four can be considered realistically. If an option is with little doubt illegal, immoral, impractical, has no merit, or would be hard to justify, why even consider it? The options you consider should be imaginative, practical, and realistic and should be developed in sufficient detail so that it is clear how they would be carried out.

 ## Step 4: Assessing the Consequences

Step 4 of the weight-of-reasons approach, assessing consequences, is where the "weighing" in the weight-of-reasons approach actually takes place. In this step, you must figure out the various parties who have a stake in your decision and the extent to which they will benefit or be harmed. Doing so is not easy, because again, you will most likely be inclined to rely on past experience rather than consider the consequences with fresh eyes. If you have done a good job of identifying the issue in Step 1, then you should already have ideas about the stakeholders who should be incorporated into your thinking and how they will be affected. Still, at Step 4, it makes sense to revisit the matter to make sure nobody has been left out.

One complication that arises in this step is that the consequences of an action are often unpredictable. You must always keep in mind *the law of unintended consequences*—that actions always have unanticipated effects, especially in complex, fast-moving situations.[16] Furthermore, for any affected party or stakeholder, there are many consequences to consider. You must try to be aware of long-term as well as short-term consequences. For a company, you have to consider not just immediate quantifiable outcomes, such as cost and revenue impacts, but also things like long-term reputational effects.

Try quantifying the consequences, even though doing so is likely to be frustrating. Start with verbal logic that articulates what you think the outcome might be, and why, and then move to quantifying the costs and benefits. Do not be deluded by quantification; you should not assume that because you have put things in numbers you are done analyzing the problem. Numbers provide only part of the picture, and the numbers you use may be no better than rough estimation.

If you are time constrained, as is often the case when addressing an issue, your goal is to do a satisfactory analysis in the time available. Acknowledge that uncertainties will remain. To know all the consequences is not possible. In further iterations, if this opportunity presents itself, you can become more precise. Keep asking others for their opinions. Do not be fooled that you have solved the problem of understanding the consequences once and for all. You still may be relying on many assumptions, some of them questionable.

### *The Weight of Reasons: A Table of Pros and Cons*

To evaluate the likely consequences of the options on stakeholders, you can prepare a table like Table 1.2, which depicts the pluses [+] and the minuses [–] of each of the options on stakeholders. You can find an example for the Medical Products case in Table 1.2.

- When filling out the table, use these designations: If an effect is *positive*, apply the symbol +, + +, *or* + + + for low, medium, and high positive. If it is *negative*, apply the symbol –, – –, *or* – – – for low, medium, and high negative. If you cannot determine if the effect is positive or negative, insert a question mark (?) or many question marks (???). How many pluses and minuses to give and how much weight to assign to short-term versus long-term outcomes is difficult.

  Be careful of biases in filling out the table. Consider both immediate and long-term effects. A consequence may be both positive and negative when one considers both the short term and the long term. For example, making working conditions better could cost money in the short term but lead to a better reputation and more sales in the long term (as well as benefitting employees). Thus, in the same box, you can have both pluses (+) and minuses (–). Separate them by a /. Mark the short-term impacts first and the long-term impacts next. Thus, if your intent is to convey that the short-term impact is negative while the long-term impact is positive, you would mark a –/+. If you mark a + +/–, you are relating that the short-term impact is very positive, while the long-term impact is negative.

- For each box in the table, summarize the reasoning that you have used to arrive at your conclusions in just a few words. Try not to just copy and paste the same words from box to box. The reasoning in each box should be unique and accurately summarize your justification for the symbols that precede it.

**TABLE 1.2**    **Pros and Cons Table for the Medical Products Case**

| Options | Consequences | | | | |
|---|---|---|---|---|---|
| | Patient | Surgeon | Company (Shareholders) | Salesperson (You) | Conclusion |
| 1. Use the company's product | – –/– – – Risk of complications<br><br>+ Takes relatively little time | + Increased revenue | + Profit of $10,800 | + Commission of $3,600 | – Risk of complications now and in future outweighs financial benefits though using company's product takes less time |
| 2. Send patient to surgeon who uses alternative procedure | – +/+ + + + Less invasive and risky surgery<br><br>More time-consuming surgery | – – Foregone revenue | – – Foregone profit of $10,800 | – – Foregone commission of $3,600 | –/+ Foregone revenue, profit, and commission and time-consuming surgery may be offset by less long-term invasiveness and risk |
| 3. Delay until more information is available | –/+ + + + + More informed comparison of options<br><br>Patient's health not immediately endangered | – Delayed or foregone revenue | – Delayed or foregone profit of $10,800 | – Delayed or foregone commission of $3,600 | –/+ + Foregone revenue, profit, and commission probably offset by no danger to patient and more informed comparison of options in future |

- Reach, to the extent possible, a bottom-line conclusion (the last column). If you do not have a bottom line, then you have not completed your work. Ben Franklin suggested a canceling method, in which positives and negatives that seem to be roughly equivalent are eliminated. Eliminating offsetting items in this way makes it easier to see if the positives outweigh the negatives, or vice versa.

## Step 5: Applying Principles

While calculating the "weight of reasons" (i.e., the consequences—Step 4) may provide you with comfort that you have thoroughly analyzed the dilemma, your analysis is not complete. Your goal should not be just to create a systematic analysis of the pros and cons of particular actions; you need to also reflect on how these actions would enable or prevent you from realizing your principles. One reason to incorporate principles into your analysis is that they provide a different view of what it means to take an ethical action. Calculating benefits and harms is important, but so are other considerations such as rights, fairness, and compassion. In Chapter 2, we will discuss such perspectives on ethics in further detail.

A second reason to bring in principles is that as noted, you *probably do not know and probably cannot know all the consequences* of your actions. Since your analysis of consequences is probably incomplete and flawed, it makes sense to bring in other viewpoints too. If you could determine for certain what all the consequences would be, perhaps principles could play a smaller role.

Finally, principles are important because pros and cons can be manipulated to find the "right"—that is, easy and convenient—answer. This is because the consequences of an action are so extensive and hard to predict.[17] Applying principles keeps you honest. As such, it guides you toward a more ethical choice and away from justifying initial intuitions without reflection.

In deciding what principles to apply, you might start by consulting an organization's public declarations of values, such as its mission statement. These help clarify the organization's priorities. Which stakeholders should you serve first? Customers? Patients, in the Medical Products case? Or should it be shareholders? Or someone else?

Following the adage that your principles consist of what you do "when other people are looking," it is worthwhile in clarifying your principles to step back and ask questions such as the following:

- Can I defend these principles to the company's board of directors?

- Can I explain them in court?

- Can I explain them to the media?

- Can I explain them to my fellow workers?

- Can I explain them to my family?

- As a consequence of following these principles, how will I feel about this decision a year from now?

- Would this decision seem right 20 years from now when someone writes my biography or a history of my organization?

These questions are worth pondering, but they also are very general. Therefore, it is also important to *apply principles appropriate and specific to the dilemma at hand*. These more contextual statements of principles should be short, precise, and to the point; no more than a single phrase may be needed. The principle applied in the Medical Products case above, to provide the patient with as much information as possible, is both abstract enough that it could be applied to any number of ethical dilemmas and also very relevant to the situation at hand.

After applying principles, it becomes clearer what to do. The preliminary bottom line based on the weighing of consequences may be reinforced or rejected. Your principles should give you greater assurance about what you should do. Assessing consequences is just a first step. Applying principles leads to the development of a course of action.

Even as we apply ethical principles, our intuitions are still in play. As we discuss in detail in Chapter 3, humans have evolved to possess intuitions that correspond to ethical principles. We have intuitions to care for and protect others, treat them with dignity, and protect them from harm. Paradoxically, though, while our ethical intuitions help us make quick decisions, through rationalization they can also lead us to take unethical actions. Furthermore, most of us rely on and develop particular ethical intuitions but not others. This means that by applying principles to an ethical dilemma, we can improve on our intuitions. We may surface ethical principles that our intuitions did not evoke, or we may reach conclusions and develop solutions that contradict our initial intuitions. Even when analysis based on principles confirms our intuitions, it is still useful because it helps us articulate them and explain them to others.

##  Step 6: Taking a Course of Action

Once the action options identified in Step 3 have been evaluated based on consequences and principles, you are ready to identify a course of action. While this plan can draw on the options identified in Step 3, it need not be confined to them. Your analysis of consequences and application of principles may stimulate new thinking; you may find that rather than choosing one option from those already identified, you must creatively combine options or develop new options that incorporate elements of the already-identified ones. As you examine options and see the strengths and weaknesses associated with them, other ideas will come to mind about how to modify or combine them. While you need not continue identifying options until you have found the perfect solution, if you see ways to generate a new option, then do so.

The more carefully you craft your plan of action, the more effective you are likely to be. At the same time, if you are operating within a very uncertain environment, one that is very complex and rapidly changing, it will make sense to plan only one or a few moves and consider how the actions turn out.[18] In identifying concrete action steps to implement your plan, consider how others might respond and how to obtain additional critical missing information.

Short-term quick fixes may be difficult to develop and implement. You should expect to make mistakes; when dealing with complex dilemmas that you do not fully understand, you might have to change direction as you implement your plan and learn more. As discussed in Chapter 5, experimentation and trial-and-error learning is a part of the process. Be flexible once you start, and learn from the feedback you receive. It may not make sense to "throw good money after bad," so avoid making significant resource—and psychological—commitments.[19]

Be aware as well of the political opportunity structure.[20] Unless you prefer being a martyr to being effective, there is no point in identifying a course of action that is not politically feasible. In considering what is politically feasible, you must consider your own sources of power and your ability to make change. With whom can you form a coalition to accumulate sufficient collective power to address the ethical dilemma effectively? Unless you are a very powerful actor, you are likely to accomplish little alone. In Chapter 4, we discuss the politics of carrying out ethical actions despite likely resistance.

In responding to a pressing ethical dilemma, your "quick fix" is a temporary solution that may prevent harm from occurring but does not address the underlying problem. The problem could be a deficient organizational culture, unethical leadership, or outside pressure from stakeholders with conflicting interests (e.g., shareholders who want maximum quarterly profits, while government or activists insist that you abandon a project or make big new investments). While the issues you face demand a short-term response, you cannot stop there.

 ## Step 7: From Short-Term Fix to Long-Term Solution

The quick fix is not the end of the decision-making process but rather a first step in developing a long-term approach. The quick fix should lead you in the direction of the root cause. You need to get underneath the presenting issue and search for the underlying causes and a way to manage them. A root cause analysis typically carries a business forward to making changes in strategy—thus, connecting ethics and strategy. In the Medical Products case, the company should come to the realization that it might have to withdraw the product in question from the market and do the requisite R&D to find a good replacement. In Chapter 9, we further explore the link between ethics and strategy.

In other words, you should not allow ethical problems to be *recurring and unstoppable events.* If you do face a never-ending series of similar events, then it means there is something that must be addressed more fundamentally.

It is unlikely that you can undertake a thorough and systematic process of getting at root causes by yourself. Such an effort necessitates a collaborative approach with many parties within the organization as well as outside stakeholders. When organizations approach ethical problems in this way, it is more likely they will be able to avoid the individual and group decision-making errors we discuss in Chapters 3 and 4. It is more likely they can uncover and address underlying causes that, if not addressed, fester and appear again and again, perhaps not in the exact same form but originating in the same sets of causes.

As you move from quick fixes to long-term solutions, you must take on the role of change agent, seeking to stimulate more impactful actions that address the underlying issues. In this role, you may find yourself doing the difficult work of establishing new stakeholder relationships and partnerships, building coalitions, and assembling resources in an effort to catalyze fundamental organizational changes, start new ventures, and even stimulate public policy changes. Such work requires dogged persistence as well as creativity, as you address seemingly irreconcilable conflicts and paradoxes. In later chapters, we discuss in more detail the difficult work of moving from quick fixes to long-term solutions. In Chapter 5, we examine how to work with others in your organization to build toward long-term solutions, and in Chapter 8 we discuss how to work with outside stakeholders.

##  Step 8: Learning From Experience

A critical, final step in applying the weight-of-reasons framework is "closing the loop"—that is, translating the lessons learned from addressing the ethical problem into an approach that can be drawn on the next time a similar problem arises. As noted, when you first address an ethical problem, you may have conflicting intuitions about how to address the problem. The weight-of-reasons approach may disconfirm initial intuitions and help you develop new ones that you will draw on as you face problems in the future.

In addition to refining your intuitions, learning from experience means creating a database of ongoing solutions that you can consult. This database can be both mental and organizational. Organizations use blogs, wikis, project reporting systems, and other tools to record knowledge they have gained over time so that it can be transferred around the organization to whoever needs it. By consulting these resources, managers can make more informed decisions when new ethical problems arise.

## Use the Framework Organically

Although Figure 1.1 presents the weight-of-reasons approach as a linear process, in fact, the approach works best when done iteratively. Follow your stream of consciousness, and let the process develop organically. Brainstorm the sequence of steps you take with a group, if you are able to work with others, before systematically organizing your thoughts. In the end, go back and rearrange your impressions into a logical pattern that conforms to the framework.

How you arrive at this pattern is likely to be complicated; it will not necessarily roll out in an orderly way. Working with others can help eliminate your biases and help you check tendencies that can lead to dead ends. Trusted partners can assist you in imagining possibilities you would not contemplate yourself. Perhaps you and those with whom you work choose to start with the facts. You might then move to a plan of action, and as you do, you come to better understand the issue you are facing. Or you might list options and their likely impacts, realizing as you go that you need to clarify the facts and gather missing information. Still another approach is to start with principles. You may decide upfront that because of your principles there are certain actions that you would not take, meaning they need not be considered in Step 3. Or you may decide that some stakeholders are your highest priority, which will shape how the approach to assessing consequences in Step 4.

There are many possibilities. The key is to try to ultimately cover all of the steps. Research shows that many decision-makers have a bias for action, which means that they start to pursue a course of action (Step 6) without ever really defining the problem (Step 1) or considering and evaluating the alternatives (Steps 3–5). The best of all possible worlds is when you and others in your organization use the entire weight-of-reasons framework to guide your responses to ethical problems. However, under time pressures and other constraints, using every element in the framework may not be possible. Even if you are not able to push yourself and others in your organization to thoroughly examine every element in the framework, each question is useful by itself. Even *partial use of the framework* will improve the quality of the decisions you and the other people in the organization make.

To stimulate a better response to an ethical problem, consider which element in the framework so far has been deficient or is missing. Then you must have the mettle to raise a red flag by asking *any one of these questions*:

- Have we identified the issue correctly?

- Do we have the relevant facts?

- Have we considered all the options?

- Do we understand where these options might lead?

- What are the principles guiding us?

- What is our immediate plan of action?

- What are the deeper issues underlying the presenting issue, and what can we do about them?

- What can we learn from this experience?

After asking one question, ask another. Then if there is still time, keep going until all the elements in the framework have been considered.

An advantage of using a framework such as the weight of reasons is that it can help you prepare for difficult conversations you must have in addressing an ethical problem. The elements of the framework can be used as a script to rehearse these conversations. In the Medical Products case, you (the salesperson) could use the weight-of-reasons framework to organize and practice your conversations with the surgeon and supervisor before they take place. Rehearsing the script helps improve your analysis by enabling you to identify weaknesses and potential objections. It prepares you to stay on message if the actual discussion you have veers off course.

The cases at the end of this chapter and throughout the book should give you practice in using the framework to address short-term presenting incidents and their deep-rooted causes. You should consider how to adjust business and corporate strategies in response to ethical issues. They are the warning sirens that your corporation must make some fundamental changes in how it conducts its business. In the Medical Products case, it is not just a matter of responding to the physician. It is a question of what kind of products the company is going to sell and how it is going to sell them.

## SUMMARY AND CONCLUSION

Addressing ethical dilemmas and applying the weight-of-reasons framework is challenging. We have limited thinking capacity, we often do not have all the information we need, and we cannot predict the consequences of our actions. Sometimes we have a hard time even recognizing that an ethical dilemma exists, let alone thinking in fresh ways about our options for addressing it. Often, it seems we are far removed from the kinds of questions Socrates would have us ask, such as those posed at the beginning of the chapter: Am I living an examined life? Am I acting according to my principles?

This book is intended to help you with this problem. Each chapter of the book is dedicated to helping you understand some of the complexities of addressing ethical problems and providing you with tools for addressing them. As we move through these chapters, we will explore their implications for applying the weight-of-reasons framework.

A big takeaway from this chapter is that ethics is hard. You may already hate this whole topic. Yet when ethical problems confront you, you do not want to be filled with regret that you immediately abandoned your principles and did not do "the right thing." Greed, ignorance, and weakness provide a few reasons why you might not engage with an ethical dilemma, but they are not the whole story. Reflecting on ethical issues is inherently difficult. This chapter introduced you to the "weight-of-reasons" framework that should assist you in making better ethical choices. It acknowledges that this framework does not easily provide an optimum solution to ethical conundrums. It can be abused if you just use it to justify what you were going to do anyway. Its best use is to apply it in an imaginative light to understand a situation in its full complexity. Doing so means unearthing facts and options you might not otherwise have considered, imagining a full host of consequences arising from these options, sticking to principles you and your organization hold sacred, and planning to deal not only with presenting a problem but its underlying root causes. Rely on this commonsense approach to practical judgment to check and refine your initial intuitions and learn lessons each time you apply the approach so that you get better at doing it.

While this book has much to say about the context in which business organizations operate, in the end, it is about you and your responsibilities as an ethical decision-maker. The aim is to improve *your ability* to make good choices. For those among you who think that such a goal cannot be accomplished because our ethical dispositions are determined by our genes and how we are raised, the research suggests that you are mistaken. According to experiments that psychologist Richard Nisbett has carried out, your ethics are not set in stone forever by your character and upbringing.[21] Rather, people can be taught to make better decisions, including better ethical decisions. However, getting better at ethical decision-making requires working at it. It requires diligence and humility. We want to avoid regret to the extent we are able, so it is incumbent on us to use frameworks such as the weight of reasons. Then, after we have made a decision, we have to rethink what we have done and assess as best we can whether it was the "right thing." If we follow this practice, then gradually, each of our successive choices should be more ethical than the last.

# KEY TERMS AND CONCEPTS

Bounded rationality  5

Cognitive dissonance  16

Decision  4

Decision process  4

Dilemma  5

Ethical decision  4

Framing  16

Sensebreaking  15

Sensemaking  16

Unstructured decision  4

# CASE APPLICATIONS

For each case, apply the weight-of-reasons approach to develop a course of action for addressing the ethical dilemma. Identify the issue, state the facts, identify possible courses of action, assess the expected consequences of each, apply your principles, and come up with a quick-fix action to address the issue. In addition, consider steps you could take to develop a long-term course of action that addresses the underlying cause of the problem and reflect on the lessons you have learned from engaging in this process.

## Case 1.1: Getting Funded

It's hard to be a start-up. To get funding from major venture capitalists with deep pockets requires having a good story. NOTHAM Foods's story had two parts that the company's charismatic founder Daniel Certech regularly pitched to investors. The first was about its rapid growth in sales. The second dealt with the scientific advances it was making in the use of plant proteins that could be used to feed the 9 billion people who would inhabit the planet by 2050. However, Jane Ireland, a newly hired accounting employee, noticed that to boost sales the company was systematically buying back its own inventory, expensing the buybacks as marketing costs under the category of Inventory Consumed for Samples and Internal Testing. This practice did not seem right, though she did not know if it was illegal. In the company lunchroom, she remarked to Anne Spinoza, a colleague and a friend who did research on plant proteins, "It's just a matter of time when there will be consequences. Investors will figure this out when they scrutinize our accounting. They could pull financing and we would not have the cash to keep going. What if they thought they were duped and brought a fraud case against us?" Anne replied, "You know, the yellow pea protein project on which I am working hasn't yielded any results, but Daniel keeps touting it as a winner." What should Jane and Anne do?

## Case 1.2: Recommending an Acquisition

Ira Koslowsky, a star employee, was on the fast track at Grandiose Private Equity, Inc. On his own he had borrowed money, creating a stake for himself of about $1 million in LUBICATe, an up-and-coming chemical company. Koslowsky studied the company carefully. It had patents on an exclusive catalytic process, for which other firms surely would be willing to pay top dollar. In addition, he believed its management were experienced pros who had done prior successful start-ups. He understood that they were now ready to sell LUBICATe and move on. He wanted to recommend the sale of LUBICATe to Grandiose. If Grandiose decided to buy the company, his investment in LUBICATe was likely to more than triple in value. He did not think there was anything illegal in making the recommendation, but he worried about how his bosses at Grandiose might respond if they found out about his stake in the company. At the top of the organization he was pretty sure this kind of inside dealing commonly took place, but nobody talked about it. From where he stood in the organization, the company seemed awfully fussy about potential conflicts of interest. What should Ira do?

## Case 1.3: A Fleet of Autonomous Vehicles

The year is 2025, and nearly 20% of all vehicles on the road are autonomously driven (self-driving). The government has established strict guidelines for the algorithms that run these vehicles. In the event that there is a choice between saving a few occupants in a vehicle and many pedestrians and occupants in other vehicles, the autonomous vehicles must be programmed to swerve to avoid harm to pedestrians and to the occupants of other vehicles. The justification for the policy is that the public interest is to have the fewest number of people harmed in traffic accidents. You are outraged by this policy. You have been a vociferous critic. This policy violates every principle you hold dear. Your company, Boogalie, employs some of the most talented people in the country. Its young, gifted, scientific, and technical workers are working on society's most pressing problem—how to prolong life and permit people to increase their productivity as they age. Boogalie just purchased a new fleet of 200 autonomous vehicles to chauffeur its employees from their homes to corporate labs scattered throughout the region and shuttle them between labs as needed. After the vehicles arrive, you have

about three days when you can arrange to have them reprogrammed so that they will save the vehicles' occupants before pedestrians and occupants of other vehicles. What should you do?

## Case 1.4: Secure Motors

You are directly responsible for boosting Secure's sales. You are on a short leash as management has little patience with employees who don't produce. The Secure Motor Corporation is widely recognized as making one of the safest family cars in the market. Independent tests by various automobile associations consistently rated its family sedan and wagon the best in terms of impact resistance and safety. The company has signed up with a new advertising agency, Satchel and Bag, which has devised a campaign built on Secure's reputation for safety. To highlight this point, it lined up a range of typical family vehicles, bumper to bumper with Secure's car in the middle, and then it drove an all-terrain vehicle, over the tops of the cars. In all cases, except the Secure car, the passenger cabins were crushed, then the motto appeared "You are Secure in Secure." Previews of the campaign tested on focus groups had excellent results. Satchel and Bag estimated that the campaign might result in sales increases in excess of 15% to 20%. As a manager for Secure, you were part of the team that negotiated the contract with Satchel and Bag, and you have an ongoing liaison role with the advertiser. You, along with several executives, have been invited to a private showing of the new campaign. As you are watching, you could not help but be impressed with the ad's powerful and evocative image, the message, and the initial market forecasts. Then one of Satchel and Bag's key advertising people sitting next to you leans across the table and in a whisper chuckles, "Pretty impressive isn't it? I'll let you in on a secret though, we reinforced the struts on the cabin, maybe we didn't have to, but just to be on the safe side you understand . . . great campaign isn't it?" What do you do?

## Case 1.5: Paying for a Life-Saving Drug

Dearborn and Dyehardt (D&D) has just put Forzosein on the market, a new compound that may be able to save the lives of people who suffer from cancer. D&D charges hundreds of times what it cost the company to make Forzosein to recoup the extremely high R&D expenses it bore to test the compound and get it approved. Darren Talbot is an executive in the Baldwin Corporation, the company that distributes Forzosein for D&D. Doctors say that Anna Bryan suffers from a rare form of cancer and has just a few months to live. Forzosein is a controversial choice for treating her cancer and is not covered by Amalgamated, her insurance company. To have hope for recovery Anna will need as many as 40 doses, but each dose of Forzosein costs $10,000. Anna is just 36 years old and has three young children. Her husband, Lester, asked D&D if it could make an exception in Anna's case and charge less for the drug, but the company refused. He pleaded with Amalgamated to expand its coverage but it turned him down. He tried to take out a loan from the Tarrytown Bank, using his house as collateral, but the maximum amount the bank would loan him was $25,000. He went to friends and family to borrow money and raised an additional $15,000. Desperate, he begged Darren for the doses of Forzosein he needed for his wife. He would hand over the $40,000 he had raised and try, if he could, to pay the rest later. What should Darren do?

## NOTES

1.  Mintzberg, H., Raisinghani, D., & Théorêt, A. (1976). The structure of "unstructured" decision processes. *Administrative Science Quarterly, 21,* 246–275.

2.  Cyert, R. M., & March, J. G. (1963). *A behavioral theory of the firm.* Englewood Ciiffs, N.J.: Prentice-Hall; Cyert, R. M., Simon, H. A., & Trow, D. B. (1956). Observation of a business decision. *Journal of Business, 29,* 237–248.

3.  Simon, H. A. (1957). *Models of man: Social and rational* (1st ed.). New York, NY: Wiley.

4.  This video depicts a variation on Simons and Chabris's "invisible gorilla" experiment. Chabris, C., & Simons, D. (2011). *The invisible gorilla: How our intuitions deceive us.* New York, NY: Harmony.

5.  Haidt, J. (2012). *The righteous mind: Why good people are divided by politics and religion.* New York, NY: Vintage Books.

6.  Willcox, W. B. (Ed.). (1975). *The papers of Benjamin Franklin: Vol. 19. January 1 through December 31,* *1772* (pp. 299–300). New Haven, CT: Yale University Press.

7.  Weick, K. E. (1993). The collapse of sensemaking in organizations: The Mann Gulch disaster. *Administrative Science Quarterly, 38*(4), 628–652.

8.  Hammond, K. (1996). *Human judgment and social policy: Irreducible uncertainty, inevitable error, unavoidable injustice.* Oxford, UK: Oxford University Press.

9.  Simon, H. A., & March, J. (1976). *Administrative behavior.* New York, NY: Free Press.

10. For Peirce's pragmatic maxim, see Peirce, C. S. (1878). How to make our ideas clear. *Popular Science Monthly, 12,* 286–302.

11. Pratt, M. G. (2000). The good, the bad and the ambivalent: Managing identification among Amway distributors. *Administrative Science Quarterly, 45*(3), 456–493.

12. Festinger, L. (1962). *A theory of cognitive dissonance.* Palo Alto, CA: Stanford University Press.

13. Goffman, E. (1974). *Frame analysis: An essay on the organization of experience*. Cambridge, MA: Harvard University Press.

14. Wason, P. C. (1960). On the failure to eliminate hypotheses in a conceptual task. *Quarterly Journal of Experimental Psychology, 12*(3), 129–140.

15. Heider, F. (1958). *The psychology of interpersonal relations*. New York, NY: Wiley.

16. Merton, R. K. (1936). The unanticipated consequences of purposive social action. *American Sociological Review, 1*(6), 904.

17. Williams, B., & Smart, J. J. C. (1973). *Utilitarianism: For and against*. Cambridge, UK: Cambridge University Press.

18. See Mintzberg et al. (1976).

19. Staw, B. M. (1976). Knee-deep in the big muddy: a study of escalating commitment to a chosen course of action. *Organizational Behavior and Human Performance, 16*(1), 27–44.

20. McAdam, D., Tarrow, S., & Tilly, C. (2001). *Dynamics of contention*. Cambridge, UK: Cambridge University Press.

21. Nisbett, R. E. (2015). *Mindware: Tools for smart thinking*. New York, NY: Farrar, Straus & Giroux.

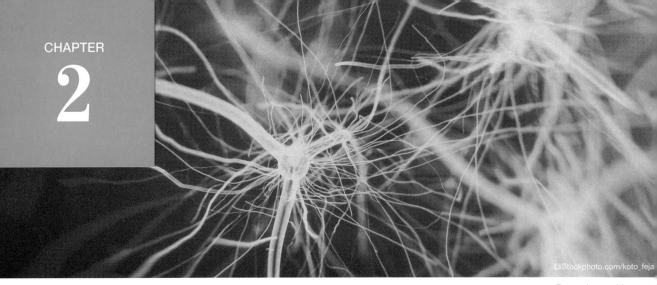

©iStockphoto.com/koto_feja

Reasoning enables us to understand and address the complex ethical dilemmas we face.

# Using Ethical Reasoning

## Learning Objectives

On completion of this chapter, the reader should be able to do the following:

LO 2.1: Understand the major approaches to ethical reasoning.

LO 2.2: Identify the strengths and limitations of utilitarianism as an ethical philosophy.

LO 2.3: Identify the strengths and limitations of deontology as an ethical philosophy.

LO 2.4: Recognize the contradictions and conflicts between utilitarianism and deontology and move toward reconciling their differences using the weight-of-reasons framework for ethical decision-making.

LO 2.5: Discuss the tenets of virtue ethics, understanding how it differs from deontology and utilitarianism.

LO 2.6: Discuss the role of contract theory and the ethics of care in working through the differences between utilitarianism and deontology.

" *If the hypothesis were offered us of a world in which . . . millions kept permanently happy on the one simple condition that a certain lost soul on the far-off edge of things should lead a life of lonely torture . . . even though an impulse arose within us to clutch at the happiness so offered how hideous a thing would be its enjoyment when deliberately accepted as the fruit of such a bargain.* 🙶

**—William James**,
19th-century American philosopher and psychologist

## Introduction: Approaches to Ethics

LO 2.1: Understand the major approaches to ethical reasoning.

This chapter reviews two major approaches to ethical reasoning—the ways in which people think about what it means to be ethical. These approaches are considered the cornerstones of ethical inquiry. One of these is utilitarianism, sometimes called teleology or consequentialism, and the other is deontology, or the rights-based or Kantian approach. For a utilitarian, the focus is on *the ends* or consequences of action. The most ethical action one can take is that which creates the greatest surplus of good over bad. If the end results of an action are positive, then they justify the means. For deontologists, on the other hand, *the means* are what matter. The means used to pursue a goal cannot transgress a person's basic rights without his or her consent. Taken together, utilitarianism and deontology raise two related and important questions for deciding the ethical course of action:

**Utilitarianism**
An ethical approach focusing on the ends or consequences of actions; also known as teleology or consequentialism

**Deontology**
An ethical approach focusing on the means of actions; also known as the rights-based or Kantian approach

- Is the action right or wrong (deontology)?

- Is the action good or bad (utilitarianism)?

The history of ethical study provides examples of thinkers who have been primarily concerned with one or the other of these questions. At the same time, much of the thinking about ethics cannot easily be categorized into one school or the other. While the deontological model is often associated with the Western religious traditions of Judaism and Christianity, these religions are also concerned with good results. And while the teleological model is often associated with classical Greek thought, Greek writers such as Plato often concerned themselves with duty. Ethical inquiry requires reflecting on both what is right or wrong *and* what is good or bad. This chapter starts by explaining, contrasting, and critiquing utilitarianism and deontology. It shows that neither is perfect by itself but in combination they can be very powerful approaches to business ethics. Utilitarianism corresponds to Step 4 of the weight-of-reasons framework, which calls on you to estimate the benefits and costs of an action, while deontology corresponds to Step 5 of the framework, which calls on you to act based on the principles of right and wrong regardless of the consequences.

Is the action right or wrong, good or bad?

**Virtue theory**
An approach to ethical reasoning focusing on qualities of ethical excellence, such as integrity and honesty

**Contract theory (or social contract theory)**
An approach to ethics that assesses the morality of an action based on whether it conforms to a set of social rules that preserve the basic rights and freedoms of all

**Consequentialism**
The theory that the ethics of an action should be based on its consequences

**Teleology**
The theory that a thing can be explained in terms of its purpose or goal

The chapter then introduces virtue theory, which is often considered the third major approach to ethical reasoning. Virtue theory is concerned with how we cultivate qualities of ethical excellence, such as integrity and honesty. While it espouses taking virtuous actions that demonstrate character, virtue theory also recognizes that virtues pushed too far become vices; for example, when taken to extremes, honesty becomes insensitive rudeness, bravery becomes foolish risk taking, and so on. Thus, virtue theory strives for attaining a "golden mean"—the appropriate midpoint between extremes. Finding the golden mean is a crucial aspect of Step 6 of the weight of reasons—deciding on a course of action. It helps reconcile utilitarianism (Step 4 of the framework) with deontology (Step 5) by embracing both but pushing neither of them too far. Applying virtue theory, one can identify a course of action that is concerned with creating as much good as possible, while also respecting individuals' rights and dignity. Virtue theory stresses improving our capacity for deliberating about ethical issues through practice—we can become better at finding the golden mean over time.

We end the chapter by considering two other important ethical frameworks. One of these is contract theory (or social contract theory). Contract theory, often, is not distinguished from deontology because it emphasizes respecting the rights of individuals. What is different, though, about contract theory is that it is concerned with ensuring the fairness of the processes and arrangements by which we reach a consensus on who has what rights. Following our discussion of contract theories, we turn our attention to the feminist ethic of care, which defines ethics in terms of compassion and the nurturing of relationships. This is an important consideration in applying the weight-of-reasons framework.

## Utilitarianism

**LO 2.2:** Identify the strengths and limitations of utilitarianism as an ethical philosophy.

Consequentialism is an ethical theory whereby the ethics of actions is judged based on their consequences (Figure 2.1). Consequentialists are concerned not with the ethics of an action itself but rather with the ends of the action and whether it causes more good than bad. Consequentialist theories sometimes are referred to as teleological theories. The term teleology is derived from the Greek word *telos*, which means "end," "purpose," or "goal." Consequentialism comes into play in the weight-of-reasons framework in Step 4, which asks you to estimate the consequences of the actions you are considering carrying out.

**FIGURE 2.1**

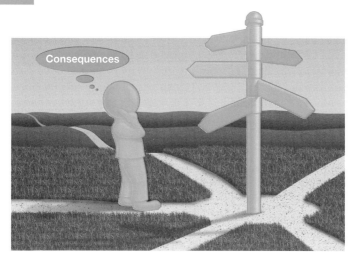

Utilitarianism assesses an action's ethics based on its consequences.

John Dewey, the 20th-century American philosopher and educator, was a major proponent of a pragmatic school of ethics that argued for deliberating on our actions' consequences. He wrote, "We are reasonable when we estimate the import or significance of any present desire or impulse by forecasting what it would come or amount to if carried out."[1] Dewey advised deliberating on consequences through an "imaginative rehearsal." People should consider the result of their actions in terms of their "likes and dislikes . . . desires and aversions," developing within themselves "a running commentary" based on their values of "good or evil."[2] As Dewey explained,

> We give way, in our mind, to some impulse; we try in our mind some plan. Following its career through various steps, we find ourselves in imagination in the presence of the consequences that would follow; and as we then like and approve, or dislike and disapprove, these consequences, we find the original impulse or plan good or bad.[3]

## Defining Good and Bad Consequences

Consequentialist theories define "good" and "bad" consequences in many different ways. The word *good* is used in different contexts: a good meal, a good job, a good feeling, and so on. The Ancient Greeks (Plato, Protagoras, Aristotle) distinguished intrinsic goods, which have inherent value—that is, are "good" in and of themselves—from extrinsic goods, which derive their value from what they can lead to—what they are "good for."[4] Extrinsic goods are means to an end rather than ends unto themselves. We go to the dentist not because doing so is an intrinsic (or "final") good but because it allows us to achieve some other, more important aim—like a nice

**Intrinsic goods**
Goods that have inherent value—that is, are "good" in and of themselves

**Extrinsic goods**
Goods that derive their value from what they can lead to—what they are "good for"

smile or the avoidance of pain. Or we may take a "good" job solely to provide for ourselves and our children and to improve the quality of our lives, not because we inherently value the work.

Assessing actions according to whether they achieve ends such as human survival or liberty are other examples of forms of consequentialism. So is ethical egoism, which sees self-interest as the basis of morality. Philosophers such as Friedrich Nietzsche and Ayn Rand argued that not only *do* people act out of self-interest but they *should* act out of self-interest because doing so makes society as a whole better off.

**Ethical egoism**
The philosophy that self-interest is the basis of morality

## Two Versions of Utility

Utilitarianism is the best-known form of consequentialism. Its primary focus is on utility, or the practical value or usefulness resulting from our choices. To a utilitarian, the action that produces the greatest net utility is the right one, regardless of who benefits and who is harmed. Jeremy Bentham,[5] the 18th-century English philosopher, maintained,

**Utility**
Usefulness, value, benefit, pleasure

> An action is right from an ethical point of view if and only if the sum total of utilities produced by that act is greater than the sum total of utilities produced by any other act the agent could have performed in its place.[6]

To a utilitarian, an action is ethical even it if causes pain, suffering, or other adverse consequences for *some* people, as long as it increases the *total utility of all*—that is, if the good outweighs the bad, or in the aggregate the pleasure outweighs the pain. According to this principle, the calculation of utility should be done impartially and include all the stakeholders who would be affected by the decision. Utilitarian philosopher Peter Singer refers to this as the "equal consideration of interests"; no person's utility, including the decision-maker's, is to be given higher priority than any other person's.[7] Hence, utilitarianism rejects both relativism and egoism.

Utilitarian philosophers have thought about utility in different ways. According to Bentham's hedonistic utilitarianism, utility derives only from an act's capacity to cause pleasure and pain. Bentham wrote, "Nature has placed mankind under the governance of two sovereign masters, pain and pleasure. It is for them alone to point out what we ought to do as well as to determine what we shall do."[8] Bentham believed that all actions are commensurable; that is, they can be measured and compared based on how much pleasure and pain they can be expected to cause. According to his version of utilitarianism, as a society, we should add together quantitative units of pleasure and subtract quantitative units of pain to arrive at a measure of total utility. Such a calculation, according to Bentham, would enable us to make more rational decisions. At the level of public policy, his approach would mean using cost–benefit analysis to analyze how much a proposed policy would increase or decrease economic indicators such as gross national product. At the corporate level, it could mean using financial measures such as return on investment to calculate how much wealth an action would produce. These measures fail to identify specific stakeholder impacts. The weight-of-reasons approach is designed to correct for this defect.

John Stuart Mill, a 19th-century economist and philosopher, had a different view of utility. Unlike Bentham, who thought that all actions could be measured in common units, Mill distinguished and ranked actions according to the degrees and types of happiness they provide. Like the Greeks, he saw long-term fulfillment and flourishing as a higher form of happiness than short-term satiation.[9] Whereas Bentham would have argued that the utility of drinking beer and going to parties could be measured on the same scale as and compared with the utility of reading a profound work of moral philosophy or attending a symphonic concert, Mill would say that the two should not be compared with each other because the former provides a lower form of happiness than the latter. Mill saw the pleasures of the mind that are uniquely human as higher than the physical pleasures humans share with other animals. He famously quipped that it was better to be an unsatisfied human than a satisfied pig, or an unsatisfied Socrates than a satisfied fool.[10] Some consider Mill an elitist. Nonetheless, the 20th-century English philosopher G. E. Moore took a view similar to that of Mill and maintained that pleasure comes from maximizing values such as freedom, knowledge, justice, friendship, love, and beauty, and not bodily pleasures alone.[11] The implication of the perspectives of Mill and Moore for business is to focus on building durable organizations challenging people to learn, grow, and fulfill their intrinsic human needs to flourish.

## Criticisms of Utilitarianism[12]

Utilitarianism is criticized on many grounds. A primary critique is that utilitarian decisions, with their emphasis on the greater good, violate the basic respect to which each *individual* is entitled. That possibility is poignantly illustrated in the quote by William James at the beginning of the chapter. If a group decides that its happiness justifies an individual's suffering, can the group easily live with this decision? Its happiness would be muted by the consciousness of the unhappy bargain it has had to strike. What if you were the lost soul on the "far-off edge of things" leading "a life of lonely torture"? Would you be willing to make this sacrifice for the good of the many? Yet this sacrifice is theoretically justifiable for a utilitarian. Deontology, discussed in the next section, takes up this problem, viewing freedom and equal treatment as fundamental rights and humans as ends in themselves. From a deontological perspective, the greater good must be achieved *only with means that respect people's rights*.

Another practical criticism of utilitarianism is that it is difficult to define and calculate the consequences of an action. Should all consequences be measured in terms of pleasure and pain, or should some types of goods and bads, like wisdom or friendship, be given greater weight? In addition, the capacity that humans have for foretelling the consequences of an action is limited. The consequences of actions—both who will be affected and how much—are hard to predict; the future is uncertain even to the most astute among us, and it is filled with unintended consequences. The insight of **complexity theory** is that small actions can have very large impacts through feedback loops that cannot be anticipated. An executive who is considering closing a factory and outsourcing the work cannot really estimate how the decision will affect every stakeholder now and in the future—workers, their families, communities, other companies, financial institutions, and others.

**Complexity theory**
The theory that explains the behavior of one element of a complex system and the system itself in terms of that element's interdependencies with other system elements

An additional criticism of utilitarianism relates to the question of who decides—that is, who has the right to calculate the benefits and harms of an action. The person or group that calculates may have conflicts of interests and biases. This person or group may choose to include stakeholders they favor and exclude those for which they have little regard. Theoretically, this problem should not exist because, according to a utilitarian, decision-makers are objective calculators who have no biases for or against particular stakeholders. Practically, utilitarian calculations often do not work in this way. As mentioned in Chapter 1, managers frame ethical issues in particular ways that may not account for all stakeholders. They may come from homogeneous and well-off groups and lack sympathy for the lives of the people whom their decisions touch.

Bentham and Mill recognized this issue and envisioned a quasi-democratic approach for deciding, but democracy is vulnerable to the "tyranny of majority": The rights and interests of minorities are often violated by the majority. To prevent this problem in the American political system, the founders established a complex system of checks and balances to protect minority interests. Similar principles can be applied in organizations. In Chapters 5 and 8, we revisit the issue of establishing mechanisms that give voice to diverse stakeholders.

# THE FORD PINTO CASE: A TELEOLOGICAL ERROR[13]

The Ford Pinto case provides an infamous example of an ethical breakdown arising from the misapplication of utilitarian analysis. As you read the case, ask yourself whether the unethical decision was made because utilitarianism was improperly applied or because utilitarianism should not have been used in the first place.

In the late 1960s, smaller and cheaper foreign cars started to make serious inroads into the market share of U.S. automobile makers. Ford's top executives hatched a plan to meet the competition head on: develop, build, and sell an automobile "weighing no more than 2,000 pounds and costing no more than $2,000." This car was called the Pinto. To meet the deadline of the 1971 model year and get a jump on the competition, the firm decided to compress the normal design-to-production time to two years from the usual schedule of four years. The compressed schedule meant that tooling for production occurred simultaneously with design, curtailing the ability to accommodate design changes along the way. When production was completed, some crash testing of the models proved problematic, with ruptured gas tanks and leaks occurring at various speeds of impact. The main reason was the location of the gas tank. Modification of the design to change its location would require retooling, which would mean spending more money, less trunk space, and a later introduction of the car. These outcomes were not acceptable to management, which wanted to beat back the Japanese challenge, earn higher profits, and save U.S. jobs. Customers were not represented in the decision-making process. The company did do customer surveys but never asked about the potential problems in the gas tank placement. Management took the view that when compared with other autos on the road at the time, such as the VW Beetle, the Pinto was a safe vehicle.

Not unexpectedly, in the first seven years after the introduction of the Pinto, many deaths occurred. The company was sued because of the design problem. Ford engineers testified that they understood that 95% of the fatalities could have been prevented if they had relocated the fuel tank. The company justified its decision not to move the fuel tank based on cost–benefit analysis. It had calculated that the financial benefits of the Pinto's early introduction outweighed the costs, which it knew was likely to be 180 deaths and 180 injuries. The value of the time and money saved from not relocating the fuel tanks was estimated to be greater than the cost of expected injuries and deaths. Furthermore, Ford had lobbied against the National Highway Transportation Safety Agency tightening the crash safety standards. It argued that the Pinto was "no more unsafe" than other vehicles of its time and met federally established standards for crash safety. In the end, Ford lost sales, and its reputation for quality was tarnished. It had to recall the Pinto, pay large sums in personal injury lawsuits related to crashes in which people were maimed and killed, and settle many more lawsuits.

The Pinto case holds important lessons for assessing the consequences of decisions (Step 4 of the weight-of-reasons framework). First, and most obviously, the case illustrates the dangers of framing issues too narrowly. Because the managers at Ford saw the Pinto decision as a financial decision and not an ethical one, they missed many of the decision's most significant impacts. Had they challenged their own assumptions, imagined the decision from the perspective of the drivers and their loved ones, and taken a longer-term view of the costs and benefits of the decision for the company, their calculation would have been different. Part of the problem seems to have been that the decision-makers knew what outcomes they wanted from the beginning (to get a cheap car to market quickly) and were committed to making these outcomes happen. As a result they did not make their decision objectively. We discuss this decision bias, which is known as escalation of commitment, in Chapter 3.

A second and related implication of the case is that one must take care to avoid being mesmerized by the false certainty of quantification. Because Ford's decision-makers made a cost–benefit analysis, they felt they had thought of everything. They made the mistake of thinking that the cost–benefit analysis was the entire decision process, when ideally it is just one tool that is used in making a decision. It may be more important to engage in dialogue with stakeholders to surface their perspectives than to make a (seemingly) precise calculation of consequences. The analysis will only be as good as the assumptions that go into it. Unfortunately, the case of the Pinto demonstrates the problem of "garbage in, garbage out."

Tools such as cost–benefit analysis must be used cautiously and with restraint. One must recognize that there are many ways to assess consequences. This could mean starting with an analysis based on Bentham's view, which accounts for obvious, tangible benefits and harms, such as money gained and spent, jobs created and lost, and people harmed. Then in successive probes, one can move toward a fuller analysis that incorporates higher-level goods, such as creating a flourishing organization dedicated to employee development, the elimination of unnecessary total harm, and the doing of good by strengthening communities, protecting nature, and creating a more just society.

## Deontology: Rights and Duties

**LO 2.3:** Identify the strengths and limitations of deontology as an ethical philosophy.

Deontology is the other major approach to assessing ethical choices. It is built into the weight of reasons as Step 5, application of principles. For deontologists, the end results are less important than the actions taken to achieve the goal. There may be actions you should *not* pursue no matter how worthy the goal.

Deontology is fundamentally about rights and duties, what we ought to do regardless of the consequences. Its claim is that each of us has certain rights, such as the right to respect for our dignity, as well as a moral duty to respect the rights of other individuals. One cannot take actions that violate these basic rights regardless of what purpose might be served. Whereas utilitarianism is associated with the overall good, deontology prioritizes the right over the good.

There are many different deontological theories of ethics, but deontology is most closely associated with Immanuel Kant, the 18th-century German philosopher. He wrote the following:

> Every rational being exists as an end in himself and not merely as a means to be arbitrarily used by this or that will. In all his actions, whether they are directed to himself or to other rational beings, a human being must always be regarded at the same time as an end . . . i.e. an object of respect.[14]

A famous critique of utilitarianism from a Kantian perspective is that utilitarianism allows one to take a person's body parts against his or her will and divide them up among other individuals who need them and whose lives have greater merit. Kant, who asserted that each person has inherent value, would never assent to this type of action. Thus, deontology addresses one of the main problems of utilitarianism, which is that it seems to permit doing tremendous harm to some if offsetting benefits are produced for others. Not only did Kant oppose hurting someone else for the greater good, he also opposed harming oneself or taking one's own life, even, for example, if the person were miserable because of some incurable disease and was an obvious burden to others. Despite the fact that the benefits might be greater than the costs in this instance, or the pain of the person continuing to live outweighs the pleasure, Kant would not allow it. He believed that individuals must have the utmost respect for *themselves* as well as others and thus are obligated to do everything they can to resist suicide and preserve their lives no matter how much discomfort they have and how much suffering they cause others.

The deontological emphasis on taking the right action is found in many of the world's great religions. For example, Buddhism's Noble Eightfold Path and its adage "Hurt not others with that which pains yourself" are expressions of deontological principles. So too are the Ten Commandments and the Judeo-Christian "Golden Rule" of doing unto others as you would have them do unto you. In the New Testament, Jesus set a very demanding deontological standard when he called on his followers to love not only their neighbors but also their *enemies*:

I say unto you love your enemies, bless them that curse you, do good to them that hate you, and pray for them that despitefully use you and persecute you. . . . For if you love those who love you, what reward have you? Do not even the common people do the same? Be you therefore perfect . . .
(Matthew 5:44, King James Version)

While this rule has inspired many, philosophers also have pointed to a logical problem. Specifically, they note that the Golden Rule contains an implicit premise that other people want *the same* treatment that we do. However, "stepping into someone else's shoes" requires not just considering what would be preferable to us but what would be preferable if we were someone other than ourselves. Following the Golden Rule, a sadomasochist who desires to hurt others and be hurt could rationalize that he has a right to harm others because he desires that others harm him. Similarly, a businessperson following the Golden Rule might believe that he was permitted to lie to others and commit fraud because he or she expects others to do the same to him in the "dog-eat-dog" business world they occupy.

## The Categorical Imperative

Immanuel Kant recognized this problem that the Golden Rule could be perversely applied. To counteract the problem, Kant developed the *categorical imperative*, which he formulated in three different ways. Each was an attempt to capture the Golden Rule in a more logically precise way.[15]

### The First Formulation

Kant's *first formulation* of the categorical imperative states that we should take an action only if it is consistent with universally accepted duties and obligations that are absolute and cannot be violated, regardless of the circumstances. As such, this formulation enables us to identify the principles we think everybody should live by all the time. When considering an action, we must ask ourselves if the proposed action is based on a principle that "could become a universal law." Examples of universal obligations related to business might include the duties to not physically or psychologically coerce employees and other stakeholders, to not sexually harass them, to be honest in your dealings, to deliver products you promised to deliver, and to follow the law.

In applying Kant's first categorical imperative, the question that arises when considering an action is "Would you be willing to live in a world where *everyone* behaved in this manner?" For example, if you are considering lying, cheating, or paying a bribe, you must ask yourself what would happen if everyone lied, cheated, and paid bribes. Would you want to live in that world? The first formulation is meant to prevent hypocrisy—that is, establishing one set of rules for ourselves and a different set of rules for others. You cannot expect others to treat you with dignity if you do not treat them with dignity. If you allow yourself to break a promise, then you must permit others to do so as well.[16]

### The Second Formulation

Kant's *second formulation* of the categorical imperative is that we should treat others as having intrinsic value, as ends in themselves and not merely as means to our ends. According to Kant, *all* people have a basic right as rational human beings to be treated with respect. They deserve respect because they are rational and capable of making intelligent choices. The obligation to treat others as ends and not merely as means is unconditional; however, with the term *not merely*, Kant admits the pragmatic inevitability that to some extent we all sometimes treat and are treated by others as mere means to the achievement of ends. From a deontological perspective, we may be treated as a means to an end only if we consent to this treatment and retain the right to decide when, to what extent, and in exchange for what. In the medical products case in Chapter 1, that is the point of giving the patient as much information as possible about her treatment options and allowing her to make the final choice.

Underlying Kant's second formulation of the categorical imperative is the idea that our ability to reason and make decisions for ourselves gives us our potential

for morality and makes us worthy of respect. We have the ability to give reasons for what we do; to act against instinct; to not be governed by pleasure and pain, as Bentham put it; and to act based on the reasons we give. For Kant, doing what we are *inclined* to do is not moral action. If you do what is right not because of reason but rather out of habit, based on impulse or mere intuition, or because you will receive a reward or avoid a punishment, you do not deserve esteem for being ethical. The emotions of sympathy, empathy, caring, and love are not relevant according to Kant's reckoning, even when they lead us in the direction of positive behavior. Rather, for Kant, morality resides in the mind's capacity to control and prevail over our sentiments and emotions. The mind should discipline the body, according to Kant. For him, an action is moral only when it is based on reasoning that enables you to act against your inclinations. The essence of our freedom is that we are not governed by pain and pleasure, and we are deserving of respect because of this capacity.

Kant lived and wrote at the time of the American and the French revolutions, and his ideas are in large measure in accord with some of the main Enlightenment ideas of this period. For

The French Revolution (like the American one) was fought for principles similar to those espoused by Immanuel Kant.

instance, the U.S. Declaration of Independence holds "these truths to be self-evident . . . that all men are created equal . . . they are endowed by their Creator with certain alienable rights . . . among these are life, liberty, and the pursuit of happiness." (Unfortunately, this did not include Black people, most of whom were enslaved in the U.S. at the time, or women.) The leaders of the French Revolution similarly proclaimed human beings to have natural rights to "liberty, property, security, and resistance to oppression." Like Kant, the leaders of the American and French revolutions believed that individuals in addition have the rights to free consent, privacy, freedom of conscience, and freedom of speech, and of due process provided they do not injure others. In many democracies today, in theory if not always in practice, these rights are accorded to all individuals regardless of religion, race, national origin, ethnicity, or sexual orientation.

### The Third Formulation

Kant's *third formulation* of the categorical imperative follows from the first two. It states that we must decide for ourselves on how to take actions that are in accordance with universal principles (the first formulation) and respect the inherent dignity of others (the second formulation). Roughly, this means that although the world in which we live does not necessarily conform to our ideals, we could bring the world closer to the desired condition if we demand the highest conduct of ourselves and live our lives as examples to others. When doing business among unethical individuals or in societies where fraud and dishonesty are rampant, it is the *duty* of companies not to fall to the level of the lowest common denominator but instead by example try to uplift the standards of everyone. In many well-known and successful companies, this principle has seen some application as companies try to treat employees, customers, suppliers, shareholders, and other stakeholders with respect. Kant did not care about the payoffs to such behavior, yet the payoffs for companies can come in many ways, in the form of a better reputation, the ability to attract talented and motivated workers, and the ability to thrive financially.[17] We discuss this point further in Chapter 7.

Kant was an idealistic thinker—he believed in how the world *should be*, not necessarily how the world actually is. Along with other Enlightenment thinkers, he proposed a series of ideals toward which we should aspire. Because they may be under threat or are not practiced universally, we should be especially diligent in our efforts to realize them. It is our *duty* to try to make them real. In business, actualizing these values means not using the excuse that "everybody does it" and "everybody is corrupt" and therefore "I have no choice"; rather, one must attempt to live up to a higher standard, to aim to be a model for the behavior of others. Set an example of moving forward toward a more moral world.

## Criticisms of Deontology

One major criticism of deontological ethics is that it actually allows decision-makers to take actions that make the world worse off than other choices would have. Because deontological approaches to ethics can involve the establishment of basic "moral minimums"[18]—lowest common denominator standards that must be followed always, such as not committing violence against others, not violating basic human rights, and dealing with others honestly and fairly—paradoxically, they permit actors to choose alternatives that meet this low bar but at the same time are only second- or third-best options from a consequentialist perspective.[19] Imagine a manager running a factory that both provides poor working conditions and creates a lot of water

FIGURE 2.2

A criticism of deontology is that the "road to hell is paved with good intentions" (i.e., good intentions may lead to bad consequences).

pollution. Whereas a utilitarian perspective would require the manager to consider many alternatives, including ones that would vastly improve working conditions and minimize pollution, the deontological approach might tolerate the manager meeting minimum labor and environmental standards and not considering options that could lead to improvements. We discuss moral minimums again in Chapter 7.

A second, and related, problem is that because of the focus on motives, deontological approaches to ethical decision-making can lead to actions with negative and even catastrophic outcomes (Figure 2.2). A well-known hypothetical example illustrates this problem. Imagine you were a Christian living in Germany during World War II and were hiding a Jewish family in a secret compartment in your home. Imagine now that Nazi officers came to your door and asked whether there were any Jews in your house. For almost all people, the ethical response would be to lie, because the consequences of telling the truth would be so terrible (the almost certain deaths of the Jewish family). According to Kant, however, you should follow the universal obligation to not lie. Kant saw lying and deception of any kind as *always* wrong because they violate the right to dignity and respect of other rational human beings, as well as your own dignity and respect. In short, following seemingly universal principles without regard to consequences may result in awful consequences. The rigid application of Kant's morality is clearly unacceptable.

A third problem deontological approaches face is that conflicts can arise among one's duties. Although Kant claimed that "a conflict of duties is inconceivable,"[20] this obviously is not always the case. The example of Nazi Germany above illustrates this problem as well, in that one feels torn between the duty to be honest and the duty to respect the dignity of the Jewish family members. As a company, how do you choose among duties to different stakeholder groups if respecting one hurts another? If your respect for shareholders overshadows your respect for workers, you will feel no compunction about making massive layoffs to preserve shareholder returns. In formulating the principles you apply to an ethical dilemma, as Step 5 of the weight-of-reasons framework, you must make choices about which set of duties you consider most important. We return to this topic in Chapter 7.

Finally, a criticism of Kantian ethics is that living up to absolute Kantian ideals can have negative consequences. In other words, perhaps under certain circumstances, the ends do justify the means—even when the means do not respect the dignity of all. Machiavelli first raised the possibility that to achieve great ends like establishing the Florentine Republic, it was justified for a leader to deceive and manipulate people. The modern political philosopher Michael Walzer[21] takes up the concept of "dirty hands" from Machiavelli and applies it to the justness of modern wars. He tries to make very careful distinctions about when a war is morally right, based on a proportionality between the ends a country is trying to achieve and the means it is willing to use. He delves into the problem of collateral damage, for instance. Usually, he maintains, no ends justify collateral damage, or the harming of innocent civilians in warfare. He argues that every action must be taken to protect innocent civilians, even if it endangers a nation's soldiers or civilian population. Yet to some degree, there may be no choice but to inflict harm in warfare on innocent civilians if there is no other way for a nation to protect its citizens from aggression. According to Walzer, if a country is attacked and its existence is in jeopardy, it does have the right to defend itself, especially when the enemy has no compunction about indiscriminately hurting the country's citizens.

It is a tall order to use Kant's absolutist's ideals to identify duties that apply without exception across all of time, in all places, and in all situations. The monstrous behavior of killing an innocent person may be justified under very extreme conditions of duress, such as when a thousand lives can be saved by the taking of one. Scholars of moral imagination argue that the Kantian approach of applying simple moral rules to ethical decision-making applies only to simple circumstances and that complex, ethical decision-making demands customized, contextual, imaginative decision-making.[22] In Chapter 5, we further discuss imaginative ethical decision-making.

While living up to Kantian ideals may be difficult, the difficulty is no excuse for the wrong means that businesses use to accomplish goals of little value that can be achieved without resorting to these means. Every day, we are inundated with advertising that intentionally deceives. Breyer's ice cream, for instance, declares on its package that it is "fat free." While this technically might be correct, it can be seen as deceptive because it suggests that we can consume a half-gallon container of ice cream without consequences. This sort of abuse of the truth is not as unethical as the outright lying that takes place in many marketing campaigns. A humor website recently demonstrated this on its YouTube channel, "The 6 Most Blatant Lies Companies Based Entire Ads On." It shows that Activia Yogurt does *not* improve our power to regulate our digestive systems; one-a-day multivitamins with selenium do *not* prevent prostate cancer, and could actually make it worse for a person who already had this type of cancer; and Five-Hour Energy is no more than concentrated caffeine that yields the same crash that any high dose of caffeine produces when it wears out.[23]  What would Kant think of violation of the categorical imperative in these cases? What are your thoughts?

## Deontology and the Weight-of-Reasons Framework

The weight-of-reasons framework incorporates deontological ethics in Step 5, the application of principles. It is no accident that the framework calls for considering principles after one has first gathered the facts (Step 2 of the framework). One should identify the principles at stake only after becoming familiar with the issue at hand and the situation in which it plays out. In other words, principles should be specific to the case rather than universal and general in nature, such as Kant's imperatives. Whereas Kantian rules prescribe behavior without regard to context, principles are flexible summaries of collective moral insight that direct behavior. They provide the flexibility to imaginatively explore possibilities for constructive action within a given context.[24] In the Pinto case, had the company relied on the weight-of-reasons framework, the principle would have been to not cause unnecessary and correctible harm to customers. This application of principles is different from a universal Kantian rule, which would have required one to *never, ever*, under *any* circumstance inflict damage to customers regardless of the consequences. In the auto industry, this injunction would be impossible to carry out. It would mean ceasing operations. A seller of autos never can be absolutely certain that a vehicle it made or sold could meet these conditions. In sum, use principles that are flexible and relevant to the case-at-hand, rather than general rules in Stage 5 of the weight-of-reasons framework. Using flexible principles rather than rigid rules is a practical way to help you choose a plan of action. In Chapter 5, we further discuss imaginative actions and the role of principles in identifying them.

## Combining Utilitarianism and Deontology

**LO 2.4:** Recognize the contradictions and conflicts between utilitarianism and deontology and move toward reconciling their differences using the weight-of-reasons framework for ethical decision-making.

As discussed, the fundamental difference between utilitarianism and deontology is in the way they treat ends and means. In teleological reasoning, the focus is on *ends*. If the end result yields a surplus of good over bad that is greater than that associated with competing options, then that end result justifies the means. For deontologists, on the other hand, *the means* of our actions, or how we go about achieving our goals, are what matter. People are entitled to be treated as ends in themselves, not merely as means. The means used to pursue a goal cannot transgress a person's basic rights without his or her consent. For deontologists, positive results do not justify denying or infringing on those rights.

Tension often arises between utilitarianism and deontological perspectives. Most people want to do what is right *and* what is good. They want to respect others' rights, keep their promises, obey the law, be fair, and not lie or cheat, and at the same time, they want to achieve goals such as providing the maximum number of people with employment or providing them with the goods and services they need to obtain a healthy and fulfilling life.

Conflicts between utilitarian and deontological perspectives often play out between people and groups representing these perspectives. People with different roles in an organization, for example, tend to view ethical dilemmas from differing points of view (Figure 2.3). Managers are more likely to adopt a teleological ethics emphasizing the "greatest good" for the organization as a whole. Although they may feel discomfort about actions such as job cuts and layoffs, their primary concern is likely to the organization's survival. They tend to frame ethical questions as broad policy issues involving the organization's welfare rather than the welfare of particular individuals. Other people in the organization may stand for a deontological ethics that calls for treating all people with respect. They will frame ethical questions in terms of the welfare of individuals. They care about their friends and colleagues in

FIGURE 2.3

The role we play in an organization can influence whether we take a utilitarian or a deontological approach.

the organization who may be hurt by decisions made at the top and resent when people they know and respect are laid off.

Differences between utilitarian and Kantian thinkers are also found among an organization's stakeholders. For example, the leaders of a company building a large infrastructure project such as a dam or oil pipeline may believe that their project should go forward because it will make society better off and that the inconvenience or harm caused to particular landowners or communities is justified. On the other hand, those landowners and communities may feel that their rights have not been honored. Vladimir Lenin, the Bolshevik leader and founder of the Soviet Union, purportedly declared that to make an exquisite omelet, that is, to create a communist utopia, one has to break a few eggs, that is, kill a great many people.[25] Those who were killed, of course, had a different point of view.

So what should you do when you experience a conflict between deontological and teleological perspectives? One obvious answer is to choose one over the other. Agreeing that the "ends justify the means" means you have chosen utilitarianism over deontology. On the other hand, you can choose deontology over teleology, even though this could mean accepting tragic and even catastrophic results so long as you comply with a universal rule. As noted, Kant took a very rigid approach to ethics and countenanced no deviations from such rules. He famously quipped that "better the whole people should perish" than that they deviate from these rules.[26]

Another approach to reconciling utilitarianism with deontology is to rely on what philosophers refer to as "threshold deontology." According to this approach, one follows deontological rules even if the consequences are negative, up to the point where the consequences reach a certain level that cannot be tolerated. According to the formulation, the means of your actions are more important than the ends, unless and until ignoring the ends becomes problematic.[27] This approach, however, is hard to apply, and in many ways, like all moral maxims, is aspirational in nature.

The cases at the end of this chapter will provide you practice in wrestling with means–ends dilemmas that the conflict between consequentialism and teleology poses. We return to the issue of balancing utilitarianism and deontology in our discussion of virtue ethics.

# LOCKHEED BRIBERY: ANOTHER TELEOLOGICAL BLUNDER?[28]

Like the Ford Pinto case, another classic case in business ethics where deontological principles conflict with teleological ones is the 1970s instance in which U.S. defense contractor Lockheed bribed Japanese government officials to win a large contract for airplanes. The Lockheed bribery scandal provides an example of a company wrestling with the question of whether the ends justify the means. If you were a leader of this company, what would you do?

In the early 1970s, Lockheed was in desperate straits. It had just been bailed out by the federal government, and its existence was at stake. Many jobs would be lost if the company did not obtain a sufficient number of orders for its L-1011 Tristar commercial aircraft. Lockheed had attempted and failed to obtain contracts for the L-1011 from Italy, Germany, and Sweden. A large order was essential to bring unit sales close to the break-even point and to repay the expense of designing and building the aircraft. A contract with the Japanese company All Nippon Airways (ANA) was viewed as essential by Carl Kotchian, Lockheed's president. ANA was considering purchasing either the L-1011 Tristar or the competitor McDonnell Douglass's DC-10. If the ANA order, which meant more than $430 million in revenues, was not forthcoming, it would mean a slowdown in new design projects and layoffs for many Lockheed engineers and production workers.

Kotchian did not go to Japan intending to bribe Japanese officials. Although he was directly responsible for the negotiations for the sale of the planes, he did not speak Japanese and had to rely on advice and representation from executives of a Japanese company that had been retained as an agent for Lockheed. This company represented Lockheed in all deliberations with the prime minister and the prime minister's office, so Kotchian did not have direct contact with the government officials who would make the actual decision. His contact was limited to the technical and functional representatives of Japan's airlines. The negotiations extended over a period of 70 days, during which time Kotchian stayed in a hotel room in downtown Tokyo. He received continual suggestions that the decision would soon be made, except that an unnamed "something" (which he gradually came to realize was a bribe) was not in place. Kotchian had no firm knowledge of whether his competitors had supplied that unnamed "something," but he suspected they had or would be willing to do so.

Lockheed maintained a large workforce in Burbank, California, which Kotchian felt obligated to protect. If Lockheed lost its fourth foreign order in a row, not only would the jobs of these workers in Burbank be in danger but Kotchian's own job would be in jeopardy. Kotchian felt that "something"—a bribe of less than 1% of the face value of the order—was a small price to pay when so much else was at stake. Ultimately, Kotchian authorized Lockheed's payment of $3.8 million in bribes to Japanese officials. These included the Japanese prime minister Kakuei Tanaka and organized crime kingpin Yoshio Kodama.

Business ethicist Mark Pastin[29] has justified Kotchian's decision using a utilitarian perspective. He argued that the positive ends of winning the Japanese contract and preserving Lockheed jobs (and perhaps its very existence) justified the unethical means of bribery. Is this a misuse of utilitarianism? Does it fail even on utilitarian grounds because it does not consider all the costs and benefits? The employees, communities, and other stakeholders of McDonnell Douglas (Lockheed's competitor) must be considered to the same extent as Lockheed's. One must also consider whether Japanese citizens received the best value for their money or instead received a second-best airplane. Also, there is the problem that Lockheed executives miscalculated the actual costs and benefits. Ultimately, the company itself suffered more costs from its choice than any short-term benefits it may have received. Lockheed lost the contract and had to shut down production of the L-1011. The cost–benefit reasoning of the company simply was not very well carried out.

The decision to pay the bribes obviously fails from a deontological perspective. By paying bribes, Lockheed violated the rights of its shareholders and lenders to have their capital spent by legal means, as well as the right of its competitor McDonnell Douglas to fair competition. Even if one accepts that a rule against bribery might sometimes lead to negative consequences and that ethics would be better served by a principle such as "Do what you can to save your employees' jobs," which Pastin used to justify Kotchian's actions, it is unclear that Kotchian even lived up to this principle. A pattern of bribery payments made by Lockheed in the 1950s to 1970s to officials in West Germany, Italy, the Netherlands, and Saudi Arabia (in addition to Japan) suggests that bribery may have been a norm at Lockheed rather than a one-time desperate attempt to save jobs.

What do you think? How would you respond if you were a member of Lockheed's board of directors at the time? Try applying the weight-of-reasons framework to this case.

## Virtue Theory

**LO 2.5:** Discuss the tenets of virtue ethics, understanding how it differs from deontology and utilitarianism.

Virtue theory provides another perspective for considering ethics—and one that provides a means of reconciling deontology with utilitarianism. Virtue ethics is often viewed as the third main approach to business ethics, along with utilitarianism and deontology. Virtue ethicists take the view that ethics is about engaging in conduct that builds our character and wisdom. In the West, virtue theory is traced back to the Ancient Greeks, principally Plato and Aristotle, while in the East, virtue theory often is associated with Confucius. "Virtues" are traits of moral excellence, dispositions and character traits that enable us to develop our potential to become wise. Examples of virtues we should cultivate include honesty, courage, compassion, generosity, fidelity, integrity, fairness, self-control, and prudence.[30]

Plato, Aristotle, and other classical philosophers believed that the highest good is wisdom and that we acquire wisdom through virtuous behavior. They also recognized, however, that virtuous behavior could be taken to extremes and actually lead to unwise and unethical behavior—virtues can become vices. For example, when pushed too far, courage can lead to foolhardy risk taking, and honesty can lead to unnecessarily hurting others' feelings. Therefore, according to Aristotle, to engage in virtuous behavior, a person must act with moderation and find the "golden mean"—the desirable middle ground in between the extremes. One should not, for example, be timid or excessively bold. One should be prudent and have the confidence to take prudent risks but not be foolish. Although virtues are "in the middle," they do not represent mediocrity; rather, virtues such as temperance, harmony, and balance provide a path to the highest good. The Ancient Greeks referred to the wisdom about how to take virtuous and practical action as *phronesis*.[31]

**Golden mean**
According to Aristotle, the desirable point that finds the middle between excess and deficiency of a virtue

Finding the mean between a deficiency and an overabundance of a virtue can be tricky. Aristotle believed that virtuous behavior develops through practice; one becomes habituated in the practice of virtues (just as one becomes habituated in the practice of vices) by repeating them, learning, and improving in their practice over time.[32] Just as the ability to run a marathon develops through training and practice, so too does our ability to act fairly, courageously, compassionately, and wisely. Aristotle compared the application of virtue theory to an archer trying repeatedly to hit the center of a target. The more the archer practices, the better he or she gets at hitting the target. The archer has many misses before coming close to perfection.

The Ancient Greeks stressed that through the consistent practice of acting virtuously our characters become virtuous. Repeat an action enough, and it becomes characteristic of your being. The honest person becomes honest by being honest again and again. The courageous person becomes courageous by acting courageously again and again.

Virtue theory has important lessons for ethical decision-making in business and the application of the weight-of-reasons framework. First, virtue ethics suggests that in taking Step 3 of the framework, identifying courses of action, we must "step up to the plate" and identify courses of action of which we can be proud.

These are actions that challenge us to become better (more virtuous) people. Rather than ruling out a course of action because it would require an act of bravery or a candid conversation that you are not sure you have within you, challenge yourself to become brave and honest by acting bravely and honestly.

Second, virtue ethics' emphasis on self-development through practice suggests that over time you can improve your ability to apply the weight-of-reasons framework and make ethical decisions. As indicated, through repeated practice of the framework, you will "move up the learning curve"—develop mastery of the framework so that identifying ethical problems and taking practical, beneficial actions that are consistent with your principles become second nature. While you may not get it perfectly right the first time, do not despair. Try and try again.

Third, virtue ethics provides a means of identifying actions (Step 6 of the framework) that reconcile the tension between deontology and utilitarianism. It suggests eschewing the extremes and aiming for a middle position that embraces both deontology and utilitarianism but does not push either one of them too far. One seeks a position that is consistent with Kantian principles and also sensitive to consequences. Virtue ethics, then, implies an approach to applying the weight of reasons in which the decision-maker identifies action options in Step 3, applies utilitarianism to assess consequences in Step 4, applies principles from a deontological perspective in Step 5, and then identifies a course of action by applying virtue ethics' concept of the golden mean in Step 6. While virtue ethics does not provide a formula for how to reconcile deontology and utilitarianism, it does suggest that decision-makers get better over time as they try to do so.

## Other Ethical Perspectives

**LO 2.6:** Discuss the role of contract theory and the ethics of care in working through the differences between utilitarianism and deontology.

Teleology, deontology, and virtue ethics are the dominant perspectives in ethical theory, which is why they are built into the weight-of-reasons framework. However, there are other accepted approaches to ethics. We now briefly review some of these theories and touch on their implications for applying the weight-of-reasons framework. We introduce contract theory and then delve into the ethics of care.

### Contract Theory: Justice and Fairness

Like deontology, contract theory is concerned with rights and obligations. What is different about contract theory, however, is that it focuses on the arrangements by which actors agree to these rights and obligations. Contractarians are concerned with making the basic structure of society, for example, its legal and political systems, as fair as possible. Enlightenment philosophers such as Rousseau imagined a time before organized society—a "state of nature"—in which people were born equal in their basic freedoms and rationality, but individually were without the means to secure these rights for themselves. Under these conditions, contractarians argue, people would knowingly and voluntarily enter into a social contract, a set of rules that would preserve the basic freedoms and security of all.[33]

Moral philosopher John Rawls wrote that society would be fairer if rule makers deliberated as if they were behind a "veil of ignorance"—that is, they didn't know their own or anyone else's position in society.

Much of modern contract theory comes from the writings of John Rawls, who was concerned with making the process of determining society's arrangements as fair as possible. Rawls wrote that this process would be fairest if all persons involved deliberated as if behind a "veil of ignorance"—as if each had no knowledge of his or her position in society. Rawls posited that if the rules governing society were established through a process in which individuals knew nothing about their or anyone else's wealth, status, and distinguishing characteristics, talents, and shortcomings, then the arrangements would be fair.[34] Thus, Rawls issued an admonition to those with the privilege and authority to make ethical decisions to be blind to their personal status and position and to try to overcome the prejudices and biases that arise from their place in society. Whether in reality decision-makers make this leap is questionable.

In addition to addressing the *process* of making society's arrangements, Rawls considered the *nature* of these arrangements. He argued that all parties should be granted equal rights to the most extensive basic liberty that would be compatible with a similar liberty for others. Social and economic inequalities were acceptable as long as (a) they could reasonably be expected to be to everyone's advantage and (b) the most favorable positions were open to all. So, for example, according to Rawls, it would be morally acceptable for some members in a society to have high-paying positions of authority as long as society as a whole benefited and they used their advantages to make everyone better off than they would have been otherwise.

Contract theory has strong implications for applying the weight-of-reasons framework and for ethical decision-making generally. Specifically, contract theory suggests that, ideally, the weight-of-reasons approach should *not* be applied by a single decision-maker or a small set of powerful actors, but rather it should involve all relevant parties coming together freely to jointly make practical agreements about how to address the ethical problems they face. In addition, contract theory—in particular the "veil of ignorance" concept—suggests that managers should try not to favor their own narrow interests over others'. Rather than using their wealth and power to benefit themselves, they should follow Elvis Presley's advice to "walk a mile in [others'] shoes"; they should try to imagine how other stakeholders think and feel and what they would like to see done.

### Pay Inequality

Many current ethical issues in the workplace can be analyzed from a Rawlsian perspective. Examples include pay inequality; racial, gender, and other forms of discrimination; and sexual harassment. Here we provide a brief consideration of the issue of pay inequality.

Pay inequality and the concentration of wealth is a global phenomenon. The gap between the top of the wealth pyramid and the bottom is very large. *Forbes Magazine* identified 2,208 billionaires worldwide in 2018; their combined wealth was $9.1 trillion, up 18% since 2017. To be among the wealthiest half of the world's population, a person needed $3,210 in assets in 2015, to be in the top 10% required $668,800, and to be in the top 1% required close to $760,000. The wealthiest 10% owned 87% of the world's assets, the top 1% owned close to 50%, and the bottom half of the population owned less than 1%.

Before adjusting for taxes and income transfers, U.S. income inequality has become the highest in the world among developed countries. The proportion of total U.S. output that the richest 1% of earners obtained more than doubled between 1970 and 2008. In 1928, the top 1% earned 24% of all income; in 1944, these individuals earned 11%. By 2012, the top 1% was earning 23% of the nation's income, about the same as in 1928. Capital's share of income—whether in the form of corporate profits, dividends, rents, or sales of property—has grown after steadily falling since before World War I. Corporate profits have increased, while wages, including those for highly educated people, have not. Since the early 1970s, real wages for most U.S. workers hardly went up, but those for the top 1% of earners increased substantially.[35]

One reason why the wealth of the highest earners has increased dramatically is that companies have granted their executives stock options, or the option to buy future shares at a fixed price. Companies gave top executives options to align the executives' interests with those of shareholders. (We discuss this "principal–agent" relationship in Chapter 7.) One can question, however, whether executives have earned the stock options they have been granted. In 1930, when Babe Ruth was asked why he earned more than President Herbert Hoover, he replied, "Because I had a better year." But can the same be said of chief executive officers (CEOs) of major U.S. corporations? The pay packages of corporate executives have not been closely tied to the performance of their firms. Some executives have earned large salaries and bonuses even though their companies' financial performance was poor.[36]

A Rawlsian perspective requires us to ask whether vast incomes and wealth inequality are just and fair. More precisely, it requires us to ask not only whether inequality is unjust but also whether the structural arrangements that produce inequality are just. Do the many laws influencing the production and distribution of wealth provide everyone with the same opportunities? Have they been established and are they implemented through fair processes in which those involved act as if behind a veil of ignorance that makes them as concerned for the opportunities and welfare of others as they are for their own?

To the extent that the structures in place favor particular individuals, groups, classes, or nations, a contractarian would conclude that these structures are unjust. From a corporate perspective, the implications are that companies should lobby for laws creating greater income equality and more opportunity for people to advance in society.

We note that libertarian philosophers take a very different view of inequality. Whereas the highest good for Rawls is justice, for philosophers such as Robert Nozick,

The ethics of care views ethics in terms of building relationships and caring for others.

it is liberty. These philosophers stress the rights of people to acquire property and forge their own destinies without interference. Nozick maintains that a person who legitimately obtains wealth is entitled to it regardless of how it affects equality or inequality. Nozick also stressed the importance of having a fair system where talent and merit could rise to the top. While Rawls would defend the right of individuals to legally acquire and maintain property, he would also ask whether the system of laws in which these individuals operate is impartial.[37]

## The Ethics of Care

**Ethics of care**
An approach to ethical reasoning that emphasizes caring for those with whom we have interpersonal relationships

The **ethics of care** provides another take on what it means to be ethical, although some philosophers suggest that it is a subset of virtue ethics. Care ethics takes a feminist perspective, with a foundation in the idea that ethical decision-making should be thought of as involving not only rational, objective calculation and rule application but also subjective, emotional judgments that give priority to caring for others. Whereas a Kantian would say that one should treat all others equally based on the same objective rules and a utilitarian would say that one should give all individuals equal weight when calculating benefits and harms, care ethicists take the view that one need not be so objective. Rather, they start from the premise that human beings are fundamentally a social species who live and find meaning in their lives in relationships, and that living an ethical life means nurturing those relationships. For care ethicists, putting your loved ones first is not a selfish thing to do but, rather, the *right* thing to do.

The ethics of care is typically traced back to psychologist Carol Gilligan and her 1982 book *In a Different Voice*.[38] Gilligan was a student of the Harvard educational psychologist Lawrence Kohlberg, who established a well-known model of moral development.[39] According to this model, moral development occurs though a process in which the individual progressively becomes more autonomous. This means being willing to make decisions on grounds other than avoiding punishment or receiving rewards, breaking free of the rules and norms of society, developing one's own worldview and principles about what is just and fair, and coming to base actions on impartial reasoning using those principles. Gilligan noticed that Kohlberg's model was developed based on a study of males only, and she was dismayed that when Kohlberg's scale was administered, women as a whole scored lower than men. Gilligan began to question and critique Kohlberg's model. She concluded that Kohlberg's work failed to capture women's experience of morality, which emphasizes caring for others and nurturing relationships rather than abstract rule application. Gilligan developed her own model of human moral development, in which one first is concerned about oneself, then cares most about others, and, finally, comes to see the world in terms of relationships between self and others.

On the surface, the weight-of-reasons framework is just the sort of abstract approach to ethical decision-making that Gilligan has criticized. Such a critique does not mean the framework is wrong, however, for the choice between objective calculation and concern for relationships is not an either/or one. Clearly, ethical decisions should involve both reasoning and care. Concern for relationships may enter into the weight-of-reasons framework at numerous points. Most fundamentally, it gives decision-makers permission to pay attention to their feelings and resist the idea that business decisions should be made solely based on bottom-line concerns. The ethics of care even suggests that in assessing the consequences of actions (Step 4 of the weight of reasons) and identifying core principles (Step 5), decision-makers are justified in giving priority to those whom they care for the most.

The ethics of care argues for a relational approach to ethical decision-making. It makes the point that decision-makers look at their businesses through the lens of stakeholder relationships where some stakeholders matter more than others because of the personal ties that the decision-makers have with these stakeholders and not just through a transactional lens. They work with those stakeholders and are likely to draw on them when they apply the weight-of-reasons framework. Applying the weight of reasons in this sense can be a relationship-building exercise.

## SUMMARY AND CONCLUSION

This chapter has presented key features of the major approaches to ethical reasoning found in Western philosophy. These are the utilitarian (teleological, consequentialist), deontological (Kantian, rights based), and virtue (character building) approaches. They are built into the weight-of-reasons framework as Steps 4, 5, and 6, respectively. Each of these approaches has its strengths and limitations. This chapter mainly has been concerned with the strengths and limitations of the utilitarian and deontological approaches, as well as of virtue theory as a means of reconciling the tensions between these approaches.

*Utilitarian* perspectives focus on the consequences of our actions and require us to think about the consequences not just for ourselves but for all relevant parties. They require us to take actions that would provide a surplus of good over bad, benefit over harm. One practical problem with teleological approaches is that they can be subjectively applied, so that we reach the conclusions we want to reach, counting

some benefits and costs but not others and including some stakeholders while ignoring others. Another problem with teleological approaches is that they permit us to commit unspeakable atrocities against particular individuals as long as those actions provide more than offsetting benefits to others. Yet another problem is that we can never know all the consequences of our actions, in the short and long terms. In applying Step 4 of the weight-of-reasons framework, try to do the best you can to account for all stakeholders and consequences, but also accept that given time and resource constraints, you are not likely to be able to account for everything the first time. In fact, doing a perfectly thorough and complete accounting is impossible. In addressing ongoing or recurring ethical problems, you should try to progressively improve your assessment of consequences.

*Deontological* approaches take a perspective that is conceptually opposite to that of teleological approaches. They focus on our intentions and ask us to live our lives according to universal ethical rules respecting the rights and dignity of all, without regard to consequences. Of course, this approach too is problematic; one has to wonder whether an action that complies with ethical rules but has devastatingly negative consequences is actually ethical. To address this problem when applying Step 5 of the weight-of-reasons framework, rather than applying abstract and general ethical rules that can be too broad and rather rigid, you should rely on ethical principles relevant to the dilemma you are confronting. Principles, rather than rules, provide the flexibility to devise practical solutions that address the complexities and uncertainties of the situations you confront.

The tension between utilitarianism and deontology, means and ends, is constantly encountered in business and, indeed, throughout life. There is no simple way to address it. In this chapter we noted that one way to do so is to combine the two approaches by taking a threshold approach. Taking this approach, one acts according to rights-based principles even if there are negative consequences up to the point where the negative consequences become unacceptably high. The weight of reasons incorporates an approach to calculating the consequences of alternative courses of action and then ruling out those choices that have positive utility but are inconsistent with your principles. An equally appropriate way to proceed would be, in Step 3 of the framework, to identify only courses of action that do not violate the basic decency of all others and then choose the course of action that is expected to produce the most positive consequences. Ultimately, what is most important is that you surface the tensions between utilitarian and deontological approaches and, where circumstances permit, develop deeper understandings over time of these tensions and how to address them. We pick up this theme in Chapter 5.

*Virtue ethics*, which is often seen as the third major approach to philosophical ethics, provides another means of addressing the tension between deontology and utilitarianism. It emphasizes the importance of character-building in ethical decision-making.

Virtue ethics suggests that you hold yourself to high standards as you consider the courses of actions you might take. You become a better ethical decision-maker—and a better person—by making frameworks such as the weight-of-reasons approach a habit. Cultivating virtues so they become intuitive to and a part of your character will enable you to make solid ethical decisions even when you do not have the time to fully apply the weight-of-reasons framework. Full application still is necessary in unfamiliar situations. Virtue ethics plays an important role in Step 6 of the framework because it helps one to navigate a course of action that accounts for both consequences (utilitarianism, Step 4) and principles (deontology, Step 5).

Two other approaches to ethical reasoning reviewed in this chapter provide further insights into applying the weight-of-reasons framework. *Contract theory* is primarily concerned with the processes by which rights are decided and allocated within a society. According to the contractarian perspective of Rawls, it is right for an action to benefit some more than others so long as all benefit and the decision process does not favor some over others. Rawls wants us to ask ourselves whether we would think that the arrangements governing society were fair if we were operating behind a veil of ignorance and had no biases, that we were neutral and objective observers. The main implication of contract theory is that we should work with stakeholders in applying the weight-of-reasons framework. We should set up fair processes which involve them.

*The ethics of care* also has implications for applying the weight-of-reasons framework. It forces us to reconsider one of the major premises of this chapter, which is that reasoning based on established ethical frameworks can lead to improved ethical decision-making. For most of this chapter, we have implicitly invoked Immanuel Kant, who insisted on the centrality of reason to ethics. His conception of ethics was based on the idea of reason controlling and dominating the passions. Without the governance of reason, Kant argued, there can be no ethics. The ethics of care leads us to a different conclusion, in which emotions are integrated into reasoning about ethics. It holds that emotions, such as our feelings for those we care about, should come into play when we consider options, assess consequences, and apply principles. It even suggests that feelings may enable us to surface ethical problems that pure reason would not surface.

These conclusions bring us back to the important theme from Chapter 1 that ethical decision-making often starts with but should not be driven by intuitions alone. While we embrace the ethics of care's insistence on the validity of emotions and its concern for building and deepening relationships, we also suggest that emotions by themselves do not constitute a complete approach to ethics. Trusting our intuitions is a good starting point for making ethical decisions under some circumstances, but doing so does not always lead to ethical choices. In the next chapter we further explore the relationship between ethics and emotions in ethical decision-making.

## KEY TERMS AND CONCEPTS

Complexity theory  37
Consequentialism  34
Contract theory (or social
  contract theory)  34
Deontology  33

Ethical egoism  36
Ethics of care  54
Extrinsic goods  35
Golden mean  50
Intrinsic goods  35

Teleology  34
Utilitarianism  33
Utility  36
Virtue theory  34

## CASE APPLICATIONS

The following short cases provide you with the opportunity to apply the weight-of-reasons framework to address difficult means–ends dilemmas. First, define the issue, and then identify the relevant facts and some preliminary options (Steps 1–3 of the framework). Then use utilitarianism to analyze the consequences (Step 4), apply deontological principles (Step 5), and identify the tension between ends and means. In Steps 6 and 7, decide what you should do in the short term to address the presenting problem and in the long term to get at the root causes

of that problem. Draw on virtue ethics to identify a course of action that considers both ends and means and also helps you develop a more virtuous character.

### Case 2.1: A Tight Schedule

A war is raging, and your job is to deliver battlefield trucks and fighter jet parts to the military on a tight schedule. The government had been extremely dissatisfied with late delivery by a prior supplier and has chosen to work with your company chiefly because it promised to deliver the goods on time.

The specifications provided by the government require work from a certified welder. Unfortunately, your welders are unavailable; one is on vacation, and the other, who has a history of unexplained absences, called in sick. You are in luck, however, because an apprentice welder is available. He has worked for your company for a number of years, and you believe his work is excellent. It is superior to the work of the certified welders; you trust him completely. You allow him to weld key components without certified welder supervision, and though you are not a certified welder yourself, you check to see if the job is done right. X-ray inspections suggest perfect work.

Government rules specify that you perform 100 hours of inspection time. As closing time approaches, more than 90 of the required 100 inspection hours are completed. The components have to be shipped to the next company in the supply chain by the end of the day to avoid production bottlenecks. You believe the 100-hour inspection requirement is arbitrary and 90 hours plus is just as good. The driver in your carpool is ready to leave. You start to sign the certification papers, apply the inspection sticker, and call shipping to come pick up the welded components. You look forward to the bonus you will get for meeting the deadline. But you start to have second thoughts. Maybe you should call the manufacturer that is to receive the shipment of the parts or maybe your supervisor, or maybe the government should be informed. If you cannot get through to any of these people, should you just send the shipment anyhow? Should you contact them tomorrow? If you don't contact them now, would it better not to contact them at all?

## Case 2.2: Pegasus's Global Expansion

With a focus on innovation, Pegasus is a company committed to "technology leadership in the new millennium." Its systems and products are selling well in markets throughout the world. The CEO wants the company to succeed, to maximize shareholder value, and to keep her job; and she wants to be a model of ethical leadership. She has made an effort to build a corporate culture characterized not only by aggressive R&D (research and development) and growth but also by integrity, honesty, teamwork, and respect for the individual. The company enjoys an excellent reputation among its customers and suppliers, employee morale is high, and ethics is a very high priority.

Pegasus is eager to grow its global business. At a strategy session, the CEO and the division managers explore the potential for further expansion globally. It is noted that China is likely to continue to develop a huge market for the firm's products but a significant "payoff" is usually required to get this business. The CEO says, "A lot of companies do business with China. How do they get around the problem?" A division manager says, "Most companies contract with agents. What the agents do is their own business. The CEOs sign disclosure statements that no bribery has taken place." The CEO says, "Isn't that paying someone else to do something unethical? I'm not comfortable with it. What if we held back in our efforts to expand in China?" Another division manager responds, "The country represents millions of dollars of potential sales. When you consider what we have to gain, what do we have to lose if our local contractors make payoffs every now and then?"

The CEO next turns to her division managers and asks, "Can you tell me what you found during your recent visits to our foreign affiliates?" She hears three reports:

1. One manager says, "In Lima, Peru, we reviewed financial records and discovered that the commission expenses for the branch were unusually high. We pay our salespeople commissions for the sales they make. Some companies pay unusually high sales commissions to disguise the fact that the sales personnel pay kickbacks for contracts.

When we confronted the Lima district manager and questioned him about the high commissions, he responded, 'We've got a job to do. If the company wants results, we've got to get things moving any way we can.'"

2. Another manager says, "In Stockholm, Sweden, we noted a number of college-age student employees who seemed to have little work to do. We questioned the district manager, who responded, 'Sure, Magnus is the son of a telecommunications regulator. Caryl is the daughter of a judge who handles regulatory appeals in utilities. Andre is a nephew of the head of the governing party. They're bright kids, and the contacts don't hurt us. In Scandinavia, this is a part of doing business.'"

3. A third manager says, "In Mumbai, India, we noted that many payments had been made to the government and government officials. When we voiced this concern, the district manager responded, 'I can explain every payment. On this one, we needed the utilities [water and electricity] for our offices turned on. We could have waited our turn and had no services for 90 days, or we could pay to get moved to the top of the list and have our utilities turned on within 48 hours. On the check for licensing, again, we could have waited six months to get licensed or pay to expedite it and be licensed.'"

The CEO then turns to the company's compliance officer: "Are these practices legal?" He responds, "The United States and European Union permit 'facilitation' or 'grease' payments, but they prohibit outright bribes. Facilitation opens doors or expedites processes; the aim is not to influence outcomes. For violating these laws, IBM and Siemens were recently held accountable in big scandals that made the headlines in the *Financial Times*."

The CEO then turns to you and asks, "What should we do?" How do you respond?

### Case 2.3: Garment Company's Labor Practices

You are on the management team of a rapidly growing apparel company that had $780 million in sales last year and is projecting an additional $150 million in sales this year. You have been invited to a meeting of the CEO and other members of the top management team to discuss the company's employment practices. The company has succeeded by targeting a niche market that pays more for fashionable styles, making speed and flexibility of operations more important than price. The company also is unique in its employee policies. Poor working conditions are common at many apparel factories, and the industry is besieged by public criticism of how labor is treated. Yet a fundamental tenet of the company has been the belief that apparel manufacturing should be profitable without exploiting workers. Management has worked hard since the company's inception to treat its employees as well as possible. The company is respected within the industry for its labor practices.

At the meeting to which you have been invited, there are a number of items on the agenda.

- *Agenda Item 1—Seasonal employment:* This summer, the company was not able to keep pace with the orders; thus, it added a second shift and hired 750 new employees, bringing the total number of its employees to 3,500. During the summer months, all the employees worked full-time (8-hour shifts, five days per week), and often overtime, to meet the sales needs and replenish the dwindling inventories. But the company's inventories are growing too large, and it must determine how to reduce production over the next 20 weeks to only two thirds of full capacity. Typical industry practice would be to lay off excess workers under such circumstances, with no severance pay or other assistance and no promise of being rehired. However, if the garment company made such a move, it would violate its code of conduct, which calls on it to treat its employees as "valued partners." Also, it has invested several thousand dollars in training each employee, and if workers are laid off, there is no guarantee it can rehire the same people when they will be needed again in spring.

- *Agenda Item 2—Expanding production abroad:* Should the company start to produce more of its goods abroad? Until now the company has made almost all of its apparel in the United States. Because it sells fashionable items, price has not been the primary concern. However, it is unsure how long it can stick to this policy. Given the company's values, this presents a problem. The media has been filled with stories about other garment companies exploiting child labor. A practice that is common in other countries where this company may go is that children aged 10 to 14 years work in filthy factories 50 or more hours per week. Their wages help their families to survive. School in these countries is viewed as a luxury, and a child attends only until he or she is able to work in one of the country's many factories. Competitors like Levi Strauss, The Gap, Esprit, and Leslie Fay have received considerable negative publicity for contracting out their production to factories in such countries. They have lost sales because of the revelations about their child labor practices.

When asked at the meeting, what do you recommend the garment company should do to address these issues?

## Case 2.4: Telecommunication Company's Lost Business

ACI is a leading supplier of components for the telecommunications industry. It sells components to companies like Alcatel, Northern Telecom, and Ericsson, who put the components into the equipment they make. ACI's annual sales are around $1.5 billion. It has more than 2,500 U.S. employees as well as another 3,000 employees about evenly divided between Mexico, Taiwan, and Ireland. All of these hourly employees are represented by an international union. The Mexican operations were launched to take advantage of the low labor costs. Those in Taiwan make use of that country's very skilled laborers. The Ireland plants give the company access to the European market and relief from the onerous European tariffs.

One day, ACI's CEO gets a phone call from Alcatel that it is canceling all orders. Apparently, Alcatel's customers are slowing their acquisition of new equipment, and Alcatel is taking the opportunity to shift all of its business to a French company that is an ACI competitor. This French firm, the caller from Alcatel says, has a reputation for higher product quality than ACI. The CEO decides he can avoid large-scale layoffs only by implementing a 4-day work week, which spreads the pain evenly among his global workforce. He mentions this to the head of the U.S. union, who tells him, "No one likes to lose part of their paycheck, but if your plan treats management the same as blue-collar workers, we might support it."

The CEO then hears additional bad news. He obtains a report from a consulting group that says the telecommunications industry is in for "a long and deep slump." The CEO now believes Alcatel's canceled orders are likely to be only the beginning of many more canceled orders that will affect ACI's businesses worldwide. The canceled orders are likely to extend to all of ACI's major customers. Now, the CEO believes his idea of a 4-day work week will not be sufficient. There will have to be major layoffs. But how should they be carried out? In what order should the layoffs be announced? Who should be the first to go, and why? From the union leader, the CEO receives an e-mail with the following article: "Telecomponents, Inc. Keeps Its Jobs in the U.S. Despite a Major Industry Meltdown: In a Struggling Domestic Economy This Manufacturer Shines as a Bright Light." The CEO sends out an e-mail to the Leadership Council prior to a meeting.

How should ACI handle the layoffs, if in fact they are necessary?

- If major layoffs cannot be avoided, which parts of the organization should be hit the hardest?

- Who should be protected? For example, should we lay off foreign or domestic workers first? Should we just lay off blue-collar workers and not management?

- Should we rely on our performance appraisal system to decide which employees to let go? If

we do this, to what extent should seniority be considered?

- How should we communicate what we are about to do? To our workers? To the union? To the community? To the shareholders? To customers and suppliers?

- What should we do if the union turns against us? How do we avoid a major confrontation with the union?

- And what about the media? Might there not be an adverse reaction in the media if we have large-scale layoffs? And will not the media reaction snowball and we will lose considerable good will?

At the meeting, the CEO turns to your team and asks for your advice. How do you respond?

# NOTES

1.  See pp. 292–293, in Dewey, J. (1983). *The middle works, 1899–1924* (Vol. 5). Carbondale: Southern Illinois University Press.
2.  Ibid.
3.  Ibid.
4.  Aristotle. (2014). *The Nichomachean ethics* (C. D. C. Reeve, Trans.). Indianapolis, IN: Hackett. (Original work published 350 BCE)
5.  Bentham, J. (1988). *The principles of morals and legislation.* New York, NY: Prometheus Books. (Original work published 1789)
6.  See p. 39, in Johnson, O. A. (2003). *Ethics: Selections from classic and contemporary writers.* New York, NY: Holt, Rinehart, & Winston.
7.  Bentham, J. (1988). *The principles of morals and legislation.* New York, NY: Prometheus Books. (Original work published 1789). See also Singer, P. (1993). *Practical ethics* (2nd ed.). Cambridge, UK: Cambridge University Press. (Original work published 1979)

8.  See p. 39, in Johnson (2003).
9.  Mill, J. S. (2014). *Utilitarianism.* Cambridge, UK: Cambridge University Press. (Original work published 1861)
10. Ibid.
11. Moore, G. E. (2004). *Principia ethica* [Principles of ethics]. Mineola, NY: Dover. (Original work published 1903)
12. James, W. (1891). The moral philosopher and the moral life. *The International Journal of Ethics, 1*(3), 330–354.
13. See pp. 294–306, in Marcus, A. A., & Kaiser, S. (2006). *Managing beyond compliance: The ethical and legal dimensions of corporate responsibility.* Northbrook, IL: Northcoast.
14. See p. 36, in Kant, I. (2012). *Groundwork of the metaphysics of morals* (2nd ed.; M. Gregor & J. Timmermann, Trans.). Cambridge, UK: Cambridge University Press. (Original work published 1780)
15. Ibid.

16. Some philosophers object to this interpretation of Kant's first categorical imperative. They note that the question "How would things turn out if everyone did it?" reflects a consequentialist rather than a deontological perspective on ethics. We agree with this objection but also feel that the question has some commonsense value in understanding deontology.

17. Peters, T., & Waterman, R. H., Jr. (2004). *In search of excellence*. New York, NY: HarperCollins. (Original work published 1982)

18. Werhane, P. H. (1999). *Moral imagination in management decision-making* (The Ruffin Series in Business Ethics). Oxford, UK: Oxford University Press.

19. *Stanford encyclopedia of philosophy*. (n.d.). Deontology. Retrieved from https://plato.stanford.edu/entries/ethics-deontological/

20. Kant, I. (1999). *The metaphysical elements of justice*: Part I of the *metaphysics of morals* (J. Ladd, Trans., 2nd ed.). Indianapolis, IN: Hackett. (Original work published 1797)

21. Walzer, M. (2015). *Just and unjust wars: A moral argument with historical illustrations*. New York, NY: Basic Books.

22. Johnson, M. (1993). *Moral imagination: Implications of cognitive science for ethics*. Chicago, IL: University of Chicago Press; Werhane, P. H. (1999). *Moral imagination in management decision-making* (The Ruffin Series in Business Ethics). Oxford, UK: Oxford University Press

23. Cracked. (2015, December 10). *The 6 Most Blatant Lies Companies Based Entire Ads On*. Retrieved from https://www.youtube.com/watch?v=BFVOXgZYuSY.

24. See p. 105, in Johnson, M. (1993).

25. This saying is variously attributed to Lenin, Napoleon, Robespierre, Robert Louis Stevenson, and others.

26. See p. 100, in Kant (2012).

27. Moore, M. (1997). *Placing blame: A general theory of the criminal law*. Oxford, UK: Oxford University Press.

28. See pp. 18–19, in Marcus and Kaiser (2006).

29. Pastin, M. (1986). *The hard problems of management: Gaining the ethics edge*. San Francisco, CA: Jossey-Bass.

30. Plato. (2012). *The republic* (C. Rowe, Trans.). London, UK: Penguin Books. (Original work published 381 BCE); Aristotle (350 BCE/2014).

31. Aristotle (350 BCE/2014).

32. The authors are keen to note that this implies that the young should venerate the elderly because they presumably have more experience.

33. Rousseau, J.-J. (2014). *On the social contract: Or principles of political right* (I. Johnston, Trans.). Arlington, VA: Richer Resources. (Original work published 1762)

34. Rawls, J. (1971). *A theory of justice*. Cambridge, MA: Harvard University Press.

35. Piketty, T. (2015). About capital in the twenty-first century. *American Economic Review, 105*(5), 48–53.

36. Cooper, M. J., Gulen, H., & Rau, P. R. (2010). *Performance for pay? The relation between CEO incentive compensation and future stock price performance*, https://papers.ssrn.com/sol3/papers.cfm?abstract_id=1572085

37. Nozick, R. (1974). *Anarchy, state, and utopia*. New York, NY: Basic Books.

38. Gilligan, C. (1982). *In a different voice: Psychological theory and women's development*. Cambridge, MA: Harvard University Press.

39. Kohlberg, L. (1931). *The philosophy of moral development: Moral stages and the idea of justice*. San Francisco, CA: Harper & Row.

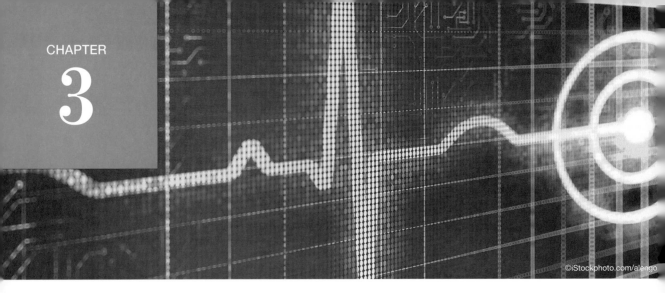
©iStockphoto.com/alengo

# Thinking, Fast and Slow
## ETHICAL INTUITIONS AND REASONING

## Learning Objectives

On completion of this chapter, the reader should be able to do the following:

LO 3.1:  Understand the relationship between intuition and reason by distinguishing between fast and slow thinking.

LO 3.2:  Identify the complexities of self-interest.

LO 3.3:  Explain the cognitive limitations and biases that prevent human beings from making rational decisions.

LO 3.4:  Recognize the role intuitions play in ethical decision-making.

LO 3.5:  Apply the weight-of-reasons framework to check the role that after-the-fact rationalization plays in ethical choices.

*We humans . . . are selfish primates who long to be of something larger and nobler than ourselves. We are 90 percent chimp and 10 percent bee.*

**—Jonathan Haidt,**
*The Righteous Mind* (2012, p. 255)

# Introduction

**LO 3.1:** Understand the relationship between intuition and reason by distinguishing between fast and slow thinking.

The previous chapter presented recognized approaches to thinking about ethics, focusing on deontology and utilitarianism and showing how they are built into the weight-of-reasons approach, Steps 4 and 5 in particular. Yet, as discussed in Chapter 1, some modern-day thinkers doubt whether reason really governs ethical choices. They point to an intuitive approach to ethical decision-making in which people instinctively act based on what they sense to be right and wrong or good and bad and use logic only to justify what their innate sentiments tell them to do. These thinkers maintain that people find it difficult to formulate and articulate logical arguments to defend their ethical choices. People generally do not impartially weigh the evidence and apply rules of logic when they make ethical choices; rather, logic stays in the background, and to the extent that people rely on it, it serves as an after-the-fact justification for choices already made.

This chapter addresses this challenge to the primacy of logic in ethical decision-making by considering the relationship between intuition and reason. The rapid, intuitive approach to making ethical choices is *fast thinking*, while the use of logic is *slow thinking*. We identify the traps associated with fast thinking and argue that slow thinking, of which applying the weight of reasons is an example, need not be subordinate to nor a rationalization of fast thinking. Slow thinking can help us recognize and correct our innate biases and leads us to refine and improve on intuitions so that we make better choices.

# Fast Versus Slow Thinking in Ethics

In the book *Thinking, Fast and Slow*, psychologist and economics Nobel Prize winner Daniel Kahneman distinguishes between System 1 and System 2 thinking (Figure 3.1).[1] Kahneman borrowed the term from brain scientists Keith Stanovich and Richard West.[2] **Fast thinking**, or System 1 thinking, is a rapid, automatic, unconscious, effortless, and intuitive approach. Through it one can know or understand something nearly immediately, without doing any conscious, intentional reasoning. Professors Richard Thaler and Cass Sunstein call System 1 "the automatic system."[3] People rely on fast thinking almost constantly to respond to events in their environment. When we swat a fly, we rely on fast thinking. In fact, there are times when people make very consequential decisions in their lives based on fast thinking, even decisions they should make carefully (e.g., taking a new job, buying a house, making a big capital investment decision for a company, or investing in a stock).

In contrast, **slow thinking**, or System 2 thinking, is an analytical approach, where reason and not intuition dominates. Slow thinking is controlled, deliberate, and effortful. Thaler and Sunstein refer to System 2 as "the reflective system."[4]

**Fast thinking** Thinking that is automatic, effortless, and intuitive (also known as System 1 thinking)

**Slow thinking** Thinking that is controlled, deliberate, effortful, and involving reasoning

**FIGURE 3.1**    Fast Thinking (System 1) and Slow Thinking (System 2).

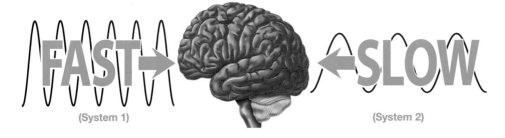

(System 1)                                                    (System 2)

People use slow thinking much less frequently than fast thinking. Applying the weight-of-reasons framework is an example of slow thinking. The reason we engage in fast thinking more than slow thinking is that we have *bounded rationality*, a term we introduced in Chapter 1 that refers to our limited cognitive capacity. We do not have the mental capacity to deliberately make sense of all the information in our environments. In addition to leading us to rely on fast thinking, bounded rationality also leads us to take shortcuts rather than doing full-blown analysis when we engage in slow thinking.

Among psychologists, there is debate about the relationship between fast and slow thinking. **Dual-process theory** in psychology proponents see intuitions and reasoning as separate and operating in entirely different parts of the brain. Each is triggered according to different circumstances; sometimes one will be triggered, sometimes the other, and sometimes both simultaneously.[5] Kahneman and his colleague Shane Frederick view the relationship between System 1 (fast) and System 2 (slow) thinking like this: "System 1 quickly proposes intuitive answers to judgment problems as they arise, and System 2 monitors the quality of these proposals, which it may endorse, correct, or override."[6] As a form of System 2 thinking, the weight–of-reasons framework can be usefully employed as a check on System 1's snap judgments.

Proponents of an **integrated theory** in psychology such as Jonathan Haidt take a different view of the relationship between fast and slow thinking. They support the insights of David Hume, the 18th-century Scottish philosopher who wrote that "reason is . . . the slave of the passions" and can only "serve and obey them."[7] According to Haidt, humans are not designed to heed the voice of reason. Their ethical reflections are simply self-serving rationalizations created after the fact to justify their actions to other people.[8] Haidt's view is that humans are not information processing machines collecting data through their senses and then making objective, rational calculations about how to use this information. Rather, Haidt and his colleagues have found that people are born with innate intuitions of what is ethical and, whether they admit it or not, mostly make rapid-fire System 1 ethical decisions based on these intuitions.[9] The research of Haidt and his colleagues shows that people sometimes consider certain behaviors unethical because the behaviors arouse an innate feeling of disgust, not because they are able to make rigorous arguments that the behaviors have negative consequences or violate other human

**Dual-process theory**
A theory that proposes that intuition and reasoning are separate and occur in different parts of the brain

**Integrated theory**
A theory that sees fast and slow thinking as originating from a single system— fast thinking occurs first and is predominant, and slow thinking justifies the decisions of fast thinking

beings' basic rights. Haidt's viewpoint is that fast and slow thinking are parts of a single system in which people rely on fast thinking to make ethical decisions and slow thinking to defend these decisions.[10]

Haidt's perspective would seem to undermine the value of using the utilitarian and deontological approaches to ethical reasoning central to moral philosophy. If people act based only on what they intuitively feel, what purpose do these approaches serve? Efforts to employ logic in making ethical choices are rather pointless and are just a clever cover for sentiments such as disgust, revulsion, sympathy, and compassion, which actually govern what people do. In their marketing campaigns, companies often exploit this tendency of people to choose based on feelings rather than logic. Toymakers, for instance, manipulate people into loving and taking care of inanimate objects such as dolls and teddy bears. Meanwhile, because of feelings of disgust and revulsion, the same people may stigmatize and dehumanize drug addicts and the homeless, who, unlike dolls and teddy bears, are human beings. Haidt suggests that people make the Dalai Lama into a "rock star" not because of rational arguments but because of the *emotions* the Dalai Lama elicits to sympathize with victims of tragedies and be concerned with the plight of strangers.[11] Dual-process theorists disagree with Haidt's view that feelings always prevail over reason. System 1 is powerful, they acknowledge, but System 2 also plays an important role. They argue that although sometimes people are driven by their moral intuitions to the exclusion of System 2, sometimes System 2 dominates and people choose carefully based on deliberation and reflection.

The main point of this chapter is that both fast and slow thinking—intuitions and reason—are involved in ethical choices in business. Intuitions enable us to carry out information processing efficiently and are useful in responding to simple and familiar ethical dilemmas. In such cases, careful deliberation may not be necessary. However, when problems are complex and unfamiliar, relying on fast thinking alone can be a trap. It can lead to decisions made by force of habit, social shame and guilt, the rewards and punishments of authorities, and rigid adherence to legal standards. In these cases, approaches to slow thinking such as the weight-of-reasons framework are needed. Inevitably, although you will start your consideration of ethical dilemmas with intuitions, use of these frameworks enables you to take a second look, clarify alternatives, establish priorities, craft values, and find better solutions. An approach to slow thinking such as the weight of reasons, by acting as a check on emotions, can improve our choices. We can turn to the weight-of-reasons framework for guidance to prevent harm and to do good.

## Self-Interest

**LO 3.2:** Identify the complexities of self-interest.

**LO 3.3:** Explain the cognitive limitations and biases that prevent human beings from making rational decisions.

Many models of human decision-making start with the premise that we act based on fast thinking to advance our **self-interest**. According to these models, no action is really ever taken entirely out of concern for others or to adhere to an abstract principle. Rather, people engage in acts of kindness because they expect to benefit.

**Self-interest**
The motivation to take actions that benefit oneself

The evolutionary biologist Richard Dawkins wrote in 1976 that we have "selfish genes."[12] That is, according to Dawkins, people have evolved to be fundamentally concerned about themselves because that is what has enabled us as individuals to survive.[13]

The inclination toward self-interest generates cooperative transactions that are fundamental to capitalism. Adam Smith (1723–1790), who is recognized as the originator of modern economics and the intellectual forebear of capitalism, identified self-interest as the mechanism (the "invisible hand") that guides societies toward a more desirable state than that which would be attained if individuals acted purely altruistically and with the intent to directly benefit others. In a famous passage of *The Wealth of Nations*, Smith wrote that

> it is not from the benevolence of the butcher, the brewer, or the baker, that we expect our dinner, but from their regard to their own interest. We address ourselves, not to their humanity, but to their self-love, and never talk to them of our own necessities but of their advantages.[14]

This passage suggests that for Smith, a person satisfies her or his self-interest by having sympathy for the self-interests of others. Smith posited that humans must often look to others for help and that they receive this help by engaging in trades that enlist the "self-love" of others for their benefit. In other words, to get what you want in business and in life, you must be able to clearly demonstrate that you can provide others what they want.

Smith's conceptualization of self-interest is quite broad. In *The Theory of Moral Sentiments*, he describes humans as having many passions: bodily passions, such as hunger and the desire for sex; imaginative passions, such as love; unsocial passions, such as resentment and hatred; social passions, such as generosity, kindness, and compassion; and purely selfish passions of joy and grief. According to Smith, the market is not a neutral setting for rational calculation but rather a place where all these emotions play a role. For Smith, these passions enter into the intimate relations that people have with others in the market. Smith believed that to be successful in the marketplace one must have sympathy, which he defined as "fellow-feeling with . . . passion."[15] He argued that the self-interest displayed toward others cannot be coarse and narrow. If others are to trust and want to do business with you, you cannot base your relations with them on the one-sided wish to take advantage of them.

Adam Smith saw deep understanding of others as an important element of self-interest.

Psychologists have uncovered additional insights into the complexities of self-interest, demonstrating that there is more to it than getting as much money or pleasure as possible. We now discuss four of these complexities. They are (1) the tension between short- and long-term gratification; (2) the inclination to advance our interests by cheating, but as we shall see, only a little; (3) our concern not for actually being ethical but rather for other people thinking that we are ethical; and (4) the cognitive biases that prevent us from making decisions that actually benefit us.

## Short-Term and Long-Term Gratification

Fast thinking drives us toward both immediate and long-term gratification. In Walter Mischel's famous 1963 marshmallow experiments, children were offered an appetizing treat—for example, a marshmallow, cookie, or pretzel—and told that they could either eat it immediately or wait and have two portions later. Mischel found that about one-third of children were able to delay their immediate gratification and obtain an extra treat. Mischel also conducted a follow-up study in which he assessed how the participating children fared later in life. He found that children who delayed their gratification tended to be happier, wealthier, and even wiser (as measured by SAT scores). On the other hand, the children who quickly indulged tended to experience later outcomes such as incarceration and drug use. This research suggests that long-term business success requires instilling in yourself and your company the inclination to delay gratification.[16]

The implication of the marshmallow experiments for applying the weight-of-reasons framework is that in assessing the consequences of possible courses of action (Step 4 of the framework), managers should consider both short- and long-term consequences. The experiments also suggest that managers should hire employees who have strong self-discipline and establish incentives and a working environment that encourages acting on long-term rather than short-term inclinations.

The results of the marshmallow experiments must be interpreted carefully, because numerous factors could influence subjects' decisions. For example, according to a follow-up study, children who delayed gratification tended to be from families that were already wealthy; therefore, they were not anxious that a second portion wouldn't come. Poor children, in contrast, tended to indulge immediately since they had no faith that future rewards would come.[17] In Chapters 4 and 6, we further discuss the influence of local and organizational influences on ethical choices.

# THE CASE OF THE WHITE-COLLAR CRIMINAL WALTER PAVLO

White-collar criminals almost always fail to delay their gratification; as a consequence, they sometimes end up in places they do not want to end up, such as in prison. An instructive case is that of Walter Pavlo. In a segment of the Moth radio show, he describes a personal odyssey filled with misery and regret. Pavlo always thought of himself as a good person who did the right thing. From a Catholic family, he went to religious schools and was an altar boy. His parents expected a lot from him as he was the first in his family to attend college. He earned an engineering degree and an MBA.

*(Continued)*

(Continued)

At the age of 29, he moved into a gated community in Atlanta with his wife and two young sons. He worked for a telecommunications company, where he quickly became a department manager. This required that he collect long distance bills from clients.

Some of Pavlo's clients were fly-by-night operators involved in criminal activities like gambling, money laundering, and prostitution. Often, when he tried to collect from them, all he found was a vacant laundromat or college dorm room. As long as his company's financial performance was good, he was well regarded and rewarded for his efforts, but when the company's financial performance started to weaken, he came under greater pressure. If he could not collect all the debts, his superiors told him, he should cover them up to keep the bad news from shareholders. Pavlo figured out a creative way to do what his superiors asked and masked millions of dollars of uncollectible debts owed to the company. Yet he started to hate himself and discussed quitting. He mentioned his dilemma to a high-flying friend who had become wealthy quickly. According to Pavlo, the friend said to him,

> Don't quit. Give me the lists of customers that owe your company money and I will represent myself as a middle man and negotiate partial payments. You cover up the debts as usual and we can split the money, depositing it in Cayman Islands banks.

His friend then added, "Everyone cheats. How do you think people get ahead?"

Pavlo first resisted his friend's proposal but then succumbed and gave his friend the name of a creditor. The friend collected $250,000 and deposited the money in an offshore bank account he shared with Pavlo. Pavlo cleared the debt from company books. Cheating six customers in six months, Pavlo and his friend put away more than $6 million, but Pavlo was miserable, frightened, near to having a nervous breakdown, downing pills, drinking heavily, and avoiding contact with people with whom he usually socialized. Then, his supervisor discovered the debts he had cleared. Put under a U.S. attorney's investigation, Pavlo feared the FBI (Federal Bureau of Investigation) was watching him, following his every move, listening to phone calls, and recording his conversations.

Distraught, Pavlo went on a three-day drinking binge and collapsed, knowing he would have to go to prison. Convicted of money laundering, wire fraud, and obstruction of justice, he spent more than two years in jail. When Pavlo reentered society, his wife divorced him. Penniless at the age of 40, he had to move into his parents' home and try to start over. His short-term scheme to get rich quick led to long-term pain and suffering. He became a lecturer for the FBI, appearing at top business schools and accounting firms with the following message: "All of us are capable of such a crime, nobody is immune. I did it, and you can do it. So let's be honest . . . about what can happen to anyone in . . . business."[18]

Pavlo's story illustrates what can happen if the short-term inclination to pursue narrowly defined self-interest overtakes what is in one's long-term best interests.

## Cheating, but Just a Little

Another way in which self-interest is complex is that for most people the inclination to get what they want is in tension with their self-image of being honest. This tension manifests as a tendency to cheat in small ways. Research by social psychologist Dan Ariely suggests that almost everyone engages in cheating, but typically just a little because we are also constrained by the need to be able to look in the mirror and feel good about ourselves.[19] Most people are not psychopaths or complete "bad apples"; they have limits on how far they will go in pursuing narrow self-interest. They do not get out of control entirely like Pavlo did and cheat a lot. Our internal desire for integrity works to keep us from acting in grossly immoral ways. At the organizational level, it prevents the normalizing of deviance and unethical behavior from getting totally out of control.

Ariely devised an experiment in which he gave 20 simple math problems to students to solve in 5 minutes. On average, the students correctly solved four problems. Then, Ariely gave the same problems to another group of students. This time he asked the students to do their own grading and tell him how many problems they had solved. For each answer they got right, they received a monetary reward. The students were told to tear up the answer sheets so that there would be no evidence of their cheating. Ariely found that the students on average reported that they got seven answers right. They cheated, but just a little. Very few of the students were complete "bad apples," claiming to get all the answers right. Ariely explains that the results show that people tend to take advantage of small opportunities to cheat, but doing more would be an affront to the need to maintain an ethical self-image. Our inclination to maximize our benefit is constrained by opposing sentiments of shame and guilt if we move beyond certain self-imposed limits.

Ariely tried different variants of this experiment. He tested an economist's "rational-actor" perspective that people would cheat less if cheating came with higher penalties or the probability of getting caught increased, but he found no change in behavior. The participants in his experiments still cheated just a little, suggesting that the internal inclination for integrity tends to be a stronger restraint than the prospect of punishment in some situations. Ariely also tried another approach to see if an appeal to morality would change people's behavior. Prior to the experiment, he asked some participants what the Ten Commandments were, and he asked other participants to name the previous 10 books they had read. Ariely found that the participants asked to recall the Ten Commandments tended not to cheat, while those asked to recall the books that they had read continued to cheat. As a further test, he told a group of participants at MIT (the Massachusetts Institute of Technology) and Princeton University to recall their school's ethics codes. At both schools, students who were reminded of their school's ethics codes cheated less than those who did not receive the reminder. The reminder worked even at MIT, which did not actually have an ethics code. Ariely concludes that a reminder of morality makes a difference because it makes it harder for us to feel good about ourselves when we cheat.

Ariely suggests that these experiments apply to behavior in corporations. Few employees are complete "bad apples." However, most "game the system," finding ways to take advantage of inconsistencies and imperfections in the way rules are written. We have flexible psychological makeups that enable us to continue to feel good about ourselves even if we cheat just a little. This tendency to cheat can be problematic for organizations, because many small acts of cheating can result in large-scale ethical breaches in aggregate. This is why it is so important for organizations to make it absolutely clear that certain behaviors are completely unacceptable, no exceptions. They must regularly remind their employees of their ethical obligations if they hope to evoke the boundaries of acceptable norms and suppress the narrow pursuit of self-interest. If these reminders are to be effective, they cannot be stale. They must be fresh or else they will have little impact.

Ariely's studies show that the amount to which people cheat varies by circumstance. For example, it increases with "psychological distance"—the distance between people physically, socially, or in time. Ariely finds that bankers are more likely to cheat borrowers where there is great physical distance between themselves and the people whose lives they affect. Another example is pirating Internet music. Because people are distant from the musicians to whom they listen, they are able to rationalize that the musicians want people to hear their music even if they don't pay for it, that record company executives are corrupt, and that they would not download the music if they had had to pay for it. Downloaders, according to Ariely, see themselves as freedom fighters not as thieves.[20] On the other hand, illegal downloading likely would decrease a great deal if the downloaders knew the musicians or had to interact with them frequently. In the next chapter, we provide additional discussions of how contextual factors such as psychological distance influence ethical decision-making.

In sum, research shows that people are at war with themselves when they act on the basis of their self-interest. They are driven simultaneously by the desire to gain something that is not rightfully theirs and the desire to uphold the self-image of being an honorable person. Most people are constrained by ethics, at least to some degree, even when nobody else is looking.

## Perception of Being Ethical

So far, we have presented two insights about self-interest: first, that it has short- and long-term aspects, which may conflict with each other, and second, that it includes both a desire for gain (even if illicit) and a sense of morality, which also can be in conflict. A third complexity, and one that has important ethical implications, is that we recognize that we can advance our self-interest not by being honest and fair but rather by managing other people's perceptions so that they think that we are honest and fair. Psychologist Philip Tetlock argues that we are *intuitive politicians*, concerned with our reputations rather than representing ourselves accurately. We try to persuade others of our honesty regardless of how we actually behave.[21] In other words, sometimes we advance our self-interest by lying.

What is lying? In the previous chapter, we raised this question of whether advertisements for fat-free ice cream that aim to mislead, while being literally true, are lies. Lying, according to psychologists, is the effort to *deliberately* mislead; thus, a person can lie even when telling a literal truth, if the intent is to create the wrong impression. Many product labels and advertisements lie with a literal truth.

Psychologists have demonstrated that people lie frequently. Professor Bella DePaulo had participants record in a notebook how many times they lied each day. They admitted to doing so at least once a day.[22] Another psychology professor, Robert Feldman videotaped college students getting to know one another. He had the students watch the videos to figure out how much they had lied. On average, he found, they lied three times a minute. Feldman concludes that lying is part of the fabric of everyday life.[23] Children learn to do it from their parents; for example, a father may tell a child to tell a caller he is not home.

Few people are wholly honest all the time and often "shade the truth." For example, companies "manage" their quarterly earnings to make their performance look better than it actually is, and people on the job market construct their résumés in ways that exaggerate their past accomplishments. Politicians "spin" the truth or lie outright, such as when they present ideas or proposals in ways that conceal negative or controversial aspects. In sports, such as basketball or football, coaches teach

©iStockphoto.com/AndreyPopov

We want people to believe that we are honest even if we are not.

deception—a head fake to make a basket, for example. Some lies are not unethical if they occur in a context in which they are accepted such as the head fake, while other lies actually are innocuous and agreeable. Most people accept the "little white lies" of everyday life if they are meant to prevent discomfort, embarrassment, or shame. If people were totally blunt, then social interactions might become much more unpleasant and unproductive. (Recall Aristotle's golden mean; honesty becomes a vice when pushed to the extreme.) If the ends justify the means and the lies cause no harm or do some good, from a utilitarian perspective they would be allowed, but based on Immanuel Kant's absolute morality they are never tolerated.

DePaulo's research makes an important distinction. She examines the difference between lies told for the benefit of others and lies told solely for our own benefit. Do we lie to spare other people's feelings, avoid conflict, and prevent embarrassment, or do we lie to look better, feel better, and get what we want even at others' expense? DePaulo's research shows that people are twice as likely to engage in self-serving as opposed to altruistic lies. Yet she makes another important distinction. She also finds that the main reason people engage in self-serving lies is not material reward. Rather, their main motive in lying is to be respected, impress other people, be liked, and avoid embarrassment. Note again how complex and contradictory self-interest is. Even when it seems on the surface that people lie for monetary gain, such as in the Wells Fargo fraud scandal mentioned in Chapter 1, they may be expressing deeper motivations related to the need for power, acceptance, and respect.

In sum, self-interest is complex and full of contradictions. There is no reason to assume that the pursuit of self-interest necessarily corresponds with monetary rewards or maximizing returns to shareholders. As we act in our self-interest, we navigate between the tensions of the short term and the long term, between material gain and self-image, and between self-regard and the regard of others. As Freud argued long ago, conflicting motivations tear us apart.[24] You may believe that if you act in ways that are unethical so long as you can live with yourself and not get caught, it is not a problem; but if you slow down and engage in ethical reasoning, you may reach a different conclusion.

## Cognitive Biases

Another complexity of self-interest is that in making decisions about how to act in our own best interests, we often make mistakes. Although economic models tend to portray humans as rational actors who make intentional decisions that advance their self-interest, as we have already noted, this is not an accurate portrayal of how we make many decisions. Behavioral psychologists have demonstrated that we rely on numerous cognitive biases that lead us to make decisions that do not maximize our self-interest.

To use our bounded rationality (finite cognitive capacity) efficiently, we often rely on **heuristics** when making decisions. Heuristics are decision-making shortcuts or "rules of thumb."[25] We use some heuristics unconsciously when doing fast thinking, while other heuristics are conscious strategies that we apply when engaging in slow thinking. Heuristics can be useful in solving problems and achieving our aims. Psychologist Gerd Gigerenzer has demonstrated that under certain conditions, such as when people don't know much about the problem they face, heuristics enable them to make decisions not only more quickly but also more accurately than more systematic, information-intensive, slow-thinking decision-making processes.[26] Gigerenzer considers heuristics to be an important part of human beings' cognitive "adaptive toolbox."[27]

Unfortunately, though, heuristics can manifest as **cognitive biases**, which are systematic decision-making errors that lead us to make less than rational self-benefitting choices. Psychologists such as Kahneman and Tversky have identified dozens of cognitive biases. Some have important implications for ethical decision-making:

- **Fundamental attribution error**, referred to in Chapter 1, occurs when we attribute someone else's behavior or performance to their internal characteristics while ignoring external factors. An example would be when a manager blames an ethical violation on a particular individual, while failing to address the systemic factors (organizational culture, pressure from a boss, perverse incentives) that contributed to the violation. One would be committing fundamental attribution error if one blamed the manager alone for the disastrous Ford Pinto decision highlighted in Chapter 2 but ignored the culture and pressures inside the company. (This is not to say that the manager bore no responsibility.) Senior officials at Wells Fargo committed fundamental attribution error when they blamed the unethical behaviors that took place in the company solely on the employees while ignoring the context they created.

- **Confirmation bias**, also mentioned in Chapter 1, occurs when one places too much emphasis on information that confirms one's existing beliefs while ignoring or dismissing disconfirming information. It is the problem of "seeing only what we want to see" rather than making sense of reality objectively. An example of confirmation bias related to ethics would be refusing to acknowledge evidence that an employee was dishonest because of a preconceived notion that she or he was a good person.

- **Escalation of commitment** is the inclination to continue following a course of action because of a commitment to that course, even though continuing to follow the course will lead to negative outcomes. The commitment can be financial (e.g., when one has spent a lot of money on a course of action) or psychological (e.g., when one has made a commitment to seeing a project succeed). Again, the Ford Pinto example is relevant: Once Ford had committed to the Pinto project, it was unable to back out even though evidence suggested that it should have. It may have been that Ford's cost–benefit analysis was a way of rationalizing the decision it had already made to see the project through.

The owners of the hands in this picture may be committing fundamental attribution error.

- **Status quo bias** is the preference to maintain the current state of affairs even when a change of course should be considered. Managers who continue to allow sexual harassment in the workplace even after they are aware of problems commit status quo bias. (See the mini-cases at the end of this chapter that pose ethical dilemmas related to sexual harassment.)

- A **stereotype** is a belief that one has about an individual because that person belongs to a particular social category. Stereotypes may be true in general about the people in a category, but they are unlikely to be true about every individual in the category, and they may not be true at all. Stereotyping is a cognitive bias because it can lead to inaccurate—and unethical—assessments and decisions. For example, a manager who decided an employee was of low character and should not be promoted because she or he belonged to a particular religion might be guilty of making an inaccurate judgment, treating the employee unfairly, and harming the company's performance.

**Status quo bias**
The cognitive bias in which one prefers to maintain the current state of affairs even when a change of course should be considered

**Stereotype**
The cognitive bias in which one has a generalized belief about people of a particular social category

Situational factors exacerbate cognitive biases. A strong group culture forces dissenters to suppress their doubts. Time and resource constraints lead managers to analyze only the most obvious possible courses of action and to reach conclusions based on little analysis in a self-serving way. Decision-making biases are likely to be overlooked, ignored, excused, or even celebrated if they validate powerful actors' political agendas. The next chapter further examines the influence of situational factors.

## Ethical Intuitions

LO 3.4: Recognize the role intuitions play in ethical decision-making.

Thus far, this chapter has explored the ways in which the self-serving intuitions of people express themselves. While the temptation at this point may be to conclude that human beings are selfish by nature, keep in mind Smith's broad view that self-interest includes moral sentiments such as generosity and kindness. Evolutionary psychology supports the view that there is more to self-interest than simple selfishness. People have innate **ethical intuitions** to

**Ethical intuitions**
Intuitions to take
actions that benefit
others

- care for others and protect them from harm;

- be concerned about fairness;

- be loyal to those in one's group;

- follow necessary rules and the dictates of authority;

- protect what is considered sacred and pure;

- value liberty;

- oppose oppression; and

- avoid environmental degradation.[28]

Note that although all these intuitions benefit others, they are nevertheless self-interested; we developed them through evolutionary processes because they helped us as individuals to survive and adapt. Among our ancestors, individuals who had these qualities increased their chances of survival.[29]

In addition to having intuitions to benefit ourselves by benefitting others, we also possess ethical intuitions that are not self-interested at all—intuitions to take actions to help the group survive but at our own expense. Not only have we evolved to outcompete others in the same group; we have also evolved to help our groups outcompete other groups. Haidt notes that Charles Darwin recognized this in his development of evolutionary theory, writing that "a tribe that has a great number of courageous, sympathetic and faithful members, . . . always ready to warn each other of danger, to aid and defend each other . . . would succeed better."[30] Because humans have characteristics such as a desire to interact with others, a sense of reciprocity ("I'll scratch your back if you scratch mine"), generosity, a concern for others' opinions of us, and, more fundamentally, the ability to understand that other members of the group to which they belong perceive the world the same way that they do, they have been able to cooperate on a large scale, create complex societies, and flourish as a species. Humans, as the quote from Haidt at the beginning of this chapter argues, are "90 percent chimp

©iStockphoto.com/DanielPrudek

Human beings are a little bit like bees—designed to sometimes do what is best for the group rather than for the self.

and 10 percent bee."[31] In his view, all people are a little bit, more or less, like the bee, which is genetically programmed to work with other bees.

The research on ethical intuitions raises the question of whether we have evolved to possess the intuition to act based on utilitarianism or deontology (the two main approaches to ethical reasoning discussed in Chapter 2). After all, there would be little reason to hope that ethical decision-making frameworks such as the weight of reasons will be useful if they are fundamentally incompatible with our fast-thinking intuitions about how to act ethically. Haidt's and related research suggests, in fact, that we have evolved to possess intuitions to care for others and prevent harm that correspond to utilitarianism, as well as those to promote liberty and oppose oppression that correspond to deontology and contract theory. Psychologist and philosopher Joshua Greene provides experimental evidence that we engage in *fast* deontological and *fast* teleological thinking and that we use the two at different times. The evidence comes from his analysis of the well-known trolley experiments.[32]

# THE TROLLEY EXPERIMENTS
## Fast Deontological and Utilitarian Thinking

The trolley experiments were first proposed by the British philosopher Philippa Foot in 1967 and have been built on by philosophers, psychologists, and neuroscientists ever since.[33] In Version 1 of the experiment, you are to assume you work for a railroad and are near the train tracks. You see a train rushing down the tracks heading for a group of five workers with their backs to the train and nowhere to go. You control a lever that can divert the train down another set of tracks. If you pull the lever, you can save the lives of the workers. The problem with engaging the lever is that the train will now head directly for another worker who has his back to the train and nowhere to go. You have no time to think and have to act quickly; you cannot use the weight of reasons or any other ethical decision-making framework and must decide based on fast thinking. What do you do?

In Version 2 of the experiment, you are to imagine you just happen to be standing on a bridge overlooking the train tracks. Again, you see a train rushing down the tracks heading right for a group of five workers with their backs to the train and nowhere to go. In this version, standing right next to you on the bridge is a large man perched precariously on the rail of the bridge, also looking at the oncoming train. You can give this man a slight nudge and he is almost sure to fall on the tracks and stop the train from killing the five workers. The only problem is that by pushing the large man in front of the train you are likely to kill him. Again, you do not have much time for reflection. You must use fast thinking. What do you do?

Psychologists have asked these questions to thousands of people. Nearly 90% would pull the lever killing one man to save five (Version 1), while nearly 90% would not shove the large man into the oncoming train killing one to save five (Version 2). Each scenario has the same result (one dead worker or five), yet the intuitions people have about them and the ways they respond are different. In Version 1, most people act on an intuition based on utilitarianism, while in Version 2 most act on an intuition that corresponds to deontology.

Professor Joshua Greene and his colleagues have investigated the neurocognitive processes underlying the different responses to the two versions of the trolley experiment.[34] His research suggests that utilitarianism and deontology are situated in different parts of the brain. Using fMRI (functional magnetic resonance imaging of the brain) he finds that participants process the two questions in different parts. When participants experience a situation as personal (Version 2), they use a part of the brain that corresponds to deontology, whereas when they experience a situation as more impersonal, they are more likely to use a part of the brain corresponding to teleology. Greene, who advocates dual-process theory, concludes that people's responses to ethical questions are not guided by a unified system. Rather, we call on fast-thinking deontology in some situations and slow-thinking utilitarianism in others.

To further explore this idea, Greene tried another experiment similar to Version 2 of the trolley experiment. In this experiment, adapted from the last episode of the TV show *Mash*, it is war time and you and the hundred other members of your village are hiding in the basement of a house. An enemy killing squad is advancing. Its orders are to kill anyone it finds in its path. The problem is that you have your baby in your arms, and the baby has a very bad cough that is sure to alert the death squad to where the villagers and you are hiding. Do you smother your child and save the villagers or save your child and endanger 100 people? When Greene asked people this question while under brain imaging, he observed the two regions of the brain lighting up at the same time and further that about half of the participants said that they would kill the baby and about half would not. This evidence shows that some situations elicit both utilitarian and deontological fast thinking. People are divided within by intuitions that match both of these philosophical conceptions when facing ethical choices.[35]

## Ethical Intuitions and Ethical Behavior

While it is comforting to learn that people have evolved to have the ethical intuitions that psychologists, neuroscientists, and philosophers have identified, it is necessary to keep in mind that having these intuitions does not mean people always act on them. There are many reasons why people do not act in these ways.

First, while people are born with ethical intuitions, they may not be developed. Neuroscientist Gary Marcus (no relation to the lead author of this book) argues that while people are not born as "blank slates" with nothing in their minds at all, nor are they "hard-wired." Rather, he argues, they come "pre-wired"—with certain built-in characteristics that may or may not be activated. Hence, while all people may be born with particular ethical intuitions, whether these intuitions are developed or not depends on culture and upbringing.[36] Thus, it is possible, as Haidt and his colleagues show, that some people have developed one set of moral intuitions at the expense of others.

Second, and seemingly paradoxically, people's ethical intuitions may be triggered in unethical ways. The world is unfortunately full of examples of people who have undertaken destructive acts for what they believed were good causes—for example, white supremacists, religious fundamentalists, and antiabortion and environmental activists who take life to preserve what they see as sacred or pure. The intuition to preserve the sacred and to be loyal can lead to unethical behavior. Many of us probably can think of a time when we wanted to be loyal to a friend or a group member but knew doing so would produce harm or violate the rights of someone else. Greene has written in the book *Moral Tribes* that because people are tribal at heart, they are capable of carrying out actions for the good of the group that have terrible impacts on people outside it. Human history shows that this tribal intuition, acted on for the good of the group, can rise to the level of brutal subjection of other peoples, war, and genocide.[37]

Third, ethical intuitions may not clearly lead to ethical behavior because conflicts arise between ethical intuitions. One intuition will point us to one action, while another intuition will point us to another. In the previous example, loyalty suggested one behavior while a contrary intuition, the desire to not harm and protect the rights of others, suggested another behavior. Or, as the trolley experiments indicate, a desire to create the most benefits for a group or society can be in tension with a desire to respect the rights and dignity of each individual. American conservatives tend to be comfortable with the idea of obeying authority and following rules even if the rules disadvantage certain groups because that is what they believe is best for society as a whole, while in contrast, liberals are not comfortable with this idea and believe that rules that disadvantage certain groups should be changed.[38] Acting on ethical intuitions is difficult because these intuitions may be contradictory, leaving us confused and uncertain about what to do.

A final reason why our ethical intuitions may not lead to ethical behavior is that they may be in conflict with our selfish intuitions. We are all familiar with the iconography of the confused individual with an angel perched on one shoulder and a devil perched on the other, torn between temptation and restraint. What should a person do in such situations? This returns us to the matter of reputation: Humans are not necessarily wired to conform to norms and do what is most ethical but rather to *look as if* they were acting in this way. They navigate between what they selfishly want to do and what society expects them to do. Hence, they find themselves trying to do both at the same time, telling small lies, and cheating just a little, so long as they do not tarnish their reputations too much. Corporations behave in the same way. In sum, while we are born with ethical intuitions, we cannot always be counted on to produce ethical behavior. The world—and our own proclivities—is far too complicated for that.

## Combining Fast and Slow Thinking: The Weight-of-Reasons Framework

LO 3.5: Apply the weight-of-reasons framework to check the role that after-the-fact rationalization plays in ethical choices.

Given that fast thinking—even ethical intuitions—can lead people astray, what can we do to improve ethical decision-making? The answer is simply to use approaches to slow thinking such as the weight-of-reasons framework. Fast thinking will lead us to frame issues in particular ways, see certain facts, consider well-known action alternatives, be aware of specific consequences, apply particular principles, and apply well-worn decision-making shortcuts. Frameworks such as the weight of reasons can help us slow down and improve our thinking at each of these steps in this process.

But can reasoning really help us correct for and improve on intuitions? Many people take for granted that reasoning (i.e., System 2 thinking) is superior to intuitions and emotion (i.e., System 1 thinking). Reason has enabled humans to flourish, producing more order and liberty, less violence, and higher standards of living than ever before.

In contrast, societies that get carried away by emotions such as anger and fear and lose their capacity for collective critical thinking make poor decisions and even inflict horrors on their own citizens and other people. Slow thinking can and should be a corrective. It can be more than a justification of decisions already made based on a set of intuitions and can help us improve our ethical decisions. While it may be true that slow thinking may serve only to justify intuition in cases where snap moral choices must be made, it is also true that by undertaking more deliberate decision-making processes, we can sort through our intuitions, critique them, correct for their biases and refine them, and ultimately make better ethical decisions. Not only that, we can learn from these decisions, develop better decision-making intuitions, and make better decisions the next time around as well. Just as virtue theory suggests, through the repeated practice of good ethical decision-making, we can become good ethical decision makers.

Researchers such as developmental psychologist Darcia Narvaez have advanced this insight that through reasoning we can improve our ethical intuitions. She argues that people can develop "mature moral functioning," which enables them to learn to act more ethically over time as they repeatedly reason through ethical dilemmas. Through slow ethical thinking, we develop improved habits of fast ethical thinking.[39]

Business ethics professor Eugene Sadler-Smith also maintains that reasoning can lead to the improvement of ethical intuitions and more ethical behavior. He sees the ethical intuitions identified by social psychologists as corresponding to the virtues identified by Aristotle and other philosophers, and he argues that people can refine their ethical intuitions over time through practice. The process of refining our ethical intuitions ideally should be shaped by supportive norms and rules in the communities of which we are a part. The toughest part of the development process, according to Sadler-Smith, is that people face conflicting and competing claims; what we feel is right may not be consistent with what our role in an organization allows us to do, what others in the organization want, or societal expectations. We may want to do what is right but lack the power to do so. As we refine our intuitions through experience, we should become better able at navigating this problem.[40]

The implication of the work of Narvaez, Sadler-Smith, and others is that practice in applying the weight-of-reasons approach can lead to better ethical choices. At the same time, we must be aware of the danger of using the framework to confirm our preexisting intuitive biases. Applying the framework means relying on slow thinking to surface, articulate, and challenge ethical intuitions, not rationalize them. It should be a process that is as objective as possible rather than one driven by preconceived notions and some ethical intuitions and not others. At every step in the weight-of-reasons process—identifying the issue, getting the facts, considering the action alternatives, considering benefits and harm, applying principles, and making a decision—multiple perspectives should be considered and juxtaposed before moving to the next step; tensions must be wrestled with and biases overcome. Once a decision is made, there should be a follow-up so that we learn from what we have done and refine our intuitions so that we make a better ethical decision next time.

Using the framework this way is not easy. Intuitions are fundamental to how people make sense of the world, and it is incredibly difficult to recognize and challenge them. Thus, it is important to carefully structure the weight-of-reasons decision-making process and guide it appropriately as it unfolds. As discussed in

Chapters 5 and 6, organizations can adopt decision-making practices as well as policies and programs that support better ethical decision-making. And as discussed in Chapter 8, they can engage their stakeholders in group learning processes that produce innovative solutions to ethical dilemmas. Haidt makes a similar argument in *The Righteous Mind* where he observes,

> If you put individuals together in the right way, such that some individuals can use their reasoning powers to disconfirm the claims of others, and all individuals feel some common bond or shared fate that allows them to interact civilly, you can create a group that ends up producing good reasoning as an emergent property of the social system. This is why it's so important to have intellectual and ideological diversity within any group or institution whose goal is to find truth.[41]

## SUMMARY AND CONCLUSION

This chapter has shown that thinking is a process with two parts, fast and slow. Fast thinking is intuitive and automatic, while slow thinking is deliberate and rational. For at least 25 centuries, philosophers, theologians, and other people of wisdom from many cultures have taught us to think about ethics slowly as utilitarians and deontologists. Modern psychological research shows that within the human mind do in fact lie these two deep tendencies in the Western intellectual tradition. We have intuitions that correspond to the major approaches to ethical reasoning as well as many other types of ethical intuitions. The weight-of-reasons framework provides an approach to slow thinking that incorporates both utilitarianism and deontology. Therein lies its potential to improve ethical decision-making.

Another conclusion of this chapter is that most of our intuitions are self-interested, but self-interest is a complicated phenomenon. Psychological studies of the fast thinking that colors ethical responses show that the pursuit of self-interest—the fundamental inclination that Smith found at the hub of markets—is a commanding instinct in business and other interactions, but the directions in which

it takes us are not at all obvious. People seek both short- and long-term gratification (Mischel's studies). They seek gain but also want to look in the mirror and feel good about themselves, which means that they are ready to tolerate their own cheating only up to a point (Ariely's studies). They lie to achieve benefits for themselves, but the gain they seek is not necessarily economic advancement and may instead be respect and self-esteem (DePaulo's studies). When and how they pursue self-interest is limited by cognitive biases that distort the ability to achieve what they want or even figure out what they wish to do.

Supporting the view of philosophers such as Smith, research shows that self-interest is more than selfishness; most people other than outright psychopaths have strong ethical intuitions. The desire to do good for ourselves depends critically on our sympathy for others. People have self-interested desires to care for other people, treat them fairly, and see that others do the same. Psychological research also suggests that some ethical intuitions are not self-interested at all; they direct us to do what is best for others even at our own expense. As Darwin recognized long ago, we have thrived as a species in part because people have evolved the capacity for generosity and cooperation.

A key point of this chapter is that intuitions, even ethical ones, do not necessarily lead to ethical actions. The chapter enumerated some of the reasons why: Ethical intuitions may not be triggered in the real world, they may lead people to take actions that seem right but cause harm, they conflict with one another (e.g., we regularly wonder whether the ends justify the means), or they may conflict with more immediate self-interest. Moreover, this chapter has shown and warned against the fact that decisions are prone to rationalization and biases, which the weight-of-reasons framework may reduce. This is where frameworks for slow thinking such as the weight of reasons come in; while we are aware that slow thinking can serve as mere justification of human intuitions, it can do more.

Fast and slow thinking play complementary roles in how people respond to ethical issues. If frameworks such as the weight of reasons are applied properly, they can help us identify and correct for intuitive ethical biases. Taking a more developmental approach, slow thinking can even help us refine and improve our ethical intuitions over time so that we think fast more ethically the next time around.

## KEY TERMS AND CONCEPTS

Cognitive biases  74
Confirmation bias  74
Dual-process theory  66
Escalation of commitment  74
Ethical intuitions  76

Fast thinking  65
Fundamental attribution
   error  74
Heuristics  74
Integrated theory  66

Self-interest  67
Slow thinking  65
Status quo bias  75
Stereotype  75

## CASES RELATED TO THE READING

Consider reading all of the cases found in Chapter 10 to gain experience in applying the concepts presented in this chapter. In every case, managers' bounded rationality and cognitive biases lead them to frame and address ethical dilemmas in partial, limited ways.

## CASE APPLICATIONS

Return to the cases at the end of Chapter 2. Did you reason your way to your conclusions, or did you begin with an intuition that you then justified? Did your initial intuitions about what to do match up with your conclusions after applying the weight-of-reasons framework?

Now use the weight of reasons to try working through the following cases, which illustrate the conflicts people have between their intuitions and logic.

## Case 3.1: Child Care at Atlantic Information Systems

Since the time that companies began to hire full-time diversity managers, they often have tried to make their organizations more hospitable to people of all sexes. Atlantic Information Systems Inc. is a medium-size firm with two complementary lines of business. Its 700 professionals advise other organizations about data storage and processing systems. They also produce and market customized software systems for a variety of business functions. In addition to its professional staff, the firm includes 100 employees whose work is administrative, clerical, or janitorial.

When Lester Barks, the founder and CEO (chief executive officer) of Atlantic, started his business, he recognized that he would require employees with both high-level technical skills and sophisticated communication skills. He recruited well and was able to infuse the staff with his own energy and appetite for work and getting the job done. As a result, the firm grew rapidly, developing a strong reputation for innovative designs and good customer service. From the beginning, Barks had strong beliefs about rewarding people for their work, but he also tried to keep fixed costs to an absolute minimum. Thus, although he had established a generous profit-sharing plan, he tried to hold the line against the expansion of employee benefits programs. This policy had been working reasonably well. As long as the company's young, well-educated employees kept getting their substantial paychecks, they seemed content to solve their own personal and career problems. Bark's view of his company was that it was not a social service agency.

As the firm and its employees matured, however, sentiment toward the firm's personnel policies seemed to shift. The people who have the skills and experience Barks needs to run his business also have young families to care for. The conflicting

demands of jobs and families are proving to be problematic for many people. Several employees recently approached Barteau Weber, the vice president for personnel, with a strongly worded request that Atlantic consider opening a company-sponsored child care center. These employees argued that the company should establish and support a high-quality child care center as a way of reducing demands on their time that detract from their ability to focus on their jobs. In addition, they point out that predicted changes in the structure of the work force are likely to make such a center a prerequisite for recruiting and retaining qualified employees in the future. Their company should show empathy toward them, not only as employees but also as people with families and young children for whom they have to care.

Weber knows that this request is not the product of a few overly demanding whiners. Indeed, it has been put together by a self-appointed committee consisting of half a dozen of the firm's most respected employees and has been signed by more than 50 people. Furthermore, Weber knows that, within just the past three months, two highly valued senior systems designers quit rather than returning to work after the six-week parental leave the company allowed. They told Weber that they were unable to arrange for suitable child care and that they thought the company did not give a damn about them. Weber has overheard many informal conversations that echo this view.

Weber understands that many companies have established child care centers, but he has little technical knowledge of how they are structured or how much they cost. Moreover, he wonders if his feeling for these employees should override his feelings for employees who do not have families, who would have to share in the costs of setting up a child care facility at the company. Finally, he is certain that Barks, the company's founder, will resist the idea of getting involved in such a venture. He has never seen Barks express the sentiment that family life should come before the hard work of maintaining the firm and making it financially viable. He feels as if he has a responsibility to bring the matter to Barks's attention, but he is very apprehensive about what will take place.

When he brings the issue to Barks's attention, the CEO immediately blurts out,

> I just don't get it. It does not feel right to me. This problem only affects a part of our work force. Some people have no children at all, and others have children they are managing to raise without any help from us. How are these employees going to react if they see the company spending its money on an expensive program that benefits only a few people? I have absolutely no sympathy for these people asking for a child care facility, none. I did not get any special protection from my employers earlier in my life when I worked for others. My gut says to just turn down those who are asking for this benefit and not to let this issue simmer any further. Let's squelch it now before it gets out of hand.

Use the weight-of-reasons framework to decide what you would do next if you were Weber. How does your decision compare with your initial intuition about what Weber should do?

### Case 3.2: Transforming the Soul of Business

Darlington Foods is an integrated wholesaler and retailer of high-quality food products. It provides gourmet foods to supermarket chains and specialty stores in the United States and Europe under the well-known brand names of "Fuller Flavor," "Good-For-You," and "Healthy Delite." Partly through acquisition, its sales have more than doubled in the past 10 years, but profits have been disappointing. The founder of the company and the former CFO (chief financial officer) were forced to resign because of the company's poor performance (Table 3.1).

| TABLE 3.1 | Darlington Foods: Performance | | |
|---|---|---|---|
| Year | Sales | Operating Income | Net Loss |
| 2015 | 28,380 | 1,554 | 1,043 |
| 2016 | 35,595 | 6,351 | 10,353 |
| 2017 | 49,020 | 4,155 | 6,975 |

Note: All values are in thousands of dollars.

The top management team now consists of company president and CEO Robert Dennis, 49, an engineering graduate with a PhD in educational administration from the University of Kansas; executive vice president Carl Martin, 47, who attended the University of Utah and worked for the Albertson and Super Value grocery chains; retail sales vice president Kevin J. O'Brien, 31, a graduate of the Harvard Business School; and CFO Benson Siegel, 59, a certified public accountant from the University of California, Berkeley, who used to run his own business. As the operations and marketing director of the firm, you are the newest member of the executive team. You have an MBA from the University of Minnesota Carlson School and formerly worked for the Target Company.

Before the monthly executive team meeting, O'Brien has proposed to send five senior employees to a conference on "Transforming the Soul of Business: Profit, Competition, and Conscience on the New Frontier," which would be held in Hilton Head Island, South Carolina, next winter. This proposal is part of O'Brien's ongoing effort to make the company more socially responsible. O'Brien feels deeply that the key to restoring Darlington's profitability is to align it with upscale consumers that appreciate a socially conscious profile. He is fond of saying, "This company should be governed by a conscience. It should not be a slave to short-term profits." The total cost of sending the five employees to Hilton Head will be more than $30,000.

Benson Siegel, whose office is right next door to yours, has been looking over the conference brochure. On the title page, it advertises "Innovative Techniques for Making a Profit While Making a Difference" and "How to Make Your Business a Positive Agent for Social Change." The mission of the conference sponsor, the National Institute for a New Corporate Vision, is "to foster an evolution that encourages balance: a thriving corporate life, self-fulfillment, and meaningful personal relationships." Many other companies that sell socially conscious goods and services will be at the conference. It promises sessions that address topics such as extraordinary customer service, incentives that appeal to employees' hearts, worker empowerment, caring for the plight of the global poor, fostering creativity through empathy, employee belonging and well-being, collaborative communication, engaging the human spirit in the workforce through love, and giving back to the community.

Siegel tells you that he does not know what to think. A liberal Democrat, a successful entrepreneur, and philanthropist, he also was known as a hard-driving executive when he owned his own business. He feels that people should keep their priorities straight: "When in the office, use your head—leave your heart at home." He tells you that this always has been his motto and communicates that to you in no uncertain terms. From his perspective, these ideas of O'Brien are a "no-go." They are "dead on arrival." But Siegel is unsure how other members of the executive team stand. He tells you that O'Brien is a "flake." What he is trying is inconsistent with the shareholder interests Siegel must protect. He comments that O'Brien is "too dogmatic, fixed in his ways . . . bright, but arrogant and self-righteous," qualities he detests. A "fanatic"—"no telling how far he might go," Siegel proclaims. You are not quite certain where your allegiances lie, for while you like Siegel, you have been charmed as well by O'Brien, who has been very supportive of your work.

Siegel reads an article about how several socially conscious businesses have not lived up to their ideals. They deserted their vaunted pay scales in which top management could not earn much more than wage earners. They took their factories from inner-city locations and shipped jobs to low-wage countries. They sullied the environment and had quality control problems, which led to the selling of contaminated products. At the same time, they proclaimed that they were a force of good, working for the future of the planet, and committed to an enlightened capitalism in order to improve society. Outraged by the hypocrisy of these firms, Siegel sends the article to the top management team at Darlington.

Meanwhile, O'Brien invites a guest to your executive committee meeting, Laura Scher, a former classmate of his, a person he believes "represents the best of the new capitalism." Scher graduated near the top of her MBA class but did not choose the path to easy and quick riches. She refused a lucrative Wall Street offer and created her own company, Working Assets Funding Service, the purpose of which is "to do well by doing good." The company offers a donation-linked credit card and charity-connected long-distance phone service that allows people to donate to causes. *Inc.* magazine named the company one of the 500 fastest-growing privately held companies in the United States. O'Brien tells you that the "soul" of your company is at stake.

The ongoing conflict between Siegel and O'Brien makes you very nervous. Their emotions are running way too high. Is there some way to intervene? You are afraid your company is going to collapse because of the conflict between two people you essentially like and respect. You vaguely recall an ethical framework you learned to use in a class at the Carlson School. It was called "Weighing the Reasons," or something like that. Would now be the time to invoke it, but how and to what end? (*Note:* We also discuss managers' duty to shareholders, corporate social responsibility, and related topics in Chapter 7.)

### Case 3.3: Mini-Cases on Sexual Harassment

The two classes of sexual harassment defined under the Equal Employment Opportunity Commission guidelines are (1) requests by a supervisor for sexual favors in return for job benefits and (2) a hostile work environment. Sexually harassing conduct in the workplace that creates an offensive work environment includes the following: physical or verbal harassment; repeated offensive or unwelcome sexual flirtations, advances, and propositions; continual or repeated verbal abuse of a sexual nature; graphic verbal commentaries about an individual's body; the use of sexually degrading words to describe an individual; and the display in the workplace of sexually suggestive objects or pictures. Since there are usually neither witnesses nor physical evidence, and it is difficult to show that advances were not wanted, fact-finding can be complicated, and it is important to know whether the victim told the accused person that the advances were not welcome.

Barteau Weber of Atlantic Information Systems, last seen in Case 3.1 of this chapter, now faces a series of sexual harassment cases. To what extent can he use the weight-of-reasons framework to help manage these dilemmas? Again be sure to compare your decision based on the weight of reasons with your initial intuitions.

### a. The Business Trip

Three people from Atlantic go on a business trip. The male partner is in his mid-40s and is married. The third-year analyst is in her early 30s, and the newly hired MBA is in her mid-20s. The business trip is a success; the employees secure a new project that will bring millions of dollars of business. That evening they celebrate. The male partner has too much to drink and asks questions about the female analyst's sex life. He moves closer to her and puts his arm around her. She is visibly shaken. She moves away from the male partner, reminding him that she has just become engaged, and tries to change the subject. The newly hired MBA is upset about what she has witnessed. The next day, she urges the analyst to file a complaint, but the analyst refuses. She says that the male partner is simply having a midlife crisis: "That's the way it is. I don't want to be branded a troublemaker." On her own, the MBA brings the incident to the attention of the human resources department. It makes some discreet inquiries and learns that the partner in the firm has a reputation for occasional heavy drinking and, apparently, has had consensual affairs with other junior employees. However, no one has ever brought a formal complaint against him. The human resources staff tell the MBA she cannot file a formal complaint herself but must convince the analyst to do so.

### b. No Touching

Atlantic Information Systems has an explicit policy of "no sexual touching" between employees. Helen, a member of John's staff, has received poor performance reviews, but nonetheless she believes she should be promoted. She files a letter of complaint with the human resources department, alleging that John embraced his secretary Emily on company property. The department begins an investigation by interviewing people in the company. It asks them for complete confidentiality, but leaks occur, and word of the inquiry spreads, hurting the reputations of both John and Emily and making it difficult for them to carry out their jobs. Their department is at a standstill with bitterness and acrimony on all sides. Helen complains that other employees are siding with John and Emily and that she is being ostracized. Emily's story is that she received a phone call about her niece's death in an automobile accident and that John was only comforting her.

### c. "Boys Will Be Boys"

After having lunch with a customer, a salesperson claims that the customer made unwelcome offensive comments followed by physical contact to which she objected. She expects her company to take immediate legal action. If it fails to protect her, she will sue. When confronted, the customer claims that "boys will be boys" and that what happened was "nothing more than a joke," an "innocent flirtation," and perhaps a "chance for a relationship." This customer represents an organization that constitutes one quarter of the company's business. The company discovers that this salesperson complained many times of sexual harassment in her previous employment.

# NOTES

1. Kahneman, D. (2011). *Thinking, fast and slow.* New York, NY: Farrar, Strauss, & Giroux.

2. Stanovich, K. E., & West, R. F. (2000). Individual differences in reasoning: Implications for the rationality debate? *Behavioral and Brain Sciences, 23*(5), 645–665.

3. Thaler, R. H., & Sunstein, C. R. (2008). *Nudge: Improving decisions about health, wealth, and happiness.* New York, NY: Penguin Books.

4. Ibid.

5. Evans, J. St. B. T. (2003). In two minds: Dual process accounts of reasoning. *Trends in Cognitive Sciences, 7,* 454–459; Evans, J. (2007). On the resolution of conflict in dual process theories of reasoning. *Thinking & Reasoning, 13*(4), 321–339; Greene, J. (2014). Beyond point-and-shoot morality: Why cognitive (neuro) science matters for ethics. *Ethics, 124*(4), 695–726. doi:10.1086/675875; Greene, J. D., Morelli, S. A., Lowenberg, K., Nystrom, L. E., & Cohen, J. D. (2008). Cognitive load selectively interferes with utilitarian moral judgment. *Cognition, 107,* 1144–1154.

6. See p. 51, in Kahneman, D., & Frederick, S. (2002). Representativeness revisited: Attribute substitution in intuitive judgment. In T. Gilovich, D. Griffin, & D. Kahneman (Eds.), *Heuristics and biases: The psychology of intuitive judgment* (pp. 49–81). Cambridge, UK: Cambridge University Press.

7. See Treatise 2.3.3., p. 415, in Hume, D. (1960). *An enquiry concerning the principles of morals.* LaSalle, IL: Open Court. (Original work published 1777)

8. Haidt, J. (2001). The emotional dog and its rational tail: A social intuitionist approach to moral judgment. *Psychological Review, 108,* 814–834; Haidt, J. (2007). The new synthesis in moral psychology. *Science, 316,* 998–1002.

9. Haidt, J., Koller, S. H., & Dias, M. E. (1993). Affect, culture, and morality, or is it wrong to eat your dog? *Journal of Personality and Social Psychology, 65,* 613–628.

10. Moll, J., & de Oliveira, R. (2007). Response to Greene: Moral sentiments and reason: Friends or foes? *Trends in Cognitive Sciences, 11*(8), 323–324; Moll, J., de Oliveira-Souza, R., & Zahn, R. (2008). The neural basis of moral cognition: Sentiments, concepts, and values. *Annals of the New York Academy of Sciences, 1124,* 161–180.

11. Sherman, G. D., & Haidt, J. (2011). Cuteness and disgust: The humanizing and dehumanizing effects of emotion. *Emotion Review, 3*(3), 245–251.

12. Dawkins, R. (1976). *The selfish gene.* New York, NY: Oxford University Press.

13. Sherman and Haidt (2011).

14. See pp. 23–24, Smith, A. (2003). *The wealth of nations.* New York, NY: Bantam Books. (Original work published 1776)

15. See p. 5, in Smith, A. (2006). *The theory of moral sentiments.* Mineola, NY: Dover. (Original work published 1759)

16. Mischel, W. (1968). *Personality and assessment.* New York, NY: Wiley; Mischel, W., & Ayduk, O. (2004). Willpower in a cognitive-affective processing system: The dynamics of delay of gratification. In R. F. Baumeister & K. D. Vohs (Eds.), *Handbook of self-regulation: Research, theory, and applications* (pp. 99–129). New York, NY: Guilford Press.

17. Calarco, J. M. C. (2018, June 1). Why Rich Kids Are So Good at the Marshmallow Test. Retrieved from https://www.theatlantic.com/family/archive/2018/06/marshmallow-test/561779/.

18. Pavlo, W. (n.d.). *Embezzled.* Retrieved from https://themoth.org/storytellers/walter-pavlo

19. See also Bing, M. N., Davison, H. K., Vitell, S. J., Ammeter, A. P., Garner, B. L., & Novicevic, M. M.

(2012). An experimental investigation of an interactive model of academic cheating among business school students. *Academy of Management Learning & Education, 11,* 28–48; Mazar, N., & Ariely, D. (2006). Dishonesty in everyday life and its policy implications. *Journal of Public Policy & Marketing, 25*(1), 117–126.

20.  Ariely, D. (2008). *Predictably irrational: The hidden forces that shape our decisions.* New York, NY: HarperCollins; Ariely, D. (2012). *The honest truth about dishonesty.* New York, NY: HarperCollins.

21.  Tetlock, P. E. (2002). Social functionalist frameworks for judgment and choice: Intuitive politicians, theologians, and prosecutors. *Psychological review, 109,* 451–457.

22.  DePaulo, B. M., Kashy, D. A., Kirkendol, S. E., Wyer, M. M., & Epstein, J. A. (1996). Lying in everyday life. *Journal of Personality and Social Psychology, 70*(5), 979.

23.  Feldman, R. (2013). *Liar: The truth about lying.* New York, NY: Random House.

24.  Freud, S. (1989). *The ego and the id.* New York, NY: W. W. Norton. (Original work published 1923)

25.  Simon, H. (1997). *Administrative behavior: A study of decision-making processes in administrative organization* (4th ed.). New York, NY: Free Press; Tversky, A., & Kahneman, D. (1989). Rational choice and the framing of decisions. In B. Karpak & S. Zionts (Eds.), *Multiple criteria decision making and risk analysis using microcomputers* (pp. 81–126). Berlin, Germany: Springer.

26.  Gigerenzer, G., & Todd, P. M. (1999). *Simple heuristics that make us smart.* New York, NY: Oxford University Press; Gigerenzer, G., & Brighton, H. (2009). Homo heuristicus: Why biased minds make better inferences. *Topics in Cognitive Science, 1*(1), 107–143; Gigerenzer, G., & Gaissmaier, W. (2011). Heuristic decision making. *Annual Review of Psychology, 62,* 451–482.

27.  Gigerenzer, G., & Selten, R. (2001). Rethinking rationality. In G. Gigerenzer & R. Selten (Eds.), *Bounded rationality: The adaptive toolbox* (pp. 1–12). Cambridge: MIT Press.

28.  Haidt, J. (2012). *The righteous mind.* London, UK: Penguin Books.

29.  Ibid.

30.  Darwin, C. (1998). *The descent of man, and selection in relation to sex.* New York, NY: Prometheus Books. (Original work published 1971), cited in Haidt, 2012, p. 223.

31.  Haidt (2012).

32.  In their research, Greene and his colleagues actually make the case that the deontological judgments made in their experiments involve fast thinking while the teleological judgments require more cognitive work and essentially involve slow thinking. Despite this, here we treat the teleological judgments made in the experiments as "fast thinking" because they do not involve conscious, deliberate application of an ethical framework. While the teleological judgments made in Greene et al.'s experiments may be slow compared with the deontological judgments made in the experiments, they are nevertheless still quite fast relative to deliberate, step-by-step, ethical reasoning.

33.  Foot, P. (1967). The problem of abortion and the doctrine of double effect. *Oxford Review, 5,* 5–15; Bleich, J. D. (2010). Sacrificing the few to save the many. *Tradition, 43*(1), 78–86.

34.  Greene, J. (2013). *Moral tribes: Emotion, reason and the gap between us and them.* London, UK: Penguin Books; Greene, J. D. (2016). Solving the trolley problem. In J. Sytsma & W. Buckwalter (Eds.), *A companion to experimental philosophy* (pp. 175–188). Malden, MA: Wiley-Blackwell; Greene, J., Sommerville, R., Nystrom, L., Darley, J., & Cohen, J. D. (2001). An fMRI investigation of emotional engagement in moral judgment. *Science, 293,* 2105–2108.

35.  Greene (2013).

36.  Marcus, G. (2004). *The birth of the mind.* New York, NY: Basic Books.

37.  Greene, J. (2013).

38.  Haidt, J. (2012). *The righteous mind.* London, UK: Penguin Books; Haidt, J., Graham, J., & Joseph, C. (2009). Above and below left–right: Ideological narratives and moral foundations. *Psychological Inquiry, 20,* 110–119.

39.  Narvaez, D. (2010). Moral complexity: The fatal attraction of truthiness and the importance of mature moral functioning. *Perspectives on Psychological Science, 5,* 163–181.

40.  Sadler-Smith, E. (2012). Before virtue: Biology, brain, behavior, and the "moral sense." *Business Ethical Quarterly, 22,* 351–376.

41.  See p. 103, in Haidt (2012).

# The Organizational Context for Ethical Decision-Making

PART

II

©iStockphoto.com/gazanfer

Our ethical decision-making is affected by what those around us think and do.

# Managing Social Influences on Ethical Decision-Making

## Learning Objectives

On completion of this chapter, the reader should be able to do the following:

LO 4.1:   Explain the impact of obedience, authority, and groupthink on ethical decision-making.

LO 4.2:   Understand Kohlberg's theory of moral development and describe its implications for how managers address organizational pressures to act unethically.

LO 4.3:   Explain why individuals tend to obey authority figures, based on Milgram's Obedience experiments.

LO 4.4:   Describe the characteristics of groupthink and the impacts of groupthink on ethical decision-making.

LO 4.5:   Discuss the options an individual has to challenge unethical behavior.

LO 4.6:   Apply the weight-of-reasons framework for ethical decision-making as an effective tool in helping to close the circle.

> *Courage is not the absence of fear, but the triumph over it. The brave man is not he who does not feel afraid, but he who conquers that fear.*
>
> —Nelson Mandela

## Introduction

LO 4.1: Explain the impact of obedience, authority, and groupthink on ethical decision-making.

Let's briefly review some of the book's main takeaways so far:

- You now should have a better capacity to identify an *ethical dilemma*. It is a situation in which there can be harm to others and yourself. No simple way exists to avoid this harm.

- You should understand the difference between fast and slow thinking. *Fast thinking* involves intuition. It involves responding instinctively without much reflection. It triggers emotions such as sympathy, anger, love, disgust, fear, confusion, and regret. *Slow thinking*, in contrast, involves stepping back from intuition and engaging in reflection.

- The tool we have presented for engaging in slow thinking is the commonsense *weight-of-reasons framework*. To apply this framework, one identifies the issue, assembles the facts, considers action options and their consequences, applies principles, and formulates an immediate and long-term response to the issue. The long-term solution should aim to deal with the issue's *root causes*. It is also necessary to incorporate ongoing lessons from engaging in ethical issues.

- In applying principles (Step 5 of the weight of reasons), be aware of *conflicts among them*. Often, a focus on consequences and the aim of doing the greatest good for the greatest number (utilitarianism) conflicts with a focus on principles and the duty to treat each person with respect and not lie, cheat, or deceive others (the deontological perspective).

- Also, be aware of the role that *virtue* ethics can play in resolving ethical dilemmas. With practice, you can get better at navigating these dilemmas. To act with greater integrity, you can work to develop your *character*.

These lessons from the first three chapters all focus on you as an individual. However, in the real world, you do not operate in isolation. You do not make important ethical decisions in business by yourself, and based solely on your own intuitions and beliefs. Rather, you make these decisions within the confines of, and working with the members of, groups and organizations. The beliefs, norms, cultures, and rules of groups and organizations influence the decisions you make.

The purpose of this chapter is to examine more carefully how organizations influence ethical decision-making. Tensions often arise between what we as individuals are inclined to do and believe is right, and the behavior our organization suggests or demands we take. While there are many ways in which organizations influence our choices, we focus on two types of influence that can lead us to take unethical action or

**Obedience to authority**
Conformity with a request or demand from an authority figure

**Groupthink**
A collective decision-making process characterized by a bias for conformity and consensus rather than creativity and critical thinking

**Truth to power**
To insist on an ethical and truthful response from those who hold authority

condone unethical behavior. These two are obedience to authority and groupthink. While the pressure to conform as a result of these factors can be very strong, if we face an ethical dilemma and determine that the course of action favored by the organization is unethical, we must not sit idly by. We need to exercise our voice. In some cases, this means speaking truth to power.

Speaking truth to power is not sufficient by itself, however. A second major takeaway of this chapter is that to effectively address an ethical dilemma, you may need to become an agent of change and move your organization to take action. In addition to speaking up, you must also *close the circle*—that is, gain power and motivate others with power to address the ethical dilemma and change the organization's or group's questionable behavior. Just making your point of view known is insufficient.

We cannot always be silent despite the discomfort we may feel. The weight-of-reasons framework provides an analytical tool you can use to assess situations. Then, use it as a tool to persuade those with power to close the circle. Understand with whom you must work to create positive change within your organization, both in the short term and the long term.

To explain how organizational context influences ethical decision-making, we first address the problem of conformity. Research and experience show that people are prone to undertake unethical actions that go against their consciences, and which they might never consider, were it not for group and organizational pressures. To examine pressures for conformity that organizations exert on all of us, we first refer to the classic Milgram experiments on obedience. We then discuss the problem of groupthink, in which the pressure for you to conform comes not just from a boss or a supervisor but from the entire group. Throughout the chapter, we analyze instances such as the *Challenger* space shuttle disaster, in which employees provided ample warning that ethical lapses were occurring or could occur, but were unable to close the circle because others dismissed and belittled them. This chapter asks you to consider why such instances occur and what can be done to avert them. We outline some of the political tactics that you can use to "close the circle"—how you should call attention to an emerging ethical issue, take ownership, and take the steps needed to effectively address it. Speaking up when you observe something amiss can be hard enough, but it is only the start. You must also persuade others in groups and organizations and build coalitions of people who *together* have the power to address what has gone wrong.

## The Problem of Conformity

**LO 4.2:** Understand Kohlberg's theory of moral development and describe its implications for how managers address organizational pressures to act unethically.

We tend to think of decision-making as an individual affair, in which a person ponders a situation and then chooses what to do. In fact, the decisions we make are influenced by the world around us. In many instances, this influence comes through the interactions we have with the people with whom we regularly come in contact. Even when we think for ourselves, our thoughts and decisions are influenced by our social interactions. They are based on information others provide and beliefs that come from outside of ourselves, often from institutions such as religion, schools, and the family.[1] Indeed, our very selves are composed of social beliefs and habits. Pragmatist philosopher and psychologist George Herbert Mead wrote "that mind can never find expression, and could never have come into existence at all, except in terms of a social environment."[2] While you may think of yourself as a lone person pursuing your individual self-interest as a student, gamer, musician, accountant, or other role you play, what you actually do is based on understandings you learned from other people or sometimes created with them, and which normally were furnished by society. Nearly 400 years ago, the English poet John Donne captured this idea when he intoned that "no man is an island entire of itself; every man is a piece of the continent, a part of the main."[3]

There are many ways in which organizations influence the decisions that organizational members make. One reason why organizations exist is to influence people's behavior in the direction of meeting shared goals. While you may not think of organizations as instruments of control, almost all of the elements of organizations have the function of producing conformity in your behavior. An organization's mission statement, leadership, culture, structure, incentive systems, socialization processes such as training programs, and performance measurement systems affect the decisions you make. Organizations are designed to produce order and stability. Even in organizations that empower employees to make their own decisions, they do so with the aim of channeling behavior toward the achievement of a shared mission and goals.

> **Conformity**
> Compliance with the behaviors others expect one to perform

What are the ethical implications of conformity within organizations? On the one hand, employees (including top executives and managers) have a legal duty to act on behalf of the organization and its owners. The owners are the "principals" and the employees are their "agents." (We discuss the principal–agent relationship further in Chapter 7.) Agents must follow reasonable instructions, act within the limits of the authority they have been conferred, not improperly delegate their responsibilities to others, and obey the law. While the responsibility of agents to principals is broad and inclusive, agents do *not* have a fiduciary obligation to obey illegal or unethical direction. There are limits to what agents must do on behalf of principals. Indeed, when you, as an employee, know of an illegal or unethical act within your company, or even the intent to commit one, your failure to reveal it and to act against those who have initiated it can be construed as a crime. Your legal and ethical obligation to prevent harm overrides any duty of loyalty you owe to the organization's principals.

Yet the tendency on the part of many people in organizations is to check the ethical questions about what they have been told to do at the door. They may rationalize that business is a competitive, dog-eat-dog world where if they did not act unethically in accord with the expectations of their organizations, they would lose out in the competition for promotions and higher salaries, and could lose their jobs. An ability to compartmentalize ethics and view what organizations expect us to do as separate and different from the rest of our lives has allowed otherwise seemingly upstanding citizens to engage in what is now recognized as scandalous behavior. Kenneth Lay, who was CEO (chief executive officer) and Chairman of the Board at Enron, was convicted on six counts of fraud and conspiracy for his role in the company's financial scandal, yet he was a respected pillar of Houston society and benefactor of charities.

©iStockphoto.com/cosmin4000

This problem of seeing personal ethics and the ethics within a business organization as separate can be particularly acute in large, bureaucratic organizations.[4] In these organizations, we tend to do specialized tasks that come with written rules, and we are not given much discretion to make decisions on our own. In many instances, we are expected to do our jobs and obey orders rather than seeing "the bigger picture" and taking independent initiative. As a result, if ethical dilemmas arise, we neither feel responsible for addressing them nor

Sometimes, people do not challenge authority and address ethical problems because they feel that they are a small cog in a big machine.

feel accountable for doing so. Moreover, we may have reached the conclusion, perhaps erroneously, from observing the behavior that the most effective way to move up in the organization is not through integrity and resourcefulness, but rather by being a "good team player" and being loyal to our superiors regardless of what they ask us to do.[5] This conformity that stems from loyalty is only compounded by the feeling of being a small peg in a very large machine, powerless to challenge authority and effectively address the ethical dilemmas that an organization inevitably faces.

# THE TALE OF HEALTHSOUTH FOUNDER AND CEO RICHARD SCRUSHY[6]

From 1992 to 2002, HealthSouth, a leading provider of rehabilitation services and outpatient surgery, met the earnings expectations of Wall Street analysts nearly every quarter. At the end of each quarter, the company's assistant controller submitted the company's actual results, while inside the company, participants in a group called the "family" committed accounting fraud, finding the "dirt" they needed to fill the "hole" in top executives' desired earnings-per-share numbers. The "family" falsified accounting entries and inflated the company's assets by more than $1 billion. Meanwhile, CEO Scrushy acted as a model citizen and made millions of dollars off the inflated stock. A former gas station attendant, Scrushy recruited employees from humble backgrounds like his own. He went into the small towns

and campuses of rural Alabama looking for people he could "trust." Scrushy endlessly emphasized the value of teamwork. In 1985, shortly after he started the company, he told his employees that regardless of the situation they would have to "circle the wagons" and pull for one another. Indeed, a sculpture of a wagon sat on the lawn of company headquarters. In March of 2003, this charade came to an end. The U.S. Securities and Exchange Commission (SEC) sued the company for overstating profits by more than $1 billion, and Scrushy eventually went to prison for bribery and mail fraud. His swindle came to a horrible end. This case illustrates the problems that can arise from following a leader who discourages personal responsibility and emphasizes being a good team player.

In retrospect, HealthSouth's deceit was obvious, but in many situations the negative effects of conformity are not as clear-cut. The stakeholders who are affected are not fully recognized, and the consequences of different courses of action are not as clear-cut as in the *Challenger* shuttle case highlighted at the end of the chapter where decision-makers were pressured into making poor choices. It is your duty to try to prevent such situations by recognizing and addressing social influences on decision-making.

## The Psychological Foundations of Conformity

### Kohlberg's Theory

Noted Harvard psychologist Lawrence Kohlberg explored the factors that led human beings to conform. According to his theory, which was based on the work of noted psychologist Jean Piaget,[7] human moral development occurs through a six-stage process. The stages are often grouped into three levels, each with two stages (see Table 4.1).[8]

- At the *preconventional* level, Kohlberg maintained, people, typically children, at first seek to gain rewards and avoid punishments (Stage 1). Later, they are motivated by self-interest, very narrowly construed (Stage 2). At the preconventional level, Kohlberg maintained that people have little thought for others and little capacity for independent thought.

- At the *conventional* level, individuals still are not likely to think independently about moral matters. Rather, they are motivated by desire for others' approval (Stage 3) or a desire to maintain order (Stage 4). People at this stage, often adolescents, but many adults as well, fit into this category, act according to social conventions, and rarely ask why. They obey rules but do not have the capacity to challenge them or understand why they exist.

- Only at the *postconventional* level, Kohlberg argued, are people able to make conscious ethical choices. At Stage 5, they have a social contract orientation. They think carefully about the purpose and function of society's rules and follow those rules, even when they disagree with them, when they believe that the rules are reasonable and fair. They are willing to accept constraints on their behavior with the recognition that if everyone does so all will be made better off. Those at Stage 6, in contrast, are not motivated by keeping the social contract but rather by universal principles concerning what is just and fair. Note the correspondence of postconventional moral development to deontological ethics and contract theory discussed in Chapter 2.

According to Kohlberg, only individuals functioning at the postconventional level have the capacity to undertake moral inquiry and give a rational defense of their actions. They do not conform to the pressures of society simply because that is what

| TABLE 4.1 | Kohlberg's Levels and Stages of Moral Development[9] |
|---|---|
| *Level 1:* Preconventional | *Stage 1:* Obtain reward and avoid punishment |
| | *Stage 2:* Act on basis of self-interest (what's in it for me?) |
| *Level 2:* Conventional | *Stage 3:* Desire for others' approval |
| | *Stage 4:* Desire to maintain order and a willingness to abide by the rules |
| *Level 3:* Postconventional | *Stage 5:* Accept utilitarianism and the social contract; consciously obey laws and norms that seek to provide the greatest good for the greatest number |
| | *Stage 6:* Recognize, understand, and act in accordance with principles regardless of societal norms |

*Source:* Adapted from Lawrence Kohlberg, 1984. *The Psychology of Moral Development: The Nature and Validity of Moral Stages* (Essays on Moral Development, Volume 2). Harper & Row, New York.

is expected of them. Their autonomy enables them to challenge authority if it is unjust. While Kohlberg thought of the postconventional level as the adult level of moral development, not all adults actually reach this level. In fact, it has been found that only 10% to 15% of people reach the postconventional level of moral development and that some children may display it while adults do not.

Subsequent work in psychology has questioned the way in which Kohlberg conceived of moral development. One critique is that the process of moral development is not as linear as Kohlberg maintains. Research shows that people are not consistent. Sometimes, they behave at higher stages, but sometimes they regress to lower levels. Over our lives, we may move back and forth between levels depending on our mood and the situation we face. A person can reason from universal principles in one situation but act in a very narrowly self-interested way in another.[10] Scholars have also questioned whether abstract reasoning with a focus on justice is the highest stage. As noted in Chapter 2, Carol Gilligan and other feminist scholars argue that ethics involves compassion and that Kohlberg's understanding of moral development is male-oriented and culturally specific.[11]

These issues notwithstanding, Kohlberg's theory of moral development is still relevant today. In doing moral reasoning, too many adults stick to perspectives Kohlberg associates with children and adolescents. They respond primarily to the stimuli of reward and punishment, pursue self-interest, spend their time and energy trying to obtain others' approval, and follow the rules they are asked to obey without much reflection. To advance to a higher stage where they have more autonomy, they may need help. It is hard to get there by yourself. A very supportive environment may be necessary. Without a context that encourages us to exhibit our freedom, we may be unlikely to suppress the inclination to speak out. This is why managers must employ the weight-of-reasons framework and use appropriate decision-making approaches and techniques to build ethical organizations. We discuss these organizations further in Chapter 6.

# Obedience to Authority

LO 4.3: Explain why individuals tend to obey authority figures, based on Milgram's Obedience experiments.

Unfortunately, as already mentioned, too many organizations value conformity rather than autonomy and critical thinking. They are set up to encourage and reward obedience to authority. As a result, employees are put in compromising situations where their personal values conflict with organizational practices. In these situations, it is not easy to decide what to do. In many cases, we give in and "just follow orders," even when we feel that the orders are unjust. We obey when we do not understand the purpose of the orders, do not know how or do not have the courage to challenge them, and feel the pressure to conform.

This rationale of "just following orders" took on a sinister and chilling tone when Nazi war criminals regularly used it as a defense during the Nuremberg trials. After the World War II, many writers tried to understand how ordinary people could engage in systematic atrocities. Why did so many German citizens allow themselves to become the tools of repressive regimes that systematically slaughtered their citizens? Hannah Arendt identified this phenomenon as "the banality of evil" after covering the Nazi Adolf Eichmann's war crimes trial in Jerusalem.[12] She observed that people can carry out the most heinous evil without feeling particular moral anguish, provided they have the excuse that they are just obeying the orders of some authority above them. Contemporary writers continue to try to understand why ordinary people engage in atrocities. They contemplate this question with regard to mass murders that have taken place in Rwanda, Bosnia, Tibet, Chechnya, Myanmar, and other sites of genocide. Why is it that so many people who get involved in these situations lack the courage to extricate themselves from such appalling evildoing?

©iStockphoto.com/Gelia

## Milgram's Experiments

In a series of experiments conducted in the early 1960s, social psychologist Stanley Milgram considered the tension between individual conscience and organizational pressure. More than 1,000 participants were involved in these experiments, which were replicated with variations in numerous universities. In the experiments, an authority figure, apparently a scientist, directed a "teacher" to administer electric shocks to a "learner" whenever the learner answered a question incorrectly. With each incorrect answer, the teacher was instructed to increase the level of electric shock given to the learner. The electric shocks were simulated, and the "learner" actually was a professional actor, as was the authority figure.

The horrors of World War II led to a surge of scholarly interest in obedience to authority.

The purpose of the experiments was to determine how far ordinary people (the teachers) would go in inflicting increasing pain on a protesting victim. The researchers wanted to see whether ordinary people would continue inflicting pain as they heard the learners progressively grunt, complain, demand to be released, make vehement and emotional protests, scream in agonizing pain, and, finally, go silent, presumably because they had fallen unconscious or died. The results of Milgram's Obedience experiments were disturbing: Over one-half of the participants continued to administer the electric shocks even after they thought that they had caused horrible pain and possibly death. The exact level of obedience of the participants varied with variations in the experimental design.

The people in Milgram's studies did not take pleasure in delivering electric shocks to others. They were not psychopaths or sadists. They experienced emotional distress, which they displayed by putting their hands to their heads, slumping in their chairs, grimacing, tapping the desk in front of them, sweating, laughing nervously, pushing the shock switch lightly and for as little time as possible, arguing with the authority figure, and delaying the experiment until commanded by the authority figure to continue. Far from enjoying the experiment or continuing mindlessly and unemotionally, many of the participants experienced "learned helplessness," which involves surrendering and enduring a painful experience when one feels powerless and unable to escape.[13] Many of the participants simply gave up and tried to get the experience over with as quickly as possible.

### *Reasons for Obedience*

What explains this apparent willingness of so many people to inflict pain on others? Milgram concluded from these experiments that normal and otherwise reasonable people can engage in abhorrent, immoral behavior when commanded to do so by authority figures. The experiments tended to validate the arguments made by Hannah Arendt about average people giving into the demands of authority and Solomon Asch's theory of *social conformism*, which states that people tend to conform to norms when making decisions, especially when they are in unfamiliar situations and have no expertise.[14] Under these conditions, people search for social cues about behavioral expectations rather than listening to their own consciences. In the experiment, many of the participants took their cues from the authority figure and failed to disobey him.

Milgram's experiments show that when people become involved in a task, they tend to lose a sense of responsibility. They feel themselves to be simply the *agents of an authority figure*. They are just carrying out their duties and feel that the authority figure bears the moral responsibility for the consequences of their actions. It is all too common that subordinate employees in large organizations take this point of view. They do not independently analyze the consequences of their behavior, as the commonsense weight-of-reasons and other ethical decision-making frameworks require.

Another and related reason for obedience is that people are *committed to doing their jobs well*, even when the destructive consequences of what they are doing is clear to them. They understand that organizations and society are made up of a variety of narrow and specialized roles, and they want to be viewed as competent performers. They are not concerned with broader tasks of setting goals and assessing the morality of behaviors, because they assume that other people, far more competent than themselves, play those roles. Next, people continue to obey authority even when they recognize that what they are doing is wrong because of what Milgram referred to as *binding factors*. These factors, such as a desire to uphold the promise to conduct the experiment and the awkwardness of a withdrawal, lock people into the situation.

Finally, Milgram argued that people also tend to obey authority because they come to share the authority figures' beliefs, even if at first they do not. They do not just comply with the orders they are given; rather, they *internalize the justifications* for those orders in terms of what they perceive to be the views the authority figures have. That is, people sometimes engage in activities that cause harm to or violate the fundamental rights of others because they have come to believe that they are doing so for a just cause. The end, in their eyes, justifies the means. The participants in the Obedience experiments believed that the experiments, and science more broadly, are worthwhile and useful to society, and their benefits justify the negative impacts that any particular person suffers.

A number of cognitive biases (see Chapter 3) abet obedience. People selectively perceive evidence that supports their deep beliefs, they escalate their commitment to the path they have started to go down, and they exhibit great perseverance in beliefs that are patently absurd.[15]

This conclusion that people are able to ignore harm for what they perceive to be a just cause is a particularly troubling implication of the Obedience and related experiments. It suggests that people do not commit harm simply because they are under pressure and are unable to speak truth to power, but rather that they willingly and even gladly commit harm because they come to believe that it is the right thing to do. Just as some people in Nazi Germany, Bosnia, and Rwanda slaughtered innocents out of a sense of righteousness and duty, so too employees in business sometimes "cook the books," pay bribes, and cheat their customers for what they see as greater goods, such as keeping the company afloat and preserving their jobs.

### Situational Factors

Milgram carried out the Obedience experiments under a range of different conditions. He found that the degree to which the participants obeyed the commands of the authority figure varied significantly with experimental conditions. It is not the case that we always obey authority figures; rather, whether we do or not depends on the precise nature of the situation in which we operate. Human nature is exceptionally flexible; we are all to greater and lesser degrees capable of being compassionate and benevolent under one set of circumstances but also capable of doing harm to others under other circumstances. This conclusion applies to nearly everyone.

Indeed, Milgram identified a number of situational factors that had a significant influence on the behavior of the participants in his experiments. One of these was the *proximity and characteristics of the authority figure*. People were more

©iStockphoto.com/Orban Alija

People are more likely to take unethical actions when the victims of their actions are remote to them, just dots in a picture or numbers on a page.

likely to obey orders to undertake unethical activities when the authority figure was physically very near to them, and when the person had a strong, dominating personality and bearing. One can see how this would be important in a workplace; an employee is more likely to disobey orders from a boss to act unethically if the boss is not nearby, not seen very often, or easy to challenge.

A second situational factor Milgram identified was the *salience of the victim*. People are more likely to knowingly cause harm to other people when they do not know the other persons, have no connection with them, and cannot picture them. Milgram found that participants were much more likely to administer shocks to learners when the learners were in another room, compared with when the learners were in the same room. In business decisions, managers often take harmful actions because the victims are distant and hard to picture. They lose empathy because of the distance and because the victims are not known. Would managers who cheat investors out of their money, dump toxic pollution into the water, or make workers work in dangerous conditions take these actions if the victims were their family members or loved ones?

A third factor that Milgram identified as affecting the relation between perpetrator and victim was the *behavior of others* around us. As noted above, we tend to look around for cues as to what behaviors are considered appropriate. If we see others acting independently and resisting authority, then we are more likely to also resist. On the other hand, if we see others acting without integrity and cheating suppliers and customers, then we are more likely to consider such behavior acceptable and do the same. In the Obedience experiments, Milgram found that participants were more likely to continue giving shocks if they saw another participant giving them, and to stop giving shocks if they saw other participants protesting and discontinuing the experiment. The powerful lesson to draw is that organizational culture and climate have a strong impact on whether we behave ethically.

### Individual Factors

While the Obedience experiments demonstrated that many people were willing to obey authority figures even when it meant behaving unethically, it is also important to recognize that some participants refused to continue with the experiment. During the course of the experiment, their ethical intuitions gained momentum and became stronger than their inclination to obey. At the beginning, they accepted the premises of the experiment and obeyed authority figure's commands, but as the pain of the learner became more evident they became uncomfortable with continuing to obey the authority figure and instead chose not to harm the learner any further.

The binding factors that at first made them obey broke down, and by articulating opposition to the authority figure, they were able to extricate themselves. They did not necessarily engage in slow thinking, in the complete way the weight-of-reasons framework requires, but they did articulate reasons for breaking off from the experiment. They overcame their learned helplessness and communicated with the authority, speaking truth to power. Some did so from a *utilitarian* perspective, asking how much pain they were actually inflicting, whether the learner would survive the punishment, and whether the experiment's benefits justified the pain they were causing. Others enunciated deontological principles, asserting that it was just not *right* to inflict more pain on the participant.

Differences between those who inflicted the maximum amount of pain and those who desisted before this point for the most part did not correspond to demographic differences among the participants. Factors such as age, sex, religion, and ethnicity were not correlated with a tendency to obey or not to obey authority. Milgram ran one panel in which only women participated and found that women conformed to authority to the same extent as men but felt more stress in doing so. The only demographic variable that tended in some instances to correlate with opposition to authority was education level, but this correlation was not strong or significant. Obedience experiments have been replicated numerous times since Milgram first conducted them; although later researchers have had to make some changes to the experiments for ethical reasons, the replications have largely confirmed Milgram's initial findings.[16]

## Consequences of Obedience to Authority

Although obedience to authority may be a safe strategy for maintaining employment, it can come with feelings of terrible guilt and shame. Moreover, the price of obedience if the actions in which one engages are illegal can be criminal indictment. Indeed, lower-level employees can be more vulnerable to prosecution than their superiors, as their superiors seek to "push blame down" and claim "plausible deniability." The typical response of superiors is that they have no knowledge of the misdeeds of their subordinates, who are to blame. Even when investigators suspect that senior executives are involved, they sometimes indict lower-level employees first with the hope that these employees will testify against higher-ups on management in exchange for a light sentence or even immunity from prosecution.

In the massive fraud at WorldCom (described in more detail later in the chapter), several relatively minor players in the scandal faced significant time in prison. One was Betty Vinson, who was a midlevel accountant at a small long-distance company that WorldCom took over. While at first she balked when her bosses at WorldCom told her to make false accounting entries, she eventually agreed in order to keep her job. Along with those higher-up in the company, she and others in similar positions within the company were indicted for accounting fraud. While the judge in her case recognized the pressure that Vinson was under, she sentenced Vinson to five months in prison and five months of house arrest. The judge opined that although Ms. Vinson was "among the least culpable members of the conspiracy at WorldCom," it was also true that "had Ms. Vinson refused to do what she was asked, it's possible this conspiracy might have been nipped in the bud."[17]

In sum, the Obedience experiments teach us that while most, if not all, of us like to think that we would do the right thing and speak truth to power when necessary, in fact, we often do not. We are social animals who follow rules and norms. We tend not to question authority figures and accepted beliefs. We often look for cues as to what is right and wrong in others rather than trusting ourselves. When we do feel discomfort because our conscience is telling us that something is wrong, we tend to resolve the tension by doing what is easy and not what is difficult and right. Our inclination to obey can lead to negative personal and legal consequences down the road.

Milgram's studies depict people experiencing fast-thinking cognitive dissonance. Due to the nature of the experiments, none of the participants switched entirely to slow thinking and engaged in ethical deliberation. Had the participants tried to apply a framework such as the weight of reasons (which admittedly would have been difficult in the experimental setting), they might have realized that they were going down a path that had rotten consequences and contradicted their principles. They might instead have made an effort to act on the basis of their conscience and proceed relying on inner virtues such as integrity and bravery.

Thus, a key lesson of the Milgram experiments is to try to articulate your objections to immoral authority by switching from a fast-thinking to a slow-thinking mode. Listen to your ethical intuitions, communicate them, and express them—but also be willing to critique them and recognize their limitations. When you are in an unfamiliar situation or have conflicting intuitions, as did the participants in the Obedience experiments, use frameworks such as the weight of reasons to sort through your intuitions and identify the most ethical action to take, rather than simply conforming to the pressure you encounter. The weight-of-reasons framework can be a tool for challenging unjust authority and can provide you with the capacity to speak truth to power.

Another important lesson from the Obedience experiments is that managers must seek to create a work environment in which there is a culture that makes it easier for their employees to do the right thing. Employees respond to the cues around them. If they are told to act unethically, see other people acting unethically, and are rewarded for doing so, they are unlikely to desist. If, on the other hand, the organization has strong ethical values that the employees comply with every day, they are likely to do the right thing instead.

## Conformity Due to Groupthink

**LO 4.4:** Describe the characteristics of groupthink and the impacts of groupthink on ethical decision-making.

Sometimes, individuals in organizations engage in unethical and tragic behavior not because of direct pressure from an authority figure but rather because the dynamics of group decision-making processes push them toward conformity rather than toward conscious, engaged, and critical (System 2) decision-making (Figure 4.1). This bias toward conformity and consensus in group decision-making rather than careful evaluation of alternatives is known as groupthink. Irving Janis, the scholar most closely associated with the study of groupthink, wrote that in cases of

FIGURE 4.1

In groupthink, team members quickly and uncritically agree on an answer, but that answer could be wrong.

groupthink, "*concurrence-seeking* becomes so dominant in a cohesive in-group that it tends to override realistic appraisal of alternative courses of action."[18]

One of Janis's major insights is that groupthink is a by-product of group cohesiveness. A group is cohesive when the members of the group feel a strong bond with one another and with the group as a whole. While group cohesiveness is one of the major factors driving team effectiveness, it also has a dark side. Though you enjoy being on a tight-knit team, you must question whether the team is so tight-knit that it sticks to its thought and behaviors without entertaining needed fresh ideas.

In his research, Janis identified three types of symptoms of groupthink, all of which trace back to group cohesiveness. The first symptom is that the team members tend to *overestimate the group* and its effectiveness, power, and morality. When a team suffers from groupthink, its members feel that the team can do no wrong and is morally superior. Another symptom of groupthink is *closed-mindedness*. In a team suffering from groupthink, the members are not open to new ideas, rationalize poor results rather than critically examining their implications, and even negatively stereotype other groups (e.g., competitors and other departments within the company). Finally, groupthink is characterized by the *pressure to conform*. The "group-thinking" members of teams actively oppose and suppress dissenting viewpoints and opinions to preserve a perception of consensus. As a result, team members who hold dissident viewpoints and opinions are afraid to speak up because they feel that they will be seen as disloyal and disaffected.

While in some cases of groupthink, team members experience direct pressure not to speak up, in other cases, their response is more unconscious and automatic. The team members never even think to question unethical behavior. They are so certain of the rightness of the group's beliefs that they thoughtlessly act on them despite

the obvious immorality of doing so. Unfortunately, history provides endless examples of atrocious behaviors rooted in shared but misplaced ideological certainty. Both obedience to authority and groupthink help in explaining horrific events such as the Holocaust and other acts of genocide.

William H. Whyte Jr., a noted organizational scholar who coined the term *groupthink*, captured its essence when he noted that it involves not instinctive conformity as seen in the Milgram experiments but rather "rationalized conformity"—a conscious, shared belief that "group values are not only expedient but right and good as well."[19] This problem is more insidious than pressure from an authority figure. When groupthink is present, team members do not speak truth to power because they must confront not only their bosses but an entire team. Worse, they may believe that the command to take unethical action is legitimate and correct.

Dismissing and suppressing alternative viewpoints are symptoms of groupthink.

# PENN STATE FOOTBALL SEX ABUSE SCANDAL

In 2012, Pennsylvania State University (Penn State) assistant football coach Jerry Sandusky was convicted on 45 counts of rape, sexual abuse, and related charges.[20] Legendary football coach Joe Paterno apparently knew years before Sandusky's arrest that his longtime assistant might be sexually abusing children. In 2001, Mike McQueary, a one-time Paterno assistant, told Paterno of an incident between Sandusky and a young boy he witnessed in the locker room shower. Paterno allegedly replied that the claim was not the first he received. Paterno told McQueary that Sandusky "was a sick guy." Other documents suggest that Paterno had heard complaints as early as the 1970s. Two men asserted that they reported their abuse directly to Paterno at that time, and one of them alleged that the coach dismissed the reports, saying that he had "a football season" for which to prepare.

In 2011, Paterno did what he thought was the right thing to do and he sent the information McQueary

gave him to Penn State Athletic Director Tim Curley and Senior Vice President for Finance and Business Gary Schultz. These officials chose to handle the matter by advising Sandusky to get professional help, but did no more. After Paterno lost his coaching job of 46 years, he admitted that he should have followed up and made sure that Sandusky no longer was preying on children. Indeed, an independent investigation concluded that Paterno had convinced Curley, Schultz, and University President Graham Spanier *not* to report Sandusky to the police.[21] In the end, Sandusky was sentenced to 30 to 60 years in prison, effectively a life sentence given his advanced age. Curley and Schultz pleaded guilty to charges of endangering the welfare of children, and Spanier was convicted of the same charge after a trial. Paterno's legacy was irreparably tarnished and his statue in front of Penn State's football stadium torn down.

McQueary, Paterno, and top Penn State officials were guilty of groupthink. Rather than trying to stop Sandusky, they willfully concealed and condoned his unethical actions. According to an independent investigation, these men shared the belief that the Penn State football program had to be protected from bad publicity. They failed to acknowledge the child abuse and how it harmed young people, and they showed a "striking lack of empathy" for the victims. Moreover, the investigation concluded that Spanier, who was then the university president, fostered a climate that "discouraged discussion and debate." The problem of groupthink even extended far beyond university leaders; the independent report blamed the scandal on "a culture of reverence for the football program . . . ingrained at all levels of the campus community."[22] The *Challenger* space shuttle case presented later in this chapter documents another case of groupthink that led to tragedy.

## Challenging Unethical Behavior in Organizations: Voice, Whistle-Blowing, and Exiting

LO 4.5: Discuss the options an individual has to challenge unethical behavior.

What can you do when you feel pressure, whether from an authority or a group, to take unethical action? If you decide to speak truth to power, what will you say? In the best of circumstances, you should apply a formal decision-making framework such as the weight-of-reasons. But doing so is not always possible. In a situation such as that depicted in the Obedience experiments, you can neither do an exhaustive analysis of your options and their consequences nor recognize all the relevant principles. Hopefully, though, you will be able to look beyond your conflicted feelings and recognize that you do not have to conform. When there is more time, you can then, working with others, do a more thorough analysis that challenges the basic premises of the situation and produces a longer-term solution that gets at the root of the problem. For example, an employee feeling pressure from a boss might come to recognize that the problem is not so much the boss but rather the company's culture and business model.

In using good decision-making techniques such as the weight-of-reasons framework, there is a *pragmatic* element. When framing an issue and considering alternatives for addressing it, you also have to understand how to address unjust demands such as groupthink, which obstruct finding a solution, and you must consider how to be an effective actor within an organization. There is a need to develop principled "solutions" that can be realized on the ground.

Political economist Albert Hirschman theorized that individuals struggling with the quandary of an organization pressuring them to take unethical action have two choices: exit and voice. Exit means to withdraw from the situation—for example, leave the organization or request a transfer. Voice means to speak up, to communicate one's opinions and try to improve or change the situation. Hirschman noted that the choice between exit and voice is affected by the degree of one's loyalty to the organization. He observed that loyalty tends to increase the chances of voice and reduce the chances of exit.[23]

**Exit**
Withdrawing from confronting an ethical dilemma

**Voice**
Communicating one's grievance within the organization to address and change the situation

**Loyalty**
Support, devotion, faithfulness. Influences the decision to exit or use voice

Building on Hirschman's framework, we identify four options that an employee has when being pressured to accept or condone unethical behavior. These are (1) voice, (2) whistle-blowing, which is really just a special form of voice; (3) exit; and (4) obedience (discussed earlier).

## Voice

Voice refers to engaging the ethical issues one confronts and working with others to try to solve them. Part of the solution to an ethical dilemma could be confronting an authority figure who demands unethical behavior and/or resisting the pressures of a group to conform. Voice can be a difficult path to take and can lead to many unpleasant consequences, including punishment, dismissal, shunning by colleagues, transfer to uninteresting and unchallenging assignments, and banishment to distant locales.

Given that these outcomes can happen, why might you be willing to exercise your voice and challenge unethical authority? The first reason may be that you want to do the right thing, however defined, using the ethical approaches previously discussed. Especially if you have reached a postconventional level of moral development, you do not want to see others harmed or their dignity violated, and you want to take actions that are compassionate, virtuous, and fair. As depicted in Figure 4.2, there are other reasons as well. Closely related to ethics, your religious

**FIGURE 4.2**    Reasons to Exercise Voice

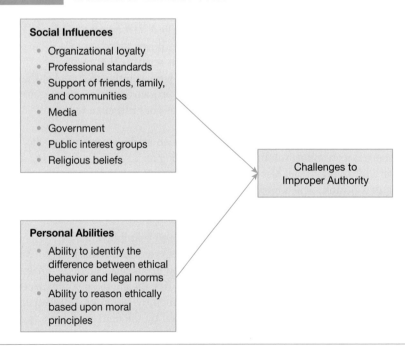

beliefs as well as the values and codes of conduct of your profession may compel you to act ethically. So might the advice of families, friends, and community members. A positive reception from the media, government, and public interest groups can also play a role.

A person's behavior when tested by a moral challenge cannot be predicted easily, yet studies have found that in many surprising and unanticipated ways people are willing to use voice and make sacrifices in order to maintain their integrity. Throughout history, people have risked their lives for others and for causes where the main rewards are helping others and an inner sense of doing what is right. Experiments have shown instances of inherently altruistic behavior. As we discussed in Chapter 2, there is more to self-interest than selfishness and greed. We often look beyond our own immediate and narrow interests, and feel good about ourselves when we do the "right thing."

### Closing the Circle

However, there is more to voice than just speaking up and presenting information. Rather, in the end, one must try to *"close the circle"*—that is, take ownership of the ethical issue and follow through by taking all the steps necessary to effectively address the issue. Closing the circle means influencing others in the organization. The "weapons of influence" one can use include, in addition to imposing authority to the degree one has it, being likable, presenting oneself as reliable, offering to do favors with the expectation that the favor will be returned ("I'll scratch your back if you scratch mine"), and pointing out that the behaviors you are recommending are the commonly accepted right thing to do.[24]

Closing the circle means that you must be willing to play organizational politics. Organizational politics is the set of activities organizational members engage in to acquire and use power in order to meet their goals. Power is the ability to carry out one's will despite resistance[25]; it is the ability to get what you want. Although politics tends to have a negative connotation because it is associated with unethical behavior for personal gain, organizational members can also play politics by ethical means for the purpose of meeting the organization's legitimate goals and accomplishing positive organizational change. You must be willing to use politics in order to solve ethical dilemmas.

Scholars have identified a range of political tactics that organizational members can use to accomplish their goals. One of the most important is coalition building. A coalition is a group of people who come together to try to achieve a common goal. While a single employee with little power may have difficulty in resisting pressure or advancing a solution to an ethical dilemma, the members of a coalition collectively may have the ability to obtain the information, expertise, decision-making authority, and persuasive ability needed to "close the circle" and resolve an ongoing ethical concern. A low-level employee who believes that groupthink is producing an unethical decision will have greater success in resisting and changing that decision if she can win over the most persuasive members of the group, the persons with special and relevant expertise, and the authorities responsible for making the final call. Furthermore, coalitions of people with diverse yet

**Closing the circle**
Taking ownership of an ethical issue and taking all the steps necessary to effectively address it

**Organizational politics**
The activities through which organizational members acquire and use power

**Power**
The ability to carry out one's will despite resistance; the ability to get what you want

**Coalition building**
Bringing individuals and groups together to work toward a common goal

complementary skill sets and perspectives also can come up with better ideas than any individual could alone.

Another important skill for closing the circle is the *ability to persuade*. In his classic text *Rhetoric*,[26] Aristotle identified three types of persuasion: (1) **ethos**, which is based on the credibility of the speaker; (2) **pathos**, which is persuasion based on an appeal to the audience's emotions; and (3) **logos**, which involves the use of logic (Table 4.2). A key insight of Aristotle's framework is that information and logic are often not enough; you will be more persuasive if you stir your audience's emotions. In closing the circle, you must not only identify the most ethical and practical course of action by applying slow thinking using the weight-of-reasons framework but also present this course of action in a way that is intuitively appealing to your audience. Your carefully considered conclusion must have an emotional appeal in addition to being logical.

An important part of persuasion is the ability to *frame ethical issues* so they have pathos. As discussed in earlier chapters, people make sense of emerging issues by categorizing them in particular ways. Managers often frame issues as "business issues," which causes them to discuss the issues in technical language and overlook their ethical dimensions. Just getting people to see the ethical dimensions of an issue can change the discussion and the decision that is made. Imagine if the Obedience experiment had been presented to participants not as an experiment in teaching and learning but rather as an experiment related to ethics and character. It is very unlikely that the participants would have persisted in shocking the learners in the way they did.

Finally, employees seeking to close the circle on an ethical issue must be able to *make deals* that align stakeholder interests. Whether when building a coalition or working with people who have opposing viewpoints, agents of change trying to close the circle on ethical issues must be flexible and willing to adjust their positions in order to achieve their goals. In his book *The Intelligence of Democracy*, political scientist Charles Lindblom used the term *mutual adjustment* to describe the ways in which actors with opposing interests coordinate their actions to reach mutually satisfactory outcomes. The adjustment techniques identified by Lindblom include negotiation, reciprocity (helping one another out), and deference (letting the other person have his or her way).[27] Each of these is appropriate under particular conditions. While deference may not seem like a good way to solve an ethical problem, it can be appropriate

**Ethos**
Persuasion based on the credibility of the speaker

**Pathos**
Persuasion based on an appeal to emotions

**Logos**
Persuasion based on the use of logic

**TABLE 4.2**   **Types of Persuasion**

| Type | Definition | Example |
|---|---|---|
| Ethos | Based on credibility | People know that you are a person of your word, you are trustworthy. |
| Pathos | Based on an appeal to emotion | You provide people with something they can identify with. |
| Logos | Based on logic | It is the ability to provide evidence of what is true. |

for a minor issue and can give you the power to be more demanding on a subsequent issue. You must understand how to "pick your battles."

In sum, identifying and raising an ethical problem is only the beginning of the process of addressing a dilemma. As hard as speaking truth to power can be, that too is just the start. To close the circle, one must make a commitment and follow through by bringing people together, by means of persuasion and negotiation. There is little joy in saying "I told you so" after tragedy occurs. It is better to proactively address and solve the ethical dilemma.

©iStockphoto.com/DjelicS

"Closing the circle" on ethical issues requires human skills such as collaborating and negotiating with people who have different viewpoints.

# SUCCESSFUL VOICE: WORLDCOM

Although exercising voice to close the circle and successfully address ethical issues is challenging, it has been done successfully. Consider the case of Cynthia Cooper at WorldCom. WorldCom started as a tiny long-distance telecommunications company in 1983 and then grew rapidly in the 1990s. In 1997, it made an unsolicited bid to take over MCI, a company more than three times its size. In 1998, *CFO Magazine* named WorldCom CFO (chief financial officer) Scott Sullivan one of the country's best CFOs. At the age of 37 years, he was earning $19.3 million a year.

By early 2001, because of overexpansion, WorldCom's earnings started to fall. Arthur Andersen (also Enron's auditor) performed the external audit of WorldCom's financial statements and verified their accuracy. Despite this, Cynthia Cooper, the vice president of internal audit at WorldCom, was skeptical. Cooper first became suspicious of accounting problems at WorldCom in 2002 when an executive told her that $400 million had been removed from a reserve account to boost the company's income.

When Cooper asked Arthur Andersen accountants about the maneuver, they told her that there was no problem. Sullivan also told her that everything was fine and to back off. Cooper was concerned that exercising her voice might jeopardize her job; nevertheless, Cooper did not trust what the firm told her and decided to put together a team to redo the audit. Cooper's team used a ruse to get into the company's restricted computer files. Working late into the night and keeping its project secret, it discovered that billions of dollars of expenses that had been characterized as capital expenditures were actually fees paid to local telephone companies to complete calls. This misclassification of the payments enabled WorldCom to turn a $662 million loss into a $2.4 billion profit in 2001.

Cooper confronted Sullivan again. He again asked her to desist, but she refused. Instead, she revealed her findings to the head of the audit committee of WorldCom's Board of Directors and challenged the company's controller, David Myers, to see if he could come up with an explanation. Cooper's

*(Continued)*

(Continued)

investigation ultimately showed that WorldCom had inflated its profits by about $9 billion—at the time the largest fraud of its kind in history. The audit committee terminated both Sullivan and Myers, who along with the CEO Bernard Ebbers ended up going to jail for fraud. Shareholders lost some $3 billion, and up to 17,000 WorldCom employees were without a job. Some fellow workers were angry with Cooper, saying that the company could have avoided bankruptcy if she had just stayed quiet. Of course, staying silent would not have been the ethical choice, and continuing to commit fraud was not a sustainable financial strategy.

Cynthia Cooper was able to close the circle. She was able to do so not only because she did a thorough investigation and had the facts on her side but also because she was able to build a coalition and use persuasion to win powerful actors over to her viewpoint.

### Difficulty of Closing the Circle

Unfortunately, business history is full of examples in which employees sought to close the circle but were unable to do so. In some cases, they failed because they lacked political skill or even the awareness that they could take ownership of an issue and try to drive change. In other cases, however, no matter how hard they tried, there may have been little they could do because their organizations were so impervious to change. Your ability to close the circle depends not only on skill but also on whether the "political opportunity structure" is open to the changes you seek.[28] When those who favor the current ways of thinking and operating hold all the strings of power and are well organized, and the organization has significant elements of groupthink, then voice may not be effective. In these cases, there may be no choice. Whistle-blowing may be the only effective approach to stopping unethical behavior. We will discuss this option next.

# EXAMPLES OF FAILED ATTEMPTS TO CLOSE THE CIRCLE

### Enron

Accounting scandals at the Houston-based energy company Enron led to the company's bankruptcy, the demise of the accounting firm Arthur Andersen, prison time for key company executives, and losses of billions of dollars for shareholders and employees. Executive Sherron Watkins became aware of accounting irregularities at Enron prior to the company's dissolution and she courageously raised the issue, but her efforts to use her voice to address the problem were unsuccessful.

Under the leadership of Chairman Kenneth Lay, CEO Jeff Skilling, and CFO Andrew Fastow, Enron morphed from a staid natural gas pipeline firm into a dynamic energy trading company. In 2001, Sherron Watkins went to work directly for Fastow and uncovered fraudulent transactions that Fastow had created to hide massive trading losses Enron had incurred. Watkins tried to get an explanation from higher-ups in the organization, though she was aware of the trouble that others had found themselves in when they challenged Fastow and Skilling. She thought of exiting Enron and started to look for a new job but planned to confront Skilling on her last day. However, Skilling abruptly quit. Watkins then expressed her concerns to Lay, writing him a confidential memo warning that the company could "implode in a wave of accounting scandals." Lay responded by telling her that he would have company attorneys look into the matter—and also confiscated her hard drive and demoted her from the executive suite.

Watkins feared for her physical safety, but she revered Lay and viewed him as a person of integrity. Her purpose in warning him of the accounting problems was to prompt him to take action. She wanted to hand him his "leadership moment." Lay did not seize the moment. Instead, he redeemed his personal stock options and assured the employees that the company's financial position never had been so strong. Six weeks later, the company announced a $618 million third-quarter loss and a $1.2 billion write-off, and a short time later, it filed for Chapter 11 bankruptcy. The efforts Sherron Watkins made to close the circle had failed.

### 9/11

On September 11, 2001, the Islamic terrorist organization al-Qaeda launched the deadliest terrorist attack in human history.[29] The group hijacked four commercial airline flights in the United States and used the planes to attack U.S. targets. The terrorists flew two of the planes into the North and South towers of the World Trade Center in New York City, and a third plane into the Pentagon building, the headquarters of the U.S. Department of Defense. The fourth plane was headed for Washington, D.C., but it crash-landed in Pennsylvania. The 9/11 attacks killed nearly 3,000 people and injured more than 6,000 others.

President George W. Bush had been briefed by intelligence 1 month before the attack about al-Qaeda leader Osama bin Laden's determination to inflict massive damage on the United States. Richard Clarke, a national security adviser to the President, as far back as January 2001, urgently requested a meeting to discuss the growing al-Qaeda threat and suggested strategies for combating it. Plots to fly airplanes into sensitive U.S. targets had been discussed in a Congressional hearing. However, National Security Adviser Condoleezza Rice demoted Clarke so he no longer had direct access to the president. Not to be deterred, in April 2001, Clarke urged the government to target bin Laden and his leadership with immediate airstrikes. At this time, Deputy Secretary of Defense Paul Wolfowitz dismissed Clarke's warning, declaring that he could not understand why "one man" should be taken so seriously. Despite Clarke's insistence that bin Laden and his network posed an imminent and serious threat to the United States, Wolfowitz maintained that Clarke was giving bin Laden "too much credit."

Just before the incident, in the summer of 2001, Clarke wrote again in briefings to high-level administration officials that he and others in the intelligence community were absolutely convinced that al-Qaeda was going to launch a pending attack on the United States, but he could not get the highest-level officials in the Bush administration to pay attention. At a July 5, 2001, White House gathering of the Federal Aviation Administration, the Coast Guard, the Federal Bureau of Investigation, and Secret Service, Clarke declared that "something really spectacular" was going "to happen soon" and warned of "1000s dead in the streets." He insisted that under similar circumstances, the Clinton administration had raised security levels at U.S. airports and that the Bush administration had to do the same. Allegedly, Bush's response to Clarke was, "All right, you have covered your ass." Sadly, although Clarke was absolutely on the mark, he did not succeed in closing the circle.

## Whistle-Blowing

When one's voice in an organization is muffled and dismissed, another option you have when confronted by pressure to ignore danger is **whistle-blowing**. Whistle-blowing can be defined as calling attention to unethical organizational conduct by informing someone outside the organization, be it a government regulator, law

**Whistle-blowing** Calling attention to unethical behavior by informing someone outside the organization

**Whistle-blower**
An organizational member who informs someone outside the organization of an organization's ethical behavior

enforcement official, media reporter, or the public directly. Later chapters discuss some of the laws protecting whistle-blowers and the mechanisms that companies have in place to report unethical behavior. This section focuses on the very difficult decision a person might have to make to blow the whistle when nearly all the other options of warning members in an organization are exhausted.

The choice between exercising voice and blowing the whistle clearly is not an easy one. In general, the decision to blow the whistle is a based on a political calculation of how one can be most effective in addressing unethical behavior. In general, voice is typically preferable because it provides an opportunity for collective problem-solving to correct such behavior. In general, employees should engage in whistle-blowing only after they have exhausted all efforts to use voice but the organization has failed to address its dubious activities and has shown a strong determination to stifle dissenting points of view. If the organization has established reliable internal mechanisms for preempting and addressing questionable behavior, then in theory there should be no reason for whistle-blowing.

Whistle-blowing should not be equated with disloyalty. Research has found that whistle-blowers are people who actually are dedicated to the work they do and the organizations they serve, and they challenge their organizations from a position of principle. Often, whistle-blowers feel that they are defending the organization's true mission, from which the organization has deviated.

Indeed, loyalty to the organization and to ethical values may be why whistle-blowers are willing to bear the great personal cost that comes with taking such an action. Whistle-blowers can face many different kinds of retaliation, including demotion, dismissal, transfer, personal harassment, and blacklisting (identification as a person to be avoided). Up to 90% of whistle-blowers, it has been estimated, suffer reprisal—nearly half are fired, half of those lose their homes, and half suffer a separation or divorce. Rarely is the ending happy. When challenged with an accusation, many corporations swing into a defensive mode instead of critically examining the charges raised. Even if the whistle-blower is not fired, he or she is generally no longer trusted and thus must give up the hope of ever succeeding in the organization.

An important reason why retaliation against whistle-blowers is prevalent is that a foundational principle of U.S. labor law is the "at-will" doctrine, which states that employers are free to hire and fire employees as they see fit. It is important to note, though, that the law does provide some whistle-blower protections. We discuss "at-will" employee and legal protections for whistle-blowers in later chapters.

Whistle-blowers should take a number of precautions to improve the chances of success and mitigate the possibility of retaliation:

- They should make sure that they are motivated by a desire to address unethical behavior rather than just personal animosity. In reality, it may be difficult to separate the two because motives are often mixed. What is crucial is that the case for whistle-blowing is objectively strong and not just a result of bitterness.

- The whistle-blower should verify and document evidence as much as possible and, if it must be obtained or revealed illegally, they should be sure that the potential harm posed by nondisclosure would justify the misappropriation.

- The whistle-blower must be able to make specific allegations and document them. Making untrue or unprovable claims opens up the possibility of a suit for defamation.

- The whistle-blower should be sure to both anticipate and document any retaliation.

- The whistle-blower should consult and retain an attorney to prepare and document the case and provide protection from retaliation.

In sum, although sometimes seen as traitors within the organization, a situation that can also befall those who exercise voice, a whistle-blower is likely to be a courageous and principled individual who has concluded that the best and perhaps only way to stop or resist wrongdoing within an organization is to bring it to the attention of those outside the organization. In doing so, the whistle-blower must plan her or his moves carefully and be willing to bear a potentially high personal cost.

## Exiting

An additional approach to opposing or resisting unethical behavior is simply to exit the organization. It is understandable why an employee under pressure would decide to quit. If you feel uncomfortable about obedience, have tried unsuccessfully to use voice, and concluded that whistle-blowing is not viable because the costs are too high or the chances of success are too low, then you might feel you have no other choice but to exit.

As with whistle-blowing, the costs of exit can be high. One might be unemployed or underemployed for some time, which can have significant personal and financial ramifications. Moreover, even if you leave, authorities may suspect that you have knowledge of the unethical behavior and pressure you to reveal what you know. Being under this type of suspicion is especially likely if you leave the organization around the time it is under scrutiny. Jeffrey Skilling, CEO of Enron, thought that he could exit without consequences because he left Enron before its worst troubles began. He claimed innocence of all knowledge and involvement in Enron's fraud and deceptions, but government attorneys did not accept this defense and conducted a rigorous investigation. Skilling was convicted of federal felony charges relating to Enron's collapse and sentenced to 14 years in prison.

As is clear to anyone who watches the business news, and as the Obedience experiments predict, managers often do not effectively resist pressures to engage in dubious activity. The case of the toxic leak at the Union Carbide pesticide plant in Bhopal, India, in 1984 provides an example of a situation in which voice and whistle-blowing failed. The Bhopal leak caused nearly 4,000 deaths and more than half a million nonfatal injuries. It is still considered the worst industrial accident in history.

# THE BHOPAL LEAK

Union Carbide's pesticide plant in Bhopal, India, had several safety systems designed to handle accidental leaks, including a vent gas scrubber that neutralized toxic gases with a caustic soda solution; a flare tower that could burn off the gases; a refrigeration system to keep the chemical at low, stable temperatures; and a set of water spray pipes that could control escaping gases or extinguish fires. None of these systems mattered on the night of the accident, however. The vent gas scrubber was undergoing maintenance and would not have been effective even if it had been operational because the temperature of the escaping gas was at least 100 °F hotter than what the system had been designed to handle. The flare tower also was being repaired and was missing a 4-foot section, and officials were afraid to turn it on during the leak anyway for fear of igniting the large cloud of gas that had enveloped the plant. Likewise, the coolant in the refrigeration system had been drained weeks before to be used in another part of the plant. The officials considered routing the escaping gas into an empty storage tank, but there were no empty tanks available, contrary to established safety procedures.

What makes these lapses inexcusable from an ethics perspective is that management at the plant and in Union Carbide's U.S. headquarters in Danbury, Connecticut, knew of these problems beforehand but had not acted to fix them. A series of articles written in 1982 by journalist Rajkumar Keswani detailed the death of a friend of his that was caused by a chemical leak at the plant. The articles warned of the possibility of a catastrophe, but neither the plant management nor the government took action, even after Keswani warned the state's chief minister of the danger. A top government official who requested that the plant be moved to another location because it posed a threat to neighboring residents was transferred to another post. Keswani was able to write his stories only because he received internal documents from two plant employees who had been fired. These two employees effectively turned whistleblowers after losing their jobs. Still, their efforts were not enough to prevent the tragedy.[30]

Sometimes vigilant external stakeholders try to expose corporate wrongdoing not because they have been tipped off by a whistle-blower, but because their own experiences led them to suspect the unethical behavior. Like whistle-blowers, these actors are sometimes but not always successful. In the fraud case of New York investor Bernard (Bernie) Madoff, government authorities were unwilling to act even after one of Madoff's competitors made a clear and compelling case that Madoff was engaging in illegal behavior.

# BERNIE MADOFF

The Ponzi scheme that Bernie Madoff ran was the biggest white-collar crime in U.S. history. A Ponzi scheme is a type of fraud in which an individual or organization pays quick and regular returns to investors by transferring money collected from other investors, rather than actually managing the money as promised. The illusion that investors are earning strong, steady returns enables those running the Ponzi scheme to attract even more investment. Using such a scheme, Madoff stole more than $65 billion from individuals, charities, and universities. In 2008, he confessed to his crimes and the next year was sentenced to 150 years in prison. Had the Great Financial Crisis not occurred and Madoff investors not demanded their money in greater amounts than they did typically (a Ponzi scheme can last only as long as investors hand over new money to pay existing investors), the scam would not have been uncovered. The government refused to act previously despite numerous well-documented warnings.

One of these warnings came from Harry Markopolos, an investment manager at a competing firm who understood that Madoff was running a Ponzi Scheme.[31] On three occasions, in 2000, 2001, and 2005, Markopolos brought a well-documented case against Madoff to the SEC so it could bring charges against Madoff, but the SEC refused to listen.

From 1991 to 2004, Markopolos was a portfolio manager at Boston-based options trading company called Rampart Investment Management, where he became its chief investment officer. In 1999, he learned from an associate that Rampart had dealings with a hedge fund manager who consistently delivered returns of 1% to 2% a month regardless of the overall market conditions. Markopolos's reaction was that this outcome was absolutely "too good to be true." Tasking himself the job of figuring out how Madoff did it, Markopolos almost immediately concluded that the only possibility was that Madoff was running a Ponzi scheme in which he paid established clients with new clients' money. According to Markopolos, anyone who understood market volatility would immediately have understood that Madoff was a fraud. If he was not running a Ponzi scheme, the only other possibility was that he was a massive inside trader getting regular illegal tips. Markopolos could find no evidence that Madoff even invested the money people gave him.

Indeed, on inspection, the accounting statements Madoff sent to investors often literally did not add up; they sometimes contained simple mathematical errors. The sophisticated institutions that invested in Madoff were willing to ignore these obvious signs of fraud because of the consistent returns Madoff delivered. In essence, they became the co-conspirators in his crime. Knowing that Madoff's investors included people with ties to organized crime, Markopolos even became concerned for his physical safety. In 2002, when he anonymously provided an investigative file to an aide of the then New York Attorney General Eliot Spitzer, he wore a pair of white gloves to prevent leaving fingerprints.

In 2005, still determined to expose Madoff, Markopolos sent a detailed document to the Boston branch of the SEC. The document, which was titled "The World's Largest Hedge Fund Is a Fraud," raised 30 red flags showing that Madoff's returns could not possibly be legitimate. In his 2009 testimony to Congress, Markopolos heavily criticized the SEC for ignoring his warnings. The SEC's excuse was that since the jurisdiction of its Boston office did not extend to New York City, Markopolos was not dealing with the right branch of the agency. Markopolos shot back that SEC lawyers were inept and their financial illiteracy was astounding. In his statement to Congress, Markopolos wrote,

> It is time the nation woke up and realized that it's not the armed robbers or drug dealers who cause the most economic harm, it's the white collar criminals. . . . They steal our pensions, bankrupt our companies, and destroy thousands of jobs, ruining countless lives.

## Applying the Weight-of-Reasons Framework to Close the Circle

**LO 4.6:** Apply the weight-of-reasons framework for ethical decision-making as an effective tool in helping to close the circle.

We now examine the space shuttle *Challenger* disaster to further exemplify the concepts of cognitive biases discussed in Chapter 3, the problem of groupthink, and the difficulties of exercising voice and closing the circle. Then we apply the weight-of-reasons framework to the case to determine if it would have helped prevent such an event.

# THE *CHALLENGER* SPACE SHUTTLE DISASTER

On January 28, 1986, the Space Shuttle *Challenger* shattered after only 73 seconds in the air. Its seven-person crew was lost when the vehicle fell into the sea. The failure of the solid rocket booster's O-ring seal that was responsible for this tragedy highlighted the National Aeronautics and Space Administration's (NASA) ongoing decision-making problems. These problems surfaced again in 2003 in the *Columbia* space shuttle disaster.

## The "Help" Memo

NASA declared 1986 the "Year of the Shuttle" and planned launches nearly every month of the year. However, in the summer of 1985, engineers at Morton Thiokol, the company that supplied the solid rocket boosters to NASA, expressed concerns about the O-ring seal of the *Challenger* rocket. There was very early evidence of serious O-ring erosion in space shuttle missions, but NASA, contrary to its own regulations, did not make the problem known outside Thiokol circles. The 1984 *Discovery* shuttle launch suggested that the problem was worse than initially thought, since it extended beyond the primary O-ring to the backup system that had to function in the event of O-ring failure. Thiokol engineers analyzed the issue, considered it relatively small, and concluded that the damage to the secondary system was an acceptable risk. But in 1985, when seven of nine launches showed O-ring erosion and the backup system heating and potentially malfunctioning, engineers understood that the problem was far worse than what they had first thought and could have catastrophic potential. Thiokol engineer Bob Ebeling wrote a memo in October 1985 revealing that a failure was most likely to occur if a launch was made at very low temperatures. He titled his memo "Help!" since he believed that senior management at Thiokol were not paying sufficient attention to the matter.

## Prior Delays

The *Challenger* space flight of January 28, 1986, was originally scheduled to take place two days earlier but was delayed twice. On January 26, the Kennedy Space Center chose to postpone the liftoff due to a weather forecast calling for strong winds and rain. The next day, a screw in the shuttle's crew hatch malfunctioned, and the battery in the drill that NASA used to fix this problem did not have power. NASA had set aside nine additional batteries as backups, but they also did not function. NASA was clearly frustrated that it was not getting the launch off in time. The next day's forecast, January 28, called for exceptionally cold temperatures. The temperature on the morning of the scheduled launch was predicted to be 24 °F.

## "A Big Gray Area"

Aware that Thiokol had raised concerns about low temperature launches, NASA consulted Bob Ebeling, who had written the "Help" memo, and asked him what temperature qualified for a safe launch. Ebeling assembled his O-ring task force team, and nearly everyone on the team agreed that a launch below 40°F could be "catastrophic." Yet they had never tested O-rings at the below freezing temperatures that were forecast for January 28. Ebeling responded that NASA should not think of making a launch at a temperature as low as was expected on January 28, since it was a "big gray area" and Thiokol did not have good data to answer NASA's question of whether the launch would be safe under prevailing conditions.

Ebeling called NASA's Marshall Space Flight Center in Alabama to make his team's misgivings known. NASA's senior manager Jud Lovingood maintained that Thiokol had counseled NASA to wait until later in the day, since by noon the weather might warm up, but he was not satisfied with this response. Lovingood insisted on a specific temperature in which Thiokol would endorse a liftoff and asked that Thiokol be available for a formal teleconference 2 hours later involving Marshall Space Flight Center employees in Alabama, Kennedy Space Center employees in Florida, and Thiokol employees in Utah. The meeting would be held that evening, 15 hours before the planned launch. Thiokol was to be prepared to defend its position about whether NASA should launch that morning.

Roger Boisjoly and Arnie Thompson were Thiokol's senior O-ring experts. Boisjoly was tasked with making the presentation to NASA. This moment was the one for which he had been waiting. He grabbed all the paperwork he had accumulated in his office to make his case, but there was no time to do a dry run and coordinate what he would say to Thiokol management. Contractors like Thiokol had the right to make a recommendation to delay a launch, but they were hesitant to exercise this power if NASA had a strong desire to meet its launch schedule. A contractor had never before prevented a planned liftoff.

Boisjoly tried to demonstrate as best he could that a low-temperature liftoff would slow the sealing of the O-ring's primary seal. An O-ring, Boisjoly maintained, had less "squeeze" and more "hardness" at low temperatures and its "actuation time" went up. If the actuation time increases, the "threshold of secondary seal pressurization capability is approached" and the O-ring might not be capable of pressurization. Boisjoly held that the "probability" was "high," based on the tests Thiokol had done, that the secondary seal designed to back up the primary one would not function correctly. Under these circumstances, there was the likelihood of hot gas leakage and a possible explosion.

Boisjoly was relieved that the other members of the Thiokol team appeared to support his position. They gave NASA what it wanted: a specific temperature below which a launch was unacceptable. They told NASA that they considered a launch below 53 °F unacceptable. Boisjoly thought that the issue might be settled. However, Lovingood, NASA's senior manager, was not convinced, and he thought that Thiokol lacked the data to support this position. Thiokol's guidance, according to Lovingood, was based on emotion and fear. Other NASA engineers saw an opening and stepped in and tried to take apart what Boisjoly had said. Afterward, Boisjoly said that he felt as if he were "hammered," but Lovingood maintained that he considered NASA's questioning to be mild compared with its typical interrogation of a contractor.

The controversy between the two sides escalated. NASA tried to show that the factual basis for upending its ambitious launch schedule was not adequate, yet it could not under the circumstances oppose a contractor's recommendation. NASA, according to Lovingood, was at Thiokol's "mercy." One NASA official told Thiokol, "I am appalled. I am appalled by your recommendation." Another official proclaimed, "My God, Thiokol! When do you want us to launch—next April?"

## A Time-Out

Thiokol managers called for a time-out to further consider the matter on their own. Boisjoly told them to look at the photographs he previously had shown them and repeated that "the more black that you see between the seals, the lower the temperature, the closer you are to a disaster." Boisjoly screamed at them to just look at the photographs, but Thiokol's managers shut out Boisjoly and Thompson from the discussion and sought no further input from them.

Not deterred, Thompson entered the managers' discussion without permission and emphatically supported what Boisjoly had said. He had no doubts that allowing NASA to proceed with the launch would be a disaster. Later, Thompson recalled that he tried to do what he could. He told the managers what he knew but understood that the ultimate choice was in their hands. He could do no more.

With Boisjoly and Thompson, the two engineers most knowledgeable about the O-rings out of the way, Thiokol's general manager turned to the three senior Thiokol managers at the table and asked them for their opinion. Two agreed that it would be OK to launch, but one hesitated. The general manager then turned to him and said, "Take off your engineering hat and put on your management hat." According to Boisjoly, as soon as the general manager made that statement, it was obvious that Thiokol would change its recommendation to accommodate NASA. It would endorse a launch because NASA was its main customer. Just 30 minutes previously, the same Thiokol manager had opposed a launch, but now under pressure from NASA, Thiokol had reversed its position. When the teleconference resumed and NASA heard that Thiokol now favored the launch, NASA did not ask why the change took place. Lovingood later admitted, "That was stupid on our part." NASA should have asked Thiokol what led to the change.

*(Continued)*

(Continued)

## No One Opposed

Before coming to a conclusion, NASA asked everyone who participated in the meeting if they opposed a launch. No one, including Boisjoly and Thompson, raised their hands in opposition. They thought that it was too late. They had been defeated. Boisjoly recalled that he went home that morning after the long all-night meeting looking sullen and not saying a word to his wife. When she asked what was wrong, he told her, "Oh nothing honey, it was a great day, we just had a meeting to go launch tomorrow and kill the astronauts, but outside of that it was a great day."

The next morning, NASA cleared the ice from the spacecraft. It thought that it was taking a prudent step. Clearing the ice meant that the liftoff was delayed to almost noon, a time when the weather was slightly warmer. It started the countdown, and Boisjoly and Thompson watched. They were very relieved that the shuttle did not blow up on the launch pad as they expected, but soon thereafter, the O-rings did fail. *Challenger's* computers desperately tried to counter the forces driving the rocket into the sea with extreme steering commands, but there was nothing NASA could do at this point to save the shuttle's astronauts. They died when the cabin they had occupied plunged into ocean at a speed of more than 200 miles per hour.

## The Postaccident Investigation

The disaster resulted in a 32-month hiatus in the shuttle program. NASA could not meet its ambitious schedule. President Reagan created the Rogers Commission to investigate the incident. It put the blame for the disaster on NASA, Thiokol, and the faulty O-rings. In his testimony before the Rogers Commission, Boisjoly walked through the heated confrontation and debate that had taken place on the eve of the launch. He maintained that Thiokol and NASA had knowingly assumed the risk. He testified that Thiokol engineers understood the potential for the explosion and had tried to persuade NASA to delay the launch but to no avail.

The Rogers Commission found that a combination of downplaying the risk and suppressing dissent stifled ethical concerns for human lives. NASA had placed the astronauts at risk for the sake of maintaining good appearances and staying on schedule. The culture at NASA was hierarchical, secretive, and internally competitive. Information did not flow through the proper channels, and concern for deadlines and securing appropriations far outweighed concerns about safety.

At Thiokol, Boisjoly was relegated to assignments unrelated to the space program that were far from his former status and position. Managers within the company accused him of airing its "dirty laundry" and asserted that he could not be trusted. Boisjoly himself suffered from post-traumatic stress disorder because he felt guilty about his inability to prevent the astronauts' deaths. NASA's ambitious schedule for human space voyages came to a screeching halt, and Thiokol ultimately went bankrupt.

## A Repeat: The *Columbia* Disaster[32]

Sadly, NASA did not learn the lessons from the *Challenger* disaster. On February 1, 2003, the world again watched in horror as the space shuttle *Columbia* self-destructed—this time on entry, not launch. Broken pieces of the shuttle's insulating foam, damaged on launch, caused the disaster. The final report of the Columbia Accident Investigation Board acknowledged the foam as the likely catalyst for the disaster, but the board cited that NASA had again ignored numerous warnings and a bureaucratic culture that disregarded human life and allowed the disaster to occur. It characterized the agency as continuing to have a "broken safety culture," and it concluded that the accident "was probably not an anomalous, random event . . . but rather likely rooted to some degree in NASA's history and the human space flight program's culture." Findings in the board's 250-page report held,

> while it would be inaccurate to say that NASA managed the space shuttle program at the time of the *Columbia* accident in the same manner it did prior to *Challenger*, there are unfortunate similarities between the agency's performance and safety practices in both periods.

## Closing the Circle: Could the *Challenger* Disaster Have Been Averted?

The *Challenger* accident provides a clear and tragic case of obedience to authority and groupthink. The parties to the decision to launch clearly *overestimated themselves*; because of their prior successful launches, they did not take seriously enough the possibility of a launch failure. Moreover, they had a deep belief in the importance of the space program and, although not articulated, believed that launching was not only a scheduling imperative but also the morally correct thing to do. As a result, key decision-makers were *closed-minded*. NASA officials like Lovingood had a strong commitment to launching on schedule and were dismissive of the concerns of O-ring engineers Boisjoly and Thompson. Finally, the launch decision process was marked by a great *pressure to obey and conform*. NASA officials discredited Boisjoly and Thompson's work and intimidated them and Thiokol's managers. Most tellingly, Boisjoly and Thompson self-censored. They remained silent at key moments when voice was necessary. The *Challenger* shuttle decision was also marked by cognitive biases discussed in the prior chapter, including confirmation bias, status quo bias, and escalation of commitment.

The seven members of the *Challenger* crew as they headed out to the launch pad.

While it is easy with hindsight to criticize Boisjoly, it is important to remember that in many respects he was an admirable individual filled with good intentions. He had a strong conscience and a desire to speak out and do what was right. He did try to voice his concerns, and he had a sense of responsibility and an intense feeling of guilt after the tragedy. Nonetheless, in this critical instance in his life, when he was severely tested, he was not able to close the circle. He had ethos (credibility) because he was the O-ring expert, but he was not able to fully take advantage of it. He was unable to employ pathos to persuade NASA decision-makers. Imagine if Boisjoly, rather than assenting to the launch decision, had banged his fist on the table, vigorously maintained that he opposed the launch, and even threatened to blow the whistle. Could NASA decision-makers have just walked away from the table and proceeded with the launch?

Although he had O-ring expertise, Boisjoly also failed to use logos. He and Thompson would have had more success if they had been able to translate their knowledge into a firm decision rule such as an automatic stop that below some temperature no launches should be permitted, period, end of discussion. NASA has many such rules as does any organization that deals with safety, such as airlines. NASA, the night before launch, was looking for such a stop rule. If a definitive stop rule had been in place, it most likely would have led to no agonizing on the part of NASA and Thiokol about whether or not to go ahead.

Had they also invoked virtues such as courage, integrity, and compassion and decided to become agents of change, Morton Thiokol's engineers would have employed political strategies to change the decision process, close the circle, and avoid the tragic deaths of *Challenger's* astronauts. They would have framed the decision differently for the group, making it clear to all involved that the decision was an ethical one—a matter of life and death—as well as an operational and technical one. They would have employed logos and pathos as well as ethos to persuade NASA decision-makers to view the decision differently, and they would have developed a coalition-building strategy for winning enough decision-makers over to their side. Perhaps if they could have convinced only one Morton Thiokol executive who had a strong relationship with a key NASA executive, they could have started to change minds. They might have been more effective if they had viewed their dilemma as a political problem as well as an ethical and operational one.

## Using the Framework and Closing the Circle

As a thought experiment, imagine that the parties to the launch decision had used the weight-of-reasons framework—identifying the issue and facts clearly, asking those assembled to consider conscientiously the options and consequence, urging them to rely on principles such as the value of a human life, seeking both a short-term response with respect to the delay that day and a long-term plan of better criteria of when and when not to proceed, and drawing on their experience and the lessons of past launches to make their decision. If they had done so, they might have

- conceived of the presenting *issue* (Step 1) as one of astronaut safety rather than in terms of engineering specifications and meeting deadlines;

- gathered a fuller set of *facts* (Step 2), specifically about how O-rings perform at low temperatures;

- analyzed a set of *action options* (Step 3) that went beyond launching or not launching in the morning as clearly they had a third option, which was to delay the launch;

- assessed a much broader set of *consequences* (Step 4). They really only assessed whether NASA would meet its deadline and Thiokol would keep its contract with NASA. A utilitarian ethics approach demands much more. The impacts of a disaster on the lives of the Shuttle's astronauts, their loved ones, and communities were not openly discussed. Even from a bottom-line perspective, the analysis was incomplete; the public relations disaster that engulfed NASA and Thiokol was ignored;

- considered astronaut safety to be their guiding *principle* (Step 5). Instead, carrying out a task on deadline seemed to be the operant principle for NASA personnel, while maintaining business ties to its main customer was the guiding principle at Morton Thiokol;

- taken safety more seriously and realized that they were addressing an ethical issue; the NASA/Thiokol team may have chosen to delay the launch and then implemented a *short-term plan* (Step 6) for implementing that decision. The plan may have included a thorough investigation of the O-ring problem, development of a new policy such as a stop rule for handling such problems, the rescheduling of the launch, and a stakeholder communication plan for explaining the decision to the public and oversight bodies such as the U.S. Congress;

- recognized that NASA had a fundamental organizational problem, which included undertaking activities that were inherently risky but making decisions in a bureaucratic, time-sensitive fashion that undervalued safety. On recognizing this problem, decision-makers could have made a *long-term plan* (Step 7) to change NASA's organizational structure, culture, and decision-making processes so personnel would be more comfortable in exercising their voices. The plan would include steps for closing the circle and consideration of how to play politics in the organization in order to make positive change; and

- *learned* from implementing the short-term and long-term plans (Step 8) that through the process of addressing the O-ring problem, and rescheduling the launch, NASA would be more sensitive to safety. Launch teams would be in a better position to effectively address emerging ethical issues. Proof that it did not learn, despite the thorough Rogers Commission report, was that the *Columbia* disaster was eerily similar to the *Challenger* disaster.

The *Challenger* disaster underscores the insidious nature of obedience to authority and groupthink. They are pervasive. Later chapters discuss approaches to decision-making and organizational design that attempt to counter these problems.

## SUMMARY AND CONCLUSION

The key point of this chapter is that situational factors influence the ethical decisions individuals make, and can lead them to make unethical decisions. While we might like to believe that we are ethical people who control our own behaviors, in fact, in many situations, many of us will conform to pressures to engage in unethical behavior. Social factors influence the courses of action we identify, the consequences we consider, the principles we apply, and even whether we see an issue as "ethical."

In describing Kohlberg's stage model of human moral development, we noted that many people do not think independently about ethical issues (although they might think they do), but rather are motivated to seek the approval of others to maintain order. They equate moral agency with following the accepted rules of their groups, organizations, and societies.

We discussed two types of social influences that feed on the tendency toward conformity and can produce unethical behavior. We discussed the lessons of Milgram's Obedience experiments, which showed that people have a strong tendency to obey authority. Rather than following their own moral compasses, people obey orders when asked to take unethical actions, especially if those orders come from an authority figure who is perceived to be legitimate. They transfer responsibility for their actions to the authority figure. The probability of obeying unjust orders increases when the authority figure is nearby and has a commanding nature, the suffering of the victim is remote, and others around them are obeying orders. But not all people obey orders to act unethically when pressured to do so. We noted that although it may be difficult, the individual has the duty to "speak truth to power" when confronted by pressure to act unethically.

We then discussed groupthink. When it occurs, the pressure to conform comes not just from a single authority figure but rather from the entire group. Individuals have difficulty acting on their beliefs when doing so requires them to oppose a tightly knit group of people who have lost their minds to alternative viewpoints. A team may be caught up in its own success, get stuck in its ways, and not be able to recognize and address ethical problems.

We then discussed the strategies organizational members can use to resist taking unethical actions. It is your job, everybody's job, to speak up rather than being a "good soldier." Rely on tools such as the weight-of-reasons framework. Using it will enable you to redefine issues so their ethical dimensions become more evident and you will gather different sets of facts, identify a broader range of action options, assess consequences for stakeholders you might not otherwise have considered, and apply principles that might have been disregarded.

Applying the weight of reasons is no academic exercise; it involves a pragmatic calculation about how to "close the circle." Voice and whistle-blowing are ways of "closing the circle." Voice is not just speaking up but relying on organizational politics to make sure that action follows. The politics of persuasion, coalition building, and deal-making are needed. Be like the leader of a social movement, an agent of change who can persuade others to advance an agenda. If voice does not or is unlikely to work, you may have no alternative but to "blow the whistle." Whistle-blowers often are principled people compelled to address wrongdoing, even if doing so is stressful and dangerous.

Ultimately, organizations can do more to ensure that the social influences in an organization move employees toward ethical behavior. That is where we are going in the next two chapters. We describe approaches to decision-making to stimulate healthy debate, counter groupthink, and develop imaginative solutions. Managers can instill ethical behavior through leadership, establishing values-based ethics programs, and designing structures, cultures, and incentives that reward ethical behavior. "Ethical organizations" with these features institutionalize use of the weight-of-reasons framework and make ethical behavior easier for individuals.

From an ethical perspective, you are accountable for your actions even when you are under pressure to act unethically. Few of us are like Socrates or Jesus, who were willing to die for their beliefs. Still, when we become aware that an ethical boundary has been crossed, we must try to close the circle. Avoid the regret that the participants in the *Challenger* decision had.

## KEY TERMS AND CONCEPTS

Closing the circle  107
Coalition building  107
Conformity  93
Ethos  108
Exit  105
Groupthink  92

Logos  108
Loyalty  105
Obedience to authority  92
Organizational politics  107
Pathos  108
Power  107

Truth to power  92
Voice  105
Whistle-blower  112
Whistle-blowing  111

## CASES RELATED TO THE READING

Consider reading the following cases found in Chapter 10 that apply to the concepts presented in this chapter:

- BP: The Big Oil Spill: What Went Wrong

- Dow–DuPont: The Bhopal Disaster

- Google: Doing No Harm

- VW: Dieselgate

## CASE APPLICATIONS

Use the weight-of-reasons framework to figure out what you would do in the following instances. As you do so, apply the lessons from this chapter. Identify the social influences on your decision, and in identifying possible courses of action, consider whether you should exercise voice, blow the whistle, or exit (where they are applicable). If you choose voice, consider the political tactics needed to "close the circle."

### Case 4.1: Ethical Dilemma at High Value Discount Appliances

The High Value (HV) chain of discount appliance stores, started in 1988 with the merger of three smaller chains, achieved sales in excess of $28 billion under the respected leadership of its CEO, John Sutherland. Investors included major banks, insurance companies, real estate developers, and investment banking houses. HV was touted by the media as one of the most outstanding companies in the United States. It was especially praised for its culture, which has been described as being "fresh, dynamic, and exciting." Fortune chose HV as one of the 10 best companies to work for in the United States.

John Sutherland came from a prominent U.S. family and was a pillar of society. An active supporter of many prominent causes, he was considered one of the most influential and respected U.S. philanthropists and a patron of the arts. He was also a major contributor to political parties and part-owner of two professional sport franchises, the Dallas Ravens (in basketball) and the Miami Bulldogs (in football). A star ski bowler in his college years at Dartmouth, Sutherland had devoted considerable time to making it a national sport in the United States. In 1989, he founded the U.S. Ski Bowling Association (USSBA), which now has eight teams. As USSBA's main corporate sponsor, HV attached its name to nearly all the league's activities. HV's brand and the USSBA were nearly indistinguishable.

In 2001, you had the chance to meet Sutherland at a ski bowling match. You too had been a star ski bowler in college and had even been a good professional player before tearing your ankle tendons in a career-ending injury. Although nearly 20 years his junior, you immediately developed a rapport with Sutherland. It so happened that your wife's cousin was a close associate of Sutherland's and an investor in a number of Sutherland's businesses.

In 2005, you ran into Sutherland again. He invited you to play golf and tennis and go boating with him near his home in Long Island. After a game of tennis, Sutherland asked whether you would like to join HV Discount Appliances as his personal assistant. "Why don't you come and work for me?" He offered you a generous salary, which was important to you because you had a spouse and two young children to support. You like not only Sutherland

but also the group of young, athletic, and talented men and women whom Sutherland gathered around him. You fit right in with this crowd of hard-working, fun-loving people. In contrast, you were bored stiff with your current banking job, and your career there was going nowhere. The bank had never felt like home. The decision was not difficult: You accepted Sutherland's offer.

After starting work at HV, you were assigned your portfolio of duties as Sutherland's assistant. One was quite unique and perfectly suited to you: You were to be the company's liaison to U.S. ski bowling. In this position, you were able to capitalize on the fact that many customers recalled your college and professional ski bowling exploits.

On July 4, 2014, after a tennis game with Sutherland at his estate, he asked you to pick up some files from his office and then bring them to him. While in Sutherland's office, you accidentally dropped the files and scattered their contents across the floor. On picking them up, you inadvertently saw a memo from Sutherland to the company's CFO, with whom you had become close through your work. The memo read,

> There are no irregularities in the statements of inventory or accounts receivable, as Gomez alleges. These are judgment calls, as we all know. There is no reason to be conservative in making these calls and to make it appear as if our profits are any less than they are. You realize as well as I that every year we are subject to an independent audit by the respected firm of McDuffey and Spather. How can we fool such experienced auditors into believing that our inventory and accounts receivable are less than reported? Explain the situation to Gomez, thank him for his diligence, transfer him to a part of the company

where he no longer can be concerned with these matters, and provide him with appropriate remuneration for his efforts. The so-called irregularities do not exist, as we both know.

The past year had not been good for appliance companies. The industry was in a tailspin—too many competitors and insufficient profits. Most investors thought that HV would weather the storm; however, Brian Bagley, an analyst from an obscure brokerage, had started to question why the company continued to be successful. He thought HV had opened too many stores and that many of them would not be profitable. "The numbers," Bagley claimed, "do not add up." Sutherland was furious whenever he heard Bagley's name. "A nobody who did not know what he was talking about" is what Sutherland said of Bagley. Bagley's analysis led other analysts to start questioning HV's finances. Yet year after year, HV's reported profits never seemed to falter. Sutherland earned one substantial bonus after another and was able to cash in on large stock options worth millions.

The Ski Bowling league, on the other hand, was having difficulties. It was not taking off in the United States. Sutherland had regularly dipped into his personal fortune to provide the league with infusions of cash. Your future was tied to the USSBA. You feared that if it was going nowhere, the same was true of you. Attendance was down, and most teams were near bankruptcy. Without more money, the league might fold. Sutherland had been on the telephone for days trying to persuade his wealthy friends to give more money, but they saw the league as a losing proposition and refused to help. They saw no reason to prop it up and keep it going.

After your tennis match with Sutherland, you found him in an uncharacteristically bad mood. He sadly said,

There is not much more I can do. My bonus and stock options this coming year will be nowhere near what they were in the past. From now on High Value will have to start playing it much closer to the vest. I don't want the league to fold, but I have sunk as much cash as I can into it. We both know, though, that we could temporarily borrow $500 to 600 million from the company and no one would have to know. What do you think?

What do you make of Sutherland's remarks? Use the weight-of-reasons framework to decide how you should address the ethical dilemma you face. In doing so, consider not just what is right but also how you can use political tactics to close the circle. What will you say to Sutherland, and what will you then do?

### Case 4.2: Polishing an Image

You have just received your MBA and for the past year and a half, you have worked as a financial accountant for a company that is conducting talks about a proposed merger with another firm. A director of the company approaches you to enlist your support in "polishing the company's image" for the upcoming merger talks. She asks for "some terrific forecasts of industry growth and market share" to give her "some leverage" in the talk. She says, "Be a good team player and do what I say, and it will all work out for the best." You are not naive. You know that the figures you choose as the basis for the forecasts and the approach and techniques you employ can influence the results. On the one hand, you could massage the data to paint a fairly rosy picture of the company's future. On the other hand, you could analyze the data to show pitfalls ahead and the prospects of rough going. While accounting standards exist for all accountants, the interpretation of how those standards apply varies. The rules applying to the numbers a person brings to the table in merger talks seem to give you substantial leeway. You like the job and the company. You have formed many close ties with the people involved, including the director, who is a role model for you. What should you do?

## Case 4.3: Down the Drain

After a yearlong search, you finally have a job in the industry of your choice. The industry is high-status and dynamic, with excellent growth potential. Landing a job in this industry makes you the envy of your fellow graduates in the MBA program. However, you discover that the company is using a recently banned chemical as a cleansing agent, which is then flushed down the drain. When you ask why the company is acting in this fashion, you are told that it has a large supply of the chemical in storage and it is only using up the remaining amount—to toss what is left would be silly. To safely dispose of the cleansing agent is a bother, and the alternative compound proposed by the government is very expensive. Moreover, you are told that the company officials believe that the government has been overly cautious in banning the chemical because the company has had no past reported health problems related to it. Your supervisor tells you, "Don't be naive. Real companies operate differently than you expect. If you want to succeed in this company, you'll have to go along." What should you do?

## Case 4.4: A Tight-Knit Group of Brokers

You have worked together with three other stock brokers in the same company for the past 12 years. The four of you are the best of friends, with strong personal ties going back 30 years; you grew up with these people, know their families, and go to the same elementary school and same church. Nevertheless, it is a surprise when one of the four reveals that he has been successfully trading on "tips" from an unmentioned source. You know that your friend has been having personal financial difficulties, but things seemed to be improving. Now you think you know why. Your friend invites you and the other members of the group to join in the trades based on the tips. You, too, face financial challenges as your children approach college age and apply to private schools with high price tags. Your parents are aging and face a deteriorating financial situation. You have recently become concerned about dipping into your savings merely to meet monthly living expenses. One of your friends eagerly accepts the offer to trade based on the tips, but another argues that doing so may be against the law. She says that the trades are not worth the risk of getting caught, and she is in no way interested in hurting her family or career. You suspect that she might not participate in a cover-up if an investigation occurs. Your trader friend explains his scheme. It seems foolproof, though perhaps of doubtful legality. The risks of getting caught appear minimal. What should you do?

## NOTES

1. Berger, P. L., & Luckmann, T. (1991). *The social construction of reality: A treatise in the sociology of knowledge.* London, UK: Penguin Books.
2. See p. 246, in Mead, G. H. (1964). *On social psychology: Selected papers* (A. Strauss, Ed.). Chicago, IL: University of Chicago Press.
3. See p. 1624, in Donne, J. (1959). *Devotions upon emergent occasions.* Ann Arbor: University of Michigan Press.
4. "The separation thesis" in business ethics is discussed by Freeman, R. E. (1994). The politics of stakeholder theory: Some future directions.

*Business Ethics Quarterly, 4*(4), 409–421; Freeman, R. E. (1999). Divergent stakeholder theory. *Academy of Management Review, 24*, 233–236; Freeman, R. E., Wicks, A. C., & Parmar, B. (2004). Stakeholder theory and the corporate objective revisited. *Organization Science, 15*, 364–369; Harris, J. D., & Freeman, R. E. (2008). The impossibility of the separation thesis. *Business Ethics Quarterly, 18*, 541–548.

5. Jackall, R. (1988). *Moral mazes: The world of corporate managers.* New York, NY: Oxford University Press.

6. See https://www.nytimes.com/topic/person/richard-m-scrushy.

7. Piaget, J. (1932). *The moral judgment of the child.* London, UK: Kegan Paul, Trench, Trubner.

8. Kohlberg, L. (1958). *The development of modes of thinking and choices in years 10 to 16* (Doctoral dissertation). University of Chicago, IL. Retrieved from https://www.worldcat.org/title/development-of-modes-of-moral-thinking-and-choice-in-the-years-10-to-16/oclc/4612732; Kohlberg, L. (1984). Essays on moral development: Vol. 2. *The psychology of moral development: The nature and validity of moral stages.* New York, NY: Harper & Row.

9. Adapted from Kohlberg (1958, 1984).

10. Parke, R., Gauvain, M., & Schmuckler, M. (2009). *Child psychology: A contemporary.* New York, NY: McGraw-Hill; Carpendale, J. I. (2000). Kohlberg and Piaget on stages and moral reasoning. *Developmental Review, 20*(2), 181–205; Krebs, D. L., & Denton, K. (2005). Toward a more pragmatic approach to morality: A critical evaluation of Kohlberg's model. *Psychological Review, 112*(3), 629–649.

11. Gilligan, C. (1977). In a different voice: Women's conceptions of self and of morality. *Harvard Educational Review, 47*(4), 481–517.

12. Arendt, H. (1964). *Eichmann in Jerusalem.* New York, NY: Viking Press.

13. Seligman, M. (1975). *Helplessness: On depression, development, and death.* San Francisco, CA: W. H. Freeman.

14. Asch, S. E. (1956). Studies of independence and conformity: I. A minority of one against a unanimous majority. *Psychological Monographs: General and Applied, 70*(9), 1–70.

15. Festinger, L., Riecken, H. W., & Schachter, S. (1956). *When prophecy fails.* Minneapolis: University of Minnesota.

16. Burger, J. M. (2009). Replicating Milgram: Would people still obey today? *American Psychologist, 64*(1), 1–11; Sheridan, C. L., & King, R. G. (1972). Obedience to authority with an authentic victim. In *Proceedings of the annual convention of the American Psychological Association* (Vol. 7, Pt. 1, pp. 165–166). Washington, DC: American Psychological Association; Elliott, T. (2012, April 26). Dark legacy left by shock tactics. *Sydney Morning Herald.*

17. The Associated Press. (2005, August 6). AuEx-WorldCom accountant gets prison term. *The New York Times.* Retrieved from https://www.nytimes.com/2005/08/06/business/exworldcom-accountant-gets-prison-term.html

18. See p. 335, in Janis, I. L. (1971). Groupthink. *Psychology Today, 5*(6), 43–46, 74–76.

19. Whyte, W. H., Jr. (2012, July 22). Groupthink (Fortune 1952). *Fortune.* Retrieved from http://fortune.com/2012/07/22/groupthink-fortune-1952/

20. Penn State Scandal Fast Facts. (2019, May 8). *CNN.* Retrieved from https://www.cnn.com/2013/10/28/us/penn-state-scandal-fast-facts/index.html

21. Belson, K. (2012, July 12). Abuse scandal inquiry damns Paterno and Penn State. *The New York Times.* Retrieved from https://www.nytimes.com/2012/07/13/sports/ncaafootball/13pennstate.html

22. Freeh Sporkin & Sullivan, LLP. (2012). *Report of the Special Investigative Counsel regarding the actions of The Pennsylvania State University related to the child sexual abuse committed by Gerald A. Sandusky* (pp. 16–17). Retrieved from http://www.bishop-accountability.org/reports/2012_07_12_Freeh_Penn_State_Report.pdf

23. Hirschman, A. (1970). *Exit, voice, and loyalty: Responses to decline in firms, organizations, and states.* Cambridge, MA: Harvard University Press.

24. Cialdini, R. B. (2001). *Influence: Science and practice* (4th ed.). Boston, MA: Allyn & Bacon.

25. Weber, M. (1978). *Economy and society: An outline of interpretive sociology.* Berkeley: University of California Press.

26. Aristotle. (1991). *The art of rhetoric* (H. C. Lawson-Tancred, Trans.). New York, NY: Penguin Books.

27. Lindblom, C. E. (1965). *The intelligence of democracy: Decision making through mutual adjustment.* New York, NY: Free Press.

28. McAdam, D., McCarthy, J. D., & Zald, M. N. (1996). Introduction: Opportunities, mobilizing structures, and framing processes: Toward a synthetic, comparative perspective on social movements. In D. McAdam, J. D. McCarthy, & M. N. Zald (Eds.), *Comparative perspectives on social movements: Political opportunities, mobilizing structures and cultural framings* (pp. 1–20). New York, NY: Cambridge University Press.

29. Graham, G. (2009). *By his own rules: The ambitions, successes, and ultimate failures of Donald Rumsfeld*. New York, NY: Perseus Books.

30. Bhopal gas tragedy: The man who tried to expose Union Carbide and the warnings that were ignored. (2014, December 8). *News18.com*. Retrieved from https://www.news18.com/videos/india/bhopal-gas-tragedy-7-730177.html

31. Markopolos, H. (2010). *No one would listen: A true financial thriller*. Hoboken, NJ: Wiley.

32. Starbuck, W., & Farjoun, M. (Eds.). (2009). *Organization at the limit: Lessons from the Columbia disaster*. New York, NY: Wiley.

In addressing ethical dilemmas, managers must be aware of time constraints but also keep in mind the bigger picture.

# From Short-Term Fixes to Long-Term Solutions

## Learning Objectives

On completion of this chapter, the reader should be able to do the following:

LO 5.1:  Explain single-, double-, and triple-loop learning.

LO 5.2:  Understand the importance of making learning a part of the decision process.

LO 5.3:  Apply systems thinking to ethical problems to investigate solutions to those problems.

LO 5.4:  Use both/and thinking to recognize and address the contradictions at the core of many ethical issues.

LO 5.5:  Use moral imagination to develop imaginative solutions to complex ethical dilemmas.

LO 5.6:  Establish team-based processes to employ inquiry and advocacy in making effective ethical decisions.

LO 5.7:  Use tools such as trial-and-error and experimental learning to deal with uncertainty in ethical decision-making.

LO 5.8:  Recognize how organizations can undertake learning spirals to continuously improve their ability to address ethical dilemmas.

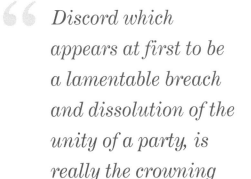

*Discord which appears at first to be a lamentable breach and dissolution of the unity of a party, is really the crowning proof of its success.*

—**G. W. F. Hegel**, *Phenomenology of Spirit* (1807)

# Introduction

**LO 5.1:** Explain single-, double-, and triple-loop learning.

Thus far, this book has familiarized you with the weight-of-reasons framework for making ethical decisions. We have shown that for relatively simple ethical issues that are not symptomatic of deeper tensions and problems, a fast decision made at Step 6 (short-term solution) of the framework often is adequate. For many ethical problems, however, short-term solutions are not sufficient because they address symptoms but not the underlying problems that produce these symptoms. Factors such as cognitive biases and social pressures to conform—discussed in Chapters 3 and 4—get in the way of developing lasting solutions. In the short term, decision-makers may not have all the facts they would like to have. They may not have the time and resources required to diagnose deeper issues and problems and understand all of their action options, and they may be unable to predict the consequences of those actions. They also may have to push aside important, "bigger-picture" difficulties such as basic disagreements about whether the organization has the right mission, priorities, leadership, structure, and so on. In the short term, decision-makers also may have bargained, compromised, or let someone else have his or her way rather than deal with tough issues. To get beyond all of these decision-making limitations, organizations must move from Step 6 of the weight-of-reasons framework to Step 7.

At Step 7, to build a deeper understanding of and achieve long-term solutions to ethical problems, managers must view decision-making as a *process*, a journey, rather than a *one-time fix*. A key way to transition to longer-term solutions is to recognize patterns and understand why ethical problems recur. In other words, it is incumbent on decision makers to engage in **organizational learning**. It is especially important for them to move from **single-loop learning**, where they may question their courses of action but not challenge organizational assumptions and goals, to **double-loop learning**, where they do question them (Figure 5.1). They must not only search for relevant facts but also find and address the patterns underlying them.[1]

Take, for example, a company that has a code of conduct requiring supply chain managers to review foreign country supplier working conditions once every 2 years. A manager engaging in single-loop learning would ask, "When was the last time we reviewed our suppliers? It's time for another review." In contrast, a manager engaging in double-loop learning would say, "We keep having persistent problems with worker mistreatment among our suppliers. We must reconsider how we do the reviews. Do we follow up to make sure our suppliers

©iStockphoto.com/DrAfter123

**Organizational learning**
The ability to recognize repeated patterns to affect change

**Single-loop learning**
Learning that occurs through questioning actions

**Double-loop learning**
Learning that occurs through questioning underlying goals and assumptions

It is necessary to recognize patterns to be able to address recurring ethical issues.

FIGURE 5.1    Single- and Double-Loop Learning

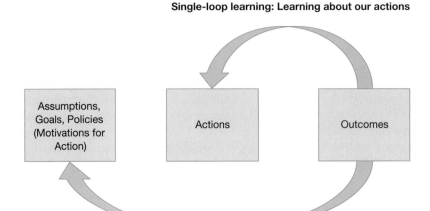

**Single-loop learning: Learning about our actions**

Assumptions, Goals, Policies (Motivations for Action)

Actions

Outcomes

**Double-loop learning: Learning about the goals, assumptions, and other motivations for our actions**

comply with recommendations? What do we do if a supplier is not in compliance? Would we be willing to stop working with that supplier? We cannot simply cite suppliers for noncompliance. We have to collaborate with them to improve their performance." When you recognize and examine not only issues and facts but also assumptions, goals, policies, and motivations for actions, you engage in double-loop learning.[2] You must be willing to question a company's procedures and the logic behind them (Figure 5.1).

Organizations can go even further than double-loop learning and engage in **triple-loop learning**. In triple-loop learning, individuals not only examine their actions, goals, and heuristics; they also question the deep assumptions and values of their cultures and also may come to accept the validity of other cultures.[3] A supply chain manager practicing triple-loop learning would examine the working conditions among suppliers and also assess the cultural norms and values in home countries that regularly produce abuses. A manager engaging in triple-loop learning might say, "We must reexamine our business model. Why do we rely on suppliers in this part of the world? Would we be better off if we no longer contracted the work out to these suppliers and did it inside the company?" To develop a long-term solution to a seemingly intractable problem, then, an organization must reassess how it carries out its business. Does it have the right business model? Its ethical problems are strategic ones. Recurrent workplace abuses should lead an organization to rethink how it does business.

The purpose of this chapter, therefore, is to flesh out Step 7 of the weight-of-reasons framework. It describes the nature of effective decision processes that will allow you to get to the bottom of complex, recurring ethical problems. Double- and

**Triple-loop learning** Learning that occurs through questioning underlying cultural assumptions and values and by being open to other cultural assumptions and values

triple-loop learning assist in this process. They provide a deeper understanding of why ethical lapses take place. The learning processes discussed in this chapter should enable you to better define issues, uncover additional facts, reconsider options and consequences, and reexamine and move beyond short-term fixes. Figure 5.2 captures this, showing that developing long-term solutions means constantly working through the weight-of-reasons framework.

## Building Learning Into Decision Processes

LO 5.2: Understand the importance of making learning a part of the decision process.

Learning needs to be built into an organization's decision processes in order to produce better ethical decisions. Thus, this chapter takes up systems thinking, a form of double-loop learning in which decision-makers develop a deeper understanding of the context in which their decisions are made. Systems thinking enables you to better understand the underlying roots of problems and to envision actions that address underlying causes. It allows you to connect the ethical dilemmas you have identified to an organization's broader context and strategies.

**Systems thinking**
Thinking to understand the nature of a system

**FIGURE 5.2**

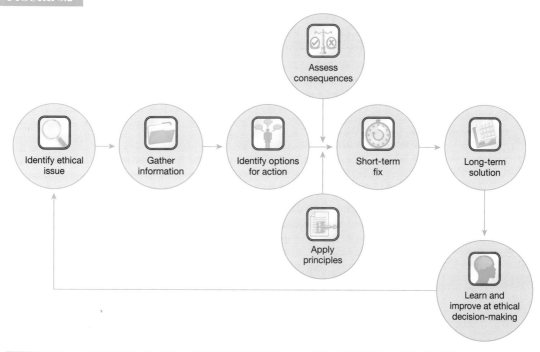

Developing long-term solutions to ethical problems requires visiting all the prior steps in the weight-of-reasons framework.

Next, we consider *both/and thinking*. Often it is difficult to develop long-term solutions to ethical issues because of organizational tensions that seem irreconcilable. In some instances, these tensions truly cannot be reconciled, in which case managers must accept them and use strategies such as compromise to manage them. In other cases, though, if decision-makers are willing to probe deeply and develop a more profound understanding of what is taking place, they may be able to develop long-term solutions that reconcile the elements in tension. An example would be when a company such as Costco, which has developed a business model that emphasizes worker satisfaction and at the same time, increases productivity and profits in the process by increasing motivation and reducing absenteeism, turnover, and hiring costs.

Another important tool in developing long-term solutions is *moral imagination*, which involves surfacing and challenging ethical beliefs and assumptions, considering alternative viewpoints, and creative ethical problem-solving. Managers employing moral imagination will look beyond the usual in every step of the weight-of-reasons framework. Moral imagination takes the decision-maker beyond double-loop learning because it involves not only challenging assumptions but also developing innovative solutions.

**Team-based decision-making process**
A process in which members of a team work together to make decisions

**Incremental decision-making process**
A decision-making, process in which a major decision is made over time through a series of smaller decisions

**Learning spiral**
A continuous learning process in which the organization moves toward ever-higher levels of knowledge

Decision-making approaches such as systems thinking, both/and thinking, and moral imagination can improve ethical decision-making in theory, but due to bounded rationality and cognitive biases, managers are likely to have difficulty putting them into practice. Team-based decision-making processes, if they are structured and carried out properly to avoid groupthink and similar problems, can address these problems. It is important to discuss how teams that engage in constructive conflict can develop effective long-term solutions to ethical issues. We also explain that teams trying to develop long-term solutions to ethical problems can use incremental decision-making processes that employ rapid feedback and learning to address uncertainties they face. Incremental decision-making processes help managers to gradually move toward bold long-term solutions by taking a series of smaller steps.

The idea behind learning spirals is that ethical decision-making is more effective when it is a continuous process of learning by using systems thinking, both/and thinking, moral imagination, and uncertainty reduction techniques such as incremental decision-making. It is important to keep in mind, though, that there is nothing inevitable about learning spirals. Because of the impediments discussed in Chapters 3 and 4—the difficulties we face in understanding and achieving our self-interest, groupthink, organizational politics, and others—organizations can fail to learn. The challenge is to use tools such as those this chapter provides to overcome these difficulties.

While the tools described here require time, discipline, and slow thinking and can be difficult for managers to use, they are worthwhile because they produce more ethical decisions. Moreover, by using these tools, managers may ultimately economize on their bounded rationality and save themselves time and effort. By actually developing long-term solutions to the ethical problems they face, these managers can avoid spending their time fixing errors, changing course, and revisiting problems they have already addressed.

# Systems Thinking

LO 5.3: Apply systems thinking to ethical problems to investigate solutions to those problems.

Systems thinking is an important tool managers can use to overcome their limited understanding of ethical problems and their options for addressing them. Systems thinkers focus not on particular actors or actions but rather on the systems in which the actors and actions are a part. A system is a group of interdependent parts organized into a coherent, unified whole, which exists for a specific purpose.[4] Systems thinkers analyze the forest rather than the trees. Systems thinking can help you overcome the cognitive and social biases described in earlier chapters.[5]

The interdependence of parts characterizes systems (Figure 5.3). This interdependence means that each element influences and is influenced by other elements. For example, the work of a particular employee influences and is influenced by that of other employees in the department, as well as by that of individuals in other departments and organizations. An accounting executive responsible for preparing a company's monthly financial statements cannot do the job without exchanging information with people in the company's sales, logistics, manufacturing, design, engineering, and other departments.

A system's structure is the set of rules and arrangements that influence the activities of actors within the system. An organization's structure determines which work units or departments it has, the roles people play, the assignment of authority and accountability, and the flow of information. An accounting executive has the responsibility to prepare monthly financial statements, the authority to decide how to prepare them, and the right to delegate responsibility for tasks to others. She may assign responsibility for collecting sales information to one person, accounts receivable information to someone else, and accounts payable information to still another employee.

Systems processes are another important aspect of systems. They are sequences of activities that predictably recur over time. The accounting department, for example, is likely to have an established sequence in which the other departments submit preliminary information and the accounting department generates preliminary financial statements. Then it makes adjustments, reviews the monthly financial statements, and finally releases them. When they are released, they have effects on the broader systems of which the company is a part, such as the industry and society.

An important insight of systems thinking is that one should not attribute behavior to a single person in the system. Rather, that person's behavior emerges from

**System**
A group of interdependent parts that is organized into a coherent, unified whole and exists for a specific purpose

**Interdependence**
The mutual dependence of the parts of a system

**Systems structure**
The rules and arrangements that influence the activities that occur within the system

**System processes**
The patterns of activities that recur over time within the system

**FIGURE 5.3**

A system consists of many interrelated parts making up a whole.

a web of interconnections.[6] While a company might hold an accounting manager responsible for whether she or he delivers honest and factual monthly financial statements, whether she does so in fact depends on the actions of many people in the organization and outside it. (If there is fundamental attribution error, which we discussed in Chapter 3, they would fail to realize this and blame accounting misstatements entirely on the accounting manager.)

The Wells Fargo case in Chapter 10 illustrates the point that behavior emerges from within a system. In that case, the bank's employees created new accounts for existing customers and charged these customers fees without their knowledge or consent, illegally generating millions of dollars in revenue. Systems thinking helps us to see that this illegal behavior was not simply the fault of unethical employees taking advantage of the opportunity to boost their performance numbers. Rather, the employees were under great pressure from the company's top management, who imposed performance criteria that were impossible to meet and created a culture that tolerated and even rewarded unethical behavior. The employees' behavior cannot be understood without understanding the broader system in which they operated.

**Feedback loops**
Behaviors of a system in which one action affects additional actions

The behaviors of a system are determined by whether feedback loops are positive or negative. Positive loops take place when changes reinforce one another. For example, there would be a positive feedback loop if an accounting manager's lack of concern for details came on top of the human resources (HR) department's tendency to hire careless employees. In this case, sloppy financial records and statements would be the product of neither HR nor the accounting manager alone but rather would occur because the behaviors reinforced each other.

In contrast, negative or balancing feedback can act as a check on the momentum that positive feedback generates. Changes in the actions of one element in the system can offset or diminish changes in another. This type of feedback stabilizes the system because changes in one element are contained. They do not reverberate throughout the system and are less likely to lead to catastrophic results. An example of negative feedback would be when an organization offsets the hiring of careless accountants with a thorough training program and internal controls that ensure that the organization is able to catch and correct the errors new accountants make.

©iStockphoto.com/DNY59

Developing lasting solutions to ethical problems requires seeing the forest as well as the trees.

Systems thinking can help decision-makers to develop long-term solutions to ethical problems by helping them dig deeper at every step in the weight-of-reasons framework. A systems perspective may be most helpful in identifying action options and assessing their expected consequences (Steps 3 and 4 of the framework). When decision-makers recognize the interconnections between actors within a system, and understand whether activities involving these systems and actors generate positive or negative feedback loops, they can begin to visualize how specific courses of action will reverberate throughout the system. Using systems thinking might lead to the conclusion, for example, that punishing managers who "fudge the numbers" is not a long-term solution, because there are many elements of the system that influence managers' behaviors. Even if particular managers are punished, other managers will continue to cheat because the system provides incentives for cheating.

Take, for example, a manager who creates a fake invoice to inflate revenues. Perhaps this manager was threatened by a boss, who himself was not a "bad person" but rather was under pressure from his boss, who felt the company's stock price would drop if the company did not show higher profits than its competitors. Furthermore, perhaps the manager faked the invoice because of a perceived legal duty she had to the company's shareholders. The reason for this belief is that the company and its competitors are part of a global network of markets and institutions that encourage higher profits. While a single manager ultimately may be held responsible for falsifying accounting records, from a systems perspective the cause of the action is much more complicated, and the problem of falsifying records will not go away until all of the significant factors contributing to the problem are addressed. Systems thinking, therefore, may lead managers to realize that the problem they need to solve is not the one they originally thought it was (Step 1 of the weight-of-reasons framework). For example, they may realize that their problem is not an unethical manager but rather the company's policies and strategies. Rather than being a case of a dishonest accountant, the core issue involves leadership, culture, incentives, and corporate governance.

Systems thinking brings to light an uncomfortable truth about ethical decision-making, which is that although managers must take responsibility for addressing ethical issues, they may not control all of the elements causing the issues to arise in the first place. Changing a whole system is likely to be beyond the power or resources of any individual. Managers may feel frustrated and powerless because they realize that the ethical problems they must address are only symptoms of deeper problems that they are unable to address. A manager who is being pressured by her boss to fudge the numbers does not want to hear that the problem is not her boss but rather the system that pressures and encourages people like her and her boss to cut corners. The manager of an employee who lied may realize that the employee was under great pressure, but the manager may not be able to do anything to relieve the pressure, although she still has to discipline that employee.

This awareness does not mean, however, that managers should give up entirely on developing systematic long-term solutions to ethical problems. Just because a manager cannot control the entire system does not mean she should be satisfied with simplistic short-term fixes, such as affixing blame on individual offenders. Managers can start by trying to effect change in the parts of the system they can influence (e.g., work groups, departments) and then work toward making change throughout the system, such as in organizations and industries. Using an incremental approach (discussed later in the chapter), managers can begin to gradually build toward systems change using political tactics such as those discussed in the previous chapter. Eventually, they can attempt to make systems change by setting up decision processes that include all the relevant stakeholders from within and outside the organization and then working through frameworks such as the weight of reasons with them. Developing a long-term solution to a problem such as pervasive accounting malfeasance ultimately may require establishing a learning process that involves many stakeholders—competitors, regulators, professional associations, corporate governance scholars, and others. In Chapter 8, we will discuss cross-sector partnerships and other tools to bring about systems-level changes.

## Both/And Thinking

**LO 5.4:** Use both/and thinking to recognize and address the contradictions at the core of many ethical issues.

Sometimes ethical decisions are challenging because the problems seem hopelessly intractable. What do you do when satisfying your obligations to all parties to a decision appears to be impossible and painful trade-offs are inevitable? For example, what should you do if it appears that there is no other way to keep your company afloat than shutting down factories and terminating the employment of thousands of workers? What if every course of action with positive consequences for the organization (Step 4 of the weight of reasons) is inconsistent with the principle of respecting individual rights (Step 5)? It is important to recognize that such situations are inherent in life; they may not be avoidable.

**Contradiction**
A dynamic tension between opposite elements that together form a unity and logically presuppose each other for their very existence and meanings

### Contradictions

According to Western philosophy, from the Ancient Greeks through Hegel to the modern day, as well as in Eastern philosophical traditions such as Taoism, human knowledge consists of contradictions (Figure 5.4). A contradiction is a dynamic tension between opposing elements that together constitute a whole and that depend on each other for their meaning and existence.[7]

Humans understand the world in terms of opposites. Good is meaningless without bad, light makes no sense without darkness, and fast is incomprehensible without slow. Inside makes no sense without outside, stability cannot be understood without change, and means cannot exist without ends.[8] The example of the factory closing, which pits managers' fiduciary duty to shareholders against their ethical obligations to workers, involves a contradiction between teleology, or ends (Step 4 in the weight-of-reasons framework), and deontology, or means (Step 5 in the framework). Teleology suggests that the manager must save the organization, while deontology posits an absolute duty to protect every worker.

When contradictions are based in physical reality, there is not much we can do to overcome them. In these

**FIGURE 5.4**

The idea that reality is made up of interdependent opposites is found in both Western and Eastern philosophical traditions.

cases, it is impossible to satisfy each side fully. It is a reality that one dose of a life-saving medicine can be given to only a single patient and that another suffering person must go without a cure. The decision-maker is unable to fulfill a duty to both persons. On the other hand, managers often perceive trade-offs and conclude that one side must suffer, when in fact a stark choice does not need to be made. How managers understand contradictions is important. If you consider all contradictions as dualisms, and view the contradictory elements as separate and adversarial, you have little choice. You must favor one party or interest at the expense of another. In contrast, if you understand contradictions as dualities, then you are able to accept that the opposing elements are interdependent and complementary, and you do not necessarily have to privilege one element at the expense of the other.[9]

When we view a contradiction as a duality, it becomes possible to explore actions and arrangements that satisfy the needs of all opposing parties. The doctor who made the choice to give medicine to one patient and left the other to die may have falsely perceived the choice in either/or terms, when in fact it may have been possible to save both patients. For example, perhaps the doctor could have given the medicine to one patient and provided some other form of treatment to the other patient. And perhaps the manager who believed that she had but two choices—either fudging the numbers at the request of her boss or getting fired—ignored an option to handle the task ethically, for example, by going around the boss and appealing to a higher company authority. Recall the WorldCom case recounted in Chapter 4. An employee can argue that the purpose of reporting the numbers accurately is to ensure that the company is not damaged by a scandal in which its reputation is irreparably sullied. The main takeaway is that we must be careful about how we frame ethical dilemmas (Step 1 of the weight of reasons), and in particular not jump to the conclusion that the situation is impossible and that only tragic outcomes can result.

## Applying Both/And Thinking

One way to manage ethical contradictions is to treat them as paradoxes. A paradox is made up of "contradictory yet interrelated elements that seem logical in isolation but absurd and irrational when appearing simultaneously."[10] When a manager treats opposing elements as paradoxical, she accepts that they coexist but cannot be reconciled. Treating a contradiction as a paradox is the first step in exploring the possibility that opposing objectives can be met simultaneously. They may even support each other.

Research shows that when first encountering contradictions, managers tend to embrace one side and resist the other; they perceive a dualism. For example, a plant manager may conclude that because safety measures hurt the bottom line, the company's goal will be to spend as little as possible on safety. Due to pressure, the manager may compromise, spend a bit more than she wants, and accept a small if unwanted hit to the company's profits. One reason managers tend to see only one side of a contradiction is bounded rationality (discussed in Chapter 3). Because people come from particular backgrounds, have had particular formative experiences, and are strongly influenced by contextual factors such as incentives and organizational culture, they have taken-for-granted ethical assumptions and resist contradictory viewpoints. The famous case of Nike's reliance on "sweatshop labor" illustrates

**Dualism**
The division of a thing into two separate and opposed elements

**Duality**
The division of a thing into two interdependent and complementary elements

**Paradox**
A statement made up of contradictory yet interrelated elements that seem logical in isolation but absurd and irrational when appearing simultaneously

this point. Prior to public shaming of the company, Nike's managers had not adequately considered that they bore any responsibility for working conditions in their subcontractors' facilities.[11]

Over time, however, one can challenge the assumption that contradictions are dualisms and that opposing objectives are irreconcilable.[12] Through a form of double-loop learning known as both/and thinking, one can come to understand that it may be possible to satisfy seemingly irreconcilable objectives. For example, the plant manager mentioned earlier may realize that if her company introduces safety measures, it will end up being more profitable. In the short run, the company's profits may suffer, but in the long run, they may flourish. This is because workers will be more motivated when they see that the company cares for their safety and because introducing safety measures may reset and reconfigure work processes so they are more efficient. Similarly, the manager of a retail store might see that paying workers higher salaries and benefits actually can improve the bottom line, because of less absenteeism and turnover, a better reputation with customers and other stakeholders, and greater productivity. Costco, mentioned at the start of the chapter, pays its hourly staff substantially more than Sam's Club does and also does better financially than Sam's Club (see Table 5.1). Both/and thinking can produce transformative solutions to ethical problems and win–win results that ease or erase tensions.

**Both/and thinking**
The cognition that two seemingly irreconcilable objectives can be reconciled; the framing of a contradiction as a duality rather than a dualism

**TABLE 5.1    Comparing the Performance of Costco and Sam's Club**

|  | Costco | Sam's Club |
|---|---|---|
| Average hourly wage ($) | 15.97 | 11.52 |
| Annual health care costs per worker ($) | 5,735 | 3,500 |
| Annual retirement costs per worker ($) | 1,330 | 747 |
| Percentage of workers covered by retirement plans | 82 | 47 |
| Employee turnover per year (%) | 6 | 21 |
| Labor and overhead costs as a percentage of sales | 9.80 | 17 |
| Profits per employee ($) | 13,647 | 11,039 |
| Sales per square foot ($) | 795 | 516 |
| Estimated gross income per similar-sized store ($) | 18,040 | 2,837 |

*Source:* Patel, H. (2016, August 8). *Costco domination of Sam's Club.* Retrieved from https://seekingalpha.com/article/3997233-costco-domination-sams-club

Both/and thinking plays a role in applying the weight-of-reasons framework, particularly in the first step of identifying the issue and in the last one of coming to a more lasting solution. When facing a dilemma, if you start by defining the problem as a dualism (e.g., "It is impossible to meet the numbers promised to Wall Street and behave entirely ethically"), then you are highly unlikely to find an innovative approach. On the other hand, if you seek to frame the problem differently, carefully defining the problem and goals from the perspective that contradictory and opposite goals may actually be complementary, then new options can open up. You may see, for example, that the choice between cooking the books and not making the numbers is false and that reporting results honestly has many benefits. Such an accommodating perception of opposites takes time to develop. Don't be hard on yourself if you at first see difficult problems in an either/or light and do not right away recognize possible complementarities.

In sum, just as managers can use systems thinking to develop long-term solutions to ethical problems, so they can also use both/and thinking. The immediate problems managers face may be symptomatic of much deeper contradictions. If managers see the problems they face as posing either/or choices between contradictory elements, they will almost certainly take actions that cause some harm or violate someone's rights. If, on the other hand, they accept that the two elements will continue to coexist, they may be able to find ways to satisfy both.

## Moral Imagination

**LO 5.5:** Use moral imagination to develop imaginative solutions to complex ethical dilemmas.

Ethical decisions are tough to make, not only because of seemingly impossible choices but also because of novel and unfamiliar problems. When we meet complex problems we have not seen before, we do not have readymade solutions on which to draw. We often try to solve problems by relying on heuristics (see Chapter 3), but especially when the situation we face is novel, then the heuristic we use may be mistaken. In these situations where we lack good precedent, we must move in directions not tried before.

One way to solve novel ethical problems is to use moral imagination. Werhane defines moral imagination as "the ability in particular circumstances to discover and evaluate possibilities not merely determined by that circumstance, or limited by its operative mental models, or merely framed by a set of rules or rule-governed concerns."[13] Moral imagination is an approach to slow thinking to overcome cognitive and organizational limitations. It is a means of making sense of ethical issues creatively rather than based on habit, instinct, and rules.

**Moral imagination** The ability to discover and evaluate new and unique ethical responses to ethical dilemmas

### The Process of Moral Imagination

Moral imagination is a three-step process in which one (1) immerses oneself in the ethical issue at hand, (2) detaches from the issue and considers various perspectives on it, and (3) reimmerses oneself in the issue and develops creative, feasible, and morally justifiable solutions to it.[14] Developing creative solutions to novel ethical

©iStockphoto.com/Alexpunker

An important part of moral imagination is stepping back and seeing the situation from a distance.

problems requires imagination—very practical and directed imagination. The American pragmatist Dewey wrote that free reflection is based on "a warm and intimate taking in of the full scope of a situation" and does not involve "imaginary flight" [15]

Dewey took the view that engaging in moral imagination involves picturing ourselves carrying out our various action alternatives:

> In deliberation, . . . we singly or collectively hunt for ways to settle difficulties and ambiguities by scoping out alternatives and picturing ourselves taking part in them. Imagination continues until we are stimulated to act by a course that appears to harmonize pressing interests, needs, and other factors of the situation.[16]

Dewey recognized that in identifying imaginative solutions, we start with known options and then modify them. Although cartoons showing light bulbs above a thinker's head suggest otherwise, we do not, nor can we, create new options from nothing. Rather, we consider the limitations of known alternatives, extend them, and combine them.

## The Added Value of Moral Imagination

As already noted, moral imagination is a form of slow thinking, and it also is a form of double-loop learning because it involves challenging the assumptions behind our actions. It may even be a form of triple-loop learning when it involves challenging our deep cultural assumptions. But what does the concept of moral imagination add beyond these other concepts related to cognition and learning?

©iStockphoto.com/Brostock

When making an ethical decision, you can think of yourself as playing the role of a particular character. Which character are you, and what would your character do?

First, moral imagination emphasizes that we should try to consciously step back from our typical roles and ways of thinking. It involves not just slow thinking but slow thinking from outside of our own self-interest, as if we were an "impartial spectator"[17] making decisions from behind a "veil of ignorance."[18] The concept of moral imagination sets a very high bar, maybe one that is impossible to clear, for challenging our own assumptions.

Second, the literature on moral imagination provides a very practical piece of advice for those trying to develop innovative solutions to ethical problems. This is to apply general **ethical principles** rather than specific rules that allow and disallow particular behaviors. Whereas universal rules, such as those proposed by Kant (see Chapter 2), require particular actions regardless of the circumstances, principles provide flexibility to address complex problems that do not have "one-size-fits-all" answers.

Recall the example in Chapter 2. If confronted by Nazi officers who asked whether you were hiding any Jews in your house, would you follow a rule that you should never lie under any conditions, when the almost certain consequence would be the death of a family? If you were hiding a fugitive slave in the period prior to the U.S. Civil War, would you tell the truth to bounty hunters trying to return slaves to their owners? Applying general ethical principles is a more commonsense approach that is more likely to lead to ethical outcomes than relying on absolute rules.

## Moral Imagination and the Weight-of-Reasons Framework

The first step of moral imagination, immersion in the details, applies mainly to Steps 1 and 2 of the weight-of-reasons framework, identifying the issue and gathering facts, respectively. Once you take a "deep dive" into the issue, you will find many facts of which you were not initially aware and come to understand that your framing of the issue is just one way of seeing it. While it may seem obvious that ethical decision-making should involve a deep dive, for reasons such as bounded rationality and group-think, discussed earlier, decision-makers often do not fully understand the situations they are in or are unable to analyze the ethical dilemmas they face. Unfortunately, there are many examples of this. The *Challenger* case considered in the Chapter 4 is one such example. Similarly, leading up to the 2008 Great Financial Crisis, the bankers who put together mortgage deals had no understanding of their decisions' negative effects. They were preoccupied with getting deals done more quickly than their competitors. Even though they didn't understand it, analysts accepted Enron's business model rather than asking tough questions about it. The #metoo movement has surfaced one story after another about claims of workplace sexual harassment and assault that decision-makers took too lightly, rationalized, or flat out denied.

The second step of moral imagination, disengagement and consideration of alternative viewpoints, applies to every step of the weight-of-reasons framework. After taking a step back, decision-makers often realize that there are many valid ways of framing an issue, possible courses of action, and perspectives on what the ethical thing to do is. In this step, managers should try to make sense of the issue from the perspective of other key stakeholders. How does the issue look from the vantage point of employees, customers, suppliers, communities, government, and the media? How would members of your family understand the issue? What consequences would they be most concerned about, and what principles would they see at stake? Which courses of action would they agree are tolerable, and which would they see as downright unacceptable?

Asking and answering these questions by ourselves is quite difficult because we are all constrained by the bounds on our rationality. We have only so much ability to take other viewpoints. This is why it is helpful to make decisions in teams, as we discuss in the next section.

The final step of moral imagination, identifying novel courses of ethical action, or what Werhane has referred to as free reflection,[19] applies to Steps 3, 6, and 7 of the

**Ethical principles** General propositions or guidelines that can be applied differently in different situations

weight-of-reasons framework. These are the action steps of the framework. The key point is simply that in identifying and choosing a course of action, you must take your thinking beyond the obvious choices, especially if the issue you face is novel. While tried-and-true approaches offer a good starting point, they must be modified to fit the situation at hand. For any difficult ethical challenge, managers will have a hard time getting from quick fixes to long-term solutions without engaging in free reflection.

Free reflection also is an important component of Step 4 of the framework, envisioning the expected consequences of actions. Free reflection ensures not taking too narrow a view when assessing the consequences of alternative courses of action. In evaluating consequences, you should not simply calculate the discounted value of future cash flows, as if ethics were a simple financial problem. Do not stick to immediate pleasure and pain as outcomes, as a utilitarian like Bentham would recommend. Rather, consider higher forms of utility as well (see the discussion of J. S. Mill in Chapter 2). In assessing consequences, reflect on the following: Will your actions make the world a better place for all people now and in the future?

In sum, ethical problem-solving using the weight-of-reasons framework rarely will involve easy choices based on tried-and-true rules. You cannot choose your actions from a playbook. Rather, you must use moral imagination at every step of the framework. Become intimately familiar with the issue, stand back and assess it from afar, and then dive back into the details to imagine courses of action and their consequences.

## Team Decision-Making

**LO 5.6:** Establish team-based processes to employ inquiry and advocacy in making effective ethical decisions.

In more individualistic societies, such as the United States, people tend to believe that tough decisions are made by the individuals that sit at the top. Decision-making is one of the key tasks that leaders and high-level managers perform when no one else knows what to do and is willing to step to the forefront and make the "tough calls." President George W. Bush famously referred to himself as the "decider." According to this view, asking others for advice is a sign of weakness. In some cases, there are advantages to individual decision-making. It assigns responsibility. It promotes accountability. People at the top rungs have no one else to blame for their choices but themselves. At other levels, when decisions are relatively simple or one person has the specialized knowledge and the relevant expertise, there may be no need for teams to be involved in the choices made. Sometimes one person really does have the best understanding of what to do and should be granted the authority to proceed regardless of what others think.

Developing long-term solutions to complex ethical issues, on the other hand, is likely to be best handled by teams rather than individuals, for many of the reasons discussed in this and prior chapters. Individuals have particular and biased viewpoints and cannot understand or imagine other people's perspectives. They may have a limited view of a dilemma and the factors behind it. They may not see a situation as an ethical dilemma at all, or they may have a limited repertoire of options for addressing it. By themselves, individuals are unlikely to possess the resources needed to gather more information and understand the facts, especially if circumstances are changing. Moreover, it is often the case that an individual by herself or himself would not have the power to implement a solution. It is unlikely that a lone individual can close the circle. Even when individuals engage in systems thinking, both/and thinking, and moral imagination, they are likely to run into these limitations. We simply are not aware of our own mental habits and assumptions. They are like water to a fish.

Team decision-making can help address these limitations. As discussed in Chapter 4, teams have their own limitations, such as groupthink. They will not produce effective solutions to ethical problems unless their members, individually and collectively, are open to ideas and are willing to scrutinize, challenge, combine, and improve them. When done correctly, however, team decision-making can improve on individual decision-making. While typically we do not see our own mental biases and limitations, we can bring them to the surface in teams. Teams are likely to be able to get at the roots of problems and address them better than individuals. Team decision-making can be a double- or triple-loop learning process, in which actors examine, challenge, and juxtapose diverse beliefs and assumptions and generate new ways of thinking and possible courses of action. In addition to creating better ideas, team decision-making also can serve as a way of building chemistry and generating the commitment needed to implement solutions.[20]

Making decisions through teams enables decision-makers to more thoroughly apply the weight-of-reasons framework and develop long-term solutions to ethical challenges. Over the course of a decision-making process, team members can take the time to gather the needed information, assess the consequences of possible courses of action, and make corrections to current courses of action. Through the process, they may come to clarify guiding principles, better define ethical issues, uncover hidden assumptions about the nature and causes of these issues, and develop novel, more morally imaginative solutions. In short, team-based decision processes can enable and contribute to continuous learning and problem-solving.

## Inquiry and Advocacy

Team-based decision processes are more likely to avoid groupthink and produce long-term solutions to ethical issues when they involve a mix of *inquiry and advocacy*.[21] In this section, we first define inquiry and advocacy and discuss how they come together to produce constructive conflict. We then describe the organizational conditions that can lead to effective inquiry and advocacy. These conditions are empowerment, cognitive diversity, psychological safety, and trust. All of these conditions were lacking in the *Challenger* space shuttle case presented in the last chapter.

Inquiry-based decision-making involves an open exchange of viewpoints and the generation of ideas. It is a form of collaboration. Participants in inquiry-based decision-making come to the decision process with the idea of helping the team make the best possible decision. Advocacy-based decision-making, in contrast, is more of a contest; those involved seek to persuade others that they are correct. They want to win rather than contribute.

While your first intuition may be that inquiry will lead to better solutions than advocacy, this often is not the case. Effective team decision-making processes

**Inquiry-based decision-making** Team-based decision-making that is collaborative and involves open exchange of viewpoints and the generation of new ideas

**Advocacy-based decision-making** Team decision-making that involves conflict, and in which each participant seeks to persuade others that his or her way is the best

include elements of both inquiry and advocacy. When advocacy takes place within a spirit of inquiry, team members both vigorously advocate their ideas and also scrutinize them from the viewpoint of whether they serve the team. Furthermore, they are less likely to feel personally attacked and more willing to do what is best for the team when they perceive others to have sincere intentions to do the same. Argyris and Schön found that when participants combine inquiry and advocacy and set out together to make an informed choice based on valid information, they become open rather than defensive, share an orientation to grow and learn, and become willing to take risks. This combination leads to the challenging of fundamental beliefs and the opening up of new possibilities for action that no single person could have come up with alone.[22]

Inquiry and advocacy together produce constructive conflict. Team conflict takes place when some members of the team have beliefs or take actions that are unacceptable to other members of the team and the opposing sides perceive that they cannot both have their way. They cannot put their differences aside because they perceive that trying to achieve one party's goals will block the achievement of the other party's goals.

Although we tend to favor peace, harmony, and cooperation because they give us a feeling of comfort, conflict can be beneficial because it stimulates greater engagement, creativity, and innovation.[23] Since conflict is an inherent feature of decision processes and can be beneficial, team decision-making is more effective when decision-makers do not deny it but rather embrace it, even stimulate it, and try to use it productively. Conflict is more constructive when it is task related rather than interpersonal (or relationship oriented). Task (or task-related) conflict involves disagreement about the team's goals and the tasks for accomplishing them. (This does not mean that it lacks emotion.)

In contrast, interpersonal (or relationship-oriented) conflict is personal; the people engaged in it perceive *themselves* and not just their ideas as being in conflict. Whereas interpersonal conflict breeds animosity and defensiveness, task conflict can lead to an exchange and examination of ideas and the development of new ones. The challenge, then, is to get all team members to advocate their viewpoints but to separate task from interpersonal conflict. Creating a climate of inquiry helps them do this.[24]

Garvin and Roberto outline a number of practical steps teams can take to stimulate debate that productively combines inquiry and advocacy. They suggest that in situations where there is concern about groupthink, team leaders should (a) appoint one participant to serve as "devil's advocate" and challenge the consensus; (b) refrain from expressing their opinions so as not to influence other participants;

**Constructive conflict** Conflict in which participants have the intention of making the best decision for the team. Occurs when inquiry and advocacy are combined

**Task (or task-related) conflict** Conflict in which there is disagreement about tasks and goals

**Interpersonal (or relationship-oriented) conflict** Conflict that is personal, in which those involved view themselves as in conflict with one another

©iStockphoto.com/laflor

Conflict can be beneficial to team decision-making because it brings out emotional energy and leads to new ideas.

(c) encourage outsiders who are not typically part of the team to participate in the decision-making, because they are more apt to bring a fresh perspective; and, above all, (d) be considerate of others.[25] We should always remember to listen and really hear what others are saying, not just tune out or wait for them to stop talking so that we can start talking again.

## Conditions for Effective Inquiry and Advocacy

Processes of inquiry and advocacy are more likely to produce innovative ideas when the participants are *empowered* to participate in the decision-making process. Team decisions take many different forms. When decisions are made through consensus or unanimous consent, all participants have a voice in the decision. In contrast, in unilateral decision-making, a single team leader or boss makes the decision, with little input from others. While participatory approaches that empower people, such as consensus and unanimous consent, are time-consuming, they tend to lead to more inquiry and advocacy and therefore to better decisions. One big benefit of empowering individuals to participate in decision-making is buy-in. Individuals are more likely to support and implement decisions in which they have participated.[26]

Inquiry and advocacy are also more likely to lead to better decisions when the team members collectively are characterized by cognitive diversity. Individuals often have very different and even conflicting beliefs, perspectives, and sets of facts that inform their decisions. Individuals from different functions within the organization (e.g., marketing, manufacturing, finance) tend to come from different "thought worlds."[27] As a result, they frame issues differently and have different opinions about what the best decision is. Furthermore, some people focus on the social aspects of a situation, while others focus on the technical; some are risk seeking, while others are averse to change; and so on. With respect to ethical frameworks, some people tend to take a utilitarian approach, while others tend to apply principles or an ethic of care. Often these differences can be traced to differences in organizational roles and life experiences, as well as differences in age, gender, and other demographic categories. Such differences need not undermine the team, however. Cognitive diversity is likely to lead to a greater range of ideas, deeper exploration of ideas, and greater ability to see the linkages among ideas.[28]

Inquiry and advocacy also lead to the development of creative approaches to complex problems when they take place within a context of psychological safety. A psychologically safe environment is one in which team members do not fear negative consequences from sharing their viewpoints. When individuals feel that it is safe to speak up, they are more motivated to contribute to the team and express their ideas, even risky and unconventional ones.[29] Psychological safety is an important precursor to constructive conflict. Research shows that a climate of psychological safety is more likely to exist when team members have clear roles on the team and strong relationships.[30] Such safety did not exist in the *Challenger* case.

Another important antecedent of psychological safety is trust among teammates.[31] Trust is defined as the a willingness to be vulnerable because of a lack of fear or concern about others' intentions.[32] Trust comes about when there is risk and interdependence. When A's and B's actions influence one another, it is possible that one's

**Cognitive diversity**
The state in which the members of a group have different perspectives and ways of thinking

**Psychological safety**
The belief that an environment provides a safe place for interpersonal risk-taking

**Trust**
The willingness to be vulnerable based on the belief that others' behaviors will have positive (or at least not negative) outcomes for you

actions could harm the other. Trust alleviates this risk. A does not feel at risk when she expects that B's actions will benefit, or at least not harm, her. Because it provides them with psychological safety, trust allows team members to listen more carefully to one another, share information, propose risky ideas, and confront one another.

In addition to increasing psychological safety, trust also contributes directly to better team decision-making. Trust helps ensure that conflict is task related rather than interpersonal. Trust also motivates individuals to contribute to the team, and it helps them maintain their relationships even as they disagree, and stick together and stay committed when they face a difficult situation and are uncertain about how to address it.[33] Furthermore, trust makes things cheaper. When one person trusts another, he does not have to monitor the other person to make sure she is keeping her word.[34]

## Team Decision-Making and the Weight of Reasons

The above lessons about the benefits of team decision-making inform every step of the weight-of-reasons framework. Empowered, cognitively diverse, psychologically safe, trusting team members combining inquiry and advocacy to address ethical issues can

- identify, discuss, and evaluate different ways of understanding the key ethical issues that must be addressed in a situation, and select the key issues to focus on (Step 1 of the weight-of-reasons framework);

- compile and consider a broader range of relevant facts than any single team member could individually (Step 2);

- identify a comprehensive range of options for action and thoroughly evaluate their expected consequences (Steps 3 and 4);

- debate and select their guiding principles and short-term and long-term courses of action (Steps 5 through 7); and

- thoroughly identify key lessons that will help the team when it addresses similar ethical problems and issues in the future (Step 8).

In sum, team decision-making processes that involve both inquiry and advocacy significantly improve ethical decisions. Individuals have great difficulty in doing double- and triple-loop learning—identifying and challenging their own assumptions and considering other assumptions—by themselves. Through dialogue in a psychologically safe environment (this is critical), individuals with diverse viewpoints who trust one another can work together to recognize that an ethical issue may be framed in various ways, that there are multiple valid principles at stake, that no single person is likely to have all the relevant facts, and that the best action option is probably something that no individual could devise alone.

Using inquiry and advocacy to address ethical issues may seem like an unattainable ideal to some. It is certainly true that some organizational environments discourage dialogue and that some people are not well suited to participating in constructive conflict. Furthermore, sadly, it is also true that sometimes in organizations people take unethical actions even after a team has made an ethical decision, and that people who speak the truth for the sake of inquiry (e.g., calling out bad behavior) are subjected to retaliation for doing so. For these reasons, it is important to create an organizational environment that supports rather than discourages constructive ethical team decision-making. We take up this subject in the next chapter.

## Ethical Decision-Making and Uncertainty: The Incremental Approach

**LO 5.7:** Use tools such as trial-and-error and experimental learning to deal with uncertainty in ethical decision-making.

As noted in previous chapters, complexity and rapid change introduce uncertainty into decision-making. Uncertainty can be a significant barrier to the development of long-term solutions to ethical problems. Decision-makers may feel that they do not have adequate information to define the dilemmas they face, let alone evaluate decision alternatives and their consequences. Under such circumstances, decision-makers are not willing to make the major commitments that are often needed to get at the problems underlying an ethical issue and implement solutions to them. For example, a large company facing numerous workplace harassment and discrimination complaints would not be willing to initiate remedial measures before it understood why the complaints were arising. Was it hiring the wrong employees? Not providing them with the right training? Was there a lack of leadership? If the company cannot answer these questions, it cannot address the complaints.

Henry Mintzberg, a leading management scholar, and his colleagues recognized that managers address this problem of uncertainty through an incremental decision-making process.[35] In these cases, managers realize that they do not have an adequate definition of the issue and that they need more information and a better understanding of the options and their expected consequences. Moreover, they recognize that the situation may change. Thus, they do not attempt to make a major decision all at once. Rather, over time they make a series of small decisions that ultimately produce a major one. With each small decision, they arrive at a better understanding of the larger problem they face and how to resolve it. They do so without making big resource commitments so they can more easily revise their course of action as they learn more and circumstances change.

An important part of the incremental decision-making process is trial-and-error learning. When team members face a novel situation, they do not know what will work; they may have difficulty in predicting the consequences of particular courses of action or even identifying actions. In these circumstances, rather than trying to identify an optimal solution, they may simply try different courses of action to see what happens. Doing so provides useful information about how to move toward a solution.[36] One weakness of trial-and-error learning is that it may demonstrate that a particular action option seems effective but not make clear *why* that option worked.[37] An example of trial-and-error learning related to ethics would be a plant manager monitoring the impacts on costs, productivity, and job satisfaction of establishing better working conditions or a supply chain manager

**Trial-and-error learning** Learning that occurs by trying different courses of action and observing the outcomes

keeping track of the impacts on a supplier of imposing new labor and environmental requirements. Even if the outcomes are beneficial, the reasons for the positive results may not be known.

Unlike simple trial-and-error learning, experimentation (or experimental learning) can enhance the incremental decision-making process by clarifying why particular actions are effective. Experimentation differs from trial-and-error in that it is more scientific. Whereas trial-and-error learning takes place as part of the organization's ongoing work, experimentation happens "off-line"—that is, in a controlled situation away from the company's operations. Unlike trial-and-error learning, experimentation is a form of hypothesis testing. Whereas in trial-and-error learning you start with no clear idea about what will happen, in experimentation you use what you know to develop "if-then" statements about the relationship between inputs and outcomes and then test these statements.[38] Firms generally try to experiment cheaply so they can learn without expending significant resources. An example of low-cost experimentation to address an ethical issue would be testing the prototype of a new environmentally friendly product with a select group of customers or using a focus group to find out if particular customers would like the new product.

An important feature of Mintzberg's incremental decision-making model is that the process does not follow a smooth path from start to finish; rather, at points that Mintzberg refers to as "decision interrupts," decision-makers gain new information, resolve uncertainty, and revisit their decision. Examples of what may take place at decision interrupts include the emergence of new action options or new data about the consequences of a possible action, recognition that a particular option will not work, or the arrival of new leadership that wants to go in a different direction. As a result of a decision interrupt, the decision-maker may have to go back to earlier steps in the decision process. For example, if a manager found out through trial-and-error learning that a new procedure designed to increase workplace safety actually decreased it, he would have to go back and identify new action options.

## Incremental Decision-Making and the Weight of Reasons

When decision-makers trying to develop long-term solutions to ethical issues face significant uncertainty, they need to apply an incremental process to the weight-of-reasons framework. In complex, fast-moving contexts, decision-makers may need to do trial-and-error and experimental learning before committing to a long-term approach to a recurring ethical problem. As the members of a decision-making team consider their action options (Step 4 of the weight-of-reasons framework), they may realize that they need more data (Step 2); or as they consider the facts, they may realize that there are deeper issues than the ones they initially identified (Step 1). Perhaps after identifying a short-term course of action (Step 6), someone in the team will have a nagging feeling that an important principle is being violated, taking the team back to Step 5. Whether individually or in teams, decision-makers are likely to learn more about the early steps of the weight-of-reasons framework as they undertake the later ones. Therefore, they must be ready to regularly revisit the earlier steps.

## Ethical Learning Spirals

**LO 5.8:** Recognize how organizations can undertake learning spirals to continuously improve their ability to address ethical dilemmas.

The purpose of the tools discussed thus far in this chapter is to help decision-makers develop long-term solutions to ethical problems (Step 7 of the weight-of-reasons framework). It is natural to think of the long-term solution as the end of the process. It is. At the same time, however, it is also the beginning of the process. No long-term solution lasts forever. In fact, long-term solutions create their own problems, which must be addressed. Organizational scholars have described a never-ending learning process in which organizations identify new arrangements and courses of action, find that these new approaches are inadequate, again identify new courses of action, and so on. Through these processes, the organization moves toward ever-higher levels of knowledge. Organizations that undertake these processes can move increasingly closer to developing long-term solutions that address the root tensions driving repeated ethical problems. For example, a company that thought there was a trade-off between being "green" and earning profits might, through an ongoing learning process, be able to completely reinvent its production processes and products to have zero negative and even beneficial environmental impacts.

The cyclical process of developing transformative long-term solutions to ethical problems typically begins with decision-makers taking a narrow "either/or" view of the ethical issue at hand. A decision-maker might think it is too bad that her company pollutes a river, but she can't worry about that because she has to "make the numbers." Another decision-maker might think, "I don't care if it costs more money, we are not dumping that stuff in the river." Such approaches tend not to last, however, because those who are left out of the decision are motivated to change the situation. For example, the environmentalists and the water users harmed by the river pollution would organize to stop the pollution. Moreover, taking action that favors one side at the expense of the other can actually undermine the action. For example, striving for good environmental performance but neglecting profitability could eventually undermine environmental performance by reducing the funds available for environmentally friendly investments and improvements. Or the opposite could happen: Emphasizing profits while ignoring environmental impacts could ultimately reduce profits by harming the company's reputation and opening it up to lawsuits.

When those taking different sides on an ethical issue both have power, then the stage is set for a learning spiral that leads to the development of a long-term solution. At this point, the two sides recognize that they cannot get rid of each other, try to empathize with each other, and come together to find ways to achieve mutually beneficial goals. For example, high-level executives motivated by profits alone realize that they must also try to meet their ethical obligations to workers; accountants realize that they have to find ways to "meet the numbers" without pressuring employees to act unethically; salespeople understand that they have to increase the firm's revenues without systematically deceiving customers; shareholders accept the need to make environmentally friendly investments; and environmentalists realize that their demands must not drive companies out of business.

Once they have come together, the opposing sides can use the tools discussed in this chapter to develop long-term solutions to their shared ethical problem. The process may be messy at first as the two sides get used to working together and try to understand each other's viewpoints. Nevertheless, through inquiry and advocacy, systems thinking, both/and thinking, and moral imagination, they can challenge their own (and each other's) definitions of the issues they face, decide what principles are most important to them, and reconsider what information they need to assess the situation, what their action options are, and what the expected consequences of these options may be. By avoiding big commitments and engaging in trial-and-error and experimental learning, they can first identify actions that provide short-term solutions to the ethical issue (Step 6 of the weight of reasons).[39] Then over time as the learning spiral continues, they can attempt to get at the deeper tensions at the root of the issue and arrive at a more stable and long-term outcome.

The global food company Nestlé provides an example of a learning spiral that produced a transformative long-term solution to an ethical problem. Nestlé first favored short-term profits for its shareholders over creating long-term value for society. Then the company shifted to managing the tension between the two by creating separate business units for each, and eventually, it adopted a "shared-value" vision that encompassed both and treated them as complementary.

The learning spiral never really ends. Even as you arrive at an elegant long-term solution, it may be shown to be antiquated and inadequate as additional contradictions surface. Almost every solution is partial and is subject to the law of unintended consequences. As an example, the Toyota Prius produces fewer greenhouse gases and air pollution than conventional autos, but the manufacture of its batteries produces toxic waste. Moreover, if the electricity to power the vehicles is made by burning coal, then the pollution and greenhouse gases may actually increase and have merely been transferred from the roadside to the power plant. The introduction of electrified transportation options has many advantages over the alternatives, but it is not foolproof in addressing the issues it aims to address. One long-term solution leaves another problem in its wake. We cannot delude ourselves that our long-term solutions to ethical problems will be trouble-free. Never-ending learning processes provide long-term but not permanent solutions to ethical problems; serious challenges will remain. Sadly, there is no ethical utopia even if we develop more and more sophisticated understandings of how to address ethical dilemmas.[40]

That said, we can still use frameworks such as the weight of reasons to address the ethical issues we face. If we work in teams and use systems thinking, both/and thinking, and moral imagination as we go, we may be able to develop long-term solutions. The fact that the solutions don't last forever should not deter us.

# ENRON: LEARNING FROM THE SCANDAL[41]

The start of the 21st century was marked by one accounting scandal after another. The table "Accounting Scandals in the 21st Century" lists some of the most significant scandals (along with the names of the accounting firms).

## Accounting Scandals in the 21st Century

| Company | Year | Accounting Firm |
| --- | --- | --- |
| Enron | 2001 | Arthur Andersen |
| AOL | 2002 | Ernst & Young |
| Bristol-Myers Squibb | 2002 | PricewaterhouseCoopers |
| Duke Energy | 2002 | Deloitte & Touche |
| Vivendi Universal | 2002 | Arthur Andersen |
| Dynegy | 2002 | Arthur Andersen |
| El Paso Corporation | 2002 | Deloitte & Touche |
| Freddie Mac | 2002 | PricewaterhouseCoopers |
| Global Crossing | 2002 | Arthur Andersen |
| Halliburton | 2002 | Arthur Andersen |
| ImClone Systems | 2002 | KPMG |
| Kmart | 2002 | PricewaterhouseCoopers |
| Merck & Co. | 2002 | PricewaterhouseCoopers |
| Merrill Lynch | 2002 | Deloitte & Touche |
| Tyco International | 2002 | PricewaterhouseCoopers |
| WorldCom | 2002 | Arthur Andersen |
| HealthSouth Corporation | 2003 | Ernst & Young |
| Nortel | 2003 | Deloitte & Touche |
| Chiquita Brands International | 2004 | Ernst & Young |
| AIG | 2004 | PricewaterhouseCoopers |
| Monsanto | 2009 | Deloitte |

*(Continued)*

(Continued)

| Kinross Gold | 2010 | KPMG |
|---|---|---|
| Lehman Brothers | 2010 | Ernst & Young |
| Olympus Corporation | 2011 | Ernst & Young |
| Autonomy Corporation | 2012 | Deloitte & Touche |
| Toshiba | 2015 | Ernst & Young |
| Valeant Pharmaceuticals | 2015 | PricewaterhouseCoopers |

Perhaps the most notorious of the scandals was that involving Enron, a once high-flying energy trading company that was exposed as a multibillion dollar financial hoax. (We briefly discussed this scandal in Chapter 4.) The scandal cost employees and investors billions of dollars and the company was forced to go into bankruptcy. The scandal also brought down Enron's accounting firm, Arthur Andersen. While Arthur Andersen was not implicated in directly assisting Enron in falsifying its financial statements, it was found to have been negligent in its role of overseeing and auditing Enron's financials. Additionally, Andersen was found guilty of obstruction of justice because it shredded documents related to its audits of Enron.

### An Enron History

With the deregulation of the natural gas industry, Enron executives developed a business in trading natural gas as well as supplying it. As the profits from the trading business overtook those from building pipelines and drilling wells, the company's emphasis moved away from the nuts and bolts of providing the resource and into the realm of developing innovative financial devices and arrangements to buy and sell the product. Enron management adopted an "asset-light" strategy for the business, emphasizing intellectual capital over hard assets.

In the mid- to late 1990s, the company decided to expand its financial expertise to diverse areas—water, coal, broadband, fiber-optic capacity, and several others. Enron's stock price rose steadily, and it became a favorite with Wall Street as well as with its own employees, many of whom invested their entire retirement savings in company stock through the company-maintained 401(k) plan. For the most part, however, these new ventures were not profitable for the company. Accordingly, the company took aggressive advantage of complicated loopholes in the accounting laws to keep these losses from public view. It also embarked on a scheme to structure its riskier ventures in entities that would not have to be reported on its balance sheet (these were called "special-purpose entities," or SPEs).

Enron executives, as individuals, were partners in several of these entities. Enron's CFO (chief financial officer), Andrew Fastow, collected more than $30 million as a partner in SPEs that he himself had engineered. Michael Kopper, another Enron executive, garnered a return of more than $10 million. Enron's Board of Directors twice suspended the corporation's code of ethics to approve the self-dealing. No information regarding the existence of these SPEs, holding hundreds of millions of dollars of Enron debt, was made public to Enron's investors.

At the beginning of 2001, Enron's stock was trading in excess of $80 per share. By early summer, the stock price had fallen to the $50 to $60 range, a point that would trigger the repayment provisions for several of the off–balance sheet partnerships that were keeping hundreds of millions of dollars of debt off Enron's public books. In mid-August, Jeffrey Skilling, Enron's CEO (chief executive officer) of 6 months, abruptly resigned, citing personal reasons. Enron's Chairman of the Board, Kenneth Lay, who served as CEO prior to Skilling's appointment, resumed the CEO position. The day after Skilling's departure, Sherron Watkins, vice president of corporate development, sent a confidential memo to Lay outlining the problems with the off–balance sheet financial structures. The memo warned that the company would "implode in a wave of accounting scandals." Based on a cursory review of Watkins's allegations, Enron's lawyers opined that there was no cause for concern. See the previous chapter, where Watkins's role was also discussed.

Enron's stock continued to decline in the aftermath of the September 11 terrorist attacks, although Lay and other executives actively sought to reassure outside investors and employee investors that the company was in great shape and "the third quarter is looking great." In October, Enron reported a third-quarter loss of more than $600 million, and the following day, the company restated its balance sheet, reducing its reported assets by more than $1 billion. The same day, the company froze all assets in the employees' 401(k) plan, preventing employees from selling the company stock in their retirement portfolios. The employees would not regain the right to sell Enron stock until its value had fallen to pennies per share. Within days, the U.S. Securities and Exchange Commission initiated an investigation into Enron's accounting and financial practices, the CFO was fired, and Enron reported overstated profits of nearly $600 million in the previous financial statements. After the stock plummeted to near zero, in the beginning of December, Enron filed for federal bankruptcy protection from its creditors and investors.

The breadth and depth of investigations into Enron's implosion "in a wave of accounting scandals" were considerable. Soon after opening its investigation of Enron, the Securities and Exchange Commission expanded its investigation to Enron's auditor, Arthur Andersen. Evidence of secret destruction of Enron's financial records and documents by Andersen personnel led to a criminal indictment of the accounting firm by the U.S. Department of Justice. Enron executives and members of the Board of Directors were under investigation by a variety of federal agencies and were named defendants in dozens of lawsuits by shareholders, employees, and creditors.

The investigations revealed that officers of the corporation had worked with the accountants and law firms hired to represent the company to hide from the owners of the company the true status of the corporation's financial affairs. Many of the executives personally profited from the deception. The CFO and others made tens of millions of dollars from the off–balance sheet partnerships, and top Enron executives made profits of more than $100 million from selling their stock while continuing to publicly reassure investors on the soundness of the company. Internal controls that should have caught the problems did not. Enron's auditor, Andersen, and the law firm Vinson & Elkins helped structure and then signed off on the questionable deals. Enron's Board of Directors failed to use the prudent care required of directors to inform itself about the transactions. The Board's audit committee failed to diligently examine the transactions, and the full Board, when presented with transactions that clearly violated the company's policy on self-dealing by corporate officers, twice waived Enron's corporate code of ethics.

Enron's collapse harmed many stakeholders. Enron's shareholders lost more than $60 billion from the beginning of 2001 to the bankruptcy filing in December that year. Perhaps the most negatively affected stakeholder group in the Enron scandal was its employees. More than 5,000 of them lost their jobs at the outset of the bankruptcy, and more than 20,000 lost their retirement savings in Enron stock. Enron's trading partners suffered several billions of dollars in losses, and Enron's bondholders also lost several billions of dollars. Suppliers, large and small, were not paid. A negative ripple effect was experienced by the energy sector generally. The city of Houston, already reeling from the economic downturn, lost a major employer, a city icon, and the sponsor of its premier sports venue, Enron Field.

Enron's collapse was not the result of missteps by one rogue actor. Many within Enron's executive ranks, managers and directors, and many of Enron's advisors were privy to the trick accounting arrangements being used to cook the corporate books. Impropriety to the degree exhibited in the Enron case requires a corporate environment that rewards results by any means necessary. Skilling had nurtured a corporate environment where risk-taking and creative, if shaky, deal-making that enhanced the immediate bottom line were rewarded with large bonuses and positive reviews, whereas concern for long-term growth and shareholder value was marginalized.

*(Continued)*

(Continued)

Enron executives, including Lay, Skilling, and Fastow, who were interviewed prior to the scandal described the culture. Skilling said the aim was to be "the world's coolest company," and Lay called for a "superstar in every position." Ambitious "Type A" employees from the world's leading business schools were given the freedom to move toward opportunities. The "weirdest people" were the "best," according to Skilling. He described Enron's culture as being an innovative one, with few bureaucratic "choke points" that could block entrepreneurial energy. Skilling maintained that he had "no idea what is going on down there" and reportedly surrounded himself with "yes men." In such an environment, critical thinking was absent.

Nonetheless, there were some people at Enron willing to point out the problems. Enron's treasurer, Jeffrey McMahon (who took over as chief operating officer of the company during Enron's bankruptcy), was reported to have raised issues regarding the propriety of the partnerships when they were initially established. He was promptly transferred to London. In early spring of 2001, Jordan Mintz, an in-house Enron lawyer, raised issue with the chief accounting officer and the chief risk officer of the company regarding the propriety of the off–balance sheet arrangements. He was told to stay out of it. Later that spring, Mintz arranged for an independent review of some of the transactions by outside counsel. Watkins submitted a powerful confidential memo to Lay the day after Skilling's resignation, outlining the nature of the off-the-books entities and the potentially devastating financial problems they presented. Presciently, she warned of the imminent implosion of Enron due to the accounting artifice. Watkins's memo was passed on to Enron's lawyers and was promptly deemed to be of no real concern.

### Enron and the Weight-of-Reasons Framework

What went wrong at Enron? What could Enron's managers have done differently? ("Everything" is not a sufficient answer.) Use the weight-of-reasons approach to develop your answer. In doing so, consider how the decision-making tools discussed in this chapter could have helped Enron move from its short-term problems toward an ethical and profitable long-term business model. How does systems thinking help you understand what went wrong at Enron and consider possible solutions? Were the Enron executives engaged in either/or thinking? How could both/and thinking have helped them run their business differently? If you were a concerned employee such as Watkins, how would you have used moral imagination to creatively address the problems at Enron?

## SUMMARY AND CONCLUSION

Decision-makers often do not have the time or resources to get to the roots of the ethical problems they must address. In such cases, they come up with short-term fixes; they do the best they can to address the symptoms of the problem. Because they do not get to the root causes of the problem, however, the problems they face are likely to recur. When they do have the time and resources to address the root causes of ethical problems, decision-makers, of course, should do so. This chapter has introduced a number of decision-making approaches that help decision-makers develop long-term solutions to ethical issues. All of the approaches involve slow thinking and double- or even triple-loop learning.

First, the chapter described systems thinking. Systems thinking can provide you with a better understanding of what it means to "get to the root of the problem." A given ethical issue may seem relatively uncomplicated. However, underneath the surface is a network of interconnected actors, arrangements, and processes. Systems thinking helps us untangle this complexity; it helps us see that although there may be one decision point or one unethical actor, an entire system produces an ethical problem—and its solution. Understanding the system will help you understand the problem, what actions may be useful for addressing it, and what the unintended consequences of those actions may be. One of the hard lessons from systems thinking is that you are not able to control all the factors that contribute to a problem.

Next, this chapter discussed the management of contradictions and the importance of both/and thinking. Often it is difficult to develop long-term solutions to ethical issues because there is a tension at the heart of the issue that seems irreconcilable. It may seem impossible to solve the problems your organization faces because doing so means satisfying two opposing objectives simultaneously. A first step in dealing with apparently irreconcilable contradictions is reframing them. View the contradictions as paradoxes. Recognize their interdependence and complementarities, and start to develop strategies for resolving both sides of the contradiction. The process of managing paradoxes often follows a pattern from defensiveness and resistance to adopting short-term coping strategies (e.g., "Let's do a little of this and a little of that"), to finding long-term solutions based on understanding of how the elements fit together. Paradox management is a process in which you recognize a core tension at the heart of the system, gradually learn more about how the elements of the tension relate to one another, and then investigate solutions.

The chapter also discussed moral imagination as a tool for overcoming bounded rationality. Moral imagination takes us beyond double- and triple-loop learning because it helps us to not only uncover and critique our own assumptions but also develop novel long-term solutions. Moral imagination involves deep immersion in the problem, stepping back from the problem to see it from different perspectives, and re-immersion. It involves the application of general principles rather than specific rules.

Another topic of the chapter was team decision-making. In team processes involving inquiry and advocacy, you can draw on the other tools discussed in this chapter—systems thinking, both/and thinking, and moral imagination—to overcome the decision-making problems discussed in prior chapters, such as cognitive biases and groupthink. Inquiry and advocacy are likely to be effective under conditions of empowerment, cognitive diversity, psychological safety, and trust.

Next this chapter introduced incremental decision-making as a way to address decision-making uncertainty. Uncertainty hinders the development of long-term solutions to ethical problems; decision-makers cannot invest in solutions to an ethical problem if they are not sure what the issue, facts, options, consequences, and principles are. Incremental decision-making allows you to transform a big decision into a series of small ones that over time add up to a big one. Through methods such as trial-and-error learning and experimentation, you can try to resolve uncertainties step-by-step and move closer to a long-term solution.

Finally, this chapter presented the concept of learning spirals to tie together the other concepts in the chapter. Because even long-term solutions inevitably have unintended consequences and create their own sets of dilemmas, ethical problem-solving must be an ongoing learning process. By means of this process, it might be possible to move toward better and better solutions.

Although decision-making tools such as both/and thinking, systems thinking, and moral imagination require slow thinking, do not make the mistake of thinking that you do not have the time to use them. On the contrary, we suggest that addressing complex ethical problems by using slow thinking can ultimately conserve time and effort. This is simply because managers will make better decisions upfront and not have to go back and correct their errors. Using the tools described in this chapter is not necessarily more mental work; it is just more effective mental work.

## KEY TERMS AND CONCEPTS

Advocacy-based
   decision-making  145
Both/and thinking  140
Cognitive diversity  147
Constructive conflict  146
Contradiction  138
Double-loop learning  131
Dualism  139
Duality  139
Ethical principles  143
Experimentation (or
   experimental learning)  150

Feedback loops  136
Incremental decision-making
   process  134
Inquiry-based
   decision-making  145
Interdependence  135
Interpersonal (or relationship-
   oriented) conflict  146
Learning spiral  134
Moral imagination  141
Organizational learning  131
Paradox  139

Psychological safety  147
Single-loop learning  131
System  135
System processes  135
Systems structure  135
Systems thinking  133
Task (or task-related) conflict  146
Team-based decision-making
   process  134
Trial-and-error learning  149
Triple-loop learning  132
Trust  148

## CASES RELATED TO THE READING

Consider reading the following cases, found in Chapter 10, that apply to the concepts presented in this chapter:

- Bayer: The Acquisition of Monsanto
- BP: The Big Oil Spill: What Went Wrong?
- Facebook: Privacy and the Public Interest

- Ford: Safety Recalls
- General Mills: Nutrition
- Google: Doing No Harm
- Mallinckrodt: The Opioid Crisis
- VW: Dieselgate

## CASE APPLICATIONS

Apply the weight-of-reasons framework to address the following cases. In making your decisions, consider how you can use the tools described in this chapter, including systems thinking, both/and thinking, moral imagination, inquiry and advocacy, and incremental decision-making.

### Case 5.1: Managing New Ventures

You work for Brighten Enterprises, a Fortune 500 company with annual sales of more than $23 billion. Your company has been on the cutting edge in new product innovation. It has grown rapidly and has produced many good jobs that help stimulate the local economy. Recently, you persuaded a small company, Sunshine Electronic Devices and Precision Equipment, to purchase, finance, install, and maintain new equipment that would be used almost exclusively to produce components for Brighten. You told Sunshine, which has about $10 million in annual sales, that it could possibly earn $70 million in sales over a number of years. The total cost of the equipment was about $15 million. It was a big step for Sunshine but one it was eager to take. You got along well with Sunshine's managers and looked forward to working with them. The negotiations lasted more than 10 months, and you were pleased with the capability of Sunshine's people. The equipment was now more than 85% installed.

Brighten Enterprises was then hit with some bad news. Marketing forecasts were not met, and revenues were much lower than anticipated. Your unit was the hardest hit; sales were down by 31%. Although your business is cyclical, these numbers surprised you. Top management at Brighten decided your unit could not afford any new investments at this point. All new projects were terminated immediately until a fuller evaluation could be carried out and decisions made about restructuring. Though your job was secure because of your strong track record in product development, Sunshine was sure to suffer. Without the Brighten contracts, Sunshine could not service its debt. It faced bankruptcy. More than 300 Sunshine workers might lose their jobs. To your mind, Sunshine had taken a chance, while Brighten, cautious as usual, had cut its losses. This was the best way to manage the risk of new ventures. Brighten is the local powerhouse, the engine that gives dynamism to the economy and provides many people with jobs. Its impact is also large at the national and international levels, and its health is more important than that of Sunshine. Sunshine can be sacrificed, or so you think.

What are the issues at stake in this case, and how should you address them? What can you do to navigate from a quick fix to a long-term solution?

### Case 5.2: Where Highways Dare Not Go

You are a marketing professional who is offered a promotion that would place you as the leader of a team developing a new recreational vehicle. This vehicle has a rough ride and few amenities but can travel at high speeds and take people to places "where highways dare not go." The vehicle will be marketed to young people interested in thrills and adventure. The product will have to sell at a low price, so there will be severe limits on engineering and material costs. The vehicle might have to sacrifice safety to keep its price low. Foreign competition has created financial difficulties, but your company is betting on this product becoming very profitable. Accepting the promotion would put you in line for a top management spot. Should you take the job? Why or why not? What should you do?

### Case 5.3: Reengineering Phantom

CEO Marina Delatorre was in trouble with the Board of Directors for her reluctance to move quickly in reengineering Phantom Savings and Loan. The company's stock was selling far below its true value, according to board members, because Delatorre had not demonstrated her willingness to implement a reengineering effort that would recalibrate all the bank's processes for enhanced productivity. The board suspected that Delatorre was dragging her feet because of an aversion to laying off employees. The company's president, Eugene Trascher, had no such wariness. He had brought in a team of consultants from the well-regarded TACK firm to help him achieve his goal of a 20% reduction in operating expenses. TACK had already completed much of the study. Instead of examining the company by division, department, or function, it had divided the company into core processes, such as customer operations, customer support, and customer contact. Then it made direct process observations. TACK also sent consultants and company personnel to visit other companies that had lowered their costs. Lessons from these visits were molded into the final recommendations. Some of the findings were appalling; for example, Phantom bought many different brands of computers each year.

The consultants now wanted to proceed beyond the first-phase diagnostics to broad-scale implementation. They had written the script for the reengineering exercise and wanted to continue guiding the effort. They talked of finding the optimal solutions for crafting new process platforms and engaging in phase-out diagnostics. TACK produced a thick book of 350 changes it wanted to make, from consolidating work centers to simplifying procedures for approving customer service. TACK said that if its fixes were implemented they would generate a high internal rate of return and a payback on investment in 2 years. If the consulting achieved only one quarter of its goals, the company still would see a 3-year payback. Board members enthusiastically received these numbers.

When questioned about the human side of the layoffs, one of the TACK consultants replied that employees would be retrained with survival skills related to initiative, teamwork, accountability, and open communications. They would need these "whether they stayed at Phantom or ended up somewhere else." In the year the restructuring was considered, Phantom had $151 million in losses compared with a profit of $356 million the previous year. Phantom had a large multistate branch network and employed 26,432 people; TACK sought to cut up to 7,000 employees from the payroll. Phantom said the details of the buyout packages would be announced·shortly. If enough people did not voluntarily accept the packages, the company would have to let them go.

Delatorre thought that TACK's plan was probably necessary. After previous cutbacks, 160 employees had banded together to bring a class-action suit against Phantom for age discrimination. Delatorre asked the HR to determine how many of the laid-off employees had new jobs. After 3 years, more than half were still unemployed. Delatorre wondered about the commitment and loyalty of the remaining employees if the layoffs were carried out. When she addressed the various concerns she had to Trascher, he replied, "If we don't lay off these people, our losses will only mount, and the longer we delay, the worse it will be." She then brought together a small group of managers from various divisions to solicit their opinions. You are one of these managers. What should you tell Delatorre to do? How would you use the approaches introduced in this chapter to address this dilemma?

## NOTES

1. Argyris, C., & Schön, D. A. (1978). *Organizational learning: A theory of action perspective.* Reading, MA: Addison-Wesley.
2. Ibid.
3. Nielsen, R. P. (1996). *The politics of ethics: Methods for acting, learning, and sometimes fighting, with others in addressing ethics problems in organizational life* (The Ruffin Series in Business Ethics). Oxford, UK: Oxford University Press.
4. Kim, A. (1999). *Introduction to systems thinking.* Retrieved from https://thesystemsthinker.com/introduction-to-systems-thinking/. *Note:* It is not strictly true that natural systems are designed with a specific purpose in mind.
5. Ashby, W. R. (1956). *An introduction to cybernetics.* London, UK: Chapman & Hall; Boulding, K. E. (1956). General systems theory: The skeleton of science. *Management Science, 2,* 197–208.

6.  In fact, one can say that the system itself emerges; it is produced through actions even as it influences those actions. For more on this topic, see Giddens, A. (1984). *The constitution of society*. Berkeley: University of California Press.

7.  Werner, C. M., & Baxter, L. A. (1994). Temporal qualities of relationships: Organismic, transactional, and dialectical views. In M. Knapp & G. Miller (Eds.), *Handbook of interpersonal communication* (2nd ed., pp. 323–379). Thousand Oaks, CA: SAGE.

8.  Lewis, M. W. (2000). Exploring paradox: Toward a more comprehensive guide. *Academy of Management Review, 25*, 760–776; Peng, K., & Nisbett, R. E. (1999). Culture, dialectics, and reasoning about contradiction. *American Psychologist, 54*(9), 741–754.

9.  Farjoun, M. (2010). Beyond dualism: Stability and change as a duality. *Academy of Management Review, 35*, 202–225.

10. See p. 760, in Lewis (2000).

11. Arnold, D. G., & Hartman, L. P. (2003). Moral imagination and the future of sweatshops. *Business and Society Review, 108*, 425–461.

12. Hargrave, T. J., & Van de Ven, A. H. (2017). Integrating dialectical and paradox perspectives on managing contradictions in organizations. *Organization Studies, 38*(3–4), 319–339. Smith, W. K., Lewis, M. W. (2011). Toward a theory of paradox: A dynamic equilibrium model of organizing. *Academy of Management Review, 36*, 381–403.

13. See p. 93, in Werhane, P. H. (1999). *Moral imagination and management decision-making*. New York, NY: Oxford University Press.

14. Werhane (1999).

15. Dewey, 1980, cited in p. 66, in Fesmire, S. (2003). *John Dewey and moral imagination*. Bloomington: Indiana University Press.

16. Dewey, 1980, cited in p. 70, in Fesmire (2003).

17. See p. 5, in Smith, A. (2006). *The theory of moral sentiments*. Mineola, NY: Dover. (Original work published 1759)

18. See Chapter 2, in Rawls, J. (1971). *A theory of justice*. Cambridge, MA: Harvard University Press.

19. Werhane (1999).

20. See Chapter 11, in Senge, P. M. (2006). *The fifth discipline: The art and practice of the learning organization*. New York, NY: Doubleday. (Original work published 1990)

21. Garvin, D. A., & Roberto, M. A. (2001). What you don't know about making decisions. *Harvard Business Review, 79*(8), 108–116.

22. Argyris and Schön (1978).

23. Coser, L. A. (1957). Social conflict and the theory of social change. *British Journal of Sociology, 8*, 197–207.

24. When we say that conflict should be task-related but not interpersonal, we are not saying that it should be devoid of emotion. As noted above, we think that emotion can add vitality to team decision-making. It just must be channeled to serve the ends of the team.

25. Garvin and Roberto (2001).

26. Lee, A., Willis, S., & Tian, A. W. (2018, March 2). When empowering employees works and when it doesn't (Online). *Harvard Business Review*. Retrieved from https://hbr.org/2018/03/when-empowering-employees-works-and-when-it-doesnt

27. Dahlin, K. B., Weingart, L. R., & Hinds, P. J. (2006). Team diversity and information use. *Academy of Management Journal, 48*, 1107–1123.

28. Ibid.

29. Edmondson, A. (1999). Psychological safety and learning behavior in work teams. *Administrative Science Quarterly, 44*(2), 350–383.

30. Edmondson, A. C., Bohmer, R. M., & Pisano, G. P. (2001). Disrupted routines: Team learning and new technology implementation in hospitals. *Administrative Science Quarterly, 46*(4), 685–716; Carmeli, A., & Gittell, J. H. (2009). High-quality relationships, psychological safety, and learning from failures in work organizations. *Journal of Organizational Behavior, 30*(6), 709–729.

31. Ring, P. S., & Van de Ven, A. H. (1992). Structuring cooperative relationships between organizations. *Strategic Management Journal, 13*, 483–498.

32. Rousseau, D. M., Sitkin, S. B., Burt, R. S., & Camerer, C. (1998). Not so different after all: A cross-discipline view of trust. *Academy of Management Review, 23*, 393–404; Mayer, R. C., Davis, J. H., & Schoorman, F. D. (1995). An integrative model of organizational trust. *Academy of Management Review, 20*, 709–734; Baier, A. (1986). Trust and antitrust. *Ethics, 96*, 231–260.

33. Bradach, J. L., & Eccles, R. G. (1989). Price, authority, and trust: From ideal types to plural forms. *Annual Review of Sociology, 15*, 97–118; Gambetta, D.

(1988). *Trust: Making and breaking cooperative relations*. New York, NY: Basil Blackwell; Ring and Van de Ven (1992).

34.  Jones, T. M. (1995). Instrumental stakeholder theory: A synthesis of economics and ethics. *Academy of Management Review, 20,* 404–437; Bromiley, P., & Cummings, L. L. (1995). Transaction costs in organizations with trust. In R. J. Bies, R. J. Lewicki, & B. H. Sheppard (Eds.), *Research on negotiation in organizations* (Vol. 5, pp. 219–247). Stanford, CT: JAI Press.

35.  Mintzberg, H., Raisinghani, D., & Théorêt, A. (1976). The "structure" of "unstructured" decision processes. *Administrative Science Quarterly, 21,* 246–275.

36.  Argyris and Schön (1978); Baum, J. A. C., & Dahlin, K. B. (2007). Aspiration performance and railroads' patterns of learning from train wrecks and crashes. *Organization Science, 18,* 368–385; Haunschild, P. R., & Sullivan, B. N. (2002). Learning from complexity: Effects of prior accidents and incidents on airlines' learning. *Administrative Science Quarterly, 47,* 609–643.

37.  Bingham, C. B., & Davis, J. P. (2012). Learning sequences: Their existence, effect, and evolution. *Academy of Management Journal, 55*(3), 611–641.

38.  Bingham and Davis (2012); Miner, A. S., Bassoff, P., & Moorman, C. (2001). Organizational improvisation and learning: A field study. *Administrative Science Quarterly, 46,* 304–337.

39.  See p. 228, in Lüscher, L. S., & Lewis, M. W. (2008). Organizational change and managerial sensemaking: Working through paradox. *Academy of Management Journal, 51,* 221–240.

40.  Hegel, G. W. F. (1969). *The science of logic*. London, UK: Allen & Unwin. (Original work published 1812)

41.  Adapted from Marcus, A. A., & Kaiser, S. (2006). *Managing beyond compliance: The ethical and legal dimensions of corporate responsibility*. Northbrook, IL: Northcoast. See also McLean, B., & Elkin, P. (2004). *The smartest guys in the room: The amazing rise and scandalous fall of Enron*. New York, NY: Portfolio Trade. This book was made into a film in 2005 directed by Alex Gibney.

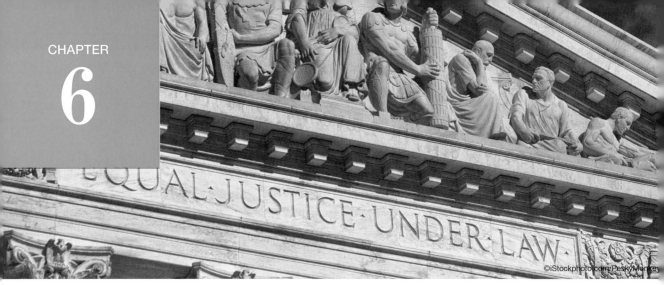

In organizations, ethical behavior depends on many people coordinating their actions.

# Building Ethical Organizations

## Learning Objectives

After reading this chapter, the student should be able to do the following:

LO 6.1: Understand the impact of organizational design on the ethical behavior of employees.

LO 6.2: Identify the elements of effective ethics programs.

LO 6.3: Distinguish compliance-based from values-based ethics programs.

LO 6.4: Explain workplace diversity and discrimination.

LO 6.5: Describe how the weight-of-reasons approach to decision-making can be integrated and used within ethics programs.

LO 6.6: Establish formal and informal organizational elements such as structure, culture, leadership, human resources systems, performance measurement systems, and reward systems so that they boost ethical behavior.

> *The more we care for the happiness of others, the greater our own sense of well-being becomes.*
>
> **—The Dalai Lama**

## Introduction

Thus far, we have presented the weight-of-reasons framework for ethical decision-making, discussed closing the circle when addressing ethical issues (Chapter 4), and described learning-based approaches such as systems thinking and moral imagination that decision-makers can use to move beyond short-term fixes toward comprehensive long-term solutions (Chapter 5). Will business decision-makers actually use these approaches? After all, using them requires time and mental effort. It is more convenient, at least in the short term, to make decisions based on habit than to take ownership of ethical issues and engage in double- and triple-loop learning. The answer to the question is that decision-makers will be more likely to employ these approaches if their organizations are set up to encourage them to do so. The purpose of this chapter is to flesh out this answer. We discuss how leaders can design organizational structures and processes to motivate more ethical decision-making. Like Chapter 4, this chapter starts from the premise that organizational context has a big influence on ethical decision-making. But whereas Chapter 4 showed how organizations can stymie ethical decision-making, in this chapter, we show how organizations can stimulate ethical decision-making.

First, we discuss organizational *ethics programs*, which typically include features such as ethics officers, ethics training programs, and codes of conduct. We conclude, as many have before us, that such programs are most useful when they motivate workers to follow shared ethical values instead of rigidly following rules. Ethics programs are not sufficient by themselves, however. To provide workers incentives to adopt core ethical values, organizational leaders must attempt to build these values into every aspect of the organization, including the structure, culture, performance measurement system, and other elements that promote and reinforce the ethical behavior for which an organization aims. This chapter reveals how to build these elements into an organization.

The takeaway from this chapter is that if an organization is to consistently improve the ethical decision-making of managers and employees, it must establish a context that makes it easy for them to address the impediments to ethical decision-making. Without this context, managers and employees will feel pressured to ignore ethics and to take unethical actions. They will be unable to effectively apply the weight-of-reasons framework for ethical decision-making. With this context in place, they will be more encouraged to use the weight-of-reasons framework to develop long-term solutions that can be implemented and sustained.

# Ethics Programs

**LO 6.2:** Identify the elements of effective ethics programs.

Almost every company has an **ethics program**. In the United States, the push to establish corporate ethics programs began in the 1970s with the passage of the **Foreign Corrupt Practices Act (FCPA)**. The U.S. Congress passed this law after investigations revealed that numerous companies were paying bribes to foreign government officials in exchange for business favors. In addition to making **bribery** illegal, the FCPA requires public companies to maintain adequate internal accounting systems and accurate records of its transactions.

U.S. companies increasingly established ethics programs after the enactment of the **Federal Sentencing Guidelines for Organizations (FSGO)** in 1991. These guidelines were established to ensure that the sentences imposed for corporate crimes were consistent across cases and to provide companies with an incentive to detect and prevent corporate crime. The most common corporate crimes include fraud, illegal environmental pollution, breaking tax laws, and antitrust violations. Companies cannot go to prison, but they can be fined, ordered to compensate their victims, and required to issue public notices that they have been convicted of crimes. Companies can be found guilty and held liable for the actions of their employees, and their employees can go to prison.

To prevent companies from being punished for illegal behavior by their rogue employees, the Federal Sentencing Guidelines stipulate that fines can be substantially reduced—by as much as 95%—if the company can show that it has an effective ethics program in place, and as long as the illegal behavior is promptly reported and was not committed by high-level employees.[1] The 2014 update of the FSGO identified the following characteristics of effective ethics programs:

©iStockphoto.com/People Images

Bribery is a pervasive ethical problem in business.

- Policies and procedures to detect and prevent criminal conduct

- Oversight of the ethics program by senior personnel

- High-level supervision of personnel responsible for implementing the program

- Provision of ample resources and power to those personnel

- Effective communication of policies and procedures to all levels of employees, through training programs and other mechanisms

- Systems for monitoring, auditing, and reporting program effectiveness

- "Whistle-blower" mechanisms for reporting suspected wrongdoing without fear of retaliation

- Incentives for compliance and disciplinary actions for noncompliance

- Ongoing updating of the program to reduce the risk of criminal conduct[2]

In practice, companies have met the requirements of the Federal Sentencing Guidelines and other laws by having ethics programs with the following components: codes of conduct, ethics officers, ethics training, ethics communication systems, and systems for producing accurate financial statements.[3]

## Codes of Conduct

A corporate code of conduct describes acceptable and unacceptable behaviors in specific types of situations that arise as employees go about their work. In general, they direct employees to conduct themselves with integrity. Companies have also adopted codes of conduct for stakeholders they do business with such as their suppliers. For instance, Ford provides trainings in corporate social responsibility and human rights to the more than 11,000 supplier companies on which it depends.

The codes of conduct that companies have in place vary in the range of situations they cover and how prescriptive they are about appropriate behavior. The Starbucks code of conduct, for instance, provides guidance across a range of ethical issues, including human rights, harassment, wages and work hours, conflicts of interest, giving and receiving gifts, bribery and interactions with government officials, sales and advertising practices, unfair competition, insider trading, intellectual property, and disclosure of personal information.[4] It generally does not specify the particular actions employees should take in these situations, however.

The New York Stock Exchange suggests its member companies adopt codes of conduct that require employees to

- do what is in the best interests of the company when they face a conflict between their own interests and those of the company;

- not take advantage of opportunities to use corporate information and resources for personal gain;

- not disclose nonpublic information that could benefit competitors or harm the organization;

- not unfairly treat any of the company's stakeholders—for example, lie to them or conceal information from them;

- use the company's assets efficiently, prevent their theft, and not use them carelessly or wastefully;

- comply with all applicable laws, rules, and regulations; and

- encourage the reporting of any illegal or unethical behavior.[5]

**Federal Sentencing Guidelines for Organizations (FSGO)**
Guidelines to ensure that sentences imposed for corporate crimes are consistent for all organizations, and to establish incentives for organizations to detect and prevent corporate crimes

**Code of conduct**
A set of rules, principles, standards, and policies regarding acceptable and unacceptable behavior by organizational members

The Starbucks code of conduct provides employees guidance for handling a range of ethical issues. Howard Schultz, former Chairman and Chief Executive Officer of Starbucks, states, "Conducting business ethically, with integrity and transparency, is essential to preserving our culture and protecting our brand."[6]

A specific topic frequently covered in codes of conduct is how to handle bribes. There is a fine line between business gifts and bribery; the former can be a genuine token of appreciation and a means of building a strong business relationship, while the latter is done to illegally steer business in the company's direction. Distinguishing between the two typically has to do with the value of what is given. It has been found that the more specifically a code of conduct addresses this distinction, the more likely it is to prevent bribery.

Another topic that is gaining increasing attention is the use of email and other modes of communication at work. Computers and cell phones should be used only for company business, and the company has the right to monitor how they are used. It can prescribe what constitutes acceptable and unacceptable communication. For example, it can specify that ageist, racist, and sexist communications are prohibited. Many employees seem unaware that their communications using company resources are not private and must meet the code of conduct. Companies should regularly update their codes of conduct to keep pace with new situations and issues.

Codes of conduct may also include policies about employees' social media presence and use. Employees use social media in ways that benefit their employers; for instance, they build their professional networks and relationships, enhance their professional profiles and reputations, stay in touch with clients, and keep up with events and trends in their industries. However, they can also use social media in ways that harm the company, including criticizing the company and making offensive statements. Many companies have adopted social media use policies to address such problems. In general, such policies should seek to strike a balance between protecting the company's legitimate business interests and respecting employees' rights to privacy and freedom of speech.

Legally, companies generally can ban social media use in the workplace, and they are able to protect their reputations by setting standards for employees' social media posts. They can, for example, prohibit speech they feel will offend stakeholders or reflect badly on the company. A judge in Virginia recently upheld a company's decision to fire an employee who posted a picture of herself "giving the finger" to President Trump's motorcade as it passed her.[7] At the same time, in many states companies are not allowed to demand access to employees' social media accounts, and they must be careful to not prohibit speech that is protected under federal law. The prohibitions include complaints about wages and working conditions, efforts to organize workers, and information about labor activities such as strikes.[8]

## Chief Ethics Officers

The Federal Sentencing Guidelines provide an incentive for companies to assign responsibility for ensuring ethical behavior. Many companies have assigned this responsibility to an ethics officer, sometimes referred to as a compliance officer or ethics and compliance officer. Carrying out this responsibility means establishing and maintaining the code of conduct, systems for monitoring and measuring corporate ethical performance, and appropriate incentives for ethical behavior and penalties for unethical behavior. It also entails oversight of ethics training programs and the ethics communication system. More informally, the **chief ethics officer** and her staff serve as the "go-to" people on ethical issues. While in an ideal world, employees would be able to go to their managers to address these issues, sometimes this type of communication is not feasible and can be ineffective. The chief ethics officer should provide a "safe haven" for employees seeking help in addressing the ethical problems they face. Table 6.1 outlines the functions of the ethics officer.

**Chief ethics officer**
The employee with primary responsibility for ensuring ethical behavior by and within the organization

Ethics officers also play an important external role. They are likely to be involved in handling legal cases in areas involving the code of conduct, such as bribery and harassment, and typically have or share responsibility for producing reports in areas such as corporate social responsibility and corporate citizenship. More broadly, ethics officers can play an important strategic role in the company by interacting and building relationships with stakeholders. By playing this role, ethics officers and their staff signal to stakeholders that the company is a good business partner because it takes ethics seriously and has integrity.

To be successful, ethics officers must possess adequate power, status, and resources within the company. If top ethics officers are seen as close confidantes of the CEO (chief executive officer) and other senior managers and are designated as senior executives, then their efforts are taken more seriously in the company. Ethics officers must have the power to investigate and punish unethical behavior and establish new corporate initiatives that fulfill ethical obligations to stakeholders. Without sufficient power and resources, ethics officers will be unable to "close the circle."

## Reporting and Communication Systems

The Federal Sentencing Guidelines state that an effective ethics program includes mechanisms that allow for "anonymity or confidentiality" in reporting ethical

| TABLE 6.1 | The Functions of the Ethics Officer |
|---|---|

- Establish and maintain the code of conduct
- Establish systems for measuring and monitoring ethical performance
- Establish appropriate incentives for ethical behavior and punishments for unethical behavior
- Oversee ethics training program
- Establish and maintain ethics communication systems—assist line, ombudsperson, whistle-blowing mechanism
- Provide a safe haven for ethics discussions

problems that are encountered at work.[9] Similarly, the U.S. Securities and Exchange Commission (SEC), the government body that seeks to ensure companies provide investors with clear and accurate information, requires public companies to have systems for reporting ethical violations. Effective ethics reporting and communication systems often include ethics assist lines, ombudspersons, and "whistle-blower" protections.

## Ethics Assist Lines

**Ethics assist line (or ethics hotline)**
A mechanism that employees can use to seek advice on handling ethical issues and to report unethical behavior in the workplace

Ethics assist lines (or ethics hotlines) provide employees with an avenue for addressing ethical questions and issues that arise in their work. Sometimes employees use ethics assist lines to report unethical behavior in the workplace, but more often, they seek assistance in addressing an ethical dilemma or guidance on what is permissible under the code of conduct. To be effective, ethics assist lines must guarantee the anonymity or confidentiality of employees. If employees don't trust them, they won't use them.

## Ombudsperson

**Ombudsperson**
An employee who has been designated to hear anonymous or confidential claims of ethics violations, investigate these claims, decide how the claim should be handled, and implement appropriate changes

Another important element of an ethics communication and reporting system is the ombudsperson. An ombudsperson is someone who has been designated by the company to hear anonymous or confidential claims of ethics violations, investigate the claim without revealing the claimant's identity, make a decision about how the claim should be handled, and then implement appropriate changes. According to their own professional code of ethics, ombudspersons must operate independently within the organization, be impartial, maintain employee confidentiality, and address claims outside of the company's formal processes. When they act according to these standards, ombudspersons provide employees with an effective means of addressing their grievances.

## Whistle-Blower Protections

Finally, perhaps the best-known part of effective ethics communication and reporting systems is whistle-blower protection (also discussed in Chapters 4 and 7). As discussed in Chapter 4, whistle-blowers are individuals who go outside the organization to call attention to unethical conduct. Companies typically seek to make whistle-blowing unnecessary by providing employees with avenues to address ethical issues internally, for example, by using ethics hotlines to report unethical behavior to a supervisor, ethics officer, or the human resources department. While companies prefer to address whistle-blower claims internally, so that the unethical behavior is not visible to the public, research shows that external whistle-blowers are more effective in changing unethical behaviors.[10]

In the United States, an assortment of federal and state laws protect whistle-blowers, although whistle-blowers are not protected in all states and not all types of whistle-blowing are protected. A provision in the Sarbanes–Oxley Act of 2002 (often referred to as SOX) imposes criminal penalties of up to 10 years in prison for retaliation against whistle-blowers in all publicly traded companies and their subcontractors.

A 2014 Supreme Court decision held that the Sarbanes–Oxley whistle-blower pro-tections covered employees of privately held companies as well. The U.S. Internal Revenue Service operates a program that rewards 15% to 30% of recovered unpaid taxes to those who provide information about tax fraud. Similarly, the Dodd–Frank Act of 2008 rewards a share of funds recovered to those who provide information about violations of securities law. Numerous older federal laws protecting whistle-blowers exist in areas including civil rights, workplace safety, and workplace organizing.

Despite these legal protections, whistle-blowers often take a real risk when they decide to shine the light on unethical behavior. As discussed in Chapter 4, whis-tle-blowers often face retaliation that can come in the form of being demoted, fired, and physically threatened. They may gain a reputation for being uncooperative or a traitor, which harms their ability to find future employment. Whistle-blowers must carefully balance the benefits of addressing ethical issues against practical consid-erations such as their physical safety (and that of their family) and their ability to continue to earn a living. While we do not take these risks lightly, we would also say that whistle-blowers can reduce the chances of these outcomes by engaging in moral imagination and using political tactics to effectively close the circle.

# WHISTLE-BLOWING AT THE SEC

Recall from Chapter 4 that although investment manager Bernard "Bernie" Madoff was eventually sentenced to 150 years in prison for defrauding investors, the SEC initially failed to follow up on evi-dence provided by rival investor Harry Markopolos that Madoff was running a Ponzi scheme. Evidence shows that this failure to investigate Madoff fits into a larger pattern of the SEC not heeding whistle-blower investigations.

In 2007, Kathleen Furey, a lawyer in the SEC's New York Regional Office (NYRO), began to pursue an investigation against Value Line, a mutual fund group that she suspected was defrauding investors. Furey was unable to get her superiors to approve an investigation, however. When she complained to Assistant Regional Director George Stepaniuk, he told her, "We do not do IM [investment manage-ment] cases." Upset that the SEC simply was not conducting investigations under two laws it was charged with enforcing (the Investment Advisers Act of 1940 and the Investment Company Act of

1940), Furey went up the chain of command. She first went to David Rosenfeld and then to NYRO director Mark Schonfeld, but they too refused to take action. Schonfeld told Furey that she had two choices: She could either withdraw her complaint or go outside the NYRO and take the complaint to the SEC's Office of Inspector General (OIG). Rather than trying to productively address Furey's concerns, Schonfeld essentially told her to be quiet or become a whistle-blower.

Shortly thereafter, in late 2007, Furey did take her case to the OIG. In her complaint, she provided evidence that the SEC had not filed a single invest-ment management case between 2002 and 2009. It appears that filing the complaint led to the blocking of Furey's career advancement, and on March 31, 2008, she was transferred from the SEC's Enforcement Bureau to its Office of Compliance Inspections and Examinations.

At first Furey thrived in her new position, receiving a pay raise and praise from her boss. This progress

*(Continued)*

(Continued)

was halted, however, when the Madoff scandal arose. When the story first broke, NYRO came under pressure from members of Congress (which controls the SEC's budget), who were outraged that NYRO had failed to detect the scandal, especially after all of the warnings from Harry Markopolos (see Chapter 4). Furey's charge that the SEC was not investigating investment management cases fed into the narrative that the SEC was not doing its job. While Furey coincidentally had initially been assigned to the Madoff case, she was quickly removed. She was also given the responsibilities of workers at a higher pay grade (SK-16) than the one she was paid at (SK-14).

Furey was able to handle her new duties, and her boss praised her in performance evaluations and recommended her for promotion from SK-14 to SK-16. She did not receive a promotion, however. The reason why became clear at a 2010 meeting between Furey and NYRO Director George Canellos. When Furey asked if she was being held back from promotion for having blown the whistle, Canellos responded that there were people in NYRO who were "not fans" of the steps she had taken. She had made enemies by becoming a whistle-blower.

Frustrated by not receiving a promotion to SK-16 while doing the requisite work, and having received three promotions between 2004 and 2007, Furey requested a desk audit. (A desk audit is a procedure in which an outside auditor examines an employee's duties and determines whether that employee should be advanced to a higher grade or pay level.) The auditor concluded that Furey was indeed working at level SK-16 and in fact should be promoted above it. Despite this conclusion, Furey still did not receive a promotion. Unable to even obtain a copy of the desk audit, Furey brought a complaint to the OIG. This led to further reprisal by Canellos, who stripped Furey of some of her duties. When the SEC's Office of Human Resources decided, based on the results of the desk audit, to promote Furey, Canellos overrode the decision.

In 2012, Furey filed a whistle-blower complaint with the U.S. government's Office of Special Counsel and then filed an amended complaint in 2013. Unable to obtain the documents needed to sustain her complaint despite having made numerous requests under the Freedom of Information Act, Furey brought a lawsuit against the SEC in 2013. Furey and the SEC settled this case under confidential terms in 2014. Furey's attorney for her legal actions was Gary Aguirre, a former SEC prosecutor who won a $755,000 settlement of his own whistle-blower case against the SEC. Aguirre was fired for trying to pursue an insider trading case against prominent investment banker John Mack. The case of Kathleen Furey demonstrates that despite the legal protections in place, whistle-blowing can come at a very high cost even when the facts are on your side.[11]

## Ethics Training

Another element of many ethics programs is training. Usually ethics trainings take the form of workshops and seminars. One of the main purposes of ethics training programs is to teach employees about laws relevant to their jobs, the company's code of conduct, and other elements of the ethics program such as whistle-blower provisions.

Ethics training should be conducted for both new hires as part of their onboarding and also for experienced employees to make sure they are aware of new developments and issues and also to ensure they have not developed bad habits. It can be especially important to provide training to middle managers and supervisors because they have the most influence on the behavior of frontline employees. In addition, they often feel a high level of pressure to engage in unethical behavior since they must try to achieve challenging goals set by senior managers while operating with limited resources.

## Financial Reporting Systems

As noted, many ethical violations that occur in companies have to do with financial records and systems. Crimes associated with producing and reporting financial information include fraud, bribery, embezzlement, money laundering, and tax evasion. Although the financial accounting and reporting system is not typically considered a part of an ethics program, maintaining the integrity of this system is absolutely essential to ensuring ethical behavior. Strong systems of internal accounting and financial controls prevent or detect many of the ethical violations that occur in companies. Simple features like separating accounting duties among different personnel, requiring double signatures on checks, and prior approval by senior managers of payments over a certain size, standardized documentation, and ongoing internal audits can help prevent and detect financial crimes. Companies should hire certified accountants to audit their books and help them with financial and tax reporting. Ethical problems related to financial systems can also be minimized if the board of directors has a strong audit committee and members who have financial expertise.

Numerous laws require companies to have strong accounting and reporting systems. Sarbanes–Oxley, mentioned above, requires

- senior executives to take individual responsibility for the accuracy and completeness of the firm's financial statements;

- strong internal controls, and audits of those controls;

- reporting of "off–balance sheet" transactions (significant transactions involving assets and liabilities that do not show up on the company's balance sheet);

- prompt reporting of significant changes in the company's financial condition; and

- restrictions on the auditors that companies hire to try to ensure that the auditors are independent of the company and have no conflicts of interest.

The Enron case presented in Chapter 5 addresses the issue of accounting misstatements. Also see the case involving Arthur Andersen and David Duncan at the end of this chapter.

## Compliance-Based and Values-Based Ethics Programs

**LO 6.3:** Distinguish compliance-based from values-based ethics programs.

Ethics programs can take two forms: compliance based and values based. The goal of compliance-based ethics programs is to make sure employees are complying with the rules set forth in the code of conduct and other ethics-related policies, as well as the laws of the jurisdictions in which the company operates. They take a legalistic, "law-and-order" approach to ethics, setting out rules for behavior, giving employees little discretion, and punishing failure to follow those rules.

**Fraud**
Illegal deception for the purpose of financial or other personal gain

**Embezzlement**
Theft of anyone's identity and core beliefs, and how it lives them out systematically through its activities and engagement with stakeholders

**Money laundering**
The concealment of illegally obtained money, typically by transferring it through a seemingly legitimate transaction

**Tax evasion**
The illegal nonpayment or underpayment of taxes owed

**Compliance-based ethics program**
An ethics program that sets out rules for behavior and punishes failure to comply with those rules

**Values-based ethics program**
An ethics program (also known as an integrity-based program) that emphasizes living up to shared ethical values in addition to compliance with laws

In contrast, rather than taking the "checklist" approach to ethics that compliance-based programs do, values-based ethics programs (also known as integrity-based programs) bring ethics to life in the organization. These programs emphasize taking action based on shared ethical values rather than detection and punishment of legal and regulatory violations.[12] They communicate the organization's shared ethical values, counsel employees and support them in acting according to those values and building them into their decision-making, and evaluate employee performance based on adherence to those values and their willingness to use frameworks such as the weight of reasons.[13] Values-based programs are necessary because codes of conduct, norms, and laws cannot possibly address all of the different types of ethical issues that arise in organizations.[14]

Values-based ethics programs are not a substitute for compliance-based systems; they build on them. They have a compliance-based component that holds employees accountable for following rules as well as a component that motivates employees to take positive actions based on shared values. Both pieces are important; the values-based component would not work by itself. This is because employees who are motivated by shared values expect ethical violations to be punished. They can come to feel that stated values are not taken seriously in the organization if they are not punished.[15]

**Mission**
The organization's purpose; what it is and why it exists

**Vision**
The organization's objective; the state it hopes to attain

**Values statement**
A formal statement of the core beliefs, principles, and priorities that are shared within an organization

**Values**
The principles by which the organization will conduct itself as it seeks to achieve its vision

**Ethical values**
The organization's values that explicitly pertain to ethics; the principles that govern behavior in addressing ethical issues

Values-based ethics programs begin with a statement of the company's core values. Often, when companies develop their mission and vision statements, they also develop values statements. Whereas a mission statement is generally viewed as a statement of the organization's identity and purpose and the vision statement expresses the organization's objectives and what it hopes to become, the values statement indicates the principles that the company intends to live by as it carries out its mission and seeks to achieve its vision. Values are the standards of behavior organizations intend to maintain in their conduct.

Gravity Payments, a credit card processing company in Seattle, provides an example of a company that seeks to achieve its vision by living up to its values. Following from his lifelong commitment to serving others, Gravity's CEO Dan Price set the company's minimum wage at $70,000 per year. Gravity's mission statement declares that the company puts "purpose and people above profit." The company's values statement asserts that "the only way to do business is to serve others, do more for them, and charge less." It further enumerates three core values that guide the company: (1) creative leadership, (2) a passion for progress, and (3) responsibility.[16]

To ensure ethical behavior, values statements should include ethical values, which are simply the subset of an organization's core values that are explicitly ethical. Ethical values can relate to the perspectives presented in Chapter 2; for example, they can include respect for individual rights (deontology), serving the greater good (teleology), acting with integrity and being fair (virtue ethics), and treating others with care. Ethical behavior is more likely if the organization officially subscribes to such values. Would you expect ethical behavior in a company that stated that it valued callousness, winning at all costs, and doing things the easy way?

Values-based ethics programs typically have many of the same elements as compliance-based programs, but these elements have a different purpose and take a different form. For example, whereas a compliance-based ethics training session would teach employees about the code of conduct and relevant laws, a values-based ethics training might be aimed at helping employees to make better ethical decisions and more effectively address the complex ethical dilemmas they come across as they do their jobs. In addition to having lectures from ethics experts sharing their knowledge, they might also involve employees interacting with and learning from one another. Taking a virtues approach, De Colle and Werhane suggest that rather than teaching employees about general ethical frameworks such as teleology and deontology, ethics workshops should instead involve employees having conversations about case studies and current issues they face.[17]

While more compliance-oriented features of ethics programs such as codes of conduct and whistle-blower protections are a part of values-based ethics programs, they play a smaller role in bringing about ethical behavior than they do in compliance-based programs. When employees address ethical issues by trying to live up to shared values rather than following rules, they have less need for mechanisms designed to detect, prevent, and address their unethical behavior.

Research indicates that values-based compliance programs do in fact lead to more ethical behavior in organizations. While compliance-based programs are "associated with higher levels of ethical awareness, reporting of misconduct, and employee integrity, and lower levels of observed misconduct and perceived role conflict," the effects are even stronger in values-based programs.[18] In an important research finding, Weaver and colleagues found that while compliance-based ethics programs influence behavior, their content actually does not matter; what matters is that the program is undertaken within the context of a strong ethical culture. Employees are inclined to behave ethically if the organizational leaders behave ethically, they perceive that other employees are treated fairly, and ethical issues are discussed openly in the organization rather than marginalized.[19] They behave ethically when they trust that the company's stated values are actually meaningful within the organization and especially when those values include autonomy—the freedom to decide for oneself how to address a problem, rather than following rules.[20] Hence values-based ethics programs are more effective when they are used in ethical organizations, which we discuss below. Table 6.2 provides a comparison of compliance-based and values-based ethics programs.

**TABLE 6.2**  Compliance-Based and Values-Based Ethics Programs

| Organizational Element | Compliance Based | Values Based |
| --- | --- | --- |
| Organizational goal | Compliance with code of conduct and other policies | Ethical behavior consistent with core values |
| Managerial approach | Control: Prevent, detect, punish | Empower: Raise awareness, support, counsel |
| Employee behavior | Follow rules | Identify and solve problems |
| Example | Ethics training: Review code of conduct | Ethics training: Discuss real-life ethical dilemma |

# DIESELGATE: EMISSIONS TESTING AT VOLKSWAGEN

The Volkswagen (VW) "Dieselgate" scandal provides an excellent yet saddening example of why values-based ethics programs are necessary. In 2015, the U.S. Environmental Protection Agency (EPA) discovered that starting seven years earlier, the company had illegally installed "defeat device" software activating pollution control equipment in many of its diesel vehicles when the vehicles were undergoing emissions testing but shut them off when the vehicles were being driven. The cars with defeat device software released pollution up to 40 times greater than that allowed under U.S. law. VW had installed the software in virtually all the diesel cars it manufactured between 2009 and 2015. The cheating occurred in eight models: the Jetta, Golf, Passat, Beetle, Touareg, Audi 7, Audi 8, and Porsche Cayenne. (Audi and Porsche are subsidiaries of VW.)

The EPA accused VW of installing defeat devices in September 2015. While VW CEO Martin Winterkorn first stated that he was unaware of the defeat device software, by the end of the month, he had resigned and the company had admitted that the devices had been installed in more than 2 million of its vehicles. In January 2016, the U.S. government followed up with further action. This time the U.S. Department of Justice sued VW and its subsidiaries for using defeat devices, as well as for violating greenhouse gas emissions rules. Eventually, under two settlements, one reached with the U.S. Department of Justice and the State of California and the other with the U.S. Federal Trade Commission, VW agreed to pay approximately $11.5 billion in compensation to purchasers of VW's diesel vehicles. In addition, the company agreed to invest $2 billion in zero-emission vehicle infrastructure, access, and education and another $1.2 billion on projects to reduce $NO_x$ emissions.[21] ($NO_x$ emissions result in smog.)

The U.S. government brought criminal charges against top-level executives as well as the company. A VW engineer, James Liang, pleaded guilty to being involved in the scandal and agreed to cooperate with the government in the prosecution of others in exchange for a delay in his sentencing. Based partly on what Liang revealed, a U.S. federal grand jury indicted seven other VW employees for fraud. Many lived in Germany and refused to come to the United States to face charges. However, the FBI was able to seize one employee, Oliver Schmidt, as he was getting ready to return to Germany. Schmidt pleaded guilty, received a sentence of up to seven years in prison, and was ordered to pay a fine of US$400,000.

Because of its tight relationship with the automakers, the government of Germany initially took a very different approach to Dieselgate. It first demanded that the company recall 2.5 million diesel vehicles (VW voluntarily expanded the recall to include 8.5 million cars across Europe), and it proposed a national program to install an emissions-reducing software update in diesel vehicles. This more accommodating approach caused a backlash, with citizens seeking to hold the company accountable. For example, many cities including Frankfurt, Hamburg, and Stuttgart have imposed bans on diesel cars. Furthermore, VW investors have filed a lawsuit seeking compensation for the drop in the company's share price caused by the scandal. The public outcry has led the government to get tougher on the company by levying a fine of 1.2 billion euros. In addition, prosecutors in Munich arrested and jailed Audi CEO Rupert Stadler for his role in the scandal.[22]

It appears that Dieselgate can be traced back to the company's quest to dominate the global auto industry and its culture and decision-making processes, which emphasized results over everything else.[23] Under Ferdinand Piëch, chairman of VW's board, ex-CEO, and grandson of Ferdinand Porsche, VW surpassed Ford in global sales in 2008, GM in 2014, and then Toyota in 2015. Piëch had a domineering style that made employees afraid to fail.

Martin Winterkorn followed in Piëch's footsteps. He expected employees to follow orders and not ask questions and made all important decisions himself. VW under his reign was once described as "North Korea without the labour camps."

Another factor driving Dieselgate was VW's failure to develop pollution-control technology for diesel engines. Going back to the 1970s, the company had unsuccessfully attempted to develop this technology but resorted to defeat devices to evade pollution control laws. The EPA fined VW for disabling emission control devices in 1973 and then reached a billion-dollar settlement with the company in 1998 for the same practices.

The Dieselgate scandal has led to a major change of course in VW's strategy, operations, and culture. While Martin Winterkorn's successor Matthias Müller first dismissed the scandal as the fault of a small group of renegade engineers, he also recognized Dieselgate as an opportunity to take the company in a new direction. Müller stated the crisis "actually worked as a kind of accelerator to address issues that, before, were unable to be addressed." Most notably, Müller moved the company toward electric vehicles, promising to introduce 50 all-electric car models by 2025. The company has also been able to achieve major cost reductions, so much so that it has actually been able to pay most of its Dieselgate penalties through increased profits. (The company was also helped by a rebound in the auto market.) Müller's successor Herbert Diess has continued to move the company in these directions.[24]

VW also has instituted major changes in its culture and decision-making in response to Dieselgate. Müller decentralized decision-making at VW and encouraged workers to take on innovative projects. The company also established its Together4Integrity program, which aims not only to detect ethical and legal compliance risks early and quickly remediate them but more broadly to establish a culture that values integrity, speaking up about ethical concerns, and accountability. The company's leadership has recognized that it cannot achieve its growth goals unless it attaches greater importance to its social responsibilities and deepens its commitment to behaving ethically.[25]

VW executives cannot afford to be complacent about ethics, however, for organizational change is difficult to make for all the reasons discussed in Chapters 3 and 4. Furthermore, Dieselgate has not gone away. In April 2019, German prosecutors charged Martin Winterkorn with fraud, breach of fair competition laws, and breach of trust for not informing regulators and customers as soon as he became aware that the defeat devices had been installed. In addition, the SEC has charged VW as well as Winterkorn personally with fraud for raising billions of dollars in the corporate bond market while knowing the company was deceptively advertising its diesel fleet as "clean." Furthermore, more than 300,000 VW diesel car owners have filed a class-action lawsuit against the company.[26] Most ominously, regulators are pursuing their suspicion that the Dieselgate scandal is much bigger than VW. In September 2018, the European Commission opened an investigation into whether VW along with BMW, Daimler, Audi, and Porsche began to collude as far back as the 1990s to limit the development and use of emissions reductions technologies. (Audi and Porsche were not owned by VW in the 1990s as they are today.)[27]

The Dieselgate case demonstrates the limitations of compliance-based ethics programs. VW had an ethics program with all of the features described in this chapter—for example, a code of conduct and ethics trainings. However, this ethics program neither prevented the scandal from arising nor effectively addressed it once it did. Because of pressure from above to achieve results and a fear of speaking up, the company's employees engaged in fraudulent, harmful behavior over the course of many years. VW employees were obedient to authority and succumbed to groupthink. They failed to speak truth to power and close the circle. While responsibility for Dieselgate starts at the top of the company, employees also contributed.[28]

Chapter 10 has a detailed case that presents a more extensive look at Dieselgate and ethical problems at VW.

# Diversity Programs

**LO 6.4:** Explain workplace diversity and discrimination.

An important way companies can bring about more ethical behavior is to establish diversity programs. Their purpose is to ensure that individuals within the organization are not treated differently because of irrelevant differences in their personal characteristics. More positively, another purpose of a diversity program is to increase individuals' awareness and knowledge of people within the organization who are different from them and, ultimately, to establish communication, build relationships, and increase teamwork among these diverse people.

People are diverse in many different ways. They differ in terms of

- more stable and enduring characteristics, such as race, ethnicity, age (date of birth), gender, and sexual orientation;

**Diversity**
The state of having variety (different elements)

- evolving characteristics including physical dis/ability, physical characteristics such as height and weight, levels and types of education, religion, marital status, and social categories such as what interests they have and what clubs they are in;

**Discrimination**
The act of treating a person unfairly based on the social category one puts that person into

- personality characteristics, such as whether they are introverted, agreeable, and conscientious; and

- organizational roles, such as job title, department, and level of seniority.

©iStockphoto.com/Bastiaan Slabbers

Bill Cosby is just one of many entertainment industry personalities who have recently been accused of, admitted to, and/or been found guilty of sexual misconduct.

All of these forms of diversity may serve as the basis for discrimination. Discrimination occurs when one person treats another person unfairly based on the social category she or he puts that person into. In the United States, laws exist to prohibit many forms of discrimination. The Civil Rights Act of 1964 and related amendments prohibit businesses from discriminating based on gender, race, ethnicity, religion, age, national origin, physical and mental disability, sexual orientation, and gender identity. Nevertheless, workplace discrimination has a long history and continues to this day. As noted earlier in the book, the #metoo movement has called attention to many instances of sexual misconduct in the workplace and elsewhere, and it stigmatizes this behavior and seeks to support its victims.

Many instances of workplace discrimination may be traced to cognitive factors discussed in Chapter 3. Individuals tend to make rapid, intuitive (Systems 1 or "fast thinking") judgments about other people based on stereotypes rather than based on their individual merits. These stereotypes can translate into workplace discrimination. For example, one person might fail to give a challenging assignment to another based on a stereotype that the other individual was not strong, intelligent, or dedicated enough to do a job well because of that individual's age, gender, or race. Equally, a person might consciously or unconsciously favor another individual whom she or he perceived to be a member of the same social category as herself or himself. Stereotypes often are incorrect and unfair. The Implicit Association Test is a research tool that can be used to reveal implicit attitudes such as stereotypes (see Figure 6.1).

Just because people have intuitive biases does not mean they have to act on them, however. Indeed, we can use frameworks such as the weight of reasons to make better ethical choices than our intuitions would lead us to make. Firms can design their ethics programs to address diversity issues. Codes of conduct should specify that discrimination is prohibited, and ethics assist lines and ombudspersons should provide ways of addressing discrimination when it does occur. Ethics trainings can help build awareness of discrimination and inform employees of tools available for addressing it.

In addition to taking these compliance-oriented steps, companies should take a values-based approach to diversity. Diversity and discrimination are not just compliance issues; they go to the core questions of what the organization's purpose is and the values it seeks to uphold. Companies' statements of core values can speak about the importance of diversity, and ethics workshops can, in addition to teaching employees' about discrimination laws and policies, help them become aware of their own implicit biases, discuss tough issues related to diversity, and apply decision frameworks to address ethical dilemmas.

Values-based ethics programs can be designed to deliver the message that diversity is a potential source of innovation and strength. Chapter 5 showed how cognitive diversity leads to better ethical decisions. Demographic diversity—that is, diversity in people's backgrounds and experiences, in general—corresponds to cognitive diversity. Decision-making processes involving inquiry and advocacy, moral imagination,

**FIGURE 6.1**      The Implicit Association Test[29]

Research shows that unfavorable mental judgments about people whom we perceive to be different are inevitable. As discussed in Chapter 3, this is because we have evolved to make fast judgments. The Implicit Association Test (IAT) is a tool used in psychology to assess the associations that individuals make between different objects in their memory and, particularly, the extent to which people implicitly view personal characteristics (e.g., race, age, weight, sex) as good or bad. It was first introduced in the 1990s by researchers Anthony Greenwald, Debbie McGhee, and Jordan Schwartz, and it has been employed most notably by Project Implicit, which was founded in 1998 by Greenwald and psychologists Mahzarin Banaji and Brian Nosek. The IAT is a computer-based measure that enables researchers to detect implicit biases that cannot be detected through methods such as surveys. These include biases that subjects may not be willing to admit to publicly and that may lead to discrimination, such as a preference for people of one race or gender over another.

The IAT is widely used but also has been subject to some criticisms, including the charge that the implicit biases the test reveals cannot be shown to translate into biased behavior.

and other decision-making techniques described in Chapter 5 are likely to produce more double-loop learning and new ideas when diverse people are involved. Diversity from an ethics standpoint is an opportunity not a problem.

# BALL CORPORATION

Ball Corporation (designated a "winner" in a previous book by Marcus called *Big Winners and Big Losers*) is an example of a company that takes diversity and inclusion seriously. The company is in the packaging and aerospace industries. Based on an analysis of anonymous employee surveys, *Forbes* magazine ranked Ball as its Best Employer for Diversity for 2019, and the Human Rights Campaign named the company one of the Best Places to Work for LGBT (lesbian, gay, bisexual, transgender) Equality. The company's Vice President of Diversity and Inclusion, Manette Snow, reports directly to CEO John Hayes rather than to the head of the company's human resources department. This signals the importance of diversity and inclusion to the company and provides workers with a means to close the circle on diversity and inclusion issues that arise.

Ball has established nine Ball Resource Groups (BRGs) that engage in activities that promote and support diversity and inclusion within Ball. The nine are the Abilities, African American, Asian, Cultural Awareness of the Religions of Employees (CARE), Hispanic, LGBTA (the A is for Allies), Veterans, Women's, and Young Professionals resource groups. Each group must be sponsored by at least two senior executives at Ball and receives company funding to carry out its activities.

The BRGs provide employees with a sense of family within the company and also provide workers with resources and help them develop skills and networks that contribute to career development. Notably, Ball employees can join resource groups that do not attach to their identities. For example, the Veterans BRG includes nonveterans who are interested in learning more about veterans' issues, and women make up only about half of the Women's BRG. Ball has used the BRGs as conduits to organizations that can help the company expand its diverse talent pool, including the National Society of Black Engineers, the Society of Asian Scientists and Engineers, the Society of Hispanic Professional Engineers, and the Society of Women Engineers.

Ball CEO John Hayes explains why nurturing diversity and inclusion at the company is both the most ethical thing to do and the best choice for the bottom line when he states,

> With different perspectives come different solutions to help our customers win in the marketplace. We will drive growth and economic value through our deliberate and intentional efforts to create a more diverse workforce and inclusive culture.

We will return to the topic of whether and how ethics and profits go hand in hand in Chapter 7.[30]

## Ethics Programs and the Weight of Reasons

**LO 6.5:** Describe how the weight-of-reasons approach to decision-making can be integrated and used within ethics programs.

Ethics programs can provide a context that rewards the application of the weight-of-reasons frameworks. Ethics assist lines and ombudspersons provide managers access to experienced individuals who can provide input and help managers work through the framework. As noted above, companies can use ethics training workshops and seminars to teach employees the weight-of-reasons framework and give them the opportunity to experiment with it in a safe setting. If an organization has an ethics officer who has put into place systems for monitoring, measuring, and rewarding ethical performance, then employees have more incentives to use the framework to address difficult ethical dilemmas.

Values-based ethics programs provide a more conducive environment for using the weight-of-reasons framework than do compliance-based programs. In the latter, there is the risk that employees will be disinclined to use the framework because they feel no need to do more than necessary to comply with rules and laws. In contrast, in organizations with values-based programs, they feel stimulated to "go the extra mile." When employees are motivated by the values of integrity, honesty, and concern for stakeholders, they can come to see the use of the weight-of-reasons framework as a normal part of doing their jobs.

## Ethical Organizations

**LO 6.6:** Establish formal and informal organizational elements such as structure, culture, leadership, human resources systems, performance measurement systems, and reward systems so that they boost ethical behavior.

Values-based ethics programs facilitate and reward ethical behavior in organizations by trying to ensure that employees are motivated by shared values and a desire to act ethically, rather than an obligation to follow rules. Unethical behavior can still take place in organizations with values-based programs, however. One reason is that there are other influences within the organization that encourage such behavior. These influences include demands from unethical leaders and norms of unethical behavior. To further ensure that employees consistently act in an ethical fashion, organizations should, in addition to establishing values-based ethics programs, seek to build ethics into all aspects of the organization. These include the organization's structure, culture, leadership, human resources systems, performance measurement systems, and rewards systems.[31] An organization that thoroughly embodies ethics in this way can be called an **ethical organization**.[32]

In ethical organizations, employees are inclined to use frameworks such as the weight of reasons because multiple factors encourage them to use it. Members perceive that ethical behavior is normal, and they discuss ethical issues and work with one another to solve ethical problems. They see other people including leaders using the framework, trying to act ethically, and being rewarded for doing so. Ethical organizations are designed so there are many influences leading employees in the same direction: to act ethically.

**Ethical organization**
An organization into which ethical values have been built into every element

### The Formal Elements of an Ethical Organization

Ethical organizations incorporate ethics into their formal elements, which are those that have been explicitly defined and articulated. The formal elements include organizational structure, hiring processes, and performance measurement and reward systems.

## *Organizational Structure*

**Organizational structure**

The arrangement of employees, groupings, tasks, and authority within an organization

**Organizational structure** refers to how work is divided up and coordinated within an organization. The organizational structure determines how employees are grouped (e.g., what departments are needed and what jobs must be done in them), the assignment of tasks, and formal reporting relationships (who works for whom). An organizational structure determines who has authority to control the work of others, who is accountable for results, and who has the right to make and delegate decisions.[33] Typically, it is represented in an organizational chart (Figure 6.2).

When managers design a structure, they must make four key decisions.

- First, they must decide on the *division of labor*. Should employees have highly specialized jobs, where they do one or a few tasks repeatedly, or should their jobs include many different tasks?

**FIGURE 6.2**    University Facility Operations Organizational Chart

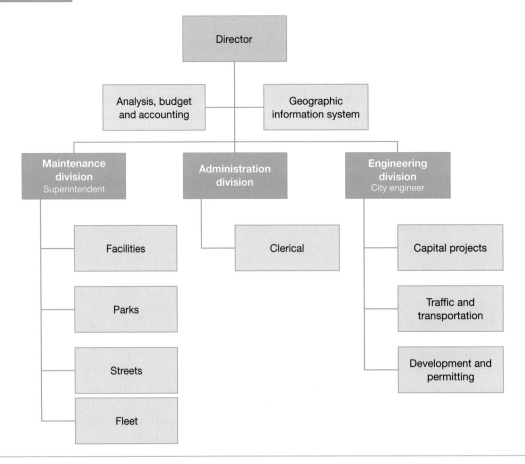

- Second, managers must decide on the extent to which work should be *formalized*—that is, the degree to which an organization's policies, procedures, job descriptions, and rules must be written and explicitly articulated.[34] When jobs are highly formalized, employees know exactly what tasks they are supposed to do and how to do them, but have little autonomy; they do not decide for themselves how to accomplish their work and meet their goals or even what their goals are.

- Third, in designing an organizational structure, managers must choose the extent to which decision-making should be *centralized* or decentralized. In centralized organizations, decision-making is concentrated at higher levels in the organization. In contrast, in decentralized organizations, senior managers make relatively few decisions, and employees at lower levels are empowered; they are given more authority and autonomy to make decisions and solve problems.

- Finally, managers must decide on the organization's *hierarchy*, and whether it will be tall or flat. Tall organizations have many different levels of management, and each manager closely manages the work of relatively few employees. In contrast, flat organizations have few levels of management, and each manager has potentially many employees reporting to her. This generally means that managers do not closely monitor and control the work of each employee.[35]

Based on these factors, one can distinguish mechanistic organizations from organic organizations. Mechanistic organizations are characterized by highly specialized and formalized work, centralized decision-making, and a tall hierarchy. They function like machines; they operate very precisely and efficiently. Employees in them do a narrow set of tasks, following orders and rules that have proven to be effective and efficient. The main weakness of mechanistic organizations is that they are not able to adapt to changing circumstances.

In contrast, organic organizations are characterized by low degrees of specialization and formalization, decentralized decision-making, and a flat hierarchy. They tend to operate less efficiently and reliably than mechanistic organizations, but they are better able to adapt to change. This is because the employees in these organizations do not so much follow rules and do what they are told but decide for themselves what needs to be done and how to do it without receiving approvals from superiors.[36] A pin factory would be an example of a mechanistic organization, while an advertising agency would be an example of an organic organization (Figure 6.3).

As a general rule, organic organizations are more likely to support the use of the weight-of-reasons framework. (There are exceptions to the rule, however.) This is because using the framework involves complex thinking, creativity, and teamwork; typically, it is not a matter of simply following rules. Managers in organic organizations have more control over their own work; therefore, they will have more opportunity to apply the weight of reasons or similar frameworks. They can more deeply examine ethical dilemmas they confront and exercise moral imagination to a greater extent than employees in more mechanistic organizations who are expected to follow rules and obey

**Mechanistic organizations** Organizations that operate precisely and efficiently. They are characterized by highly specialized and formalized work, centralized decision-making, and a tall hierarchy

**Organic organizations** Organizations that are able to adapt to their environments. They are characterized by low degrees of specialization and formalization, decentralized decision-making, and a flat hierarchy

**FIGURE 6.3**

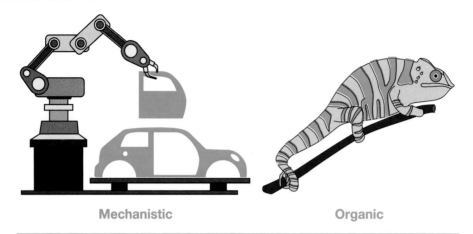

**Mechanistic**                    **Organic**

Mechanistic organizations are like machines; they can accomplish predictable tasks efficiently and effectively. In contrast, organic organizations are like species such as the chameleon that can adapt to changes in their environments.

authorities. Since communication is more fluid in organic organizations, employees are more likely to seek out others who can help them understand and address dilemmas than can employees in mechanistic organizations. They may even reach beyond the organization's boundaries, pulling in relevant stakeholders. (In Chapter 8, we further discuss stakeholder engagement.) Jason Stansbury captures the importance of an organic organizational structure for ethical decision-making when he writes that "valid moral discourse is likely to be promoted by organizational structures that encourage collaborative inquiry when employees are faced with moral problems."[37]

The ethics program is the part of an organization's structure that provides a mechanism for coordinating ethics-related activities. A values-based ethics program is likely to be especially effective if it is implemented within an organic organization. When employees are free to decide for themselves how to do their jobs and have the authority to make decisions for themselves, they will be more likely to address ethical issues by trying to live up to shared values rather than trying to just comply with rules.

### Hiring Processes

Another formal element of the organization that can be designed to support ethical behavior is hiring. Simply put, organizations who hire ethical people are more likely to exhibit ethical behavior. There are many ways to build ethics into the hiring process.[38]

- First, job descriptions and announcements should include ethics screens—they should strongly indicate that ethics are important within the organization.

Ethics screens should go beyond noting that the company complies with laws and speak to the company's shared ethical values.

- Second, the organization should be sure to comply with applicable hiring laws and live up to its shared values during the hiring process. This means, for example, ensuring that all employees who participate in the interview process are aware of the types of questions they legally and ethically can and cannot ask in interviews, and employee group decision-making to ensure that interviewers do not fall prey to their own decision-making biases and discriminate against particular types of job candidates.

- Third, companies should use a variety of instruments to gather information about candidates' ethical behavior and dispositions. These instruments typically include evaluating résumés, checking references, conducting background checks, and administering integrity or honesty tests. In these tests, job candidates usually are asked questions about whether they have ever engaged in illegal activity, how they feel about particular types or instances of dishonesty, or how they would handle a hypothetical situation involving dishonesty. These tests have been shown to help companies distinguish individuals who act honestly from those who do not, although they do pose the risk that they may screen out some job candidates who would have behaved honestly. For this reason, these tests should be used in conjunction with other ethics screens.

- Fourth, companies can administer personality tests to gauge job candidates' ethical qualities and, more broadly, their fit with the organization and their prospective jobs. A number of personality traits are correlated with ethical behavior, including conscientiousness, organizational citizenship behavior, and social dominance. *Conscientiousness* refers to whether an individual is responsible, dependable, and hardworking. It is a strong predictor of not only ethical behavior but also job performance. It is strongly associated with empathy, which is the ability to understand how other people feel. *Organizational citizenship behavior* refers to the willingness to engage in helping behaviors outside of one's job description. Individuals who are willing to "go the extra mile" for the team and the organization tend to be people who behave ethically. Finally, a *social dominance orientation* is negatively associated with ethical behavior. Social dominance orientation is the personality trait of being predisposed to see the dominance of some social groups and individuals over others as natural and good.[39] It is positively associated with unethical behaviors such as racism and sexism.

- Finally, some companies also use postinterview tests such as drug tests to screen out job applicants. They typically do not use polygraph (lie detector) tests, which are illegal both during the screening process and during employment, in most industries.[40] Employers are permitted under U.S. law to administer drug tests during the hiring process, and drug testing is required in some industries with strong public safety risks such as transportation (airlines, trucking, railroads). Drug testing is seen by many as invasive of job candidates' privacy, however. Whether or not to use drug testing is itself an ethical dilemma that requires careful consideration.

### Performance Evaluation and Reward Systems

Other formal elements of the organization that can be designed to motivate ethical behavior include performance evaluation and reward systems. At some level, every person responds to expected rewards and punishments. If workers are rewarded for ethical behavior and punished for unethical behavior, then all things being equal they will act more ethically. Note that rewards can be extrinsic or intrinsic. Extrinsic rewards are tangible rewards that are given by someone else, such as compensation and benefits, while intrinsic rewards are those that arise inside the employee such as a sense of fulfillment and the opportunity to solve problems. Both types of rewards may be used to motivate ethical behavior, with the right mix of rewards depending on the employee.

The measures that a firm can employ to assess whether an employee has behaved ethically range from the simple and objective to the complex and more subjective. At its most basic, ethics appraisal can simply assess whether an employee has attended ethics trainings, has had ethics complaints brought against her, or has been found to violate the company's code of conduct. More subjectively, employees can be evaluated based on whether they have conducted themselves according to the company's shared values. Acting in conformance with shared values means evaluating employees not just on the outcomes they achieved (e.g., no legal violations, good environmental performance) but also on the processes by which they achieved those outcomes. Do they treat fellow employees with respect, ask questions about how they can do their jobs more ethically, and listen to stakeholders? Organizations also can reward employees for proactively addressing ethical dilemmas by using tools such as the weight-of-reasons framework.

One way to ensure that assessments are fair is to use 360-degree appraisal, which involves getting feedback from everyone who interacts with the employee, including co-employees, supervisors, subordinates, and stakeholders such as customers and suppliers. Figure 6.4 illustrates the 360-degree appraisal process.

Just as important as rewarding ethical behavior is not rewarding unethical behavior. Sometimes rewarding unethical behavior happens unintentionally: Well-intended policies such as giving bonuses or stock options to those who achieve strong financial performance may inadvertently motivate managers to take actions such as disregarding environmental and safety laws and "fudging the numbers." If CEOs are rewarded for increasing the stock price of the company, they may try to drive the stock price higher by artificially inflating the company's profits. Rewarding executives based solely or primarily on financial performance can create a "bottom-line" mentality that leads to unethical behavior. Harris and Bromiley show that the greater the extent to which a CEO's compensation comes in the form of stock options, the more likely a company is to engage in financial misconduct.[41]

## The Informal Elements of an Ethical Organization

Designing an organization so that it stimulates ethical behavior also involves managing the informal elements of the organization as well as the formal ones. Fundamentally, organizations are places where like-minded people gather and interact to achieve collective and individual goals. While the ways in which they go about

**FIGURE 6.4**

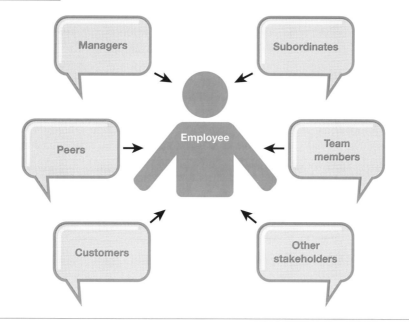

360-degree performance evaluations can produce fairer assessments of employees and uncover ethical and unethical behavior.

doing so are influenced by explicit elements such as the organization chart, codes of conduct, and reward systems, they are also—and perhaps even more—influenced by the shared ways of thinking and doing things that may never have been written down. These include organizational culture, leadership, and climate.

## Organizational Culture

**Organizational culture** consists of shared assumptions and values regarding the appropriate ways to think and behave within an organization, as well as the material artifacts that express these assumptions and values.[42] Hence while culture exists in our minds and the symbols we use to express our thoughts, it is also composed of art, furniture, dress, ceremonies, and other objects.[43] One can tell a lot about what the members of an organization believe by looking at the pictures on the wall, what members wear, how they interact with one another, and what they celebrate. Culture binds the members of organizations together by providing them with an understanding of the correct way of thinking, being, and doing. When you hear a person say, "That's just the way we do things around here," you have encountered evidence of a strong organizational culture.[44]

Treviño and colleagues find evidence that culture influences ethical behavior. Their survey of American companies shows that ethical behavior is associated with cultures in which leaders are ethical, employees perceive the workplace to be fair, ethical issues are openly discussed, and ethical behavior is rewarded. Treviño and

**Organizational culture** Shared assumptions and values regarding the appropriate ways to think and behave and the artifacts that express them

colleagues also conclude that lower levels of ethical behavior are associated with cultures of unquestioning obedience and a focus on self-interest.[45] Emphasizing this point, Johnson recommends that ethical behavior is likely to be higher when employees are comfortable using ethical terms rather than trying to "hide ethics" by talking about ethical issues in technical and financial language.[46]

Managers seeking to build an ethical culture must try to embed shared core assumptions and values into workers' everyday activities. They must make sure the stories that are told in the organizations, the arrangement of office space, the policies about work breaks, and the organization's ceremonies and other events reflect core assumptions and values. If a company's stated values include honesty and hard work, then the stories that are told in the company's official history and repeated often should celebrate honesty and hard work, and not the opposite (see Figure 6.5). If the company's stated values include teamwork, then monthly employee awards should be given out based on teamwork.

Managers must be sure their efforts to express ethical values through organizational artifacts are thorough and comprehensive. A manager who puts a motivational poster on the wall that has a slogan related to integrity accompanied by an inspiring picture will not succeed in building a culture of "integrity" if that is all she or he does; the manager must personally demonstrate integrity and celebrate and reward it.

**Ethical leadership**
The process of taking ethical actions to influence others to act ethically to achieve organizational goals

### Leadership

Leadership is another aspect of the organization that influences whether ethical behavior occurs and whether the use of ethical decision-making frameworks such as the weight of reasons is supported. **Ethical leadership** is "the demonstration

**FIGURE 6.5**    Stories Embody Corporate Culture[47]

Four Seasons Hotels and Resorts is a company with a rich reservoir of stories that reflect its core values. Stories about the Power of Personal Service are used to illustrate what this term means in real examples that anyone in the organization can understand and use. One story, for example, tells of an employee who accidentally overheard a guest telling his wife how embarrassed he felt as he was the only one without a black tie at a black-tie function. The employee pulled him aside and said he thought he might have a solution. After asking the man to take a seat in his office, he went into a back room, took off his own tuxedo, put on his civilian clothes, rushed to the laundry to clean his tuxedo, and then called in the seamstress to fit the cleaned tux to the guest. What makes this story so rich is that it teaches the values management wants shared by all of Four Seasons's employees. It also shows clearly the connection between customer service and two important business outcomes. First, the guest turned out to be the chairman and CEO of a leading consulting organization, who after this experience directed all his company's business, worth millions in food and lodging, to Four Seasons. Second, the man took every opportunity to tell people in his speeches and conversations what Four Seasons did for him. These testimonials from a leading businessman proved to be priceless word-of-mouth advertising. Teaching the culture through stories can leave a lasting impression on employees as they come to see how the abstract idea of customer service translates into specific employee actions that lead to outcomes that benefit both their company and them.

of normatively appropriate conduct through personal actions and inter-personal relationships, and the pro-motion of such conduct to followers through two-way communication, rein-forcement, and decision-making."[48] In addition to conducting themselves in an ethical fashion, ethical lead-ers stay attuned to ethical issues in their organizations, motivate other organizational members to act ethically, and hold them accountable. Ethical leadership also involves designing an ethical organization.

Managers of Recreational Equipment, Inc. (REI) have exhibited ethical leadership.

Kevin Hagen was formerly the director of corporate social responsibility at outdoor gear and clothing company Recreational Equipment, Inc. (REI). Hagen established difficult goals for both environmental performance and financial perfor-mance and accepted no trade-offs between them. This led to "radical collaboration" throughout the company to develop innovative new approaches to doing business. Hagen's success in driving change at REI can be attributed not only to establishing tough goals but also to Hagen's personal salesmanship and the strong support he enjoyed from REI CEO Sally Jewell.[49]

Some of the behaviors associated with ethical leadership include the following:

- *Role modeling:* If a leader exhibits ethical behavior by being conscientious, caring, and honest, then employees are more likely to be as well. In contrast, unethical behaviors by leaders are likely to beget unethical behaviors by employees. Leaders can talk about integrity all they want; if they are known to blame subordinates for their mistakes and cheat on their expense reports, then employees will find their talk to be meaningless and hypocritical.

- *Exercising multiple types of power:* Managers enjoy many different types of power. These include formal authority (the power that comes with the job title, such as the ability to delegate tasks to employees); the control of rewards and punishments; referent power, which is the ability to influence people's behavior through personal characteristics such as charm; and the ability to influence behavior by demonstrating expertise.[50] Ethical leaders who rely on authority and coercion alone tend not to inspire ethical behavior among their subordinates; on the other hand, leaders who possess expertise and winning personalities are more likely to induce ethical behavior among their employees.

- *Matching leadership style to the employee and situation:* Contemporary leadership theory stresses that effective leaders match their leadership style to the individuals they lead. According to one of these theories, path–goal theory, leaders should match their leadership style, first, to the characteristics and needs of the employees they are managing—for example, whether they are highly competent and whether they are comfortable with certainty; and, second, to the characteristics of the task and environment—for example, whether the task is complex and whether the work environment is friendly and supportive.[51] Path–goal theory identifies four types of leadership styles: directive, supportive, participative, and achievement-oriented. Each is appropriate for leading a particular type of employee. Path–goal leadership is an ethical approach to leadership because it involves understanding employees' needs and guiding them, showing concern for them, and unlocking their potential as appropriate. Path–goal leadership expresses the ethic of care, respects the rights and dignity of employees, helps employees develop their virtues, and ultimately creates the most good for the most people because it helps organizations to effectively achieve their goals.

**Servant leadership**
The leadership philosophy that emphasizes putting others first and helping them develop and perform at their best

Numerous other contemporary leadership theories align with a concern about ethics because they emphasize understanding, building relationships with, and inspiring followers. One such theory is servant leadership, which posits that leaders help their organizations achieve their goals by serving the needs of others. Robert Greenleaf, the American executive who first developed servant leadership theory, wrote that its starting point is the desire first to serve before aiming to lead.[52] Servant leaders tend to

- be motivated by service;
- focus on followers rather than themselves;
- see themselves as "first among equals"—as having a leadership role, yet as no higher or lower in status than the rest of the team;
- empower others;
- be empathetic,
- hold themselves accountable;
- be authentic (understand and act on their personal convictions); and
- be humble.

Rather than demanding obedience and controlling employees' work, servant leaders emphasize setting a vision, listening and building trust with employees, and serving them in meeting their needs and goals in a way that serves the needs of the organization.

**Ethical climate**
The atmosphere of an organization regarding how to address ethical issues

### Ethical Climate

A final informal element of the organization that influences ethical behavior in organizations is ethical climate. Pioneering scholars Bart Victor and John Cullen define ethical climate as "the shared perception of what is correct behavior, and how ethical issues should be handled in an organization."[53] Climate has a strong immediate impact on behavior because it is essentially the atmosphere in which behavior takes place.

Ethical climate is a product of many of the other elements of the organization discussed in this chapter. The organization's structure, culture, socialization processes, and leadership and other factors combine to produce a shared understanding of how to address ethical dilemmas.[54] Thus, there is no easy way for a manager to create an ethical climate. Rather, she or he must build an ethical organization so that workers operate in ethical climates. Focusing on leadership, Grojean and colleagues argue that role modeling ethical behavior, recognizing and rewarding ethical behavior, and strong training and mentoring in ethics help produce a strong ethical climate.[55]

Victor and Cullen's research identified five types of ethical climates:

- In *instrumental* ethical climates, employees are encouraged to act out of narrow self-interest (i.e., not very ethically at all).

- *Caring* ethical climates compel employees to "look out for each other's good."[56]

- Companies with *rules-based* ethical climates are ones in which employees are expected to "go by the book,"—that is, strictly follow all of the company's policies and procedures.

- *Law and code* ethical climates also encourage strict adherence to rules, but they influence employees to follow external sets of rules like professional codes or state laws, rather than internal policies and procedures.

- *Independence* ethical climates encourage employees to follow their own beliefs and make their own decisions about how to handle ethical issues.

Research indicates that law and code climates and rules-based climates reduce unethical behavior and that professionals prefer to work in these climates; employee satisfaction is higher in independence ethical climates; employees feel a higher degree of organizational commitment in caring ethical climates; and unethical behavior is highest in instrumental ethical climates. Independence climates are likely to be supportive of employees facing complex ethical dilemmas, if the organization is guided by strong ethical values. In situations where rule-following is insufficient and frameworks such as the weight of reasons are needed, a climate of independence is the most suitable.

## Ethical Organizations: Bringing It All Together

Ethics programs are helpful for establishing and promoting ethical behavior, but they are not sufficient by themselves.[57] All aspects of the organization—structure, culture, leadership, incentives, and others—influence how organizational members act and whether they live up to shared ethical values. The components of an organization must align with and reinforce one another so that an ethical climate exists. The signals that members receive about how to behave must be consistent. If these signals are inconsistent, then members of organizations will experience confusion and cognitive dissonance and probably take actions that are inconsistent with shared ethical values. The implication, a main point of Chapter 4, is that behavior is as much a function of context as of internal desire.

Imagine, for example, an organizational member that values (or purports to value) integrity and "organizational citizenship behavior" (doing tasks that help the organization but are not part of her or his job description). Now imagine that the leaders of the organizations are known to be deceptive and dishonest, that employees can earn pay raises and promotions by lying about their performance, that there are no awards or other incentives for teamwork, and that training sessions barely mention ethics. In such an organization, one would not be surprised if most of the members failed to live up to espoused values. Even if these employees felt a desire to do so, many of them probably would not. The organization has been designed to suppress this desire and to act contrary to it.

While all the elements of the organization can be important influences on behavior, informal elements such as leadership, culture, and hence climate tend to have the most impact. People's behaviors are more affected by what they see and feel actually happening around them than by rules and policies. They tend to live according to an organization's shared ethical values and will apply the weight-of-reasons framework only when they see that others consider it normal and appropriate. As the leader of an organization, an important part of your job is to build an organization that values ethics.

Many scholars have presented models of ethical organizations. Lynn Paine was one of the first to do so. According to her integrity-based approach to management, ethics becomes the organization's driving force.[58] Core ethical values shape how managers design the organization, make decisions, and motivate their workers, and they empower these workers to use their own discretion and judgment in addressing ethical dilemmas. Paine concludes that integrity strategies can not only prevent unethical behavior but also "tap into powerful human impulses for moral thought and action."[59]

# ENRON: THE ACCOUNTANTS—DAVID DUNCAN AND ARTHUR ANDERSEN[60]

As noted in the case at the end of Chapter 5, the accounting firm Arthur Andersen went out of business due to its role in the Enron scandal. David Duncan was Andersen's partner in charge of the Enron account. He was considered a typical Andersen employee; his values were in sync with where Andersen wanted to go. All accounting firms want to keep their clients happy to maintain their business and earn higher fees. Duncan came to Andersen in 1981 from Texas A&M University, a

school whose graduates had the reputation for loyalty and an unparalleled work ethic. Duncan was an ambitious, courteous, and respectful person who blended in and wanted to be liked, played by the rules, and did not question the firm.

At Andersen, Duncan became a partner (the highest level one can reach). His work there was highly acclaimed, and after 20 years at the firm, he was earning more than $1 million a year. He had worked on the Enron account for more than 10 years and had been the lead partner on it for five. His ties with Enron were close. He had an office in Enron's building, often had lunch with its accountants, and regularly attended major golfing tournaments accompanied by Enron accountants and other top ranking officials at Enron. Many of them, like Duncan, had gone to Texas A&M. His loyalty to his Enron friends was intense and led him to dismiss warnings he heard from Andersen accounting-standards specialists that Enron's approaches to its off-book partnerships were problematic.

Andrew Fastow, Enron's CFO (chief financial officer), first approached Duncan about setting up these partnerships. Fastow called them "special-purpose entities" (or "special-purpose vehicles"). The first one, LJM1, was a partnership giving Fastow millions of dollars in compensation and allowed Enron to keep millions of dollars of debt off of its balance sheet. LJM1 was followed by LJM2 and other partnerships of this nature. To approve the partnerships, Duncan had to consult with Andersen's Professional Standards Group. When Duncan first asked for advice from this group, one of the members raised a number of objections, stating that Enron should not record gains from the sale of its assets to LJM and that the venture should not be managed by Fastow because of conflicts of interest. Duncan replied that though he was not completely comfortable with the arrangements, there was little he could do. He did ask Fastow to obtain permission for the partnerships from Enron's CEO and its board. Fastow got permission, the matter seemed settled, and Andersen's Enron-related fees increased by nearly 20%. Carl Bass, a member of Andersen's Professional Standards Group, objected, and Duncan removed him from the account. Bass went to a senior partner at Andersen, complaining the removal was unfair. Duncan responded that Bass had been removed because Enron had given him a negative review.

Members of Andersen's Professional Standards Group remained unconvinced of the partnerships' legality. They wanted to know if the partnerships met a "nonconsolidation" test. What would happen if Enron had to merge the partnerships' results with its own? The partnerships were running huge losses and so could significantly harm Enron's financial statements. Duncan maintained that the special-purpose vehicles would not have to be amalgamated into Enron's financial statements so long as they had independent external ownership of at least 3% and that the Enron's partnerships met this test. However, a member of Duncan's team, Debra Cash, told the standards group that she did not agree and that Enron would not be able to hide its losses in the special-purpose entities. Enron and the standards group were "miles apart." Duncan stood up for Enron because of concern that Andersen could lose the account.

The Enron scandal proved to be Duncan's—and Arthur Andersen's—downfall. After Enron received a request from the SEC for information, Duncan led an effort to do away with as many sensitive Enron documents as possible. In 2002, he was fired for shredding Enron-related documents and pleaded guilty to obstruction of justice. He admitted that he had destroyed critical audit documents that might have incriminated his client, Enron.

At "Andersen U.," the campus where Arthur Andersen trained new employees, the firm had an exhibit dedicated to its history of ethical behavior. In 1914, months after Arthur Andersen founded the company, a client demanded that he approve a transaction that would lower expenses and boost earnings, but Andersen said there was "not enough money in the city of Chicago" to make him do it. The client promptly fired the company. Leonard Spacek, head of Andersen from 1947 to 1963, led a campaign to clean up the accounting industry, with the main focus being to eliminate conflicts of interest. Despite this history, Andersen was involved in many scandals in the 1990s other than Enron, from Sunbeam Corp. to Waste Management Inc. It faced obstruction-of-justice charges in the Enron case and was failing as a company, a sad ending for a firm that had been one of the world's most successful accounting firms. Its 85,000 employees, who had generated $9.3 billion in revenue in 2002, were the ones who had to deal with the consequences.

What went wrong for David Duncan and Arthur Andersen in the Enron scandal? What cognitive biases and social influences led to poor decision-making? How could Arthur Andersen have used the lessons from this chapter to create a more ethical decision-making environment?

## SUMMARY AND CONCLUSION

This chapter argues that to fortify the use of the weight-of-reasons approach in organizations, there is a need for a supportive context that motivates, supports, and promotes ethical decision-making. The chapter describes the typical ethics programs found in many organizations that are composed of codes of conduct, workshops, whistle-blowing mechanisms, and other elements. Two types of ethics program have been identified: compliance-based and values-based. Compliance-based programs focus on obeying laws and policies, and preventing, detecting, and punishing unethical behavior. In contrast, values-based ethics programs emphasize acting in accordance with shared ethical ideals. This chapter has argued that, all else being equal, values-based programs are likely to lead to more ethical behavior than ones based solely on compliance.

Next, the chapter unpacked the full range of elements that make up ethical organizations. These are formal elements such as structure, hiring practices, and performance measurement systems and informal elements such as culture and leadership. In ethical organizations, individuals are more likely to apply frameworks such as the weight-of-reasons approach and rely on double- and triple-loop learning, systems thinking, moral imagination, team inquiry and advocacy, and incremental learning and spiral learning because every aspect of the organization supports and promotes their doing so.

## KEY TERMS AND CONCEPTS

Bribery  166

Chief ethics officer  169

Code of conduct  167

Compliance-based ethics
    program  173

Discrimination  178

Diversity  178

Embezzlement  173

Ethical climate  190

Ethical leadership  188

Ethical organization  181

Ethical values  174

Ethics assist line
    (or ethics hotline)  170

Ethics program  166

Federal Sentencing Guidelines
    for Organizations (FSGO)  167

Foreign Corrupt Practices
    Act (FCPA)  166

Fraud  173

Mechanistic organizations  183

Mission  174

Money laundering  173

Ombudsperson  170

Organic organizations  183

Organizational culture  187

Organizational structure  182

Servant leadership  190

Tax evasion  173

Values  174

Values statement  174

Values-based ethics program  174

Vision  174

## CASES RELATED TO THE READING

Consider reading the following cases found in Chapter 10 that apply to the concepts presented in this chapter:

- BP: The Big Oil Spill: What Went Wrong?

- Dow–DuPont: The Bhopal Disaster

- Ford: Safety Recalls
- Google: Doing No Harm
- Merck and J&J: Problems With Consumer Safety

- Microsoft: Addressing Bribery
- VW: Dieselgate
- Walmart: Sustainability
- Wells Fargo: Can It Come Back?

# CASE APPLICATIONS

Apply the weight-of-reasons framework to address the following cases. In making your decisions, consider how you can use tools described in this chapter as well as concepts from the last chapter, including systems thinking, both/and thinking, moral imagination, inquiry and advocacy, and incremental decision-making.

## Case 6.1: Stealing at Hawthorne Manufacturing

Mayo Elton is the chief ethics officer at Hawthorne Manufacturing. He has established a code of conduct that prohibits stealing supplies and equipment from the factory floor and also imposes strict punishments up to, and including, being fired and prosecuted. Elton ensures that these policies and procedures are communicated to all new hires at an annual ethics training. Despite this, theft is persistently high at the plant, so much so that it is making a noticeable dent in profits. Elton is very disappointed by this, especially because he constantly refers to and tries to live up to Hawthorne's core values, which include integrity.

Elton offers to hire you for a handsome sum to resolve the theft problem at his plant. After accepting Elton's offer, you get to work gathering data to try to understand the underlying reasons the code of conduct on stealing is not working at Hawthorne (step 2 of the weight-of-reasons framework.) Based on the lessons of this chapter, identify three plausible reasons that theft is taking place. Use the weight-of-reasons framework to recommend solutions to the problem.

## Case 6.2: Chief Ethics Officer's Job

Arete Corporation manufactures and sells industrial cleaning products. It has factories, warehouses, and sales teams spread throughout the United States. Arete once had a sterling reputation for integrity, so much so that its chief strength relative to its competitors was that it was known for its reliably high-quality products and for dealing honestly and fairly with its customers and suppliers. Over time, though, cutting corners has become commonplace. In fact, unsafe products, questionable sales practices, and rude customer service have become the norm.

Realizing that the company's future is in doubt because of its ethics problems, Arete's president Dewit Wright has decided to create the job of Chief Ethics Officer. He has offered you the position. You are interested in taking it but will do so only if you have a reasonable chance of succeeding. What conditions should you put on Wright's offer? If you were to accept the job and then come in and establish an ethics program, what organizational elements would need to be in place for the program to successfully develop long-term solutions to the company's ethics problems?

## Case 6.3: Diversity Debate

Pithos Internet Company is known for its innovative software products. The secret to Pithos's success is in large part its ability to create a climate in which its smart and ambitious employees are motivated to work together to develop new ideas, products, and services.

One consequence of the emphasis on freedom of expression at Pithos is a very open conversation among employees about the company's diversity and inclusion programs. Some employees are very supportive of the programs, others think the programs should be more aggressive in trying to make the Pithos workforce more diverse, and yet others do not support the programs at all. Employees in this last group think the reason that nearly three fourths of the company's employees are white and Asian men is that workers in these categories are simply more deserving of and better at their jobs. The diversity debate at Pithos is not mere water cooler talk. Much like the broader national debate in which it is taking place, it has become very hostile.

Assume you are a senior human resources manager at Pithos. You embrace the company's core values of collaboration, sharing of ideas, and freedom of expression, but you also wonder whether the diversity debate needs to be managed. Employing the lessons of this chapter, use the weight-of-reasons framework to identify steps you could take to ensure that the diversity debate at Pithos is healthy and productive.

# NOTES

1. U.S. Sentencing Commission. (n.d.). *Organizational guidelines*. Retrieved from https://www.ussc.gov/guidelines/organizational-guidelines

2. U.S. Sentencing Commission.(2018). *2018 Federal sentencing guidelines (FSG). Guidelines manual* (Chapter 8: Sentencing of Organizations). Retrieved from https://www.ussc.gov/guidelines/2016-guidelines-manual/2016-chapter-8

3. Weaver, G. R., Treviño, L. K., & Cochran, P. L. (1999a). Corporate ethics practices in the mid-1990s: An empirical study of the Fortune 1000. *Journal of Business Ethics, 18*, 283–294.

4. Living our values. (n.d.). *Starbucks Standards of Business Conduct*. Retrieved from https://livingourvalues.starbucks.com/

5. See p. 63, in Collins, D. (2019). *Business ethics: Best practices for designing and managing ethical organizations* (2nd ed.). Thousand Oaks, CA: SAGE.

6. Message from Howard. (n.d.). *Starbucks Standards of Business Conduct*. Retrieved from https://livingourvalues.starbucks.com/letter-from-howard

7. Weiss, D. C. (2018). *Judge tosses wrongful termination claim by woman forced to resign after flipping off Trump motorcade*. Retrieved from http://www.abajournal.com/news/article/wrongful_termination_claim_trump_motorcade

8. Pryme Group. (2018, January 25). *7 Ways employee privacy laws impact social media in the workplace*. Retrieved from https://allpryme.com/employee-privacy-laws/employee-privacy-laws/; Social Networking & Computer Privacy. (n.d.). *Workplace fairness*. Retrieved from https://www.workplacefairness.org/social-network-computer-privacy-workplace#11

9. U.S. Sentencing Commission. (2009). *Federal sentencing guidelines* (Section 8B2.1(b)(5)(c). Retrieved from https://guidelines.ussc.gov/gl/%C2%A78B2.1

10. Dworkin, T. M., & Baucus, M. S. (1998). Internal vs. external whistleblowers: A comparison of whistle blowing processes. *Journal of Business Ethics, 17*, 281–298.

11. Divito, N. (2013, September 6). SEC attorney lowers the boom on the agency. *Courthouse News Service*. Retrieved from https://www.courthousenews.com/sec-attorney-lowers-the-boom-on-the-agency/; Cohan, W. D. (2013a, May 15). How bad can it be for SEC whistle-blowers? *Bloomberg*. Retrieved from https://www.bloomberg.com/opinion/articles/2013-05-15/the-saga-of-one-sec-whistle-blower-william-d-cohan-correct-; Taibbi, M. (2013, May 31). Why didn't the SEC catch madoff? It might have been policy not to. *Rolling Stone*. Retrieved from https://www.rollingstone.com/politics/politics-news/why-didnt-the-sec-catch-madoff-it-might-have-been-policy-not-to-86356/; Furey against the SEC. (2013, May 29). *Corporate Crime Reporter*. Retrieved from https://www.corporatecrimereporter.com/news/200/fureyagainstthesec0529201/. (For legal documents related to the case, go to www.pacermonitor.com and then search for case 6081748.); Cohan, W. D. (2013b, May 15). SEC whistle-blower says she was frozen out by new enforcement chief. *Investment News*. Retrieved from https://www.investmentnews.com/article/20130515/FREE/130519955/sec-whistle-blower-says-she-was-frozen-out-by-new-enforcement-chief

12. See p. 245, in Stansbury, J., & Barry, B. (2007). Ethics programs and the paradox of control. *Business Ethics Quarterly, 17,* 239–261. See also Weaver, G. R., & Treviño, L. K. (1999). Compliance and values oriented ethics programs: Influences on employees' attitudes and behavior. *Business Ethics Quarterly, 9,* 315–335; Weaver, G. R., Treviño, L. K., & Cochran, P. L. (1999b). Corporate ethics programs as control systems: Influences of executive commitment and environmental factors. *Academy of Management Journal, 42,* 41–57.

13. Stansbury and Barry (2007); Weaver and Treviño (1999).

14. Paine, L. S. (1994). Managing for organizational integrity. *Harvard Business Review, 72*(2), 106–119.

15. Stansbury and Barry (2007); Weaver et al. (1999b); Weaver and Treviño (1999).

16. About Gravity payments: Leveling the playing field for community businesses of all sizes. (n.d.). *Gravity Payments.* Retrieved from https://gravitypayments.com/about/

17. See p. 758, in De Colle, S., & Werhane, P. (2008). Moral motivation across ethical theories: What can we learn for designing corporate ethics programs? *Journal of Business Ethics, 81,* 751–764.

18. See p. 246, in Stansbury and Barry (2007), citing Weaver and Treviño (1999).

19. See p. 131–132, in Treviño, L. K., Weaver, G. R., Gibson, D. G., & Toffler, B. L. (1999). Managing ethics and legal compliance: What works and what hurts. *California Management Review, 4*(2), 131–151.

20. See p. 206, in Verhezen, P. (2010). Giving voice in a culture of silence. From a culture of compliance to a culture of integrity. *Journal of Business Ethics, 96,* 187–206.

21. U.S. Department of Justice, Office of Public Affairs. (2016, June 28). *Volkswagen to spend up to $14.7 billion to settle allegations of cheating emissions tests and deceiving customers on 2.0 liter diesel vehicles.* Retrieved from https://www.justice.gov/opa/pr/volkswagen-spend-147-billion-settle-allegations-cheating-emissions-tests-and-deceiving

22. Audi Chief Rupert Stadler arrested in diesel emissions probe. (2018, June 18). *BBC News.* Retrieved from https://www.bbc.com/news/business-44517753

23. Smith, G., & Parloff, R. (2016, March 7). Hoaxwagen: How the massive diesel fraud incinerated VW's reputation—and will hobble the company for years to come. *Fortune.* Retrieved from http://fortune.com/inside-volkswagen-emissions-scandal/

24. McGee, P. (2018, January 18). What went so right with Volkswagen's restructuring? *Financial Times.* Retrieved from https://www.ft.com/content/a12ec7e2-fa01-11e7-9b32-d7d59aace167; MacDuffie, J. P., & Zaring, D. (2019, March 21). Exhausted by scandal: "Dieselgate" continues to haunt Volkswagen. *Knowledge@Wharton.* Retrieved from https://knowledge.wharton.upenn.edu/article/volkswagen-diesel-scandal/

25. Volkswagen. (2019). *Volkswagen sets the pace for cultural change.* Retrieved from http://inside.volkswagen.com/New-Cultural-Change-Program.html

26. Amelang, S., & Wehrmann, B. (2019, July 2). "Dieselgate": A timeline of Germany's car emissions fraud scandal. *Clean Energy Wire.* Retrieved from https://www.cleanenergywire.org/factsheets/dieselgate-timeline-germanys-car-emissions-fraud-scandal

27. European Commission. (2019, April 5). *Antitrust: Commission sends Statement of Objections to BMW, Daimler and VW for restricting competition on emission cleaning technology.* Retrieved from http://europa.eu/rapid/press-release_IP-19-2008_en.htm; Kerler, W. (2018, September 18). You thought Dieselgate was over? It's not. *The Verge.* Retrieved from https://www.theverge.com/2018/9/18/17876012/dieselgate-volkswagen-vw-diesel-emissions-test-epa-german-auto-industry-mercedes-benz-bmw; Amelang and Wehrmann (2019); MacDuffie and Zaring (2019).

28. Halfond, J. (2016, July 11). Speaking ethics to power: Lessons from Dieselgate. *Huffington Post.* Retrieved from https://www.huffpost.com/entry/speaking-ethics-to-power_b_10880852

29. Project Implicit. (2011). *Education.* Retrieved from https://implicit.harvard.edu/implicit/education.html; Goldhill, O. (2017, December 3). *The world is relying on a flawed psychological test to fight racism.* Retrieved from https://qz.com/1144504/the-world-is-relying-on-a-flawed-psychological-test-to-fight-racism/

30. Ball Corporation. (n.d.-a). *Creating diverse and inclusive environment.* Retrieved from https://www.ball.com/na/about-ball/careers/diversity-inclusion/business-resource-groups; Ball Corporation. (n.d.-b). *Our passion and purpose!* Retrieved from https://www.ball.com/na; Valet, V. (2019, January 15). America's best employers for diversity, 2019. *Forbes.* https://www.forbes.com/sites/vickyvalet/2019/01/15/americas-best-employers-for-diversity-2019/#4176334a2bda

31. See Chapter 3, in Daft, R. (2016). *Organizational theory and design* (12th ed.). Boston, MA: Cengage Learning; Tushman, M. L., & O'Reilly, C. A., III (1997). *Winning through innovation: A practical*

*guide to leading organizational change and renewal.* Boston, MA: Harvard Business Review Press.

32. Baucus, M. S., & Beck-Dudley, C. L. (2005). Designing ethical organizations: Avoiding the long-term negative effects of rewards and punishments. *Journal of Business Ethics, 56,* 355–370.

33. Daft (2016).

34. Ibid.

35. Ibid.

36. Burns, T., & Stalker, G. M. (1961). *Management of innovation.* London, UK: Tavistock; Lawrence, P. R., & Lorsch, J. W. (1967). Differentiation and integration in complex organizations. *Administrative Science Quarterly, 12,* 1–47.

37. See p. 50, in Stansbury, J. (2009). Reasoned moral agreement: Applying discourse ethics within organizations. *Business Ethics Quarterly, 19,* 33–56.

38. See Chapter 3, in Collins (2019).

39. Sidanius, J., & Pratto, F. (1999). *Social dominance: An intergroup theory of social hierarchy and oppression.* Cambridge, UK: Cambridge University Press.

40. U.S. Department of Labor, Wage and Hour Division. (n.d.). Employee Polygraph Protection Act (EPPA). Retrieved from https://www.dol.gov/whd/polygraph/

41. Harris, J., & Bromiley, P. (2007). Incentives to cheat: The influence of executive compensation and firm performance on financial misrepresentation. *Organization Science, 18,* 350–367.

42. Schein, E. H. (2004). *Organizational culture and leadership* (4th ed.). San Francisco, CA: Jossey-Bass.

43. Schein (2004); James, H. S., Jr. (2000). Reinforcing ethical decisionmaking through organizational structure. *Journal of Business Ethics, 28,* 43–58.

44. Note, though, that there is an enduring debate about the extent to which organizational members buy into organizational culture in an unthinking, taken-for-granted way, as opposed to exercising agency as they enact culture. Following Chapter 4, we take the view that there is no single answer to this question; rather, the extent to which actors enact culture consciously or unconsciously depends upon the person and the situation.

45. Treviño et al. (1999).

46. See p. 274, in Johnson, C. E. (2018). *Organizational ethics: A practical approach* (4th ed.). Thousand Oaks, CA: SAGE.

47. Ford, R. C., & Struman, M. C. (2020). *Managing hospitality organizations* (2nd ed.). Thousand Oaks, CA: SAGE.

48. See p. 120, in Brown, M. E., Treviño, L., & Harrison, D. A. (2005). Ethical leadership: A social learning theory perspective for construct development. *Organizational Behavior and Human Decision Processes, 97,* 117–134.

49. Sustainability at REI. (2012). Stanford Graduate School of Business case SM-196.

50. French, J. R. P., & Raven, B. (1959). The bases of social power. In D. Cartwright & A. Zander (Eds.), *Studies in social power* (pp. 15–167). Ann Arbor: University of Michigan Institute of Social Research.

51. House, R. J., & Mitchell, T. R. (1974). Path–goal theory of leadership. *Journal of Contemporary Business, 3,* 81–97; House, R. J. (1996). Path–goal theory of leadership: Lessons, legacy, and a reformulated theory. *Leadership Quarterly, 7*(3), 323–352.

52. Greenleaf, R. K. (1970). *The servant as leader.* South Orange, NJ: Greenleaf Center for Servant Leadership.

53. See p. 51, Victor, B., & Cullen, J. B. (1987). A theory and measure of ethical climate in organizations. *Research in Corporate Social Performance and Policy, 9,* 51–71.

54. Victor, B., & Cullen, J. B. (1988). The organizational basis of ethical work climates. *Administrative Science Quarterly, 33,* 101–125; Grojean, M. W., Resick, C. J., Dickson, M. W., & Smith, D. B. (2004). Leaders, values and organizational climate: Examining leadership strategies for establishing an organizational climate regarding ethic. *Journal of Business Ethics, 55,* 223–241.

55. Grojean et al. (2004).

56. See p. 111, in Victor and Cullen (1988).

57. Stansbury and Barry (2007); James (2000).

58. Paine (1994).

59. See p. 67, in Paine (1994).

60. Adapted from Marcus, A. A., & Kaiser, S. (2006). *Managing beyond compliance: The ethical and legal dimensions of corporate responsibility.* Northbrook, IL: Northcoast. See also McLean, B., & Elkin, P. (2004). *The smartest guys in the room: The amazing rise and scandalous fall of Enron.* New York, NY: Penguin Books; Raghavan, A. (2002, May 15). How a bright star at Andersen fell along with Enron. *The Wall Street Journal.* Retrieved from https://www.wsj.com/articles/SB1021425497254672480

# The Societal Context for Ethical Decision-Making

PART

III

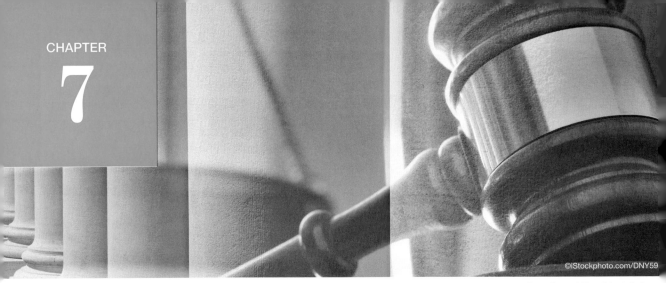

Laws impact the ethical choices that managers face and how they make these choices.

# Legal Compliance and Beyond

## Learning Objectives

On completion of this chapter, the reader should be able to do the following:

LO 7.1: Incorporate legal considerations and an appreciation of the interests of stakeholders into the weight-of-reasons ethical decision-making framework.

LO 7.2: State the major U.S. laws that exist to protect the rights and interests of stakeholder groups.

LO 7.3: Explain the relationship of ethics to the law, that is, that ethics requires us to go "beyond compliance."

LO 7.4: Describe various approaches to "going beyond the law," including moral minimums, corporate social responsibility, corporate citizenship, and sustainability.

> " *One has not only a legal, but a moral responsibility to obey just laws. Conversely, one has a moral responsibility to disobey unjust laws.* "
>
> —Dr. Martin Luther King Jr.,
> *Letter from the Birmingham Jail*

# Introduction

This chapter discusses the relationship between ethical decision-making and the legal environment. The focus is on the laws of the United States. Laws capture many of the ethical values and aspirations of a society. As such, they protect the rights and interests of stakeholders and require companies to meet their ethical obligations to these stakeholders. For example, laws prevent firms from providing dangerous working conditions for their employees, selling unsafe products to their customers, providing inaccurate financial information to their lenders and investors, and releasing toxic emissions into the air and water.

In the next section of this chapter, we discuss companies' legal obligations to their stakeholders. Stakeholders are the individuals and organizations that influence or are influenced by the company. We detail the major U.S. laws that exist to protect the rights and interests of shareholders, employees, customers, suppliers, communities, and the natural environment.

While firms must follow the law, mere legal compliance often is not sufficient from an ethical standpoint. There are many reasons why the law and ethics may diverge, including the time it takes to pass legislation, imperfections in the political process that prevent the enactment of laws to codify understandings of what is ethical, and that laws tend to specify what persons (including companies) are not allowed to do, rather than the positive actions they could undertake. The law does not require virtuous behavior or caring for loved ones; rather, it specifies the minimum requirements for behavior. To act ethically, one, therefore, must often go "beyond compliance" with the law.

This chapter then enumerates approaches that companies can take to going beyond compliance. One of these is *corporate social responsibility* (CSR), which is a mode of business in which companies seek to earn profits and, in addition, have a positive impact on some of their other stakeholders. Another is *corporate citizenship*, which is a special case of CSR in which companies not only exceed the law in treating stakeholders ethically but also take the lead in addressing pressing social and environmental issues. A final approach to going beyond the law's limits is *sustainability*, in which businesses seek to achieve excellent performance on economic, social, and environmental criteria as well as financial criteria.

# Legal Considerations and the Interests of Stakeholders

LO 7.1: Incorporate legal considerations and an appreciation of the interests of stakeholders into the weight-of-reasons ethical decision-making framework.

Stakeholders are individuals and organizations that influence and are influenced by the organization. Companies have many different types of stakeholders. These include the primary stakeholders with which the company has regular commercial interactions, such as customers, employees, suppliers, and capital providers (e.g., banks, shareholders). A company would be powerless without the contributions of

**Stakeholder**
An individual or organization that influences and is influenced by the company

**Primary stakeholders**
Stakeholders with which the company has regular commercial interactions

these stakeholders; it would cease to exist if it had no employees, customers, or investment capital. In addition, companies have **secondary stakeholders**. These are the stakeholders with which the company has less frequent interactions and ones that often are not commercial. They include governments, community representatives, social and environmental activist organizations, the media, and even future generations.[1] Although primary stakeholders tend to receive more attention from management, both types of stakeholders are important from an ethical and legal perspective. These stakeholders and the company can have big impacts on one another.

Specific laws govern the relationships between companies and their stakeholders. In estimating the consequences of options and deciding on a course of action (Steps 4, 6, and 7 of the weight-of-reasons framework), organizations must take account of these legal requirements. In the United States, well-developed laws, regulations, and a long history of court cases govern the ties companies have with their stakeholders, often in quite explicit ways. Organizations that violate these laws may be subject to fines, penalties, and punishments. They may also suffer public disgrace and lose the trust of stakeholders on which they rely. This book provides many examples of such companies, including Johnson & Johnson, Merck, Volkswagen, and Wells Fargo (see Chapter 10).

It is true that U.S. laws sometimes are selectively enforced; that is, companies are not always punished for breaking the law. Furthermore, it is also the case that the laws of other countries are often not as stringent as those in the United States and that managers legally can engage in practices that would be illegal in the United States. Indeed, the laws of other countries are sometimes more stringent than those of the United States, as in the case of European antitrust laws. While we do not wish to make light of the social costs and implications of selective enforcement or the difficulties that managers face in navigating cross-national legal and cultural differences, we see these issues as ultimately not as significant with respect to ethical decision-making. Indeed, one of the main points of this chapter, which we develop further below, is that managers should try to make ethical decisions regardless of what the law requires in the U.S. and elsewhere, and *what they can get away with*.

It also should be kept in mind that companies can suffer commercial harm for engaging in activities that are legal but widely seen as unethical. For example, Apple has come under great scrutiny for contracting with the Taiwanese company Foxconn (formally, Hon Hai Precision Industry Co.) to assemble its iPhones. Critics charge that poor wages and working conditions are responsible for a spate of suicides among workers at Foxconn's Shenzen, China plant. The fact that Foxconn's wages and conditions comply with Chinese law is beside the point since Apple's reputation has been harmed.[2] Society may hold you and your company accountable even when the law does not.

## Existing Laws That Protect the Rights and Interests of Stakeholders

**LO 7.2:** State the major U.S. laws that exist to protect the rights and interests of stakeholder groups.

We now discuss the laws that address firms' ethical responsibilities to their various stakeholder groups. The stakeholder groups we consider are shareholders, employees, customers, suppliers, communities, and the natural environment. Our purpose is not to provide a comprehensive guide of all the laws to which companies are subject but rather to provide a broad overview of some of the most important laws. In Chapter 8, we further discuss companies' relationships with their stakeholders, how stakeholders fit into ethical decision-making, and how companies can work with stakeholders in making ethical decisions.

## Shareholders

A company's owners or shareholders are one of its most influential stakeholder groups. For businesses that are publicly traded and have issued common stock, they are particularly influential. Typically, they provide investment capital and assume the company's financial risk; if the company goes bankrupt and is liquidated, shareholders can lose their entire investment. They are owners and the residual claimants—that is, the last to be paid back in the case of bankruptcy— and therefore have a position of primacy among stakeholders. (We discuss this topic of stakeholder primacy at length in Chapter 8.) In return for the high level of risk shareholders take, they receive some portion of the company's profits in the form of dividends, and they can also benefit from increases in the company's stock price.

Shareholders of public companies typically do not participate in the everyday management of the business. Instead, they elect a board of directors to oversee the company. The directors who serve on the board then appoint senior managers including the CEO (chief executive officer) to carry out the day-to-day management and operations of the company. Senior managers then delegate authority and responsibility to their subordinates and so on. This system of hierarchical control of the firm is the essence of a corporate governance system. Although shareholders have delegated day-to-day management of the company to the board of directors, they retain, in theory at least, the ultimate right to control the company's direction and decisions. In addition to the right to receive dividends and elect the board of directors, they also enjoy the right to vote on major decisions as well as the right to sue when they believe that the company and its officers are not carrying out their obligations to shareholders.

### *Fiduciary Duty to Shareholders*

In law, company directors and managers have a fiduciary duty to use all available means to make informed and prudent decisions that are intended to benefit shareholders. Fiduciary duty simply means a duty of trust. While company leaders have been entrusted to act in the best interests of the shareholders, there is no guarantee that their decisions will in fact work out in favor of the shareholders. The fiduciary duty of company decision-makers to shareholders is referred to as a principal–agent relationship. Shareholders are the "principals" (people of importance), and the directors and managers are their "agents" (people who have a duty to work on behalf of the principals). Chapter 4 discussed the principal–agent relationship between employees and owners.

Since the *Dodge v. Ford Motor Co.* case of 1919, the managers of publicly traded companies in most U.S. states—including Delaware, where the majority of U.S. firms are incorporated—have a legal duty to put the interests of shareholders ahead

**Shareholder**
A person who owns shares in a company. Typically has the right to elect the board of directors, receive dividends, participate in major decisions, and sue the company and its officers

**Residual claimant**
The person who has the last claim on a company's net cash flow after the deduction of all other persons' claims

**Corporate governance**
The structures and processes used to direct and control a corporation

**Fiduciary duty**
A duty of trust

**Principal–agent relationship**
The fiduciary relationship between the board of directors and managers that oversee the company to act as agents of shareholders (principals)

of that of other stakeholders.[3] It should be noted, though, that according to the "business judgment rule," managers are presumed to have acted in the best interests of the corporation unless it can be shown otherwise (e.g., that they have embezzled money or committed fraud).[4] The business judgment rule is important from an ethical perspective because it means that managers are not legally vulnerable to the charge that they have violated their fiduciary duty to shareholders when they spend money to benefit other stakeholders (e.g., by donating corporate money to charity or paying above-market wages), as long as they can make the case that these expenditures are in the shareholder's long-term interest.

# DODGE v. FORD MOTOR CO.

In this case, two shareholders of the Ford Motor Company, John F. and Horace E. Dodge, brought a lawsuit against the company. They objected to Henry Ford's plan to pay smaller dividends to shareholders and instead invest more in auto production and pay workers higher wages. In 1919, the Michigan Supreme Court decided in favor of the Dodge brothers, stating that shareholder profit should be the primary concern of Henry Ford and other company directors. The effects of the *Dodge v. Ford Motor Co.* ruling, however, have been ameliorated by the business judgment rule, which gives corporate managers broad discretion in deciding what is best for the corporation.

**Principal–agent problem**

The problem that a director or a manager of a corporation does not fulfill his or her fiduciary duty to work on behalf of the shareholders

**Managerial capitalism**

A form of capitalism in which directors and managers, rather than shareholders, control the company's decisions and direction

In practice, managers sometimes do not faithfully represent the interests of owners. The principal–agent problem, also known as the agency problem, develops when directors and managers work on their own behalf rather than in the interests of shareholders. This problem arises because of the separation of company ownership from its control; those who own the company don't make day-to-day decisions for it. The control of the company by managers rather than shareholders is also referred to as managerial capitalism.

Managerial capitalism was long the norm. As far back as 1932, Berle and Means noticed the principal–agent problem and observed that it occurs because managers take an active interest in and have great knowledge of the company, while most shareholders are only passively involved in the company's affairs.[5] This problem is compounded by the fact that boards of directors also are not involved in the company's daily affairs. In part because they feel that the managers understand the company and its business better than they do, they tend to be sympathetic to managers' perspectives and "rubber-stamp" their plans and decisions, rather than providing effective oversight and protecting shareholders' interests. Also, because board members are often recommended for their seats by management, they feel indebted to management for the benefits that come from being on the board. Thus, they are reluctant to challenge the decisions of management.

Recognizing that companies sometimes were not being run in their best interests, shareholders started to exert more control over the companies they owned in the 1980s. Shareholders who seek to influence managers and directors are known as "activist shareholders." Activist shareholders often seek election to the board of directors so they can participate directly in major decisions, challenge the nominations of directors who they think will not represent them well, seek to purchase a majority of the company's stock so they can elect a majority of the board's directors, and use other means to influence company management. The period from the 1980s to the present therefore is often referred to as the era of shareholder capitalism, in contrast to the period of managerial capitalism that preceded it.[6]

Critics now argue that shareholders have too much power over corporate decision-making and that shareholders are exercising their power to the detriment of other stakeholders.[7]

*Shareholder capitalism* A form of capitalism in which shareholders, rather than directors and managers, control the company's decisions and direction

### *Securities Laws and Insider Trading*

Numerous U.S. laws have been passed to ensure that directors and managers work on behalf of shareholders rather than themselves. Securities laws, for instance, require companies to provide full and accurate information about their financial position on an annual basis and when they offer stock to the public. The main securities laws in the United States were enacted in response to the stock market crash of 1929 and the ensuing Depression. When an individual purchases shares in a company, nearly the only guarantee that she receives about the company's current and projected future performance is what she can find in the quarterly and annual publicly audited financial statements and reports. For a company to lie or mislead the investing public in these reports is a serious crime that can come with severe penalties.

In response to a wave of financial scandals, Congress passed the Sarbanes–Oxley Corporate Fraud Accountability Act of 2002 (sometimes referred to simply as "Sarbanes–Oxley," "Sarbox," or just "SOX"). Prior chapters and cases briefly introduced this act and pointed out its importance. Sarbanes–Oxley was designed "to protect investors by improving the accuracy and reliability of corporate disclosures made pursuant to the securities laws." Among other things, it requires the board of directors to provide thorough oversight of firms' financial reports and the company's CEO and CFO (chief financial officer) to certify the accuracy of the company's financial statements and other financial filings.[8]

U.S. laws also aim to prevent managers and board members from engaging in "insider trading"—that is, profiting from their knowledge of significant nonpublic information about the company by buying or selling company stock. Laws against insider trading derive directly from the fiduciary duty of managers and the board to shareholders. They are not allowed to use their "insider information" for their own benefit and to the detriment of shareholders. For instance, it is illegal for them to sell their stock if they are aware of looming financial difficulties that are unknown to the general investing public. While insider trading may seem like a victimless crime, it is not; the victim is the person with whom the insider is trading—either a current or soon-to-be shareholder whom the manager or board member has a fiduciary duty to serve. The underlying reason why insider trading represents a violation of fiduciary duty is that the "inside information" on which the manager or board member trades belongs to (is "proprietary" to) the company rather than these persons. Any value associated with the information belongs to the shareholders, not to the manager or board member who possesses it. For an example of insider trading, see the case of Martha Stewart and ImClone.

# MARTHA STEWART AND INSIDER TRADING

In 2004, food and lifestyle businesswoman and television personality Martha Stewart was convicted of lying to a federal agent, conspiracy, and obstruction of justice in a case related to Sam Waksal, the founder of biopharmaceutical company ImClone. Waksal sold off a substantial portion of his ImClone stock because he had inside information that an imminent ruling from the Food and Drug Administration on one of ImClone's most promising drug discoveries was going to be unfavorable. Waksal eventually was found guilty on numerous charges for trading on this inside information including securities fraud and was sentenced to more than seven years in prison.

The story does not end here, however. On learning of Waksal's sales of ImClone, Waksal's stock broker Peter Bacanovic of Merrill Lynch asked his assistant to notify Stewart so that she could also sell her stock and profit from the inside information. Stewart was a friend of Waksal's and also a client of Bacanovic. Bacanovic argued that Stewart's trade was legitimate, and he produced documents showing that Stewart had put in an order to sell any time that ImClone stock dipped below $60 per share. The government successfully showed, however, that Bacanovic made the notations regarding Stewart's sell order after the investigation started in an attempt to cover up the insider trade.

The government indicted Stewart and Bacanovic on nine counts, including obstruction of justice, conspiracy to obstruct justice, making false statements, committing perjury, making and using false documents, and, finally, against Stewart, for securities fraud in her capacity as the head of her publicly traded company Martha Stewart Living Omnimedia (MSLO). The theory of this charge was that MSLO derived much of its intangible corporate value from the reputation of Martha Stewart and that Stewart made misleading public statements about her ImClone trades to maintain MSLO's share value. Jurors convicted Stewart and Bacanovic on the charges of obstructing justice, conspiracy, and making false statements to federal officials. Both Stewart and Waksal went to jail.

## Employees

Employees are another important stakeholder group. Whether managers or nonmanagers, employees are agents of the company and its shareholders. The relationship between employees and shareholders can be complementary; when managers work to create positive economic returns for the company, they not only fulfill their fiduciary duty to shareholders but also benefit themselves by increasing their chances for promotions and higher pay. If they own stock in the company, perhaps through stock options, they benefit as well from dividends and higher stock prices. Moreover, rising pay and better working conditions benefit workers and can also benefit shareholders by increasing employee productivity. They do so by increasing employee satisfaction and motivation and reducing problems such as absenteeism and turnover.

Issaquah, Washington-based merchandiser Costco, mentioned in an earlier chapter, provides an excellent example of a company that has achieved financial success for shareholders in part by treating its employees well. In 2017, *Forbes* magazine named Costco the best employer in the United States.[9] The company provides higher wages and benefits than its competitors, which not only makes employees

happy but also means a better shopping experience for customers and less
money spent on hiring and training
new employees.[10]

While the interests of shareholders and employees sometimes are
aligned, they can also be adversarial.
Employees wish to maximize wages
and work under ideal conditions, but
managers, as agents of shareholders,
are interested in minimizing labor costs
in order to increase profits. In recognition that the interests of management
and labor are opposed and that man-

©iStockphoto.com/milanvirijevic

agement tends to enjoy greater bargaining power than workers, U.S. laws impose
significant obligations on employers and grant particular rights to employees. One
of the goals of these laws is to ensure that employees work under safe conditions and
are paid enough to provide a good life for themselves when they do not have bargaining power to negotiate for themselves. Another goal of the law is to give workers the
chance to increase their bargaining power vis-à-vis their employers. The rights that
employees enjoy under U.S. law are discussed next.

Laws administered by OSHA are designed to protect the health and safety of workers.

### Right to a Safe Workplace

In the United States, the Occupational Safety and Health Administration (OSHA)
develops and enforces rules on workplace health and safety, what workers can be
exposed to, and what notices and warnings employers are required to give them.
The mission of OSHA is "to save lives, prevent injuries and protect the health of
America's workers." OSHA was established under the Occupational Safety and
Health Act, passed in 1970. This law requires employers with 10 or more employees to provide a workplace that is free from known hazards posing serious health
risks. OSHA has the authority to inspect workplaces, cite violations, and impose
penalties and fines for noncompliance. The agency does not have the ability to
require immediate abatement of hazards or shut down a noncompliant workplace
without a court order.[11]

While federal law imposes on employers the duty to prevent avoidable harm
and fully inform workers of known risks, it does not address the issue of compen-
sating employees for harm caused in the workplace. This obligation is left to state
law. All 50 states have some form of workers' compensation system. Eligibility for
workers' compensation benefits and the amount available to injured workers vary
from state to state.

### Right to Fair Pay

Numerous laws establish and protect workers' right to be compensated fairly. These
laws are seen as necessary because workers often do not have the power to bargain
individually for fair compensation. Today, fair pay is often discussed in terms of a

"living wage"—one that enables workers to meet their basic needs. The concept of a living wage has deep roots in philosophy; for example, Aristotle wrote that government had a responsibility for ensuring that all people attain happiness and self-sufficiency.[12] The Amazon case at the end of this chapter deals with the issue of fair pay.

The federal Fair Labor Standards Act (FLSA) imposes a minimum hourly wage rate for workers covered by the act. It also mandates overtime pay for hours worked in excess of daily and weekly maximums. Numerous states and municipalities have enacted their own minimum wage laws that require some employers to pay more than the federal minimum wage. For example, at the time of the writing of this book, the U.S. minimum wage was $7.25 per hour for covered workers; in the state of Washington, however, it was $12.00; and in the city of Seattle, $15.00 for small employers and $16.00 for large employers.[13]

A robust debate persists about whether minimum wage laws are unethical, that is, whether they benefit or harm workers. Activists tend to believe that minimum wage laws are necessary and should be set at a level that provides at least a living wage. However, many economists argue that such laws harm workers by inducing companies to hire fewer workers, especially low-skilled ones; replace workers with automation; find cheaper labor elsewhere; or simply close their doors. Other economists acknowledge these costs but question the magnitude of their impacts and argue that they are more than offset by the benefits to workers who are paid more than they would have received otherwise.[14]

### Right to the Opportunity to Work

Historically, though much less so today, an unwritten social contract existed between employers and employees. According to this contract, employees expected secure, long-term employment in exchange for their loyalty and commitment to the company.[15] This idea that employees have a right to their jobs is at odds with the fundamental principle of U.S. labor law, however, which is that employment is "at-will." The term **at-will employment** means that employees are hired and may be fired at the will (discretion) of their employers without providing a reason (having a "**just cause**") for termination. The principle behind at-will employment law is that employers should be able to dismiss employees just as employees may voluntarily leave their employers. This principle has little practical value in the many cases where employers have more bargaining power than employees—that is, when employers have many workers to choose from and workers have few employment options. Such cases often involve unskilled and low-skilled workers.[16] While "at-will" employment has become a fundamental principle in the United States, in many other countries this principle is not in effect, and employees have rights that prohibit their termination other than for good reasons.

Even in the United States, there are numerous exceptions to the rule of at-will employment. First, employers cannot dismiss employees for reasons that are illegal. In addition, workers cannot be fired because they belong to a union or engage in some types of whistle-blowing as discussed in Chapter 4. It is also important to note that in many cases employers and employees agree to terms that are not based on at-will employment. Approximately one third of U.S. workers have contracts

**At-will employment**
The principle of U.S. labor law that employers may fire employees at their discretion—that is, that employees hold their jobs at the will of their employers

**Just cause**
An exception to at-will employment, specifying that an employer must have a good reason for firing an employee

that include "just cause" provisions or otherwise specify that employees may be dismissed only for objectively fair reasons.[17]

U.S. law also recognizes that all people should have an equal opportunity to work and to fair treatment in the workplace. The Equal Employment Opportunity Commission is the U.S. federal agency that enforces laws related to workplace discrimination. Its mandate is to investigate cases of discrimination based on race, national origin, religion, sex, age, disability, sexual orientation, gender identity, genetic information, and children (whether or not one has them, and whether they need care).[18] The EEOC enforces numerous U.S. laws, including Title VII of the Civil Rights Act of 1964, the Age Discrimination in Employment Act of 1967, the Americans with Disabilities Act of 1990, and the ADA Amendments Act of 2008. It handles more than 100,000 workplace discrimination cases each year; however, workers have received compensation in only 18% of these cases. One important reason for this is that the EEOC does not have the resources it needs to properly investigate cases. The agency closes most cases without having determined whether discrimination actually occurred. Another reason very few cases result in compensation is that discrimination is hard to prove. It takes place in subtle ways, such as being given inferior work assignments or unfair performance evaluations.[19]

### *Right to Organize and Bargain Collectively*

As indicated above, U.S. law provides workers the right to organize. (The same is true in many other countries as well.) Under the U.S. laws that together constitute the National Labor Relations Act (NLRA), employees have the right to establish and operate labor unions and collectively bargain with their employers. Labor unions are simply organizations that represent workers, and "collective bargaining" refers to unionized workers working together to negotiate terms of employment with employers. The NLRA and related regulations prohibit employers from interfering with employees' rights to organize and collectively bargain, controlling unions, discriminating or retaliating against employees for union or whistle-blower activities, and failing to negotiate in good faith with unions.

At the same time, labor laws and regulations contain provisions that prohibit some union activities. Unions are not allowed to coerce employees to join a union or to restrain them from organizing and collectively bargaining through means other than a union. Unions also must negotiate with employers in good faith and hold fair elections to select union representatives. They are not allowed to engage in racketeering, that is, use their power to illegally earn money or demand favors from union members or employers. They cannot conduct some types of strikes or other activities. The managers of labor unions are subject to the same fiduciary duties of care and loyalty as are the directors and officers of a corporation.

The right to organize and collectively bargain is widely recognized as a fundamental human right.[20] With this right, workers can achieve greater bargaining power and attain better pay and working conditions. While one employee often does not have the power to negotiate a favorable agreement with an employer by herself or himself, employees working together may achieve this power. They can obtain this power because they can threaten to collectively withdraw from the labor pool, leaving the employer without an adequate workforce. When a labor union acts in the best interests of its members and enjoys equal bargaining power with the management of the company, the two sides can negotiate employment arrangements that are acceptable to both—the minimum that each is willing to accept and the maximum it is willing to concede.

While our focus has been on U.S. employment laws, we recognize that today it is common practice for companies to "offshore" jobs—that is, outsource them to foreign countries. There are many reasons that companies engage in outsourcing, including lower wage rates and less stringent labor laws. Of course, companies should comply with the laws of the countries in which they operate, but whether mere compliance in a country with weak employee protections is sufficient from an ethical perspective is an important question. Should companies have double standards and treat domestic workers differently than workers in other countries? Ethics requires companies to confront this question and to choose to go beyond legal compliance if necessary. We address this point at length later in the chapter.

It is also important to recognize that the employment laws designed to protect workers often are not followed in the United States and elsewhere. At the extreme, businesses have engaged in labor trafficking, which is using force, coercion, or fraud to compel individuals to work and provide services.[21] This type of behavior is essentially slavery, and unfortunately, it is not a relic of the past. It still takes place throughout the world, including the United States in agriculture, restaurants, cleaning services, and other settings. Numerous cases of human trafficking in U.S. agriculture have led to criminal convictions.[22]

## Customers

Companies could not exist without their customers. Customers provide companies with the revenues that sustain them, and they receive valued goods and services in exchange. As indicated, many companies make customers their top priority. As with other stakeholders, customers' relationship with the company is both cooperative and adversarial. In general, companies would like to charge the highest price they can for their products, while customers generally would like lower prices or more value, such as enhanced features for the price they pay. Under the best of circumstances, the sale of a good or service represents a mutually beneficial agreement where both sides are satisfied with what they receive in exchange for what they provide.

### *Tort Law, Negligence, and Product Liability*[23]

The purchase and sale of goods and services historically has been viewed as a matter of legal contract, even if the terms of such a sale are not specified in a written agreement. Such contracts and thus the sale of virtually all goods and services are generally seen as valid and enforceable as long as the parties enter into them knowingly, voluntarily, and without duress, deceit, or manipulation. The contracts would be valid even if they seemed unfair or careless to others who were not a party to the deal. Only certain types of contracts must be in writing, such as those for the purchase and sale of land.

According to the doctrine of privity, which emerged in England in the 19th century, contracts may impose benefits and harms only on the parties to the contract. Following this doctrine, a party that is harmed by a product but not directly involved in the transaction would have little recourse. In the case of *Winterbottom v. Wright*, decided in England in 1842, the court held that a wagon driver (Winterbottom) who suffered an injury due to a faulty wagon wheel had no right to sue the wagon manufacturer (Wright) because there was privity of contract between Wright and Winterbottom's employer, but not between Wright and Winterbottom himself.

Because privity of contract was widely seen as unfair to third parties (e.g., Winterbottom), tort law began to develop. The purpose of tort law is to impose legal liability on those who inflict harm on others and to provide remedy to those who are harmed. Tort law covers a range of harms, including those caused intentionally and unintentionally, and those that are the result of negligence. An important case in the development of U.S. case law as it relates to negligence was *MacPherson v. Buick Motor Co*, decided in 1916 by the New York Court of Appeals.[24] In this case, which also involved injury caused by a faulty wheel, MacPherson sued Buick for producing a defective car. Noted jurist Benjamin Cardozo ruled in favor of MacPherson even though he had purchased the car from a dealer and not directly from Buick.

The critical element in negligence cases is often the foreseeability of harm. Manufacturers must offer products that are not defective and do not pose dangers they reasonably should have anticipated. Another important element in negligence cases is proximate cause. The plaintiff must be able to show that the harm they suffered resulted from a defect or dangerous condition stemming from the defendant's negligence. An example of establishing proximate cause is provided by the case of *Escola v. Coca-Cola*, where a jury determined that the serious injuries suffered by a waitress when a bottle of Coca-Cola exploded could be traced to the company's negligence.

Two other factors that come into play in tort cases are contributory negligence and assumption of risk. According to the doctrine of contributory negligence, plaintiffs cannot recover awards if their own negligence contributed to their injury. Many states, however, seek to apportion legal responsibility in cases where both the defendant and the plaintiff were negligent, a doctrine known as comparative negligence. Like contributory negligence, assumption of risk is a defense against tort claims. Assumption of risk is the defense that the plaintiff was aware of the defects or risks associated with a product and still voluntarily went ahead and used it.

A landmark case involving assumption of risk was *Cipollone v. Liggett Group*.[25] In the case, a federal jury in Newark, New Jersey, awarded $400,000 to Anthony Cipollone, whose wife had died of lung cancer in 1964—before tobacco companies were first legally required to put warning labels on cigarette packages. Liggett argued that Mrs. Cipollone had knowingly assumed the risks of smoking. The jury found, however, that Liggett's ads had wrongly implied that cigarettes were safe and that the company knew of and should have warned customers about the dangers of cigarette smoking.

In some cases, companies can be held liable for harm their products cause when the companies had no intent to harm and were not negligent. According to the doctrine of strict liability, parties are held liable when they sell defective products or

---

**Privity of contract**
The legal doctrine that a contract may impose benefits and harms only on the parties to the contract and not on third parties

**Tort law**
The area of law that imposes legal liability on those who cause harm to others and provides relief to those who are harmed (a tort is an act that causes harm)

**Liability**
In tort cases, the responsibility of a defendant to reimburse the plaintiff for harm caused to him or her

**Negligence**
The failure to exercise appropriate care

**Foreseeability of harm**
The ability to reasonably anticipate or predict the negative consequences of an action (proving foreseeability is a requirement in tort cases)

**Proximate cause**
In a tort case, an event that is deemed to have caused an injury

**Contributory negligence**
The defense to a tort claim that the plaintiff's negligence contributed to his or her injury; an approach in tort law that apportions responsibility between the plaintiff and the defendant when both are found to have been negligent

**Assumption of risk**
The defense in tort cases that the plaintiff was aware of and voluntarily assumed the risks associated with a product or service

**Strict liability**
The legal doctrine that a person or organization can be found legally liable for the consequences of their actions even when they are not at fault

**Right to safe products and services**
The consumer right to products that present no foreseeable harm to health and life

**Right to be informed**
The right of consumers to complete and truthful information about products and services, including their foreseeable consequences, so that they may make informed choices about whether to use or consume them

**Informed consent**
Permission to provide a service based on a customer or patient's acknowledgment that she or he is aware of and accepts the foreseeable consequences of receiving that service

engage in inherently dangerous activities such as keeping wild animals, firing test rockets, and transporting toxic waste. The rationale behind strict liability is that it forces those undertaking such activities to take all necessary precautions. The doctrine of strict liability, which has been adopted in some form in almost every jurisdiction in the United States, however, does recognize as valid contributory negligence, comparative negligence, and assumption of risk defenses.

## Consumer Bill of Rights

In 1962, U.S. President John F. Kennedy gave a speech in which he identified four basic customer (consumer) rights. The first of these is the right to safe products and services. Companies must offer products that are not defective and do not present foreseeable dangers. Companies that offer unsafe products may be sued for negligence or held liable for damages. Ryobi provides just one example of a company that was held liable for selling a defective and dangerous product. In 2015, a Virginia jury awarded damages of $2.5 million to the family of a man who was killed when riding a Ryobi lawn mower that caught fire and exploded. The man had been riding a mower built in 2005. The following year, Ryobi began to offer a safer mower but did not recall older ones.[26] It was liable because it did not replace the old mowers with the new and safer ones, and knew of the dangers involved in operating its old mowers but neither adequately informed customers nor told them how to protect themselves.

In the United States, no single office protects consumer rights; rather, this duty is distributed across numerous federal agencies. With respect to customer safety, the Consumer Product Safety Commission (CPSC) plays an important role. The CPSC is an independent federal agency set up under the Consumer Product Safety Act of 1972.[27] It is responsible for "protecting the public from unreasonable risks of injury or death" associated with a wide array of consumer products.[28] For example, the CPSC enforces laws that require refrigerators to be designed so that people cannot become trapped inside them, poisonous household products to be contained in child-resistant packaging, and many children's products to come with warning labels.[29] Another important product safety agency is the U.S. Food and Drug Administration (FDA), which is responsible for ensuring the safety of food products, pharmaceuticals, medical devices, and cosmetics.[30]

The second right identified by President Kennedy was the right to be informed. Customers have the right to the information they need to make an informed decision, and the information that companies provide them must be truthful so customers are not vulnerable to false and misleading claims about the products they buy. An example of a U.S. law that protects customers' right to be informed is the Truth in Lending Act of 1968, which requires providers of consumer credit (e.g., credit card companies) to provide full and easy-to-understand information about the cost and terms of credit. Similarly, medical providers must obtain the informed consent of their patients, meaning that they must provide patients with all relevant information, judge that they are capable of understanding it, and obtain their acknowledgment that they are aware of and accept the possible consequences of the treatments they receive.[31] Provisions such as informed consent agreements embody a deontological ethical perspective by protecting the dignity and autonomy of patients. Informed consent is an important part of the assumption of risk defense a seller of a product or service can invoke if damages take place. It is meant to assure that buyers are aware of the risks they confront and that they voluntarily agree to these risks.

In response to the widespread misleading, unfair, and predatory behavior in the financial sector that contributed to the financial crisis of 2007 and 2008, the U.S. Congress created the Consumer Financial Protection Bureau.[32] The CFPB protects consumers' right to be informed in a wide range of financial sectors including commercial banking, investment banking, mortgage lending and servicing, credit cards, payday lending, and debt collection. The law creating the CFPB sought to consolidate responsibility for consumer financial protection in one agency, whereas before it had been spread across seven.[33] In its early years, the CFPB was led forcefully by Elizabeth Warren. However, in recent years, the CFPB's leadership has largely failed to carry out the agency mandate due to ideological opposition to that mandate.[34]

The right to choose was the third right President Kennedy identified in his "Consumer Bill of Rights." The U.S. government has sought to protect this right by establishing a range of laws designed to ensure a competitive marketplace in which a variety of products is available to customers at competitive prices. These include laws preventing tactics that unfairly harm customers, such as price gouging (charging customers exorbitantly high prices when they have no other options), and laws protecting competitors against unfair practices such as "dumping" products onto the market at below cost. They also include antitrust laws that prevent corporate collusion, cartels, and mergers and acquisitions that consolidate corporate power and potentially reduce competition and increase prices.

The main U.S. federal agency that is responsible for ensuring customers' right to choose is the Federal Trade Commission (FTC).[35] This agency's origins go back to the Progressive Era at the start of the 20th century. The FTC's Bureau of Competition enforces antitrust laws that are designed to protect customer choice.[36] Their approach to enforcing antitrust laws has varied. Some federal administrations have taken the view that government should be concerned about corporate power only when it leads to higher prices for customers, while others have taken the view that antitrust regulation should also address the impacts of the concentration of power on competitors, workers, and society more broadly. This debate is currently playing out with regard to Facebook. Some argue that the company engages in unfair business practices that give it inordinate influence on American political discourse, while others, including the head of the FTC's Antitrust Division, take the view that Facebook's actions do not harm its users (see the case on Facebook in Chapter 10).[37]

Finally, the fourth consumer right President Kennedy identified was the right to be heard. By this right, the President meant the right to raise concerns about products and have those concerns resolved in a fair and timely manner. The right to be heard also refers to the right of consumer advocates to participate in the policy-making process so that the interests of consumers are reflected in the law.[38] Many of the federal agencies already mentioned in this section provide mechanisms for customers to voice their concerns. For example, the FTC's Bureau of Consumer Protection conducts investigations of consumer complaints in areas such as identity theft and false advertising,[39] and the CFPB investigates complaints about aggressive and unfair debt collection.[40]

**Right to choose**
The right of consumers to choose from among a variety of options; the right to transact in a competitive rather than an anticompetitive marketplace

**Collusion**
Illegal cooperation between companies

**Cartel**
A group of seemingly independent companies that collude to set prices or restrict output for the purpose of increasing profits

**Mergers and acquisitions**
Types of transactions in which the ownership of businesses is combined

**Right to be heard**
The right of consumers to voice their concerns about products and services and to have those concerns resolved in a fair and timely manner

### *Right to Privacy*

**Right to privacy**
The right to have one's personal information protected from public view

Another consumer right that is gaining increasing attention with advances in information and communication technologies is the **right to privacy**. While the right to privacy may seem intuitively simple to understand, scholars have struggled to define it. In U.S. law, recognition of an individual's right to privacy is typically traced back to an 1890 article by Samuel Warren and Louis Brandeis, which defined the right to privacy simply as "the right to be let alone."[41] The right to privacy is often construed as the right to have information about one's identity and personal affairs protected from public view. Some definitions emphasize that individuals should be able to control what personal information can be accessed by others.[42]

Customers have a reasonable expectation of a right to privacy. They expect that the information they provide to companies about themselves through transactions and other communications will be protected unless they authorize the sharing of it, and they are concerned that once their personal information is shared, it will be misused (e.g., used by others to make unauthorized purchases). In a number of recent cases, companies have failed to honor this expectation. One reason is a lack of data security; computer hackers have stolen the information. A high-profile case of such a data breach involved Equifax, one of the largest consumer credit scoring and reporting companies in the United States. In this case, the company failed to protect the personal information of nearly 150 million customers. The disclosed information included not only telephone numbers and email addresses but also social security numbers, credit card numbers, and driver's license numbers. A U.S. investigation concluded that the breach occurred because of Equifax's inadequate internal controls and failure to use best practices in data privacy. One reason that the breach drew the ire of the public was that Equifax did not disclose it until six weeks after it happened.[43]

Consumers' right to privacy has been violated by hackers and the failure of companies to protect against them.

A second reason that companies share customers' personal information is simply that they profit from doing so, and even that doing so is central to their business models. Internet companies generate revenues by selling advertising, which they target based on personal information. In addition, they allow third-party applications to access personal information in order to use it and sell it.[44] Providing personal information to third parties is legal if consumers authorize it when they accept the companies' privacy policies and user agreements. Often, however, consumers do not realize that they are authorizing the sharing of their personal information because these agreements are lengthy and contain legal language that is difficult to understand.

To address these issues, the European Union adopted the General Data Protection Regulation (GDPR). The GDPR, which was adopted in 2016 and came into effect in 2018, requires companies to make short and clear user agreements;

©iStockphoto.com/iLexx

allows customers to access their personal information and see how it is being shared; gives customers more control over their data by requiring them to "opt in" (consent) to each of the various types of uses of their data, rather than having them provide blanket consent for all uses of their information and then "opting out" of the uses to which they do not consent; and makes it easier for customers to withdraw their consent to data sharing. In addition, the GDPR requires companies that experience significant data breaches to report them within 72 hours. It imposes significant penalties on companies that are not in compliance.[45]

The U.S. does not have a comprehensive law governing data privacy. The failure to have such a law is in part due to the strenuous efforts of companies such as Facebook and Google to prevent such laws. Numerous states have established data privacy laws, however. The most significant of these is California's Consumer Privacy Act. This law includes many provisions similar to those in the GDPR, but it is narrower in scope. For example, it applies only to companies with revenues above $25 million that sell data on more than 50 million customers, or that earn over half of their revenues from selling information.[46]

While our focus has been on customers' right to privacy when transacting with businesses, we note that the right to privacy is a more sweeping issue that goes beyond customer-related issues and is of great concern to citizens across the world. The United Nations Universal Declaration of Human Rights recognizes the right to privacy as a fundamental human right.[47] Of particular concern to many is government use of advanced technology to access personal information and monitor individuals' activities, often for reasons of law enforcement and national security. Concern about government intrusions on privacy came to the fore with the case of Edward Snowden, who, while working for a government contractor, provided reporters with thousands of documents revealing the existence of numerous government global surveillance programs. A fundamental question that society is now grappling with is how to balance the right to privacy against the need for government to acquire the information necessary to protect safety and security. This issue implicates business, because government surveillance requires the cooperation of telecommunications companies.

## Suppliers

Suppliers are another vital stakeholder group. Companies could not achieve their goals without the partners who provide them with the raw materials, components, and services that go into the production of their products and services. The supply chain for even a seemingly simple product can be very long; for example, the shirt you are wearing (if you are wearing one) may have been made possible by cotton farmers, textile producers, button makers, and sewing facilities—not to mention the manufacturers of the tools and equipment used by these suppliers.[48] We have already covered the laws relevant to supplier interactions and relationships in the last section, because suppliers are simply on the other side of customer transactions. A company purchasing goods and services from suppliers is a customer.

What is perhaps most interesting from the standpoint of ethics about the laws related to suppliers is how few there are beyond contract law. This deficiency is partially due to the fact that many suppliers are located in countries with little regulation. As a result, the supply chains of many products sold in the United States have been associated with a range of unethical activities that were customary and legal in the countries where they took place.

# RANA BUILDING COLLAPSE

One tragic event of this type occurred in Bangladesh in 2013, when the Rana Plaza building in Dhaka collapsed, killing more than 1,100 workers.[49] The building was intended for use as shops and offices, but it also housed a number of garment factories that it could not support structurally.[50] It also was three stories taller than allowed by permit, was built on wetlands, and used substandard construction materials.[51] After significant cracks developed in the building, but before the collapse, a Bangladeshi government official declared the building safe.[52] The garment factories produced clothing for a number of well-known Western companies including Wal-Mart and Benetton. Due to the scrutiny they received as a result of the Rana Plaza collapse, many clothing retailers developed an agreement to improve working conditions in Bangladeshi factories. Wal-Mart, however, refused to sign the agreement because it did not want to commit to paying for building improvements.[53]

## Communities

Businesses rely on and influence the communities in which they operate. These include not only geographic communities, such as neighborhoods, towns, and cities, but also virtual communities (e.g., social networking forums in which the company participates). Communities provide many important resources to companies, including workers, raw materials, and the infrastructure that makes business possible, such as water, electricity, roads, and bridges. They also shape the business environment through: income, sales, and property tax rates; fees of various kinds; permitting processes; zoning laws; and other factors that affect the ability of companies to earn profits and execute their strategies. They also enact laws that influence the quality of the local workforce, such as laws related to education and job training.[54] In exchange, communities typically seek to attract businesses because they create jobs, attract complementary businesses, and pay taxes. Communities also expect businesses to act as good citizens would—by contributing to the community in various ways, such as supporting local schools, parks, social programs, charities, and other civic activities.

As with other stakeholders, the relationship between communities and businesses is at once adversarial and complementary: On the one hand, company growth and profits can mean more jobs and a bigger tax base, and corporate civic engagement benefits not only the community but the company as well in the form of improved public reputation and worker pride and loyalty. At the same time, companies tend to want to pay lower taxes and wages, make smaller investments, and receive subsidies from communities.

Companies must follow the laws of the communities in which they operate, but they also shape those laws by participating in local and state political processes. Large businesses often influence the laws of a community before they even arrive.

They do so by stimulating competition among the many communities that prize the jobs, tax revenues, and other benefits that a corporate presence can bring. These communities compete with one another by offering businesses subsidies and other incentives to choose them as their location. Often, companies can "shop for the best deal" by promising to locate in communities that provide them the best combination of workforce, business environment, incentives, and other resources.

The extent to which businesses and communities mutually benefit is often a matter of bargaining power. The greater the benefits that a company can provide to a community, the greater its power to extract incentives and influence political processes. Businesses have less power in communities that have a strong economic foundation, an attractive business environment, and a skilled, desirable workforce.[55] As noted below, New York City ultimately did not support Amazon's proposal to receive subsidies in return for locating one of its headquarters there. On the other hand, "fracking" (the production of oil and gas through hydraulic fracturing of underground rock) tends to take place disproportionately in poor communities. While fracking can provide economic benefits to these communities, it also has had numerous negative impacts, including air and water pollution and associated health problems.[56] Fracking, and the disposal of waste fluids produced from it, can induce earthquakes.[57] The state of Oklahoma experiences hundreds of fracking-related small earthquakes each year.[58]

Amazon's decision about where to locate its second corporate headquarters ("HQ2") provides a vivid and extreme example of the power that companies have to influence laws that shape the business landscape. In September 2017, the company announced its plans to expand beyond its Seattle headquarters by establishing a second head-quarters (HQ2). It stated that it expected HQ2 to house 50,000 workers and require $5 billion in new construction. More than 200 cities submitted bids to host HQ2, many of them making extensive promotional campaigns. These cities offered extensive tax breaks, streamlined building approval processes, infrastructure improvements, and other incentives in a bid to woo Amazon.[59] After narrowing the list of finalists, Amazon ultimately elected to divide HQ2 between two cities: New York City and Arlington, Virginia (a suburb of Washington, D.C.).[60] (Amazon later withdrew from New York City amid widespread protests that the city received little value in exchange for the generous subsidies it was prepared to give Amazon.) The winning Virginia package included approximately $600 million in tax and cash incentives from local and state governments.[61] Critics argued that the driving purpose behind Amazon's HQ2 decision was to gather information about the relative benefits and costs of the many commu-nities in which it might operate in the future. Urban studies scholar Richard Florida stated that the HQ2 decision was not really about a second headquarters. Rather, Florida argued, the decision was about a locational strategy in many future cities.[62] In other words, the bidding process enabled Amazon to "crowdsource" the gathering of information about variety of factors that drive its location decisions.

## The Natural Environment

The natural environment and the human beings who advocate for its protection and sustenance also are stakeholders of all businesses. Companies could not survive without "natural capital"—the stocks of geological, air, water, and living resources that serve as raw materials and energy sources for businesses. These stocks provide "ecosystem services" such as productive soils, breathable air, and clean water that make human life possible.[63]

Through the consumption of materials and production of waste, businesses have an impact on the natural environment—impacts that can be detrimental to companies and individuals alike. The impact of humans on the natural environment has now become so extensive that many scientists argue that we have entered a new era of geological history known as the **Anthropocene**, a period that is distinguished by the role of human beings as the most dominant force of change on the natural world.[64] Some scientists date the Anthropocene to the beginning of human agriculture, while others see it as beginning with the dawn of the Industrial Revolution.[65]

One of the surest—and most distressing—signs we live in the Anthropocene is that we are now pushing up against and in some cases exceeding **planetary boundaries**— the ability of Earth to support human life. The idea behind the planetary boundaries framework is that human activity must take place within a safe space for humanity. Nine interconnected earth system processes make human life possible and are affected by human activity. The nine processes are (1) climate change, (2) biodiversity loss, (3) biogeochemical processes that include the impacts of human activity, primarily agriculture, on global nitrogen and phosphorus cycles, (4) ocean acidification, (5) land use changes like deforestation, (6) water consumption, (7) stratospheric ozone depletion, (8) particulate emissions to the atmosphere, and (9) chemical pollution such as the loading of plastics, toxic chemicals, and radioactive contamination into the air and water (see Figure 7.1). For each of these processes, there is a threshold level at which dangerous and even disastrous change happen. Two of the nine planetary boundaries already have been exceeded, and we are at risk of exceeding others. The two crossed boundaries are climate change and biodiversity loss, which is measured as the rate of species extinction.[66]

The United States first made a concerted and comprehensive effort to address environmental issues in the 1970s. In 1970, the U.S. Congress enacted a suite of environmental protection laws and established the Environmental Protection Agency (EPA) to administer and enforce these laws. Major U.S. environmental laws include the following:

- The *Clean Air Act* seeks to achieve air quality standards by establishing maximum allowable concentrations of various air pollutants that contribute to the development of smog. It also establishes emissions limitations on sources of pollutants. The Clean Air Act was passed in 1970 and then amended in 1990 to address the problems of acid rain and depletion of the stratospheric ozone layer.[67]

- The *Clean Water Act* aims to restore and maintain the chemical, physical, and biological integrity of the nation's waters. The EPA uses a permitting system to restrict the discharge of pollution into navigable waters.[68] A separate statute, the Safe Drinking Water Act (SDWA), regulates drinking water. The EPA sets the standards for public water supplies by establishing limits on bacterial and chemical contaminants and by regulating the underground

---

**Anthropocene**
The current geological period, in which human activity is the dominant force of change on the Earth's climate and environment

**Planetary boundaries**
A theoretical framework that identifies earth systems processes that make human life possible, specifies the threshold levels at which human activity would exceed the capacities of these processes to continue to support human life, and assesses whether human activities are exceeding these thresholds

**FIGURE 7.1**

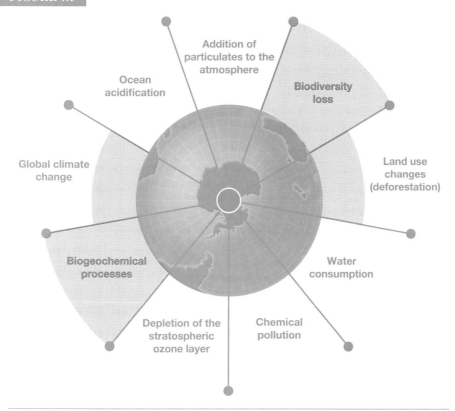

Ocean
acidification

Addition of
particulates to the
atmosphere

Biodiversity
loss

Global climate
change

Land use
changes
(deforestation)

Biogeochemical
processes

Water
consumption

Depletion of the
stratospheric
ozone layer

Chemical
pollution

The planetary boundaries framework identifies nine ecological processes and specifies thresholds at which dangerous and even catastrophic change could occur. Scientific evidence suggests that we have already crossed two of the boundaries. We have also crossed the threshold of the nitrogen cycle, which is part of the biogeochemical boundary.

injection of contaminants into groundwater that contributes to public drinking water sources.[69]

- The *Resource Conservation and Recovery Act* (RCRA) is a comprehensive national program for systematic control of hazardous waste. Before it was passed, disposal of hazardous waste was a matter of state regulation, as is the case with solid waste, including garbage. Under RCRA, the generator of waste has *cradle-to-grave* liability; it is responsible for storage, transportation, and final treatment or disposal.[70]

- The *Comprehensive Environmental Response, Compensation, and Liability Act* (CERCLA) is typically referred to as "Superfund." It addresses the cleanup of sites that have been contaminated with hazardous waste. It permits the EPA to clean up the sites and require those responsible for the waste to either participate in the cleanup or reimburse EPA for cleanup costs. Those responsible include everyone in the chain of activity who created the hazardous waste, including those who owned or operated the property at the time of the offensive activity and those who currently own or operate the property.[71]

- The *Toxic Substances Control Act* (TSCA) gives the EPA the power to require that chemicals be registered and screened for toxicity before being used. The statute covers toxic substances used in everyday products and their by-products. TSCA put the burden of proof of a chemical's safety on those proposing to use it. Prior to passage of TSCA, chemicals were presumed to be innocuous until harm had been caused.[72]

- The *Endangered Species Act* (ESA) was established in 1973 and is designed to protect endangered flora and fauna from extinction. Under the ESA, species are designated as either endangered, which means that they are in danger of extinction, or threatened (likely to become endangered). The ESA requires that the "critical habitat" of endangered species be protected. Critical habitat refers to all land, water, and air that a species needs for recovery. The ESA is administered by the U.S. Fish and Wildlife Service and the National Marine Fisheries Service.[73]

During the Trump presidency, enforcement of environmental laws by the U.S. EPA has been at best selective. In 2018, EPA prosecutions of environmental crimes were the lowest in 30 years.[74] The Trump administration has eliminated almost 50 environmental regulations and stopped enforcing many others. It has lifted requirements that manufacturers use technologies that reduce emissions of carcinogenic air pollutants and has also removed a ban on the use of an agricultural pesticide, chlorpyrifos, which has been linked to neurological, developmental, and autoimmune disorders.[75]

## Ethics Means Going Beyond Compliance

**LO 7.3:** Explain the relationship of ethics to the law, that is, that ethics requires us to go "beyond compliance."

What do all of these laws protecting stakeholders mean for ethical decision-making in business? The simple answer is that considering the law is an important step in ethical decision-making processes. Generally, the law is a reflection and codification of a society's ethical beliefs and understandings. Many of the laws just discussed correspond closely with the ethical obligations to stakeholders that the ethical frameworks discussed in Chapter 2 imply. For example, the fiduciary duty of corporate directors and managers to shareholders embodies the deontological perspective that an agent must treat the principal as an ends and not merely as a means. Similarly, the obligation to provide a reasonably safe workplace embodies the deontological viewpoint that workers' dignity must be respected.

Workplace safety laws also may be justified on utilitarian principles. Workers exposed to fewer hazards in their jobs are likely to be more satisfied and motivated workers who suffer fewer injuries. The result is not only less harm to the workers (increasing their utility) but also lower turnover, absenteeism, and workers' compensation premiums for employers (thereby increasing their utility).

Often, however, the law and ethics have a weak correspondence. In these cases, ethics typically imposes a higher obligation than the law does. In some cases, laws not only fail to meet basic ethical standards but actually require unethical behavior. An example is provided by the Fugitive Slave Act of 1850, a U.S. law that imposed a fine and jail sentence on any individual who provided food or shelter to a runaway slave.[76]

The behavior required by law and the behavior required by ethics can differ for a number of reasons. First, laws often set minimum standards of behavior rather than representing the moral "high ground." They often define behaviors that we are not allowed to engage in rather than specifying the ethical behavior we should engage in. Making a product so it is not unsafe or simply complying with the terms of a contract are a far cry from meeting the exacting standards of moral philosophers like Kant, Rawls, Aristotle, Mill, Gilligan, and others, whose ideas we discussed in Chapter 2.

Second, adherence to ethics requires more than obedience to the law because there is a time lag between a change in accepted views about what behaviors are ethical or unethical, and when that change becomes codified in the law. For many issues, the process of identifying, analyzing, and understanding a problem; developing solutions to that problem; and, finally, enacting laws and regulations takes a considerable amount of time. Finding better ways to control the spread of automatic weapons to individuals who might use them to murder other people or themselves is only one example of an issue where the time lag between recognizing a problem is severe and enacting legislation to deal with the problem is great. Furthermore, in some industries, especially new ones that rely on complex technologies not well understood by lawmakers, the pace of innovation is much greater than the pace of the legislative process, so new, ethically questionable practices can become commonplace even before legislators understand them and take action. Many of the schemes used to defraud investors and creditors during the financial crisis of the 2000s were not specifically prohibited by tax and securities regulations or accounting standards that prevailed at the time.

Another reason the laws do not perfectly reflect accepted ethical standards is that legislative processes are inherently political; the laws that legislative processes produce are essentially negotiated settlements that reflect the relative power of the participants in the process. While it may be comforting to think that legislative processes and rulemaking procedures produce a solution that perfectly reflects citizens' values, laws are often not effective, efficient, or fair. In addition, they may reflect the interests and beliefs of individuals and organizations that enjoy disproportionate power at a particular point in time. An example is the issue of climate change. Although the vast preponderance of evidence suggests that global climate change is occurring, could be catastrophic, and has been caused by human activity, and a majority of Americans support action to address it, the U.S. Congress has never enacted legislation to reduce the greenhouse gas emissions that cause climate change.[77]

Finally, a divergence between laws and ethical standards can arise because of the difficulty of making effective policy, even when all involved agree on a problem and have the best intentions of solving it. Being committed to solving a problem and designing a policy that effectively addresses it are different. Since predicting the effects that policies will have once they have been enacted is very difficult, laws tend to have unintended consequences. This is especially the case for issues that are complex and fast-moving.

Many examples exist of well-intended laws and policies that have not achieved their objectives and had significant unintended consequences. One example involves the Energy Independence and Security Act (EISA), which was passed in 2007. This law required U.S. fuel producers to mix vegetable oils (e.g., soy and palm oil) and ethanol made from corn and sugar into gasoline, the purpose being to reduce U.S. oil imports, stimulate demand for agricultural products, and reduce emissions of greenhouse gases by reducing oil use. An unintended consequence of the law, however, has been massive deforestation in Indonesia and Malaysia to make room for palm oil plantations. This deforestation has increased rather than decreased greenhouse gas emissions, harmed villagers, and destroyed the habitats of endangered species including orangutans.[78]

When ethics requires more than the law demands, one must go beyond mere compliance with the law. Managers too often approach the decision-making process by asking what the law requires; in contrast, operating in an ethically responsible manner requires recognition that although some moral obligations have not been codified, observing them is nevertheless imperative. Managers also must move beyond the mentality of "gaming the system" (manipulating the law to gain an advantage rather than complying with the spirit of the law) and seeing what they can get away with. Rather, they should apply a framework such as the weight-of-reasons. The law's prescriptions and proscriptions come into play in Step 2 of the framework, establishing the facts, Step 3, identifying alternative courses of action, but ethical decision-making involves asking the full set of questions the framework includes.

**Civil disobedience** Activities in which individuals intentionally fail to comply with laws they believe are unethical as a form of protest against those laws

It is important to recognize that saying that managers should go beyond complying with the law is not to say that they must always comply. In cases where the law requires unethical behavior, you should conclude that you have no choice but noncompliance. (The quote at the beginning of this chapter speaks to this point.) History provides many examples of civil disobedience, in which individuals knowingly broke laws they saw as unethical and willingly paid the price for doing so. U.S. history shows that the country was born out of acts of civil disobedience such as the Boston Tea Party and

Photo by Michael Ochs Archives/Getty Images

Dr. Martin Luther King Jr. was an ethical leader and a proponent of civil disobedience.

that the tradition of civil disobedience runs through Henry David Thoreau, who opposed slavery and the Mexican–American War; suffragette Susan B. Anthony; Martin Luther King Jr. and other civil rights and peace movement leaders of the 1960s, and continues today. This history neither means that one has an ethical duty to break every law one disagrees with nor that every person who breaks the law has a moral reason to do so. The decision to break the law out of principle must be taken cautiously only after serious reflection and consideration of the alternatives, for respect for the law itself is an important principle.

## Approaches to Going Beyond Compliance

**LO 7.4:** Describe various approaches to "going beyond the law," including moral minimums, corporate social responsibility, corporate citizenship, and sustainability.

There are numerous approaches companies can take that involve going beyond compliance to meet their ethical obligations to stakeholders other than shareholders. This section touches on the following approaches: (a) moral minimums, (b) CSR, (c) corporate citizenship, and (d) sustainable business.

### Moral Minimums

To address the problem that managers can take actions that are legal yet nevertheless unethical, scholars have developed theories of **moral minimums**. These theories accept shareholder primacy but also seek to establish a "moral floor"—a set of minimum ethical standards that profit-maximizing firms should seek to adhere to in all circumstances, regardless of their impact on their financial performance.

Moral minimums do not establish an affirmative duty for firms to engage in higher levels of ethical behavior, for example, to show love and compassion, to act virtuously, or to maximize utility for a broad range of stakeholders. Rather, they are framed in negative terms, as injunctions against causing harm or violating basic human rights unless explicit voluntary consent is given, even if there is a compelling overriding moral reason to do so. The moral minimum approach is captured in ancient Greek physician Hippocrates's famous phrase "First, do no harm." The moral minimum was at the core of Google's mission statement at its founding, when it adopted the motto "don't be evil." We discuss Google and this motto further in a case in Chapter 10.

> **Moral minimums** Sets of minimum ethical standards that persons should follow in all circumstances; moral minimums are typically posed as injunctions against unethical behavior rather than as obligations to engage in ethical behavior

### Corporate Social Responsibility

The basic idea behind **corporate social responsibility (CSR),** as its name makes clear, is that corporations have a responsibility to make society better off. This very broad definition can accommodate many different approaches to business. Some see CSR as essentially synonymous with corporate philanthropy, others define CSR in terms of following a code of ethics, and yet others see CSR as akin to stakeholder management (discussed in Chapter 8), where nonshareholder stakeholders (e.g., employees, the environment) are actively incorporated into the company's core strategy and operations. As we discuss in Chapter 8, some argue that the social responsibility of business is simply to fulfill its economic purpose of generating wealth for shareholders.

> **Corporate social responsibility (CSR)** An approach to business characterized by exceeding legal compliance in order to make stakeholders and society better off

We take the concept of CSR to refer to the corporate policy of exceeding legal compliance in order to make stakeholders and society as a whole better off. This definition suggests that creating benefits for some stakeholders cannot come at the cost of greater harm to other stakeholders. While below we treat corporate citizenship and sustainable business as distinct from CSR, our broad definition of CSR suggests that these other approaches can be viewed as forms of CSR. The same can be said for the concepts of shared value and base of the pyramid development, discussed in Chapter 9.

CSR is not without its critics. Some argue that CSR actually is counterproductive for society because it legitimates the amoral pursuit of self-interest. The basis for this critique, which we believe is fair in some cases and not in others, is that companies practice CSR by undertaking one set of activities to earn profits for shareholders and another set of activities to benefit other stakeholders, rather than running their companies so that their activities benefit all stakeholders. When this type of separation between profits and CSR happens, CSR becomes a marginalized, unimportant set of activities that is unrelated to the company's core business. Corporate philanthropy undertaken solely to improve the company's reputation and not for community betterment falls into this category.

Some critical theorists take the view that CSR is a means of distracting attention from the negative effects of corporate behavior. According to this view, corporations have disproportionate political power and are responsible for an array of social and environmental problems, but they use CSR to present themselves as productive members of society. These critics see the purpose of CSR as being to sustain the legitimacy of business and its ability to act autonomously without society's interference while preventing and putting to the side demands that arise for more fundamental change in law and how capitalism is practiced.[79]

There is little doubt that in practice CSR can involve a set of ancillary activities done to improve a company's public reputation, even as the company's core operations impose harms on society. CSR can be a sort of legerdemain designed to get people to focus on one thing while distracting them from another. Altria, for example, the largest tobacco company in the world, is very well-known for its charitable activities. Many universities, museums, and other cultural bodies of great merit owe a considerable amount to Altria for its generous donations, but does corporate giving excuse the harm that the company has otherwise caused? The Sackler family—the founders and main owners of Purdue Pharmacy, one of the world's biggest promoters of opioids and beneficiaries of the use and abuse of these drugs—were major philanthropists, and their name is attached to important institutions throughout the world.

Nonetheless, these criticisms do not undermine the basic soundness and usefulness of the concept of CSR. There is value in the idea that corporations should do more than follow the law and more than the minimum required by ethics.

**Corporate citizenship**
An approach to business in which corporations take a lead role in fulfilling the rights of a society's citizens

## Corporate Citizenship

Another concept that relates to going beyond compliance is **corporate citizenship**. Historically, the term has been practically synonymous with CSR, in that it connoted being honest, considerate, and involved in improving the community. More recently, the concept has taken on a political flavor that distinguishes it from other forms of CSR. Corporate citizenship scholars now use the term to refer to corporations taking an important and even primary role in fulfilling the rights of citizenship and addressing pressing social and environmental problems. These scholars argue that with power comes responsibility; they take the view that because large multinational corporations have vastly greater resources, scope, and influence than the governments of the jurisdictions in which they operate, they are ungovernable and are subject only to the rules they impose on themselves. With this power, the argument goes, they should also assume the lead and be held accountable for providing for the common good.[80]

In effect, the concept of corporate citizenship advocates that companies start to play the role of government in places where government cannot or does not serve its citizens. Scholars argue that some multinationals are already playing this role, engaging in activities that traditionally have been the purview of government.[81] These activities include public health, education, social security, and protection of human rights. Often companies take up these activities in countries where governments have failed and are incapable of providing even the basics of social order for their citizens. In countries where states have failed corporations may step into the void and address social ills such as AIDS, malnutrition, homelessness, and illiteracy. They may on their own protect the natural environment, when governments do not do the job.[82]

Self-regulation is meant to fill the gaps in legal regulation and moral orientation and create peace and stability when governments fail. This role of stepping in and filling the gaps when governments fail no longer is reserved for developing countries where such failure often takes place. Rather, today it also may apply to developed countries whose state budgets are stretched thin and who are beset by ideological conflicts that fray the fabric and incapacitate these governments from carrying out these vital functions that increasingly might have to be taken up by business.

Corporate citizenship thus requires companies to view themselves as an important part of the global governance system that also includes states, international institutions such as the United Nations, and civil society groups. Rather than advocating for narrow interests, these companies should instead participate in and convene democratic deliberative processes that establish societal arrangements that work for all. We discuss such processes further in the following chapter.

## Sustainable Business

Sustainability provides another lens for approaching ethics and going beyond compliance. The concept of sustainability typically is traced to a 1987 report by the United Nations–appointed Brundtland Commission, which defined sustainable development as "development that meets the needs of the present without compromising the ability of future generations to meet their own needs."[83] Unlike other approaches to going beyond compliance, sustainability is explicitly oriented toward making people better off not just today and tomorrow but for the very long term.

The concept of sustainability has permeated the business world; hence the term sustainable business has become popular. Businesses are increasingly expected

**Sustainable business**
An approach to business in which companies seek to have a positive impact on the economy, society, and the natural environment

to operate sustainably, that is, with the interests of future generations in mind. In practice, sustainable business has three interrelated spheres: (1) the environmental, (2) the social, and (3) the economic (Figure 7.2). (Together, these three are referred to as the "triple bottom line" or sometimes "people, planets, profit.") The current Global Reporting Initiative sustainability reporting guidelines, which provide one of the leading approaches to assessing and reporting a firm's sustainability performance, describe these spheres as follows[84]:

- *Social (people):* The social dimension of sustainability refers to an organization's impacts on "the social systems within which it operates." These include impacts on employees, customers, communities, supply chains, and legal and political systems. The GRI social performance criteria include measures of a wide range of social impacts in these areas: workplace safety; labor relations (e.g., stance toward unions and collective bargaining); discrimination in hiring, pay, and opportunities; use of child labor and forced labor (slavery) in operations and supply chain; respect for the rights of indigenous peoples; engagement with local communities; charitable contributions; customer safety and privacy; and legal compliance and impacts on political systems (e.g., through campaign contributions).

- *Environmental (planet):* Organizations create environmental impacts at the local, national, regional, international, and global levels. The GRI's environmental reporting system aim is to measure a company's impacts on land, water, air, and other natural systems. Specific environmental disclosures included in GRI environmental reporting refer to the volume of raw materials used; the use of recycled material and the takeback and reuse of products and components; energy consumption, and whether energy sources are renewable or nonrenewable; efforts to reduce energy use; water used and discharged, and treatment of discharged water; impacts on habitat, biodiversity, and threatened and endangered species; emissions of pollutants to the atmosphere, including greenhouse gases; waste (including hazardous waste) created and how it is disposed; compliance with environmental laws; and assessment of suppliers' environmental performance.

- *Economic (profit):* Organizations affect the economic conditions of their stakeholders as well as the local, regional, national, and global economies. They do so in many ways including, but not limited to, their creation of wealth for their shareholders, but there is more to the economic dimension than just profit. Using the GRI economic reporting framework, companies report on the profits they generate, their contributions to workers' pensions, the wages they pay, whether they receive government subsidies (which is seen as having a negative impact), the extent to which they use local suppliers, their ability to create jobs and pay taxes, and whether they engage in anticompetitive and corrupt behavior.

Sustainable business activity has increased dramatically in recent decades. According to GRI, more than 13,000 organizations now file GRI reports, including

93% of the world's 250 largest corporations.[85] And business's involvement in sustainability goes beyond reporting. Many companies have adopted voluntary codes and standards to regulate and improve their sustainability performance, and they also participate in voluntary industry initiatives and certifications related to social and environmental issues. Large corporations engaged in sustainable business, however, are vulnerable to the charge raised above (fair or not) that they do so primarily to improve their reputations and divert attention from the harms they are causing.

In addition to the efforts of existing companies, many entrepreneurs are now establishing new companies for the explicit purpose of addressing sustainability problems. Since the establishment of Ashoka in 1980 and the registration of Grameen Bank as an independent bank in 1983, there has been an explosion of "social enterprises" that use commercial strategies to address social and environmental needs. Much of this activity takes place at the base or bottom of the pyramid,[86] that is, it serves the billions of people whose needs are not served by the conventional business and financial sectors. In addition to entrepreneurs, established businesses such as Unilever have begun to undertake such activities. We discuss base of the pyramid strategies further in Chapter 9.

Another testament to the rise of sustainable business is the emergence of benefit corporations. Benefit corporations are for-profit corporations that are legally recognized as having the goal of positively affecting society and the environment, in addition to earning profits for shareholders. Thirty-three states now authorize benefit corporations. Having benefit corporation status protects companies against the claim that they are not putting shareholders above other stakeholders.[87] "B corporations" are very similar to benefit corporations. (In fact, one company can be both.) B corporations are companies that have been certified by the private, independent B Lab to "meet the highest standards of verified, overall social and environment performance, public transparency, and legal accountability." Many B corporations adopt benefit corporation status into their articles of incorporation and governance structures to signal that they "are purpose-driven and created to benefit for all stakeholders, not just shareholders." As of 2019, there were 2,800 B corporations operating in 150 industries and 60 countries.[88]

In sum, companies take many paths in their efforts to go beyond compliance in order to meet their ethical obligations to stakeholders. These range from the very narrow, such as following moral minimums, to the very broad, such as trying to contribute to long-term economic, social, and environmental sustainability. Society increasingly expects companies to make a significant contribution, especially in places where government does not.

FIGURE 7.2

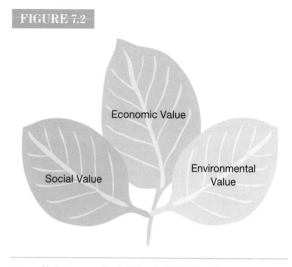

*Source:* Venkataraman, R., & Pinto, J. (2018). *Operations management: Managing global supply chains*. Thousand Oaks, CA: SAGE (p. 35, Figure 2.2).

# AMAZON: IMPROVING THE WORK ENVIRONMENT

With a fortune worth well over $100 billion by conservative estimates, Jeff Bezos is generally acknowledged to be the world's richest person.[89] Most of his wealth is derived from his 16% stake in Amazon, the publicly traded Seattle firm he started. While other early Internet companies like AOL and Yahoo faded and ultimately died, Amazon's rise was relentless. In 2019, it had the highest value of any firm traded on global stock markets. An online marketplace for nearly every imaginable product, the company also ran Amazon Web Services (AWS), the cloud storage company, which was the main source of its profits, meager though they were.

Bezos's mantra was to "Get Big Fast," which meant that only after the company achieved a certain scale would profits follow. The company's soaring stock market value was mainly attributable to the rapid rise in its revenue, not its profits, since in most years it had not earned profits (Figure 7.3).[90] Amazon employed more than half a million workers in the United States.[91]

**FIGURE 7.3**     Amazon's Annual Revenues and Profits, 2014 to 2017

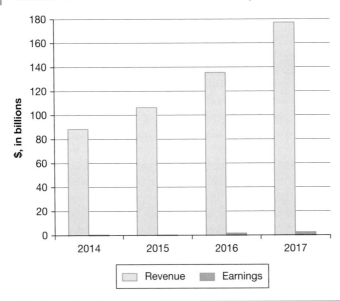

Bezos owns multiple homes in fashionable Seattle, Beverly Hills, and Manhattan neighborhoods, and also has large tracts of land in his native Texas. In 2013, he bought the *Washington Post* newspaper for $250 million. Though for many years it was reported that he drove a Honda Accord, he also possessed a $65 million Gulfstream private jet.

Unlike fellow billionaires Warren Buffett and Bill Gates, who promised to donate the majority of their money to charity, he was not known for his philanthropy. However, he did support his alma mater, Princeton University; the University of Washington; employment training; a homeless shelter; and cancer research in Seattle.[92]

## Pushing Hard

Bezos has pushed himself very hard. In 2015, an exposé in *The New York Times* described the work culture at Amazon as brutal and nearly Darwinian in nature. According to *The New York Times*, employees were instructed to discard "poor habits" they had acquired at prior jobs, and when they "hit the wall" from the unrelenting pressure, they were supposed to "climb the wall." They have to sign lengthy confidentiality agreements, their behavior is continuously monitored and measured, and they are incited to rip apart one another's ideas and work late into the night, with the expectation that the emails received after midnight will be answered then.

Turnover is high at Amazon, and many employees have refused to stick with the system. They have had to send secret complaints about peers to supervisors with sample texts to convey concerns about peers who were not completing their tasks or being inflexible. Those with illnesses or other personal issues sometimes have received unfavorable evaluations and felt compelled to leave.

Other companies have done away with the practice of "rank and yank," as it often ended in the termination of talented people to meet quotas, but team members at Amazon are regularly rated and those at the bottom released. Many believe the competition-and-elimination system to be biased against women. Unlike other tech companies, there were no women in the top leadership team as of 2015. Balancing raising children with the demands of the job is difficult.[93]

Yet many employees have thrived in this atmosphere. They loved that Amazon is willing to embrace risk and that relatively junior employees can make important contributions and advance quickly. Everyone's ideas, even those who are most senior in the company, are subject to serious criticism. Some employees consider the company to be an ideal meritocracy. *The New York Times* article cited above quotes Susan Harker, Amazon's top recruiter, as saying that Amazon is "shooting for the moon," implying that Amazon was not the right place for a person of limited ambition and mediocre talent or commitment. The bias is for "action" and for people who have "big" ideas. Apparently Amazon is meant only for an elite corps of driven white-collar workers.[94]

## Blue-Collar Workers

Bezos has strived to establish a hard-driving culture throughout the company and not only among its white-collar employees. As a result, the company requires as much of its blue-collar workers, who fulfill orders in its warehouses, as it does of white-collar workers. Legendary is the story that workers in an eastern Pennsylvania warehouse toiled in more than 100 °F temperatures in 2011, and when they collapsed from the intense temperatures, waiting ambulances were there to take them away to a hospital. Only after being criticized in a local newspaper did the company agree to install air-conditioning.

The company is data-driven in all that it does, including blue-collar working conditions. Very detailed metrics control its relationship with the workers in the same way that they dictate relationships with their customers. The warehouses monitor employees with sophisticated electronic systems to guarantee that they pack enough boxes every hour. Blue-collar employees are subject to intensive reviews and are held accountable by the numbers.[95]

Since its founding, Amazon had successfully fended off any hint of employee unionization. If workers show signs of unionizing, it might shut down a facility and lay them off rather than allow them to form a union. In Europe, the lack of unionization has been less tolerated than it has been in the United States. German, Polish, and Spanish workers have participated in demonstrations and labor strikes to draw awareness to their lack of rights, their low compensation, and the unsatisfactory working conditions they are convinced prevail in Amazon warehouses.

Amazon has been adamant and maintained that strikes will not affect the fulfillment of customers' orders. It has presented itself as being "a fair and responsible employer" that maintains "an open and direct dialogue with associates." It provides "good jobs with highly competitive pay, full benefits, and

*(Continued)*

(Continued)

innovative training programs." According to the company, its working conditions were both safe and positive.[96]

## Sanders's Criticism

Democratic presidential candidate Bernie Sanders sees the situation very differently. He criticized the company during his 2016 presidential campaign for the way in which it treats its workers. He brought attention to the fact that many were poorly paid and subject to unsafe working conditions. He introduced a bill in the U.S. Senate called the Stop Bad Employers by Zeroing Out Subsidies Act, the STOP BEZOS Act. The bill called for ending food stamps, Medicaid, and public housing benefits for employees of large companies such as Amazon and requiring the companies themselves to provide those benefits to its employees instead.[97]

Amazon reacted by raising its minimum wage to $15 for its U.S. employees.[98] However, it was discovered that one of its contractors, California Cartage Co., has continued to violate California state's minimum wage laws.

In his critique of the company, Sanders also pointed to incidents where workers had been injured or killed. The National Council for Occupational Safety and Health reported that seven workers have died since 2013. Then, in 2017, the Indiana Department of Labor started an investigation after a worker was fatally crushed when a forklift's lift fell on him while he was doing maintenance. In the same year, OSHA investigated the death of another warehouse worker in Pennsylvania who was crushed to death by a truck near the fulfillment center loading dock. It was alleged that the company refused to accept worker's compensation claims from employees who were injured on the job and that several workers who had refused the company's settlement offers had their jobs terminated, after which they confronted homelessness.

In one lawsuit against the company, workers claimed that during periods of excessive heat they were not given time to rest and that the company retaliated against those who complained. There were also stories of employees urinating in soda cans and water bottles rather than taking the time to walk to a restroom, because the company's break system allows them only 30 minutes for lunch and three other quarter-hour free-time periods during a shift. Amazon warehouses are mammoth, and the number of toilets tend to be few in number. Between scanning and packing an item, the distances that employees have to travel can be great, which means that workers often are seen running to meet their quotas. Due to long shifts and few breaks, many employees have complained of back pain, heart problems, and other aches and injuries. Reporters have found that employees who have needed emergency help due to health concerns could not call for help directly but instead had to contact Amazon security guards first, resulting in delays that could cost them their lives. The company has also subjected workers to demeaning and overly time-consuming security checks without pay so they did not steal goods from the company.[99]

## Amazon's Response

On its blog, Amazon has declared that such criticisms about low pay and poor workplace are "inaccurate and misleading." The Vice President of North American Operations has maintained that the company has "goals for employees in regards to performance metrics," and a team regularly examines the metrics to ensure that they are "safe, fair, and attainable." Amazon announced that its workers already earning $15 an hour would get raises of $1 per hour. Additionally, it introduced a cash bonus of $1,500 to $3,000 for tenure milestones when workers reach 5, 10, 15, and 20 years with the company. Furthermore, Amazon has indicated that workers with good attendance in the month of December—the busiest month of the year—would be eligible to receive an extra $100 bonus. As noted in the chapter, the federal minimum wage currently is $7.25 per hour.

Amazon has proclaimed that ensuring safety is its "number one priority." It has "safety metrics and audits" integrated into every program, and it expects continuous improvements in safety results through better equipment, standards, training, coaching, reporting, and systems to track and audit progress. Nonetheless, former employees continue to say that they sometimes find human waste in trash cans because workers feel that they cannot take the time to go to the bathroom. They hold that the focus on efficiency makes them feel like "robots" who are expected to do only one thing, and do it very quickly. The company has continually dismissed such reports as "unsubstantiated anecdotes."[100]

Amazon continues to rely as much as it can on automation to reduce costs. While its warehouses already are highly automated and are emulated by other companies for their efficiency, the company has been considering going even further. For example, it has considered having employees wear wristbands to track their movements and nudge them with vibrations if they are working in ways that are inefficient or dangerous.[101]

Work practices such as these often are distressing to workers, and some have been heard to say that they have had to pack boxes for the richest man in the world but that his wealth is not making their lives any better. As the company continues to rapidly grow its business, erecting warehouses around the world to keep pace with demand, it seems obvious

that it will have to come up with new solutions to such problems—or will it?

Use the weight-of-reasons framework to analyze Amazon's dilemma.

- What is the ethical issue the company is facing?
- What do you consider to be the relevant facts?
- What options does the company have for addressing the issue, and what are the expected consequences of pursuing these options?
- What principles should it apply, and what actions should it take in the short term and long term to deal with its dilemmas?
- And what should Amazon learn from its experience?

In addressing these questions, focus on Amazon's legal and ethical duties to its employees. Is the company in compliance with relevant laws? What duties, if any, does it have to go "beyond compliance?" What actions should it take to meet these duties? Are concepts such as moral minimums, CSR, corporate citizenship, and sustainability useful for understanding how Amazon should move forward?

## SUMMARY AND CONCLUSION

This chapter has focused on the relationship between ethics and the law. It has reviewed the laws that pertain to firms' obligations to various stakeholder groups. A major implication of this chapter is that managers must take existing laws and policies into consideration when applying the weight-of-reasons framework. Laws are an input into the decision-making process. In some cases, they specify exactly the actions that should be taken.

However, while it is important for managers to follow the law except in very exceptional circumstances, following the law often does not equate to

acting ethically. The laws cannot possibly capture the full range of ethical values to which a corporation should conform. Managers will always be called on to make judgments about right and wrong even after they have consulted the law.

Just following the law is likely to fall short from an ethical perspective. To act ethically, managers must go "beyond compliance." This chapter described various ways of going beyond compliance, including adhering to moral minimums, CSR, corporate citizenship, and sustainable business that you should take into account.

## KEY TERMS AND CONCEPTS

Anthropocene  218
Assumption of risk  212
At-will employment  208
Cartel  213
Civil disobedience  222
Collusion  213
Contributory negligence  211
Corporate citizenship  224
Corporate governance  203
Corporate social
  responsibility (CSR)  223
Fiduciary duty  203
Foreseeability of harm  211
Informed consent  212

Just cause  208
Liability  211
Managerial capitalism  204
Mergers and acquisitions  213
Moral minimums  223
Negligence  211
Planetary boundaries  218
Primary stakeholders  201
Principal–agent problem  204
Principal–agent relationship  203
Privity of contract  211
Proximate cause  211
Residual claimant  203
Right to be heard  213

Right to be informed  212
Right to choose  213
Right to privacy  214
Right to safe products and
  services  212
Secondary stakeholders  202
Shareholder capitalism  205
Shareholder  203
Stakeholder  201
Strict liability  212
Sustainable business  225
Tort law  211

## CASES RELATED TO THE READING

Consider reading the following cases found in Chapter 10 that apply to the concepts presented in this chapter:

- BP: The Big Oil Spill: What Went Wrong?
- Dow–DuPont: The Bhopal Disaster
- Facebook: Privacy and the Public Interest
- Google: Doing No Harm
- Mallinckrodt: The Opioid Crisis
- Merck and J&J: Problems With Consumer Safety
- VW: Dieselgate
- Walmart: Sustainability
- Whole Foods: Conscious Capitalism

## CASE APPLICATIONS

For each of these cases, use the weight-of-reasons framework to make a decision that addresses the dilemma. Think about what the issue is (Step 1 of the framework), what the facts are (Step 2), what your action alternatives are (Step 3), what the possible consequences of those actions will be (Step 4), and what principles matter to you in deciding (Step 5). The action alternatives you consider should be short (Step 6) and long (Step 7) term, and you should consider what are the relevant lessons an organization should learn from dealing with the dilemma (Step 8). Include in your deliberation what the law requires you to do as well as alternatives that go beyond compliance. Use both/and thinking and moral imagination in generating and choosing the alternatives.

## Case 7.1: Unionizing Your Factory

You are a plant manager at a manufacturing company. Relationship between your management team and factory workers is generally harmonious. You and the other managers have worked your way up through the company so you understand the demands of your workers' jobs, and you have done your best to create a culture of togetherness at the plant.

While in the break room one afternoon, you find out that one of the line workers, Mary Chan, has started talking to other employees about unionizing the factory. She wants to start an organizing committee to discuss labor issues at the plant and figure out how the plant's workers could start or join a union. You have nothing against unions, but you don't understand why one would be necessary at your plant. You are worried that having a union would create a lot of tension in the plant and create a more adversarial environment that would ultimately result in lower productivity and profits.

You feel really disappointed because everyone seemed so happy. You are thinking about inviting Mary out to lunch to dissuade her from her union effort. Should you do this? If so, what should you say to Mary?

## Case 7.2: Paying Workers Under the Table

Imagine again that you are the plant manager in the unionizing your factory case. Your factory is located in a declining industrial city where jobs are hard to come by. The state in which the plant is located has a minimum wage of $15 per hour.

You need to hire some workers and know that there are plenty of people in the local workforce who would work for much less than the minimum wage. It occurs to you that you could hire these people "under the table", that is, secretly, without putting them on your official payroll and accounting for their salaries in the company's financial statements. The company would save money, and the workers would have jobs. Should you do it? Why or why not?

## Case 7.3: Real Estate Deal

You live in a city where real estate prices are skyrocketing. Home prices and rental prices are expected to go up for the foreseeable future. You decide to borrow money and buy an apartment building. Your plan is to evict the building's elderly and low-income residents, many of whom have lived there for a long time; refurbish the building; and then rent the apartments out at a higher price to more well-to-do people who have just moved to the city to take high-paying jobs.

Your plan is legal according to local law. Based on the frameworks described in Chapter 2, is it also ethical? Speculate about how you might develop a plan that would enable you to take advantage of the financial opportunity you see while also accounting for the welfare of those who would be evicted.

## Case 7.4: Working With ICE[102]

You work at the front desk of a hotel in a small town near the border between the United States and Mexico. When you check in guests, you ask them to show identification and provide the make, model, and license plate numbers of their cars. You guarantee your customers that you will protect their privacy.

One evening, an agent from the U.S. Immigration and Customs Enforcement (ICE) comes to the hotel. He asks you to provide the names of all guests who have Hispanic surnames and the license plate numbers of their cars. The U.S. Supreme Court has held that hotel operators are not required to provide such information but can do so voluntarily. You go ahead and provide the information.[103]

A few weeks later, you are talking with one of your friends in local law enforcement. She tells you based on credible information that ICE has used the information you gave it to track down the hotel's guests and question them about whether they have entered the United States lawfully (i.e., entered at an authorized check point and gone through the required screening). Based on their answers and failure to provide the required proof, some of these guests have been detained or deported to Mexico.

Did you do the right thing in handing over information to the ICE? If you were in hotel management, what policy should you develop to address these situations?

# NOTES

1. There is a robust debate among scholars about whether some secondary stakeholders such as the public and natural environment actually should count as stakeholders. While some consider them stakeholders because they can impact and be affected by the firm, others reserve stakeholder status for those actors that have reciprocal obligations with the firm. See, for example, Phillips, R. (2003). *Stakeholder theory and organizational ethics*. San Francisco, CA: Berrett-Koehler.

2. Merchant, B. (2017, June 18). Life and death in Apple's forbidden city. *The Guardian*. Retrieved from https://www.theguardian.com/technology/2017/jun/18/foxconn-life-death-forbidden-city-longhua-suicide-apple-iphone-brian-merchant-one-device-extract. Based on B. Merchant: *The one device: The secret history of the iPhone. 2017*. London, UK: Bantam Press; Heffernan, M. (2013, August 7). *What happened after the Foxconn suicides*. Retrieved from https://www.cbsnews.com/news/what-happened-after-the-foxconn-suicides/; Barboza, D. (2010, June 6). After suicides, scrutiny of China's grim factories. *The New York Times*. Retrieved from https://www.nytimes.com/2010/06/07/business/global/07suicide.html

3. Stout, L. (2012). *The shareholder value myth: How putting shareholders first harms investors, corporations, and the public*. San Francisco, CA: Berrett-Koehler.

4. Sharfman, B. S. (2017). *The importance of the business judgment rule*. Cambridge, MA: Harvard Law School Forum on Corporate Governance and Financial Regulation.

5. Berle, A., & Means, G. (1932). *The modern corporation and private property*. New York, NY: Macmillan.

6. Stout (2012).

7. Stout (2012); Heracleous, L., & Lan, L. (2010, April). The myth of shareholder capitalism. *Harvard Business Review*. Reviewed from https://hbr.org/2010/04/the-myth-of-shareholder-capitalism; Bower, J. L., & Paine, L. S. (2017, May–June). The error at the heart of corporate leadership. *Harvard Business Review*. Retrieved from https://hbr.org/2017/05/managing-for-the-long-term#the-error-at-the-heart-of-corporate-leadership

8. Public Law 107-204, 116 Statute 745, 2002. Commonly referred to as the Sarbanes–Oxley Act.

9. McCarthy, N. (2017). *Costco named America's Best Employer 2017*. Retrieved from https://www.forbes.com/sites/niallmccarthy/2017/05/10/costco-named-americas-best-employer-2017-infographic/#4bd84f416022

10. Stone, B. (2013, June 7). Costco CEO Craig Jelinek leads the cheapest and happiest company in the world. *Bloomberg*. Retrieved from https://www.bloomberg.com/news/articles/2013-06-06/costco-ceo-craig-jelinek-leads-the-cheapest-happiest

-company-in-the-world; LeCain, E. (2014, April 22). *A revolution in retail: Treat workers well to boost profits*. Retrieved from https://www.huffingtonpost.com/eleanor-lecain/a-revolution-in-retail-tr_b_4823429.html; Ton, Z. (2014). *The good jobs strategy: How the smartest companies invest in employees to lower costs & boost profits*. New York, NY: Houghton Mifflin Harcourt.

11.  U.S. Department of Labor. (n.d.). *About OSHA*. Retrieved from https://www.osha.gov/about.html

12.  Aristotle. (2009). *The Nicomachean ethics* (Oxford World's Classics) (W. D. Ross, Trans. & L. Brown, Ed.). Oxford, UK: Oxford University Press.

13.  Office of Labor Standards. (n.d.). *Minimum wage ordinance*. Retrieved from https://www.seattle.gov/laborstandards/ordinances/minimum-wage

14.  For a recent synopsis of this debate, see Weissmann, J. (2019, February 25). How I learned to stop worrying and maybe love the minimum wage. *Slate*. Retrieved from https://slate.com/business/2019/02/new-research-15-dollar-minimum-wage-good-for-workers.html. Also see Millsap, A. (2018, September 28). *How higher minimum wages impact employment*. Retrieved from https://www.forbes.com/sites/adammillsap/2018/09/28/how-higher-minimum-wages-impact-employment/#6cb6c3071e7d. For recent studies, see Beaudry, P., Green, D. A., & Sand, B. M. (2018). In search of labor demand. *American Economic Review, 108*, 2714–2757; also see Congress of the United States, Congressional Budget Office. (2014). The effects of a minimum-wage increase on employment and family income. Retrieved from http://www.cbo.gov/sites/default/files/cbofiles/attachments/44995-MinimumWage.pdf

15.  The Treaty of Detroit provides an example of a long-term agreement between companies and workers. See Barnard, J. (1983). *Walter Reuther and the rise of the auto workers*. Boston, MA: Little, Brown.

16.  Guerin, L. (n.d.). *Employment at will: What does it mean?* Retrieved from https://www.nolo.com/legal-encyclopedia/employment-at-will-definition-30022.html

17.  Verkerke, J. H. (2009). Discharge. In K. G. Dau-Schmidt, S. D. Harris, & O. Lobel (Eds.), *Labor and employment law and economics: Vol. 2. Encyclopedia of law and economics* (2nd ed., pp. 447–479). Northampton, UK: Edward Elgar.

18.  U.S. Equal Employment Opportunity Commission. (n.d.). *Discrimination by type*. Retrieved from https://www.eeoc.gov/laws/types/index.cfm

19.  Center for Public Integrity. (2019, February 25). *Despite protections, most workers who face discrimination are on their own*. Retrieved from https://publicintegrity.org/workers-rights/workplace-inequities/injustice-at-work/workplace-discrimination-cases/; Jameel, M., & Yerardi, J. (2019, February 28). *Workplace discrimination is illegal but our data show it's still a huge problem*. Retrieved from Vox. https://www.vox.com/policy-and-politics/2019/2/28/18241973workplace-discrimination-cpi-investigation-eeoc

20.  UN Human Rights Office of the High Commissioner. (1949). *Right to Organise and Collective Bargaining Convention, 1949*. Retrieved from https://www.ohchr.org/EN/ProfessionalInterest/Pages/RightToOrganise.aspx

21.  Polaris. (n.d.). *Human trafficking*. Retrieved from https://polarisproject.org/human-trafficking

22.  Food Empowerment Project. (n.d.). *Slavery in the US*. Retrieved from http://www.foodispower.org/slavery-in-the-us/; Vanden Heuvel, K. (2010, March 29). The nation: Florida's modern slavery . . . The museum. *NPR*. Retrieved from http://www.npr.org/templates/story/story.php?storyId=125296794; U.S. District Court for the Northern District of Florida Gainesville Division. Federal Indictment. *United States of America v Carline Ceneus*. (2010). Retrieved from https://assets.documentcloud.org/documents/2177327/carline-hot-pickers-superceding-indictment.txt; Watanabe, T. (2010, September 4). Federal grand jury indicts associates of Beverly Hills firm in human-trafficking case. *Los Angeles Times*. Retrieved from https://www.latimes.com/archives/la-xpm-2010-sep-04-la-me-0904-human-trafficking-20100904-story.html

23.  Adapted from Marcus, A. A., & Kaiser, S. (2006). *Managing beyond compliance: The ethical and legal dimensions of corporate responsibility*. Northbrook, IL: Northcoast.

24.  New York Court of Appeals. (1916). *MacPherson v. Buick Motor Company*. 111 N.E. 1050. Retrieved from https://www.courtlistener.com/opinion/3616523/macpherson-v-buick-motor-co/

25. Cipollone v. Liggett Group, 505 U.S. 504 (1992). Retrieved from https://supreme.justia.com/cases/federal/us/505/504/

26. Wrongful Death Law. (2015, July 20). *Five deaths that occurred due to defective products*. Retrieved from https://www.wrongfuldeathcaselaw.com/five-defective-products/

27. U.S. Consumer Product Safety Commission. (n.d.-b). *Statutes*. Retrieved from https://www.cpsc.gov/Regulations-Laws--Standards/Statutes/#consumer-product-safety-act-cpsa

28. U.S. Consumer Product Safety Commission. (n.d.-a). *About CPSC*. Retrieved from https://www.cpsc.gov/About-CPSC

29. U.S. Consumer Product Safety Commission. (n.d.-b).

30. U.S. Food and Drug Administration. (2018). *What we do*. Retrieved from https://www.fda.gov/about-fda/what-we-do

31. American Medical Association. (n.d.). *Informed consent*. Retrieved from https://www.ama-assn.org/delivering-care/ethics/informed-consent

32. Eaglesham, J. (2011, February 9). Warning shot on financial protection. *The Wall Street Journal*. Retrieved from https://www.wsj.com/articles/SB10001424052748703507804576130370862263258

33. The White House President Barack Obama. (2012, January 4). *Consumer Financial Protection Bureau 101: Why we need a consumer watchdog*. Retrieved from https://obamawhitehouse.archives.gov/blog/2012/01/04/consumer-financial-protection-bureau-101-why-we-need-consumer-watchdog

34. Confessore, N. (2019, April 16). Mick Mulvaney's master class in destroying a bureaucracy from within. *The New York Times Magazine*. Retrieved from https://www.nytimes.com/2019/04/16/magazine/consumer-financial-protection-bureau-trump.html

35. U.S. Federal Trade Commission. (n.d.-b). *About the FTC*. Retrieved from https://www.ftc.gov/about-ftc

36. U.S. Federal Trade Commission. (n.d.-c). *Bureaus and offices*. Retrieved from https://www.ftc.gov/about-ftc/bureaus-offices

37. Hughes, C. (2019, May 9). It's time to break up Facebook. *The New York Times*. Retrieved from https://www.nytimes.com/2019/05/09/opinion/sunday/chris-hughes-facebook-zuckerberg.html; Buck, M., & Vaheesan, S. (2019, March 6). Trump's big tech bluster. *The New York Times*. Retrieved from https://www.nytimes.com/2019/03/06/opinion/trump-antitrust-laws.html

38. In this context, we are not referring to the "right to be heard" as defined in the United Nations Convention on the Rights of the Child or to the legal principle that all participants in legal proceedings should be able to argue and present evidence in court.

39. U.S. Federal Trade Commission. (n.d.-a). *About the Bureau of Consumer Protection*. Retrieved from https://www.ftc.gov/about-ftc/bureaus-offices/bureau-consumer-protection/about-bureau-consumer-protection

40. Gordon, A. (2015, July 6). *You have the right to be heard*. Retrieved from https://www.consumerfinance.gov/about-us/blog/you-have-the-right-to-be-heard/

41. Warren, S. D., & Brandeis, L. D. (1890, December 15). The right to privacy. *Harvard Law Review*. Retrieved from http://faculty.uml.edu/sgallagher/Brandeisprivacy.htm

42. Onn, Y., & Team of 14 authors. (2005). *Privacy in the digital environment* (N. Elkin-Koren & M. Birnhack, Eds.). Haifa, Israel: Haifa Center for Law & Technology.

43. Fleishman, G. (2018, September 8). *Equifax data breach one year later: Obvious errors and no real changes, new report says*. Retrieved from http://fortune.com/2018/09/07/equifax-data-breach-one-year-anniversary/; CBS News. (2018, September 11). *Equifax data breach was a year ago: What has DC done about it?* Retrieved from https://www.cbsnews.com/news/equifax-data-breach-was-a-year-ago-what-has-dc-done-about-it/; U.S. Federal Trade Commission. (2019, July). *The Equifax data breach*. Retrieved from https://www.ftc.gov/equifax-data-breach

44. Korosec, K. (2018, March 21). *This is the personal data that Facebook collects—and sometimes sells*. Retrieved from http://fortune.com/2018/03/21/facebook-personal-data-cambridge-analytica/

45. Kharpal, A. (2018, May 25). *Everything you need to know about a new EU data law that could shake up big US tech*. Retrieved from https://www.cnbc.com/2018/03/30/gdpr-everything-you-need-to-know.html; EU GDPR.org. (n.d.). *The EU General Data Protection Regulation (GDPR) is the most*

*important change in data privacy regulation in 20 years*. Retrieved from https://eugdpr.org/

46. Confessore, N. (2018, August 14). The unlikely activists who took on Silicon Valley—and won. *The New York Times*. Retrieved from https://www.nytimes.com/2018/08/14/magazine/facebook-google-privacy-data.html; Burt, A. (2018, August 21). States are leading the way on data privacy. *The Hill*. Retrieved from https://thehill.com/opinion/technology/402775-states-are-leading-the-way-on-data-privacy

47. United Nations. (n.d.). *Universal Declaration of Human Rights*. Retrieved from https://www.un.org/en/universal-declaration-human-rights/

48. Aumann, T. (2014, July 9). *Supply Chain 101: The journey of a T-shirt*. Retrieved from https://www.slideshare.net/TimAumann/supply-chain-101-journey-of-a-tshirt

49. Manik, J. A., & Yardley, J. (2013, April 24). Building collapse in Bangladesh leaves scores dead. *The New York Times*. Retrieved from https://www.nytimes.com/2013/04/25/world/asia/bangladesh-building-collapse.html; Thomas, D. (2018, April 24). Why won't we learn from the survivors of the Rana Plaza disaster? *The New York Times*. Retrieved from https://www.nytimes.com/2018/04/24/style/survivors-of-rana-plaza-disaster.html

50. Bergman, D., & Blair, D. (2013, May 3). Bangladesh Rana Plaza architect says building was never meant for factories. *The Telegraph*. Retrieved from https://www.telegraph.co.uk/news/worldnews/asia/bangladesh/10036546/Bangladesh-Rana-Plaza-architect-says-building-was-never-meant-for-factories.html; BBC News. (2013, May 3). *Power generators linked to Dhaka building collapse*. Retrieved from https://www.bbc.com/news/world-asia-22404461

51. Tipu, M. S. I. (2017, April 19). Rana Plaza collapse: Order on charge framing against Sohel Rana, others May 8. *Dhaka Tribune*. Retrieved from https://www.dhakatribune.com/bangladesh/court/2017/04/19/rana-plaza-charge-framing-may-8/

52. al-Mahmood, S. Z. (2013, April 27). Nexus of politics, corruption doomed Rana Plaza. *Dhaka Tribune*. Retrieved from https://web.archive.org/web/20160306015544/http://www.dhakatribune.com/politics/2013/apr/26/nexus-politics-corruption-doomed-rana-plaza

53. Greenhouse, S. (2013, May 14). As firms line up on factories, Wal-mart plans solo effort. *The New York Times*. Retrieved from https://www.nytimes.com/2013/05/15/business/six-retailers-join-bangladesh-factory-pact.html

54. Buss, T. F. (2001). The effect of state tax incentives on economic growth and firm location decisions: An overview of the literature. *Economic Development Quarterly, 15*, 90–105; Hayter, R. (1997). *The dynamics of industrial location: The factory, the firm and the production system*. New York, NY: Wiley; Luce, T. F. (1994). Local taxes, public services, and the intrametropolitan location of firms and households. *Public Finance Quarterly, 22*, 139–167; O'Mara, M. A. (1999). Strategic drivers of location decisions for information-age companies. *Journal of Real Estate Research, 17*, 365–386.

55. Rogers, C. L. (2013). How competition to attract businesses leads to economic losses for cities and states. *Scholars Strategy Network*. Retrieved from https://scholars.org/brief/how-competition-attract-businesses-leads-economic-losses-cities-and-states; Zaretsky, A. M. (1994). Are states giving away the store? Attracting jobs can be a costly venture. *Federal Reserve Bank of St. Louis*. Retrieved from https://www.stlouisfed.org/publications/regional-economist/january-1994/are-states-giving-away-the-store-attracting-jobs-can-be-a-costly-adventure; Berle and Means (1932).

56. Bienkowski, B. (2015, May 6). Poor communities bear greatest burden from fracking. *Scientific American*. Retrieved from https://www.scientificamerican.com/article/poor-communities-bear-greatest-burden-from-fracking/; Union of Concerned Scientists. (2015, Fall). *Fracking: Science, policy, and people*. Retrieved from https://www.ucsusa.org/center-science-and-democracy/bringing-science-critical-issues/fracking-science-policy-people

57. U.S. Geological Service. (n.d.). *Induced earthquakes*. Retrieved from https://earthquake.usgs.gov/research/induced/myths.php

58. Francis, M. (2015, June 18). This oil extraction process is causing earthquakes in Oklahoma. *Forbes*. Retrieved from https://www.forbes.com/sites/matthewfrancis/2015/06/18/oil-byproduct-practices-to-blame-for-oklahoma-earthquakes/#9ca90f012a10; Oskin, B. (2014, May 2). Fracking-linked earthquakes may strike far from wells. *Live Science*. Retrieved from https://www.livescience

.com/45322-fracking-wastewater-farther-earth
quakes.html

59. Day, M. (2018b, August 31). Mum's the word as Amazon nears one year anniversary of HQ2. *Seattle Times*. Retrieved from https://www.seattletimes.com/business/amazon/mums-the-word-as-amazon-nears-one-year-anniversary-of-hq2-quest/

60. Day, M. (2018c, November 13). Amazon shifts its sights to the East Coast; two new headquarters and a third site selected. *Seattle Times*. Retrieved from https://www.seattletimes.com/business/amazon/its-official-amazon-says-northern-virginia-new-york-will-get-headquarters-expansion/

61. Ibid.

62. Nickelsburg, M. (2018, November 7). *Urbanist Richard Florida on what splitting HQ2 means for cities: It never was about a second headquarters.* Retrieved from https://www.geekwire.com/2018/richard-florida-splitting-amazon-hq2-means-cities-never-second-headquarters/

63. Hawken, P., Lovins, A., & Lovins, H. (1999). *Natural capitalism: Creating the next industrial revolution.* New York, NY: Little, Brown; Daily, G. C. (1997). *Nature's services: Societal dependence on natural ecosystems.* Washington, DC: Island Press.

64. It should be noted, however, that leading geological bodies have not yet officially recognized the Anthropocene as a distinct period of geological time.

65. Zalasiewicz, J., Williams, M., Steffen, W., & Crutzen, P. (2010). The new world of the Anthropocene. *Environmental Science & Technology, 44,* 2228–2231; Crutzen, P. J., & Stoermer, E. F. (2000). The Anthropocene. *Global Change Newsletter, 41,* 17–18.

66. Steffen, W., Richardson, K., Rockström, J., Cornell, S. E., Fetzer, I., Bennett, E. M., . . . Sorlin, S. (2015). Planetary boundaries: Guiding human development on a changing planet. *Science, 347,* 1259855; Rockstrom, J., Steffen, W., Noone, K., Persson, A., Chapin, F. S., III, Lambin, E., . . . Foley, J. (2009). Planetary boundaries: The safe operating space for humanity. *Ecology and Society, 14,* 32.

67. U.S. Environmental Protection Agency. (n.d.-a). *Overview of the Clean Air Act and air pollution.* Retrieved from https://www.epa.gov/clean-air-act-overview

68. U.S. Environmental Protection Agency. (n.d.-c). *Summary of the Clean Water Act.* Retrieved from https://www.epa.gov/laws-regulations/summary-clean-water-act

69. U.S. Environmental Protection Agency. (n.d.-b). *Safe Drinking Water Act* (SDWA). Retrieved from https://www.epa.gov/sdwa

70. U.S. Environmental Protection Agency. (n.d.-e). *Summary of the Resource Conservation and Recover Act.* Retrieved from https://www.epa.gov/laws-regulations/summary-resource-conservation-and-recovery-act

71. U.S. Environmental Protection Agency. (n.d.-d). *Summary of the Comprehensive Environmental Response Compensation and Liability Act* (Superfund). Retrieved from https://www.epa.gov/laws-regulations/summary-comprehensive-environmental-response-compensation-and-liability-act

72. U.S. Environmental Protection Agency. (n.d.-f). *Summary of the Toxic Substances Control Act.* Retrieved from https://www.epa.gov/laws-regulations/summary-toxic-substances-control-act

73. U.S. Fish and Wildlife Service. (n.d.). *Endangered Species Act: Overview.* Retrieved from https://www.fws.gov/endangered/laws-policies/

74. Public Employees for Environmental Responsibility. (n.d.). *Criminal enforcement collapse at EPA.* Retrieved from https://www.peer.org/news/press-releases/criminal-enforcement-collapse-at-epa.html

75. The Week Staff. (2019, January 12). How Trump is redefining the EPA. *The Week.* Retrieved from https://theweek.com/articles/816875/how-trump-redefining-epa

76. Cobb, J. C. (2015, September 18). One of American history's worst laws was passed 165 years ago. *Time.*

77. Intergovernmental Panel on Climate Change. (2018). Summary for policymakers. In V. Masson-Delmotte, P. Zhai, H. O. Pörtner, D. Roberts, J. Skea, P. R. Shukla, . . . T. Waterfield (Eds.), *Global warming of 1.5°C: An IPCC Special Report on the impacts of global warming of 1.5°C above pre-industrial levels and related global greenhouse gas emission pathways, in the context of strengthening the global response to the threat of climate change, sustainable development, and efforts to eradicate poverty.* Geneva, Switzerland: World Meteorological Organization. Retrieved from https://report.ipcc.ch/sr15/pdf/sr15_spm_final.pdf; Marlon, J., Howe, P.,

Mildenberger, M., Leiserowitz, A., & Wang, X. (2018). *Yale climate opinion maps 2018*. Retrieved from http://climatecommunication.yale.edu/visualizations -data/ycom-us-2018/?est=happening&type=value& geo=county

78. Lustgarten, A. (2018, November 20). Palm oil was supposed to help save the planet. Instead it unleashed a catastrophe. *The New York Times*. Retrieved from https://www.nytimes.com/2018/11/20/magazine/ palm-oil-borneo-climate-catastrophe.html?login= smartlock&auth=login-smartlock

79. Levy, D. L., & Kaplan, R. (2008). Corporate social responsibility and theories of global governance: Strategic contestation in global issue arenas. In A. Crane, A. McWilliams, D. Matten, J. Moon, & D. S. Siegel (Eds.), *The Oxford handbook of corporate social responsibility* (pp. 432–451). New York, NY: Oxford University Press.

80. Matten, D., & Crane, A. (2005). Corporate citizenship: Toward an extended theoretical conceptualization. *Academy of Management Review, 30*(1), 166–179.

81. Scherer, A. G., & Palazzo, G. (2011). The new political role of business in a globalized world: A review of a new perspective on CSR and its implications for the firm, governance, and democracy. *Journal of Management Studies, 48*, 899–931.

82. Ibid.

83. World Commission on Environment and Development. (1987). *Our common future: Brundtland Report*. Oxford, UK: Oxford University Press.

84. Global Reporting Initiative. (2016). *Consolidated set of GRI sustainability reporting standards*. Retrieved from https://www.globalreporting.org/ standards/gri-standards-download-center/

85. Global Reporting Initiative. (n.d.). *About GRI*. https://www.globalreporting.org/information/about -gri/Pages/default.aspx

86. Hart, S. L. (2005). *Capitalism at the crossroads: The unlimited business opportunities in solving the world's most difficult problems*. Upper Saddle River, NJ: Prentice Hall; Prahalad, C. K. (2006). *The fortune at the bottom of the pyramid: Eradicating poverty through profits*. Philadelphia, PA: Wharton School.

87. B Lab. (n.d.-a). *Benefit corporation*. Retrieved from http://benefitcorp.net/

88. B Lab. (n.d.-b). *Homepage*. Retrieved from https:// bcorporation.net/

89. Frank, R. (2018, July 16). *Jeff Bezos is now the richest man in modern history*. Retrieved from https:// www.cnbc.com/2018/07/16/jeff-bezos-is-now-the -richest-man-in-modern-history.html

90. Carr, F. (2018, February 15). *Amazon is now more valuable than Microsoft and only 2 other companies are worth more*. Retrieved from http:// fortune.com/2018/02/15/amazon-microsoft-third -most-valuable-company/

91. Bort, J. (2017, October 27). Jeff Bezos's Amazon already employs over half a million people, and it plans to hire thousands more. *Inc*. Retrieved from https://www.inc.com/business-insider/jeff-bezos -amazon-employees-hiring-spree-second-largest -company-behind-walmart.html

92. Ginsberg, L. (2017, July 27). *How Jeff Bezos, now the richest person in the world, spends his billions*. Retrieved from https://www.cnbc.com/2017/07/27/how -richest-man-alive-jeff-bezos-spends-his-billions.html

93. Kantor, J., & Streitfeld, D. (2015, August 15). *Inside Amazon: Wrestling big ideas in a bruising workplace*. Retrieved from https://www.nytimes.com/ 2015/08/16/technology/inside-amazon-wrestling -big-ideas-in-a-bruising-workplace.html

94. Ibid.

95. Kantor and Streitfeld (2015); Hartmans, A. (2018, October 9). I took a rare look inside one of Amazon's giant warehouses right before the company hiked workers' wages: Here's what I saw. *Business Insider*. Retrieved from http://www.businessinsider .com/amazon-warehouse-tour-in-kent-washington -pictures-2018-10#employees-will-take-a-bin-off -the-belt-scan-it-and-unpack-it-then-the-system -will-tell-them-what-type-of-box-they-need-an -employee-will-assemble-the-correct-box-fill-it-and -send-it-on-its-way-10

96. Saez, A. (2018, April 13). *Advantages and disadvantage of labor unions*. Retrieved from https://yourbusiness.azcentral.com/advantages -disadvantage-labor-unions-3553.html; Sainato, M. (2018a, July 8). Exploited Amazon workers need a union. When will they get one? *The Guardian*. Retrieved from https://www.theguardian.com/ commentisfree/2018/jul/08/amazon-jeff-bezos -unionize-working-conditions

97.  Lieber, C. (2018a, August 30). Amazon and Bernie Sanders are sparring over warehouse workers' treatment. *Vox*. Retrieved from https://www.vox.com/2018/8/30/17797786/amazon-warehouse-conditions-bernie-sanders; Bhattarai, A. (2018, September 5). *Bernie Sanders introduces "Stop Bezos Act."* Retrieved from https://www.washingtonpost.com/business/2018/09/05/bernie-sanders-introduces-stop-bezos-act-senate/?utm_term=.cf6ce925c01b

98.  Chappell, B., & Wamsley, L. (2018, October 2). Amazon sets $15 minimum wage for employees, including temps. *NPR*. Retrieved from https://www.npr.org/2018/10/02/653597466/amazon-sets-15-minimum-wage-for-u-s-employees-including-.temps

99.  For sources regarding poor conditions at Amazon warehouses, see Eidelson, J. (2018, June 22). Amazon contractor settles warehouse conditions lawsuit. *Bloomberg*. Retrieved from http://www.bloomberg.com/news/articles/2018-06-22/amazon-contractor-settles-warehouse-conditions-lawsuit; Ghosh, S. (2018, April 16). Undercover author finds Amazon warehouse workers in UK "peed in bottles" over fears of being punished for taking a break. *Business Insider*. Retrieved from https://www.businessinsider.com/amazon-warehouse-workers-have-to-pee-into-bottles-2018-4; Green, D. (2018, April 28). Seven people have died on the job in Amazon's warehouses since 2014: Here's what happened. *Business Insider*. Retrieved from https://www.businessinsider.com/amazon-warehouse-safety-and-deaths-2018-4; Hawkins, J., & Fortson, L. (2016, January 12). Amazon fulfillment center receives $7K fine, hazard alert letters after OSHA investigates workplace safety complaint. *OSHA*. Retrieved from http://www.osha.gov/news/newsreleases/region3/01122016; Jamieson, D. (2013, May 8). How miserable is it working in an Amazon warehouse? *Huffington Post*. Retrieved from https://www.huffingtonpost.com/2013/05/08/amazon-warehouse-lawsuit-security-checkpoints_n_3232644.html; Jamieson, D. (n.d.). The life and death of an Amazon warehouse temp. *Huffington Post*. Retrieved from https://highline.huffingtonpost.com/articles/en/life-and-death-amazon-temp/; Liao, S. (2018, April 16).

Amazon warehouse workers skip bathroom breaks to keep their jobs, says report. *Verge*. Retrieved from http://www.theverge.com/2018/4/16/17243026/amazon-warehouse-jobs-worker-conditions-bathroom-breaks; Lieber, C. (2018b, November 23). Inside an Amazon warehouse on Black Friday. *Vox*. Retrieved from https://www.vox.com/the-goods/2018/11/20/18103516/black-friday-cyber-monday-amazon-fulfillment-center; National Council for Occupational Safety and Health. (2018, April 25). *National COSH announces "Dirty Dozen" employers*. Retrieved from http://www.coshnetwork.org/national-cosh-announces-"dirty-dozen"-employers-0; Rey, J. D. (2017, November 10). Amazon faces fines following the death of a warehouse worker, the second in the same month. *CNBC*. Retrieved from http://www.cnbc.com/2017/11/10/amazon-fined-in-indiana-over-death-of-worker-phillip-terry.html; Sainato, M. (2018b, July 30). Accidents at Amazon: Workers left to suffer after warehouse injuries. *The Guardian*. Retrieved from http://www.theguardian.com/technology/2018/jul/30/accidents-at-amazon-workers-left-to-suffer-after-warehouse-injuries; and Soper, S. (2018, October 10). Amazon pledges to compensate its warehouse workers more following criticism. *Time*. Retrieved from http://time.com/5421061/amazon-warehouse-workers-more-pay/.

100. For sources regarding Amazon's response to criticism, see Day, M. (2018a, August 29). Amazon fires back at Bernie Sanders' "inaccurate" claims about its warehouse working conditions. *Seattle Times*. Retrieved from http://www.seattletimes.com/business/amazon/amazon-fires-back-at-bernie-sanders-inaccurate-claims-about-its-warehouse-working-conditions/; Long, H. (2018, October 10). Amazon tells Bernie Sanders: All workers will earn more despite bonuses and stock grants going away. *The Washington Post*. Retrieved from http://www.washingtonpost.com/business/2018/10/10/amazon-tells-bernie-sanders-all-workers-will-earn-more-despite-bonuses-stock-grants-going-away/?noredirect=on&utm_term=.b9ade143ba3f, and Soper, T. (2018, August 25). Amazon pays employees to tweet about how much they like working inside fulfillment centers. *Geekwire*. Retrieved from http://www.geekwire.com/2018/

amazon-pays-employees-tweet-much-like-working-inside-fulfillment-centers/

101.  Yeginsu, C. (2018, February 1). If workers slack off, the wristband will know. (And Amazon has a patent for it.) *The New York Times*. Retrieved from https://www.nytimes.com/2018/02/01/technology/amazon-wristband-tracking-privacy.html

102.  Based on similar cases involving Motel 6. See Jacobs, J. (2018, November 6). Motel 6 agrees to pay $8.9 million to settle claims it helped ICE arrest guests. *The New York Times*. Retrieved from https://www.nytimes.com/2018/11/06/us/motel-6-lawsuit-ice-settlement.html and Farzan, A. N., & Flaherty, J. (2017, September 13). Attorneys suspect Motel 6 calling ICE on undocumented guests. *Phoenix Times*. Retrieved from https://www.phoenixnewtimes.com/news/motel-6-calling-ice-undocumented-guests-phoenix-immigration-lawyers-9683244

103.  U.S. Supreme Court. (2015). *City of Los Angeles v. Patel*. Retrieved from https://www.scotusblog.com/case-files/cases/city-of-los-angeles-v-patel/

©iStockphoto.com/faithiecannoise

Engaging many diverse stakeholders is often an important part of addressing ethical dilemmas.

# The Role of Stakeholders in Ethical Decision-Making

## Learning Objectives

On completion of this chapter, the reader should be able to do the following:

LO 8.1: Discuss the relationship between stakeholders' interests and ethical decision-making.

LO 8.2: Recognize that the interests of some stakeholders are interdependent, and therefore that a company's actions to benefit one stakeholder can benefit or harm other stakeholders.

LO 8.3: Explain shareholder theory, its justifications, and challenges to it.

LO 8.4: Explain stakeholder theory, its justifications, and challenges to it.

LO 8.5: Assess the impacts of ethical decisions that go beyond compliance with the law on the firm's financial performance (i.e., whether it "pays to be good" and the reasons why or why not).

LO 8.6: State the reasons for, characteristics of, and benefits of interactive stakeholder management.

LO 8.7: Incorporate stakeholder and shareholder interests into the weight-of-reasons framework for ethical decision-making.

*Capitalism . . . is primarily a cooperative system of innovation, value creation, and exchange. Indeed, it is the most powerful form of social cooperation we have ever invented.*

—Freeman, Harrison, and Wicks[1]

# Introduction

The previous chapter discussed companies' ethical obligations to their stakeholders and the laws that—partially—require companies to meet these obligations. It also described some of the ways companies go "beyond compliance"—that is, do more than what the law requires to meet their ethical obligations to stakeholders.

In reality, as firms consider their ethical obligations to their stakeholders, they often find that it is difficult to satisfy them all. The inability to satisfy all stakeholder interests is especially true in the short term and can be true in the long term, even after you have used the approaches to effective ethical decision-making discussed in Chapter 5. Hence, managers often have to prioritize their ethical obligations to various stakeholders. When they do so, who should come first? Should it be employees? Customers? Or those who invested money in the business? Is it possible for managers to satisfy the firm's ethical obligations to one stakeholder group without violating the obligations to others? The next section of this chapter considers this problem. The chapter is about the reciprocal obligations of businesses to stakeholders and the interdependent nature of stakeholder interests.

Following this introduction, we examine two well-known positions on how managers should prioritize their ethical obligations to stakeholders. According to one of these, known as shareholder theory, companies should meet their legal duties to all their stakeholders, as described in Chapter 7, but put the interests of one stakeholder group—shareholders—ahead of the others. According to the shareholder approach, companies need not go beyond compliance with the law and commonly accepted ethical norms to create value for stakeholders other than shareholders. In some cases, this approach means maximizing benefits for shareholders by doing the least amount legally permissible and morally acceptable to benefit other stakeholder groups. We discuss the conceptual underpinnings behind this "shareholder primacy" perspective as well as the perspective's limitations.

This chapter also presents an alternative viewpoint known as stakeholder theory, which posits that firms have an ethical duty to create value not only for shareholders but for other stakeholders as well. According to this approach, stakeholder management is both the right thing to do from an ethical perspective and also good business. Adherents of the stakeholder approach argue that there is no trade-off between serving other stakeholders and serving shareholders, and in fact, doing the former—treating your stakeholders well—tends to create equivalent value for shareholders as well.

Indeed, most firms today have little choice but to carry out both approaches simultaneously; there is scarcely a company that does not try to earn high profits while it simultaneously addresses its social and environmental impacts on other stakeholders.

After reviewing stakeholder theory, this chapter takes a closer look at whether companies that practice stakeholder management and go beyond compliance to meet their ethical obligations to diverse stakeholders actually do produce enhanced benefits for shareholders. Is taking a stakeholder approach a viable or even the *best way* to satisfy obligations to shareholders?

This chapter reviews reasons that "being good" (acting ethically) can affect revenues, expenses, and profits, and the empirical evidence regarding this relationship. We conclude that the majority of evidence suggests that acting ethically does not *guarantee* better financial results but that it can lead to better financial performance when undertaken in particular ways in some circumstances. In other words, it is contingent on how stakeholder management is practiced and the contingencies that surround how it is carried out. We do not want to create the false impression that "being good" always works out best for shareholders. Nonetheless, in this chapter we echo the message from Chapter 5 that achieving good financial performance and fulfilling the firm's obligations to all its stakeholders necessitates using decision-making approaches such as both/and thinking and moral imagination. Without these, it would be difficult to avoid tragic situations in which the interests of one stakeholder group are favored at the expense of another. If managers begin with the assumption that the interests of shareholders and other stakeholders are always contradictory, they cannot hope to act ethically and also earn exceptional returns for shareholders.

This chapter also discusses the importance of understanding how best to manage the firm's relationships with its stakeholders. We identify four approaches to such engagement—inactive (or passive), reactive, proactive, and interactive—and make the case that mechanisms for interactive stakeholder engagement such as multisector partnerships (MSPs) can be an effective approach to developing long-term solutions to complex and dynamic ethical issues while creating value for all stakeholders including shareholders. When managers engage with stakeholders interactively, the decision-making approaches discussed in Chapter 5—inquiry and advocacy, both/and thinking, moral imagination, and systems thinking—become collective processes that can lead to the development and implementation of innovative ideas for tackling ethical dilemmas. The important point is that in many cases, the most effective means of ethical decision-making is to include stakeholders in the decision-making process. The chapter ends with a brief analysis of how stakeholder considerations fit into the weight-of-reasons framework.

## Stakeholders, Ethics, and Priorities

LO 8.2: Recognize that the interests of some stakeholders are interdependent, and therefore that a company's actions to benefit one stakeholder can benefit or harm other stakeholders.

As noted in Chapter 7, a stakeholder is an individual or a group that can affect or be affected by a focal organization.[2] Managers have obligation to act ethically toward all their stakeholders even when the law does not require it. Thus, ethical decision-making and meeting ethical obligations to stakeholders are synonymous, and ethical decision-making is nothing other than making decisions that meet the organization's ethical obligations to stakeholders.[3]

Because of this close correspondence, the weight-of-reasons framework incorporates stakeholders into every step. Stakeholder considerations are part of defining an issue (Step 1), establishing the facts (Step 2), identifying options (Step 3), analyzing impacts (Step 4), establishing principles (Step 5), devising short- and long-term solutions (Steps 6 and 7), and learning lessons from engaging in this process (Step 8).

Stakeholder considerations play an especially important role in Step 4 when it is necessary to list affected stakeholders, and reflect on options for creating value for them in both the short and long term. They also play an important role in Step 5, where it may be necessary to establish preferences among affected stakeholder groups based on the ethical principles deemed appropriate for the dilemma a company faces. The interests of some stakeholders may have to take precedence over the interests of others, at least in the short run. In the long run, the disadvantaged stakeholders perhaps can be compensated for sacrifices they may not have made voluntarily.

Companies' interactions and relationships with their stakeholders are *reciprocal*; they involve mutual obligations. As shown in Table 8.1, stakeholders receive *inducements* to make their *contributions* to the company. For example, employees contribute their labor to the company in exchange for the inducement of a paycheck, benefits, status, and intrinsic goods such as strong relationships and invigorating challenges. Since most stakeholders voluntarily associate with the company, they can withdraw if they find the inducements unacceptable, and they can reduce and revoke their commitment to the organization.[4] Without their ongoing contributions, the company cannot function.

The interests of various stakeholder groups often are interdependent. Company activities that affect one stakeholder affect other stakeholders. If the interests of interdependent stakeholder groups can be seen as complementary, then addressing

**TABLE 8.1**    Reciprocal Duties of Companies and Stakeholders

| Stakeholder Group | Inducement Offered by the Company | Contribution Provided by the Stakeholder |
|---|---|---|
| Shareholders | Financial gain (e.g., dividends, increase in stock price) | Capital resources |
| Employees | Wages, benefits, job security, opportunities, other | Skills, labor, and loyalty |
| Customers | Reliable, affordable, quality products and services | Financial payments (company revenues) |
| Communities and their members | Taxes, jobs, other economic, social, and environmental benefits | Facilities, infrastructure, competent workforce, operating environment conducive to profitability |

the interests of one stakeholder group is likely to benefit another group. An example of such a "win–win" relationship, already given, is that paying workers more and providing them with better working conditions can lead to higher profits for shareholders and better products and services for customers because workers are more productive and loyal. They may miss work less often, stay with the company longer, and become more committed to the company's goals and vision.

What should managers do, though, when they perceive that they must make trade-offs among the various stakeholders' interests? What if it is nearly inevitable that one stakeholder group will benefit at the expense of another? Circumstances often do arise where win–win results do not seem possible, even after techniques discussed in Chapter 5 such as moral imagination and both/and thinking have been used. For example, in some cases when wages rise beyond a certain level, prices to customers increase and/or dividends to shareholders decrease. Similarly, a company that reduces its prices may not be able to provide its employees with promised raises.

Dick's Sporting Goods provides an example of a company that faced such a trade-off. To its great credit, its management was willing to take the short-term hit to revenue and earnings that followed from its decision to stop selling assault-style weapons in its stores. Its reason for this decision was to prevent gun violence in the communities it serves.[5]

The case about working conditions in Amazon's warehouses at the end of Chapter 7 is another example. That case pits the interests of shareholders (profits) and customers (low prices) against the best interests of the warehouse workers. How should managers prioritize their obligations to these different stakeholder groups? This question about prioritizing stakeholder obligations raises the fundamental issue of why companies exist and what purpose they serve in society. Nearly every time you ponder your principles when engaged in Step 5 of the framework, you are called on to reflect on this question.

There are two dominant perspectives on how to answer this question. According to the shareholder approach, managers should make the interests of shareholders their first priority, and they should not go beyond compliance with the law and the minimums of moral custom in meeting ethical obligations to other stakeholders, if doing so comes at the expense of shareholders. A second view, the stakeholder perspective, is that companies should try to meet their ethical obligations to a wider range of their stakeholders, in some cases even if doing so comes at shareholders' expense. We now present these two approaches in turn.

## Shareholder Theory

**Shareholder theory**
The theory that the sole responsibility of business is to earn maximum returns for shareholders, within the boundaries of society's laws and customs

LO 8.3: Explain shareholder theory, its justifications, and challenges to it.

**Shareholder theory,** as classically articulated by the economist Milton Friedman (1912–2006), holds that the sole responsibility of business is to earn maximum return for shareholders, within the boundaries of society's laws and customs. As noted in Chapter 7, U.S. law in most states has established that corporate managers have a legal duty to make the interests of shareholders their highest priority. With Friedman's article, "The Social Responsibility of Business Is to Increase Its

Profits," the primacy of the shareholder moved from a legal precept to an ethical one. In this article, Friedman argued that corporate managers have a social responsibility to "make as much money as possible while conforming to the basic rules of society, both those embodied in law and those embodied in ethical custom."[6]

Friedman maintained that it is irresponsible for the employees of a corporation to do more than the law requires to address issues such as controlling pollution and training the unemployed. He argued that it is the job of government rather than business to take care of these issues. The job of business, on the other hand, is to earn profits for shareholders within the framework of laws and customs laid down by society. Friedman believed that managers have a moral duty to maximize returns to shareholders because, as discussed in Chapter 7, shareholders are the firm's owners, the risk bearers, and residual claimants in the event of bankruptcy. To Friedman, using company resources for reasons other than benefitting shareholders would violate the principal–agent relationship. (See the discussion of this relationship in Chapter 7.)

While Friedman argued that it was the job of government rather than business to address social problems, he felt that government should exercise caution and restraint in playing this role. He believed that in instances where it might seem warranted, as in the case of pollution, government involvement was likely to be ineffective or even harmful.[7] On the other hand, Friedman felt that government functions such as maintaining security and law and order were necessary prerequisites for a free market system.

## Challenges to Shareholder Theory

Many commentators have challenged shareholder theory and its principle that corporate managers should do no more than obey the law to increase the well-being of shareholders, even if necessary at the expense of other stakeholders. One important criticism of shareholder theory, which we discussed in Chapter 7, is that simply following laws and regulations is not sufficient from an ethical standpoint because they often do not fully embody accepted ethical standards. Even in the best of circumstances, where government officials are concerned about citizens and are able to act on their behalf, there are gaps between law and ethics because of limited resources, time lags, imperfections in the political process, and the difficulties of implementing the laws on the books, no matter how well formulated they may be.

When the gap between ethics and law is wide, what should managers do? Should they, for example, degrade the natural environment and employ slave labor when the laws of countries either do not prohibit them or are not enforced effectively? Friedman's view was that in general, businesses should not take the lead in addressing such issues because it was not their role in society to do so. His hope was that governments over time would enact laws needed to protect stakeholder interests and close the gap between law and ethics—at which point, companies should follow the new laws. This view is hard to reconcile with the ethical perspectives presented in Chapter 2.

A second and related problem with shareholder theory is that it can blind managers to their legal and ethical obligations to other stakeholders. This issue is

©iStockphoto.com/saiyood

Should a company use slavery (forced labor) when doing so is legal? Slavery is still practiced in many parts of the world.

one of bounded rationality (Chapter 3); a singular focus on shareholders means less management attention to other stakeholders. Under pressure or in their zest to earn higher profits and drive up stock prices, managers stop paying attention to their obligations to other stakeholders.

Another problem with the shareholder approach is that it does not account for the large role that companies sometimes play in making the laws to which they then abide. If companies effectively use lobbying and other political tactics to influence lawmakers to pass laws that favor shareholders over other stakeholders, then how will these stakeholders be protected? As noted, Friedman clearly distinguished the relative roles of business and government in society, with government responsible for developing and implementing a legal framework that reflects the will and ethical beliefs of citizens, and businesses focus on increasing profits while working within this framework. In practice, however, this separation of duties is frequently violated. Companies are actively involved in the political and legislative process in many ways, including lobbying and providing financial support to political campaigns. Despite complaints that nongovernmental organizations (NGOs), unions, and public interest groups are heavy spenders on political campaigns and lobbying in the United States, business clearly outspends all other groups (Figure 8.1). Companies play a large role in shaping the rules that control their own behavior, and do so in ways that favor the interests of shareholders and top executives but do not reflect the will of citizens. It is contradictory to argue that companies should do no more than follow the law because the law reflects society's preferences and at the same time work to enact laws that are contrary to these preferences.

To his credit, Friedman did criticize business for its lobbying. He was as suspicious of big business as he was of big government, once stating that

> every businessman is in favor of freedom for everybody else, but when it comes to himself that's a different question. He's always the special case. He ought to get special privileges from the government, a tariff, this, that, and the other thing.[8]

Yet another problem with a shareholder primary approach has to do with its assumption that companies should not go beyond compliance to benefit stakeholders other than shareholders because doing so would reduce shareholder wealth. Friedman had a zero-sum view of corporate expenditures; he believed that the cost of additional environmental protection or community development, for example, ultimately would be borne by shareholders. This premise is questionable, at least under some circumstances; although it is not always possible to find "both/and" solutions

FIGURE 8.1    The Top 10 Industries for Spending on Lobbying: 1998 to 2018

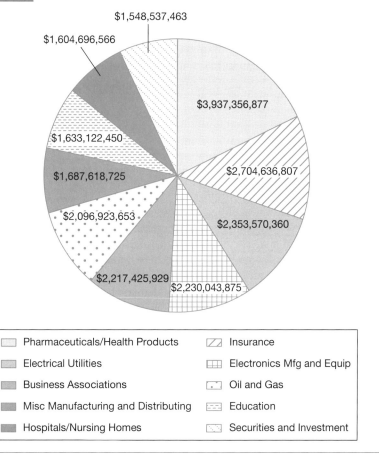

$1,548,537,463

$1,604,696,566

$3,937,356,877

$1,633,122,450

$2,704,636,807

$1,687,618,725

$2,353,570,360

$2,096,923,653

$2,217,425,929

$2,230,043,875

| | |
|---|---|
| Pharmaceuticals/Health Products | Insurance |
| Electrical Utilities | Electronics Mfg and Equip |
| Business Associations | Oil and Gas |
| Misc Manufacturing and Distributing | Education |
| Hospitals/Nursing Homes | Securities and Investment |

*Source:* opensecrets.org, Center for Responsive Politics (data as of August 2018).

that make all stakeholders better off, it is also not the case that such trade-offs are *always* necessary.

Since Friedman's time, advocates of the shareholder-first perspective have recognized that in many instances, companies can "do well by doing good"—that is, they can earn higher profits for shareholders by benefitting other stakeholders. As touched on above and in Chapter 7, the interests of various stakeholder groups are often complementary. The example of Costco provided in Chapter 5 shows that paying wages and providing benefits beyond the minimum required and even above the industry average can lead to more profits for shareholders, not less. Similarly, companies that go out of their way to optimize the customer experience often are rewarded with greater customer loyalty and increased sales, both which reverberate to shareholders' benefit. When stakeholders' interests seem to conflict, they often can be reframed as complementary through both/and thinking (Chapter 5). The ability to "do well by doing good" is taken up later in this chapter.

Finally, Friedman's view that businesses should not get ahead of the law in addressing social and environmental issues fails from a strategic perspective, in the sense that it is a reactive approach to business. Given that the law is continually evolving, mere compliance with the letter of the law can, and often does, place firms in a vulnerable position from which it is hard to recover. For example, tobacco companies did not violate the law when they failed to warn the public of the known health risks posed by cigarettes. Nonetheless, they faced billions of dollars in punitive damage judgments for their negligence.

## Stakeholder Theory

LO 8.4: Explain stakeholder theory, its justifications, and challenges to it.

**Stakeholder theory**
The theory that the responsibility of business is to create value for stakeholders, including shareholders

**Stakeholder theory** provides a different view on the question of how companies should prioritize their ethical obligations to stakeholders. It is concerned with how firms manage their relationships with and create value for a broad range of stakeholders, not just shareholders.[9] Stakeholder theorist Ed Freeman and his colleagues write that stakeholder theory is "first, and most fundamentally, a moral theory."[10] Drawing on Kant, Evan and Freeman argue that all stakeholders count and none should be treated as a means to an end[11] (also see the quote at the beginning of the chapter). Since stakeholder management involves meeting ethical obligations to numerous stakeholder groups and not just shareholders, it is a form of going "beyond compliance." Said another way, the forms of going beyond compliance discussed in Chapter 7 (corporate social responsibility, corporate citizenship, and sustainability) are forms of stakeholder management in that they all involve creating value for a range of stakeholders and not just shareholders.

According to the stakeholder approach, a company's purpose is to facilitate and coordinate interactions among cooperating stakeholder groups who are united by a shared purpose.[12] Shareholders are among these groups. Companies that practice stakeholder management are successful when they are able to develop and implement strategies that promote and harmonize the interests of the many stakeholders on which they depend.[13] By working together, each stakeholder group can end up in a better position than it would have otherwise been had it operated alone. Hence, stakeholder theory is a theory of cooperative, rather than of competitive, advantage. Stakeholder theorists believe that business is primarily a game of innovation that is best achieved through teamwork. Companies gain advantage in the marketplace not so much by beating their competitors but rather by focusing on how collaboration can create value for all of the company's stakeholders.[14]

Normatively, stakeholder theory claims that managers should honor their ethical obligations to all stakeholders, with none automatically given priority over any other. Descriptively, stakeholder theory recognizes that some companies give a high priority to particular stakeholders apart from shareholders. A company's *enterprise strategy* determines the particular stakeholder groups to which managers should give the most attention. Freeman describes enterprise strategy as the answer to the question, "What do we stand for?"[15]

Enterprise strategy is closely related to a firm's mission, vision, and values, discussed in Chapter 6. Companies that exist to provide a particular product or service or fill a particular need have narrow enterprise strategies and try to satisfy the interests of their primary stakeholders, while giving less attention to secondary stakeholders. At the other extreme, there are companies that have a broad purpose and seek to fulfill their ethical obligations to many stakeholders, and even society as a whole. Freeman and colleagues refer to these companies as having a "noble cause" enterprise strategy.[16]

One well-known company that practices stakeholder management is Johnson & Johnson. Its enterprise strategy focuses on customers. The company's "credo" makes customers its highest priority, stating, "We believe our first responsibility is to the patients, doctors and nurses, to mothers and fathers and all others who use our products and services."[17] Shareholders follow not only customers but also employees, communities, charities, and the natural environment.

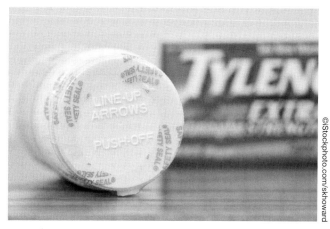

Johnson & Johnson's handling of a 1982 crisis that involved tampering with Tylenol greatly enhanced the company's reputation.

Johnson & Johnson famously lived up to its credo in its handling of a crisis in 1982. In this case, seven people died after ingesting Tylenol pills that a malevolent person had laced with the poison cyanide. The company immediately removed the pain medication from store shelves across the world to protect its customers, although the deaths were confined to metropolitan Chicago. Two months after the recall, Johnson & Johnson relaunched the product in a new tamper-resistant bottle. The company's decision to act ethically was appreciated by many, including customers: Although Tylenol's market share plummeted from 37% to 7% after the poisonings, it rebounded to 30% within a year. Furthermore, the company's stock price, though falling drastically in the short run, returned to a record high within two months.[18]

Johnson & Johnson has not always lived up to its credo, however. The company deliberately withheld important information about its DePuy hip replacement product from scores of consumers, causing them untold permanent damage. In addition, more recently it has been implicated in the U.S. opioid crisis. (See the cases in Chapter 10.)

# O'NEILL AT ALCOA

An executive who has exemplified the best qualities of stakeholder management is Paul O'Neill. O'Neill served as Alcoa's CEO from 1987 to 1999. After that, he briefly served as Treasury Secretary in the Bush administration. While at Alcoa, O'Neill made worker safety his highest priority. He proclaimed that no Alcoa employee should ever get hurt at work and that safety was a precondition rather than a priority. He maintained that pleasing Wall Street indeed was important but only after all other stakeholders

*(Continued)*

(Continued)

were satisfied. O'Neill told Alcoa managers that they should make whatever expenditures they needed to improve safety conditions, rather than arguing that they could not afford or needed to delays such expenditures.

O'Neill followed through on his safety promise, despite the skepticism of senior managers who pointed out that Alcoa already had just about the best safety performance in its industry. At Alcoa, he introduced a database with systematic information about all safety incidents, including near misses, and a detailed examination of their causes. This made it possible to proactively share safety lessons throughout the company. He also established a benchmarking system that compared managers' safety performance records not with industry averages or best practices but rather with what was he argued was theoretically possible. He saw no reason to assume that the best the company could do was to equal one of its competitors. O'Neill even shared his home phone number with his workers and told them

to call him if their managers did not make safety their highest priority.

O'Neill's approach to safety was highly successful. In every year that he was at Alcoa, the number of workdays lost due to injury and illness as a percentage of total hours work declined, and Alcoa became by far the safest company in the industry. O'Neill attributed this achievement to creating an organization where people treated one another with dignity. He took pride that Alcoa's safety record continued to improve even after he left because it signaled that he had successfully nurtured the company's commitment to safety. Safety had become deeply embedded in Alcoa's culture so it no longer mattered who led the company, whether O'Neill or another CEO. This dedication to safety paid off for shareholders, as the price of Alcoa stock climbed steeply during O'Neill's tenure. Although O'Neill maintained that he would have maintained his commitment to safety regardless of whether shareholders were doing well, shareholder gain seemed to be a byproduct of putting workers first.

While U.S. law mainly gives primacy to shareholders, there are exceptions not only in the United States but globally. In states like Delaware and Nevada, where most publicly traded firms are incorporated, the way the law is interpreted is that shareholders come first. Some other states require companies to take multiple stakeholders and not just shareholders into account, however. One such state is Minnesota, where the law requires that corporate takeovers of companies incorporated in the state must be justified in terms of their benefits to the communities in which the companies are located. Minnesota passed this incorporation law to protect the Target Corporation, which gives 5% of its profits to charity, from takeover by a Maryland company, Dart, that had indicated that it might remove this benefit if its takeover bid was successful. Furthermore, 33 states now allow companies that expressly serve society and the environment as well as shareholders to incorporate as benefit corporations (see Chapter 7).

Some countries, including Germany and Japan, have laws that require companies to include stakeholders other than shareholders in their corporate governance mechanisms. The German system of codetermination, for instance, requires that a significant number of seats on a company's board of directors go to workers, with the exact number depending on the size of the company. In general, nations with legal systems from the Anglo-Saxon tradition such as the United States, the United Kingdom, and Australia have laws of incorporation favoring shareholders, while nations outside the United States, including Germany and Japan, have laws of incorporation that require companies to take into account a broader array of stakeholders.

## Challenges to Stakeholder Theory

A main critique of stakeholder theory is that it does not sufficiently address the question of how managers should handle the trade-offs among stakeholders. Stakeholder theory is based on a "both/and" view of the world. Rather than focusing on how companies' interests do not align, proponents of a stakeholder approach to management emphasize stakeholder interdependence and search for ways to align stakeholder interests in a creative manner. Freeman and his colleagues have become major spokespersons for this position. They take the view that a stakeholder approach means not having to resort to trade-offs among stakeholders.

But to what extent is this view entirely realistic? It is a worthy goal perhaps but is it possible to achieve? As we have emphasized throughout this book, some decisions require tragic choices where at least one stakeholder group is made worse off. In many cases, these are the least powerful stakeholders. Advocates of the stakeholder approach do not adequately grapple with the issue of power among stakeholder groups and how this power influences the way in which the burdens and benefits of corporate activities are allocated.[19] Since stakeholder theory sees the purpose of the company as coordinating and harmonizing the interests of various cooperating groups, it tends to give little attention to conflicts and trade-offs between shareholders and other stakeholder groups.

Certainly in some cases, it is possible to generate solutions to ethical dilemmas that make all stakeholders better off—especially by using the weight-of-reasons framework and decision-making approaches described in Chapter 5, such as inquiry and advocacy, moral imagination, systems thinking, and both/and thinking. Nonetheless, it would be simplistic to believe that such solutions are always possible. While the stakeholder approach fairly describes some of the choices that managers make, ultimately it is an aspirational approach to management.

A related criticism of stakeholder theory is that it is difficult to implement. Shareholder theory proponents take the view that managers are more effective decision-makers when they have but a single objective to achieve and that profit maximization is the proper objective. Stakeholder theory only confuses managers, they argue, by giving them the impossible task of trying to satisfy the interests of many different stakeholders simultaneously—almost guaranteeing that no stakeholder group will be well-served. Quoting from the insightful movie *The Incredibles*, the problem with stakeholder theory is that "when everybody is special, nobody is." Some opponents of stakeholder theory take this critique one step further, arguing that by obfuscating the company's priorities, stakeholder theory provides managers with the opportunity to violate their fiduciary duty to shareholders and use company resources for their own selfish purposes (again, the principal–agent problem discussed in Chapter 7).[20]

Table 8.2 provides a summary comparison of shareholder and stakeholder theories.

**TABLE 8.2**     Comparison of Shareholder and Stakeholder Theories

|  | Shareholder Theory | Stakeholder Theory |
| --- | --- | --- |
| Purpose of company | To increase profits and shareholder wealth | To coordinate the interests of those pursuing a common purpose or goal |
| Ethical obligations | Explicit moral duty to serve owners, since they are at the most risk in case of bankruptcy | Explicit obligation to act ethically and create value for all stakeholders that contribute to achieving the company's purpose or are affected by efforts to do so |
| Ethical obligations vis-à-vis the law | Comply within the minimum and not interfere with the process of creating laws, as laws should be created in the interests of citizenry at large | Must exceed legal compliance if ethics demands it, thus providing top-level managers with considerable discretion about how they choose to allocate corporate funds |
| Relationship of shareholders' and other stakeholders' interests | Adversarial | Joint, cooperative, complementary |
| Key ethical pitfall to avoid | Exploiting stakeholders to maximize shareholder benefits | Symbolic conformity with stakeholder expectations as a means of justifying self-interested decisions by top managers |

## Does It Pay to Be "Good"?

**LO 8.5:** Assess the impacts of ethical decisions that go beyond compliance with the law on the firm's financial performance (i.e., whether it "pays to be good" and the reasons why or why not).

In discussing shareholder and stakeholder theories, the question that recurs is whether and how the two fit together. In modern business, managers are often under pressure to act according to both approaches simultaneously; they are expected to create value for shareholders and satisfy their ethical obligations to a range of other stakeholders at the same time.

We keep coming back to this question of whether it is realistic to expect that both can be accomplished simultaneously. To what extent are the interests of shareholders and other stakeholder groups opposed versus complementary? The major proponents of the shareholder and stakeholder approaches, Friedman and Freeman, respectively, take opposing views on this question. Whereas Friedman assumed that dollars spent going beyond compliance to satisfy stakeholders would come from the pockets of shareholders, Freeman emphasizes that stakeholder management is about creating as much value as possible for *all* the corporation's key stakeholders without making trade-offs. Freeman's argument in essence is that "it pays to be good," that is, a company can create more wealth for shareholders by meeting its ethical obligations to all its stakeholders. A great deal of empirical research has been done to determine whether, in fact, "being good" pays. Despite all the research, the question remains difficult to answer. One reason is that assessing all of the firm's ethical obligations to its many stakeholders can be very time-consuming and difficult. How can we adequately measure what it means to be "good" to all these stakeholders? Another reason the question is hard to resolve is that it is not straightforward to assess whether "it pays"—that is, whether and how much shareholders are made better off. Should consideration mainly be given to short-term or long-term profits? An investment in meeting obligations to stakeholders may lead to higher profits in the long term but reduce profits in the short term.

One can question whether profits are even the best way to measure shareholder value creation. Much of the research examines ratios such as return on assets (ROA) or return on equity (ROE) rather than stock market returns, which might be a more direct measure of whether shareholders benefit. Again, think of Amazon—in its history, it has rarely had positive ROA or ROE results. The company actually lost money while its stock market value soared. Young and growing companies are often unprofitable as they try to scale up, and yet, if traded on public markets, they can provide shareholders with stock price increases that are much greater than those for more established firms that are highly profitable but are in weak and in declining industries.

Rather than trying to find a single answer to the question of whether it "pays to be good" some researchers have turned toward identifying the ways that meeting ethical obligations to stakeholders can complement and positively affect a firm's financial performance. They try to trace out the *logic* of how and under what circumstances meeting ethical obligations can increase revenues or reduce costs, leading to higher profits and greater share value appreciation for shareholders.

## Increasing Revenues

One of the main ways that going beyond compliance and doing "good" can increase revenues is by providing the company with a differentiation advantage in the marketplace. **Differentiation** is defined as having a distinct status and set of attributes that set the company's products and services apart from those of other firms. A strong brand image is a common and powerful means of creating a differentiation advantage. Companies that treat their stakeholders ethically may be able to establish an image that enables them to attract new customers who are concerned with the ethical production and sourcing of products. Having a brand that distinguishes the company as socially responsible, a good corporate citizen, sustainable, or in some other way exceptionally concerned about some or all of its stakeholders is a feature that can make a company stand out, attract customers, and obtain a premium price for its products and services. Having a reputation for "being good" also reduces the risk that a company will be damaged by protests and boycotts by activists. In these ways, there is a logic that connects being "good" with strong economic performance.

**Differentiation**
The strategy of having a distinct status and set of attributes that set the company's products and services apart from those of other firms

# SUSTAINABILITY AND PROFITS AT PATAGONIA

©iStockphoto.com/Andrei Stanescu

Patagonia is a company that has a strong brand image because it makes sustainability a high priority. Seemingly paradoxically, it is a consumer products company that opposes mass consumer culture.

While there are many examples of companies that have gained a differentiation advantage by meeting their obligations to stakeholders, perhaps the outstanding example continues to be outdoor clothing and gear company Patagonia. This company has earned a reputation both for the high quality and durability of its products and for its passionate advocacy for environmental causes. On its website, the company proclaims, "We're in business to save our home planet" and "the protection and preservation of the environment isn't what we do after hours. It's the reason we're in business and every day's work." The company's charismatic and still-active founder Yvon Chouinard first got into the outdoor gear industry by fashioning his own rock climbing tools. He did so because he was not satisfied with the ones that were commercially available. Chouinard's enthusiasm for rock climbing and outdoor sports was motivated by his desire for a deep connection with nature. Caring for the environment he has demonstrated is Patagonia's distinct DNA.[21]

Sustainability seems to be woven into everything that Patagonia does. For example, it encourages its customers to repair their clothing and buy used clothing rather than purchasing the company's new products. The company has recently started its WornWear Internet line of clothing to compete with its line of new clothing (see https://wornwear.patagonia.com/). Through WornWear, customers can have their current clothes repaired or turn them in at a Patagonia store to be repaired and resold. Customers who turn in used clothes receive credit toward future WornWear purchases. The WornWear campaign features a truck that tours the United States, making stops at various cities to repair and sell clothes. It also has a truck that travels through Europe.

Other evidence that Patagonia walks the sustainability talk was its 1994 decision to eliminate chemically treated cotton and purchase only organic cotton. Patagonia moved in this direction even before the word *organic* was widely used. To do so, the company had to end its relationships with most of its cotton suppliers and develop its own private cotton supply chain. The company also offers a fair-trade line of clothing, has provided $90 million in funding to grassroots environmental activists, and now operates a service connecting customers to activist groups that work on issues about which they are passionate. When the company expands, it does not build new buildings but, rather, purchases older buildings and brings them up to the highest energy efficiency standards.

Patagonia's environmental activism has paid off for it commercially. The company's focus on making functional, sustainably produced, repairable, and durable gear and clothing has enabled it to build a strong brand image that translates into devoted customers who pay premium prices. By being an authentic "activist" company that exists to "save our home planet," Patagonia has seemingly paradoxically achieved regular financial success.[22]

Another revenue advantage of going beyond compliance is that it can lead to product innovation, which every company operating in a fast and rapidly changing industry must have. When managers take a both/and approach and push themselves to both earn high profits and "do good," they force themselves to become creative. For instance, many of Nike's innovative new shoe materials and designs come from its commitment to sustainability. The company's chief operating officer has proclaimed that it could not have been innovative if not for sustainability.[23] Procter & Gamble and many other companies are committed to sustainability because they are key drivers of innovation.[24]

## Lowering Costs

Treating stakeholders ethically can also reduce costs. Actions that benefit stakeholders and reduce costs can be taken throughout a company's operations and can take many forms. For example, activities such as reducing energy use and the amount of waste produced have a positive environmental impact and reduce energy, materials, and waste disposal costs. As discussed in Chapter 6, the outdoor gear and clothing company REI found that when it set tough financial and tough environmental goals and allowed no trade-offs between them, workers came up with numerous process improvements that both saved money and reduced the company's environmental impact.[25]

Similarly, efforts to treat employees ethically can lead to lower employee hiring and training costs and lower costs related to injury to workers. Operating improvements such as these not only reduce immediate costs but also lower the risk of regulatory fines and punishments and the initiation of prolonged and expensive court cases. Companies that treat stakeholders ethically also may have lower borrowing costs. Because these companies have a strong reputation in the marketplace and are able to reduce costs and risks, banks and other capital providers view lending to them as a good bet.

Notwithstanding these financial benefits of "doing good," it is important to keep in mind that treating stakeholders ethically can also reduce profits. There is certainly no guarantee that "being good pays." There are numerous reasons for this:

- Some expenditures that benefit other stakeholders cannot be recouped through higher prices.

- Another possibility is that relying on a stakeholder approach can reduce profits by impeding a company's ability to execute its strategy. The problem in these cases is a lack of strategic focus—as predicted by shareholder theorists. Managers who seek to benefit all their stakeholders may in the end not benefit any of them.

- A third issue is that customers are not likely to purchase products just because they are produced in an environmentally friendly way or because the company treats its workers well; these products must also provide good value for their price. Would you buy organic fair-trade chocolate if it tasted bad? Or buy a pair of shoes made by happy, well-paid workers if the shoes were expensive and uncomfortable?

- Companies that seek to "do well by doing good" will not succeed in the marketplace if the only managerial capability they have is ethics. If they do not create value for customers and investors, they will not be able to create it sustainably for workers or the environment.

As noted earlier, scholars have done a great deal of quantitative research on whether "it pays to be good." On one point, the literature seems to be clear: Overall, *it does not "pay to be bad."* Although there clearly have been instances where bad corporate actors have prospered, large-sample statistical studies suggest that these are exceptions. Mostly, unethical behavior does not work to the benefit of companies that engage in it. Sometimes, there is some justice and order in the world after all!

While it is clear that in general it does not pay to be bad, the evidence on whether it pays to be good is more ambiguous. One oft-cited meta-analysis of 167 statistical analyses that Margolis, Elfenbein, and Walsh carried out in 2009 on over 35 years of studies came to the following conclusions:[26]

- The overall effect of being good is generally *positive*. The mean improvement in firm financial performance of being "good" in some way was 14% and the median was 8%. These are very large improvements. However, the impact on financial performance depends on what type of "good" behavior the company engages in. The strongest positive impacts arise from charitable contributions, uncovering and revealing misconduct, and improvements in environmental performance. Establishing corporate ethics and transparency policies have the weakest impact.

- Moreover, the link between prior corporate financial performance and subsequent corporate social performance is stronger than the link between prior corporate social performance and subsequent corporate financial performance. In other words, it seems that companies must be "doing well" *before* they can "do good." Doing good, it seems, is a luxury that only some companies can afford.

- Despite all the studies that have been done, far more is unknown than is known about the relationship between "doing well" and "doing good." We do not know enough about the *mechanisms* that connect doing well and doing good and what actions companies can take to achieve both simultaneously.

In sum, it is a mistake to think the answer to the question of whether "it pays to be good" has a simple yes or no answer. The answer is that it depends. Some actions that companies take to make stakeholders better off help the bottom line and others do not. Some work in some situations but not others. Some work when done by one company but not by another.

While managers may not always be able to rely on moral imagination and both/ and thinking, doing so is part of their job if they wish to find ways to harmonize the interests of shareholders with their ethical obligations to other stakeholders. In the best of situations, they will be able to establish virtuous cycles in which strong financial results enable greater investments in social and environmental performance, which improve the company's reputation and lead to even better financial results, which make possible even more positive social and environmental action (Figure 8.2). Better to aim for the virtuous cycle than to engage in unethical behavior that sets off a vicious cycle in which bad behavior leads to deteriorating financial results, which in turn leads to more risk-taking and unethical behavior, which leads to even worse financial results.

## Managing Stakeholder Relationships

**LO 8.6:** State the reasons for, characteristics of, and benefits of interactive stakeholder management.

The best way to ensure that stakeholders are accounted for and treated ethically is probably to include them in the decision-making process. The ongoing process of interacting and building relationships with stakeholders to resolve problems of mutual concern is known as stakeholder engagement.

Companies vary in the way they approach stakeholder engagement. Four approaches have been identified:[27]

- Companies taking an *inactive* or passive approach to stakeholder engagement ignore their impacts on, and do not communicate with, stakeholders. This approach is obviously not an ethical approach to stakeholder engagement. Sadly, this book is full of examples of companies taking an inactive approach. These include the Ford Pinto case (Chapter 2), the Enron case (Chapter 5), and the Arthur Andersen case (Chapter 6).

- Companies taking a *reactive* approach to stakeholder engagement respond to stakeholders' concerns only when they are forced to do so, and then they do so defensively by denying and resisting concerns. An example of a reactive approach is Exxon Mobil's denial of the issue of climate change and its resistance to policies to address it (see the case at the end of Chapter 9).

- Companies taking a *proactive* approach anticipate stakeholders' concerns. They do so by communicating with their stakeholders to identify emerging issues and concerns so that they are not taken by surprise. The oil and gas company BP took a proactive approach to global climate change in the 1990s, acknowledging the importance of addressing the issue even as its competitors resisted it. BP did not maintain this proactive approach, however, as the end-of-book case on the company's Gulf of Mexico oil spill makes it clear.

- An *interactive* approach to stakeholder engagement refers to establishing relationships of trust and respect with stakeholders and engaging in dialogue with them to jointly solve problems and create stakeholder value.

FIGURE 8.2

Good financial performance

Try to create beneficent cycles

Good social performance

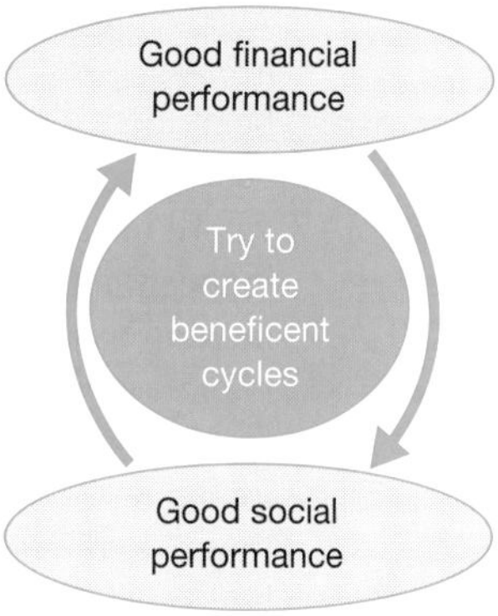

Attempts should be made to create beneficial cycles in business.

**Stakeholder engagement** The ongoing process of interacting and building relationships with stakeholders to resolve problems of mutual concern

**Cross-sector partnership**
Mechanism for cooperation between private sector, public sector, and nonprofit organizations to address an issue or problem

**Public–private partnerships**
Government–business collaborations

**Business–NGO partnerships**
Collaborations between business and nongovernmental organizations (nonprofit organizations that address social and environmental issues)

**Multisector partnerships**
Collaborations that include business, government, and nongovernmental organizations

## Cross-Sector Partnerships

The primary means of accomplishing interactive stakeholder engagement is through cross-sector partnerships. Three types of cross-sector partnerships (CSPs) have been identified: (1) public–private partnerships, in which businesses collaborate with government to address issues of concern; (2) business–NGO partnerships, where businesses work with NGOs, which are nonprofit organizations that operate independently of government and business, and exist to address social and environmental issues; and (3) multisector partnerships that include businesses, government organizations, and NGOs alike.[28]

MSPs come in a variety of forms, including roundtable discussions, where participants debate and discuss issues and try to reach consensus about ways to address them, and collaborative governance arrangements, where the participants go beyond discussion and collaborate to establish and implement policies and programs for addressing issues.[29]

MSPs are not needed when issues and problems are simple and their causes and solutions are well understood. They become necessary when addressing large, complex problems involving many different actors. Such problems often can be effectively addressed only by bringing together representatives of companies, communities, interest groups, and local, state, and federal government agencies, because no single organization has the resources, expertise, and skills needed to address such problems themselves. In many cases, companies have significant financial and operational strengths, NGOs have problem-relevant expertise and networks, and government representatives bring knowledge and contacts as well as formal decision-making authority.[30] Paul Polman, who until recently was the CEO of the multinational consumer products company Unilever, stated that MSPs are necessary because

> the issues we face are so big and the targets are so challenging that we cannot do it alone. When you look at any issue, such as food or water scarcity, it is very clear that no individual institution, government or company can provide the solution.[31]

MSPs are useful not just for pooling skills and resources but also for working out differences. In pluralistic environments (ones in which there are many opposed and diverse opinions), all the stakeholders to an issue must work together to develop a shared understanding of the issue and identify mutually acceptable actions for addressing it. MSPs arise when actors who might otherwise engage in conflict, such as companies and activists protesting the companies' activities, come to accept that they have to work together because they cannot defeat each other. Companies often participate in MSPs when they recognize that activists have the power to tarnish their reputations through information campaigns, boycotts, and protests, or that the government has the power to impose expensive new rules or penalties. In short, MSPs sometimes occur when business, government, and NGOs all agree that "if you can't beat 'em, join 'em."[32]

MSPs are more likely to lead to mutually agreeable solutions to complex ethical challenges when they are designed so that all stakeholders have a fair chance to participate in the process and shape the outcomes. Dialogue in multistakeholder processes is more likely to be productive when it is face-to-face, all may participate equally regardless of their power, and all involved are willing to consider one another's viewpoints and change their own, rather than coming to the table with fully formed and rigid preferences.[33] Under these conditions, dialogues become collective learning processes. Those participating are more likely to engage in both inquiry and advocacy, develop a systems view of the problems they face, take a both/and view, and devise morally imaginative solutions based on the quality of arguments made rather than on ignorance, power, cognitive biases, and groupthink (see Chapters 3–5).[34]

MSPs tend to operate for long periods of time due to the complexity of the problems they address. When a problem involves many interdependent actors, decision-makers experience great uncertainty. Just understanding the nature of a problem and its causes can be very time-consuming. Furthermore, the effects of possible actions to address the problem are unclear because they can have nonlinear, unpredictable, and unintended impacts as they are either muted through negative feedback cycles or amplified by positive cycles (see again the discussion of systems thinking in Chapter 5). A rapid pace of change only makes matters worse, because the problem and its possible solutions keep on changing. In such situations, MSP participants must realize that any particular solution they develop will be short-lived and will need to be adjusted or even discarded as they learn more and conditions change.[35] They will need to continuously engage in trial-and-error learning, also discussed in Chapter 5.

In complex and dynamic conditions in which uncertainty never abates, the decision-making conventions and relationships of trust that the participants in MSPs build are more important than any particular decision made or action taken. Once the participants in MSPs work out a way of addressing problems, they can solve them on an ongoing basis. MSPs ultimately succeed or fail in addressing complex problems based on their ability to

- explore differences,

- create a shared vision,

- develop norms and rules for participation and decision-making,

- build trust,

- handle conflict,

- make decisions by consensus,

- devise accountability criteria,

- share power, and

- cultivate leadership.

Interactive stakeholder engagement is a means of developing long-term solutions to ethical problems. It brings stakeholders into the decision-making approaches discussed in Chapter 5, including moral imagination, systems thinking, both/and thinking, inquiry and advocacy, trial-and-error learning, and experimental learning. As described in Chapter 5, when managers make decisions by engaging with others who have diverse viewpoints, they are more likely to more deeply understand the ethical issues they face, see these issues from multiple perspectives, and develop morally imaginative ways of addressing them.

Extensive multistakeholder engagement is now commonplace in industries that undertake large capital-intensive projects (e.g., mining, oil and gas development, hydropower development). In 2017, the World Bank, which is a major funder of such projects in developing countries, established environmental and social standards that its borrowers are required to follow.[36] The standards for stakeholder engagement require project developers to identify all project stakeholders, including those who would be disadvantaged by the project, and to provide detailed information about how they disclose project information to, consult with, and respond to the grievances of stakeholders.

Multistakeholder partnerships and other approaches to interactive stakeholder engagement, however, do not always succeed in addressing the ethical issues that arise from business activities. One reason is that the companies involved do not take stakeholder engagement seriously and approach it as no more than a cost of doing business, a box to be checked during the project development process. MSPs can also fail because the government actors take the same attitude and are more interested in siphoning money from the projects (legally through taxes and fees or illegally through corruption) than in addressing stakeholder needs. MSPs can also fail for more benign reasons, such as the inability of involved parties to find compromise solutions. They may fail to use, or inadequately use, the decision-making approaches discussed in Chapter 5.

# CHALLENGES IN MAKING MSPs WORK: THE CHAD–CAMEROON PETROLEUM DEVELOPMENT AND PIPELINE PROJECT[37]

One example of a project that has failed to address stakeholders' concerns despite extensive stakeholder engagement is the Chad–Cameroon Petroleum Development and Pipeline Project. In this project, Exxon Mobil and its partner companies signed an agreement with the governments of African nations Chad and Cameroon to develop the oil fields of southern Chad and construct a 650-mile pipeline through the countries to the Atlantic coast of Cameroon.

Due to concerns that the project would breed corruption and have negative social and environmental impacts and that the Chad government would use project royalties to repress and conduct military campaigns against its political opponents, the World Bank was brought into the project. The World Bank is an international financial institution that lends money to countries for large, capital-intensive development projects. The bank had extensive experience in negotiating with nondemocratic governments and had relationships with government officials in Chad and Cameroon.

The World Bank's board of governors approved the bank's participation in the project subject to numerous conditions. It required a comprehensive environmental assessment, an extensive stakeholder engagement process, and a plan for ensuring that royalties to the Chadian government would be used for beneficial purposes. Following thousands of meetings in hundreds of villages and the involvement of numerous NGOs, the final project design included rerouting of the pipeline, provisions for addressing impacts on indigenous populations, third-party monitoring of environmental impacts, two national parks in Cameroon, disease prevention programs, and the construction of new schools and health clinics. In addition, the project established a revenue-sharing agreement that called for the government of Chad to spend 85% of project royalties and dividends on education, health, and rural development programs and to set aside an additional 10% to finance future poverty reduction efforts. Construction of the project began in 2000, oil production began in 2003, and Chad received its first royalties in 2004.

Unfortunately, it was not long before the Chadian government sought to change the revenue management plan to allow for military spending, which led the World Bank to suspend all new lending to the country. The bank and the country then negotiated a compromise deal, but Chad failed to honor that as well. A World Bank investigation concluded that the more than $1 billion per year in revenues that Chad earned from the project was largely siphoned off by corruption, used on military spending, or simply wasted on projects that were poorly designed and implemented. Based on the report, the World Bank decided to exit the project in 2008, leaving the government free to spend the royalties however it deems fit.[38] The project's continued operation has been beset by claims of corruption and negative social and environmental impacts, including two pipeline spills in Cameroon.[39] After the World Bank's withdrawal, one activist priest stated, "We knew from the very beginning how this would end. Chad is a corrupt country with no real democracy. The government has simply enriched itself."[40] In such circumstances, thorough and sincere stakeholder engagement is no match for powerful actors bent on using their power without regard for others.

# INTEL AND CONFLICT MINERALS[41]

In contrast, the joint effort of chip manufacturer Intel and many other organizations to eradicate the use of "conflict minerals" in the Democratic Republic of Congo (DRC) provides an example of an effective multistakeholder initiative. The DRC is one of the chief producers of the minerals tantalum, tungsten, tin, and gold, which are used to make cell phones, computers, televisions, and other consumer technologies. The country also has long been the chief site of a brutal war involving nine countries and 40 rebel groups. The various warring factions vie to control the DRC's mines and use the money gained from selling the minerals produced to finance their military activities, which contribute to disease and

poverty and have been known to involve terrible crimes against humanity. By purchasing metals from these mines, Intel and other companies (and their customers, like you and me) have inadvertently financed these atrocities.

When confronted with the evidence about conflict minerals, Intel decided it wanted to be part of the solution rather than contributing to the problem; it wanted to establish a "conflict-free" supply of raw materials rather than financing conflict. After studying the problem, the company recognized that the main difficulty in addressing it was identifying the source of the metals it was purchasing. It

*(Continued)*

(Continued)

also concluded that the most effective approach to addressing this difficult problem would be to establish a smelter-level system for assessing whether or not ore came from conflict-free mines. (Smelters combine shipments of raw ore into larger batches before shipping them to refiners, which turn the ore into finished metal for sale to manufacturers such as Intel.) Intel executives recognized, however, that to establish a smelter audit system, it would need to bring together a wide range of industry, government, and nonprofit organizations. Its initiative catalyzed the establishment of the Conflict-Free Sourcing Initiative, which in turn created the Conflict-Free Smelter Program (CFSP). This program audits the sources of minerals sold to the smelters to ensure they are from conflict-free mines.

In addition to Intel, the collaborative effort to develop the CFSP includes the following organizations:

- Two industry associations, the Electronic Industry Citizenship Coalition and the Global e-Sustainability Initiative (GeSI). The Electronic Industry Citizenship Coalition works to create social, ethical, and environmental standards for the electronics industry, while the GeSI provides sustainability information, resources, and best practices to the industry. It was a research report by GeSI that identified smelters as the "choke point" in the supply chain where an audit system could feasibly be established.

- The Enough Project, a U.S.-based nonprofit organization that analyzes and establishes campaigns to address genocide and other crimes against humanity. A letter from the Enough Project spurred Intel to learn more about and address the issue of conflict minerals.

- RESOLVE, a nonprofit organization that specializes in building consensus and resolving disputes related to resource, environmental, and public health issues. RESOLVE helped develop the system for tracking minerals from the mine to the smelter, and it also worked with local communities to ensure their economic stability.

- Global Witness, a nonprofit organization dedicated to ending "environmental and human rights abuses driven by the exploitation of natural resources and corruption in the global political and economic system,"[42] Global Witness helped disseminate information about conflict minerals to the public.

- Pact, a nonprofit international development organization that worked on the ground in mining communities to promote peaceful economic development and strengthen the smelter audit system. Pact also helped implement literacy, financial management, and small business assistance programs for women in these communities.

- The U.S. Agency for International Development, a U.S. government international development agency that operates the Responsible Minerals Trade Program. This program promotes conflict-free mining and sought to protect vulnerable citizens in mining communities in the DRC and neighboring countries. The agency also sponsored the assistance programs run by Pact.

- The U.S. State Department, which successfully argued in the United Nations Security Council for bringing economic sanctions against those supporting the armed groups that took over mines and profited from selling minerals.

- The International Council of the Great Lakes Region, a group of 12 African nations that work together to promote peace and economic development in their shared region. The council contributed to the design of the system for certifying mines as conflict free.

- The United Nations, which authored influential and credible reports about conflict minerals in the DRC. These reports served as the basis for policy-making. A 2010 UN report found that nearly every mineral deposit in the country was under the control of armed groups. The United Nations also promoted democracy in the DRC, managing the country's first democratic election in 2006.

The CFSP developed by Intel and its partners serves as the basis for the conflict-free mineral standards that were adopted by the Organisation for Economic Co-operation and Development—a group of 36 countries with advanced economies that includes the United States. The program also serves as the basis for a U.S. law that requires companies to disclose their use of conflict minerals. This law was adopted as part of the Dodd–Frank Act, a piece of financial reform and consumer protection legislation passed in 2010 in response to the financial crisis of 2008. Although the Trump administration sees the conflict mineral reporting requirement as unnecessary and is not enforcing it, major companies including Intel continue to comply with the law.[43]

In summary, multistakeholder and other forms of CSPs provide a mechanism for developing long-term solutions to ethical problems that are complex and dynamic. No single actor, even large corporations or the federal government, has the knowledge, capital, scope, and other resources and capabilities needed to address these problems themselves. In many cases, the solutions that are developed by CSPs are temporary and must be revised as conditions change and more information is collected. Thus, CSPs must operate on an ongoing basis, which makes the development of a shared vision, trusting relationships, and conflict resolution mechanisms critical to success.

## Stakeholders and the Weight-of-Reasons Framework

**LO 8.7:** Incorporate stakeholder and shareholder interests into the weight-of-reasons framework for ethical decision-making.

As noted at the start of the chapter, meeting ethical obligations to stakeholders and using frameworks such as the weight-of-reasons are practically synonymous. Ethical decision-making is decision-making that accounts for the effects of decisions on stakeholders. Decision-makers can and should consider stakeholders in every step of the weight-of-reasons framework.

In Step 1 of the framework, identifying the issue, it is important to keep in mind that because of the cognitive and social factors discussed in Chapters 3 and 4, we frame issues that grab our attention in particular ways, while other stakeholders may see the same issues very differently. We may even fail to recognize that an issue affects a particular stakeholder group that is in fact very concerned about the issue. An issue may not even seem "ethical" until we recognize these stakeholders. For example, the technology companies that source "conflict minerals" probably did not consider that their design and production decisions had very significant implications for communities half way around the world. In business, it is easy to get into the mind-set that once we have done financial and competitive analysis, we are done. This thinking is insufficient from an ethical standpoint. Ethics demands that we cast a broad net in understanding the issues we are addressing and the stakeholders to them.

Once we have identified the stakeholders to an issue, we must then follow through and consider them as we gather information about the issue (Step 2 of the framework). Referring again to the Intel case, it would have been inadequate for the company to recognize that its demand for metals contributed to strife in Central Africa and then do nothing about it. Much to their credit, the company's decision-makers did not rely on hunches based on past experiences in addressing the problem of conflict minerals; rather, they made a concerted effort to understand the facts on the ground (in the ground) as well as the broader context. Rather than struggling within the limits of their bounded rationality to gather data in order to understand the problem, they reached out to many other stakeholders with knowledge and perspective on the issue.

With this information in hand, managers are then in a position to identify action alternatives that take into account many stakeholders and to assess the consequences of those alternatives (Steps 3 and 4 of the weight of reasons). Here again, Intel executives deserve great credit. Most notably, they recognized that any actions they could take by themselves would probably be futile, so they concentrated their efforts on building a coalition of actors, who together had the knowledge, resources, and skills needed to make a difference. Together these actors were able to use systems thinking to develop an understanding of the context in which the conflict minerals issue was playing out and use both/and thinking and moral imagination to envision a package of initiatives that would have beneficial consequences for many stakeholders. As they evaluated those alternatives, they were guided by the principle that they were responsible for the indirect consequences of their actions for many stakeholders and should take an interactive approach to stakeholder management (Step 5 of the weight of reasons) and should seek to develop long-term solutions rather than settle for a quick fix. Developing long-term solutions was both an ethical and a strategic imperative.

## SUMMARY AND CONCLUSION

This chapter picked up where Chapter 7 left off— by recognizing that companies must go beyond compliance to meet their obligations to their stakeholders. Doing so is often not easy because stakeholders' interests are interdependent and sometimes negatively related; what is good for one stakeholder may harm another.

What should managers do when facing a choice between benefitting one stakeholder but not, or even at the expense of, another? This chapter reviewed two approaches that address this question of how to prioritize stakeholders. These are shareholder theory and stakeholder theory. The former holds that managers should always make shareholders their highest priority because they

have a fiduciary duty to do so. Their only obligation to other stakeholders is to obey law and custom. According to this approach, going beyond compliance to benefit these stakeholders is tantamount to stealing shareholders' money and using it to solve social problems that citizens and governments, and not companies, should solve.

Stakeholder theory, in contrast, maintains that the choices managers make are not so simple. According to this approach, managers must account for the full impacts of their decisions; they cannot violate their ethical obligations to stakeholders just because they are not required by law to honor those obligations. However, according to stakeholder proponents, there is no easy answer to the question of which stakeholders come first. Managers must assess their ethical obligations to their stakeholders on a case-by-case basis, which sometimes could mean that company decisions will disadvantage shareholders.

Stakeholder theory comes in several varieties; whereas some companies' enterprise strategies call for them to concentrate on creating value for just a few stakeholder groups such as customers and employees, others consider a wider range of stakeholders, with some even taking all of society and the environment into account in their ethical decision-making processes. Stakeholder theory is an aspiration that very few companies live up to in practice. Like corporate social responsibility, it can be used to mask a lack of strategic focus or self-serving decision-making by managers.

The seemingly paradoxical reality that most managers face is that they must practice both shareholder and stakeholder theories. In this era of shareholder capitalism, the pressure to realize returns for the corporation's owners is high, while at the same time society increasingly expects companies to be good citizens and treat stakeholders well. The existence of pressures from both sides raises the question of whether practicing stakeholder theory increases or decreases returns to shareholders. This chapter reviewed the evidence and arguments regarding this question. In aggregate, studies show a positive relationship between being ethical and shareholder returns. Most are clear that "doing bad" does not pay most of the time for most companies. Going beyond compliance and behaving ethically with respect to a firm's stakeholders can have many concrete financial benefits. For instance, it can enhance the company's reputation and provide it with opportunities to charge higher prices and sell new products. It can also reduce costs. It can motivate workers. It can sustain an innovative climate where creativity flourishes.

Frameworks such as the weight-of-reasons can help managers develop innovative solutions that satisfy shareholders and other stakeholders alike.

In making ethical decisions, keep coming back to techniques discussed in Chapter 5, such as both/and thinking, systems thinking, moral imagination, and team decision-making. As the virtue perspective suggests, through practice you can become better at finding win–win solutions. Although you may shoot many arrows and fail to hit the mark many times, you can learn how to hit the mark (Figure 8.3). In the same way, developing imaginative, both/and ethical solutions to making decisions can become your habit and the foundation for developing your character.

FIGURE 8.3

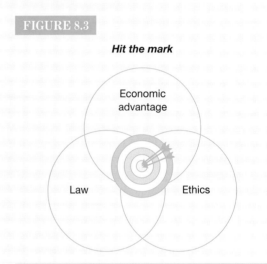

*Hit the mark*

Economic advantage

Law

Ethics

Use the tools you have learned throughout to help you manage to hit the mark when it comes to making advantageous, legal, and ethical decisions.

Also keep in mind the lessons of Chapters 3 and 5—that our ethical intuitions and other cognitive biases can lead us astray in complex and unfamiliar situations and that team decision-making can improve on individual decision-making. An important conclusion of this chapter is that to consistently make decisions that comply with the law and meet ethical obligations to shareholders and other stakeholders alike, we are best served by developing the habit of using both/and thinking, systems thinking, and moral imagination in collaboration with others, including the stakeholders we affect.

Interactive stakeholder engagement mechanisms such as MSPs enable the pooling of resources and the development of strong relationships that facilitate ongoing problem-solving.

## KEY TERMS AND CONCEPTS

Business–NGO partnerships 260
Cross-sector partnership 260
Differentiation 255

Multisector partnerships 260
Public–private partnerships 260
Shareholder theory 246

Stakeholder engagement 259
Stakeholder theory 250

## CASES RELATED TO THE READING

Consider reading the following cases found in Chapter 10 that apply to the concepts presented in this chapter:

- Dow–DuPont: The Bhopal Disaster

- Facebook: Privacy and the Public Interest

- General Mills: Nutrition

- Mallinckrodt: The Opioid Crisis

- Merck and J&J: Problems With Consumer Safety

- VW: Dieselgate

- Walmart: Sustainability

- Wells Fargo: Can It Come Back?

- Whole Foods: Conscious Capitalism

## CASE APPLICATIONS

For each case, get some practice applying the weight-of-reasons approach to develop a course of action for addressing the ethical dilemma. Identify the issue, state the facts, identify possible courses of action, assess the expected consequences of each, apply your principles, and come up with a quick-fix action to address the issue. In addition, consider steps you could take to develop a long-term course

of action that addresses the underlying cause of the problem.

### Case 8.1: USMNC's Chemical Release in the Philippines[44]

USMNC (a fictionalized company) is a major U.S. corporation in the metalworking industry. A chemical release at the company's facility in the

Philippines has resulted in 36 deaths, approximately 100 injuries, and property damage of more than $600 million. The event also has endangered the local population with a chemical cloud for a period of 36 hours. More than 25,000 people in the vicinity of the plant have had to be evacuated because of the explosion and fire that ensued, and a thin mist of the toxic pollutant, ethylene oxide, has lingered in the air for a period of more than 30 days. Workers and community members are lining up to bring lawsuits claiming they are suffering respiratory and other serious ailments as a result of their exposure to the toxic mist.

USMNC management views the incident as a wake-up call to do better, although it is not the first such experience at the company's facilities. The event challenges management's sense that the company is on the leading edge technically. It has some of the best engineers in the world, and though some of its processes are highly dangerous, management has always believed that these processes have the backups and redundancies needed to prevent serious damage to people and the environment. Talk of the risks of USMNC's activities generally has been suppressed because it challenges the prevailing narrative.

Prior to the accident, most of management's attention has been devoted to rapid expansion. The company's ambition is to create a large global enterprise having the size and scope to realize economies of scale in an industry that is extremely competitive. The conventional thinking at USMNC has been that only aggressive global expansion would permit the company to survive.

How should USMNC respond to the chemical release in the Philippines? Use the weight-of-reasons framework to answer this question. Consider all the stakeholders to your decision and the consequences of various courses of action you could take. Pay particular attention to possible financial benefits of treating stakeholders ethically

as well as to opportunities for interactive stakeholder engagement.

### Case 8.2: Safety Audit of USMNC's Nicaragua Facility

USMNC (the same company as in Case 8.1) has just purchased Latin America Metallurgy Company (LAMC) from a competitor. LAMC is located near Managua, Nicaragua. There has been rapid growth in worldwide demand for the sheet metal and coil that LAMC makes. The acquisition substantially bolsters USMNC's capacity to meet this new demand. For the acquisition of LAMC by USMNC to succeed, USMNC has to be able to move LAMC's products out of the door quickly. With worldwide demand soaring, it cannot afford delays in production.

USMNC management feels that all the company's facilities worldwide must meet or exceed the state-of-the-art U.S. standards for health, safety, and the environment. This policy was developed after the chemical release in the Philippines described in Case 8.1. After that event, the CEO called for a safety audit of all the companies' facilities worldwide. The audit showed that the company's global safety, health, and environmental practices were not as strong as they should have been. Whereas before the Philippines event the company granted USMNC's far-flung global subsidiaries substantial discretion to follow local practice, since the event, the company has tried to centralize control of safety, health, and environmental policies. In addition, it conducts regular audits to bring local affiliates into compliance with corporate policies and practices.

### The Audit at LAMC

Shortly after acquiring LAMC, USMNC conducted a health and safety audit of LAMC's plant. The main focus of the audit was on respirator use. LAMC engaged in a variety of operations that required workers to wear respirators. These operations included welding, cutting, smelting, and casting molten materials; sanding, grinding, crushing, drilling, machining, and sandblasting; and cleaning, spraying, plating, boiling, mixing, and painting various pieces of metals and metal parts that LAMC produced. These activities resulted in all kinds of fumes, dusts, and mists that could endanger human health and the environment. Gas and vapor contaminants that were present included inert gases such as helium, argon, and neon; acidic gases such as sulfur dioxide, hydrogen sulfide, and hydrogen chloride; and organometallic compounds such as tetraethyl lead and organic phosphates.

Unfortunately, the audit team found that safety policies and practices at LAMC's facility were not up to the company's standards. For example, the team discovered that there was an insufficient number of respirators at the facility and that maintenance was not being done on them on a regular basis. It appeared that many of the respirators were not functional. Even more alarming was that many workers routinely took off their respirators. Others refused to wear them under any circumstances. Supervisors did little or nothing to stop them. Even when the workers wore the respirators, it was not at all clear to the members of the audit team whether they were wearing the right respirators for the jobs they were doing. The audit team observed that a stack of respirators of various kinds were kept piled in a corner of the plant, with workers deciding for themselves if and what kind of respirator they would wear.

The audit team concluded that these problems were occurring largely because the plant management did not have any written policies in place regarding the use of respirators, did not supervise the respirator use, and failed to provide necessary training. Furthermore, there was no medical surveillance in place to ensure that workers were not having regular symptoms such as wheezing, coughing, and chronic bronchitis, nor were workers trained to recognize and address respiratory emergencies.

The safety auditors took the time to interview workers about respirator use. These interviews revealed among other things that workers felt pressure to do their jobs quickly, and that respirators could interfere with getting the job done; that they needed to remove their masks to communicate; that they could not wear the masks comfortably for long periods of time; and that they thought the risks of not wearing masks were minimal. They also said their supervisors paid them to meet production goals and treated safety concerns as secondary.

Overall, the findings of the audit team were very troubling. The final sentence of their report said that USMNC should consider shutting down the facility for a period to reassess worker safety issues and institute new policies and practices.

*Trying to Prevent Harm*

This finding posed an obvious dilemma for USMNC management. The company wanted to avoid the mistakes of the past and provide its workers with safe conditions. It was aware that the local media and activists worldwide were watching the company suspicious that it had purchased the plant in Nicaragua to save money by paying low wages and cutting corners on safety and environmental protections. USMNC already had been pilloried in the press for its accident in the Philippines and did not want more bad publicity. At the same time, temporarily closing the facility would mean missing out on a substantial amount of revenue.

If you were a top manager at USMNC, how would you approach this dilemma? What is the central issue? Do you have all the facts you need to address it? What options do you have and what would their consequences be? In formulating your answer, keep in mind the lessons of this chapter. For USMNC, might it "pay to be good"? How can USMNC build from a short-term fix to a long-term solution? How might it employ interactive stakeholder engagement to address the issues?

## Case 8.3: Keeping Out the Food Trucks[45]

You own a restaurant in a mid-sized, fairly well-to-do town. Your restaurant is located near many other restaurants in a part of town that has a lot of foot traffic and visitors day and night. You offer diners a nice experience and serve high-quality, but not, gourmet food. Reviewers on Yelp typically give your restaurant four or five stars. Prices at your restaurant are well above fast-food prices but not exorbitant ($$ on Yelp).

One day, you notice a van parked on the curb near your restaurant. Quite a few people are coming and going from it. On closer inspection, you find that the van is a food truck, and by the smell of it, the food it is selling is not half bad. You see that the truck's menu is interesting and the prices are pretty low—lower than your own. Threatened by the appearance of this food truck, you start talking to the other restaurateurs in your neighborhood. You find out that the city has been granting permits to food truck owners to locate in your neighborhood during peak lunch and dinner hours. In fact, the city council has been offering incentives to start food truck businesses because it thinks food trucks add to the character of the city.

You start to consider your options for dealing with this scary new phenomenon. One idea that arises in your mind is to try to work with your fellow restaurateurs to pass a law forbidding food trucks within 1,000 feet of existing brick-and-mortar restaurants. A quick look at the map suggests to you that this would pretty much eliminate food trucks from your part of town.

Use the weight-of-reasons framework to evaluate this idea. Is it ethical? Should you do it? Also use the framework to come up with other alternatives for dealing with the arrival of food trucks in your neighborhood. As you formulate your answer, consider your views on the role of business in community politics.

## Case 8.4: Worker Safety—Is It Worth It?

You run a die casting facility that produces metal tools used in industry. (Dies are essentially molds that are filled with superhot molten metal to make metal products.) Competition is fierce in your industry, so keeping costs down and delivering quickly on orders are important to your company's survival. There are a lot of accidents in die casting; in fact, the rate of accidents in the industry is twice the industrial average.[46] Your facility has an even worse safety record than the industry average. You are not proud of this, but look at it as "the cost of doing business." You don't see how your facility can keep costs down and delivery times short without accepting a high accident rate.

One night after work, you are browsing YouTube and come across a speech by Paul O'Neill, the former CEO of aluminum producer Alcoa. O'Neill is talking about how safety at Alcoa was not just a priority but rather a precondition. (See the discussion earlier in the chapter.) At first, you dismiss O'Neill's message but then, after setting aside your confirmation bias, decide to keep listening. The more you hear, the more intrigued you are. You start to wonder if O'Neill's message might be applicable to the die casting facility you run.

Using the weight-of-reasons framework, speculate about the benefits and costs of a new approach to die casting that emphasizes worker safety. Who are all the stakeholders that would be affected by a shift to a new, safer production method? Give special attention to how such a change might affect the company's profits.

## Case 8.5: Slavery Chocolate

You work in procurement for a large candy manufacturer. One of your main responsibilities is to locate cocoa plantations in Africa that can provide you cocoa at a reasonable price. (Cocoa is the main ingredient in chocolate.) You have found one supplier that can't be beat; its product is always of high quality, while its prices are always lower than those of the competing plantations.

One day, in accordance with company policy, you do a surprise inspection of the plantation. The inspection reveals that the reason its prices are so low is that it employs slave labor. The plantation owners traffic young men from neighboring countries against their will, do not pay them, do not allow them to leave the plantation, and make them work for endless hours under inhumane conditions.

You are horrified by what you have found. Your first instinct is to end your company's contract with the plantation. On reflection, however, you start to reconsider. Your performance as a procurement agent will certainly suffer without this plantation; if you can even replace this supplier, your costs will certainly go up and cocoa quality may suffer. And it won't be just you that is hurt; if sales decline, the company's workers and owners could also be hurt. Moreover, it dawns on you that if you stop buying from the plantation, you probably won't hurt it at all. The chocolate industry is a tough one, and you are almost certain that one of your competitors will move in and start buying the plantation's product.

Use the weight-of-reasons framework to decide how to handle this situation. What options do you have? What are their expected outcomes, and what principles should you use to decide? Which stakeholders should count the most? Is it possible to come up with an option that is ethical and keeps costs low as well?

# NOTES

1.  See p. 6, in Freeman, R. E., Harrison, J. S., & Wicks, A. C. (2007). *Managing for stakeholders: Survival, reputation, and success.* New Haven, CT: Yale University Press.

2.  Freeman, R. E. (1984). *Strategic management: A stakeholder approach.* Boston, MA: Pitman; Freeman, R. E., Harrison, J. S., Wicks, A. C., Parmar, B. L., & de Colle, S. (2010). *Stakeholder theory: The state of the art.* Cambridge, UK: Cambridge University Press.

3.  While stakeholder theorists tend to talk about stakeholder theory as a means of creating stakeholder value, this too is synonymous with meeting ethical obligations to stakeholders. One creates value for stakeholders by respecting their rights, treating them fairly and compassionately, and creating benefits for them that outweigh costs.

4.  Bridoux, F., & Stoelhorst, J. W. (2014). Microfoundations for stakeholder theory: Managing stakeholders with heterogeneous motives. *Strategic Management Journal, 35,* 107–125; Hill, C. W. L., & Jones, T. M. (1992). Stakeholder-agency theory. *Journal of Management Studies, 29,* 131–154;

Harrison, J. S., & Wicks, A. C. (2013). Stakeholder theory, value, and firm performance. *Business Ethics Quarterly, 23,* 97–124.

5.  Jones, C. (2018, November 29). Dick's Sporting Goods ban on some guns dented sales: But weaker gun market also took toll. *USA Today.* Retrieved from https://www.usatoday.com/story/money/2018/11/29/gun-ban-dents-sales-dicks-sporting-goods/2152134002/

6.  Friedman, M. (1970, September 13). The social responsibility of business is to increase its profits. *The New York Times.* Retrieved from http://umich.edu/~thecore/doc/Friedman.pdf?mod=article_inline

7.  See p. 6, in Friedman, M. (1975). *An economist's protest* (2nd ed.). Sun Lakes, AZ: Thomas Horton.

8.  Machan, M., Cobb, J., & Raico, R. (1974, December). An interview with Milton Friedman. *Reason.* Retrieved from https://reason.com/1974/12/01/an-interview-with-milton-fried/

9.  Freeman (1984); Freeman et al. (2010).

10. See p. 212, in Freeman et al. (2010). See also Freeman (1984); Jones, T. M., & Wicks, A. C.

(1999). Convergent stakeholder theory. *Academy of Management Review, 24,* 206–221.

11.  Evan, W. M., & Freeman, R. E. (1988). A stakeholder theory of the modern corporation: Kantian capitalism. In T. Beauchamp & N. Bowie (Eds.), *Ethical theory and business* (pp. 75–93). Englewood Cliffs, NJ: Prentice Hall.

12.  Bridoux and Stoelhorst (2014); Freeman (1984); Freeman, Harrison, and Wicks (2007); Freeman et al. (2010). See also Jones, T. M. (1995). Instrumental stakeholder theory: A synthesis of ethics and economics. *Academy of Management Review, 20,* 404–438; Parmar, B. L., Freeman, R. E., Harrison, J. S., Wicks, A. C., Purnell, L., & deColle, S. (2010). Stakeholder theory: The state of the art. *Academy of Management Annals, 4,* 403–445; Westermann-Behaylo, M. K., Van Buren, H. J., & Berman, S. L. (2016). Stakeholder capability enhancement as a path to promote human dignity and cooperative advantage. *Business Ethics Quarterly, 26,* 529–555.

13.  Strand, R., & Freeman, R. E. (2015). Scandinavian cooperative advantage: The theory and practice of stakeholder engagement in Scandinavia. *Journal of Business Ethics, 127,* 65–85; Westermann-Behaylo et al. (2016).

14.  Ibid.

15.  See Chapter 4, in Freeman (1984).

16.  Freeman et al. (2007).

17.  Johnson & Johnson. (n.d.). *Our credo.* Retrieved from https://www.jnj.com/credo/

18.  Rehak, J. (2002, March 23). Tylenol made a hero of Johnson & Johnson: The recall that started them all. *The New York Times.* Retrieved from https://www.nytimes.com/2002/03/23/your-money/IHT-tylenol-made-a-hero-of-johnson-johnson-the-recall-that-started.html

19.  Great attention has been given to the question of "stakeholder salience," or how managers allocate attention among stakeholders. This literature, however, does not challenge stakeholder theory's normative assumption that trade-offs among stakeholders can be avoided.

20.  Jensen, M. C. (2002). Value maximization, stakeholder theory and the corporate objective function. *Business Ethics Quarterly, 12,* 235–259.

21.  Pages from the company's website that were referenced in this discussion of Patagonia include the following: https://www.patagonia.com/company-info.html; https://www.patagonia.com/company-history.html; https://www.patagonia.com/the-activist-company.html; https://www.patagonia.com/20-years-of-organic-cotton.html; https://www.patagonia.com/actionworks/about/; and https://wornwear.patagonia.com/

22.  Social Media for Business Performance. (2015). *Patagonia's authentic self: The building of trust and reputation.* Retrieved from https://smbp.uwaterloo.ca/2015/10/patagonias-authentic-self-the-building-of-trust-and-reputation/; Beer, J. (2018). How Patagonia grows every time it amplifies its social mission. *Fast Company.* Retrieved from https://www.fastcompany.com/40525452/how-patagonia-grows-every-time-it-amplifies-its-social-mission

23.  Jones, L. (2018, June 11). "There is no innovation without sustainability," says Nike's chief operating officer. *De Zeen.* Retrieved from https://www.dezeen.com/2018/06/11/nike-eric-sprunk-interview-sustainability-flyleather-recyclable-leather/

24.  Nidumolu, R., Prahalad, C. K., & Rangaswami, M. R. (2009, September). Why sustainability is now the key driver of innovation. *Harvard Business Review.* Retrieved from https://hbr.org/2009/09/why-sustainability-is-now-the-key-driver-of-innovation

25.  Hoyt, D., & Reichelstein, S. (2011). *Environmental sustainability at REI.* Stanford, CA: Stanford Graduate School of Business.

26.  Margolis, J. D., Elfenbein, H. A., & Walsh, J. P. (2009). *Does it pay to be good . . . and does it matter? A meta-analysis of the relationship between corporate social and financial performance* (Working paper). Boston, MA: Harvard Business School.

27.  Preston, L., & Post, J. E. (1975). *Private management and public policy: The principle of public responsibility* (The Prentice Hall Series in Economic Institutions and Social Systems). Upper Saddle River, NJ: Prentice Hall.

28.  Gray, B., & Stites, J. P. (2012). *Sustainability through partnerships: Capitalizing on collaboration.* London, Ontario, Canada: Network for Business Sustainability. Retrieved from http://www.mspguide.org/sites/default/files/resource/nbs-systematic-review-partnerships.pdf

29.  Innes, J. E., & Booher, D. E. (2010). *Planning with complexity: An introduction to collaborative rationality for public policy.* London, UK: Routledge;

Koontz, T. M., Steelman, T. A., Carmin, J., Korfmacher, K. S., Moseley, C., & Thomas, C. W. (2004). *Collaborative environmental management: What roles for government?* Washington, DC: Resources for the Future; Margerum, R. D. (2011). *Beyond consensus: Improving collaborative planning and management.* Cambridge: MIT Press.

30. Hartman, L. P., & Dhanda, K. K. (2018). Cross-sector partnerships: An examination of success factors. *Business and Society Review, 123*(1), 181–214; Austin, J. E., & Seitanidi, M. M. (2012). Collaborative value creation: A review of partnering between nonprofits and businesses: Part I. Value creation spectrum and collaboration stages. *Nonprofit and Voluntary Sector Quarterly, 41,* 726–758; Dahan, N. M., Doh, J. P., Oetzel, J., & Yaziji, M. (2010). Corporate–NGO collaboration: Co-creating new business models for developing markets. *Long Range Planning, 43,* 326–342.

31. See p. 2, in Gray and Stites (2012).

32. Koontz et al. (2004).

33. Habermas, J. (1981). *The theory of communicative action: Reason and the rationalization of society.* Boston, MA: Beacon Press.

34. For examples from the natural resources, environmental management, and policy/planning literatures, see Connick, S., & Innes, J. (2003). Outcomes of collaborative water policy making: Applying complexity thinking to evaluation. *Journal of Environmental Planning and Management, 46,* 177–197; Healey, P. (1997). Collaborative planning: Shaping places in fragmented societies. London, UK: Macmillan; Innes, J. E., & Booher, D. E. (2005). Reframing public participation: Strategies for the 21st century. *Planning Theory and Practice, 5,* 419–436; Innes and Booher (2010).

35. Brunner, R., Steelman, T. A., Coe-Juell, L., Cromley, C., Edwards, C., & Tucker, D. (2005). *Adaptive governance: Integrating science, policy, and decision making.* New York, NY: Columbia University Press; Ostrom, E. (2010). Polycentric systems for coping with collective action and global environmental change. *Global Environmental Change, 20,* 550–557; Innes and Booher (2010).

36. The World Bank. (2017). *Environmental and social framework.* Washington, DC: Author. Retrieved from http://www.worldbank.org/en/projects-operations/environmental-and-social-framework

37. Based on a case study in Hargrave, T. J. (2009). Moral imagination, collective action, and the achievement of moral outcomes. *Business Ethics Quarterly, 19,* 87–104.

38. Polgreen, L. (2008, September 11). World Bank ends effort to help Chad ease poverty. *The New York Times.* Retrieved from https://www.nytimes.com/2008/09/11/world/africa/11chad.html

39. Reseau de Lutte Contre la Faim. (2010, April 27). *Another oil leak on the marine terminal of the Chad–Cameroon pipeline* (Press release). Retrieved from https://web.archive.org/web/20140222032737/http://www.relufa.org/documents/Pressreleaseoilspillapril2010.pdf; Reseau de Lutte Contre la Faim. (n.d.). *Oil spill at Chad–Cameroon pipeline's offshore terminal.* Retrieved from https://web.archive.org/web/20140222032735/http://www.relufa.org/partners/jhnewsletter/documents/KribiOilSpill.doc

40. Polgreen (2008).

41. Information about the conflict-free mineral initiative spearheaded by Intel comes from the case of España, C., Robinson, I., Bukhari, H., & Hodge, D. (2015). *Intel: Undermining the conflict mineral industry* (Case 1-429-411, Prepared under the supervision of A. Hoffman, 2015). Ann Arbor: University of Michigan, William Davidson Institute.

42. Global Witness. (n.d.). *About us.* Retrieved from https://www.globalwitness.org/en/about-us/

43. Apple, Intel carry on as SEC relaxes conflict mineral scrutiny. (2017, April 13). *Bloomberg News.* Retrieved from https://news.bloomberglaw.com/corporate-law/apple-intel-carry-on-as-sec-relaxes-conflict-minerals-scrutiny?context=article-related

44. This case and the next are fictionalized accounts based on research done by the first author.

45. This mini-case is based on real-life events in El Paso, Texas. See Needleman, S. E. (2012, August 9). Street fight: Food trucks vs. restaurants. *The Wall Street Journal.* Retrieved from https://www.wsj.com/articles/SB10000872396390443404004577576992254177540.

46. North American Die Casting Association. (n.d.). *Safety.* Retrieved from https://www.diecasting.org/wcm/Technology/Safety/wcm/Technology/Safety.aspx?hkey=a1d36be6-42ac-4365-8fed-1c32680b00c4

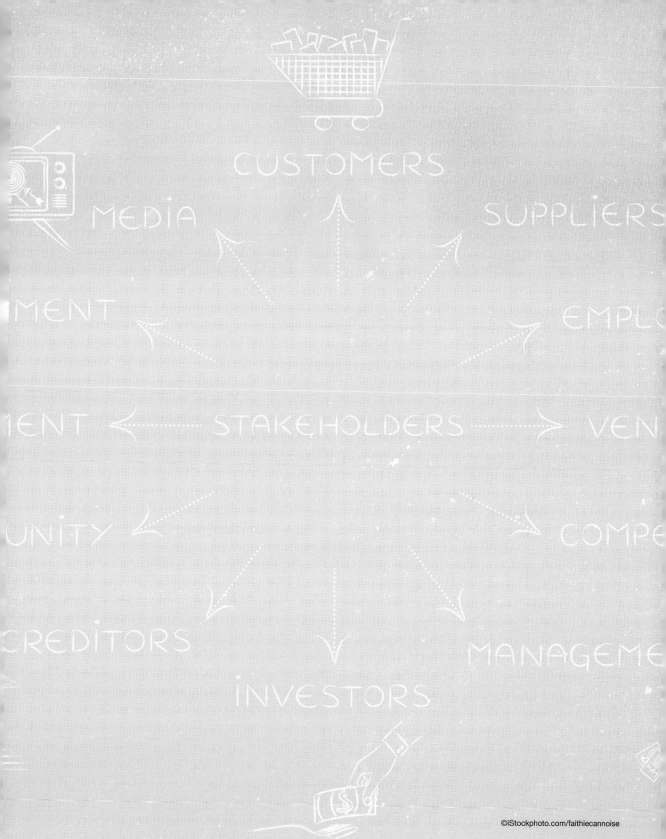

CUSTOMERS

MEDIA

SUPPLIERS

MENT

EMPL

MENT    STAKEHOLDERS    VEN

UNITY

COMPE

CREDITORS

MANAGEME

INVESTORS

©iStockphoto.com/peepo

# Ethics, Strategy, and Grand Challenges

Businesses will need tremendous skill to effectively address the grand challenges of our time in ethical ways.

## Learning Objectives

On completion of this chapter, the reader should be able to do the following:

LO 9.1: Identify the grand challenges of our time, as enumerated in the United Nations Sustainable Development Goals.

LO 9.2: Recognize that grand challenges involve difficult ethical choices and, therefore, addressing them requires ethical decision-making tools such as those presented in this book.

LO 9.3: Recognize that addressing grand challenges requires innovation and that businesses will innovate more to address grand challenges if governments establish frameworks that encourage such innovation.

LO 9.4: Identify existing innovative business approaches to addressing grand challenges, including shared value, base of the pyramid, and industry-transforming innovation.

> " *A pessimist sees the difficulty in every opportunity; an optimist sees the opportunity in every difficulty.* "
>
> —Winston Churchill

# Introduction

As discussed in Chapter 8, businesses typically prioritize some stakeholders over others when making decisions. While some companies consider a very narrow group of stakeholders, and sometimes just shareholders, others cast a broader net and try to account for many different stakeholder groups in their decisions. Consistent with this, Chapter 7 noted that some companies go far beyond the minimum requirements of the law in meeting their ethical obligations to a wide range of stakeholders, some even taking the lead in addressing pressing environmental and social problems.

This chapter takes the discussion one step further. It does so by examining the efforts that some companies are making to address the world's grand challenges. We first define grand challenges and refer to the United Nations Sustainable Development Goals to identify the major ones. Some of these, such as global climate change, have been identified in Chapter 7. We note that grand challenges are essentially ethical challenges, and tough ones at that. They involve choices about who benefits and who is harmed, questions about fundamental rights, and issues of basic fairness.

Because grand challenges are very complex and fraught with uncertainty, frameworks such as the weight-of-reasons and the other tools described in this book can be used to address them whether tacitly or explicitly. Ideally, grand challenges are approached through interactive stakeholder processes in which companies, nongovernmental organizations (NGOs), and government agencies work together to continuously learn and develop innovative, morally imaginative new products, services, policies, and practices. Governments can support this innovation by creating a business environment that promotes appropriate risk taking.

We then take a look at three innovative business approaches to addressing grand challenges. These are (1) Porter and Kramer's shared value approach, (2) Prahalad and Hart's base of the pyramid (BOP) approach (and Bill Gates's related idea of creative capitalism), and (3) industry-transforming entrepreneurship. While these three approaches are not always distinct in practice, analytically it is useful to separate them. All three are forms of going beyond compliance that are compatible with corporate citizenship and sustainable business (discussed in Chapter 7). All three involve working with stakeholders to develop innovative ways of solving big problems and at the same time earning a profit.

Companies taking the shared value approach strategically engage in a set of activities that simultaneously benefits many stakeholders, including shareholders. The BOP approach has a similar flavor, emphasizing that businesses can flourish in the long run by offering products and services that meet the needs of and are affordable to society's poorest people. Similarly, Bill Gates's creative capitalism, which is treated as synonymous with the BOP approach, calls for reorienting the firm's offerings around essential services the poor need, such as health care, nutrition, clean air and water, and energy. The third approach, industry-transforming innovation, focuses on developing new technologies that address grand challenges. We examine the examples of Shai Agassi and Elon Musk, the founders of the electric vehicle (EV) companies Better Place and Tesla, respectively; and Elizabeth Holmes, who started

Theranos, a company that intended to bring about a revolution in health care with a new diagnostic device. Agassi's company failed, Holmes was an outright fraud, and the jury is still out on Tesla.

Doing good for the world can be profitable, but often it is not. Good intentions are not enough. Addressing grand challenges requires, in addition to a desire to make the world a better place, vision, a solid strategy and business model, and the desire and ability to follow through.

Thus, a takeaway from this chapter is that in formulating strategies for addressing grand challenges, business leaders may be best served by applying an ethical decision-making framework like the weight-of-reasons. By using systems thinking, moral imagination, and other ethical decision-making tools discussed in Chapter 5 to develop innovative strategic options and assess whether they would make stakeholders better off, businesses can contribute to long-term solutions to grand challenges while also thriving financially.

A related takeaway is that to be "part of the solution" businesses must work with their stakeholders. As the quote at the beginning of this chapter emphasizes, we live at a moment in history where people must come together to address daunting challenges. No substitute exists for sitting down together and working it out.

## Addressing Grand Challenges Through Ethical Decision-Making

**LO 9.1:** Identify the grand challenges of our time, as enumerated in the United Nations Sustainable Development Goals.

**Grand challenges**
Complex global problems that affect the well-being of many people and can only be addressed through the coordinated efforts of many diverse stakeholders

**Grand challenges** are complex problems that affect the well-being of many people around the globe, and that can only be addressed through the coordinated efforts of diverse stakeholders. While a wide range of problems might be considered grand challenges, the most widely accepted are those addressed by the Sustainable Development Goals (SDGs) adopted by the United Nations in 2015. These goals, which are listed in Table 9.1, address a variety of complex economic, social, and environmental problems. If humanity were able to attain these goals, it is likely that it could live prosperously and harmoniously on a planet that could support it indefinitely. While the SDGs themselves are stated very generally, more specific targets have been established to measure progress toward meeting them.

### Grand Challenges and Business

Companies increasingly have made it their business to address grand challenges. In the language of Chapters 7 and 8, they go "beyond compliance" to treat stakeholders ethically and try to make society better off by engaging in approaches such as corporate citizenship and sustainable business. They have adopted "noble cause" enterprise strategies that explicitly establish contributing to achievement of the SDGs as

**TABLE 9.1**    United Nations Sustainable Development Goals

| | |
|---|---|
| SDG 1 | End poverty in all its forms everywhere |
| SDG 2 | End hunger, achieve food security and improved nutrition, and promote sustainable agriculture |
| SDG 3 | Ensure healthy lives, and promote well-being for all at all ages |
| SDG 4 | Ensure inclusive and equitable quality education, and promote lifelong learning opportunities for all |
| SDG 5 | Achieve gender equality, and empower all women and girls |
| SDG 6 | Ensure availability and sustainable management of water and sanitation for all |
| SDG 7 | Ensure access to affordable, reliable, sustainable, and modern energy for all |
| SDG 8 | Promote sustained, inclusive, and sustainable economic growth; full and productive employment; and decent work for all |
| SDG 9 | Build resilient infrastructure, promote inclusive and sustainable industrialization, and foster innovation |
| SDG 10 | Reduce income inequality within and among countries |
| SDG 11 | Make cities and human settlements inclusive, safe, resilient, and sustainable |
| SDG 12 | Ensure sustainable consumption and production patterns |
| SDG 13 | Take urgent action to combat climate change and its impacts by regulating emissions and promoting developments in renewable energy |
| SDG 14 | Conserve and sustainably use the oceans, seas, and marine resources for sustainable development |
| SDG 15 | Protect, restore, and promote sustainable use of terrestrial ecosystems; sustainably manage forests; combat desertification; halt and reverse land degradation; and halt biodiversity loss |
| SDG 16 | Promote peaceful and inclusive societies for sustainable development, provide access to justice for all, and build effective, accountable, and inclusive institutions at all levels |
| SDG 17 | Strengthen the means of implementation, and revitalize the global partnership for sustainable development |

*Note:* SDG = Sustainable Development Goals.

the company purpose. Muhammad Yunus, the founder of the Grameen Bank, provides an example of someone who introduced a business innovation to address a grand challenge.

# MUHAMMAD YUNUS AND GRAMEEN BANK

One of the best-known examples of a business addressing a grand challenge is the Grameen Bank, which bills itself as "a bank for the poor."[1] Grameen is a for-profit "microenterprise" lender that makes loans to the poor so they can start small businesses. Its founder Muhammad Yunus established Grameen to address poverty and end predatory lending by commercial banks in his native Bangladesh. The bank also helps address the problem of gender inequality by extending many of its loans to women. Grameen has made loans to more than 9 million borrowers and has moved beyond Bangladesh to numerous other countries, including the United States.

## Grand Challenges and the Weight of Reasons

**LO 9.2:** Recognize that grand challenges involve difficult ethical choices and, therefore, addressing them requires ethical decision-making tools such as those presented in this book.

Grand challenges are inherently ethical challenges. By their very nature, they involve questions about individuals' ability to live with dignity, enjoy basic rights and freedoms, and be treated fairly. For this reason, companies seeking to contribute to addressing grand challenges can use a framework such as the weight-of-reasons to do so.

Applying the weight of reasons to a grand challenge is no easy task, however, primarily because grand challenges are so complex. Even understanding what issue you are addressing (Step 1 of the weight-of-reasons) can be difficult. For example, a company that wanted to address poverty in a region where it operated would need to understand the economic, social, political, and many other factors (Step 2 of the weight-of-reasons) that could have led to the region being poor. Identifying all the stakeholders and gathering all of the information needed to understand the issue (Step 2) would be challenging.

Identifying actions that the company could take to help resolve the challenge (Step 3) similarly would be difficult. One of the main reasons is that no individual or organization has the resources, expertise, and skills needed to address the challenge by itself. Therefore, addressing grand challenges often requires an ambitious effort to coordinate business, government, and nongovernmental actors through mechanisms such as multisector partnerships, which we discussed in Chapter 8.

A particular difficulty in identifying courses of action to address a grand challenge is finding a way to make stakeholders better off. Because grand challenges involve so many different actors, avoiding trade-offs is difficult; almost invariably, someone will be neglected or harmed. Efforts to develop new sustainable industries could come at the expense of existing "dirtier" industries. Scarce resources may dictate that an antipoverty initiative will include some needy people but not others.

Efforts to empower the women of a community through commerce may threaten the existing power structure. Or perhaps comprehensive efforts to address a grand challenge will not add up financially, leaving the company's owners with less or no profit.

Step 4, assessing the consequences of alternative courses of action, also is very difficult for grand challenges because of decision-making uncertainty. The consequences of particular actions that could be taken to address a grand challenge can be hard to predict. In complex systems, small acts can have large unintended consequences (see Chapter 5). An example is provided by Tom's Shoes, a company that provides one free pair of shoes to youth in developing countries for every pair it sells. While the company was founded with the best of intentions, the act of giving shoes away has had the unintended consequence of undermining local shoe producers in the recipient communities and stifling their economic development.[2] To its credit, Tom's has responded to this problem by sourcing shoes locally.[3] Or see again the example given in Chapter 7 of the Energy Independence and Security Act. This U.S. law was enacted to stimulate plant-based fuel production and reduce air pollution and greenhouse gas emissions, but because of a reliance on palm oil instead has led to social and environmental disaster in Southeast Asia.

Finally, understanding what principles should serve as the criteria for decision-making (Step 5 of the weight-of-reasons) can also be complicated. This is because important ethical principles can sometimes come into conflict in addressing a grand challenge. What should one do when the option that creates the most utility infringes on fundamental rights, or the most effective solution to a problem is not fair to some?

Raising these difficulties does not mean that it is useless to try to address grand challenges. By relying on the tools presented throughout this book, companies have a better chance of contributing to solving grand challenges. Systems thinking can help them identify stakeholders and understand the consequences of different courses of action. Both/and thinking, moral imagination, and inquiry/advocacy decision-making can help them as they try to resolve conflict among stakeholders' interests in innovative ways. Incremental approaches to decision-making such as trial and error learning can help them deal with the uncertainty associated with grand challenges. Critically, collaboration through multisector partnerships can provide a platform for ongoing mutual learning and problem-solving. Political skills such as coalition building, persuasion, and deal making can enable businesses to effectively implement preferred courses of action. Clear statements of mission, vision, and values can help clarify the principles (Step 5) that decision-makers should apply and those that should be disregarded. Values-based ethics programs can help ensure that decision-makers live up to those principles.

## Creating a Supportive Societal Context

LO 9.3: Recognize that addressing grand challenges requires innovation and that businesses will innovate more to address grand challenges if governments establish frameworks that encourage such innovation.

As we have just discussed, because grand challenges are so complex, no playbook exists for addressing them. They require businesses and their stakeholders to collaborate continuously in order to develop innovations in policies, practices, and business models. Yet the success of efforts to address grand challenges is not in the hands of these actors alone. Just as individuals are influenced by their organizational environments (see Chapter 4), so businesses and their stakeholders are influenced by the rules of the societies in which they operate.

Of particular importance in addressing grand challenges are the questions of whether the business environment rewards innovation and who bears its costs and risks. In addressing grand challenges, societies must grapple with the fundamental risk management question of whether it is preferable to allow innovations that solve one problem but might have other adverse consequences, or instead stifle innovations that have unpredictable consequences to ensure that nobody is harmed. For example, should a pharmaceutical company be able to sell a new disease-preventing medicine that could help millions but may have dangerous side effects? And should it have to sell the medicine even if doing so generates losses rather than profits? Societies must make such decisions about what risks they are willing to accept and which ones they are not, and who will bear the costs.

In general, in considering the risks of innovation, most societies have adopted a teleological approach according to which harm to some is an acceptable price of actions and policies that benefit many. Indeed, some have argued that in the development of bridge building, auto transport, aviation, dams, nuclear power, and other technologies, societies have chosen to tolerate some risks even when that means a great number of mishaps and casualties.[4] The tendency to tolerate risk for the sake of innovation varies, however, between societies and even within them. In the United States, for instance, the federal government agencies EPA and OSHA have been known to apply different standards when judging the riskiness of technologies and society's willingness to tolerate that risk.

One consideration in assessing risks and rewards is who bears the risk. Governments tend to accept that innovations may have some adverse consequences for competitors and their capital providers, so long as innovating firms have competed fairly. The rationale is that society is better off when this kind of evolution occurs. The process of innovation then is one in which users sort through their options, firms offering the best ones survive and thrive, and those offering lesser options do not endure or occupy weaker marketplace positions. As discussed in Chapter 7, government's role is to ensure that competition is fair and that innovations make customers better off. Moreover, governments often take a Rawlsian view of innovation and try to address harms to those hurt—displaced employees and depressed communities through job training, economic revitalization programs, and other policies and programs.

An alternative to the teleological view of managing risk is the view that innovation should harm nobody and respect the rights of all regardless of the results. These principles have deep philosophical roots, as discussed in Chapter 2. For more than 2,000 years, the Hippocratic Oath has required doctors to not *knowingly* harm their patients. The renowned management theorist Peter Drucker proclaimed that avoiding harm was the quintessential business ethic that no firm should violate.

One well-known formulation of the principle of doing no harm is the **precautionary principle**. While the principle has been presented in many different forms, it is generally accepted to mean that new technologies and practices that have uncertain consequences should not be undertaken (Figure 9.1). The principle has been adopted into European law as well as incorporated into numerous UN environmental treaties. The precautionary principle shifts the burden of proof in risk management; rather than putting the burden on injured parties to show that they have been harmed, it places the burden on innovators to show that the risk of adverse consequences is minimal or nonexistent. The principle is captured in the popular phrase "better safe than sorry." It is meant to prevent the problem of escalation of commitment, discussed in Chapter 3, and it can be seen as an element of incremental decision-making, discussed in Chapter 5. By requiring companies and societies to delay investments until uncertainty is resolved, so the thinking goes, applying the precautionary principle helps society avoid going down paths that ultimately are very harmful. Examples of issues where activists have invoked the precautionary principle include nuclear power and human consumption of genetically modified foods.

The price to society of following the precautionary principle may be reduced innovation. With respect to scientific and technological impacts on the natural world and on human health, the precautionary principle can stall the development of new products or processes that may yield progress in solving grand challenges, but have unknown or disputed side effects. The precautionary principle forces companies to have second thoughts prior to attempting to commercialize their discoveries.

One can hope and work for outcomes in which societies do not face an either/or choice between innovations and their adverse consequences. Utilitarian philosopher John Stuart Mill, discussed in Chapter 2, took this view. According to Mill, when people are free to develop their faculties and interests in the ways they want, society ultimately benefits from the innovation and experimentation that ensue. Those who take advantage of the freedom this principle affords can branch out and try activities

**FIGURE 9.1**

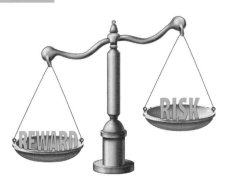
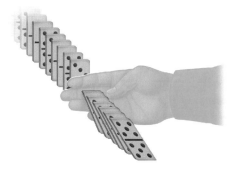

Cost–benefit analysis:
Weigh the rewards against the risks

Precautionary principle:
Eliminate all risk

The precautionary principle suggests addressing uncertainty by embracing the maxim "better safe than sorry." In contrast, utilitarianism suggests addressing uncertainty through cost–benefit analysis; if expected benefits exceed expected costs, then innovations may proceed.

that they would not otherwise endeavor to do if greater restrictions were imposed on them. At the same time, Mill recognized that innovators should take pains not to harm others. Rawls's theory of justice takes a similar view in insisting that the basic rules governing society should be acceptable to all. Applying Rawls's theory, innovation would occur only if those who might be harmed by it agree to it.

In countries taking a more utilitarian approach to risk taking and innovation, it is fundamentally important that before proceeding, firms assess the degree of harm they might cause. To balance the twin imperatives of taking risks to address grand challenges and ensuring safety, companies should operate transparently, obtain voluntary and informed consent from those who knowingly might be harmed, and do their best to mitigate the adverse consequences that they did not foresee. In addition, companies must try to resolve uncertainties about the consequences of their innovations before they undertake them. This requires them to counter cognitive biases such as escalation of commitment and organizational decision-making biases such as groupthink by using the weight-of-reasons framework and the decision-making approaches for developing long-term solutions described in Chapter 5.

As well, companies should try to build ethical organizations (Chapter 6) and engage with stakeholders in collective problem solving that benefits all (Chapter 8). By taking steps such as these, companies can be sure that they are not making light of the possible adverse consequences of their innovations to address grand challenges.

## Ethical Innovations to Address Grand Challenges: Three Approaches

LO 9.4: Identify existing innovative business approaches to addressing grand challenges, including shared value, base of the pyramid, and industry-transforming innovation.

We now turn to several different ways companies have taken a leading role in addressing grand challenges. All three involve moral imagination, an understanding of the larger systems in which the company is operating, a both/and approach to the tension between earning a profit and doing good for the world, dealing with uncertainty by adopting an incremental approach to decision-making, and engaging in serious interaction and learning with stakeholders.

### Creating Shared Value

One approach to addressing grand challenges is Porter and Kramer's shared value framework (Figure 9.2). Michael Porter is perhaps the most influential strategy scholar of the past 50 years. His ideas about industry competitiveness and business strategy are widely taught. With Michael Kramer, Porter wrote an important 2011 *Harvard Business Review* article titled "Creating Shared Value." In this work, Porter and Kramer address the perceived decline in business legitimacy. They associate this decline with business's failure to contribute to solving important global problems and the widespread perception that business has even made these problems worse.

**FIGURE 9.2**

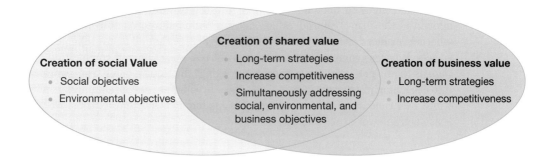

The shared value framework takes a both/and approach to the question of whether it "pays to be good."

*Source:* https://researchleap.com/wp-content/uploads/2015/02/Shared-Value-Creation.png

Porter and Kramer view corporate social responsibility (CSR) as an insufficient way to address grand challenges and propose creating shared value (CSV) instead. While careful to affirm that CSV and CSR can complement each other, Porter and Kramer contrast CSV and CSR along a number of dimensions. According to their critique, CSR programs are typically undertaken without explicit thought given to the benefits they provide to the company. They often include charitable activities that are valuable, worthy, and even noble but marginal to core profit-generating activities. In contrast, CSV mobilizes all of the firm's resources and is intended not just to aid society in solving urgent problems but also to enhance firm profitability. CSV is intended to make the firm more competitive while simultaneously advancing economic and social conditions in the world.

Porter and Kramer maintain that whereas CSR agendas are heavily determined by external demands to which companies must respond, CSV agendas are internally generated based on a company's deep understanding of its unique business value chain. In contrast to CSR, Porter and Kramer argue, CSV strategically deploys the firm's core operations to simultaneously make the world better and meet the firm's economic needs. By their very nature, CSR programs are also limited by the budget that corporations allocate to it, while CSV, because it is integral to profit maximization, can summon the entire company budget.

CSV also involves companies working collaboratively with the entire "cluster" of stakeholders in their geographic region, including related businesses, suppliers, service providers, universities, trade associations, and governments.[5] Porter and Kramer give the example of Nestlé's Nespresso brand, which Nestlé built in part by working with regional farming cooperatives, supporting agricultural extension programs, and partnering with NGOs to improve the social and environmental sustainability of coffee growing. By giving diverse stakeholders the opportunity to share their viewpoints and work together in developing plans of action, such multistakeholder engagement provides a means of identifying, preempting, and mitigating the unintended consequences of shared value activities.

**Creating shared value** An approach to business in which companies deploy their core resources and capabilities to create value for shareholders and society simultaneously

The main insight that comes from Porter and Kramer's shared value framework is that the firm should focus on areas where its business capabilities intersect with grand challenges to maximize benefits for society while also advancing the core agenda of the firm. "Shared value" takes a both/and approach to the question of whether business primarily serves shareholders or rather all of its stakeholders and society. Whereas companies often take profit maximization and competitive advantage as the targets of strategic decision-making, the shared value framework takes into account a broader set of principles and a broader set of consequences in ways in which everyone benefits. Accordingly, CSV is highly consistent with the weight-of-reasons framework.

## Serving the Base of the Pyramid

**Base of the pyramid**
An approach to business in which companies seek to earn profits by providing goods and services, and in some cases employment, economic empowerment, economic development, and other services, to the world's poorest people

Another way to approach grand challenges is to target the base of the pyramid as a company's main customer group. Scholarship on BOP traces back to a 2002 article by C. K. Prahalad and Stuart Hart. In 2004, Prahalad followed this article with his book *The Fortune at the Bottom of the Pyramid: Eradicating Poverty Through Profits*. The term *base of the pyramid* has since come to replace bottom of the pyramid. Shortly thereafter, Hart published his book *Capitalism at the Crossroads*, which also addresses BOP.

BOP researchers argue that up to 4 billion poor people in the world are underserved by the private sector and in need of new products, services, and technologies. Attending to the poor at the BOP thus offers an opportunity to expand to businesses operating outside well-saturated existing markets and that are struggling to grow (Figure 9.3). The size of the BOP market has been estimated to be as large as $5 trillion.

Helping the world's poor to elevate themselves is an opportunity to do well by doing good. While the idea of lending to the poor already had gained currency due

**FIGURE 9.3    The Base of the Pyramid**

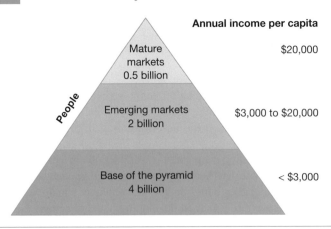

*Source:* Pennsylvania State University.[6]

to the efforts of microenterprise lenders such as Grameen Bank (mentioned earlier), Prahalad and Hart were the first to write that large, established companies in many other industries could also play a role in addressing the grand challenges facing the poor, including poverty, inequality, and discrimination.

Microsoft founder and billionaire businessman Bill Gates, under the rubric of creative capitalism, has taken up many of Prahalad and Hart's ideas. He has maintained that capitalism does a very good job of caring for the well-off, and should also use its resources and capacity for innovation to provide the world's poorest people with vital goods and services such as health care, banking, communications, and nutrition. Gates believes that over the long run, capitalism can solve some of the globe's most intractable problems, such as preventing tropical diseases, providing potable water, and supplying reliable and environmentally sound sources of energy.

Gates, like Prahalad and Hart, holds that corporations are likely to be better than governments in assisting the poor to rise above their privation.[7] While he acknowledges obstacles to doing business at the BOP such as inability to pay and a lack of infrastructure, Gates maintains that companies can work with host governments and NGOs to overcome these obstacles. He identifies many strong reasons why corporations should emphasize people at the BOP. These reasons, which mirror the arguments for why it can pay to be good presented in Chapter 7, include the following:

**Creative capitalism** An approach to business in which companies, governments, and nongovernmental organizations work together to use capitalism to address grand challenges

- Access to a very large market

- The ability to recruit idealistic, young, enthusiastic, and highly motivated workers

- Cost breakthroughs, which companies would have to find so that they are able to sell products cheaply

- Product innovations

- Enhanced brands and reputations

Some of the earliest achievements in the quest to serve the people at the bottom of the pyramid took place in the telecommunications industry. Many new firms came into existence to provide telecom services, such as Mobile Telephone Networks in South Africa, Celtel in sub-Saharan Africa, Bharti Airtel in India, and Globe Telecom in the Philippines. The spread of cell phones has been very rapid and has had many benefits for the poor. For example, having a cell phone allows small business owners to more easily find out current prices for the goods they sell and adjust the quantities they produce and to more easily order the supplies they need. Individuals and businesses alike gain more control over their lives. They become less reliant on slow and undependable postal services, are better able to complete financial transactions, get medical information more quickly, and access entertainment options that otherwise would not be available.

Early efforts to do business at the BOP also included many failures, both commercially and in terms of addressing social problems. Companies often sought to use mass production and distribution models to sell standardized products to the poor, but this effort was often unsuccessful because of inadequate infrastructure and a very

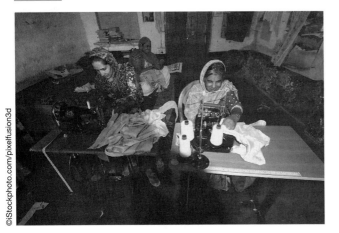

©iStockphoto.com/pixelfusion3d

BOP 2.0 involves building relationships with the poor to co-create products and services that meet their needs and improve their lives.

diverse customer base. Furthermore, these early BOP efforts, which Hart refers to as BOP 1.0, came under extensive criticism for exploiting the poor.[8] Companies were accused of viewing the poor as customers but not really understanding their needs, providing them with economic opportunities, or helping them improve their lives.[9] According to this critique, BOP activities even caused harm to the poor, including displacement of local producers and merchants by the large companies engaged in BOP activities, and vulnerability to changes in commodity prices and other global economic forces from which poor communities previously were largely isolated.

Some of the more recent efforts to serve the BOP have accounted for these problems and criticisms. In BOP 2.0, company employees interact with, and sometimes live in, poor communities; come to deeply know and understand those who live there; and cocreate new products and services that meet these people's needs and improve their lives. They engage the poor in the production and sale of these products. Hart and Sharma call this deep engagement with stakeholders "radical transactiveness." Hart has stated that engaging people in the community and co-creating products with them is probably the only way to establish a compelling value proposition.

# THE CHOTUKOOL REFRIGERATOR

Hart gives the example of the Indian company Godrej's Chotukool refrigerator. Chotukool means "little cool" in Hindi. The company's first effort to produce a "BOP refrigerator" failed because it followed the BOP 1.0 model: The company did market research, conducted focus groups, designed a product, determined its price point, and then had its salesforce and some NGO partners go out and sell it. After this product, which "looked like a little metal box, with a little freezer compartment," failed to sell, Godrej, to its credit, took a BOP 2.0 approach. Company representatives went to and lived in Indian villages and began to develop ideas with community members and enlist them as partners. Local women helped

develop, service, and sell the Chotukool, which can be moved around, doubles as a workspace, works with any energy source, and does not use a compressor for cooling. Realizing it had hit on something big, Godrej now sells the Chotukool throughout India to customers of all incomes (see https://www.chotukool .com/). The Chotukool example shows that it is possible for companies operating at the BOP to decrease poverty, reduce gender and income inequality, and even promote local, renewable energy sources, while also making a handsome profit. Working directly with the stakeholders who are most affected by grand challenges can lead to breakthrough innovations that earn money and improve lives.

## Industry Transformation Through Entrepreneurship

Increasingly, new companies are emerging for the explicit purpose of developing entirely new approaches to addressing grand challenges.[10] As ambitious as the shared value and BOP approaches to grand challenges are, perhaps even more so are the entrepreneurs who address grand challenges by trying to revolutionize global industries. These entrepreneurs come up with innovative new technologies, products, and services that transform existing industries and give birth to new ones. The entrepreneurs who succeed in developing industry-transforming innovations use moral imagination and both/and thinking to develop new products and business models that overcome the tension between making profits and addressing grand challenges. Critically, they recognize that just developing new products is not enough; they also use systems thinking and political skill to imagine and then build the supporting business context that is needed for these products to succeed. They develop networks of businesses (e.g., suppliers, distributors) with complementary resources and capabilities, and they sometimes get involved in politics to work for institutional changes (e.g., tax credits, regulatory approvals) that support their new products.[11]

**Industry-transforming innovations** Innovations that produce products and services that disrupt or destroy existing industries

We now examine the efforts of two companies that have tried to introduce electric cars on a widespread basis: Tesla and Better Place. Electric cars potentially could address a number of grand challenges, including sustainable energy, sustained economic growth, sustainable industrialization, sustainable production and consumption, and global climate change (SDGs 7, 8, 9, 12, and 13—see Table 9.1). Then we examine the case of medical technology company Theranos. None of the three companies profiled may be considered an unmitigated success at this point, and two of them went out of business. Theranos in fact was a scandalous failure. Together, the cases provide a realistic assessment of the difficulties of entrepreneurship to address grand challenges. An important, if unsurprising, conclusion of these examples is that innovating to address grand challenges requires not just a vision and the desire to do the right thing but also business acumen. When entrepreneurs start businesses to address grand challenges, they keep in mind both the basics of good management and their ambitious goals. You are unlikely to make the world a better place if your *only* motivation is profits. At the same time, you cannot make the world a better place, at least for very long, if you ignore profits. As you read these three cases, consider whether the entrepreneurs involved applied the steps of the weight-of-reasons framework and whether they have used the tools of effective ethical decision-making such as systems thinking, both/and thinking, moral imagination, experimentation, and interactive stakeholder management.

# AUTOMOBILE INDUSTRY INNOVATION TO ADDRESS GRAND CHALLENGES: BETTER PLACE AND TESLA[12]

At a 2009 TED conference, "ecopreneur" Shai Agassi declared that the mission of converting the world to electric cars was the "moral equivalent of abolishing slavery." He attested that making this conversion was like going to the moon, and that anything short of fully achieving this objective would be a failure. According to Agassi, moving to EVs would be the start of a new industrial revolution.

## Better Place

Agassi was born in 1968 and grew up outside Tel Aviv. He began his university studies at Israel's best engineering school, the Technion, at age 15. With his father, an army officer and later telecom executive, he started a software company that provided enterprise-level services for small businesses. A 1995 consulting assignment from Apple led him to Silicon Valley. Once there, he began TopTier, a company that created web portals for large Bay Area companies such as Hewlett Packard. Software giant SAP bought this company in 2001 for $400 million and asked Agassi to head global product development.

As a rising star in SAP's executive suite, Agassi was invited to be a part of the World Economic Forum's under-40 age-group in 2005. He responded to a question about how to make the world a better place by calling for research into alternative transportation models. The white paper he cowrote titled "Transforming Global Transportation" maintained that the widespread adoption of EVs would mean a revolution in the world like that of Watt's steam engine, Ford's Model T, the Apollo program, and the Internet.

In 2007, Agassi decided to leave SAP and start a company called Better Place to try to realize his vision. The company would sell EVs, but the key to its business model would be to make money by providing drivers with battery charging services at a lower cost than gasoline. Because at that time EV batteries had a range of only about 85 miles, Agassi envisioned building an infrastructure of battery charging and swapping stations.

Better Place's first investor was Maniv Energy Capital, which had been set up in 2005 by Michael Granoff to explore opportunities in new energy technologies. Granoff introduced Agassi to Idan Ofer, who at the time was the Chairman of the Board of Directors of Israel Corporation, a major industrial company that had formerly been owned by the State of Israel. Ofer decided to invest $100 million in Agassi's company. With this funding committed, further investment came shortly thereafter.

Better Place then had to find an auto company with which to partner. Carlos Ghosn, at that time the CEO (chief executive officer) of Nissan and Renault, promised Agassi that Renault would develop an electric version of the midsize passenger car Fluence for Better Place. In return, Better Place agreed to acquire 100,000 vehicles to sell in Israel and Denmark between 2011 and 2016. Better Place's early marketing efforts tried to sell fleet managers on the environmental benefits of EVs and on cutting dependence on foreign oil, but the company quickly realized that it also had to make a case for the car based on other features. From the beginning, Better Place acknowledged that limited car choice was a problem. The Fluence was a mundane family car with few features. After making the deal with Renault, Agassi approached other major automakers to introduce other vehicles and thereby increase buyer choice, but none of them agreed to supply him with cars.

One of the main challenges that Better Place faced was synchronizing the various parts of its business model. Realizing each part of the model was difficult in itself. The company had to sell enough electric Fluences in Israel and Denmark to achieve economies of scale; install thousands of charging spots in garages, retail spaces, streets, and homes; and build battery swapping stations. It also had to create software to monitor customers' energy use and bill them.

### Better Place's Lack of Focus and Its Bankruptcy

Better Place was unable to successfully take these steps. As of the start of 2012, it had orders for just 100 cars, with most of these orders coming from its own employees. While it built 30 swapping stations in Israel that covered the entire country, each cost far more than a traditional gasoline station to construct. Obtaining land and the rights to build the swapping stations led to huge cost overruns. The company did not really even start the task of building swapping stations in Denmark because the task became so overwhelming just in Israel.

The company also lost its strategic focus. Rather than taking care of operating problems and buoyed by a second investment round of $350 million, Better Place turned its attention from Israel and Denmark to starting similar initiatives in many other countries. It engaged in discussions with more than 20 countries and started projects in the San Francisco Bay Area, Hawaii, Australia, China, and elsewhere. Each location required a different operational blueprint and necessitated extensive preparations.

Faced with these problems, Better Place was losing more than half a million dollars a day at the start of 2012. Despite having raised close to $1 billion in funding, time was running out. Reluctantly, Better Place's Board of Directors asked Ofer to tell Agassi that with him at the helm the company would be unable to obtain additional funding. Ofer fired Agassi, raised another $100 million from Israel Corporation, and appointed Evan Thornley, head of the company's Australian operations, as CEO. When Thornley did not make sufficient progress, he too was quickly ousted. Dan Cohen, a former Israel Corporation executive, then replaced Thornley.

Bleeding cash, despite Cohen's best efforts, the company had no choice but to declare bankruptcy. Fluence EV owners in Israel mourned the company's demise and tried to organize to run it on their own as a cooperative, but the company had such deep economic woes that no matter what the owners did they could not figure out a way to keep Better Place afloat. Agassi's ambition to address the world's grand challenges through business innovation never came to fruition.

### Tesla

Tesla's Elon Musk exhibited similar if not more revolutionary fervor than Agassi. Musk's approach to bringing about the revolution could not have been more different, however. His celebrated 2006 blog "The Secret Tesla Motors Master Plan (just between you and me)" asserted that Tesla's "overarching purpose" was to "expedite the move" from a "mine-and-burn hydrocarbon economy" toward a solar electric economy. To bring this economy into being, Musk wrote, Tesla would enter the high end of the automotive market, where customers were prepared to pay a premium, and then move down the market as fast as possible to greater volume and lower prices with each successive model.[13] The goal was to offer Tesla's third-generation vehicle, the Model 3 (originally known as the Model E), sometime in 2017 at a base price of $35,000, excluding any tax credits from government. It would have a 200-mile plus battery range and generate an average gross margin of 15%.

### Tesla's Birth and Early Development

Musk was an early investor in Tesla and became CEO in 2008, after the company failed to meet its deadlines for producing the Roadster sports car, its first product. Agassi, in contrast, was never a direct investor in Better Place. In 2008, Tesla had limited operating history, a long history of losses, and dwindling capital. Building an all-electric car was proving to be an extremely difficult proposition. Moreover, Tesla was competing against the world's largest automakers which had a stable base of customers who were accustomed to drive gasoline-powered vehicles. Nevertheless, Musk was able to get the company on track, and the Roadster proved to be a rousing marketplace success. It sold for $109,000. Its ability to accelerate at a rate of 0 to 60 miles per hour in less than 4 seconds, faster than some Ferrari, appealed to a slim but important niche in the market.

*(Continued)*

(Continued)

A big part of the success of the Roadster was its innovative battery design. Working with Panasonic, the company designed the car's battery pack around the small-format lithium ion cells found in laptops. These cells enabled the Roadster to achieve a range of 245 miles. This accomplishment was important because earlier EVs rarely had ranges greater than 85 miles. Tesla enjoyed numerous advantages in addition to its unique battery. One of these was that it completely bypassed dealers and typical advertising strategies. Tesla sold the Roadster by word of mouth. In addition, the company benefitted like other electric car companies from the subsidies governments offered EV buyers.

Tesla's challenge was to get beyond a unique and highly priced sports car and move toward a more affordable vehicle that would appeal to the typical driver. The company took incremental steps in this direction. The Model S, its second product, sold for about $75,000. Even more so than its predecessor, this car was a huge success. *Consumer Reports* gave the Model S its highest rating ever and bestowed on it its coveted 2014 Car of the Year award. In 2013, its U.S. sales were greater than that of the Mercedes-Benz S-Class, the BMW 7 Series, the Lexus LS, and the Audi A7, among others (Table 9.2). Largely because of the introduction of the Model S, Tesla went on a very successful two-year run on Wall Street. Its stock price soared by more than 600%. The company for a time came to be worth more than either Ford or GM.

**TABLE 9.2**　**U.S. Luxury Car Sales, 2013**[14]

| Luxury Cars | 2013 Sales | Price Range |
| --- | --- | --- |
| Tesla Model S | 22,477 | $69,000 to $89,000 |
| Mercedes-Benz S-Class | 13,303 | $92,000 to $212,000 |
| BMW 7-Series | 10,932 | $73,000 to $140,000 |
| Lexus LS | 10,727 | $71,000 to $119,000 |
| Audi A7 | 8,483 | $62,000 to $105,000 |
| Mercedes-Benz CLS-Class | 8,032 | $72,000 to $95,000 |
| Audi A8 | 6,300 | $73,000 to $111,000 |
| Jaguar XJ | 5,434 | $73,000 to $116,000 |
| Porsche Panamera | 5,421 | $75,000 to $175,000 |
| Hyundai Equus | 3,578 | $59,000 to $66,000 |
| Cadillac ELR | 6 | $74,000 |

*Source:* M. Rogowsky. August 24, 2013. The Numbers Don't Lie: Tesla is Beginning to Put the Hurt on the Competition. *Forbes.*

*Tesla's Moves*

Because of the superior range of Tesla's vehicles—they had almost three times the range of the Fluences that Better Place had sold—Tesla did not have to install as many charging and swapping stations as Better Place did to achieve the same coverage for drivers. In the United States, Tesla was able to install enough charging and swapping stations for a driver to travel from the East to the West Coast and to travel up and down each seaboard without having to worry about running out of electricity.

However, the next generations of Tesla's cars, if they were to appeal to the world's middle classes, would have to be priced far lower than the Model S. Tesla's aim was to sell its third vehicle, the Model 3, at no more than $35,000. If priced at this level, however, it was not clear whether the company could earn a profit. The estimated cost of producing the Model S was approximately $60,000 per car. Even if Tesla could reduce the cost of the battery from $15,000 to $10,000, use fewer materials to eliminate another $3,000, rely on shared tooling to take off another $3,000, and save $4,000 by ordering parts in greater quantity, the cost of building the Model 3 might not go lower than $45,000, which would mean that it would lose $10,000 on each vehicle sold (Table 9.3).

**TABLE 9.3**   Could Tesla achieve a break-even point for its third-generation vehicle?[15]

| | |
|---|---|
| Estimated cost of building the basic Model S | $60,000 |
| Estimated reduction in cost of the battery due to smaller battery manufactured in Tesla's proposal battery giga-factory | −$5,000 |
| Estimated lower material costs (less aluminum, plastics, and vinyl) | −$3,000 |
| Estimated lower tooling costs due to shared production with Model S | −$3,000 |
| Estimated lower component parts from ordering in larger quantities | −$4,000 |
| Estimated cost of building the basic Model 3 | $45,000 |
| Proposed retail price of Model 3 | $35,000 |
| Expected loss per sale of each Model 3 | −$10,000 |

Source: M. Rogowsky. August 24, 2013. The Numbers Don't Lie: Tesla is Beginning to Put the Hurt on the Competition. Forbes.

The only way to make the numbers add up was vast manufacturing and technological innovation, and very quickly. Musk planned to achieve these innovations and cost reductions through mass production in the large assembly plant that Tesla had acquired from GM and Toyota in Fremont, California, and by building a large-scale battery factory, a "giga-factory" located near Reno, Nevada, that would achieve cost reductions in batteries and accelerate the pace of battery innovation. Musk sought to automate vehicle assembly and battery manufacturing entirely and the company predicted that its new factory would be able to produce batteries for 500,000 vehicles. Doubling worldwide capacity by 2020 would lower battery prices by 30%.

*Troubles Arise*

Making all the technical innovations needed for the assembly plant and the giga-factory to run well was not easy, however. Problems arose in battery manufacturing, parts acquisition, and, perhaps most important, the development of assembly lines. Tesla's oft-proclaimed goal was to build 5,000 vehicles a week, but at one point, the company was making fewer than three cars a day.

Musk, nonetheless, was dedicated to meeting the ambitious production goals he had set for the company. He was relentlessly hard driving and demanded perfection of himself and others. He regularly spent time at the factories, trying to figure out why machines did not function, parts did not align correctly, and the software crashed so often. He was overcome by the frustrations of not getting the automation to work and the robots to function in the ways he wanted. Still, he did not let up in his quest for total automation, even when this demand just added to delays and malfunctions.

(Continued)

(Continued)

Musk urged his employees to think in unconventional ways and insisted that the inconceivable could be accomplished if they reduced it to logical steps and just put in the additional time and effort needed. His unrelenting leadership style alienated as much as inspired those who worked for him, however. The Model 3, he asserted, was a bet-the-company decision, and everyone in the company had to work harder and smarter. He was unwilling to tolerate deviation from the absolute commitment he expected from his workforce. He blamed his employees for the failure to meet production targets and let go of hundreds of them for alleged performance failures. Fear pervaded the workforce and did not make it any easier for Tesla to achieve Musk's goals.

No matter how hard Musk pushed himself and the others, his factory was not meeting his ambitious production goals. The robots the company installed were unable to carry out simple tasks such as reliably recognizing and grasping different colored wires well. Musk at one point stated that the company was operating in a "manufacturing hell." Aware of the problems, some customers who had made deposits to reserve Model 3s started to ask for their money back. In interviews, Musk appeared to be angry and visibly shaken. In October 2017, Tesla announced that it had lost $671 million in the previous quarter, $1.5 billion in the first nine months of the year, and had made only 222 Model 3s.

### Foregoing Complete Automation

Musk continued to work nonstop and unremittingly. He apparently believed that the more he worked, the more likely he would be to overcome the gargantuan production problems the company faced. He slept in the factory and played a role in personally attempting to diagnose the roots of problems. Improvements came, and assembly line production started to pick up, but the vision of a nearly fully automated factory to which he stubbornly adhered simply proved to be out of reach. In the winter of 2018, as many executives left the firm in near complete frustration, Musk finally conceded. He allowed plant workers to hand carry parts to assembly lines and move them by forklift rather than using undependable robots to get the work done. Musk struggled to control his emotions. In the spring of 2018, during a conference call with investors, he broke down. When an analyst asked about the company's financial statements, he responded, "Boring. Bonehead."

Soon thereafter, Musk announced that Tesla would build a tent in the assembly plant's parking lot. In that tent, it would build an entirely new assembly line, one not burdened by the vision of total automation. That summer, Tesla was able to manufacture 5,031 Model 3 vehicles in a week, finally hitting its goal, but doing so a half year late and only after the departure of hundreds of executives and workers who could not function under Musk's demands. In that summer, Musk tweeted that Tesla finally was a real manufacturer of automobiles.

Unfortunately, Musk also continued to engage in erratic behavior, tweeting "Am considering taking Tesla private at $420. Funding secured."[16] The latter boosted the company's stock price by a large percentage, but soon it was obvious that Tesla did not have the backing to go private. It also had not obtained the necessary regulatory approvals. The Securities and Exchange Commission imposed a $20 million fine on the company for announcing that it was going private without these critical elements and required Musk to give up his post as Chairman of Tesla's Board. He was permitted to remain the Chief Executive, however. In the fall of that year, Musk raised even more questions when on the Joe Rogan Experience podcast, he publicly smoked marijuana. This was a legal act in the state of California, but questionable from the point of view of investors.

### Tesla's Cost Bind

During this ongoing turmoil, the company continued building Model 3s, getting better and faster as it went. In the third quarter of 2018, Tesla reported profits of $312 million. It seemed to have seized success from the jaws of defeat. Yet it was still far from certain whether its business model was really working and whether it could profitably sell Model 3s on an ongoing basis. Moreover, other auto companies, including many in China where EV advances were being made, were catching up with Tesla.

Tesla shareholders undeniably have done very well, but whether they will continue to do well is an open question. While Tesla may have ushered in a revolution in the auto industry, its long-term survival is uncertain. The ultimate outcome of Musk's massive attempt at innovation to address a grand challenge is far from clear.

*Learning From Better Place and Tesla*

There is much to learn from a comparison between Better Place and Tesla. The weight-of-reasons framework helps us understand the differences between the two companies' fortunes. Both Agassi and Musk were motivated by a desire to move the world away from fossil fuels in order to address climate change, pollution, and oil-related conflict (Step 1 of the framework). The two worked from reasonably similar sets of facts about the problem (Step 2) and applied roughly the same principles (Step 5). Yet they clearly had very different ideas about what the consequences of different courses of action would be and which would provide a long-term solution (Steps 3, 4, 6, and 7). Agassi accepted battery technology as it was and tried to build a battery charging and swapping station infrastructure around that technology. Though he recognized the need to offer a broader array of vehicle model types, he started with a ho-hum vehicle. In contrast, Musk accepted neither the current battery technology nor the current stock of vehicles. He wanted to revolutionize electric battery and vehicle technology. He also wanted to revolutionize EV infrastructure, but unlike Agassi, he saw this as complementary to his main task rather than the main task itself. He had a clear set of incremental goals, which he tried extremely hard to meet in a timely fashion in order to build trust and maintain credibility with the investing public. Where he encountered the most difficulty was in manufacturing and getting the cost of the vehicle down in a reasonable period of time so that it could be adopted on a wide-scale basis.

Both Agassi and Musk were motivated by an ethical vision, and both took a both/and approach to the question of whether it pays to be good. Furthermore, both engaged in systems thinking, basing their entrepreneurial actions on a big picture view of the role and impact of cars on our society and the

environment. Both also engaged in politics, trying to build the networks of actors needed to achieve their visions and "close the circle." Where Musk clearly seems to have outshined Agassi is in the area of moral imagination. He clearly has a very rare ability to question prevailing assumptions and imagine the consequences of various courses of action. Musk imagined an electric car industry and surrounding business system vastly different from prevailing ones, whereas Agassi accepted existing technology and systems and took them as his starting points. Musk's approach to bringing about the electric car revolution was better conceived than that of Agassi.

Still, it is too soon to declare that Musk is leading the world to victory in its quest to address grand challenges such as climate change and pollution. As noted above, significant competitive challenges await him. Moreover, the potential for negative unintended consequences from EV production and use is not insignificant. Concerns already have been raised that the mining, refining, and ultimate disposal of the rare earth metals used in lithium-ion batteries and electric motors can be dangerous to humans and damaging to the environment.[17] Furthermore, the production of these metals often takes place in countries that could decide to withhold them.[18] The manufacture of EVs also may produce greater greenhouse gas emissions than the manufacture of standard gasoline-powered vehicles.[19] And if EVs run on coal fired electricity, the net benefit of using them is considerably lower than if they run on renewable electricity. EVs are cleaner vehicles, not clean ones. The transition to EVs, if it happens, may provide benefits to the world, but there is little doubt that it will also come with other hard-to-predict effects.

There is another matter. The age-old ethical question, and one that is at the heart of this book, needs to be asked about Tesla. Is Musk's erratic and abusive behavior in the face of Tesla's adversity simply a cost that has to be borne in the service of addressing grand challenges? Does the noble "end" of a sustainable transportation revolution justify the "means" of his unethical behavior toward his workers and shareholders? There is no reason one cannot push hard to make change happen and treat people well at the same time. One can be ambitious and demanding yet respectful of one's employees.

# THE THERANOS SCANDAL

This chapter concludes with the cautionary tale of an entrepreneur who went badly astray in attempting to address—or pretending to address—a grand challenge. Elizabeth Holmes, the founder of Theranos, preyed on the gullibility of investors while purporting to make a revolutionary dent on the grand challenge of health and well-being (SDG-3). The company produced a semiportable device that Holmes alleged could do thousands of blood tests with a pin prick and produce results within 1 hour or less. The device would have been an extraordinary breakthrough because it would have provided users with real-time information and enable them to monitor their health and make adjustments in ways that human beings never have before. Other companies have tried but failed to solve the problem of how to conduct many different kinds of blood tests with such a small sample. This problem was one that Theranos never came close to solving, though Holmes claimed it had.

Holmes was the daughter of an ex-Enron executive and a scion of the Fleischmann family that built a food product empire. A chemical engineering dropout from Stanford, she was determined to follow in the footsteps of entrepreneurs like Steve Jobs. Her attachment to Jobs was so great that she regularly dressed in black turtlenecks in imitation of her hero. Holmes burnished her credentials by alleging that she had learned programming at an early age and started a successful business while still in high school selling C++ compilers to Chinese universities. These claims were similar to those of other entrepreneurs like Agassi and Musk. In addition, she cultivated a speaking style in which she affected a deep baritone voice in her public appearances to make her sound mature and hyperserious. This style of speaking provided her with an authoritative demeanor, which made her appear very believable. To further enhance her credibility and build her company's image, Holmes created an influential board of directors that included well-regarded diplomats, politicians, military figures, and corporate executives, including Henry Kissinger, George Shultz, William Perry, Sam Nunn, Bill Frist, James Mattis, and Dick

Kovacevich, the ex-CEO of Wells Fargo. None of these luminaries had any substantive knowledge of health care. Holmes succeeded in raising $92 million in venture capital prior to 2011 to research her blood testing concept. From the start, however, there were serious concerns from members of the medical community that what she was trying to do was impossible. The number of tests she promised from a pinprick of blood in a short period was beyond what any known technology could accomplish.

In 2013, Holmes sold the use of the device to Walgreens's stores in Arizona and California. The sale enabled the drugstore chain to have in-store blood sample collection centers. Selling the use of the device to Walgreens suggested that the device was a fully functioning innovation with great accuracy and entirely ready for commercialization. Walgreens's buy-in boosted Holmes's stature and provided her with the credibility to approach other wealthy investors for funding. In raising money, Holmes continued to avoid sophisticated Silicon Valley medical technology investors. Instead, she made her pitch to extremely rich and gullible individuals who had little experience in investing in the health sector and who lacked the sophistication to seriously investigate or challenge her claims. By all accounts, she was an exceptionally charismatic and convincing liar. She seemed very knowledgeable and beyond reproof and told a very good story. Holmes raised millions of dollars from among others the media mogul Rupert Murdoch; the Cox family, which controlled an Atlanta-based media empire; Carlos Slim, the Mexican business magnate who is one of the world's wealthiest persons; and the family of U.S. Secretary of Education Betsy DeVos, who is the daughter-in-law of Amway's billionaire cofounder Richard DeVos.

In 2014, Holmes was on the cover of *Fortune, Forbes, The New York Times Style Magazine*, and *Inc.* magazine. *Forbes* added to her renown by proclaiming that she was the world's youngest self-made female billionaire. In the magazine's list of billionaires in 2014, she ranked #110, with Forbes estimating her net worth as $9 billion. In 2015, Theranos was able to craft agreements with well-regarded medical institutions, including the Cleveland Clinic, to use its technology. Holmes's sales skills were exceptional. The problem was that her product simply did not work, a secret she tried to keep from everyone.

### Breaking the Story

In 2015, *The Wall Street Journal* reporter John Carreyrou broke the story that Holmes was lying about the product. He relied heavily on information he had obtained from Tyler Shultz, the grandson of Theranos director and former U.S. Secretary of State George Shultz. Shultz had been a Theranos employee and true believer in Holmes and her product until he realized that the enterprise in which he had become involved was a fake. In the demonstrations of the Theranos device, which Holmes called "Edison," she promised that 250 blood tests could be carried out simultaneously. Actually, Theranos technology could handle only a small subset of the tests. The company conducted most of its tests on a hacked Siemens diagnostic machine already on the market. The blood samples Edison collected were diluted to create more volume since the Siemens machines could carry out tests only on regularly sized samples. Done this way, the tests were unreliable. Healthy people might receive information that they had a disease (a "false positive"), while people who actually were sick might receive assurance that they had nothing to worry about. Had the devices actually come into regular use at Walgreens or the hospitals of the Cleveland Clinic, thousands of people would have been at risk.

When regulators from the state of California came to inspect Theranos's labs, they were not shown the Siemens equipment because it was hidden in the basement. The company, moreover, regularly told false stories to the U.S. Food and Drug Administration (FDA) about what its employees did in its labs. Holmes threatened her employees to deter them from revealing what was actually taking place. She, however, could not stop Tyler Shultz and others from talking to Carreyrou, despite the threats she made. On becoming aware that Tyler Shultz was

talking to Carreyrou, Holmes hired well-known trial lawyer David Boies, who threatened the Shultz family with bankruptcy if Tyler Shultz continued to speak to reporters. When the Carreyrou articles came out revealing the fraud, Holmes made an appearance on Jim Cramer's Mad Money show and said, "This is what happens when you work to change things, first they think you're crazy, then they fight you, and then all of a sudden you change the world."

In 2016, the Centers for Medicare and Medicaid Services confirmed that the results Theranos was producing were inaccurate and the company was relying on commercially available machines to do most of its testing. They banned Holmes from being involved in the company for two years. The company appealed to the U.S. Department of Health and Human Services, but Walgreens next stepped forward and canceled its relationship with Theranos. The state of Arizona then sued Theranos for carrying out 1.5 million bad blood tests. The company agreed to a settlement that amounted to nearly $5 million. After Arizona, the SEC sued in 2017 maintaining as part of the suit that Theranos had sold its technology to the Defense Department for use by soldiers in combat situations. Again, Theranos reached an out-of-court settlement.

Criminal charges came next, with Holmes facing up to 20 years in prison. Sunny Balwani, her ex-boyfriend and second in command at the company, also faces criminal charges. Theranos dissolved as a company and laid off all 800 of its employees. The billionaires who had funded Theranos came away with nothing, their losses reaching sums as great as $1 billion. Holmes, meanwhile, maintains her innocence and says that she is eager to have her day in court in front of a jury. The trial is currently scheduled to begin in August, 2020.

### Lessons Learned From Theranos

The lessons from the Theranos case are obviously very different from those of the Better Place and Tesla cases. Holmes clearly did not use a framework such as the weight-of-reasons. She did, however, use some of the ethical decision-making tools described in this book. The problem, it appears, was that

*(Continued)*

(Continued)

ultimately she used them to facilitate her fraudulent behavior. Holmes clearly took a both/and approach to the tension between shareholders and stakeholders; she saw addressing a grand challenge and creating great financial wealth as one and the same. Holmes also seems to have appreciated systems thinking. She understood that medical innovations take place within a larger business ecosystem that involves customers, regulators, investors, and the press, and she carefully manipulated other actors within this system to align with her. While it is hard to say, it seems that Holmes dealt with uncertainty by taking an incremental approach to decision-making. She seems to have been motivated by a blind faith that her company would overcome an insurmountable technical challenge, and in trying to get there, she was comfortable in making it up as she went along. The case brings out a very important point about ethical decision-making, which is that sophisticated decision-making tools such as those described in this book can be used unethically. This

is why Step 5 of the weight-of-reasons, principles, is so important.

The Theranos case takes us back to the cognitive biases and social influences that can taint ethical decision-making, discussed in Chapters 3 and 4. It seems that Holmes took advantage of the cognitive limitations of investors and others who bought into her scheme. She structured her interactions with her board of directors and investors so they would believe her, rather than gathering and evaluating evidence with a formal decision process. She and Balwani managed the Theranos workplace so that with a few exceptions, people like Tyler Schultz felt coerced into going along with bad behavior. Holmes herself also seems to have fallen prey to her own cognitive biases. Whether she started as a fraud or just got sucked into it by her own lies is hard to tell. Either way, it seems that Holmes escalated her commitment to her self-image as the new Steve Jobs and harmed many others in the process.

## SUMMARY AND CONCLUSION

In this chapter, we have discussed companies that go far beyond legal compliance in meeting their ethical duties to stakeholders. For these companies, ethics is not just about how they conduct themselves; rather, it is their business. The very reason they exist is to address grand challenges such as poverty, inequality, pollution, and climate change. Grand challenges are ethical challenges because they involve fundamental questions about human dignity, rights, and fairness. For companies that make it their purpose to address grand challenges, ethics and strategy become one and the same. Every important strategic decision that the company makes involves ethical reasoning. For this reason, frameworks such as the weight-of-reasons can help companies in addressing grand challenges to make strategic decisions.

Grand challenges are by definition very complex, and decisions made to address them are fraught with uncertainty. Moreover, they require decision-makers to carefully consider trade-offs among stakeholders. Most commonly, developing new approaches to grand challenges can threaten individuals and companies who are committed to and benefit from the status quo. They help some in need but not others, and they often have unclear profit potential. For these reasons, the tools described in this book can be crucial to companies that want to contribute to addressing grand challenges. The weight-of-reasons framework, both/and thinking, moral imagination, and team decision-making based on inquiry and advocacy can help companies resolve tensions between stakeholders, as well as the tension between making profit and doing good for the world.

Systems thinking can help decision-makers develop a deeper understanding of the problems they are solving, as well as think through the possible consequences of the actions they might take.

Also crucial in addressing grand challenges are incremental decision-making, political skills, and multisector partnerships. Because grand challenges are so complex, one can never truly close the circle and deliver one big solution to them. Any large-scale action could have large and negative unintended consequences. For this reason, addressing grand challenges is often an ongoing process in which companies work with many stakeholders to take small steps toward the end goal. After taking one step, they assess the outcome, make adjustments, and consider next steps. Thus, the essence of addressing grand challenges is often convening stakeholders so that they engage in dialogue, experiment together, learn, and solve problems. This works best when all stakeholders have a say and are sincerely motivated to address the grand challenge. As noted, it also works best within an institutional context that both rewards innovation and takes seriously the threat of serious unintended consequences. Within such a framework, decision-makers do thorough analysis to resolve uncertainty about the consequences of their innovations. While unintended consequences should be prevented and mitigated, it must be kept in mind that the negative consequences of not innovating can be higher than those of innovating.

This chapter examined three different approaches to addressing grand challenges. These are (1) the shared value approach, (2) the BOP approach, and (3) industry-transforming entrepreneurship. As discussed, a key idea behind the shared value approach is that companies can mobilize their resources in ways that simultaneously produce competitive advantage and address grand challenges in ways that stakeholders benefit. Similarly, the BOP approach emphasizes that serving the world's poor is both a tremendous business opportunity and a means of addressing grand challenges. Likewise,

transformative entrepreneurship involves coming up with and commercializing innovations that address grand challenges while simultaneously creating whole new industries. These three approaches are analytically but often not practically distinct, and in fact can be complementary. For example, a company engaging in entrepreneurship at the BOP could use a shared value approach to its operations. All three approaches could involve using the ethical decision-making tools profiled in this book, including the weight-of-reasons framework, both/and thinking, systems thinking, moral imagination, and interactive stakeholder engagement. The entrepreneurs and innovators profiled in this chapter tend to ask questions the weight-of-reasons would have them ask, and they use tools such as those presented in Chapters 5 through 8 to resolve these questions.

We ended the chapter by considering examples of entrepreneurs who addressed grand challenges. One of the critical points that comes from the cases is that in a capitalist economy, ethics, strategy, and sound management must come together. In other words, you will not succeed in making the world a better place if you cannot translate good intentions into winning marketplace approaches. Shai Agassi of Better Place could not match his high-level aspiration with a correspondingly strong business plan. His failure not only hurt the investors who backed him, but it also tainted the very idea of a vibrant EV sector that could ween the world from fossil fuels. Elon Musk's business model of producing attractive vehicles and not just extending vehicle range with charging stations was more sound as it met more of drivers' needs. Despite his erratic behavior, Musk has demonstrated dogged persistence as he has moved step by step in making his vision a reality, even as he has encountered unexpected obstacles. While the jury literally is still out (and in fact has not yet convened) in the case of Elizabeth Holmes, it appears that she has never had a viable business model or product but, rather, just fierce ambition and the ability to manipulate stakeholders. She provides the cautionary tale to us that we must not worship false idols in our search for answers to the world's grand challenges.

Taken together, the cases bring us back to an important point we have made throughout this book, which is that the ends—solving the world's grand challenges—do not necessarily justify the means. Ethics require us to be concerned with both means and ends. The chicanery of Holmes and the abusive management style of Musk do not have to be the costs of solving big problems. There is no

reason why one cannot persistently and even obsessively take on grand challenges in an ethical way.

We must all try to do good while also doing what is right and, as discussed in Chapter 2, being virtuous, just, and compassionate. As business leaders, you will increasingly be called on to play this role. We hope that using the tools presented in this textbook will enable you to address the grand challenges and other dilemmas you face in an effective and ethical way. Make a difference, and do so with honesty and with integrity.

## KEY TERMS AND CONCEPTS

Base of the pyramid 286
Creating shared value 285
Creative capitalism 287

Grand challenges 278
Industry-transforming
 innovations 289

Precautionary
 principle 282

## CASES RELATED TO THE READING

Consider reading the following cases found in Chapter 10 that apply to the concepts presented in this chapter:

- Bayer: The Acquisition of Monsanto
- BP: The Big Oil Spill: What Went Wrong
- Facebook: Privacy and the Public Interest

- General Mills: Nutrition
- Google: Doing No Harm
- Intel: Mobileye
- Mallinckrodt: The Opioid Crisis
- Walmart: Sustainability
- Whole Foods: Conscious Capitalism

## CASE APPLICATIONS

### Case 9.1: ExxonMobil and Climate Change[20]

Multinational oil company ExxonMobil faced many challenges related to climate change. Climate

change is taking place because of the greenhouse effect. When solar radiation passes through the atmosphere, some of it is absorbed and warms the earth, while some is reflected outward and trapped in the atmosphere. The trapping of solar radiation has made the Earth's climate tolerable in comparison with that of other planets. However, the greater the concentration of greenhouse gases, the more that solar radiation is trapped in the atmosphere, and the warmer the atmosphere becomes. The consumption of fossil fuels including coal and oil is one of the chief sources of human-produced greenhouse gases.

Scientific evidence shows that climate change is indeed taking place. The years 2014 to 2018 were the five hottest years since the time the U.S. government started to track global temperature in 1880. Climate change brought devastation to the Philippines, Vietnam, the Korean peninsula, and Tonga. Hurricanes Florence and Michael created significant damage in the United States. Wildfires erupted in Greece, Canada, California, and other areas, while floods overwhelmed Kerala, India, and forced the evacuation of more than 1.4 million people. Japan and East Africa too have had serious flooding, the likes of which they have not previously experienced. As the climate has changed, sea levels have risen and the oceans have become hotter, changing the patterns of global rainfall, evaporation, snow, stream flow, and other factors affecting water supply and quality. With record-high heat waves, record-low Arctic sea ice level, above-average tropical cyclones, and deadly wildfires, the world is now in the midst of a climate crisis.

The concentration of greenhouse gases in the atmosphere is likely to continue to increase to a point where the climate will heat up in very dangerous ways, resulting in the following:

- More extreme weather such as droughts and hurricanes

- The melting of glaciers and ice sheets

- Small island states disappearing entirely

- Wildfires growing in both number and severity

- Severe changes in plant life cycles, with negative impacts on agriculture and food production

- Unpredictable and heavy levels of rain and snow

- The destruction of coral reefs

- The disruption of animal migration

These changes are having very real impacts on people's lives. Heat waves, wildfires, extreme weather events, and rising sea levels take their toll in the form of reduced crop yields, deaths, health problems, and destruction of vital infrastructure.[21] Throughout the world, climate change has become an imminent and tangible threat to people's lives, property, and their ways of earning a living.

### Steps to Curb Emissions and Promote Renewable Energy

The world has taken a number of steps to curb greenhouse gas emissions.[22] The 1992 Rio Treaty, signed by the then U.S. President George H. W. Bush and ratified by the U.S. Congress, established a goal of "stabilization" of greenhouse gases at a level to "prevent dangerous interference with . . . (the) climate system." Each nation in the world, under this treaty, has a "common" but "differentiated" responsibility to addressing the problem, meaning that industrialized nations, who have been most responsible for the problem, had to act first, since they owed a substantial amount of their affluence to the greenhouse gases they had emitted in the past. For developing countries, the highest priority was sustainable development, in effect meaning that they should address their greenhouse gas emissions but not at the expense of economic growth.

After Rio, the next step that the world took was the Kyoto Protocol, which most nations signed in 1997 and ratified in 2005. According to the protocol, industrialized countries were to reduce their average annual emissions by 5% in the years 2008 to 2012 in comparison with 1990. To achieve these goals, they could reduce their emissions, buy emissions reduction allowances from developing countries, or buy them from one another. The United States did not ratify the Kyoto Protocol due to senators' concerns about job loss in the coal industry and the belief that developing countries were not being called on to contribute to the solution. Although the United States did not sign the protocol, the country took some steps to reduce emissions. After the election of President Barack Obama in 2009, the U.S. EPA assumed the obligation to regulate greenhouse gas emissions. Some states followed. For example, California's Air Resources Board and a consortium of states in the Northeast started cap-and-trade programs to obtain greenhouse gas reductions.

### ExxonMobil and Climate Change

In 2015, the New York Attorney General sought documents to determine whether ExxonMobil had lied to investors and consumers and kept secret information about the effects of climate change on its financial health. The pressure intensified when the Center for International Environmental Law released decades-old documents that revealed that the firm had investigated and understood the link between burning fossil fuels and climate change many years ago but tried to keep this information from the public. Attorneys general from other states demanded that the company release information about its research and its funding of climate change denial.

ExxonMobil vigorously fought these actions, calling the accusations against it inaccurate and misleading. Yet the news disturbed family members of the company's founder, John D. Rockefeller. They controlled the Rockefeller Family Fund (RFF), which was a major shareholder in the company. They were concerned that the company had concealed its prior knowledge of climate change and failed to act on it. They accused the company of not

disclosing the research it had done on the impacts and distorting the evidence.

ExxonMobil forcefully denied these charges. However, family members turned against the firm and chose to divest their holdings in the company in a public gesture that received substantial media exposure. In a public statement, members of the Rockefeller family wrote,

> Earlier this year our organization, [RFF] announced that it would divest its holdings in fossil fuel companies . . . In a public statement we singled out ExxonMobil for immediate divestment because of its "morally reprehensible conduct." For over a quarter-century the company tried to deceive policymakers and the public about the realities of climate change, protecting its profits at the cost of immense damage to life on this planet . . . Often working indirectly through front groups, it sponsored many of the scientists and think tanks that have sought to obfuscate the scientific consensus about the changing climate, and it participated in those efforts through its paid advertisements and the statements of its executives.

### The Company's 2016 Annual Meeting

At the company's 2016 annual meeting, shareholders had many reasons to be concerned. From 2014 to 2016, ExxonMobil's finances were in a free fall (Figure 9.4). The company lost about a third of its revenue and profits as oil prices fell steeply (Figure 9.5) and natural gas prices did not rebound significantly from their 2012 lows. The stock market value of all the major oil and natural gas prices, ExxonMobil included, had not kept up with the growth in the value of the other stocks listed in the S&P 500.

FIGURE 9.4    Decline in ExxonMobil Annual Revenue and Earnings: 2014 to 2016

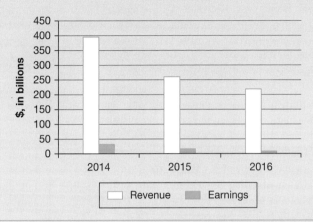

FIGURE 9.5    Oil Prices From 2012 to 2017

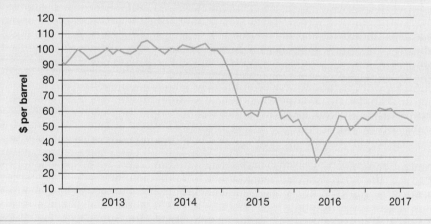

Though the company faced many challenges, the 2016 shareholder meeting was dominated by the issue of climate change. It was a raucous event in which the company was inundated with climate-related demands. The conveners had to remind those present of proper rules of conduct. Participants were prohibited from making provocative statements and distributing unauthorized literature. The security guards who patrolled the hallways had the responsibility to prevent protesters from disrupting the meeting. Knowing that civility would not be easy to maintain, the conveners wanted to be prepared. The anger against the company was palpable.

Shareholders brought forward eight proposals dealing with climate change. Only one passed, obtaining the support of 62% of the shareholders. Backing for this proposal came from some of the most prominent investment firms and organizations in the world, including BlackRock, Vanguard, State Street, and the California Public Employees' Retirement System. Without their backing, the proposal would not have passed, as they represented a majority of the company's share owners. This victory, though important, seemed hollow in the activists' eyes, who wanted much more. The proposal gave shareholders—actually only those with 3% or more of the company's shares for more than three years—the right to nominate a quarter of the firm's board of directors. The hope of activists was that this proposal would lead to the appointment of a climate advocate to the board. In a nonbinding resolution, more than 62% of shareholders also voted that the company should conduct a detailed assessment of the impacts of climate change on the firm. As climate change became more of a problem, the company's fossil fuel assets would be worth less.

### Stranded Assets

A major concern of the activists was the problem of stranded assets. In a study conducted by the research group Carbon Tracker, it concluded that oil companies were wasting trillions of dollars in investments in additional oil development. The investments would generate 380 billion tons of additional carbon dioxide by 2035, but within a decade, world governments were likely to introduce legislation limiting the amount of climate-changing gases emitted into the atmosphere and reducing the demand for oil. Oil companies like ExxonMobil would be left with petroleum assets that had decreased in value. Indeed, the study found that ExxonMobil, which had more oil reserves than any other major oil company, also would have more stranded assets than any other company.

The SEC also was uneasy about the value of the company's assets. Following an investigation, in a 2016 ruling, it compelled ExxonMobil to write down the value of its oil reserves by about one fifth. Other oil companies had taken similar actions voluntarily, but ExxonMobil refused and the SEC had to compel it to reduce its assets' value. As a result

of the investigation by securities regulators, the company had to write down the value of more than $2 billion of its assets in the United States. The reduced value of these assets was not good news for ExxonMobil's shareholders. Shareholder activists were not done and planned to bring forward additional resolutions at future shareholder meetings. They wanted ExxonMobil to do a more honest reckoning of the implications of climate change for the firm's future.

### The New CEO

In 2017, Darren Woods replaced Rex Tillerson as CEO of the company. Woods was a graduate of Texas A&M University, where he earned an engineering degree. He also had an MBA from Northwestern's Kellogg School of Management. The expectation was that he would break from ExxonMobil's past climate change policies even more than his predecessor, Tillerson, who had made many changes, and, in comparison with his predecessor, Lee Raymond, was considered rather enlightened on the climate change issue.

ExxonMobil had many initiatives in the area of climate change. Along with other companies, it was part of the Climate Leadership Council, which advocated for a gradually rising and revenue-neutral carbon tax with carbon dividend payments to be made to American families. The company also continued to participate in the activities of the U.S. National Research Council and the Intergovernmental Panel on Climate Change (IPCC), the United Nations body that was responsible for the assessment of climate change. Moreover, it had a goal of reducing its environmental footprint and had taken a number of steps to reduce emissions and lower its carbon intensity. The company was not just seeking to reduce its own emissions but was also trying to help consumers reduce theirs. It was therefore pursuing innovations in the reduction of methane emissions, internal combustion engine (ICE) efficiency, power generation technologies, automotive light weighting, reduced packaging, and industrial process efficiency.

It was carrying out research into alternative energy, carbon sequestration, and biofuels. Since 2009, it had invested $0.6 billion into an algae-based biofuels project. The company was a main sponsor of a global climate and energy project at Stanford University. In trying to create new supply options and efficiency savings, it had secured partnerships with universities and private sector companies including Georgia Tech, Purdue, Berkeley, TDA Research, ECN, Fuelcellenergy, Michigan State, the Colorado School of Mines, Synthetic Genomics, and REG. Nevertheless, company managers were concerned that international accords and regional and national greenhouse gas regulations would continue to evolve and reduce the value of the company's fossil fuel assets. The uncertain timing and outcomes of greenhouse gas control policies made it difficult to assess their business impact.

### Continued Criticism

Activists continued to target the company even as investors staged their revolt at the annual meeting. The company persistently denied the charges that it had concealed its prior knowledge of climate change and regularly pointed to its support of a carbon tax and its endorsement of the 2015 Paris Climate Agreement that called for the countries of the world to keep global temperatures below 2 °C above historic levels, but activists considered its endorsements weak. They called on the company to show that it had a plan to manage a transition away from fossil fuels. They held that the company stood out among its competitors for its failure to invest in renewable energy.

Indeed, some of the world's other large oil companies were preparing for a decline in oil demand in coming decades. BP projected slower demand growth until about 2040, and a decline in demand after that. Shell forecast a demand peak as early as 2025 and changed its long-term investment plans to diversify away from oil and invest in alternatives. ExxonMobil, however, expected that oil would be the dominant fuel source well beyond 2040, predicting that demand would pick up because of growing

incomes in Asia and lack of progress in fuel economy, electric and self-driving vehicles, and battery technology. ExxonMobil concluded that substantial need for sizable investment in oil projects remained.

The company continued to fight off the suit the New York and Massachusetts attorney generals had brought against it for seeking to neutralize and obfuscate climate change research. ExxonMobil pointed out that since 2007, it had included in its assessment of new projects a proxy cost of how much governments might charge it for carbon dioxide emissions. However, the attorney generals claimed that from 2010 to 2014 the company publicly held that it applied a $60 per ton cost, while internal documents showed that it used a $40 per ton cost—in other words, it had not built climate change into its plans to the extent it said it did.

### Investing in Shale and in the Internal Combustion Engine

ExxonMobil also announced plans to spend $50 billion to expand its U.S. shale initiatives over five years. It invested $6.5 billion into doubling its acreage in the Permian Basin's shale fields. Once a dominant player in the region, ExxonMobil had to rebuild its portfolio. Though the purchase doubled the amount of oil and gas the company held in the area to the equivalent of 6 billion barrels, its holdings were smaller than rivals Chevron and Occidental Petroleum. ExxonMobil planned to use the purchase to drill long horizontal wells that would reduce its costs by extending the drilling's reach. It planned to spend about $5.5 billion in 2017 in Texas, New Mexico, and North Dakota in tapping wells that could turn a profit at prices as low as $40 a barrel. Though the hurdles were high and costs great, ExxonMobil also tried to replicate the U.S. fracking boom in a desolate part of Patagonia in western Argentina that potentially had as much oil and gas as the biggest fields in Texas or North Dakota.

As ExxonMobil increased its investment in shale, it sought to reduce oil production and concentrate on natural gas production. The natural gas

ExxonMobil extracted from shale was a bet on a relatively low-emissions bridge from coal to renewable energy, since the greenhouse gas emissions that contribute to climate change are lower for natural gas combustion than they are for oil combustion. Nevertheless, methane, which is the main component in natural gas, was a potent greenhouse gas, and the issue of methane emissions leaks was drawing increasing attention. To reduce these leaks, ExxonMobil joined together with seven other large energy companies and created an agreement to abide by a set of principles to drive down their fugitive methane emissions.

ExxonMobil also teamed with other oil companies and automakers in an effort to help sustain the gasoline-powered auto, as tough regulation and EVs put the technology at risk. They were spending millions of dollars a year to create a new superslick oil that would make traditional engines more efficient, which would allow them to comply with stricter environmental rules and fight off the threat of zero-emission EVs.

Many countries signaled that they would ban traditional gasoline-powered vehicles in coming years and implement tough new emission standards. The European Union in 2017 came forward with a proposal to cut carbon dioxide emissions from cars and vans 30% by 2030. China called for 20% of its vehicle production and sales to be electric and hybrid by 2025. The Trump administration, on the other hand, was trying to relax U.S. efforts to tighten vehicle emissions standards. Auto companies promised to launch more EVs in the next decade, and GM pledged to sell a million annually by 2026. Oil companies other than ExxonMobil invested in gasoline-powered vehicle alternatives and in EV infrastructure.

Once defined by massive spending and ambitious exploration, ExxonMobil had to practice greater frugality. The company got praise from President Trump for $20 billion in commitments to oil, gas, and chemical infrastructure projects on the Gulf Coast. However, investments of this kind were becoming increasingly less attractive. The company had to respond to investors who demanded greater financial discipline and a more judicious approach to investing.

*Financial Performance*

Despite billions of dollars in spending cuts and a modest oil price rebound, in 2016 ExxonMobil spent nearly $7 billion more in developing new projects and paying dividends than it generated in cash. According to analysts' estimates, the company needed the price of oil to be at more than $50 a barrel in order to balance the cash it generated against the capital expenditures it made and the dividends it generated.

The company's first quarter 2018 profits missed Wall Street expectations. Seventy percent of its $8.4 billion net income in that quarter arose out of one-time Trump administration tax change benefits. Earnings declined by 2.2% on an adjusted basis that excluded the new tax law bonus. Production fell by around 130,000 barrels a day. The company's U.S. drilling operations lost money for the 12th consecutive quarter.

How should ExxonMobil address the grand challenge of climate change? What facts are relevant to its decision? What options does it have, and what are their consequences for the company's many different stakeholders? What principles should it apply? What can it do to build from a short-term fix to a more thorough long-term solution? In answering these questions, consider ExxonMobil's legal and ethical responsibilities to its various stakeholders, and whether there is a difference between them. Can the company earn higher profits by investing more in sustainable energy options? Which stakeholders should be the company's highest priority? Should it take an interactive approach to engaging stakeholders? Also consider the point made in Chapter 7 that companies do not just follow laws but also contribute to their making. What role if any should ExxonMobil take in national and international climate change policy processes? What positions should it take?

## Case 9.2: NextEra Energy and Renewable Power

Starting in the 1990s, the U.S. electric utility sector underwent a process of consolidation. Utility companies merged, acquired other utilities, and moved from their home bases in one state across state lines. Through such activities, Duke Energy, Southern Company, and NextEra Energy became the largest U.S. investor-owned utilities.[23] These three companies had different specializations.[24] Duke and Southern were the largest coal and natural gas generators in the United States, while NextEra was the largest wind and solar owner and operator, not just in the United States but in the world.

### The Shift to Renewable Energy

The types of fuels the world uses to meet electricity demand has been shifting gradually from fossil fuels to renewable energy.[25] In 1973, about 75% of the world's generation of electricity came from coal, oil, and natural gas, but in 2016, this number had fallen to 66%. Renewables went from 0.6% of electricity generated in 1973 to 7.1% in 2015 (Figure 9.6). The use of coal in the United States dropped for a number of reasons. Extensive pollution control standards put in place because of coal's negative health effects curtailed coal's growth. Another concern that led to less growth in the use of coal was the greenhouse gases that coal-fired power plants emit.

---

**FIGURE 9.6**   The Levelized Cost of Electricity

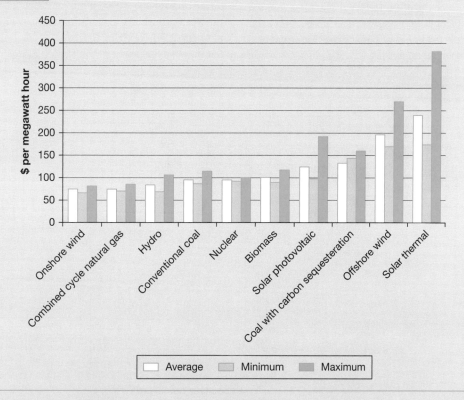

Average   Minimum   Maximum

*Source:* Derived from Stacy and Taylor.[26]

In general, generating electricity from coal became more expensive than generating it from wind or natural gas. Joined with combined-cycle natural gas, wind had become the first choice of most electric utilities when this option was available and they needed to add generation capacity to their systems.

### The Threat of Climate Change

One reason renewable energy made inroads in the United States and elsewhere was concern about climate change, described above in the Exxon Mobil case and in Chapter 7.

Concerns about climate change and other issues such as energy security led to U.S. government efforts to promote renewable energy sources such as wind and solar power. The U.S. Congress provided a wind production tax credit of 2.3 cents per kilowatt of electricity generated for any facility built before 2020, with the amount of the credit declining each year from 2017 to 2019. Congress also extended a solar investment tax credit of 30% of cost for residences and commercial establishments. How long the credit would remain in force was uncertain. Many U.S. states mandated that utilities generate more of their power from renewables. Iowa introduced the first of such mandates in 1991. By 2018, 29 states with 56% of U.S. electricity sales had such mandates in place. Government encouragement of wind and other renewables had a long history starting in the 1970s.[27]

### NextEra's Evolution as a Renewable Power Generation Leader

The U.S. electric utility industry was responsible for roughly 30% of U.S. greenhouse gas emissions.[28] NextEra had been an industry leader in addressing the issue (Figure 9.7). While the company generated about 46% of its electricity from natural gas and another 26% from nuclear power, nearly 25% came from wind and solar energy. This concentration on renewable energy made it the largest producer of electricity from wind and solar energy in the world. Its ability to capture the renewable market permitted NextEra to grow despite relatively flat demand for power in the United States.

**FIGURE 9.7**    Leading U.S. Wind Energy Operators in 2016 Based on Ownership

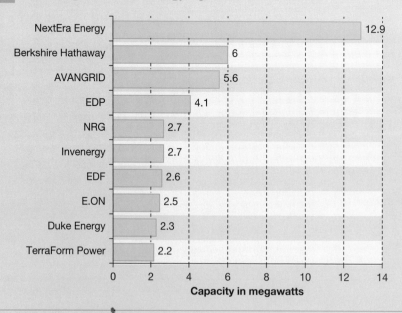

NextEra's predecessor company had started building its renewables business in the 1990s, primarily for commercial reasons. Over time, the company steadily added to its renewables portfolio. In 2006, NextEra acquired WindLogics of Minnesota. This company was largely considered the best among U.S. companies in forecasting wind patterns. NextEra found and leased some of the best wind sites in the United States. It outbid competitors on the building of wind and solar farms. By 2016, NextEra Energy and its subsidiaries owned 85 wind farms in 17 U.S. states and three Canadian provinces. It was also the co-owner and operator of Solar Energy Generating Systems, the world's largest solar power generating facility.

NextEra had grown its renewable power investments in a prudent way. For instance, it kept its debt low by funding projects with cash and credit lines that did not involve financing charges. It also built its renewable installations only after its customers (electric utilities) provided it with long-term power purchasing agreements. In this way, it avoided the debt problems that other U.S. wind energy installers such as NRG and SunEdison had experienced.[29] As a large purchaser of turbines, the company obtained good deals from the turbine manufacturers, not only GE but Vestas and Siemens.

NextEra relied heavily on federal tax credits for solar and wind power. From 2015 to 2018, NextEra made use of $401 million in federal tax credits to build wind power units. It was the country's largest beneficiary of such credits. The company CEO James Robo recognized that his company would face a substantial problem if federal wind tax credits expired in 2020.

NextEra planned to continue its move to renewables, which accounted for one third of its revenue and had been very profitable, generating $2.9 billion in net income for the company in 2018. By that year, the company had 28,000 megawatts of wind and solar projects and was aiming to expand that amount to 40,000 megawatts in two years. NextEra was in the midst of going beyond its utility customers and building wind and solar farms for companies like Google, whose cloud servers consumed huge amounts of energy and who were heavily committed to transitioning to renewable power.

Part of NextEra's plan going forward was to accumulate and control centralized renewable power facilities. It did not want to have to compete with customers who used rooftop solar panels to generate their own power. If a household or commercial establishment generated excess electricity, NextEra would have to absorb that electricity onto its transmission system and pay the customer for it. This path forward was not one NextEra wanted to take. While in general, environmentalists approved of the company's renewable energy efforts, they had been critical of what they considered to be attempts by NextEra to slow the deployment of rooftop solar.

### What Should NextEra Do Next?

Many executives at NextEra wanted to maintain the company's commitment to renewable power, but they also had an obligation to serve the company's shareholders. They could maintain the commitment to renewables only if doing so was financially prudent. NRG's CEO David Crane had been ousted by his company's board of directors for preserving the company's commitment to renewable energy even as the company was losing significant amounts of money in carrying out wind and solar projects.[30] NextEra CEO Robo recognized that federal tax credits had been critical to the growth of NextEra's renewables business and that his company would face a substantial problem if these credits expired in 2020. The company had to decide on whether the company should maintain its commitment to wind and solar.

Use the weight-of-reasons framework to identify and evaluate NextEra's strategic options. Is it possible for NextEra to address the grand challenge of climate change and earn a profit? What options does the company have in the short term and long term? How do future innovations in solar, wind, and other renewable energy options fit in? Should NextEra get involved in the political process, and in what way? Who are the stakeholders to the company's decision, and how are they likely to be affected by each option?

## Case 9.3: Sourcing Cashews

You are a new supply chain manager for a large multinational food products company. Your company insists that all of the fruit and nut products it sells are organic. The cashews your company sells are sustainably grown. They are also delicious and considered to be good for your health because they are high in protein, minerals, fiber, and unsaturated fat (the "good kind of fat"). The plantations you source from are also unusual because they pay the women who pick nuts unusually high wages for the country in which they are located and also provide excellent working conditions.

On your first trip to visit one of the plantations, you discover something that surprises you: Paychecks are issued not to the women who pick the nuts but rather to their husbands. You ask the plantation manager if this is legal, and he responds that he is not sure, but it is consistent with local tradition. One of the women who works at the plantation sidles up to you and mentions that she wishes her paychecks were issued directly to her. Her husband is abusive, she says, and spends the money foolishly. She feels that if she controlled her paycheck, she might be able to improve the conditions in her household and village.

You are not sure what to do. The situation just feels wrong to you. On the other hand, you don't know if the behavior is illegal, don't want to upset relations with this supplier, and are not sure that the paycheck issue is any of your business. Use the weight-of-reasons framework to work through this issue. Might you have options that would allow you to continue working with this supplier and also address your concerns? What principles should you use in deciding?

## Case 9.4: Winning the Community Over to Wind

You work for a company that develops wind energy projects. You are proud to work in the industry because you believe that it contributes to solving the problems of air pollution and climate change. You have identified an attractive new project site. Wind speeds are really high at the site, the topography is suitable for placing wind turbines, and the land owner is willing to locate your wind turbines on her property in exchange for reasonable royalty payments. Once the project is approved by the local county council, you will be ready to break ground on the project.

One day, you are having lunch at a restaurant near the site and are surprised to read an editorial article opposing your project. Apparently, some local citizens believe that wind turbines will ruin their view of the countryside. They have also found a study that shows that the presence of wind turbines reduces tourism to rural areas. They are planning to mobilize to oppose the project. They aim to put pressure on council members who are up for reelection. While you don't mind sitting down with people who have different views, you start to imagine a lengthy and expensive approval process that involves hiring lawyers and land use experts, and which could delay the start of the project. The project's economics start to look less solid.

Use the weight-of-reasons framework to determine how you should handle this situation. Might it be possible to develop a project approach that makes sense financially and also satisfies your opponents? What process should you adopt to work out your differences with your opponents?

## Case 9.5: Selling Soap and Saving Lives[31]

You are a regional manager for a global company that sells soaps and other personal hygiene products. You have recently read about the base of the pyramid approach to business and are intrigued by the possibility that you could use it to develop a new customer base. Your soaps and other products could really make a difference in poor and rural areas of your region because communicable diseases that cause many illnesses and deaths in the region could be prevented through handwashing and other hygienic practices. However, while you want to help people avoid these outcomes, you don't think that the people of the region can afford your product. You work for a for-profit organization, not a charity.

Use the weight-of-reasons framework to assess whether there might be a way for your company to address the health and poverty problems of the region while also earning a profit. In applying the framework, use both/and thinking, systems thinking, and moral imagination. Consider the role of multistakeholder partnerships.

### Case 9.6: Making Environmentally Friendly Furniture[32]

Your office furniture company has decided that it wants to make its furniture according to "circular economy" principles. This means that when customers are done using the furniture, they can return it to your company instead of throwing it away. Your company then disassembles the furniture products and refurbishes and reuses their parts. No parts are ever thrown away. The office furniture business is very competitive. While many customers have expressed interest in purchasing sustainably made products, they are also price sensitive.

As your company is producing its first product, an office chair, that will be built following circular economy standards, you come across a challenge. You find that it is just really difficult to produce a seating pad that is made out of reusable materials. You have two options: Use a material that can be reused after the chair is returned, or use a material that is cheaper but has to be thrown to the landfill after the chair wears out. If you use the second option, the cost of the chair to your customers will be about 2% less.

Use the weight-of-reasons framework to address this dilemma. Who are all the stakeholders to your decision? What principles will you rely on? Does it make sense to choose the more expensive but more sustainable option?

## NOTES

1. Grameen Bank. (n.d.). *Objective*. Retrieved from http://www.grameen.com/objective/
2. Davenport, C. (2012, April 10). The broken "Buy-one, give-one" model: 3 ways to save Toms Shoes. *Fast Company*. Retrieved from https://www.fastcompany.com/1679628/the-broken-buy-one-give-one-model-three-ways-to-save-toms-shoes
3. Montgomery, M. (2015, April 28). What entrepreneurs can learn from the philanthropic struggles of TOMS Shoes. *Forbes*. Retrieved from https://www.forbes.com/sites/mikemontgomery/2015/04/28/how-entrepreneurs-can-avoid-the-philanthropy-pitfalls/#766586061c38
4. Perrow, C. (2011). *Normal accidents: Living with high risk technologies* (Updated ed.). Princeton, NJ: Princeton University Press.
5. Porter, M. E., & Kramer, M. R. (2011). Creating shared value. *Harvard Business Review, 89*(January–February), 62–77.
6. Pennsylvania State University. (n.d.). *MDGs and the base of the pyramid*. Retrieved from https://sites.psu.edu/engagedscholarshiphese/mdgs-base-of-the-pyramid/

7. Hart, S. L. (2005). *Capitalism at the crossroads.* Upper Saddle River, NJ: Prentice Hall.

8. Mahajan, N. (2013, July 31). The bottom of the pyramid and beyond. *Forbes India.* Retrieved from http://www.forbesindia.com/article/ckgsb/bottom-of-the-pyramid-and-beyond/35575/1

9. Karnani, A. G. (2007). The mirage of marketing to the bottom of the pyramid: How the private sector can help alleviate poverty. *California Management Review, 49,* 90–111.

10. We use the term *industry-transforming innovation* to refer to two types of innovation described in the business literature: (1) disruptive innovation and (2) radical innovation. Disruptive innovation results in products and services that are introduced into existing industries and displace established companies, while radical innovation produces products and services that create all new industries and render existing industries obsolete. See Christensen, C. M. (1997). *The innovator's dilemma: When new technologies cause great firms to fail.* Boston, MA: Harvard Business School Press.

11. Hargrave, T. J., & Van de Ven, A. H. (2006). A collective action model of institutional innovation. *Academy of Management Review, 31*(4), 864–888.

12. Modified from Marcus, A. A. (2015). *Innovations in sustainability: Fuel and food.* Cambridge, UK: Cambridge University Press.

13. This pattern is the opposite of that normally observed for disruptive innovations, where companies introduce products at the low end of the market and then gradually move up. See Christensen (1997).

14. Rogowsky, M. (2013, August 24). The numbers don't lie: Tesla is beginning to put the hurt on the competition. *Forbes.* Retrieved from https://www.forbes.com/sites/markrogowsky/2013/08/24/numbers-dont-lie-tesla-is-beginning-to-put-the-hurt-on-the-competition/#1535ce5d7748

15. Ibid.

16. "420" is a reference in popular culture to marijuana use.

17. Margonelli, L. (2009). Clean energy's dirty little secret. *The Atlantic.* Retrieved from https://www.theatlantic.com/magazine/archive/2009/05/clean-energys-dirty-little-secret/307377/

18. See Chapter 6, in Mintzer, I. (2009). Look before you leap: Exploring the implications of advanced vehicles for import dependence and passenger safety. In D. B. Sandalow (Ed.), *Plug-in electric vehicles: What role for Washington* (pp. 107–126). Washington, DC: Brookings Institution Press.

19. Green Car Congress. (2011, June 8). *Ricardo study finds electric and hybrid cars have a higher carbon footprint during production than conventional vehicles, but still offer a lower footprint over the full life cycle.* Retrieved from https://www.greencarcongress.com/2011/06/lowcvp-20110608.html

20. Based on information contained in Chapter 8 of Marcus, A. A. (2019). *Strategies for managing uncertainty: Booms and busts in the energy industry.* Cambridge, UK: Cambridge University Press.

21. Gramling, C., & Hamers, L. (2018, November 28). *Here's how much climate change could cost the U.S.* Retrieved from https://www.sciencenews.org/article/climate-change-economic-cost-united-states

22. Marcus (2019).

23. IBIS World Industry Report. (2016). *Coal and natural gas power in the US.*

24. Ibid

25. Ibid.

26. Stacy, T. F., & Taylor, G. S. (2016). *The levelized cost of electricity from existing generation sources.* Washington, DC: Institute for Energy Research.

27. Marcus (2019).

28. U.S. Environmental Protection Agency. (n.d.). *Global greenhouse gas emissions data.* Retrieved from https://www.epa.gov/ghgemissions/global-greenhouse-gas-emissions-data

29. Gold, R. (2018, June 18). *How a Florida utility became the global king of green power.* Retrieved from https://www.wsj.com/articles/how-a-florida-utility-became-the-global-king-of-green-power-1529331001

30. Pyper, J. (2015, December 3). *David Crane steps down as NRG's CEO amidst investor pressure.* Retrieved from https://www.greentechmedia.com/articles/read/david-crane-steps-down-as-nrg#gs.cjc9t5; Pyper, J. (2016, April 29). A conversation with David Crane on getting fired from NRG and what's next for his energy plans. *gtm.* Retrieved from https://www.greentechmedia.com/articles/read/a-conversation-with-david-crane

31. Based on Unilever's efforts to start handwashing and similar campaigns in poor rural areas. See https://www.unilever.com/sustainable-living/improving-health-and-well-being/health-and-hygiene/healthy-handwashing-habits-for-life/

32. Based on the following case: Lee, D., & Bony, L. (2009). *Cradle-to-cradle design at Herman Miller: Moving toward environmental sustainability.* Boston, MA: Harvard Business School Press.

# Cases

PART

IV

# Cases

## Introduction

This chapter presents 16 cases that involve ethical dilemmas at well-known companies. Use the weight-of-reasons framework to address the questions posed in each case. Chapters 1 through 3 apply to all of the cases found in this chapter. To identify the cases most relevant to specific material found in Chapters 4 through 9, please refer to the "Cases Related to the Reading" section found near the end of the relevant chapter.

## Bayer: The Acquisition of Monsanto[1]

Bayer's $66 billion acquisition of Monsanto in 2018 was the biggest ever by the German firm (see the timeline of Monsanto's history in Table 10.1). The aim was to create a global leader that would transform agriculture. The combined Bayer and Monsanto stood out as a giant in genetic engineering. In acquiring Monsanto, Bayer was purchasing the world's leading genetic engineering firm and also, unfortunately, the most hated. At the time of the purchase, there had been significant protests against Monsanto in many parts of Europe, as Europeans had long been uneasy about the use of genetically modified organisms (GMOs) in agriculture.

**TABLE 10.1**   A Timeline of Monsanto's History

| | |
|---|---|
| 1901 | Founded in St. Louis, MO, with the first products being food additives like saccharin, caffeine, and vanillin |
| 1944 | Begins manufacturing DDT |
| 1945 | Starts producing agricultural chemicals, including 2,4-D |
| 1961 | President Kennedy authorizes the use of defoliants in the Vietnam War, including Agent Orange, which was applied from 1965 to 1971 |
| 1970 | U.S. Department of Agriculture halts the use of 2,4,5-T on all food crops except rice |
| 1972 | DDT is banned under most circumstances |
| 1974 | Puts Roundup, or glyphosate, on the market, which becomes one of the most commonly used herbicides |
| 1979 | Strikes a deal with Genentech in 1979 to license patents |
| 1980 | First U.S. Agent Orange class-action lawsuit filed for injuries to military personnel |
| 1983 | One of four groups announcing the introduction of genes into plants |
| 1985 | Purchases G. D. Searle & Company |
| 1993 | Searle files a patent for Celebrex |
| 1994 | Introduces a recombinant version of bovine somatotropin |
| 1995 | Introduces potato plants with Bt toxin, the first U.S.-approved, pest-resisting genetically modified crop |
| 1996 | Introduces genetically modified Roundup Ready soybeans, resistant to Roundup, since glyphosate can be sprayed in fields without harming crops |
| 1996 | Acquires Agracetus, a biotechnology company that generated the first transgenic varieties of cotton, soybeans, peanuts, and other crops, and from which it had been licensing technology since 1991 |
| 1997 | Spins off its industrial chemical and fiber divisions into Solutia |
| 1998 | Introduces genetically modified corn that is resistant to Roundup |
| 1999 | Merges with Pharmacia and Upjohn |
| 2000 | Pharmacia spins it off as a new company |
| 2007 | Purchases Delta & Pine Land Company, a major cotton seed breeder |
| | Divests Stoneville cotton to Bayer and Nexgen cotton to Americot and exits pig breeding |
| 2013 | Purchases San Francisco–based Climate Corp, which makes accurate local weather forecasts for farmers |
| 2013 | Worldwide protest against genetically modified organisms |
| 2015 | Rolls out seeds engineered with new herbicide resistance, releasing Dicamba-resistant cotton |
| 2016 | Bayer acquired for $66 billion |
| 2016 | Buys a license to use CRISPR/Cas9 gene-editing technology |

## Ethical Debates

Ethical debates about the genetic engineering of seeds, Monsanto's main business, were long-standing. The issues raised had included harm to human health, environmental damage, negative effects on farms and farmers, the dominance of just a few corporations in this sector, and tampering with natural processes, when genetic engineering involved uniting seeds from different species.

These issues had to be considered in light of important principles such as advancing human welfare and eliminating environmental harm. Uplifting the poor in developing countries by improving nutrition was an important outcome that, if achieved, had to be taken seriously. Lowering environmental harm by increasing the pest resistance of plants was another important benefit. Some argued that in each instance the benefits had to be weighed against the risks. It depended on the crop and the circumstances.

With the world's population estimated to approach 10 billion by the year 2050, the potential to increase yields and raise the nutritional value of foods had to be taken into account. Companies, governments, and citizens had an obligation to understand the issue and assess how to treat the technology. If genetically modified food could reduce poverty and improve the quality and quantity of the world's food supply, should it not have an important role to play? Yet applying a precautionary approach to the use of this technology still might be necessary, and questions such as the following were important..

- How and to what extent should the technology's development be controlled by governments?

- To what extent should individual consumers limit their consumption of genetically modified foods and ingredients?

Genetically modified crops like corn were consumed mainly by cows and pigs and not humans. Another use of the corn crop was to make the high-fructose corn syrup (HFC) found in many processed foods. A third use was as ethanol, as a fuel for automobiles. A question often posed was the extent to which the modification of seeds by means of moving genes from one species to another really differed from conventional breeding.

## Business Considerations

About 20% of the world's markets in seeds and agricultural traits was under Bayer's control. The company's largest competitors were other giant companies. They had been involved in major acquisitions at around the same time that Bayer purchased Monsanto. ChemChina, which bought Syngenta, had the second biggest market share in seeds and agricultural traits. DowDuPont had the third largest market share. Dow and DuPont recently had merged and had chosen to divest the crop science business as a separate firm called Corteva. ChemChina's market share in seeds and agricultural traits was about 14%, and Corteva's was about 13%. Corteva's portfolio of products was more balanced between genetically engineered seeds and agricultural traits and chemicals, while ChemChina was more an agricultural chemical company. Corteva stood in the middle between Bayer and ChemChina, more of an agricultural chemical company Corteva stood in the middle between Bayer and ChemChina, more of an agricultural chemical company than Bayer and more of a genetics company than ChemChina. With the acquisition of Monsanto, about 45% of Bayer's revenue came from crop sciences. The remaining 55% was derived from pharmaceuticals and over-the-counter medicine.

## Monsanto's Movement Into GMOs

Monsanto originally moved into GMOs in the 1990s with the hope that it could make a dent in one of the world's most pressing problems. The then CEO (chief executive officer) of the company, Robert Shapiro, in a 1996 *Harvard Business Review* article, warned that by 2050 the world's population would come close to 9 billion people. The only way to feed that number of people would be to obtain additional productivity from each acre of soil harvested. By using biotechnology to create valuable foods—with less fertilizers, pesticides, and other chemicals— Monsanto could create an agricultural revolution that would enable the world to boost soil yields with fewer inputs.

Shapiro was addressing a serious agricultural productivity problem. The great advances in agriculture that Norman Borlaug, at one time a University of Minnesota professor, had brought into being were coming to an end. The breeding technology Borlaug introduced into the world had allowed countries like China, India, and Pakistan, with their vast populations, to become virtually self-sufficient in food production, but would their self-sufficiency continue if advances like genetic engineering were curtailed?

In 1950, it took 1.7 billion acres to grow 692 million tons of grain to feed 2.2 billion people. By 1992, the total acreage in cultivation was about the same. Yet the world grew almost three times as much food, and it fed 5.6 billion people. At the same time that malnutrition declined, obesity grew. The average daily intake of calories per person increased from about 2,000 calories a day in 1950 to about 2,500 in the mid-1990s. However, the high-yield crops that Borlaug and his colleagues had created did not do well without the intensive use of fertilizers, pesticides, and other chemicals. In addition, global crop yields no longer were growing at the same pace. Shapiro's belief was that farmers again could increase yields through the application of genetic engineering.

Genetic engineering allowed scientists to alter the make-up of living organisms by cutting bits of DNA from one cell and splicing them into another. By this means, the scientists could create hardier plants that did not require the use of massive amounts of fertilizers. These plants would consume less water, resist pests without as much spraying, and had the potential to be far more nutritious. The plants these scientists engineered might be able to survive salty soil and dry conditions. Their taste might be far better than the taste of foods people currently consumed.

Under Shapiro, Monsanto became committed to using biotechnology to bring genetically modified crops to the market. The company's scientists made breakthroughs in a number of the world's most important agricultural products, including cotton, corn, soy, canola, and potatoes. They added traits that resisted pests that devastated these crops. They increased the nutritional value of both animal feed and the foods people ate.

The plants that the scientists modified also were able to survive the spraying of Monsanto's Roundup herbicide. The application of the herbicide then had the potential to raise agricultural production in two distinct ways. First, by allowing famers to eliminate weeds before they planted, the application of Roundup ensured less topsoil erosion. Second, the application of Roundup assisted farmers after new plants sprouted, as farmers could apply Roundup again, knowing it would not harm their crops while killing the dangerous weeds that threatened the crops' survival.

## Biotechnology's Take-Off

Biotechnology-based crops first took off in North and South America. DuPont and Syngenta became Monsanto's competitors, and all three companies looked forward to a brighter future. That future might involve producing bananas that had vaccines that fought against infectious diseases such as hepatitis B. It might mean breeding fish that would mature far more quickly and growing fruit and nut trees that would do the same. The feedstock for plastics and fuel might be derived from the plants the scientists engineered, in this way decreasing the world's dependence on fossil fuels, which contributed to climate change.

With the take-off of biotechnology, massive changes took place in U.S. agriculture. In the United States, industrial-grade genetically modified corn and soy were fed to almost all cattle, poultry, and livestock that people ate. Traces of genetically modified crops also were found in thousands of foods people consumed, from soy sauce to bread, pasta, ice cream, candy, meats, and corn flakes. Indeed, high fructose corn oil was a genetically modified ingredient found in nearly every processed food people bought in supermarkets.

Dissenters to the take-off of biotechnology foods did exist in the United States as well as Europe. They identified various problems and wanted more caution to be applied in the use of the technology. For example, the Union of Concerned Scientists proposed that the pests frustrated by new bioengineered plant strains eventually would adapt and, once they adapted, superpests could arise. The superpests could create a hazard that would be nearly impossible to control.

With regard to human consumption, the critics insisted that the precautionary principle be used: So long as *any* risk existed, the burden was on the introducer—firms like Monsanto—to demonstrate safety. Though there was no evidence to suggest that consuming genetically modified food was a real threat to human health, the critics were concerned that the genetically modified seeds had been rushed to the market without adequate testing.

## European Resistance

Europeans did not adopt the new technology at the same pace as Americans. The media in Europe tended to portray Monsanto in the worst possible terms as a manipulator of people's fears and creator of Frankenstein-like substances. The European media regularly appealed to people's anxieties about a technology that tampered with the food supply. Another reason for resistance in Europe was that its farmers wanted to preserve their independence. They did not want to be dependent on U.S. agribusiness for their seeds. Acknowledging the consumer's right to information to make informed choices about genetically modified ingredients, the European Union (EU) was responsive to these concerns, and in 1997, it issued a directive that made labeling obligatory on all foods containing, consisting of, or derived from GMOs. This ruling resulted in a virtual moratorium on the importation of products that contained GMOs into EU countries. Many large European food companies, including Nestlé, Unilever, and Cadbury, then came out against the use of GMOs and tried to restrict or prohibit their use in their products.

In general, U.S. consumers did not share these concerns. Yet Monsanto itself had not been without controversy in its history, as over the years it had been associated with contested products such as saccharin, fertilizers, polychlorinated biphenyls, dioxin, and the defoliant Agent Orange.

Patrick Moore, a cofounder of Greenpeace, argued that the EU's own research was dismissive of concerns about GMO foods. He argued that 81 scientific studies on GMOs, conducted by more than 400 research teams at a cost of $65 million, showed *no* evidence of negative human health effects or environmental concerns. Moore characterized the European campaign against genetically modified foods as one of fear based on fantasy and a lack of respect for science and logic.

Nonetheless, as a result of the controversy, Monsanto became one of the most hated companies in the world. A 2013 poll put Monsanto's reputation in 49th place out of 60 companies. The critics were relentless in their attacks, claiming that the company's seeds promoted pesticide resistance and increased herbicide use, spread gene contamination, expanded monoculture, and fell very far short in feeding the world's hungry. The Internet, in fact, was filled with angry sites (MonsantoSucks) and attacks against Monsanto (e.g., references to MonSatan).

## Alternatives to GMOs

Environmental organizations urged Monsanto to give up on biotech and embrace organic farming. The opposition put the company on the defensive and led to a search for alternatives to GMOs. Indeed, there were alternatives to GMOs to increase crop yields and Monsanto had started to become involved in their development. Two of the most prominent were precision agriculture and turbo-charged selective breeding:

- *Precision agriculture:* With the purchase of two companies, Precision Planting and the Climate Corporation, Monsanto was able to offer software and hardware products that gathered and processed large amounts of temperature, rain, soil, and pest data at the square yard of soil, not the farm or field, level. With precise data of this kind, the amount of chemicals and fossil fuels used could be reduced and yields improved in an environmentally sound and less energy-intensive way. Monsanto competitor DuPont also was headed in this direction.

- *Turbo-charged selective breeding:* This technique meant relying on plants with desirable traits and mating them without having to resort to gene splicing. Rather, robotic devices examined slices of DNA from thousands of plants, and scientists observed the slices to find genetic differences that could explain why some plants did better than others in dealing with conditions such as cold weather, insect suppression, drought survival, or reproduction. With this knowledge, the scientists might be able to create better plants by rapid breeding rather than genetic transfer. Monsanto had helped create a number of new vegetable and fruit varieties using this method.

## The Right Decision

Bayer was confident that its buying of Monsanto had been the right decision. Long-term megatrends were in its favor. The world population was growing, and more food, feed, and biofuel would be needed. It was projected that by 2050 people in developing nations would increase their meat consumption by 70%. The animals slaughtered for this level of consumption would have to eat something. A significant increase in agricultural productivity therefore was needed to deliver the type of food consumers wanted more efficiently.

As the need to increase per capita consumption of food drove agricultural growth, Bayer and Monsanto could draw on their combined capabilities to meet the needs of current and coming generations. Their combined capabilities were not just in genetic engineering but also in crop protection, breeding and digital technologies, as well as seeds and traits. By engaging these capabilities, the combined companies would be able to deliver the unique and customized solutions that farmers and the people who relied on farm produce needed.

As indicated, Bayer's vision was not just to rely on biotechnology to solve the problems of the future. Its integrated approach depended on these components:

- Strong genetics and breeding technologies

- Innovative chemistry for weed, pest, and disease control

- Digital farming based on extensive data collection, computation, and predictive analytics

Bayer's strategy was to dominate in all three of these areas. As a European company, it was certain that it could not only succeed in its home base and in the United States but also spread its innovations on the European continent and throughout the world.

With Monsanto's capabilities, it was in a better position to compete for the agricultural markets of the future than either ChemChina or Corteva. It was a company whose every action was based on integrity. As defined by Bayer, integrity meant being concerned about the long-term welfare of humanity. Indicative of a push beyond GMOs designed to benefit human beings in whatever way the company could was its move into the latest genetic technology, CRISPR/Cas9 gene-editing technology. It bought a license to use this technology in 2016.

## The San Francisco Jury Award

Bayer was in for a rude shock, however, which took place almost immediately after the acquisition. Its profits plunged, despite revenue growth of nearly 9%, and its stock market value fell by about a quarter. The main reason was that a San Francisco jury had awarded $289 million to school groundskeeper Dewayne Johnson for Monsanto's failure to warn him about the cancer risks of using RoundUp. The plaintiff had terminal non-Hodgkin's lymphoma, and the judge reduced the award to $78 million. Bayer, however, faced 8,700 additional suits of the same kind.

Bayer was adamant in denying that RoundUp in *any way* caused cancer. It declared emphatically that there were decades of scientific studies and real-world experience showing that the herbicide was safe. The company asserted that it would "resolutely and with all means" defend itself. It revised its legal strategy and brought in new attorneys from the law firm Arnold & Portner, which had won product liability cases Bayer had confronted as a pharmaceutical company in the past. The tactic on which Arnold & Portner relied was to try to change juror selection procedures to assure no jury bias. Bayer engaged in the following calculation. Only if its defense costs vastly exceeded the potential settlement amounts would it consider creating some type of compensation fund for the people claiming they had contracted cancer because of their use of Roundup.

The U.S. Environmental Protection Agency (EPA) chose to put additional restrictions on Roundup use. Pending further study, it was only going to allow farmers to spray Roundup in its current form for an additional two years. The agency prohibited spraying after soybean planting for 45 days and after cotton planting for 60 days and limited spraying to 1 hour after and 2 hours before sunset. The total applications of Roundup on cotton crops had to be reduced from four to two.

With this much concern about Roundup, Bayer had to make some quick decisions about what to do next. Should it settle with the plaintiffs and avoid endless jury trials, which further sullied its reputation? Should it recall Roundup or put additional warnings on its use? Or should it just fight on hoping to be ultimately vindicated in the courts?

## Not Desisting From Radical Innovation

For the time being, Bayer insisted that it would not desist from the path of radical agricultural innovation despite this setback. The world's need for its products and services was just too great. The company was dreaming of a future involving crops that were drought resistant and could deal with the ravages of climate change. It was hoping it could increase rice and wheat yields by addressing the issues these crops faced with pests and diseases. It wanted to make commercial breakthroughs in weight loss, in bacteria resistance, and in high-protein foods.

The company pledged that it would live up to the requirement for a heightened sense of corporate social responsibility (CSR). It declared that it would be fully committed to upholding the highest level of ethical standards. It would apply the same rigor to achieving its sustainability targets as its financial targets, and further reduce its environmental footprint, but at the same time it would not relent on Roundup and would defend its use. The company also had to make decisions about the type of research it would undertake, the responsibilities it had for products Monsanto already had sold on a wide-scale basis, and where it would go next in the quest to increase food security and quality for the coming generations.

As an employee of Bayer, what actions would you propose that it should take? What is the issue Bayer faces? What are the facts, the company's action options, and the expected consequences of pursuing those options? What principles should the company follow? As you apply the weight-of-reasons framework consider the following questions: Is Bayer attempting to address a grand challenge in this case? If so, what does this imply for the actions it should take? How can it move from a short-term fix to a long-term solution? Should stakeholder engagement play a role? Can the company "do well by doing good"? Can Bayer come up with a long-term strategy that is both profitable and ethical? If the company followed your advice, what key lessons do you think it would learn?

## BP: The Big Oil Spill—What Went Wrong[2]

The British multinational oil company BP (formerly known as British Petroleum) was not new to controversy. It had a reputation for taking risks and had suffered a number of safety breaches. In the 1960s, it had the worst safety record in the oil industry and was responsible for the massive Torrey Canyon oil spill off the British coast. In 1995, John Browne became CEO and moved the company in the direction of aggressive expansion. Browne also tried to improve the company's safety record; however, after the company's acquisitions of Amoco and Arco, it was strapped for cash. As a result, neither Browne nor his successor, Tony Hayward, had sufficient funds to upgrade worn-out facilities to the extent needed, and the company continued to have safety incidents:

- In 2005, 15 workers died and more than 170 workers sustained injuries in a Texas City Refinery explosion.

- In 2006, the Thunder Horse production platform in the Gulf of Mexico almost sank in a hurricane when workers installed a valve backward.

- Pipeline corrosion in the Prudhoe Bay oil field on Alaska's North Slope in the same year caused a major oil spill.

- The company's Ohio and Texas refineries accounted for 97% of the U.S. Occupational Safety and Health Administration 2007–2010 "egregious" and "willful" violations.

The 2010 Deepwater Horizon accident was therefore not very surprising when viewed from the context of these problems.

### Beyond Petroleum

While BP was associated with safety and environmental problems, it also was the first major oil company to grant the risks of global climate change. In 1996, it departed from the Global Climate Coalition, an organization that resisted actions to reduce greenhouse gas emissions, and linked up with the Business Environmental Leadership Council, which supported the Kyoto Accord. Among large integrated oil and natural gas companies, BP's CEO Browne was the first to recognize publicly the threat of global climate change. In a 1997 speech at Stanford University, he stated, "We must now focus on what can and what should be done, not because we can be certain climate change is happening, but because the possibility can't be ignored." He affirmed, "It falls to us to begin to take precautionary action now," and declared that it was necessary "to go beyond analysis to seek solutions."

In 2000, two years after the company purchased Amoco, it created the slogan "Better people, better products, beyond petroleum." It embraced a green sunburst logo and rebranded itself. The company already had started a number of initiatives in the field of alternative energy. It invested in wind energy, solar energy, biofuels, gas-fired power generation, and hydrogen. It aimed to expand its solar subsidiary fourfold by 2007 and spend billions to advance renewable energy. It tried to hire management with strong environmental convictions. From 2005 to 2011, BP spent $8.3 billion on renewable energy projects that employed, at their peak, more than 5,000 people. The American Petroleum Institute treated it as a traitor to the cause of climate change opposition and alleged that it had "left the church."

## Expansion, Explosions, and Leaks

Six years after its rebranding effort began, BP made the decision to expand capacity to process Canadian tar sands at its Whiting, Indiana, plant. Its plan was to invest $3.8 billion to expand the facility, including $1.4 billion for environmental improvements. Indiana Governor Mitch Daniels initially applauded the initiative because of the affirmative economic effects. Indiana's Department of Environmental Management and the EPA were ready to approve a water permit for the facility after BP informed county and city officials, obtained comments, and exposed the permit to multiple peer and other reviews. However, the *Chicago Tribune* published an article titled "BP Gets Break on Dumping in Lake," which led to demonstrations, organized boycotts, more probing news articles, and a petition movement against the permit.

The controversy in Indiana took place at the same time that BP received negative media attention for the explosion at its Texas City facility in 2005, which claimed the lives of 15 workers and caused injuries to more than 170 people. The explosion raised inquiries from investigators because of the company's prior legal violations. Investigators discovered that the firm's refineries in Texas, which it had inherited from Amoco, were seriously mismanaged. A company culture that relied on fear and intimidation to keep sensitive matters quiet prevented employees from openly reporting accidents or their safety concerns.

In 2006, a large oil leak took place in the firm's Alaska pipeline. Attributable to BP was up to 267,000 gallons of oil that escaped into Alaska's North Slope tundra. The steelworkers' union stated that for years it had warned the company that such an accident could take place, but the warning had been systematically ignored. In 2007, BP accepted plea bargains for the Texas City accident and the Alaska pipeline leak and admitted that it had violated laws.

## The Big Spill

The Macondo 252 well site in the Gulf of Mexico broke apart in 2010. BP's contract with Transocean Ltd. was for that company to drill the well below 5,000 feet of seawater and 13,000 feet into the seabed. BP obtained a license for the Deepwater Horizon oil rig and worked with the construction firm Halliburton on the project. With the shattering of Macondo 252, the rig went up in flames. Eleven crew members died, and 17 were seriously injured; BP and Halliburton blamed each other for the accident.

The spill was the largest in the history of the oil industry. For the accident to take place, many technical barriers had to be breached. The oil gushed out for 87 days following the explosion and the sinking of the rig, with the total discharge amounting to 4.9 million barrels, or approximately 210 million gallons of oil. The fishing and tourism industries suffered because of the widespread damage to marine and wildlife habitats. A massive effort had to be made to protect beaches, wetlands, and estuaries, yet dolphins and other marine life died in record numbers and tuna and other fish acquired deformities.

In the investigations that followed, it became apparent that the causes of the spill were technical and procedural failures and poor management oversight. The reports blamed BP for defective cement on the well and rig operator Transocean and contractor Halliburton for cost-cutting, insufficient safety systems, and neglect of root causes, which would have stopped the accident from happening.

A day before the accident, the crew had pumped cement into the bottom of the borehole. This procedure should have blocked the oil from leaking. The crew tried to make adjustments, but eight safety systems, including the cement in the borehole, failed:

1. At the bottom of the borehole, the cement did not seal.

2. Two mechanical valves that were meant to stop the flow of oil and gas did not work.

3. The crew did not correctly interpret the pressure tests, which were supposed to determine if the well had been sealed.

4. Therefore, the crew was unable to spot the leak soon enough.

5. The blowout preventer, a second valve to stop the flow of oil, did not work properly.

6. A fire started when the oil flow overcame a separator in place for the purpose of diverting mud and gas away from the rig and safely venting it through pipes on the side.

7. The gas alarm detection system should have activated the closure of the ventilation fans, which could have stopped the fire.

8. Because of a defective switch and a battery that did not have power, the blowout preventer's safety mechanisms did not shut the valves automatically.

BP pleaded guilty to federal criminal charges involving 11 counts of manslaughter, two misdemeanors, and a felony for lying to Congress in 2012. By holding it guilty of criminal responsibility, the federal government was affirming that at the time of the spill BP understood what it should be doing but did not take appropriate action. The spill was not an accident beyond the company's control. The government chose to monitor its safety practices and ethics for four years, and BP had to pay a record-setting $4.525 billion in fines and make other payments.

In 2014, a U.S. District Court judge ruled that because of gross negligence and reckless conduct the company was primarily responsible for the spill. The additional penalties the court set at that time were for $18 billion, and they had serious ramifications for BP's future.

## Financial Distress

BP was in continued financial distress because of the lasting impacts of the spill. The total payments it had to make to all parties finally exceeded $60 billion. Even for BP, one of the world's largest integrated oil companies, that amount was substantial. The only way to pay for the damages it caused was to sell about $38 billion of its assets. It made its biggest sale to the Russian oil firm Rosneft in 2012. BP obtained $12.3 billion in cash and a 19.5% stake in Rosneft, as the two parties brought a prior joint venture to a conclusion.

The costs of the Deepwater Horizon spill forced BP to reduce its commitments to green energy. It shut down BP Solar, a manufacturer and installer of photovoltaic solar cells. In 2011, BP Solar had been in operation for 40 years. Hayward, Browne's successor as CEO, alleged in a Stanford speech that renewables were a distraction. The company had to make safety its top priority. The company, however, did not give up all its alternative energy initiatives and continued to own 13 wind farms in seven U.S. states and to have partial ownership of a wind farm in Hawaii.

Bob Dudley succeeded Hayward as CEO in 2010, and he tried to improve the safety situation. Since the company would continue to carry out activities in hazardous, remote, and environmentally sensitive locations, it confronted many factors that could lead to accidents. The most prominent among them were natural disasters, extreme weather, human error, and technical failure. It was not easy to prevent a significant accident like Deepwater Horizon. Of particular concern was that most of the projects the company undertook relied on contractors and subcontractors, such as Transocean and Halliburton, over whom BP had limited control and responsibility and whose actions could lead to significant safety breaches.

BP had to make gargantuan efforts to win back trust and improve its relations with governments, nongovernmental organizations (NGOs), and local communities after the Deepwater Horizon spill. It gradually was able to make improvements in a number of important indicators, like reported recordable injury frequency, process safety events, and loss of primary containment, but it still lagged industry safety leader ExxonMobil.

To meet the financial commitments the company had because of the Deepwater Horizon spill, the company had to continue to sell assets. It disposed of these assets and used the money to help pay for the oil spill obligations. Each year from 2011 to

2013, the company kept selling additional assets. Yet even after the spill, BP possessed leading offshore positions in the Gulf of Mexico, Libya, Egypt, India, Uruguay Nova Scotia, the Arctic, Angola, Brazil, South China, and Australia. The EPA temporarily banned it from new U.S. government contracts in the Gulf of Mexico, but it continued to have seven rigs operating there.

## Still Facing Dilemmas

Even in 2017, 10 years after the spill happened, BP was not in a position where it could escape its postspill obligations as it still had to make billions of dollars of annual payments. What was even more distressing was that it continued to face occasional serious operational problems. For instance, in the Prudhoe Bay region of Alaska, where it accounted for about 55% of Alaska's oil and gas production, it had a leak in 2017 because of a damaged pressure gauge. It had to notify the mostly Native American community that lived within a 50-mile radius. BP's crews could not immediately access the site because the danger of a natural gas release persisted after the leak terminated. It was not clear how much oil had spilled and the degree to which it affected the snow-covered tundra. Ultimately, the company controlled this event before extremely serious impacts occurred. Its crews plugged the well and stopped its operation, containing the contamination without serious injury to humans or damage to wildlife.

In addition, during this time period, BP made some progress in lowering its greenhouse emissions. They went down from 59.8 million tons of $CO_2$ equivalent in 2012, to 50.3 million in 2013, to 48.7 million in 2014. However, they went back up to 49 million in 2015 and 50.1 million in 2016.

With regard to carbon pricing, BP, like other major oil companies, advocated for this policy. It wanted a well-designed carbon tax or a cap-and-trade system to limit greenhouse gas emissions. In evaluating potential projects, it factored in a range of carbon prices and stress tested its proposed investments at various prices of carbon per ton. Unlike ExxonMobil (see the case at the end of Chapter 9), it accepted that peak oil demand was likely, and it projected that demand for oil would grow only until around 2035 and after that it would flatten out and decline. This recognition affected its willingness to undertake new projects to discover oil in far-flung and dangerous areas of the globe. If the demand for this oil was not likely it was not prudent or responsible for the company to try to develop it.

Why did the Deepwater Horizon oil leak happen? In answering this question, draw on the lessons of Chapters 3 and 4 about the cognitive and organizational impediments to ethical decision-making. What should BP's leaders do now? What policies and programs could they put in place to ensure that operational failures such as the Deepwater Horizon spill don't happen again? What lessons can they learn from the spill?

Over the longer term, what are BP's strategic options, and what are the expected consequences of pursuing them? Which stakeholders should the company prioritize and engage, and what principles should it apply? In the short term and long term, what can BP do to establish a strong safety record, address climate change, and earn high profits?

# DowDuPont: The Bhopal Disaster[3]

In 1984, a toxic gas leak at a Union Carbide facility in Bhopal, India, killed more than 3,000 people and injured thousands more. After the Bhopal disaster, Union Carbide was the subject of many takeover attempts and Dow Chemical bought Union Carbide in 1999 for $8.89 billion.

In 2017, when Dow Chemical merged with DuPont to form a new firm called DowDuPont, Baskut Tuncak, the United Nations' special rapporteur on hazardous substances and wastes, indicated that he was "deeply concerned" that the Dow–DuPont merger would make it virtually impossible to see an "effective remedy" for the victims more than three decades after the tragedy. Dow did not own or operate the facility that leaked the highly toxic methyl isocyanate (MIC) but Indian citizens and courts continue to try to hold it accountable. Would the merger between the chemical giants make it more difficult for the victims and survivors of the Bhopal disaster to obtain compensation? How should the new DowDuPont respond? In deciding what to do, it reviewed what happened in the period immediately around the accident.

## Highly Toxic Chemicals

The Union Carbide plant in Bhopal, India, originally built in the 1960s, was located in open fields within 2 miles of a local commercial and transportation center. At the time of its start-up, it mixed chemical components that had been manufactured overseas and shipped them to India to be made into final pesticide formulations that would be marketed. The plant did not pose much of a threat to neighboring residential areas. However, by 1978, Union Carbide, under pressure from the Indian government to manufacture the precursors to the pesticide in India, built and began operating the facilities necessary to manufacture highly toxic compounds in India.

Although some local authorities objected to the plant's location, state and national government officials overruled them. The Indian government made no serious attempts to shield local people from the potential consequences. The plant was an important part of the economy. Among the pesticide components manufactured at the plant was the highly toxic and unstable MIC, which is used to make the active ingredient in the pesticide Sevin. It was manufactured in batches and stored in three large refrigerated concrete tanks within a few yards of each other just below the surface of the soil.

## Weak Infrastructure

The city of Bhopal was the capital of one of the least industrialized states in India. Beginning in the 1950s the government actively encouraged industrial development in the region, but it did not engage in a comprehensive planning effort. As a consequence, infrastructure and services like roads, utilities, and communications services were very poor. By the 1980s, stagnation in agricultural production in the country's rural areas drove thousands of people to cities like Bhopal to look for work. Bhopal's population increased sixfold between 1961 and 1981, almost three times the average for the country as a whole. A severe housing shortage forced migrants to build shantytowns wherever there was open space. Areas near industrial plants where work might be found were among the migrants' favorite choices. Right outside the walls of Union Carbide's Bhopal plant could be found crowded squatters' dwellings.

## An Uncontrolled Explosion

At 11:00 p.m. on the evening of December 2, 1984, everything seemed normal at the Bhopal plant. However, half an hour later, a worker noticed an MIC leak near the vent gas scrubber. Plant employees planned to fix the leak after the 12:15 a.m. tea break, but by the time the break had happened it was too late.

The pressure in one of the tanks shot up and quickly exceeded its upper limits. The thick concrete tank cracked open and unleashed poisonous gases. A white cloud of MIC smoke shot out of the vent gas tower attached to the tank and settled over the vicinity. Each tank had been equipped with pressure and temperature gauges, a high-temperature alarm, a level indicator, and high- and low-level alarms.

## Nonfunctioning Backups

What was more, there were several safety systems designed to handle accidental leaks. They included a vent gas scrubber, which neutralized toxic gases with a caustic soda solution; a flare tower, which could burn off the gases; a refrigeration system to keep the chemical at low, stable temperatures; and a set of water-spray pipes, which could control escaping gases or extinguish fires.

Within a few minutes, the fire brigade began to spray a curtain of water in the air to knock down the cloud of gas. The tower from which the gas was escaping was 120 feet high, however, and the water only reached about 100 feet in the air. The system of water spray pipes was too low to help.

The vent gas scrubber, designed for an emergency of this nature, did not function. The scrubber had been under maintenance and had not been charged with a caustic soda solution. Even if the scrubber had been operational it would have been ineffective since the temperature of the escaping gas was hotter than the system was designed to handle.

The plant operators were afraid to turn on the flare tower for fear of igniting the large cloud of gas that enveloped the plant. In any case, it too was being repaired and was missing a 4-foot section. Likewise, the coolant in the refrigeration system had been drained weeks before to be used in another part of the plant, and therefore it was useless in fighting the poisonous fume. Routing the escaping gas into an empty MIC storage tank was not possible because, contrary to established safety procedures, there were no empty tanks available.

## Trapped Victims

As the gas began to escape, the warning alarm sounded for just a few minutes before it was shut off. As the workers fled the plant in panic by foot, the four buses parked near the entrance, which were intended to be used for emergency evacuations of plant workers and nearby residents, were left standing. In the shantytowns and neighborhoods outside the plant, chaos reigned. The gas seeped into the rooms of the sleeping population, suffocating hundreds in their sleep and driving others into a panicked run through the narrow streets, where they inhaled more gas.

Blinded by the cornea-clouding effect of the gas, lungs on fire, thousands died or were injured. Long after the accident, victims suffered from breathlessness, coughs, lung diseases, eye disorders, abdominal pain and vomiting, menstrual disorders, and psychological trauma. Many women had to contend with reproductive illnesses.

## Organizational Shortcomings

In the weeks and months after the accident, a horde of reporters, Indian government officials, and Union Carbide technical experts analyzed the causes. Union Carbide contended that the accident was the result of sabotage by an unhappy employee. Yet, whatever the proximate cause of the accident, it was clear that the magnitude of deaths and injuries was the result of more than an act of sabotage. The safety policies and procedures that were intended to prevent such an accident had not been followed, and the reasons were rooted in the deteriorating financial condition of the Bhopal plant.

The Bhopal plant was an unprofitable unit in an unimportant division. The plant had lost money for three years in a row. As profits fell and budgets were cut, maintenance was deferred, employees were laid off, and training programs were scaled back. Morale was low, and many employees had voluntarily left. Safety training was inadequate—workers did not know how to deal with emergencies, and they knew little about the toxic effects of MIC.

Formal control of the plant had been turned over to an Indian subsidiary, because of Indian law. However, important day-to-day decisions still were being made by Union Carbide's top management in Connecticut. Based on the receipt of monthly reports, the Connecticut management team continued to make financial, maintenance, and personnel decisions, while Indian personnel did safety inspections.

The unpreparedness of the emergency infrastructure of the local government exacerbated the problem. The accident was not just the result of technical malfunctions in equipment but stemmed from human errors and organizational shortcomings.

## Warnings Ignored

There had been many small accidents in the past, yet the Department of Labor of the state where the accident occurred was grossly understaffed. It had only 15 inspectors for more than 8,000 industrial plants. Trained as mechanical engineers, most of the inspectors had little understanding of the hazards of a chemical plant.

When a journalist from the Bhopal area wrote a series of articles in 1982 detailing the death of an employee that was caused by a chemical leak at the plant and warned of the possibility of a catastrophe, neither the plant management nor the government took action, even after the journalist wrote a letter to the chief minister of the state to warn him of the danger. A top government bureaucrat, who requested that the plant be moved to another location because of the threat it posed to the neighboring slum residents, was transferred to another post.

## The Price of the Accident

The plant was closed and 650 high-paying jobs lost, as well as 1,500 government-related jobs. Union Carbide was hard hit. The Indian Supreme Court ordered the company to pay out $470 million to the victims and survivors, and the company's reputation came under attack. Activist groups undertook a variety of campaigns against the company. The company's stock dropped, its debt rating was reduced, and the company was sued by its shareholders for not telling them of the risks. Ultimately, it no longer could operate as a separate company, and the remaining assets were sold to Dow Chemical.

It was argued that Union Carbide could have avoided this accident if it had taken the precautions needed to run the plant in a safe way. It should have designed the plant differently, made certain that the safety equipment was running and not let financial considerations get in the way, and trained the workers in what they should do to prevent an accident. The company should have heeded the warnings of journalists and government officials that an accident could happen. These questions remained:

- To what extent were the company and the Indian government criminally responsible for what happened?

- What should DowDuPont do to ensure that an accident of similar magnitude never again occurs at its facilities?

- To what degree does it have to coordinate with government and local civic groups to warn them of hazards and prepare them for their possibility no matter how dire they might be?

Specifically, now that DowDuPont is the owner of what remained of Union Carbide, what should it do? Many activists argued vehemently that those responsible had never been held fully accountable for the toxic gas leak. They suggested that the site of the facility might still be contaminated. They rallied against corporate greed and the negligence of governments like that of India, which put economic growth above the harm that corporations could cause to common people.

Industrial accidents still regularly occur, and kill and maim people. On April 11, 2019, the Center for Chemical Process Safety listed several reported accidents (Table 10.2).

Reflecting on Chapters 3 and 4, what cognitive biases and organizational problems do you think led to the Bhopal disaster? Use the weight-of-reasons framework to identify what actions DowDuPont should take today, more than three decades after the leak. What issue does it face? What facts are relevant, and what principles are at stake? What options does the company have, and what are the consequences of pursuing these options? What are the company's legal responsibilities and ethical responsibilities? What does the company need to do to become an "ethical organization"? Can it "do well by doing good"?

| | |
|---|---|
| **TABLE 10.2** | **Industrial Accidents Reported in April 2019** |

Crews responding to oil field fire in Kilgore

Natural gas explosion overnight in Louisiana

Silo explosion at Lake County asphalt plant heard from miles away

2 injured in Wyoming oil rig explosion

Schools still closed near Texas chemical plant fire

Deer Park plant fire: Blaze extinguished, but some questions linger

One hospitalized in Greenfield chemical spill

Firefighters control fire in dust collector

Officials: Multiple fire departments respond to Glen Cove building blaze

Two workers critical after chemical spill

Woman injured by chemical explosion in filer

Explosive fire causes $1.25 million in damage to Wyoming County storage building

Structure fire at Kobe Aluminum

Air district "closely monitoring" flaring at Richmond Chevron refinery

Flint Hills to restart portion of unit following fire

Blaze hits Great Plains building

Chlorine Gas Leak Sends 50 Water Treatment Workers to Hospital

*Source:* https://www.aiche.org/ccps/chemical-accidents-news

## Facebook: Privacy and the Public Interest[4]

Facebook was launched in 2003 at Harvard College as an online directory by 19-year-old Mark Zuckerberg, along with his roommates Eduardo Saverin, Andrew McCollum, Dustin Moskovitz, and Chris Hughes. Within a couple of weeks two thirds of the school had signed up. By 2005, Facebook had expanded to become an online directory for colleges. It had 3 million users and 20 employees. From the start, it aimed high. Similar to Google, which wanted to provide access to all the world's information, Facebook's goal was to connect all the world's people.

Fascinated by hacker culture, Zuckerberg believed that software programmers could do things that would shock the world. To achieve its goal of connecting all people, Facebook would have to create status updates, photos, groups, and apps that would generate a world of its own that would intensively involve users.

In moving to Silicon Valley, Facebook shared the technological optimism of other firms that were located there. It was like the law of gravity that technology always made the world a better place. Company managers knew, however, that in building a product people loved, it might make mistakes. The Facebook motto was to "move fast and break things." Zuckerberg, who had a smidgeon of a renegade philosophy and disrespect for authority, was quoted as saying, "A lot of times people are . . . too careful. I think it's more useful to . . . make things happen and then . . . apologize later."

From the start, Facebook promised that it would not share people's information, except with those who had received permission. The intention "to do no harm" was never clearly stated, and Facebook suggested that in trying to achieve its idealistic ambition it did not have to be overly concerned with harm that might take place. The end of connecting everyone on the planet justified the price it paid.

## An Intoxicating Vision

Facebook was driven by an intoxicating vision of giving people the power to share, in the hope that it would make the world more open and better. Along with the heady vision was a lucrative business plan to get everyone on the planet on board. By 2007, Facebook already had nearly every college student in the United States signed up. Facebook then expanded to high school students. It was translated into more than 100 languages. Zuckerberg made it clear that the goal of the business was worldwide growth and expansion.

Zuckerberg was not yet satisfied in 2012, when the company announced that it had 1 billion monthly active users for the first time. He wanted to fashion what in effect was a digital nation-state, which would become the greatest experiment in free speech in human history.

The far-reaching changes and the consequences of the company's reach were not taken seriously, despite warning signs that existed before problems burst into public view. For these problems, Zuckerberg seemed honestly apologetic, willing to admit mistakes, and show that he was sorry. Yet he did not fail to hold to his paradigm-shifting, world-stirring vision. His favorite slogans almost never lacked rousing rhetoric. They included "Fortune favors the bold" and "What would you do if you weren't afraid?"

Facebook focused on the good ways in which it could be used, never really on the bad ways. Its engineers were preoccupied with figuring out how to make the user experience increasingly more engaging so more people would sign up. The mission driving nearly all Silicon Valley companies, including Facebook, was to *scale up* as quickly as possible. Obsessed with unlimited growth, the problems Facebook experienced were associated with its exceptional expansion.

## News Feed

To generate and maintain interest in the site, the company's engineers developed News Feed. News Feed analyzed all the information Facebook had about users and provided interesting information for them. The aim was to produce unending interesting content based on personalized algorithms that were uniquely customized for each person. The addition of a new "like" button in 2009 allowed News Feed to collect vast amounts of personal data about people. Facebook provided users with an end-less stream of stories, pictures, and updates, which were shared by friends, adver-tisers, and others. The intent was to have people keep going on the site, continuously looking, scrolling, and liking.

News Feed was a flywheel of engagement. It allowed Facebook to better under-stand who the people were who used the platform—to whom they related the most, what interests they cared about the most and what causes were of greatest concern to them. News Feed also permitted Facebook to figure out from which businesses its users were likely to make purchases and under what circumstances they were most likely to buy from these businesses.

In gathering this type of data, Facebook did not explicitly violate existing laws, as these laws did not hold Internet companies responsible for the content posted on their sites. Section 230 of the Communications Decency Act allowed Internet companies like Facebook to grow and thrive since it did not hold them accountable for its users making violent statements. The internal doctrine within Facebook was libertarian in that the company would not make or enforce rules that prevented people from saying whatever pleased them so long as they did not *directly* incite violence. Direct incitement clearly was out of bounds, and for that Facebook would try to remove a person from the site, but in the name of free speech, it allowed users to push up right to the edge so long as others were able to respond. The basic ground rules at Facebook were decency, no nudity, and no extremely violent or hateful speech.

The company was reluctant to impose its value system on its users out of concern that in doing so it might limit its worldwide growth. Thus, little effort was made to distinguish outright lies from the truth, and with lies having the same status as truth, the truth often was obfuscated. The company thought it could rely on people's common sense and decency to police the site.

## The Arab Spring

Facebook's attitude toward free speech was tested during the 2010 Arab Spring. Wael Ghonim, a Google employee in the Middle East, set up a Facebook page after the events that led to Tunisia's regime falling in 28 days. Ghonim's page protested the abuses of Hosni Mubarak's Egyptian regime. Along with other online activists, he called for an Egyptian revolution in 10 days. In just 3 days, more than 100,000 people joined the page. Hundreds of thousands of people filled the streets of Cairo, and Mubarak stepped down 18 days later.

Facebook had helped to achieve what seemed unimaginable in Tunisia and Egypt. It was relatively restrained about taking credit but in a certain sense it was trium-phant. Zuckerberg said, "People being able to share what they want with the people who they want is an extremely powerful thing." Facebook thought that it was an enabler of the good.

But just as it had been used for this purpose, it now fell into opposing hands, with the adversaries of democratic change then using Facebook to unravel the rev-olution. Soon, it became apparent that Egypt was beset by extreme polarization, with deadly clashes between the military police and forces of change activating the

Muslim Brotherhood, which had an entirely different interest in Mubarak's downfall than Egypt's original democratic protestors.

The tone of the Facebook posts as they related to the Egyptian revolution started to change and became more extreme and antidemocratic and less faithful to the truth. Posts accused Ghonim of insulting the Egyptian army and being an Israeli spy.

The same Facebook tool that helped liberate Egypt was used for a disinformation campaign against the original protestors. Ghonim tried to approach the people he knew in Silicon Valley and at Facebook to alert them about what was taking place. He told them that they had to invest more in trying to prevent the platform from being used for such purposes. Government officials in the region also approached Facebook about false rumors, which were abundant on the platform, but the company, with its history of relying on metrics and measurements, dismissed the information, which it considered anecdotal and did not take the warnings seriously.

## Policing the Platform

In any case, it would have been very difficult for Facebook to act because it was not staffed to police the site adequately. The people it employed, who might police the site, were very young, did not speak the language or understand the culture of the countries where the company operated, and were not well attuned to the complexities and nuances of events taking in these countries. Facebook's employees were overwhelmed. They had to make snap judgment calls, deciding if what they observed violated any of Facebook's standards or its terms of service and trying to figure out the meaning and consequences of the provocations they observed posted on the site. The responsibility they had for taking down posts was great, and they were unprepared to fulfill this responsibility.

Facebook, moreover, could not spend limitless amounts of money on these tasks as it was trying to first and foremost to grow its revenue, keep costs down, and generate additional revenue. The financing of the firm remained a primary concern. Facebook was about to have its initial public stock offering and it wanted to secure billions of dollars from investors, which was only possible if it was a ubiquitous platform that allowed people to post without any serious restrictions. Allowing people to use the site for whatever purpose they wanted was more important that imposing controls and keeping them from engaging with it.

As the company went public, it also had to show investors and advertisers that it could profit from the personal data it had on its users. To achieve this goal, Zuckerberg turned to Sheryl Sandberg, whom he hired away from Google, where she had succeeded in the same undertaking of monetizing Google's data. Sandberg brought with her many of the same people with whom she had worked at Google and built a business model that probably skirted the legal boundaries of personal privacy. Without directly going over a boundary, Facebook had to use the data in a way that was to users' benefit while at the same time assuring them that they were safe in handing over as much of their personal information as possible to the company.

## Pressure to Grow Advertising

Sandberg needed unlimited access to this personal data because she was under intense pressure to grow the company's advertising, which was the main source of its revenue. When she came to the company in 2012, revenue growth was flattening and investors were speculating that the company's growth would subside. What ensued was an intense period of experimenting in how to make the data the company had about a person, which included chats among boyfriends and girlfriends and pictures of drunken party photos from college, more useful to advertisers. None of these data were of much interest unless they could be converted into the tendencies that users had to buy particular products.

Thus, right before the initial public offering (IPO), Facebook started to purchase information about its users from data broker companies. These data revealed what people bought, where they shopped, what their families liked to do, and what political opinions they had. Facebook tracked its users' browsing intensively and matched the data from the brokers with the information it had so it could sell targeted ads. This campaign helped the company achieve a very significant spike in revenues and profitability.

The degree to which Facebook started to collect data about its users was revealed when Max Schrems, then an Austrian exchange student at Santa Clara University in Silicon Valley, sent an email to Facebook asking for a copy of the data the company had collected about him. Schrems was especially concerned since the privacy laws covering him as a European were not being enforced. Facebook sent Schrems 1,200 pages of information and Schrems was alarmed because he considered much of it sensitive, for example, information about his location, his love life, his sexuality, and the communications he had with a friend who was confined to a psychological hospital in Vienna, Austria.

Schrems sent 22 complaints to the EU's Data Protection Commission in Ireland, where Facebook's international headquarters was located. The commission had just 20 employees in Ireland at the time yet was responsible for regulating all Internet data companies, not just Facebook. Ultimately, Facebook contested Schrems's allegations and maintained that it took European privacy laws seriously; it agreed to make its policies clearer and to stop storing some kinds of user data. Though the incident made Zuckerberg very uncomfortable he did not change Facebook's policies of collecting data about the individuals who posted on Facebook and trying to monetize these data.

## The Federal Trade Commission Consent Order

The U.S. Federal Trade Commission (FTC) then took notice. It investigated the company in 2012 and found that Facebook was sharing users' personal data with third-party developers—companies that built games and apps for the platform—without the users' consent. The action the FTC brought against Facebook was for deceptive conduct, in that the company had not made clear to users that it would be sharing their data with third parties. The FTC also was concerned that Facebook was not keeping track of what the third parties did with the data. The third party developers, according to the FTC, could be foreign agents from countries like Russia. In the consent order with the FTC, Facebook promised to plug such leaks quickly so that risks to personal privacy would be eliminated.

Yet the potential gaps in its policing of privacy were extensive, and Facebook had a great deal of difficulty complying with the consent decree. The main danger it was unable to remove entirely was that a malicious agent could target someone and use Facebook information against that person. This possibility could not be entirely ruled out, and there was little that Facebook's top executive could or would do to prevent it.

After the IPO, Facebook acquired Instagram and WhatsApp; it had even more information about people that it could sell to whoever want the information. These acquisitions did not go unnoticed by the U.S. Department of Defense (DOD). The DOD was concerned that the information Facebook could be used for disinformation, deception, and many other nefarious purposes. A party with access to the information not only could try to manipulate someone into making purchases but could also influence the person's political attitudes and voting behavior. The DOD published hundreds of papers and reports about the threats that social media, including Facebook, posed of using disinformation and turning it into a weapon against national security by manipulating people. It showed how easily people could be misled by someone setting up a fake account or a large number of fake accounts and disseminating propaganda that was not in the interest of the U.S. government.

## Russia's Internet Research Agency

In Russia, a secret propaganda factory in St. Petersburg called the Internet Research Agency (IRA) had hundreds of Russian operatives using Facebook and other social media to fight a propaganda campaign against the anti-Russian government in the Ukraine. The Russian agents registered on various social media sites including Facebook using fake names and pictures. They used illustrations and other messages to sully the name of the Ukrainian government and its elected officials. The aim was to help sow distrust and fear of the Ukrainian government and inspire the pro-Russian opposition.

The Russian goal was to weaponize Facebook. It paid money to promote stories so that the stories became very popular and appeared on the top lines of Facebook's news feeds. Stories like the following regularly appeared on Facebook. They were a direct consequence of the Russian campaign:

> Cruel Ukrainian nationalist killing people or torturing them because they speak Russian. They are going to attack. They're going to burn your villages. Worry.

> Child crucified by Ukrainian soldiers. They nailed him like Jesus to the board. One nailed him while two held him down.

Dmytro Shymkiv, a top adviser to Ukraine's government, met with Facebook representatives and asked them to intervene and to stop the Russian campaign against his country. He brought proof to representatives that the Russian accounts were fake, but the company refused to take action. Facebook responded that it was prodemocracy and therefore in favor of free speech and would not exclude users from saying what they wanted on its platform except in very extreme circumstances. Facebook maintained it had an open platform, and so long as parties conformed to policy found on its website it would not take action.

As far back as 2008, Facebook was aware that different countries had engaged in disinformation campaigns on its platform. Evidence showed that it tried to take into account the evolving threats and risks from various scams, bullying, harassment, nudity, and porn, but it could not keep up. Doing so seemed not to be a priority in comparison with growing the use of the platform and the profits it could earn from the information it collected about people's wants, desires, and needs, which it could sell to advertisers and others willing to pay for this information.

## The U.S. Presidential Election

By 2016, Russia started to use the platform to introduce division and polarization into the U.S. presidential election. Zuckerberg admitted,

> As I look around, I'm starting to see people and nations turning inward against this idea of a connected world and a global community. I hear fearful voices calling for building walls and distancing people they label as "others," for blocking free expression, for slowing immigration, reducing trade and, in some cases around the world, even cutting access to the Internet.

However, Zuckerberg argued that Facebook was an element in the solution to this problem, not the source of the problem. He maintained that was why the work Facebook was doing in opening up its site to all comers and anything they wanted to post was more important than ever.

At the time of the presidential debates between Donald Trump and Hillary Clinton, 39% of people in the U.S. were obtaining most of their election news and the material they relied on for making decisions about voting from material on Facebook. Facebook was getting more than 1 billion political campaign posts, and it was touting itself as the "new town hall." People were spending more and more hours of their day consuming Facebook content. The company had become extremely popular, and this popularity allowed it to become one of the most profitable companies in the world.

Donald Trump's digital media director, Brad Parscale, knew Facebook well and he was an intense user of the platform, spending more than $100 million on Trump Facebook. With custom audiences and targeted ads, he was able to get information about the candidate precisely to the people he most wanted to receive it. Facebook was dominating the news business. Sixty-two percent of Americans reported getting their news from social media sites like Facebook. Media organizations started to publish directly on News Feed, making it a major news distributor. Zuckerberg was ecstatic. He said, "I'm personally really excited about this. I think that it has the potential to not only rethink the way that we all read news, but to rethink . . . a lot of the way that the whole news industry works."

However, Facebook, unlike a traditional media company, did not view itself as responsible for the accuracy of news and information that it released on its site. It did no serious editing of the news and was not subject to the rules of fairness and lack of bias that governed traditional media outlets. Rather, the design of its algorithms was meant to feed people the information they wanted to hear so they would come back to the Facebook site and stay on it for the longest time possible.

Zuckerberg insisted that Facebook was a tech company, not a media company, and therefore was not responsible for curating the news. Legitimate and fake purveyors of the news on Facebook did not look different to viewers and Facebook did nothing to prevent fake news from spreading.

## Rampant Misinformation

As a result, misinformation was rampant on Facebook. Much of it originated in Macedonia, where about 200 people set up fake news websites from which they could earn good incomes from ads based on the traffic the websites generated. The "news" headlines they posted included the following:

Hillary Clinton Indicted

The Pope Endorsing Trump

Clinton Selling Weapons to ISIS

This type of news got far more traffic than an honest and balanced *New York Times* investigation of Trump's tax returns. Facebook was aware of what was taking place but was reluctant to intervene because it did not want to curtail "free speech" or be regarded as a news agency rather than technology platform. If regarded as a legitimate news source, it would be subject to controls that would remove the fake news that was rampant on its platform. Enforcing those controls would be costly, not only in having to hire employees to supervise postings on the platform, but in pushing people away who wanted to engage in the lying and deceit and who went to Facebook because they wanted to hear it.

Facebook did, however, appoint Tessa Lyons, who had been chief of staff to Sandberg, to lead a team of five to fight misinformation. She later admitted that she did not think "there was a real awareness of . . . the scope of the problem and the . . . right course of action" to take at the company. Facebook began to see a plethora of hyperpartisan pages that were getting tremendous engagement, with claims like "A million migrants are coming over the wall and they're going . . . to rape your children." The counter to these charges were viewed far less. Thus, such vain and false charges, by dictate of Facebook's algorithms, went to the top of News Feed. To go against this trend was not in Facebook's business interest, as polarization was popular and Facebook benefitted above all else from its popularity. It appealed to people's low-level emotions that brought engagement, more time on the site, more sharing, and more advertising value. Roger McNamee, an early Facebook investor, wrote to Zuckerberg and Sandberg about his concerns. They responded that what he understood to be taking place was an isolated problem that they were addressing.

Parscale claimed that arguments about Facebook influencing the election were based on resentment at the outcome. The platform was free and open to all sides. The Clinton campaign simply was not successful in using Facebook sufficiently to its advantage, Parscale implied.

## Defending the Company

After the election, Zuckerberg continued to defend the company by asserting, "I think the, the idea that . . . fake news on Facebook, of which, you know, it's a very small amount . . . of the content, influenced . . . the election in any way . . . is a, a pretty crazy idea." Andrew Anker, Facebook director of product management from 2015 to 2017, said,

> I think it was very easy for all of us sitting in Menlo Park to not necessarily understand how valuable Facebook had become. I don't think any of us, Mark included, appreciated how much of an effect we might have had. And I don't even know today . . . that we really understand how much of a true effect we had.

James Clapper, director of national intelligence for the U.S. government from 2010 to 2017, maintained during the Senate hearings that "classical propaganda, disinformation, fake news . . . we only scratched the surface. . . . I didn't appreciate the full magnitude of it until well after."

Fearful that his business empire was in trouble, Zuckerberg set out on a cross-country trip to defend the platform. He announced that Alex Stamos, Facebook's chief security officer from 2015 to 2018, was tasked with investigating the fake news phenomenon, specifically what component of it was Russian in origin. Stamos and his team ended up linking a large amount of it to the Internet Research Agency of St. Petersburg, the same group that had been using Facebook to spread disinformation in the Ukraine. Russian operatives bought ads promoting political messages to entice people to become part of what appeared to be legitimate social movements. They created pro- and anti-immigration groups with extreme and polarizing messages. Their aim was to find the fault lines in U.S. society, amplify them, breed mistrust in the U.S. political system, and ultimately undermine it.

As the controversy about Facebook's role in the election heated up, Zuckerberg announced that Facebook was

> actively working with the U.S. government on its ongoing investigations into Russian interference. We've been investigating this for many months now. . . . And when we recently uncovered this activity, we provided that information to . . . Congress.

Congress then concluded that Facebook-related posts, originated either through Russian fake accounts or through paid advertising from the Russians, touched about 150 million Americans and affected their behavior. The Russians had prepared messages for every group in U.S. society—Black Lives Matter, white supremacists, gun control advocates, and gun control opponents. It did not matter. The aim was to promote divisiveness and to bring about discord, disunity, and the failure of the U.S. people to govern themselves.

## Cambridge Analytica and Zuckerberg's Mea Culpa

Whistle-blower Christopher Wylie then exposed the abuse at Cambridge Analytica, a company that specialized in rumor campaigns and seeded the Internet with misinformation on behalf of the Trump campaign. Cambridge Analytica had gained access to Facebook data from a third party without Facebook's permission. Almost all the people who had their data collected and given to Cambridge Analytica did not know about it. When the data left Facebook servers, there was no way for Facebook to track the data, know how they were used, or find out how many copies there were.

What came out was that Facebook knew what was happening for at least two years prior to this revelation. But Facebook only changed its data-sharing policies and ordered Cambridge Analytica to delete the data. After Wylie came forward, Facebook banned Cambridge Analytica from its site and announced that it was ending the controversial practice of working directly with data brokers.

The uproar was so intense that in April 2018, Zuckerberg was called before Congress, where he finally did a mea culpa and said,

> We face a number of important issues around privacy, safety, and democracy. And you will rightfully have some hard questions for me to answer. Facebook is an idealistic and optimistic company. And as Facebook has grown, people everywhere have gotten a powerful new tool for making their voices heard and for building communities and businesses. But it's clear now that we didn't do enough to prevent these tools from being used for harm as well. And that goes for fake news, for foreign interference in elections and hate speech, as well as developers and data privacy. We didn't take a broad enough view of our responsibility, and that was a big mistake. And it was my mistake. And I'm sorry.

For Facebook with its 2 billion–person platform to control, it was difficult to know what it should do, if anything, next. Unfortunately, Facebook still was finding foreign actors using the platform to spread disinformation. So Zuckerberg went on to say:

> One of my greatest regrets in running the company is that we were slow in identifying the Russian information operations in 2016. And we're going to take a, a number of measures, from building and deploying new AI [artificial intelligence] tools that take down fake news, to growing our security team to more than 20,000 people.

## Other Problems

In the Philippines, Facebook had been warned that President Rodrigo Duterte had been using a network of paid followers and fake accounts to spread lies and attack his critics since 2016. His brutal war on drugs had taken an estimated 12,000 lives, which Human Rights Watch called government-sanctioned butchery. Online state-sponsored hate was meant to silence and to intimidate Duterte's opponents. In 2016, Facebook was given the names of 26 fake accounts and asked to intervene. But the company had been focused on the growth of its platform in that country and was reluctant to introduce safeguards.

Monika Bickert, Facebook's vice president of global policy, responded to the charges that Facebook had facilitated Duterte's policies by stating,

> Any time that we think there might be a connection between violence on the ground and online speech, the first thing for us to do is . . . understand the landscape. . . . What should our role be? . . . We now have a team that is focused on how to deal with exactly that sort of situation.

In Myanmar as well, Buddhists had incited hatred and violence against Muslims using Facebook and other social media, but Facebook was slow to respond to charges that its platform had fanned the ethnic tensions. False reports appeared on the platform that a Muslim man raped a Buddhist woman, an angry mob killed two people, and massive waves of violence followed that displaced 150,000 people. Facebook had met with civil society organizations as far back as 2015. It indicated that it was gravely concerned and promised to dig into the issue and come back with substantive action. However, it maintained that at its headquarters, it did not have sufficient information and a pulse on what was happening in Southeast Asia and therefore had not acted. It hired more international people as its way to cope with the problem.

Facebook appeared to understand that it needed more people to work on safety and security and that it had not done enough historically but the reason it gave for its past failures was that it was too idealistic. What it meant by being too idealistic was it was too committed to free speech and too hopeful that people on their own would police the site. Facebook claimed that it was ready to step back, review what it should do, and take actions to address the situation. Imagine that you are part of a team called on to brief Zuckerberg and Sandberg. Use the weight-of-reasons framework to develop a long-term solution to the problems described in this case. What is the key issue, and what facts are relevant? What options do you have for addressing the issue, what consequences should you consider, and which principles should you apply?

As you apply the weight-of-reasons framework, consider which stakeholders count the most. Should the company engage with these stakeholders or try to solve the problem itself? What, if any, changes to the law should it support? What should Facebook learn from its history of having its platform used for nefarious ends? Ultimately, is there a fundamental contradiction between Facebook's business model and the goals of protecting private information and preventing misinformation? Can Facebook use systems thinking, both/and thinking, and moral imagination to create long-term solutions?

## Ford: Safety Recalls[5]

U.S. auto-making giant Ford manufactured vehicles under its own name and the Lincoln brand name. It also operated Ford Credit and previously owned Hertz, the large automobile rental company. In addition, it once manufactured vehicles under the name of Mercury and owned Jaguar, Volvo, Land Rover, and Aston Martin; it

**FIGURE 10.1**    Ford's 2018 Quarterly Revenue and Earnings

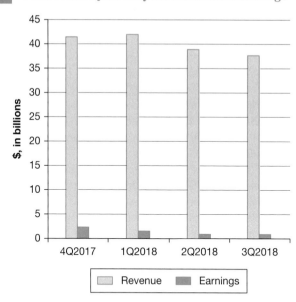

also had a controlling interest in Mazda. But it let go of all of these holdings because of its poor financial performance. Sales for its mainstay Ford and Lincoln brands were declining. They consistently lost market share. In the last quarter of 2018, Ford's financial results were far from stellar (Figure 10.1). Though it met revenue expectations, it missed its earnings projections. Its sales grew in North America, but it had losses in China and Europe, and they kept mounting. While its financial performance fell, it also faced safety issues.

## The 2018 Ford Recalls

In 2018, Ford experienced three large safety recalls. These were the largest among U.S. carmakers in that year.[6] The company had to take back 1.6 million 2015 to 2018 Ford F-150 trucks, 1.3 million 2014 to 2018 Ford Fusions and Lincoln MKZs, and 1.3 million 2012 to 2018 Ford Focus sedans.

- The F-150 trucks were recalled because the front seat belt could ignite in a crash, potentially starting a fire in the carpeting or insulation.

- The Fusions and Lincoln MKZs were recalled because a steering wheel bolt could loosen and result in it becoming detached.

- The Focus sedans were recalled because a valve could become stuck, producing a fuel system problem.

The National Highway Traffic Safety Administration (NHTSA) enforced U.S. safety standards. It had the right to investigate complaints relating to vehicle safety and to order manufacturers to recall and repair vehicles found to have safety-related defects. The cost of these recalls could be substantial, depending on the nature of the repair and the number of vehicles affected.

As if these three NHTSA-related takebacks were not enough, Ford also had to withdraw 504,000 2013 to 2016 Ford Escape SUVs (sports utility vehicles) and Fusions because their transmissions could shift to a gear different from the one selected. No other auto manufacturer came close to having the number of vehicles recalled in 2018 as Ford did. The company had to be careful not to let these safety issues balloon into crippling losses that could undermine its future. It had to assess what had happened and determine what it could learn from its recalls and those of its competitors.

## Ford's History of Safety Problems

Though all large automakers have had serious bouts with recalls, Ford stood out for what happened in 1973, when a top-selling vehicle, the Ford Pinto, generated a series of lawsuits, a federal investigation, a "60 Minutes" exposé, and a 1.5 million–vehicle recall. This incident culminated in the indictment of the company for reckless homicide in three teenage girls' deaths. Ford established an unfortunate pattern for safety incidents in which automakers have foreknowledge of the problem but do nothing about it. (The Pinto decision is profiled in Chapter 2.)

Ford did not do a good job in absorbing lessons from this incident. In 1991, it had to replace 13 million Firestone tires, mounted mostly on its Explorer vehicles where it had prior warning that a problem existed that it could have corrected. Well before the vehicles reached the market, company engineers were aware that the vehicles had issues with instability and handling. In a 1989 test, a year prior to Ford selling the vehicle, an internal report pointed out that the vehicle was prone to excessive rollovers, yet Ford chose to ignore this problem and did not make changes to correct it. Instead, it told drivers to lower their tire pressure, even though doing so reduced the vehicles' fuel economy.

The company's actions ultimately were responsible for 174 deaths and more than 700 injuries. Ford lost about $2.4 billion in damage settlements, with additional lawsuits seeking another $590 million. In 2001, the company recalled more than 300,000 vehicles and replaced more than 13 million tires at a cost of $3 billion. It could not deny that its SUVs rolled over more frequently than other automobiles, as it built most of them with pickup truck bodies, which ride higher and raise the vehicle's center of gravity. In 2002, it chose to correct the problem after the fact. It built the next Explorer 2.5 inches lower to the ground than its predecessor.

## Ford's Mounting Losses

After the Explorer problem, the company continued to have poor quality ratings. Its losses mounted as it encountered sluggish sales, intense price wars, and faltering employee morale. It closed plants, eliminated jobs, and stopped making

Mercury Cougars and the Lincoln Continental. Though it started to cut its losses, its market share fell. In 2005, the company had its bonds downgraded to junk status. To gain additional sales, it had to increase incentives and rebates, and lower interest financing.

In 2006, Ford had the largest annual loss in its history. The plan to return to profitability that it unveiled that year called for dropping the models that lost money, consolidating production lines, closing more factories, and cutting more jobs. Ford raised bankruptcy as an option, getting the United Auto Workers to agree to a historic contract settlement in 2007; in return, Ford got breaks in its retiree health care coverage.

During the Great Recession that followed, Ford did not declare bankruptcy like General Motors, nor did it ask the government for a bridge loan, but it requested and got a credit line of $9 billion as a backstop against its worsening condition. In 2010, it returned to profitability, earning $6.6 billion. In that year, the F-Series established itself as the best-selling vehicle of the United States. Ford sold 528,349 F-Series trucks, a 27.7% increase in comparison to 2009 sales. The F-Series constituted about a quarter of the company's total sales of 1.9 million vehicles in that year.

## Ford's Attempt to Introduce New Safety Features

Like its competitors, Ford was trying to introduce innovative safety features into its vehicles.

- It offered accident avoidance and driver assist technologies on select models, such as adjustable speed limiters, traffic sign recognition, stop devices, brake support, and adaptive headlights.

- It expanded its lane-keeping systems.

- It made curve control available, which slows the vehicle when it senses that a driver is taking a curve too quickly.

- Its SYNC® technology allowed drivers to use voice commands on their cell phones and MP3 players to prevent them from diverting attention from the road conditions.

- SYNC-equipped vehicles also had a nonsubscription call-for-help system.

- An SOS–Post Crash Alert System™ automatically sounded the horn and activated the emergency flashers.

Ford's aim for its global vehicle platforms was to offer superior safety. At its test facilities in Michigan and Germany, it had motion-based driving simulators that did advanced research in driver assist features, the human–machine interface, and in topics like drowsy and distracted driving. In California, at its Palo Alto Research and Innovation Center, it examined the safety implications of the driver assist technologies as well as connectivity, mobility, and autonomous vehicles. Ford was committed to a new mobility blueprint of connected transportation for transportation in

2025 and beyond, making driving safer. Connected transportation would ease traffic congestion and create substantial environmental improvements.

## NHTSA Increase in the Number of Recalls

Starting in 2014, NHTSA greatly increased the number of its safety recalls. One of the reasons was NHTSA's expansion of its definition of defects and a shift to more civil penalties, actions that adversely affected all automakers. Meeting or exceeding existing government safety standards and anticipating future standards was costly and technologically difficult. Moreover, the standards frequently conflicted with weight reductions the government wanted so that Ford and other automakers would comply with fuel economy standards.

Ford took notice that its safety initiatives were not advancing as rapidly as it wanted:

- On the one hand, the number of Ford's new models that reached NHTSA's 5-star safety rating grew to 71% in 2017. On the other hand, the company was shocked by the scope of the 2018 recalls it endured.

Dedicated to designing and building safe vehicles that met or exceeded government standards, Ford did not know what to do next. It was not alone among the large auto companies that had such issues. What could it learn from a review of Toyota's and General Motors' (GM) experiences?

## A Challenge to the Toyota Way

Toyota's automobiles consistently had ranked near the top in quality and reliability. Largely considered responsible for this was the company's management approach, referred to as the Toyota Way. The company made decisions slowly and by consensus, considering the options first in a very deliberate manner and then rapidly implementing the decisions it made. Its employees were supposed to adhere to principles involving teamwork, learning, continuous improvement, long-term thinking, respect for people, and problem-solving. They were expected to take care of problems before they grew large and out of control. The company's approach put a heavy emphasis on its employees' contributions. It was noted for emphasizing vehicle quality, lean manufacturing, and just-in-time production.

Yet Toyota had a significant setback in 2009–2010. In a series of global recalls, it took back more than 9 million vehicles and briefly had to halt all production and sales after reports that several of its cars and trucks experienced unintended acceleration. NHTSA advised the company that it had to eliminate movements that drivers experienced when floor mats slid into the accelerator and advised the company to take care of the problem of crashes caused by the floor mat incursions. It had to prevent its accelerators from sticking to the floor and causing vehicles to move on their own. Toyota had to recall 7.5 million vehicles in the United States, and in Europe and China it had to recall another 2 million vehicles. The number of deaths attributable to the problem was alleged to be 37.

U.S. media reported heavily on the problem. For the week of January 25 to 31, 2010, the story of unintended acceleration was the fifth most reported U.S. news story. Toyota dealers in the southeast of the United States pulled their advertising from newspapers in protest against what they considered to be excessive reporting.

Automotive experts, Toyota officials, and government agents contested whether the problem was as serious as the media claimed. They asked if victim reports were reliable and argued that several factors could cause sudden, unintended acceleration, including driver mistakes.

Since Toyota was trying to emerge from the recession and was already suffering from declining sales, the recalls came at a difficult time. Its dealerships in the United States lost about $2 million a month on average in revenue. In 2008, Toyota sold more automobiles in the United States than in Japan. From 2009 to 2013, this situation changed and Toyota sold fewer cars in the United States than Japan. The negative publicity had an impact.

In 2012, Toyota spent more than $1 billion and it settled a class-action lawsuit that compensated owners for the lost resale value of their vehicles. It also agreed to pay a fine of $1.2 billion for not revealing information and for misleading the public about the issue. A 2013 jury ruling concluded that the accidents involving Toyota vehicles were the result of electronic deficiencies in the vehicles. It criticized the company for conducting an incomplete investigation of the electronics and concluded that it had not followed best software practices.

Previously, the accelerators in Toyota vehicles had been entirely mechanical, but then came the advent of electronic control. Older mechanical pedals relied on friction to keep the pedal in a fixed position. With electronic accelerators, the friction was not sufficient, which made it difficult for drivers to hold the accelerator steady. Drivers tended to prefer the freer and more tactile response of the conventional system. Toyota's designers tried to emulate the tactile accelerator response with a special friction device. Juries found that the friction devices often failed, which was the root of the sudden-acceleration problems.

In 2014, the company and the U.S. Department of Justice (DOJ) reached an agreement whereby Toyota agreed to pay a $1.2 billion criminal penalty in exchange for deferred Justice Department prosecution. This agreement subjected Toyota to independent monitoring of its safety procedures and ended an investigation in which the DOJ concluded that Toyota had hidden information from the public and made deceptive statements to protect its image.

At the time, this penalty was the largest ever issued against an automotive company. Toyota called the agreement difficult to bear but necessary to put the issue behind it. Brake-override systems then became standard in all its vehicles, but the company continued to confront lawsuits for wrongful death and personal injury as a result of this problem.

## Toyota's New Quality Committee

The recalls represented a challenge to the philosophy of the Toyota Way, which previously had produced such high levels of quality. The errors, it turned out, were due to design and quality control problems. While the recall events took place, competitors like GM and others offered rebates for customers to switch from Toyota to their cars. In response, Toyota set up a new global quality committee to coordinate defect analysis and future recall announcements. It also established a Swift Market Analysis Response Team in the United States to conduct on-site vehicle inspections. It expanded its event data recorder system and the degree to which it relied on third-party quality consultation. It also expanded its driver safety education initiatives. It promised that its global quality committee would become ultraresponsive to consumer concerns. The company analyzed accidents and incorporated what it learned into vehicle development, seeking optimal systems for every driving scenario it could identify. Toyota aimed to put in place an integrated safety system that functioned before an accident, during every stage of driving, and after an accident, if it was unpreventable.

## GM's Defective Ignition Switches

GM had been the world's largest automaker from 1931 to 2007. However, in 2009, at the time of the Great Financial Crisis, its U.S. sales fell 60%, from more than 5 million vehicles in 2008 to about 2 million in 2009. This decline in sales resulted in very heavy indebtedness and the company's bankruptcy. To bail it out, the U.S. Treasury provided the company with $49.5 billion under the Troubled Asset Relief Program. To survive, the company had to eliminate brands such as Saturn, Pontiac, Oldsmobile, and Hummer, and sell Saab.

In 2010, "the new GM" emerged out of one of the world's largest IPOs. Purchasing a majority of the old firm's assets, including the *General Motors* name, the new GM took on the task of designing, assembling, marketing, and distributing vehicles, and selling parts and financial services. However, the new GM no longer commanded the title of being the world's largest motor vehicle company. Toyota and Volkswagen (VW) alternated in holding that position.

The new GM appointed Mary Barra CEO in 2013, ending a period of turmoil in which the company had three different CEOs between 2009 and 2011. Barra was 51 years old at the time of her appointment. She previously had been GM's executive vice president for the Global Product Development, Purchasing and Supply Chain and had a lifelong career at the company, rising through the ranks. Immediately after her appointment, she faced a serious test: a safety defect in the ignition switches the old GM had installed in millions of vehicles. The defect had caused 124 deaths, for which the new GM now had to compensate the survivors. The company faced 79 lawsuits seeking upward of $10 billion in damages. The NHTSA fined it $35 million in 2014 for failing to recall the brands responsible for the accidents—Cobalt, Pontiac, Saturn, and Chevrolet, which the new GM no longer made—claiming that the old GM had known for a decade or more about the faulty switches and had not acted to correct the problem.

NHTSA imposed the maximum fine it could, as evidence showed that GM's violation of safety rules had been egregious. In total, the company had to recall 2.6 million vehicles in 2014 and 2015 because a loss of electrical power in their ignition switches prevented the airbag from deploying in the event of a crash, and also because of an ignition lock cylinder problem that caused the car key to come loose when the engine was running. These problems had direct costs to GM of several billion dollars. The company's profits declined, it lost sales, its stock market value fell, and its reputation for safety and quality, not high to begin with, diminished.

## GM's In-Depth Review

In response to these problems, GM initiated a comprehensive review. The review showed that it would have to recall another 36 million vehicles. The total recall costs would amount to more than $4 billion. The impact on the company's sales and revenue were difficult to determine since of the approximately 36 million vehicles subject to recall about 10 million were subject to multiple recalls. Approximately 63% were vehicles the new GM no longer produced or sold, models the old GM had made, such as the Chevrolet Cobalt, Pontiac G5, and Saturn ION.

In conducting an in-depth review of its safety policies the company hired a former U.S. government attorney to carry out the investigation and provide recommendations. At the end of the investigation, it chose to discipline five employees, and it created a new global vice president of safety, responsible for safety performance, and a new Global Product Integrity organization within the Global Product Development department. The company made enhancements to its investigation and consumer-facing processes. It implemented new standards to facilitate information-sharing within the firm and to aid in decision-making as well as adding global technical resources to support the new processes. GM also launched a Speak Up for Safety Program to encourage employees to report on issues, and it tried to ensure that those issues were brought to the highest levels in the company.

Apply the weight-of-reasons framework for ethical decision-making to this case. Based on its own experience and that of Toyota and GM, what should Ford do to improve vehicle safety? What cognitive biases and organizational problems does the company face? If it truly desires to create a long-term solution to its safety problems, what organizational steps does it need to take? To what extent would stakeholder engagement help?

## General Mills: Nutrition[7]

General Mills had to decide to what extent it would treat so-called healthy foods as a threat or an opportunity. To what extent should the company shift its portfolio of products in this direction?

General Mills had many brands and competed vigorously for market share in a variety of food categories other than just cereals, such as yogurts (Yoplait), soups (Progresso), flour and cake mixes (Gold Medal and Betty Crocker), and snack foods (Chex Mix, Fiber One, and Gardetto's). The company also sold nature bars under the Nature Valley and Larabar labels.

Consumer tastes seemed to be shifting toward foods promoted as healthier options. For instance, consumers increasingly wanted high-protein, low-carbohydrate foods-on-the-go. General Mills for years had been trying to meet consumers' demand for more convenience but had been slow to recognize the consumer preference for added protein.

How should the company approach the trend of consumers looking for healthier food alternatives? To what extent should it copy the initiatives of Pepsi, a competitor that owned Frito Lay and was the world's leading vendor of snack foods?

## Hunger and Obesity

In 2000, Worldwatch Institute, a Washington, D.C.–based think tank, announced that for the first time in human history, the number of overweight people in the world was about equal to the number of underweight people.[8] Since 1980, the world's underfed population had declined to roughly 1.1 billion, while the number of over-weight people had increased to roughly 1.1 billion.[9] Overweight and underweight people had similar health problems—high levels of sickness and disability, curtailed life expectancies, and low productivity levels. They suffered from a lack of the essential nutrients and the dietary elements they needed for healthy living. More than half of the world's disease burden was related to eating disorders. Overnutrition and obesity were linked to cancer, heart disease, and diabetes, and stretched the capacities of the world's already overburdened health care system.

By 2016, the World Health Organization reported that this problem had only grown worse, with more overweight and obese people than ever:

- More than 1.9 billion people above the age of 18 years (39% of the world's total population) were overweight.

- More than 650 million of these people (13% of the world's total) were obese.

- Moreover, 381 million children suffered from being either overweight or obese.

Most of these people lived in countries where being overweight and obese was a greater health risk than being underweight.

## Marketing to Children

General Mills had aggressively marketed presweetened cereals to children and had been roundly criticized for it. The company relied on a host of marketing techniques in its marketing to children, including television and social media ads, in-store banners and signs, and its website. Critics pointed out that the sugar and HFC found in these cereals was a danger to children and their families about which General Mills was not providing enough warning.

General Mills countered the claims of the critics by maintaining that it had undertaken a long history of initiatives to fight obesity. As far back as 2009, it had affirmed its commitment to helping people achieve a healthy weight. It had joined together with retailers, other food and beverage manufacturers, and NGOs in the Healthy Weight Commitment Foundation, the purpose of which was to conduct a national, multiyear campaign to reduce obesity, especially among children, by promoting healthy weight through a balance of fewer calories and physical activity. General Mills's foundation had participated in other anti-obesity campaigns.

These efforts were criticized, however, because they focused on personal responsibility. They did not address the company's contributions to the problem. The concern of the Yale Rudd Center for Food Policy and Obesity was the advertising of sweetened cereals to impressionable young children by General Mills on prime time television and other media. The Yale Center maintained that General Mills was responsible for about 60% of the cereal ads aimed at children and had the most children-targeted advertising of any cereal company. The products it advertised most extensively to children (Cinnamon Toast Crunch, Honey Nut Cheerios, Lucky Charms, Cocoa Puffs, and Trix) had the *worst* combined nutrition scores of any of the cereals that were sold. The critics also maintained that the serving size on the cereal labels was very misleading. The Cheerios label, for instance, stated that it had only 100 calories per serving, but most children ate two to three cups.

General Mills responded to these critiques with the argument that cereal was one of the healthiest breakfast choices for an individual. Ready-to-eat cereals had fewer calories and less fat and cholesterol than almost all other breakfast options, including bacon, eggs, waffles, pancakes, syrups, cream cheese, jam, butter, toast, or bagels.

## Sugar, Salt, and Fat

Prior to Harvard nutrition professor Jean Mayer shaking up the industry in 1969, the only objection to sugar-coated cereals had been tooth decay. No one expected Mayer to associate cereals so directly with obesity, which he presciently called the "disease" of civilization. In a column running in newspapers throughout the country that year, he asked if popular sugar-coated cereals such as those that General Mills sold actually were candy and not food.

Michael Moss relates in his book *Salt, Sugar, and Fat* that at an industry conclave in Minneapolis, Minnesota, in 1999, Michael Mudd, at the time vice president for global corporate affairs at Kraft, made a 114-slide presentation calling on food industry companies to do far more to fight obesity. According to Moss, Stephen Sanger, the then General Mills CEO, squashed the changes Mudd was seeking by asserting that consumers wanted good-tasting food and good-tasting food was incompatible with food low in calories. Sanger asserted that the industry was acting responsibly and the obesity storm, unlike the cigarette controversy that had ravaged the tobacco industry, would blow over.

Sanger responded to Moss's book in an email to Moss, in which he wrote that General Mills "consistently placed a high priority" on improving the nutritional properties of its products by adding whole grains, fiber, and nutrients and reducing fat, salt, sugar, and calories. The company had corporate objectives for nutritional improvement. It invested in research and development (R&D) to achieve them. It tracked its progress and built metrics into the assessment of its employees to ensure that it was achieving progress. General Mills, Sanger held, had introduced a regular stream of new and reformulated products offering higher levels of nutrition, including light and low-fat yogurt, light and low-fat cakes and frostings, light and lower-salt soups, reduced-sugar and higher-fiber cereals, and whole-grain natural fruit bars. The company advertised the nutritional improvements to consumers, but not all the new products were successful. The problem, according to Sanger, was that consumers were only responsive to nutritional improvements "if they did not have to sacrifice taste to get them."

A joint 2013 article by employees of General Mills, Kellogg's, and the U.S. Department of Agriculture in the academic journal *Procedia Food Science* documented the progress cereal companies had made. Calculating the mean 2005 to 2011 sugar, salt, and fiber values for ready-to-eat breakfast cereals, they found that the sugar levels had decreased by 7.6%.

## Facing More Challenges

General Mills faced many challenges in assuring consumers about the quality, safety, and nutrition of the foods it sold. Here is a list of some of them:

- In 2012, the company introduced Nature Valley Protein bars as part of a general effort to provide more protein-rich products. Protein was seen as building muscle and helping people lose weight. However, the degree to which U.S. consumers actually needed additional protein was questionable. Most of them ate more than enough meat, giving them all the daily protein they required. The additional protein intake was likely to just contribute to weight gain.

- In 2013, General Mills' Yoplait yogurt lost its leadership position to Dannon in the valuable U.S. yogurt market. Greek yogurt rose from 2% of the overall market in 2007 to 43% in 2013. Chobani became the segment leader. Yoplait responded with its own Greek yogurt brand but could not match the taste or consistency achieved by traditional Greek yogurt makers, which thickened their product by straining it while General Mills added milk protein concentrate.

- In 2014, General Mills introduced Fiber One Protein bars and Larabar Alt protein bars. However, health-oriented websites warned that most protein bars like those of General Mills were loaded with sugar and fat. The website Everyday Health rated nine protein bars, and Nature Valley's came in last place. The Nature Valley bar had 190 calories but only 10 grams of protein. It also had 6 grams of sugar and 3.5 grams of saturated fat.

- In 2014, the company tried to dispel consumer concerns about genetically modified ingredients in its cereals. Several animal studies suggested that there were serious health risks associated with genetically modified food, including infertility, immune problems, accelerated aging, faulty insulin regulation, and changes in major organs and the gastrointestinal system.[10] General Mills announced that it was making the original Cheerios free of this content, but it was criticized for not removing these ingredients from other varieties like Honey Nut Cheerios.

- In 2014, a class-action suit attacked the company's Fruit Roll-ups, Fruit Gushers, and Fruit by the Foot for being filled with trans-fat, sugar, and food dye and being packed with additives that were harmful to children. These products did not have significant amounts of real fruit and, according to the suit, were substantively different from candy.

- In 2015, prior to its sale of Green Giant vegetables to B&G Foods, the company tried to capitalize on the brand by creating various types of vegetable chips for health-conscious consumers. However, to achieve a decent taste, the company had to include in the chips 6 to 7 grams of fat per serving.

## Competition With Pepsi

General Mills's mainstay, the ready-to-eat cereal industry, was mature, declining, and consolidating. Many U.S. consumers had turned to inexpensive generic cereal alternatives, such as Malt-O-Meal. Indeed, General Mills faced reduced demand for many of the products it sold, not just ready-to-eat cereals. Moving more aggressively into snack foods, which Pepsi dominated, could be an attractive option. The company already competed with Pepsi in cereals (Pepsi owned Quaker Oats) and granola bars. Pepsi was a much larger company, with revenue of about $65 billion in 2018 and more than 250,000 global workers. General Mills only had revenue of about $16 billion and employed just 40,000 workers globally. Pepsi outspent General Mills on marketing and advertising by a substantial amount, with General Mills' marketing and advertising expenditures trending slightly downward overall (Figure 10.2).

**FIGURE 10.2**    Pepsi and General Mills: Annual Marketing and Advertising Expenditures

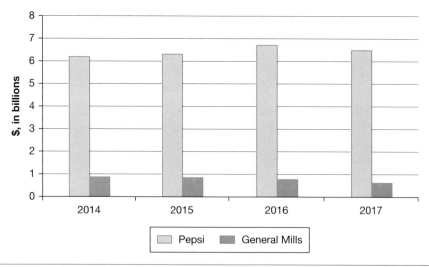

## Saturated Markets

Pepsi had experienced similar problems. The problems were similar in that they both faced saturated markets for their core products: In General Mills's case the core product was cereals, while in Pepsi's case the core product was soft drinks. In both instances, the reason was that demand for sugar-laced products was declining. Demand for sugary soft drinks had been dropping for many years. Figures like Michelle Obama and former New York mayor Michael Bloomberg attacked them. U.S. states proposed the idea of soda taxes. Whereas the American Heart Association recommended no more than 9 teaspoons of sugar per day, the equivalent of 16 teaspoons was in a 20-ounce soda serving. Diet drink consumption also was falling because of concern about how artificial sweeteners affected health.

Pepsi had long ago hedged its bets by acquiring Frito Lay and becoming a snacks company as well as a soda company. It then moved to purchase alternatives to soft drinks and snacks. Via joint ventures, acquisitions, and investments of various kinds, it went outside its mainstream businesses and started to sell these alternative products. On its website, it maintained that it was giving customers choices. It divided its products into three categories: (1) fun for you, (2) better for you, and (3) good for you. In the latter category were protein shakes, fruit juices, and fuel bars. Though promising, these investments did not yield the kinds of financial success that Pepsi attained from nonhealthy alternatives.

Pepsi's snacks dominated the global market, with major brands like Lay's and Ruffles potato chips, Doritos and Tostitos tortilla chips, Cheetos, and Fritos corn chips. More than 50% of Pepsi's total revenue came from these snacks. General Mills was a distant second in this market. Yet Pepsi faced severe nutritional challenges in the snack market in that sugar, salts, and fats were such important ingredients. Consumers were aware of the negative health effects of eating foods high in sodium. According to the U.S. Centers for Disease Control and Prevention, 90% of people in the United States ate more sodium than they needed for a healthy diet, which put them at risk for high blood pressure and cardiovascular diseases. The demand for snacks in the United States and globally was on the rise, though it was changing and consumers were increasingly asking for healthier snacks.

## Performance With a Purpose

Pepsi's CEO from 2006 to 2018 Indra Nooyi's approach to the criticism was to articulate a vision she called "performance with a purpose." A vegetarian and the first woman and non-U.S.-born person to hold the job, she did not accept Pepsi's responsibility for the obesity crisis—that she blamed on sedentary lifestyles—but she did believe that Pepsi should be part of the solution. The company should be part of the solution not by selling fewer products but by selling products that were good for people, but these products also had to taste great.

Nooyi aimed to position Pepsi for a future in which nutrition would play a much more central role. With so many people focused on health, she considered the demand for more nutritious foods an opportunity, not a threat. Healthy food categories would grow faster than less healthy categories. Pepsi had to be ready to meet this demand.

Her solution was to apply science and technology to the problem. Via the application of science and technology, Nooyi believed foods could be made healthier and they could taste good at the same time. She also believed that Pepsi's scientists could make them more affordable. The products Pepsi referred to as "good for you," those made of grains, fruit, nuts, vegetables, and dairy, ultimately would become a much larger part of Pepsi's portfolio. The company was in a transition process where its portfolio of products would shift over time from "fun for you" to "good for you." Someday, the good-for-you products would dominate, and the fun-for-you products would fade into the background.

As to when this shift exactly would occur, Nooyi was unclear. To make it happen faster, she tasked Pepsi's scientists to reengineer all its foods so they would have less salt, fat, and sugar. Pepsi employed many top-notch experts in trying to accomplish this goal. It built world-class laboratories and expanded its R&D budget. For example, its scientists developed the following:

- A salt replacement that the company tested on its Walker brand of chips in the United Kingdom

- A technology to reduce the amount of oil absorbed by potato chips

- A sophisticated method of taste-testing to experiment with sugar substitutes in the hope that they could create a natural, 0-calorie sweetener that tasted exactly like sugar

In fulfilling the goal of profit with a purpose, Nooyi promised that Pepsi would reduce the amount of salt and sugar in all its products. Still the company was cautious because, like Sanger at General Mills, it was not certain that people would be satisfied with the taste.

In addition, Pepsi became known for its other CSR initiatives. It started a major advertising campaign known as Pepsi Refresh and donated $20 million to people with uplifting ideas about how to change the world. The funded projects assisted the homeless, built school playgrounds, established education programs for teenage mothers, and carried out many worthy activities. General Mills too was known for such initiatives as its foundation made serious investments in people, neighborhoods, and education. It aimed to alleviate hunger and advance nutrition wellness for children.

Nooyi claimed that her job was not to pay attention to quarterly numbers but to gaze into the future and understand the challenges Pepsi would confront in the coming decades. Her campaign that Pepsi perform with purpose did not, however, release the company from the sting of all its health-minded critics, some of whom asserted that the best way for people to consume healthier foods was for Pepsi to go out of business.

What can General Mills learn from Pepsi? If consumers remained wary of the foods Pepsi and General Mills offered for sale, how could the companies retain existing customers and find new ones? What cognitive biases do General Mills executives have that affect the way they run their business and prevent it from moving forward? What stakeholders should they value the most? To be part of the long-term solution to the problem of obesity, does General Mills need to rethink its mission, vision, values, and strategy?

How would you apply the weight-of-reasons framework to this case? What are the issues, the facts, the options, the consequences of pursuing the options, the principles that the company should apply, its best long- and short-term actions, and the lessons it should learn from its past experience?

# Google: Doing No Harm

Google first established its well-known principle "Don't be evil" in its code of conduct in 2000. Then in 2004, the company's founders went further, recognizing that harm avoidance was not enough. They wrote, "We believe strongly that in the long term, we will be better served—as shareholders and in all other ways—by a company that does *good things for the world* [italics added] even if we forgo some short term gains."[11]

Has the company lived up to its principle of "Don't be evil"? Has it done good things for the world?

Because of its immense scope, Google affects people's lives in many ways. The company has sought to be exemplary in addressing pressing social and environmental issues. At the same time, it has suffered problems of sexual harassment in the workplace and stymied stronger data privacy laws. In addition, the company has been accused of using its power to stifle competition, not living up to its promise to operate in an environmentally sustainable fashion, and contributing to the development of autonomous weapons. This case examines whether Google has obeyed its own maxim to not be evil.

## Leadership on Social Issues

Google (and its parent company, Alphabet) are often seen as leaders in ethics and social responsibility. Forbes named it one of the world's most reputable companies in 2018.[12] The company was regarded as one of the best places to work in 2018 and again in 2019. It achieves this status partly because of the luxurious amenities it provides to employees, such as free food, workout facilities, laundry services, and massage chairs, but also because it provides more important and meaningful benefits such as access to in-house doctors and on-site child care facilities. Though the company has experienced significant problems related to sexual harassment and gender inequality, it is also considered a leader in workplace diversity. Women constitute approximately 25% of its leadership[13]—a number that reveals inequity but is far above corporate averages.[14]

Google has engaged on a number of social issues. Through its nonprofit arm Google.org, it has given billions of dollars in grants, and its employees have volunteered millions of hours to organizations that use information technology to promote inclusiveness and battle discrimination, help workers prepare for and access the job market, and provide education to children.

A hallmark of Google's work on social issues is its shared-value approach: The company seeks to create value for its stakeholders and society by employing its capabilities in data science. In addition to funding its nonprofit partners, it also helps them develop their technical capabilities so that they can execute their missions.

For example, Google.org has worked with Goodwill, the leading job training organization in the United States, to launch the Goodwill Digital Career Accelerator, which will teach computer skills and provide related career opportunities to more than 1 million people. Similarly, the company has worked with Pratham Books to develop an online open-source platform for creating free children's books.[15]

## Environmental Sustainability

Google is also a leader on environmental issues. Early in the company's life, the consensus among the top management team and employees was that it had to consider the environmental impacts of operations on its campuses. The company undertook projects related to commuting (e.g., providing employee shuttles, corporate electric car sharing, and bicycles), eating (sourcing food locally, supporting sustainable seafood, and reducing food waste), and buildings (eliminating toxic materials, smart design, and performance measurement including LEED [Leadership in Energy and Environmental Design] certifying its buildings). Employees also tried to accelerate the adoption of plug-in hybrid vehicles by means of a project called RechargeIT.

Google soon took on more ambitious environmental goals. One of these was to become "carbon neutral." The company has tried to meet this goal by reducing its energy use, switching to renewable energy, and improving its energy efficiency. In 2008, Google made a $10 million investment in the solar thermal developer Brightsource, and then in 2011, it made a $168 million investment in the company's inaugural utility-scale solar project. In 2008, Google.org also invested in the geothermal developer Potter Drilling. In 2010, the company acquired a 35% stake in the transmission infrastructure company Atlantic Wind Connection, and it invested $38.8 million in the North Dakota utility-scale wind-scale projects of NextEra (see the case at the end of Chapter 9), from which it agreed to buy carbon offsets. In 2011, Google signed a second power purchase agreement with NextEra and invested in a Clean Power Finance fund to assist homeowners in placing solar panels on their roofs, a SolarCity fund to provide lease financing for residential solar projects, and numerous Southern California wind projects. In 2013 Google invested in Makani Power, a maker of airborne, kite-mounted wind turbines. Along the way, Google continuously improved the energy efficiency of its data centers, which are now among the most energy efficient in the world. Google achieved a goal of carbon neutrality in 2007 and has been powered 100% by renewable energy since.[16]

Google also has reduced its environmental footprint by working with the Ellen MacArthur Foundation to adopt circular economy practices in its data centers. Google seeks to refurbish, remanufacture, and sell old servers and other data center machines rather than sending them to the landfill. It destroys and shreds the equipment that it cannot reuse or resell and then sends it to an electronic waste recycler. Six of Google's 14 data centers now divert 100% of their used equipment from the landfill, and the data centers' overall diversion rate is 86%.[17]

Google takes a shared-value approach to environmental issues. It has funded and worked with numerous initiatives that address environmental issues through data science. One such program is Global Fishing Watch (GFW), an online map that allows viewers to track the activities of the world's 60,000 largest fishing vessels worldwide. Google's GFW staff work with nonprofit organizations to protect critical marine mammal habitat and develop more sustainable fishing practices.[18]

Google's path to carbon neutrality and environmental sustainability has not been without bumps in the road. For example, environmental groups including Greenpeace criticized the company for keeping the details of its energy consumption and greenhouse gas emissions secret. The company claimed that this information was a trade secret that competitors could use. In 2009, however, *Harper's Magazine* ran an article asserting that the real reason for Google's secrecy was the extent of its emissions. The article claimed that the company was causing real harm because each search on its search engine contributed 7 grams of carbon dioxide to the atmosphere.[19] Google retorted that responsibility for emissions from searches should be shared with computer users and that it was only responsible for 0.2 gram of carbon dioxide per search.

However, with the growth in energy use by its data centers, the company could not stem the tide of increased criticism from environmental groups and media scrutiny. Finally, in 2011, Google relented and made public its carbon emissions and electricity consumption. It maintained that compared with other sectors in society it was not a major emitter. It reported that its servers were among the most efficient in the world and that they used half the energy of a typical center.

Even so, Google could not refute arguments that its emissions were high and that while each search was low in emissions, use of Gmail and watching videos on YouTube had very high negative carbon footprints. At the same time, Google received praise from environmentalists for its increased transparency. Partnering with organizations like the Climate Savers Foundation and the Green Grid, Google aimed to establish a set of best practices and make improvements in its data centers.

## Search Engine Dominance

The company's dominance of the search engine market raised other questions. Competitors' search engines, such as Lycos, Excite, Yahoo, AltaVista, and WebCrawler, have lost out. Google's share of the global search market has continuously hovered around 90%, with Bing and Yahoo splitting most of the remaining share.[20] The company competed fairly, and users freely made the choice to make its browser because it had superior features. In the evolutionary contest for engine dominance, most of its rivals were not as efficient as Google.

Assessing the societal impacts of Google's strong position is not easy, however. Google has been accused of using its search engine dominance to direct users to its other businesses at the expense of competitors. For example, Yelp has claimed that Google directs search users to its own product reviews rather than Yelp's. Similarly, Google has been accused of unfairly directing shoppers to its own online shopping website, Google Shopping, at the expense of competing online shopping tools.

These accusations were validated and in 2017, the European Commission fined Google $2.7 billion for unfair trade practices related to search. The Commission's research showed that on average, links to competitors' shopping websites were listed on the fourth page of search results.[21] Thus far, Google has escaped penalties in the United States, although during the Obama administration the FTC did investigate it and require it to make changes. U.S. antitrust regulators generally are more concerned about whether monopoly power leads to less choice and/or higher prices for consumers, and in comparison with the European Commission are less worried about impacts on competitors.

Another concern about monopoly power is that companies that grow big enough to dominate markets also gain inordinate power over the political system. Google and other large Internet companies have worked to thwart efforts to introduce more customer-friendly privacy laws in the United States.

## Reworking the Original Motto

In 2014, Google reworded its original "Don't be evil" motto, reformulating it as "You can make money without doing evil."[22] Then in 2015, when the company reorganized as the parent company Alphabet (with subsidiaries, the most prominent of which is Google), it officially changed the motto to "Do the right thing."

In an article in *Fast Company*, University of Michigan's business professor David Mayer praised the company's move. Echoing a theme of this textbook, he maintained that the prior standard of doing no harm was insufficient. Mayer wrote that "it's clearly important for people in organizations to avoid unethical conduct" but that "does not inspire people to take positive actions."[23] Mayer cited research by David Jones, Chelsea Willness, and Sarah Madey demonstrating that people prefer to work for companies that aim to do good and not for companies that just try to avoid evil.[24] The advantage of the "do good" standard is that it inspires employees toward organizational citizenship behavior (see Chapter 6).

## The Comeback of "Don't Be Evil"

Despite the apparent change at the time of Alphabet's formation, the "Don't be evil" maxim has not been removed from the company's code of conduct. In 2018, the principle was reformulated again as "And remember . . . don't be evil, and if you see something that you think isn't right, speak up!" This revised motto seems to reveal the ongoing tension between doing no harm and actively doing good in how the company approaches its social responsibility.

This tension is also visible in the company's work developing artificial intelligence (AI) applications for the U.S. Defense Department. The company declared that the AI algorithms it created would "do no harm," yet it also stated that it established the principle of "no harm" only to prohibit a particular kind of weapons technology, autonomous weapons, rather than for all military technologies. Google indicated that it would not turn down all defense contracts and that its position on autonomous weapons was taken in response to the protests of its employees. These protests arose in response to the use of the company's AI technology by a Department of Defense initiative called the Algorithmic Warfare Cross-Functional Team. Among other goals, this initiative aimed to improve the accuracy of drone strikes. A number of Google employees quit the company when they found out about its involvement, and many others signed a letter of protest.[25] Google's CEO, Sundar Pichai, maintained that the company's code of ethics meant benefiting society, avoiding bias, respecting privacy, testing for safety, showing accountability, and maintaining scientific rigor. Google's decision not to let its AI technology be used in the development of more accurate drones was controversial as other tech companies, including Amazon and Microsoft, did not put similar restrictions on the bids they were making to the Pentagon to be involved in billion-dollar military projects.

What is your assessment of Google's overall ethical performance? What should it do next to address social and environmental issues? In response to concerns that it engages in unfair trade practices? With respect to the use of its AI for defense applications? Who are the stakeholders in these issues, what are Google's ethical obligations to them, and how would they be affected by the various courses of action that the company could take? What ethical principles should it be guided by as it considers its alternatives? Has it been using and can it continue to use moral imagination and both/and thinking to identify ethical, profitable approaches to the issues it faces? Use the weight-of-reasons framework to answer these questions. Then turn to another problem that has plagued Google, sexual harassment.

## Google: Problems With Sexual Harassment

On October 25, 2018, *The New York Times* ran a story titled "How Google Protected Andy Rubin, the 'Father of Android'."[26] In the article, the *Times* reported that Google paid Rubin, the creator of Android, $90 million when he left the company and commended him despite an accusation of sexual misconduct. The woman with whom Rubin was having an extramarital affair claimed that Rubin forced her to have oral sex in a hotel room. This claim was just the tip of the iceberg in the story, which asserted that other Google senior executives also had been protected and were paid millions of dollars when they left the company.

The *Times* based its story on corporate and court documents and employees' accounts. Most of these employees could not reveal their names because of confidentiality agreements or wished to remain anonymous because they were concerned about retribution if they let their names be known.

Rubin shot back that the story the *Times* ran was false and was concocted by his ex-wife, who wanted to defame his character in the divorce proceeding. By paying off Rubin and the other accused men, Google protected itself from court fights and preventing the men from working for the company's rivals. In response to the article, Google maintained that it took sexual harassment very seriously and was willing to lay off high-level executives when they behaved inappropriately. As evidence, the company pointed to 48 dismissals without pay in 2017–2018.

### Prior Controversy

Even before the payout to Rubin, Google already had courted controversy in the areas of sexual harassment and discrimination. The previous year, it became public that its engineer James Damore had claimed in an internal document that women were underrepresented in the company because they were less capable than men. The CEO Pichai and Eileen Naughton, Google's vice president for people operations, responded to the incident by writing, "We are committed to ensuring that Google is a workplace where you can feel safe to do your best work and where there are serious consequences for anyone who behaves inappropriately."

The *Times* article brought forward additional charges against high-level Google executives, including ones against its founder Larry Page and the previous CEO, Eric Schmidt. Page apologized, and another employee mentioned in the *Times* article resigned without an exit package.

These actions did little to dampen the controversy, however. Less than one month after the article was published, approximately 20,000 Google employees worldwide staged a protest against the company's handling of sexual harassment cases. They demanded an end to private arbitration in cases of harassment, a transparency report, an employee board representative, and a chief diversity officer. Private arbitration was common among technology companies and limited employees from publicly speaking out about their experiences. Other tech companies had recently decided to eliminate this clause in their employee contracts.

## Policy Change

Pichai supported the employee protest and responded that he too felt "anger" and "frustration." In a change of policy, the company announced that it no longer would engage in forced arbitration in instances of alleged sexual harassment. Such arbitration, though, would remain optional. The organizers of the protest against the company, a group calling itself Walkout for Real Change, maintained that Pichai had not gone far enough in dealing with the discrimination as well as systemic racism at Google.

Neither Pichai nor Google's founders, Page and Larry Brin, were present when Naughton and Danielle Brown, the company's chief diversity officer, presented policy changes to the employees. Employees did not appear entirely satisfied, as they asked why contractors did not get the same protection as permanent employees and why their demand for a representative on the board was dismissed.

## The Meaning of Sexual Harassment and What Employers Are Expected to Do

Sexual harassment consists of actions such as inappropriate sexual comments or unwanted physical advances in an office, factory, or other workplace setting, or in a professional or social situation. It is one of the most common types of workplace harassment, which also includes bullying.

Unwelcome sexual advances, requests for sexual favors, and other verbal or physical abuse of a sexual nature violate Title VII of the Civil Rights Act of 1964. Under this law, neither victim nor abuser has to be of the opposite sex. Even a person not harassed but affected by offensive conduct can bring a complaint. Anyone with whom a person works, whether a supervisor, employer, agent of the employer, supervisor in another area, coworker, or nonemployee, can be found guilty of harassing.

Employers are expected to take steps to ensure that such harassment does not occur. They should provide training and set up a complaint or grievance process and take quick action when a complaint arises. They have to communicate clearly that sexual harassment will not be tolerated in their workplace.

The two most common types of harassment are quid pro quo and a hostile environment. Quid pro quo occurs when in either an explicit or an implied way an employee asks for sexual favors in exchange for a favorable employment decision. A hostile environment exists when a person makes unwanted sexual remarks or engages in unwelcome behavior that creates an intimidating, threatening, and abusive working environment in which it is difficult for other people to function effectively.

Employ the weight-of-reasons framework to address the issue of sexual harassment at Google. What options does it have, and what consequences would these options have? What principles should it apply? How can it build from a short-term fix to the problems that arise to a long-term solution? What should it learn from its experience? In your answer, consider the cognitive and organizational factors that contribute to the problem. Also, consider the lessons from Chapters 5 and 6 on building a long-term solution and ethical organization.

## Intel: Mobileye

In 2017, Intel acquired Mobileye, a company with which it had partnered to develop self-driving automobile technology. The acquisition, which cost $15.3 billion, put Intel in a leadership position in the emerging driverless cars industry, a market estimated to be as large as $70 billion by 2030. The combination of the two companies would allow Intel to sell end-to-end solutions from the sensor and meter part of autonomous vehicles to the connectivity through an LTE (Long Term Evolution) or 5G network and back to a data center or the cloud. Intel's plan was to supply auto manufacturers with complete platforms that combined Mobileye's computer vision chips with its processors and connectivity products.

### Mobileye's Technology

Mobileye's technology allowed self-driving cars to see the road, while Intel's processors enabled vehicles to plot the paths they would take. The company had wireless connectivity in the modem and Wi-Fi chip technologies needed for communication between the vehicle and the cloud or a data center. The company's processors then would be able to perform the complex calculations needed to act on what the Mobileye technology saw. The NAND flash technology that Intel offered would provide the fast, reliable storage that maintained the system.

Intel's competitors were not capable of achieving such a comprehensive approach. They could deliver chip-to-sensor functionality but could not take the next step in effectively connecting the vehicle to a data center or the cloud. Mobileye's relationships with nearly 30 auto manufacturers were an extremely valuable asset. For instance, Mobileye had a joint partnership with BMW on the "iNext" platform, an open standard for manufacturers to develop, produce, and deploy driverless cars.

## The Ethical Issues

With Intel now having such a large footprint in the autonomous vehicle business, it had to grapple more seriously with the ethical issues facing this industry. Mois Navon, who designed the Mobileye System-on-a-Chip—the "brain" enabling autonomous vehicles—was very concerned about these issues. He understood that autonomous vehicles could "revolutionize the world." The impact would be manifold. On the positive side, the following developments are likely in a fully driverless world:

- There would be far less traffic and pollution.

- People no longer would have to have their own cars, since robo-taxis would be ubiquitous and inexpensive.

- Commute time would be reduced because all cars would know exactly where all other cars were and be able to respond to changes immediately.

- People would be able to travel at speeds previously unimaginable because human drivers, unlike computer-driven cars, are limited by human reaction times.

- Sprawling parking lots in city centers no longer would be needed as much, and they could be replaced by housing, offices, stores, walking malls, and parks.

- Among the most promising possibilities was that the numbers of traffic deaths and fatalities might approach zero, and with accident rates reduced, insurance rates could fall drastically. Currently, 3,400 people die in traffic accidents daily, and 54,000 to 136,000 people are injured.

- In addition, the car body replacement industry would be far less needed.

But Navon also was aware of some of the negative developments possible in a fully driverless world, such as the following:

- It was not clear, at least in the short term, that autonomous vehicles could operate safely in unpredictable conditions.

- The vehicles' computers could be hacked.

- An Internet failure could bring the transportation system to a standstill.

- As a result of faster transportation, people would live farther from city centers.

- Jurisdictions that relied on traffic tickets for money would see this source of revenue dry up.

- The massive number of people who made their living as drivers of trucks and taxis would have to find other types of employment, and so would people who repaired vehicles.

As the programmer of the Mobileye System-on-a-Chip, Navon was keenly interested in the Trolley Dilemma (see Chapter 3) and another version of it called the Tunnel Dilemma.

- In the Trolley Dilemma, a trolley is making very rapid progress down a track on which five employees of the company are working, and they cannot get out of the way. The switch person for the company, observing the scene, can divert the trolley in another direction, but in doing so, an innocent pedestrian would be killed. What is the right thing to do? The utilitarian answer is clear—save five people's lives at the expense of one person, in this way achieving the greatest good for the greatest number, though this decision violates the basic right of the innocent bystander not to be killed.

- In the Tunnel Dilemma, a driver coming close to a single-lane tunnel views a pedestrian on the road. The driver does not have time to brake and is left with the choice of either running over the pedestrian or killing herself by hitting a wall. In pitting one individual against another, the quantitative aspect of the dilemma is removed. The focus is on the qualitative aspect of the value of one individual's life versus the value of another's.

As a central programmer involved in the autonomous vehicle industry, Navon was unsure how he should approach such issues. Navon wrote,

In the case of the autonomous vehicle, there is no driver, there is a program that is being executed according to some predetermined code. That code was written, days, months, or, in all likelihood, years before these dilemmas are encountered.

When programmers sit in front of their computers, what should they do? Navon was convinced that autonomous vehicles undoubtedly would save millions of lives, improve the quality of life, and serve, along with all the other phenomenal advances in AI, to fix the world in profound ways, but he understood as well that these types of ethical dilemmas would not go away that easily.

## Intel's White Paper

Intel itself was concerned and had three employees—Jack Weast, Matt Yurdana, and Adam Jordan—write a "white paper" on autonomous vehicles, which they called "A Matter of Trust." They argued for "trust interactions" that "promote confidence, control, and a sense of safety." They admitted that technology companies have struggled with trust. Too often they were not sensitive enough to how the technologies they introduced were received by people: "Many products and services have claimed to make our lives better, easier, or less stressful . . . only for the opposite to be true." With respect to autonomous vehicles, the need for trust is great because the stakes—serious injury and even death—are so high. Autonomous vehicles would be successful only if people learn to trust them.

The authors of the white paper made a number of suggestions on how the designers of autonomous vehicles could increase trust in their products. They maintained that the systems have to be able to sense pervasively what is happening in nearly every challenging condition the vehicles might face, such as night, dusk, rainstorms, and alternating bright sun and shade. They also maintained that the systems have to be able to communicate simply and clearly with passengers so that the passengers are well aware of what is happening at all times and what they are supposed to do if there is an emergency.

## Autonomous Vehicle Accidents

In 2018, two fatal accidents occurred in the United States involving semi-autonomous vehicles. These were not fully autonomous vehicles. The information about the two accidents did not assign responsibility exclusively to either human error or the technology. In one accident, Elaine Herzberg was walking over a six-lane freeway in Tempe, Arizona, with her bicycle, when she was killed by a Volvo SUV that had been modified to rely on driverless technology and was taking a test drive for Uber. The sensors in the SUV did not recognize her soon enough. In addition, the safety driver in the car failed to pay attention. Uber responded by temporarily suspending its tests of self-driving cars in Arizona. Toyota, which used the same graphic chips in its autonomous driving program as Uber did, also chose to temporarily stop tests in Arizona. Herzberg was apparently the first pedestrian victim of autonomous driving gone awry.

In another mishap that took place soon thereafter, Apple engineer Walter Huang died driving a Tesla SUV that employed auto pilot technology, as his vehicle crashed into a barrier in Mountain View, California. Huang previously had complained to Tesla that the vehicle was veering in the direction of the very same road barrier he hit. Tesla's response was that the severity of the crash was attributable to driver error and a piece missing in the road barrier, and was not the fault of the company's auto pilot feature. These crashes increased the total number of reported deaths associated with self-driving to four and made self-driving vehicle industry participants more anxious about the legal claims they might face.

Indeed, California had introduced a new permit process for autonomous vehicles that had complex and strict safeguards meant to prevent such accidents. As of the end of 2018, the state Department of Motor Vehicles had received 129 autonomous vehicle collision reports involving the vehicles of multiple companies, including Waymo, GM Cruze, Zoox, Aurora Innovation, Apple, and the Toyota Research Institute.

## Missing Out on the Mobile Revolution

The changing business landscape led Intel to decide that it had to branch out into other areas. The company could not rely just on microprocessors to sustain it. In 2014, Intel had the world's largest market share in all segments of the global microprocessor market—servers, laptops, and desktops. It controlled close to 98% of the server market, more than 90% of the laptop market, and more than 80% of the desktop market. In the desktop market, where its rival AMD was the most competitive, Intel's gross margins were more than 60%, while AMD had gross margins of only 30%. However,

FIGURE 10.3    Income, Revenue, and Market Cap in the Computer Industry, Third Quarter 2015

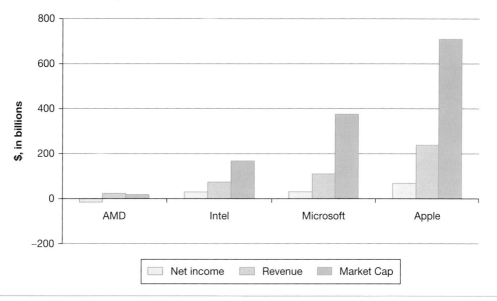

Intel did not anticipate and was not prepared for the mobile revolution. Because of the ascendance of smartphones and tablets over personal computers (PCs), Apple, and not Intel, rose to become the world's leading computer company (Figure 10.3).

Intel made several false starts to enter the smartphone and tablet markets but largely was shut out. Taiwan Semiconductor and Samsung made most of the devices, including many of Apple's, using ARM's architecture. The British company ARM Holdings developed this architecture based on a reduced instruction set computing design, which depends on far fewer transistors than the complex processors Intel created for servers, PCs, and laptops. In 2015, ARM's architecture supported more than 95% of the smartphones and tablets used in the United States.

In comparison with mobile markets, the server, laptop, and desktop markets responsible for most of Intel's revenue were in decline. Because the products that Intel could offer for mobile markets had low margins, it had been reluctant to sell them. As a supplier of CPUs (central processing units) for laptops, PCs, and servers, how could Intel ensure that it did not miss out on the next great movement in technology?

## Branching Out Into Autonomous Vehicles

With its core business not as strong as it once was, the company had to find new business opportunities. Intel spent very heavily on R&D. Its corporate venture capital also invested heavily in what it believed to be leading-edge start-ups. With PC sales flattening and weak growth in the server market, Intel started searching for new markets. In 2010, Intel made the biggest acquisition in its history. It purchased the computer security company McAfee for $7.68 billion, but it then later realized that McAfee was not a good fit and divested the company. Might Mobileye be a similar mistake, or should Intel double down and invest even more into an autonomous vehicle future?

How should Intel address the ethical issues associated with autonomous vehicles? Can Intel move into this industry and hold itself to a high ethical standard? Focus on the safety dilemmas and related ethical questions, such as those brought up by the Trolley Dilemma and Tunnel Dilemma. What options does Intel have in the short term and long term? In assessing consequences, which stakeholders should it consider? What principles should it apply—what do the various ethical frameworks discussed in Chapter 2 suggest? What should be its plans of action? Should it coordinate its efforts with other autonomous vehicle manufacturers and government agencies? What are the key lessons Intel should learn from its autonomous vehicle experience?

## Mallinckrodt: The Opioid Crisis

Mallinckrodt Pharmaceuticals, a very profitable company, had been embroiled in numerous scandals. For one, its 2013 tax inversion had been controversial. The company moved to Ireland for tax benefits, though its origins were in Saint Louis, Missouri, its operational headquarters was in the United States, and 90% of its 2017 sales came from the United States. It also faced a class-action lawsuit claiming that it overcharged for its muscular dystrophy drug, Acthar, and did not even know what was in the medication. On top of these controversies, the company was implicated in the U.S. opioid epidemic.

### Financial Performance

Despite the company's vast increase in net income in 2017—which grew from less than $300,000 to more than $2 million, mostly because of reduced income tax expenses—its stock price had been on a downward trajectory (dark blue line in the graph of Table 10.3) since the middle of 2015 in comparison with Standard & Poor's 500 stock index (light blue line in the graph of Table 10.3).

### Mallinckrodt's Sale of Generic Opioids

According to the U.S. Centers for Disease Control and Prevention, opioid abuse was out of control. In 2018, 130 Americans were dying daily from overdose.[27] Mallinckrodt was the biggest supplier of opioids in Florida. A "60 Minute" exposé maintained that the company had been responsible for 500 million oxycodone pills arriving in the state from 2008 to 2012. That was the equivalent of 25 pills for every resident of a state in which 2,900 people had died of overdoses. Dr. Barry Schulz— jailed for 157 years for drug trafficking, making $6,000 a day and dispensing 800,000 opioid pills in 16 months from his clinic's pharmacy in West Delray, Florida—obtained all his pills from Mallinckrodt.

The company, which manufactured only generic branded opioids, claimed that it had been active in preventing misuse and diversion of its products. It also defended itself by asserting that its employees had testified for the prosecution in drug diversion cases. Yet being a leading manufacturer of generic oxycodone painkillers, the DOJ had subpoenaed it in the summer of 2017, asking for information about its sales and marketing of the drug. The company responded that it would fully cooperate

## TABLE 10.3    Mallinckrodt Financial Performance

| Financial Parameter | 2017 | 2016 | 2015 | 2014 |
|---|---|---|---|---|
| Total revenue | 3,221,600 | 3,399,500 | 3,380,800 | 2,923,100 |
| Cost of revenue | 1,550,000 | 1,546,000 | 1,496,600 | 1,255,800 |
| Gross profit | 1,671,600 | 1,853,500 | 1,884,200 | 1,667,300 |
| Research development | 277,300 | 267,000 | 262,200 | 203,300 |
| Selling, general and administrative | 866,300 | 1,076,600 | 910,800 | 897,400 |
| Total operating expenses | 2,693,600 | 2,889,600 | 2,669,600 | 2,356,500 |
| Operating income or loss | 528,000 | 509,900 | 711,200 | 566,600 |
| Total other income/net expenses | −466,400 | −641,500 | −477,800 | −459,300 |
| Earnings before interest and taxes | 528,000 | 509,900 | 711,200 | 566,600 |
| Interest expense | −369,100 | −378,100 | −384,600 | −255,600 |
| Income before tax | 61,600 | −131,600 | 233,400 | 107,300 |
| Income tax expense | −1,709,600 | −340,000 | −255,600 | −129,300 |
| Net income from continuing operations | 1,771,200 | 208,400 | 489,000 | 236,600 |
| Discontinued operations | 363,200 | 71,000 | 154,700 | 88,100 |
| Net income | 2,134,400 | 279,400 | 643,700 | 324,700 |

*Note:* Figures in thousands of dollars.

## FIGURE 10.4

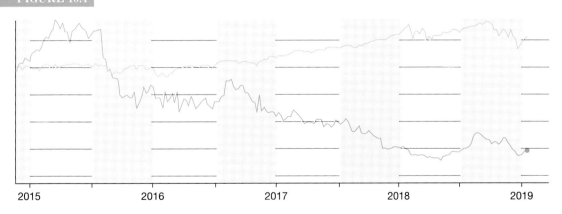

| 2015 | 2016 | 2017 | 2018 | 2019 |

with the DOJ. The company's prepared statement read as follows: "To truly make an impact on opioid abuse and misuse, all stakeholders must work together to address this national problem in a comprehensive, thoughtful manner."

Earlier that summer, the company had arrived at a $35 million settlement regarding its controlled substances monitoring program with the U.S. Drug Enforcement Administration and attorneys in Michigan and New York. It denied any wrongdoing with respect to the suspicious ordering that the authorities argued took place under its watch. In trying to prevent a suit from being filed against the company in the state of Tennessee, Mallinckrodt blamed the deaths on illicit drug dealers, some of them operating online from foreign countries. It wanted to be taken off the hook for any financial damages the state was seeking. Meanwhile, the U.S. Food and Drug Administration (FDA) was refusing to approve what Mallinckrodt claimed was an abuse-deterrent opioid painkiller that it had developed.

## Other Companies' Involvement

A number of companies, including Purdue Pharma, Endo, and Johnson & Johnson (J&J), were negotiating with state attorneys general and lawyers who represented cities and counties throughout the country in a consolidated case. A judge in Cleveland was overseeing the consolidation. He maintained that any deal had to go beyond mere monetary compensation and should address the companies' business practices. In the judge's opinion, they were the real cause of the crisis. The government was trying to obtain data from the defendants about diversion of opioids to pill mills and to doctors who oversubscribed the pills, but the companies refused to cooperate. The government argued that the companies had not used the information they had to stem the epidemic.

In addition, the state of New York passed a law by which it could collect $600 million over six years from manufacturers to help pay for the costs of the crisis. Mallinckrodt and other manufacturers contested the law for being unconstitutional. The law allocated charges to companies that sold and distributed drugs based on the volume and potency of the drugs for which they were responsible.

The companies against which the state was assessing charges included McKesson, Cardinal Health, CVSEndo, Purdue, Teva, and AmerisourceBergen. The state wanted $100 million from McKesson and $22 million from Cardinal Health. Mallinckrodt reported that the state was asking it to pay 8.2 cents for each tablet it had sold for just 4.7 cents apiece. The full list of companies involved in the trade of opioids in the state of New York is provided in Table 10.4.

## A Decline in Legitimate Sales

In almost every state in the country, sales of retail filled opioid prescriptions, while still robust, had declined significantly. Mallinckrodt declared that it had no choice. It was likely to suspend selling opioids in the state of New York despite patients' continued need for the drugs because it no longer could make money doing so. Almost all the distributors, drug makers, and others who had been involved in selling such drugs in the state might abandon New York.

What are the ethics of a company that so aggressively markets an addictive product that can get into the hands of children as well as adults and kill them? In court papers, the Drug Enforcement Administration called Mallinckrodt "the kingpin of the drug cartel."[28] An investigation of Mallinckrodt's distributors at a physician assistant's

**TABLE 10.4**    Companies Selling Opioids in New York State

- *Distributors:* A.F. Hauser Inc., AmerisourceBergen Corp., Bell Medical Services, Benco Dental Supply Co., Bloodworth Wholesale Drugs, Burlington Drug Co., Caligor Coghlan, Capital Wholesale Drug Co., Cardinal Health Inc., Catalent Inc., Eversana, Exel Inc., Genetco Inc., Golden State Medical Supply Inc., Henry Schein Inc., Independent Pharmaceutical, Independent Pharmacy Cooperative, Independent Pharmacy Distributor, Lifeline Pharmaceuticals LLC, LifeScience Logistics, McGuff Co, McKesson Corp., Patterson Companies Inc., PD-Rx Pharmaceuticals Inc., Prescription Supply Inc., QK Healthcare Inc., Quest Pharmaceuticals Inc., R&S Northeast LLC, Redmond & Greer Pharmacy Supply, Rochester Drug Cooperative, Saddle River Marketing Concepts, TopRX LLC, UPS Inc.

- *Drug makers:* AbbVie Inc., Akorn Inc., Alvogen, Amneal Pharmaceuticals LLC, Apotex Corp., Auburn Pharmaceutical Inc., Aurobindo Pharma, Endo International PLC, Epic Pharma, Glenmark Pharmaceuticals Inc., Hikma Pharmaceuticals PLC, Lannett Co. Inc., Lupin Pharmaceuticals Inc., Mallinckrodt PLC, Mylan N.V., Osmotica Pharmaceutical, Perrigo Co., Pfizer Inc., Pharmaceutical Associates Inc., Precision Dose Inc., Purdue Pharmaceuticals, Sun Pharmaceutical Industries Inc., Tagi Pharma Inc., Teva Pharmaceutical Industries Ltd., Vertice Pharma

- *Others:* Aidarex Pharmaceuticals LLC, AndersonBrecon Inc., Associated Pharmacies Inc., Bound Tree Medical LLC, Central Admixture Pharmacy, CVS Health, Darby Dental Supply, Dealmed Medical Supplies, Diamond Pharmacy Services, Fagron Inc., ICU Medical Inc., Letco Medical LLC, NYC HHC Correctional Health Services, PCCA, PuraGraft, Southern Anesthesia & Surgical Inc., Value Drug Co.

*Source:* New York State Department of Health.

Staten Island office in 2010 described a parking lot and street filled with people in cars waiting to buy drugs. The physician assistant faced charges in 2014 of conspiracy to distribute narcotics and was sentenced to 11 years in prison. In court papers filed in April 2019 by New York State Attorney General Letitia James as part of the office's lawsuit against opioid manufacturers, it was disclosed that a supervisor at Mallinckrodt told his staff that opioids were their best opportunity to make big money. Another supervisor advised his sales force to "attack," informing them that they would obtain "big bonus dollars" by standing at the doors of health care providers and giving them free trials.

## Mallinckrodt's Plan to End the Problem

For its part, Mallinckrodt announced a plan to end the drug problem, which it called a "Prescription for America's Opioid Epidemic." The initiative maintained that as a "pioneer in addressing the problem of prescription drug diversion and misuse," the company had a unique perspective on the solution. Its solution came down to the following:

- Use opioids sparingly. Alternative therapies should be used when possible, but new treatment guidelines have to be created to advance this approach.

- Provide mandated education for health care professionals.

- Enhance regulatory standards and data usage to prevent diversion and improper use of opioids.

- Strengthen prescription drug monitoring programs, and obtain more and better data on the nature of the use of opioids, legitimately and otherwise.

- Ensure proper and safe disposal and storage to prevent diversion, especially from home medicine cabinets.

- Fund community-based interventions and education, especially among youth and at-risk persons.

The company donated about 1.5 million drug disposal pouches and said it would donate another 0.5 million in 2018. Was Mallinckrodt correct? As an addictive drug, could opioids be used "sparingly"?

## Other Controversies

Mallinckrodt's main business was in the treatment of pain and related conditions. In 1982, Avon purchased the company but sold it in 1986. In 2000, Tyco bought Mallinckrodt and spun off its health care unit Covidien in 2007. Covidien then divested Mallinckrodt in 2013, after which Mallinckrodt executed the corporate tax inversion scheme in Ireland by acquiring the Irish-based Cadence. The company then made many other acquisitions. Besides painkillers and other specialty drugs, it had a medical imaging division, which contributed about a quarter of its revenue. Mallinckrodt was eligible for $450 million to $500 million in tax credits under the Tax Cuts and Jobs Act, which was passed in 2017, but some of these benefits were offset by an anti-inversion provision in this law.

In 2018, the company confronted another controversy. It came under scrutiny because it was revealed that one of its main drugs, Acthar, had become one of Medicare's highest expenditures. Acthar gel was an injectable biopharmaceutical used for the treatment of infantile spasms, multiple sclerosis, and a number of orphan diseases. Mallinckrodt had acquired the product in 2014, when it bought the company Questcor. Questcor had procured rights to the drug in 2001 and over time had increased its price from $40 a vial to $28,000 a vial when Mallinckrodt bought the company. Mallinckrodt then raised the price further to $34,000 a vial. The *Journal of the American Medical Association* published research in 2017 showing that Acthar was one of the most expensive drugs in the United States and alleging that its sales had been driven by a relatively small group of doctors who prescribed it heavily. Good alternatives were available at 2% of the price Mallinckrodt was charging for the drug. The FTC and attorneys general from five states sued Mallinckrodt for anticompetitive behavior and in 2017 the company settled, agreeing to a fine of $100 million. However, in 2018, a whistle-blower lawsuit claimed that Acthar, which had been available for 60 years and was approved under FDA's "grandfathering" rules, had an unknown formulation and its efficacy was doubtful. Clearly, Mallinckrodt had been beset by controversy after controversy. It was not just opioids to which it had to respond.

How should Mallinckrodt respond to the opioid crisis? Is its "Prescription for American's Opioid Epidemic" a sufficient response? Does it fulfill the company's obligations to its key stakeholders? Who are those stakeholders, and how should the company engage them? What principles does the plan embody? What consequences would come from implementing it? Can a single company, even one playing a role as large as Mallinckrodt's, solve a problem such as the opioid epidemic?

What other issues does Mallinckrodt face? Use the weight-of-reasons framework to address those issues? What facts are relevant, and what options does it have? What consequences would come of these options? What principles should it uphold? What actions should it take and what should it learn from its experience?

## Merck and J&J: Problems With Consumer Safety

This case documents ethical lapses at two pharmaceutical and health care companies. Merck and J&J historically have had good reputations for ethics and CSR, yet recently have faced ethical dilemmas which they confronted poorly. The problems they have encountered have similar elements and are worth comparing for the lessons that can be learned. Applying the weight-of-reasons framework for ethical decision-making, what can Merck and J&J learn from their own experiences and from the experiences of each other? What changes should they introduce to try to ensure that such problems do not recur?

### Vioxx: What Lessons Should Merck Learn?

Merck, a major pharmaceutical company, had been named one of Fortune 500's top companies several times. The company's employees have to sign a statement indicating that they accept the company's core values. These include being responsible to customers, employees and their families, the environment, and societies worldwide, and not taking professional or ethical shortcuts. At the time of this case, many of Merck's drug development efforts had not been productive. Furthermore, some of its drugs were about to lose patent protection. To compensate, Merck needed a blockbuster drug. The company began studying COX-2 drugs in the 1980s, hoping to discover a painkiller without the gastrointestinal complications associated with other painkillers. The company's studies of COX-2 drugs suggested that they produced the same benefits without the negative side effects. Vioxx, a COX-2 drug, was put through several rounds of tests, and it looked like it had great potential. However, decades ago, Garret Fitzgerald of the University of Pennsylvania showed that the COX (cyclooxygenase) enzyme, by preventing arterial blood clot formation, might harm people with damaged blood vessels.[29]

Merck excluded patients with a history of cardiovascular disease from the studies leading up to Vioxx's FDA approval. After 10 years, the FDA approved the drug for sale in 1999. In its first year on the market, Merck spent more than $160 million—more than any other pharmaceutical company that year—advertising and promoting the drug's benefits. In its first seven months on the market, doctors wrote 5 million prescriptions for Vioxx. Yet in 2000, Merck's research chief, Ed Scolnick, warned of cardiovascular complications. In an ongoing study to demonstrate Vioxx's gastrointestinal benefits, users were found to have two to five times the rate of cardiovascular problems of participants who used the generic drug naproxen. Merck reasoned that the study had been done without a placebo and it was impossible to know whether Vioxx had caused the negative results or naproxen had cardiovascular benefits.

In 2001, a study by Mukherjee et al. appeared in *The Journal of the American Medical Association* showing increased rates of heart attacks and strokes connected to Vioxx.[30] In the same year, a Merck employee leaked to *The Wall Street Journal* internal emails that suggested that the company intentionally tried to exclude heart patients from Vioxx studies so the cardiovascular problems would not surface. An FDA advisory panel accused the company of minimizing the cardiovascular findings and misrepresenting Vioxx's safety, and it recommended that Merck put a warning label on Vioxx.

Under pressure from the company, the FDA delayed the requirement. The Vioxx label provided information about the benefits and then mentioned the potential heart and stroke problems. Merck canceled a planned 2002 study to test whether patients with acute coronary syndrome who were given Vioxx would benefit. In 2003, it suspended a study to determine if Vioxx could be used for the prevention and treatment of colon polyps and colorectal and prostate cancer because the study's initial results showed a high rate of cardiovascular deaths.

Vioxx brought in $2.5 billion in revenue in 2003, 1 billion of which came from Medicaid. Advocates for Medicaid patients then started to publicly criticize the company for not withdrawing Vioxx from the market. A British medical journal, *The Lancet*, indicated that in a study in 2004 based on data from 25,000 patients and 18 clinical trials that patients taking Vioxx exhibited 2.3 times the cardiovascular risks of patients taking competitor drugs or placebos.[31] David Graham, who was carrying out an epidemiological study for the FDA, made public data that showed that using pain relievers other than Vioxx would have prevented 27,000 heart attacks and sudden cardiac deaths in the United States. Merck officially stood behind the efficacy and safety of Vioxx, but employees leaked more documents to *The Wall Street Journal*, including one called the "Vioxx Dodge Ball," which instructed sales representatives not to directly answer questions that physicians posed about Vioxx's safety.

Merck finally voluntarily recalled the painkiller in the fall of 2004. The CEO at the time maintained that he came to know of the risks only with the publication of the article in *The Lancet*. Merck's stock price fell drastically. In the fall of 2004, Senator Charles Grassley held a Congressional investigation. He blamed the FDA as well as Merck, revealing a conflict of interest in that 10 of the 32 expert committee members chosen by the FDA to evaluate Vioxx had ties to the industry, had consulted for Merck, and/or owned pharmaceutical companies' stock.

Starting in 2005, lawyers filed thousands of lawsuits against Merck. They showed that perfectly healthy people who did not have a history of weight problems, did not smoke, and had no past heart disease problems died of heart attack or stroke after taking Vioxx. An *Archives of Internal Medicine* study showed that nearly three quarters of Vioxx users took the drug unnecessarily. Physicians felt pressured into prescribing it when ordinary over-the-counter drugs like Advil and Ibuprofen would have been safer, cheaper, and just as effective.

In 2007, Merck agreed to pay $4.85 billion to settle 27,000 lawsuits. It signed a corporate integrity agreement with the government, promising to monitor its future promotional activity. In 2011, it pleaded guilty to a criminal charge of selling Vioxx and agreed to pay $950 million to the DOJ in fines. Merck's legal liabilities exceeded $18 billion for the wrongdoing it did. It is easy to be irate with the company. It killed thousands of people and pleaded guilty to criminal responsibility, yet its executives escaped without having to go to prison.

## DePuy Hip Replacement: What Lessons Should J&J Learn?

The case of the DePuy hip replacement and J&J is a similar story. J&J's credo stated that its first responsibility was to doctors, nurses, patients, children, mothers, and families who used its products and services, while stockholders were its last responsibility, to whom it only owed a "fair return" (see Chapter 8). In 1982, it lived up to these principles when, despite concerns about shareholder reaction, it initiated a very rapid recall of Tylenol after seven people died from ingesting cyanide-laced pills.

J&J acquired DePuy, the world's first commercial orthopedic manufacturer and device maker, in 1998. By 2010, this J&J subsidiary was the world's top manufacturer of hip replacements. Orthopedic surgeons were told that all-metal replacement hips like DePuy's would last longer than traditional replacement devices, which were made of plastic and metal. DePuy's products were installed in nearly 80,000 U.S. patients, and another 56,000 patients abroad. However, the metal ball-and-cup components in the products often rubbed against each other, causing friction and releasing metal debris and particles into the patient's bloodstream, which resulted in tissue damage and crippling injuries. The implants often loosened, and patients suffered joint dislocation, which required additional surgeries. The design problems came to light in Australia and England shortly after the first sales in those countries.

Internal DePuy documents revealed that at subsequent trials, a consultant to the company had warned the head of DePuy's orthopedic unit, Andrew Ekdahl, who oversaw the replacement hip's introduction, that a design flaw existed, but for years, DePuy insisted that the reason for the failures was the surgeons' poor technique. By August, 2010 with the FDA ready to take action, J&J agreed to a voluntary recall, but only after selling the remaining inventory without revealing the problems to physicians and patients. The company claimed that it acted as soon as it had definitive information. Definitive data came from the National Joint Registry of England and Wales, showing that the devices were failing prematurely and at a higher rate than competing implants. The company promised to pay the medical costs of the replacement procedures.

However, during the lawsuits, another picture emerged. Internal company documents showed that DePuy officials knew before the recall that the product's design was flawed and that it failed prematurely. In testimony, a DePuy engineer admitted that by 2008 company officials were aware of reports by an English surgeon that the hip replacement released high levels of metallic ions. Orthopedic databases to which the company subscribed showed that the systems J&J sold failed in most patients within five years, while other companies' implants had a lifetime of 15 years.

DePuy did not warn the patients. Therefore, the company confronted as many as 12,000 legal claims against it in the United States alone (see Chapter 7). In two thirds of these cases, the patients would need additional surgeries to remove and replace the original implants. DePuy settled three hip-related lawsuits in the summer of 2012 for $200,000 each. However, a 2013 court verdict ordered the company to pay the plaintiffs $8.3 million in punitive damages. Later that year, the company agreed to pay $2.5 billion to settle more than 7,500 state and federal lawsuits affecting more than 8,000 people who had to have their all-metal artificial hips removed and replaced with a safer device. Under the reimbursement plan, the typical patient obtained $250,000 before legal fees. However, it was uncertain if this settlement would satisfy most of the claimants. They had the right not to take part and sue on their own. J&J had to take a $3 billion special charge related to the medical and legal costs of the technology. It was not clear that this amount was even sufficient.

How did Merck and J&J come to have their legal and ethical problems? What cognitive biases and organizational shortcomings contributed to these problems? When running their businesses, what principles did their managers apply, and what consequences did they consider? Once the problems arose, how did they make sense of their legal and ethical responsibilities? Which stakeholders were most important to them? Were they focused on the short term or long term?

What can Merck and J&J do going forward to avoid the types of problems they have faced? How can they become ethical organizations and still earn high returns for their shareholders? Apply the commonsense weight-of-reasons framework for ethical decision-making to derive the lessons that Merck and J&J should learn from these predicaments.

## Microsoft: Addressing Bribery

Microsoft considered expanding into emerging markets to be essential to its growth. This need, however, led it to become increasingly embroiled in unsavory business practices that had come to the attention of the DOJ and the U.S. Securities and Exchange Commission (SEC). Its involvement in these practices had developed into a serious legal and reputational challenge that Microsoft wanted to prevent from getting out of hand as U.S. authorities were investigating the company over possible bribery and corruption relating to its software sales in Hungary.

In Hungary, the investigation centered on the way vendors sold software such as Word and Excel to government agencies. Microsoft provided the software to the vendors at steep discounts; then the vendors sold the products to the Hungarian government at close to the full price, using the difference to pay bribes and kickbacks to get the government officials to buy the products. Microsoft wanted to set up safeguard mechanisms within the company to prevent even the hint of this wrongdoing in the future.

### Vetting Agencies

A possible safeguard was to work with vetting agencies in order to ensure that the third parties it dealt with, like the vendors in Hungary, had sufficient integrity to be trusted. However, such due diligence was not always effective. For instance, U.S. government officials had discovered that such vetting agencies had failed to protect Panasonic Avionics. The company was fined $280 million even though it had hired an antibribery group called Trace International to check on the parties with whom it did business in Asia. Panasonic employees figured out how to do end-runs around the antibribery group. They allowed the sales agents who obtained anti-bribery clearance to hire subagents– for whose integrity Trace International could not vouch. Due diligence did not go far enough in stopping these multilevel agent–subagent agreements from taking place. They came to light only when the commissions earned by the sales agents seemed out of line and Panasonic employees revealed what was actually happening.

## Hotlines

A remedy Microsoft considered was to strengthen its use of hotlines. According to Navex Global, a company that sells ethics and compliance software and services, hotlines were becoming increasingly effective, but their effectiveness depended on companies taking the charges tipsters raised seriously and assuring employees that they would not face retaliation. More than 40% of the claims inside tipsters brought to the attention of companies proved to be correct, according to a benchmark report of 900,000 such claims from 2,400 companies that Navex Global monitored. The increase in substantiated reports was an important indication that employees took these programs seriously, and they often worked in preventing corruption. However, employees wanted assurance that they would not be subjected to retaliation, an action would be taken, and, if the charges were serious enough, that people at the highest level in an organization, including its Board of Directors, would pay attention. Companies had to take into account the time it took them to resolve an issue. Navex reported that the median time it took companies to resolve claims had gone up slightly in 2017 to 44 days from 42 days in 2016.

## Whistle-Blowing

What Microsoft wanted to avoid was to have an internal whistle-blower bypass its hotline and go directly to the U.S. or some other government. Along with internal hotlines, there had been an expansion of whistle-blowers going directly to U.S. government agencies to earn cash for their reporting of wrongdoing. At the end of 2018, the SEC's Office of the Whistleblower had paid more than $326 million to tipsters in the seven years following the Bernie Madoff fraud. Each year, the amount of tips coming into this office grew, with more than 5,200 entering the system in 2018 compared with about 3,000 in 2012. Frivolous requests for compensation still were taking place, but they were not blocking genuine tips from coming forward.

The SEC took an average two years to decide if a complaint had merit. It still was considering about 50% percent of the tips it had received. For those bringing complaints against their companies, though they faced the risk of retaliation and the uncertainty of the SEC actually deciding in their favor and providing them with compensation, the rewards could be quite large. For instance, for uncovering JP Morgan's failure to disclose its preference for investing client money in the bank's own mutual funds and hedge funds that shared fees with the bank, the whistle-blowers received $30 million from the U.S. Commodity Futures Trading Commission and were promised another payment of $48 million from the SEC.

FIGURE 10.5    **The Number of Cases Pending Payment to Whistle-Blowers and the Amount of Money Paid Out**

**Bounty Backlog**

The share of whistle-blowers waiting to hear whether they will be paid has risen over the past of four years.

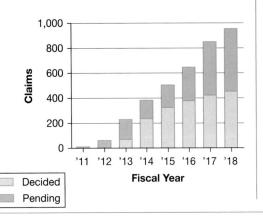

Decided
Pending

**Whistle-Blowers Windfall**

Rewards to tipsters in SEC enforcement cases rose gradually until 2018, when they more than tripled from the prior year.

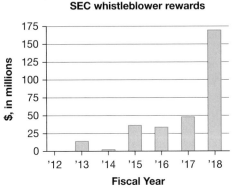

*Source:* U.S. Securities and Exchange Commission (SEC).

*Note:* 2018 data are through July.

Companies like Whistleblower Inc. had arisen to help employees bring charges to the attention of the government and share in the proceeds. Law firms also were involved. Any employee could go to SEC.gov/whistleblower and click the "Submit a Tip" icon, and after the SEC settled a case and obtained a monetary judgment, the whistle-blower could ask for compensation (Figure 10.5). The problem was that the monetary judgments often took years to be awarded.

## Cases and Fines

In 2018, the SEC brought almost 500 cases against firms and had issued fines of nearly $4 billion by September of that year in two foreign bribery cases (Figure 10.6). In one case, it fined the Brazilian oil giant Petrobras $1.7 billion, and in the other, it fined Panasonic Avionics $143 million.

## Microsoft's Standard of Business Conduct

Microsoft had a 57-page Standard of Business Conduct on its website that was available to employees and the public.[32] One of the main aims of its internal guidelines was to prevent issues from moving beyond internal hotlines and being taken up by the SEC or other government agencies. The company wanted its employees to rely on internal reporting options rather than become whistle-blowers. The company's

**FIGURE 10.6**    Number of SEC Bribery Cases and the Dollar Amount of Fines Enforced

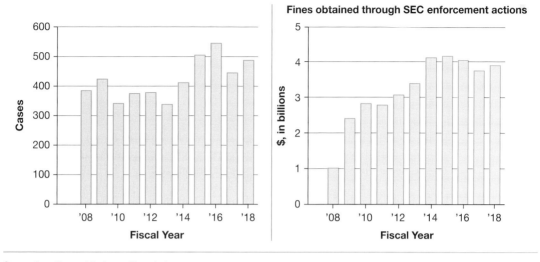

Source: Securities and Exchange Commission

Note: SEC = U.S. Securities and Exchange Commission.

Standard of Business Conduct lists five different ways an employee could report a dubious practice: email, phone (which includes an international collect number), the web, fax, and mail to the Office of Legal Compliance.

The code begins with a letter from CEO Satya Nadella, in which he declares, "You should never compromise your personal integrity or the company's reputation and trust in exchange for any short-term gain." It calls on employees, when faced with a difficult decision or situation, to "pause," "think," and "ask." The employee should talk to the Office of Legal Compliance, Finance, or Human Relations and get help. The code encourages employees to "speak up" when something is "not right" so that the company can address the problem. It assures employees that the company has "no tolerance for retaliation." It tells managers to take employee concerns seriously.

The code explicitly states that employees should not make "improper payments." It states, "In some parts of the world, paying a bribe to get business may be something that others are doing. We won't. We would rather lose the business than secure it through a bribe, kickback, or other improper benefit." The code prohibits "hidden terms or arrangements" when doing business abroad and advocates relying only on partners with "a reputation for integrity." Yet the code also allows "reasonable" gifts, hospitality, or travel to government officials or customers. When necessary, the code states, these types of payments may require preapproval.

Microsoft promises to follow the laws and customs of the countries in which it operates. However, it does not plainly indicate what the employee should do when the la and customs of the countries where it operates differ from U.S. laws and customs.

Has Microsoft done enough to address the problems of bribery, corruption, and other unsavory business practices in emerging markets? What issue does it confront, what facts are relevant, what options does it have, and what are the possible consequences of those actions? To what principles should it adhere? What should it do in the short term, how can it build toward a long-term solution, and what lessons can it learn? In addressing these questions, carefully consider the lessons from Chapter 6 on ethics programs and building ethical organizations. In the long term, what must the company do to effectively prevent and handle systemic issues such as bribery?

## VW: Dieselgate[33]

What should VW learn from its recent history (see Chapter 6)? In 2015, the EPA revealed that since 2008, VW had illegally put engine control software into its vehicles to sense when they were undergoing emissions testing, which is when the software would enable a pollution control device; otherwise, the vehicles were not in compliance with U.S. emissions standards. When driven on roads and highways, the device to control nitrogen oxide ($NO_x$) emissions shut down. The reason VW engaged in this hoax was to maintain the vehicle's fuel economy and provide the car with additional power. When the pollution control device was enabled, the VW vehicles consumed more fuel and lost power.

VW's deception was not trivial. The vehicles involved in this fraud released *40 times* more $NO_x$ emissions than U.S. law allowed. Virtually every diesel VW manufactured between 2009 and 2015 had this software, which disabled the $NO_x$ controls during actual driving. VW fought vigorously against charges that it had engaged in this charade, but ultimately it had to admit that it had installed the illegal software, and it had to take back nearly half a million cars in the United States and another half a million in Europe.

The U.S. government imposed penalties amounting to more than $18 billion, and many top-level company executives faced criminal charges. As a result of its trickery, VW in 2016 also faced a $15.3 billion class-action lawsuit, the largest an auto company ever encountered in the United States. The scandal has been called "Dieselgate." It forced VW into making massive layoffs. It had to lower its workforce by 30,000 people by 2021. The question the company had to ask was how it had allowed itself to become involved in such a blatant deceit.

### VW's History

To what extent did the company's history have a bearing on its current problem? The trade union of the Nazi Party, the German Labor Front, founded VW in 1937. The goal was to make a vehicle inexpensive enough so anyone could buy it, as at the time only the wealthiest Germans could afford a car and only 1 in 50 Germans owned one. In 1933, Ferdinand Porsche had built a prototype, a "people's car," the Volksauto (*volk* means "people" in German). The "people's car" was the model for the Beetle, a car with a rear, air-cooled engine and a distinctive shape, which became VW's trademark.

Adolf Hitler endorsed the state-owned factory, which started to make Beetles. The company shifted to military production when World War II started, for which it depended on slave labor from the Arbeitsdorf concentration camp. With Germany's defeat, VW was devastated. Little of value remained. The British offered Ford whatever assets were left, but because they were of such little value, Ford declined to accept them.

Until 1968, VW made nothing more than the Beetle, other than a van and a sports car called the Karmann Ghia. In the 1960s, Beetle sales took off in the United States, especially in California, where it had cult-like status as a symbol of freedom. Abetted by advertising and a reputation for reliability, the car also sold well in other parts of the United States. Ultimately, it surpassed the Model T as history's all-time best-seller. However, pollution control laws ended its successful run.

In 1970, the U.S. Congress passed strict, national antipollution laws and the Beetle's air-cooled engine could not achieve compliance. Without Audi, which VW acquired in 1964, the company would have gone out of existence. Audi gave it the capabilities it needed to make a standard water-cooled, front-wheel-drive vehicle. The distinctive rear, air-cooled engine of the Beetle became a relic of a bygone era.

Based on Audi technology, VW produced a number of very popular successors to the Beetle. The first was the Passat, which was launched in 1973. It shared parts with the Audi, on which it was based. The company next launched the Scirocco in 1974, aiming to compete with Ford's affordable four-seater, the Capri. It also launched the Golf in 1974, a vehicle that became the company's mainstay. VW produced many generations of the car, which was called the Rabbit in the United States and Canada. In 1978, VW set up a manufacturing facility in the United States for the Golf—in New Stanton, Pennsylvania, outside Pittsburgh—but it faced stiff competition from Japanese vehicles with similar features and lower prices; thus, U.S. sales of the Golf dropped from 293,595 units sold in 1980 to 177,709 in 1984, and VW decided to cease making cars in the United States.

The company entered the supermini market in Europe with the Polo in 1975. A stylish and spacious, three-door hatchback, the Polo competed with the Fiat 127 and Renault 5. Ford's response was the Fiesta, which it launched in 1991. VW introduced a third-generation Golf in 1992 and the Vento, called the Jetta in North America, in 1993. In 2002, Audi also brought to market many new models.

VW was known for the fuel efficiency of its vehicles. Many of them had diesel engines, which in Europe, where VW sold most of its vehicles, was preferred over the gasoline engines common in the United States. Stringent U.S. government emissions requirements made it difficult for VW to sell diesel engine vehicles in U.S. markets.

Until 2009, VW was unable to introduce a lineup of diesels in the United States that it was claiming were compatible with U.S. standards. The company at first was reluctant to introduce SUVs into the U.S. market for SUVs were not its specialty, but it did relaunch the Touareg, made in partnership with Porsche, in the United States. The Touareg was a heavy vehicle that did not have a third-row seat and had relatively poor fuel economy, but it had but modest sales. VW's distinctive selling point in the United States was its relatively fuel-efficient economy vehicles. Their unique feature in comparison with the fuel-efficient vehicles Japanese carmakers were selling was that most of them were very powerful and they were fueled by diesel engines.

The company's policy was to set up its factories in different parts of the world, manufacturing and assembling its vehicles for local markets. This policy resulted in its return to the United States to manufacture cars. In 2011, it started to make cars in a newly constructed facility in Chattanooga, Tennessee. Besides Germany and the United States, VW had factories in many countries including Mexico, China, Russia, and South Africa. Its Mexican factories, like those of other carmakers, became very closely linked to the U.S. market. All the automakers found Mexico attractive because the wages of auto workers in Mexico were a fraction of what they were in the United States.

VW's relationship with Porsche was a very important factor in creating a special engineering culture that allowed VW to design vehicles that consumers liked because of their acceleration and power. The Porsche family was a major shareholder in the company. Though the family was not allowed to exercise effective control because of German laws, it owned more than half of the company in 2009. Porsche components, including engines, gearboxes, and suspensions, found their place in many of VW's brands. As the Porsche reputation for engineering was outstanding, it had the effect of raising the status of the vehicles VW designed and built.

Over time, VW evolved into a very large holding company. In addition to the VW and Porsche brands it controlled a dozen different motor vehicle companies located in six European countries. In Germany, it owned Audi and Man as well as Porsche. Its Italian brands were Ducati, Bugatti, and Lamborghini. SEAT was the Spanish brand, ŠKODA the Czech brand, Bentley the English brand, and Scania the Swedish brand. VW was the parent company, which helped develop, make, and sell the components for these companies. With the exception of VW passenger cars and commercial vehicles, all of the auxiliary companies were independent and separately managed.

VW, with its Chinese partners, also had the largest market share among auto manufacturers in China. Because of its global reach, and despite experiencing some setbacks on the way, VW nearly doubled its global sales from 2006 to 2016, from 5.7 million units in 2006 to 10.3 million in 2016. In terms of leadership in global market share, it flip-flopped between VW and Toyota. However, the global automobile business was extremely competitive and included many strong companies, including GM, Ford, Nissan, Honda, Peugeot, and Hyundai. No firm was absolutely dominant. Outside China, the market was saturated and was not growing at a fast pace. All of the companies in the industry had a hard time keeping their margins up. They had large fixed assets, could not predict with certainty what the demand was likely to be, and often created more cars than needed, which they then sold often at a loss via discounts and incentives.

In this highly competitive industry, VW was the best performer in the years 2006 to 2016 (Figure 10.7). After 2009, it grew rapidly and maintained its position as *the* dominant player.

## Dieselgate

The incident that became known as Dieselgate was a huge blow to the company. During the years of its growth, VW got away with using the pollution control–defeating software without being detected. EU regulators started to have misgivings since

**FIGURE 10.7**    Volkswagen Global Sales Growth, 2006 to 2016

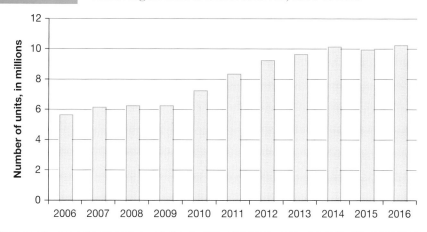

VW diesel emissions in the lab did not seem to match those observed on the road. The International Council on Clean Transportation, a European organization, devoted to causes like lower emissions and increased automotive efficiency, commissioned West Virginia University's Center for Alternative Fuels to do research because it suspected that there might be a problem with VW vehicles not performing up to the standards they claimed to be adhering to under actual driving conditions.

Suspicion that something was amiss mounted. California regulators supported the West Virginia researchers by giving them access to a state compliance-testing lab. However, neither the researchers at West Virginia University, who conducted the study, nor their sponsors expected to find cheating on the scale they discovered. They were flabbergasted when they realized the degree to which VW had rigged the system so that its vehicles would perform differently on the road than they did in the lab.

When the Center for Alternative Fuels confirmed that the problem existed in 2014, VW adamantly denied the accusations. It stuck to the story of its innocence for more than 15 months. When confronted with the results of the center's study, the company was arrogant and aloof, belittling the researchers and casting blame on them, giving lame excuses, and citing weather conditions, driving styles, and technicalities as the cause of the anomaly that the West Virginia investigators had discovered. VW asserted that the researchers from West Virginia University could not possibly comprehend the company's sophisticated engineering feat in reducing its $NO_x$ emissions. No one had a right to challenge its exceptionally brilliant engineering.

Frustrated by these denials, California regulators took additional steps to carefully scrutinize the company's software to make sure the suspected fraud in fact was real. They ultimately found the secret codes VW engineers had installed, a subroutine of parallel instructions to shut down emissions controls when the vehicles were not operating in laboratory settings.

The EPA threatened it might withhold approval of VW's 2016 cars in the United States and forbid their sale. This threat got the attention of the company and forced it to admit that it had deliberately gamed and rigged its emissions control systems to avoid complying with the law. CEO Martin Winterkorn reluctantly issued an apology in September 2015 and agreed to cooperate with the investigators.

VW admitted that it had installed the defeat device in 11 million vehicles worldwide. The next day, the company's stock price plummeted 20%, and the following day, it fell another 17%, at which point Winterkorn resigned in shame.

The EPA searched for and continued to discover more VW-made vehicles where the software only activated the pollution reduction systems when the cars were tested and shut them down under actual driving conditions. In addition, the FTC brought action against the company in 2016 for false advertising, as the company had marketed its diesel vehicles as a less polluting green alternative. It asserted that the diesels were among the world's leading clean and environmentally friendly vehicles, while it simultaneously tampered with their emission control devices, and each spewed forth more than 40 times the $NO_x$ that the law allowed.

## The Causes of the Scandal

VW had to reflect on the causes of the scandal. A 2016 *Fortune* article blamed it on the company's "overweening ambition."[34] Winterkorn's goal had been to triple U.S. sales in under a decade, a goal he sought to achieve at all costs in an effort to unseat Toyota once and for all as the world's largest automaker. His way of achieving this goal was to bet heavily on diesel-powered cars and to promote them as more fuel efficient and better for the environment than Toyota's hybrids.

VW diesels, the claim went, unlike Toyota hybrids, gave customers high mileage and low emissions, without sacrificing power or performance. Cheating rewarded VW's customers, for without disabling the emissions control devices, VW's miles per gallon would not be comparable with Toyota's hybrids. In this way, VW lied and positioned itself as being at the forefront of green technology. The hypocrisy in its stance provoked widespread outrage about a company that deceived regulators and the public blatantly.

The *Fortune* article maintained that the roots of VW's decision to cheat were in discussions the company had in 2007, when it walked away from pollution control technology for diesels that Mercedes-Benz and Bosch were creating. It chose instead to go it alone and try to create a $NO_x$ pollution control solution by itself, but it failed. Therefore, the company decided to revert to a prior practice of using defeat devices to get around pollution laws.

Indeed, in 1973, the EPA fined VW $120,000 for using the same tactic—it was not new. Again, in 1998, the EPA detected a scam that VW's truck division perpetrated, and it reached a 1-billion-dollar settlement with VW for the fraud. Regulators were astonished that VW had reverted back to the tactics it had used before, after having been exposed then and having had to pay fines.

Mercedes-Benz and Bosch recommended a technology that involved mixing urea with engine exhaust to neutralize harmful $NO_x$ pollutants in diesel. Though the method was effective, it was hard to implement, as drivers had to fill up their tanks with urea periodically. VW judged that this solution might work for trucks and heavier commercial vehicles, but it could not imagine applying it to the midsize undercar market, where buyers would shun buying VW vehicles because of the trouble they would have in maintaining the urea levels.

## The Ambition to Dominate the World Auto Industry

Ferdinand Piëch, grandson of Ferdinand Porsche, CEO from 1993 to 2002 and chairman of the firm from 2002 through the crisis, had imbued the company with the ambition and drive to dominate the world auto industry regardless of the methods used to achieve this goal. Piëch's strategy seemed to have worked as VW grew very rapidly, surpassing Ford as third in global sales in 2008, leapfrogging GM into second place in 2014, and then beating out Toyota and moving into first place in 2015.

Piëch became CEO at a time when VW had been performing poorly, and he ruthlessly enforced his will on workers and suppliers to reduce costs and grow the business. The pressure he brought to bear inside the company appeared to have no limits. Many employees believed it was unacceptable to admit that a task VW assigned, such as complying with pollution control laws, was impossible to carry out. If the employees could not achieve the task legitimately, then it was acceptable to find a ruse to get around it.

Prevarication became normalized in the company. Therefore, it was not a stretch for the company's top managers to proclaim that VW's vehicles used a $NO_x$ trap no other company had. The details did not matter as long as customers thought they were obtaining tangible performance and fuel economy benefits. VW had no choice but to confess that it had installed the defeat devices in the nearly 500,000 diesel vehicles it sold in the United States, starting in 2009, and another half a million it sold in Europe. It confessed at the very moment it publicly proclaimed its total dedication to clean diesel innovation and an environmentally friendly future.

The incident provoked rage from many of VW's loyal customers. Winterkorn accompanied his departure from the company with apologies and claimed that he had not been personally involved. Matthias Müller, who replaced him as CEO, still did not seem to comprehend fully the seriousness of what had transpired. In interviews, he continued to make lame excuses and alleged that the issue was a technical problem. The issue was an innocent misinterpretation of U.S. law, which he blamed on a handful of rogue engineers.

## Above the Law?

So intertwined with major institutions in Germany, the company long escaped serious criticism. The public thrashing that VW endured in the United States did not take place in Germany at first, as the company was considered to be above the law. In the end, even the German government saw fit to punish VW. The KBA—or Federal Vehicle Agency, an arm of the Ministry of Transport—agreed to a European recall. VW had to fix millions of affected cars in Europe as well as the United States. In total, the cheating affected eight models: the Jetta, Golf, Passat, Beetle, Touareg, Audi 7, Audi 8, and Porsche Cayenne. Yet despite the scandal and the precipitous fall in profitability, the company's growth continued, and its overall revenues continued to increase (Figure 10.8).

**FIGURE 10.8**    Volkswagen Revenue and Operating Income, 2012 to 2016

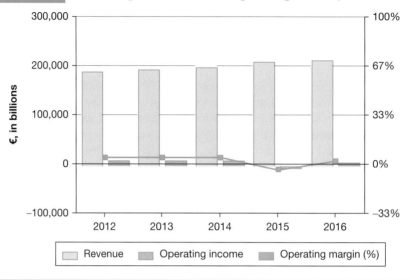

Use the lessons from this text to understand how Dieselgate occurred. What cognitive biases did VW's decision-makers have? What decision-making errors did they make? How did social pressures within VW contribute to the scandal?

What should VW's leadership do now? Rely on the weight-of-reasons framework to consider this question. What is the issue the company confronts, what are the facts, what options does it have, what would be the consequences of carrying out these options, what principles should it apply, what short- and long-term actions should it take, and what lessons should it learn from its history?

How should VW use the approaches described in Chapter 5, such as systems thinking, both/and thinking, moral imagination, and inquiry/advocacy, to go beyond a quick-fix to a long-term solution that ensures that such scandals do not occur again? What does it need to do to become an ethical organization (Chapter 6)? Which stakeholders has it prioritized in the past, and which should it prioritize in the future? How should it engage its stakeholders going forward? Can it be an ethical organization and still continue to grow its revenues and profits as much as it has in the past (Chapter 8)?

## Walmart: Sustainability

In 2018, Walmart, the world's largest retailer, operated more than 11,000 stores in many formats in many countries throughout the world. It sold its products on the Internet and in discount stores, supercenters, Sam's Clubs, small express stores, neighborhood markets, cash-and-carry warehouses, as well as the big-box stores that dotted the U.S. landscape. It made many types of goods available to customers, from food to pet supplies, to consumer electronics, which it sold at everyday low prices. Walmart claimed to give customers what they wanted, not only low prices but also a wide selection and freedom to choose.

The company moved into groceries in the early 1990s, which got its customers to come to its stores more often, as the average customer visits a food store about once a week. Walmart sold its foods at razor-thin margins to draw in this traffic. By the early part of the 21st century, it had become the largest grocer in the United States. Indeed, Americans spent about 1 in every 3 food dollars at Walmart.

Walmart put great pressure on its suppliers to keep their prices as low as possible. Since it held such a large percentage of the U.S. food market, suppliers depended heavily on Walmart for their survival.

Critics regularly attacked the company. They claimed that Walmart stores harmed local retail districts and independent retailers and grocers. They charged the company with engaging in corrupt practices to further its business interests in countries like Mexico, where it had resorted to bribes. These were just some of the faults they found with Walmart.

In addition, the company faced a number of serious sustainability challenges. One was the effort it was making to bring inexpensive organic food to its customers. Another was its ongoing relations with its workers, both those who worked directly for the company and those who were part of its extensive global supply chain. Still another was the initiatives it was taking to use less energy in its stores and to try and get companies in its supply chain, in China and elsewhere, to become more energy efficient, cut their wastes, and rely more on renewable power.

Where Walmart should go next was open to question. How should the company orient itself toward its customers, its employees, and the communities where it does business? Where should it go with its sales of organic foods, its relationship with its workforce, and its efforts to reduce the amount of energy it uses and to rely more on sustainable and renewable energy sources.

## Organic Foods

In 1990, the U.S. Department of Agriculture introduced an organic food label. This label provided consumers with the confidence that they were buying an organic product, but it label did not mean that the foods were necessarily healthier, fresh, or made of vegetables or whole grains. Rather, the purpose was to assure the consumer that the products Walmart sold did not contain artificial or sewage-based fertilizers, pesticides, genetically modified organisms, and an assortment of hormones and antibiotics.

Offering of organics by Walmart appealed to customers. Ninety-one percent were willing to buy organics from the company if the company priced the organics appropriately and the organics came from a well-respected brand.[35] Walmart shoppers made this type of purchase because they were looking for a healthier lifestyle. About a quarter of Americans in 2018 maintained they preferred buying organics as opposed to food that did not have an organic label.

Walmart was not the only grocer to enter the organics market. Besides Whole Foods, almost every conventional grocer sold organics, including supermarket chains like Kroger and Safeway. Walmart's rival, Target, had its own organic and natural product lines.

Holding back organic growth was the insufficient number of suppliers on which companies could depend to deliver large amounts of organic products at low prices reliably. With its massive scale, Walmart could stimulate the development of the supply chain and use its supply chain mastery to keep the prices low. To do so, it needed to enter into long-term contracts with growers and processors and lock them in for a considerable period.

The calculation Walmart made was that the less expensive organic food would create more demand. More demand then would stimulate further supply chain efficiencies. Ultimately, organic foods could compete with conventional foods. With the economies of scale the company introduced, it could make organic foods available at lower prices.

Most organic processors relied on production facilities that also handled conventional food. These facilities had to keep incoming and outgoing products segregated. They had to shut down and clean their facilities when a shipment of organic food arrived. If these facilities could be devoted exclusively to organic foods, producers could streamline operations and lower prices. Selling to Walmart the large volumes of organic food it needed could help them make this transition possible. Larger volumes would allow suppliers to run 100% organic all the time, which could cut their costs by as much as 20% to 30%.

However, critics posed questions. Was further consolidating the fragmented organic food supply chain under the guidance of Walmart's distribution system and giving manufacturers the chance to operate on a larger and more efficient scale *really* in customers' and suppliers' interests?

Critics also maintained that some of the organic food found in Walmart's stores was coming from abroad, where the standards for guaranteeing the authenticity of the products could be lax. When the U.S. government established guidelines for organic food, it did not include the word *local* in how it determined if a product was organic. This omission allowed Walmart to establish supply agreements for large-scale shipments of organics from faraway places. The organic tomatoes found in its stores, for instance, did not come from local farmers. Instead, the company obtained typically guaranteed purchases at low costs from large bulk shippers and growers elsewhere. Critics maintained that people should not buy organics because they cost less but because of the underlying ethical values they represented. An important value they associated with organic food was it be locally grown.

## Labor Relations

Another matter that seriously plagued Walmart was labor relations. The company employed more than 1.4 million people and was the largest employer in the world. Historically, it had a very complicated relationship with its workforce. Nonunionized employees, called associates, had to work very hard for low wages, but since they received some of their compensation in stock ownership, they became wealthy if Walmart's share price went up. Rapid rise in Walmart's stock took place in its early years, but once the company achieved scale and was a well-established firm the stock price did not increase much.

The company also had a reputation for treating its workers harshly. This reputation arose historic low wages. It also came about because the company had not granted women the same pay and promotion opportunities as men and that it had blocked every effort on the part of its workforce to unionize. In fact, Walmart ended its operations in Europe because it would have had to unionize there.

Critics also maintained that in its push for low prices, Walmart sourced most of its supplies from overseas. After an exceptionally disparaging NBC Dateline report in 1992 that uncovered the notorious use of child labor by a Walmart supplier in Bangladesh, the company fashioned a code of conduct that banned child and prison labor among its suppliers. Other large companies joined in and signed similar agreements, which in turn generated a market for auditors to inspect factories, scrutinize wage records, and interview workers in overseas factories about their work conditions.

Critics, however, questioned the auditors' effectiveness. The auditors might be bribed and assist in cheating by allowing factories to treat workers harshly, provide low pay, and endanger lives. Walmart allowed factories to outsource more than half the work, and auditing was a cat-and-mouse game where suppliers avoided detection by keeping two sets of books. One set presented an accurate picture while a second, fraudulent set was presented to auditors. The auditors observed just a small part of the activity that occurred in the factories where Walmart outsourced the work.

The company tried to introduce a number of other progressive practices. For example, it endeavored to assist the more than 60,000 women who worked for companies that supplied it from factories in India, Bangladesh, China, and Central America. It trained them in communication, hygiene, reproductive health, and occupational health and safety.

## Energy and the Environment

The company had ambitious goals in the domain of energy and the environment. It aimed to be 100% supplied by renewable energy, wanted to create zero waste, and sell products that sustained people and the environment. In 2005, CEO Lee Scott gave an address to the company's stores and suppliers in which he affirmed his belief that environmental stewardship is compatible with profits. After the speech, the company asked suppliers to condense products like laundry detergent into more easily packed and shipped containers and to reduce the amount of cardboard and plastic they used in packaging. According to Scott, these actions were worth pursuing because they saved money and also protected the environment.

Michael Duke succeeded Scott as CEO in 2009 and reaffirmed Scott's goals. He asked employees to recycle, use smarter packaging, reduce the use of plastic bags, and in general rethink the processes they used to get the work done. During Duke's tenure, Walmart succeeded in getting dairy farmers to use low-carbon cattle feed and methane digesters. It also succeeded in getting Hollywood studios to use slimmer DVD packaging. The company increased its truck fleet's efficiency by 60% and eliminated hazardous materials in most of the electronics it sold. It also built a solar power system in Hawaii.

By 2011, Walmart had reduced its wastes by 64%. It had accelerated the widespread adoption of compact fluorescent light bulbs. In 2012, it reported that it expected to eliminate all the waste it sent to U.S. landfills by 2025. The company became the top corporate user of on-site solar power in the United States. It had more than 180 renewable energy projects underway. In 2013, it reported that its wind energy projects, fuel cell installations, and zero-waste programs had added $150 million to its bottom line. The company's record, nonetheless, was not perfect. At its global stores and distribution centers, it met just half of its goal to reduce greenhouse gases by 20% by 2012.

Walmart's more than 100,000 suppliers from Alabama to Uzbekistan deposited an incalculable amount of greenhouse gases into the atmosphere. Many of these suppliers s relied heavily on shadow factories that were not directly under their control. If Walmart counted the transport of goods and services by its suppliers and the shadow factories, it would be nearly impossible to estimate the company's complete carbon footprint.

## China

China was an especially difficult challenge for the company. The country hosted more than 30,000 factories manufactured directly or indirectly for Walmart. In 2008, the then-CEO Scott met with the CEOs and managers of more than 1,000 Chinese suppliers and urged them to be responsible environmental stewards, cognizant of climate change, and preservers of energy. He insisted that meeting social and environmental standards was not optional. Walmart would not tolerate companies that did not live up to high standards. If companies did not live up to these standards, Walmart would work with them to raise their standards, but if they did not make sufficient improvements, Walmart would, after inspection by outside auditors, terminate its relations with them.

Indeed, China's government supported Walmart and seemed to be sympathetic to Scott's initiative. It said it wanted Chinese companies to be more environmentally responsible, instead of focusing on unfettered development.

However, dealing with issues in China was far harder than Walmart or the Chinese government anticipated. Coordinating the behavior of so many suppliers and subcontractors was beyond the capability of any company, even one as large as Walmart. The investment required to reduce energy, water use, and emissions demanded more of Walmart's suppliers than they were able to provide. Walmart still pressured them to lower prices by 3% to 5% per year. Operating on the thinnest of margins, the suppliers maintained that they did not have enough cash to invest in green projects. Walmart strengthened its compliance agreements with its Chinese suppliers, but it lost patience when the suppliers complained that they could not make more progress because of the company's insistence that they keep prices low.

Though the company made some strides in China, its performance was far from perfect. In 2008, it promised to boost energy efficiency by 20% per unit produced in 200 factories making goods for it in China. However, in 2011, it indicated that just 119 factories had met this goal.[36] The Environmental Defense Fund (EDF), which had been a partner in this effort, exited the program at the end of 2011 because of what it maintained was Walmart's lack of full cooperation. It was hard for Walmart to make progress in China.

## In-Store Sustainability: Energy and Products

Where Walmart had been more successful was in measuring its own energy use and the waste of its own stores. It lowered them and saved substantial amounts of money by improving operational efficiency. Walmart made many simple alterations. For example, it turned off the lights in Coke machines when they were not in use. From 2005 to 2011, the total square footage of its stores and facilities increased by 40%, and sales grew by 44%, but the company's greenhouse gas emissions expanded by just 10%.

Still not satisfied, the company tried to generate greater employee awareness and started to put in place life-cycle metrics. These metrics would help it in another round of trying to make its supply chain more sustainable. It also launched a supplier Sustainability Index that asked its suppliers questions about their operations.[37]

The company began its new sustainability drive in 2009, when it collaborated with the Sustainability Consortium, a nonprofit coalition at the University of Arkansas and Arizona State University. The consortium's aim was to provide a technical foundation for the initiative.[38] A number of other retailers—Tesco, Kroger, Ahold, and Best Buy and consumer product companies like Coke, Disney, Kellogg's, Mars—agreed to participate.

Working with the consortium, Walmart sent questions to its suppliers in about 200 product categories. Each year, it aimed to survey more of its suppliers, with the ultimate goal of including about half the products it sold in the system. The company intended to rank the suppliers from best to worst and share this information with its buyers; in turn, Walmart would compensate the suppliers in part based on their sustainability performance. The goal was to improve the environmental reputation of the company's most popular products.

Walmart asked the suppliers many questions, including the following:

- How could a supplier remove chemicals?

- How could a supplier improve the way it mined for minerals?

- How could a supplier increase the number of products with Energy Star certificates? (These certificates were the U.S. government–backed symbol for energy efficiency.)

- How could a supplier cut the amount of water it used?

A prior survey of suppliers had been too long and burdensome, and there was no follow-up. Now, the company's intention was to grade each supplier against its peers with a score of 1 to 100. In a particular category, its buyers would be able to make comparisons. In cereals, for instance, they could compare Kellogg's, General Mills, Post, and Quaker. In soft drinks, they could compare Coke, Pepsi, and Dr. Pepper. Buyers could discuss performance with the suppliers and encourage them to do better. Buyers, however, could not guarantee the rewards for the best companies or punish the laggards.

In the end, Walmart had to grant the suppliers the discretion to improve on their own. The company did not have the legal authority to compel them to make changes.

It was not a government agency. Yet in 2017, the company did promise to buy 70% of the goods it sold in U.S. stores and U.S. Sam's Clubs from suppliers who answered the Sustainability Index questions and were committed to doing better.

With regard to the farmers who also supplied the company, Walmart urged them to track fertilizer use and have optimum goals for its use. It asked them to monitor soil fertility and have goals to minimize degradation and erosion. It inquired if they could grow wheat with less water and fertilizer, and it urged wineries to grow their grapes in accordance with biodiversity plans.

Walmart received positive media attention for these initiatives, but it had to prove that that they were more than hype. Advocacy groups continued to doubt the company's sincerity.

## Much to Prove

In the realm of sustainability, Walmart still had much to prove. It was trying to increase the amount of organics it offered to customers at low prices, but this effort had not met with full success. It was trying to improve the way its own workforce and that of its suppliers throughout the world were treated, but again its success was partial. Finally, it tried to make its own stores more energy efficient and to improve the environmental and energy performance of suppliers everywhere in the world, but especially in China, but these efforts had not achieved as much as the company wanted.

Walmart had to ask itself to what extent whether it was on the right path. How could it make further progress? What more could it do? Use the weight-of-reasons framework for ethical decision-making to address these questions. Must it make tradeoffs in meeting its obligations to its various stakeholders? What principles should guide the company? Which stakeholders matter most, and how should it engage them? What actions can the company take in the short-term, and what does it need to do in the long-term? Is Walmart's long-term strategy and business model compatible with its sustainability goals?

## Wells Fargo: Can It Come Back?

Wells Fargo flourished while other banks floundered after the 2008 Great Financial Crisis. Its reputation was intact because it took fewer risks and its business was apparently built on a sounder ethical foundation. The legendary Warren Buffett remained a major investor and defender of Wells Fargo even after the cross-selling scandal, which shook this company to its very foundations. At his 2018 meeting with shareholders, he said, "I see no reason why Wells Fargo as a company . . . going forward is in any way inferior to other big banks in which it competes."[39]

### Cross-Selling

At Wells Fargo, cross-selling meant pitching a new product or service to a consumer who already had one product or service the bank provided, for example, offering a credit card or mortgage to a customer with a checking account. Richard Kovacevich,

Norwest Corporation CEO and then CEO of Wells Fargo when it acquired Norwest, championed this concept and was widely praised for implementing it.[40]

Cross-selling is not an uncommon business practice. It is a way of marketing multiple products to customers. Once a firm obtains a customer, it tries to sell her or him other products and services it offers. Kovacevich considered employees at the company's branch offices to be part of its sales teams and encouraged them to sign up clients, or customers as he referred to them, to as many of the products and services the bank offered as possible. Kovacevich evaluated employees based on their ability to cross-sell. He tried to get them to sell at least eight products or services to every customer.

## The *Los Angeles Times* Investigation

In 2013, a *Los Angeles Times* investigation brought to light the intense pressure this system put on employees.[41] The company had mathematically imposed cross-selling quotas that were nearly impossible to meet unless employees resorted to cheating. Employees had to sell as many as 20 products a day. Many responded by signing up customers for the bank's products and services without their consent and without telling them, but charging them nonetheless, in most cases by taking money out of their legitimate accounts *without their permission*. Often, employees engaged in these practices with their supervisors' knowledge and support.

The fraud they perpetrated was extremely widespread. When employees complained or resisted, typically they lost their jobs. Some maintained that the stress led to crying, vomiting, and panic attacks. They reported that the calls they made to the company's ethics hotline either were ignored or resulted in their termination.

The *Los Angeles Times* article resulted in the company introducing methods to prevent these abusive practices, but they did not end the fraud. From 2011 to 2016, the company's employees created more than 1.5 million deposit accounts and more than 0.5 million unauthorized credit card accounts. About 85,000 of the accounts opened during this period incurred unnecessary fees totaling $2 million. Because of the fake accounts, many customers saw their credit scores decline. Starting in 2016, whistle-blowers revealed that employees of the bank also had issued unwanted insurance policies. By 2017, the number of fraudulent accounts that investigators discovered grew to 3.5 million.[42]

## Trying to Contain the Damage

Wells Fargo tried to contain the damage, taking out ads in newspapers admitting that some of its sales practices had been wrong. However, the bank rejected out of hand the notion that its aggressive sales culture was primarily to blame. John Stumpf, Kovacevich's successor, took some responsibility for the scandal but refused to resign.[43] Instead, he fired more than 5,000 employees whom he declared were the guilty parties, trying to exculpate himself by blaming subordinates and saying they acted on their own without authority from the top management team. His cure for the problem was to increase supervision at local branches. He reported that the company would invest about $50 million in greater oversight and eliminate sales quotas but not totally end cross-selling.

The employees at Wells Fargo who were let go had difficulty gaining employment at other banks, since the bank issued documents with a record of their misbehavior. The defamatory documents asserted that they had been complicit in malfeasance and the creation of the unwanted accounts. The fired employees had no right to appeal the documents, which alleged that they had participated in unethical conduct, other than to file a lawsuit against the bank.

## Senate Hearings

With outrage against the company high, the Senate Banking Committee, egged on by Senator Elizabeth Warren of Massachusetts, held hearings.[44] The committee forced Stumpf to appear at the hearings in 2016. Prior to appearing, Stumpf relented to the demands of the company's board and chose to relinquish $41 million of his not yet vested stock options.

Stumpf gave prepared testimony but refused to answer many of the questions, citing lack of expertise. He received heavy criticism for the praise he had once heaped on Carrie Tolstedt, the previous head of retail banking, whom the company forced into retirement in 2016. The bank had investigated her for the way she had brought pressure on middle management to radically increase the bank's cross-sell ratio, which was the metric she had used for the number of accounts each customer had. Senator Warren called Stumpf's leadership of the bank "gutless" and told him to step down. Senator Pat Toomey of Pennsylvania doubted whether the employees the bank terminated had acted independently, without orders from supervisors or management.

After a less than spectacular defense of the company at the hearing, Stumpf did resign. Apparently, the board did not force this decision on him; rather, he maintained that it was in the company's best interest. The board then used a clawback stipulation in his employment agreement to strip him of $28 million in earnings. Tolstedt as well had to relinquish her earnings, though she continued to maintain her innocence regarding what had transpired.

## Repercussions

After the hearing, the Consumer Financial Protection Bureau fined Wells Fargo $185 million, a very small fine given the magnitude of the company's violations.[45] The following year, the Office of the Comptroller of the Currency (OCC) imposed additional penalties. It added new restrictions, subjecting the bank to oversight as if it were a troubled and insolvent institution.

Immediately after news of the scandal was revealed, the company's profits fell. Its expenses grew because of payments to lawyers and outside firms. It had to shut down more than 400 of its 6,000 branches. It cut other costs and announced that it would rely more on technology than on its sales force to grow revenue. Compared with other banks, its stock continued to perform poorly. Customers could not pursue legal action against the bank because of provisions in the agreement they had made when they opened an account that mandated that in the case of a dispute they would have to enter into private arbitration with the bank. Wells Fargo did end up paying $110 million to customers who had accounts opened in their name without permission.

In 2017, Timothy Sloan, the new CEO, agreed to rehire about 1,000 employees terminated wrongfully or who had quit because of the fraud, but not employees whom he maintained were implicated rightfully. Senator Warren charged that Sloan too should go because he had been in a top leadership position when the fraud took place. Prosecutors in New York City, San Francisco, and North Carolina started their own investigations, as did the SEC. The state of California ended its relationship with the bank, and the city of Chicago took out the money it had invested in the bank. Cities such as Philadelphia and Seattle backed away from ever having anything to do with the bank. In 2019, Sloan too was compelled to step down as the company's CEO.[46] As of September 2019, Wells Fargo still did not have a CEO. Experienced executives from other companies did not want the position.

## Fines and Other Penalties

In April 2018, Wells Fargo agreed to pay $2.09 billion in settlement of risk management claims.[47] This fine was the largest against a bank made at that point by the Trump administration. The Consumer Financial Protection Bureau and the OCC fined the bank for its inability to catch and prevent improper charges from being levied on consumers in its mortgage and auto-lending businesses. The company had to develop and submit a compensation plan for affected customers within three months. The government imposed the fines for improper fees charged in mortgage lending. It determined that the selling of unneeded auto insurance could have resulted in defaults and vehicle repossessions for up to 27,000 customers. The bank would have to obtain the OCC's approval before it appointed executives and board members and before it awarded them payment for the duties they performed. The amount of compensation customers would be awarded would be determined later, and it would be separate from the penalty.

On top of this fine, in May 2018, the company reached a preliminary $480 million settlement in a securities fraud class-action suit for opening as many as 3.5 million fake retail banking customer accounts. Union Investment, a European asset management firm, was the lead plaintiff appointed by the court in the case. It claimed that by engaging in the fraud the bank and its current and former executives and directors were able to falsely state and artificially inflate the firm's stock price from 2014 to 2016. The bank denied the charged but chose to settle in the interests of employees and investors in order to put the issue behind it.

In December 2018, the company announced a $575 million settlement with the 50 state attorneys general and the attorney general for the District of Columbia regarding its practices. Sloan, CEO at the time, said that the agreement underscored a "serious commitment to making things right" and building "a better bank."[48] Under the terms of the agreement, the company had to respond to ongoing customer inquiries and maintain a website detailing its remediation efforts. It also had to provide regular reports to the states on its progress in paying people back.

Why did the cross-selling scandal happen at Wells Fargo? How did social pressure and organizational factors (Chapters 4 and 6, respectively) influence individual employees' actions? Based on this case, what do you learn about whether it pays to be good"—or "pays to be bad" (Chapter 7)? What should Wells Fargo do next?

Use the weight-of-reasons framework in formulating your answer. What is the issue, and what are the facts and the options and consequences? Which stakeholders should it prioritize in assessing the consequences? What principles should the bank apply, and what actions should it take in the short- and the long-term? What will it take for Wells Fargo to build an ethical organization? What lessons must it learn from its experience?

## Whole Foods: Conscious Capitalism[49]

The business model that John Mackey, the charismatic founder and long-time CEO of Whole Foods, maintained he adhered to was "conscious capitalism."[50] Now that Whole Foods was a part of Amazon, to what extent should it continue to adhere to the tenets of this model? Whole Foods had to profitably grow and at the same time pursue a sustainability agenda. It had to increase the size of its market while enhancing its image for making the world the better.

The positive image that Whole Foods tried to project did not always match the reality. It touted its dedication to natural foods and proudly displayed the many environmental awards it had won on its website and elsewhere, but it had been heavily criticized for the hyperaggressive way it had expanded, leveling smaller health food chains and cooperatives. The most comprehensive and objective assessment group in the realm of social responsibility, CSRHub, rated Walmart as doing substantially better than both Whole Foods and Amazon in 2019. CSRHub evaluated 12 indicators of employee, environment, community, and governance performance and aggregated and normalized this information to create a broad and consistent set of findings. The sources on which it relied included socially responsible investing firms, NGOs, government agencies, and many lists of best and worst firms. Whole Foods had to prove to that it was truly a socially responsible company, but so did its parent Amazon (see again the case on Amazon in Chapter 7). What approach should Amazon take to Whole Foods' social responsibility now that it was a part of Amazon?

### Whole Foods' Acquisition by Amazon

When John Mackey of Whole Foods first met Jeff Bezos, CEO of Amazon, in 2017, he recalled that it felt like he was "falling in love." Amazon's acquisition of Whole Foods for $13.7 billion had come at the urging of activist investor Jana Partners. Shareholder activists wanted a takeover of Whole Foods because of a failure to live up to its potential for serving shareholder interests. Its same-store sales were down, and they had been falling for some time.

The company no longer was a unique provider of healthy food products. It faced tough competitive challenges from both mainstream grocers like Kroger's and upstarts like Sprouts Farmers Market. Even Walmart could claim to have a full line-up of the type of items Whole Foods stocked, but at substantially lower prices. Walmart, the world's largest grocer, had more than 1,600 organic items on its shelves. It was a leading seller of organic milk and sold its own organic fresh produce under the Marketside label. In the packaged organic food category, it sold everything from canned vegetables to spices like paprika, curry, and cinnamon. Whole Foods could not match Walmart's prices in this category. The reasons consumers had flocked to Whole Foods were no longer as compelling as they had been. With Whole Foods' prices out of proportion to those of its competitors, the moniker "whole wallet" applied to the company.

After the takeover by Amazon, Mackey, known as a "right wing hippie," remained CEO. Since Amazon's takeover, he admitted that he had unspecified disagreements with the parent company but that he had the confidence to push back. Amazon quickly made many changes at Whole Foods. It brought its own signature products and services, including devices like the Echo speaker, Fire TV, and Kindle. It offered exclusive discounts and promotions for Amazon Prime subscribers, including same-day delivery. The larger question was how the combined company would affect Whole Foods' image. One reason why customers were willing to pay outsize amounts for products they bought at Whole Foods was the way the company branded itself for social responsibility.

Mackey referred to his philosophy or CSR as conscious capitalism. The concept, as Mackey developed in a *Harvard Business Review* article he cowrote, meant giving equal preference to workers, vendors, customers, and the community as to shareholders and create a holistic unity.[51] As he argued, Whole Foods' purpose was not just linked to making a profit; rather, it practiced a form of capitalism in which it gave priority to all its stakeholders. The article stated that a conscious business such as Whole Foods should have "a trusting, authentic, innovative and caring culture" where working was "a source of personal growth and professional fulfillment." According to Mackey, Whole Foods' purpose was to create "financial, intellectual, social, cultural, emotional, spiritual, physical and ecological wealth" for *all* its stakeholders. In contrast, Amazon's reputation was for "squeezing" suppliers and "pushing" workers to their limits[52] (see the related case in Chapter 7, and its aim was to grow its business as fast as possible. Amazon did not belong in the group of firms like Starbucks, Trader Joe's, and Patagonia, which were recognized for their social responsibility. Amazon had to choose how it would adjust Whole Foods' approach to social responsibility, if at all, now that Whole Foods was a part of Amazon. To what extent would conscious capitalism survive the transition?

## Whole Foods as a Mission-Based Business

The mission of Whole Foods was not just to sell food but to educate its customers about their lifestyles and encourage them to adopt a set of values. The values Whole Foods celebrated included community well-being and environmental awareness, as well as healthy eating of high-quality natural and organic foods. Whole Foods also hailed win–win partnerships with its suppliers, which it claimed differentiated it from other grocers. Other grocers had more of a zero-sum relation with suppliers in which one party prevailed at the expense of the other. With regard to what it sold, Whole Foods was very careful. It banned dozens of products from its shelves that were found on the shelves of nearly every other grocer.[53] How did it choose what to bar? Many factors were involved; the company maintained that they included safety, the way the foods were manufactured, their compatibility with the company's values, and animal welfare, among others.

Whole Foods also responded to customer complaints about products with ingredients the customers did not trust. For example, it added high HFC to its list of prohibited ingredients in 2011 in response to customer complaints. Though HFC often was singled out as a cause of high obesity rates, biochemically it differed little from sugar, a substance found in abundance in Whole Foods stores. Another sweetener Whole Foods prohibited, Aspartame, had been the subject of much public debate, yet many authoritative health bodies that examined the evidence had concluded that it was safe. Moreover, the company did a lively business selling sugar-filled indulgent baked goods and deserts and prided itself on its collection of specialty chocolates. For instance, its Chocolate Sandwich Cremes were mock-ups of Oreos and rivaled the Kraft product in their lack of sound nutritional value. Indeed, customers had sued Whole Foods for vastly understating the amount of sugar in some of its products, like its store-brand yogurt.[54]

Lawyers who brought a class-action federal court case cited six tests by *Consumer Reports* on the supermarket chain's Whole Foods 365 Everyday Value Plain Greek Yogurt, which showed that this product had 11.4 grams of sugar per 170-gram serving rather than the 2 grams Whole Foods had listed on the label. The plaintiffs sought $5 million in damages. Forced to capitulate, Whole Foods removed the yogurt from its shelves and investigated the incident. Whole Foods declared that its intention was to provide customers high-quality products with accurate labeling. For those with an interest in healthier fare than its Chocolate Sandwich Cremes or its yogurt, the company gave the choice of buying Engine 2 Plant-Strong products, a line of minimally processed snacks, breakfast items, and pantry staples.

## Whole Foods' Growth

Because Whole Foods had grown so rapidly by means of acquisitions, it had forced many independent retailers and co-ops to cease to exist. Competitors the company swallowed or forced out of business included Bread & Circus, Fresh Fields, Bread of Life, Merchant of Vino, Nature's Heartland, Food for Thought, Harry's Farmers Market, and Mrs. Gooch's Natural Foods Market.

Whole Foods began in 1980 when Mackey and his then girlfriend opened Safer Way, one of a number of small health food grocers in Austin, Texas. The name "Safer Way" was a spoof on the name of the food giant Safeway. Mackey merged Safer Way with Clarksville Natural Grocery. Craig Weller and Mark Skiles, the owners of Clarksville, later charged that they had been coerced to join Whole Foods by threats Mackey made that he would put them out of business. Mackey admitted to being overly aggressive and competitive.[55] Located in a former night club, the first Whole Foods, at 12,500 square feet and with a staff of 19, was huge in comparison with other health food stores of its time. To fill the space, Mackey sold liquor and meat as well as granola and lentils.

In 1984, Whole Foods expanded to other large Texas cities, first Houston and then Dallas, where it acquired the Bluebonnet Natural Foods Grocery.[56] In 1988, it moved into New Orleans, Louisiana, where it purchased another firm that also had The Whole Food Company name. It set up operations in Palo Alto, California, buying

Mill Valley, and in 1989, it bought Wellspring Grocery, adjacent to the college towns of Chapel Hill and Durham in North Carolina. The basic idea was to be in close proximity to college campuses. With this in mind, Whole Foods acquired many more health food stores and chains in the 1990s including the following:

- Bread & Circus in Massachusetts and Rhode Island

- Mrs. Gooch's Natural Foods Markets in Los Angeles, California

- Unicorn Village in South Florida

- Bread of Life in Northern California and Florida

- Fresh Fields Markets in the Midwest and East Coast

- Merchant of Vino in Detroit, Michigan

- Nature's Heartland in Boston, Massachusetts

- Oak Street Market in Evanston, Illinois

In the next decade, Whole Foods forcefully grew via acquisition. It acquired more natural grocers including Natural Abilities in Northern California, Harry's Farmers Market in Atlanta, Georgia, and Fresh & Wild in the United Kingdom.

The advantage of becoming bigger was the clout it gave the company over its suppliers. The aim of creating this empire was to dictate terms and prices to its suppliers and to lock them into having a single outlet for the specialty foods they provided. In the process of achieving consolidation as the largest and only national natural food grocer, Whole Foods went against a fundamental tenet of the natural food movement of keeping its enterprises small and local. Whole Foods was a major national and international entity that looked and acted far differently than the typical co-op, from which it had risen.

## The Acquisition of Wild Oats

In 2007, Whole Foods attempted to acquire the Wild Oats grocery chain. This acquisition would be another critical step in its drive toward consolidation for Wild Oats at the time was the only other national challenger in its niche. However, the Bush administration fought the purchase, contending that the merged company would unfairly dominate the market.

At the same time, the SEC began an investigation of Mackey. For eight years he had been furtively logging into an Internet message board under the fictitious name of Rahodeb, which was an anagram of "Deborah," his wife's name. In 2006, he wrote a message on the board that Wild Oats "still stinks and remains grossly overvalued based on very weak fundamentals. The stock is up now but if it doesn't get sold in the next year or so it is going to plummet back down. Wait and see."[57] The panning of Wild Oats was done to lower its price so that it would be easier and less expensive for Whole Foods to acquire the chain. At the same time that Mackey panned Wild Oats on the message board, he enthusiastically praised his own company. By praising his company with such vigor, he was hoping its stock price would be at its highest at the moment Whole Foods made its bid for Wild Oat. What Mackey was doing was both unethical and illegal. In the age of Trump, it may seem trivial, but at the time it was a serious breach of ethics and law.

Thus, the FTC had no compunctions about contesting the transaction. It alleged that in secretly posting on the message board Mackey had violated federal antitrust laws. His aim, the FTC went so far as to declare, was to bring an end to competition among natural food grocers. If the agency did not prevent the transaction, Whole Foods would be able to raise prices, cut quality, and gouge customers. Though a federal district court permitted the deal, the U.S. Court of Appeals for the District of Columbia reversed the decision in 2008. It ruled that consumers who cared about social and environmental responsibility would be devastated. In the court's view, based on the evidence it had, Whole Foods' sole intention in trying to acquire Wild Oats was to raise prices. Whole Foods agreed to a settlement in 2009, selling the brand name "Wild Oats" along with 32 of the company's stores and the company's intellectual property to Luberski, a West Coast food distributor, otherwise known as Hidden Villa Ranch, while retaining the remainder of Wild Oats assets.

After Whole Foods' acquisition of Wild Oats, the great recession of 2008 took hold. Per capita disposable income declined precipitously, and consumers pulled away from the premium, organic and all-natural brands, that Whole Foods sold, which hurt the company's revenues. However, when the recession slackened, Whole Foods made a comeback. Some store revenues grew again but only temporarily, for in 2014 the company's revenues again contracted. In general, growth in the U.S. food industry was weak.[58] Buyers wanted the ethically sourced, fresh, simple nutritious foods that Whole Foods sold but not at the prices Whole Foods was charging. They wished to experiment with ethnic fare and new and exotic tastes, yet there were limits to how much they could pay. Competitors provided much of what Whole Foods offered but at far lower prices. Companies like Costco, for instance, had a wide range of products similar to those Whole Foods sold, but at far lower prices. Costco also provided many ancillary services like gas stations, pharmacies, food courts, hearing aids, and travel, which were not available at Whole Foods.

Whole Foods faced the difficult question of why customers should regularly shop at its stores. Other than die-hard Whole Foods fans, its customer base was shrinking. Nothing Mackey did seemed to be able to reverse this situation. He was not willing to lower Whole Foods' prices even though it had exceptionally high margins and there seemed to be substantial room for price reductions. Whole Foods sought to maintain its elite customers. It was concerned that if it lowered its prices it would be a sign that it was opening itself up to the mass of everyday shoppers who did not frequent Whole Foods often. Lower prices might compromise the look and feel of the stores—the company would have less money to spend on showy lighting and elaborate displays.

## A Focus on Its Values

To bring customers into the stores, Whole Foods chose to focus on its vaunted values. If customers could fully identify with those values, they would be more willing to tolerate the high prices Whole Foods charged. Thus, Whole Foods went out of its way to develop a set of value statements that it prominently displayed. For instance, on its website, it declared,

> Whole Foods Market's vision of a sustainable future means our children and grandchildren will be living in a world that values human creativity, diversity, and individual choice. Businesses will harness human and material resources without devaluing the integrity of the individual or the planet's ecosystems. Companies, governments, and institutions will be held accountable for their actions. People will better understand that all actions have repercussions. . . . It will be a world . . . where people are encouraged to discover, nurture, and share their life's passions.

Mackey promoted his celebrity. He coauthored a book called *Conscious Capitalism*, in which he proclaimed his belief that economic freedom and entrepreneurship were the way to end poverty, increase prosperity, and evolve humanity upward.[59] He maintained that both business and capitalism were fundamentally ethical and that it was possible to do a vast amount of good for humanity and at the same time make substantial sums of money. In fact, he was very proud to declare that the more money a person made the more good that person could do. Whole Foods offered itself as an alternative to solely profit-seeking corporations. Mackey asserted that by treating its employees, shareholders, customers, and suppliers so well, the company would spread goodness throughout the world. Everyone would be better off if Whole Foods had the chance to thrive. The company's core values were simple. They were to provide equitable treatment to all of its stakeholders—its customers, employees, investors, and suppliers—and to meet its obligations to the entire population of the world, to the food system, and to the earth.

A fan of Milton Friedman, Ronald Reagan, and Ayn Rand, Mackey was a committed libertarian and a firm believer in free markets. In a *Wall Street Journal* opinion article, he asserted that health problems did not arise because many people were without health care coverage—which he opposed giving to more Americans—but were self-inflicted. The government should not have to take care of the people. People should be responsible for their own health. Overweight and obese Americans were just making a series of bad choices. Mackey implied, but did not actually say, that their problems were correctible if they restricted their shopping to a noble enterprise like Whole Foods.

Pushback quickly came from many of Whole Foods' customers and suppliers, who found Mackey's point of view offensive; his comments, in fact, inspired a Boycott Whole Foods campaign. To repair the damage he had done, Whole Foods had to fight back with a message about the host of causes Mackey supported that appealed to Whole Foods' socially conscious customers. The CEO was prochoice and in favor of legalizing marijuana and gay marriages, protecting the environment, enforcing strict animal welfare protection laws, and allowing for a safety net for the poor and disabled. He was in favor of a drastically reduced defense budget and U.S. military presence, though he opposed socialism because it was undemocratic.

Whole Foods touted the many awards it had won for social responsibility.[60] They included the Natural Products Association's 2009 Socially Responsible Retailer

Award for excellence in integrating social responsibility into multiple aspects of its business. The Ethisphere Institute in 2010 recognized the company for being one of the world's most ethical. In 2013, the company ranked 19th in *Fortune* magazine's list of most admired companies. The company had a policy of donating 5% of after-tax profits to charities. A number of foundations were the recipients of its generosity. The Whole Planet Foundation gave microcredit to poor people in the communities that supplied its stores. The Whole Kids Foundation improved children's nutrition by means of grants to schools for salad bars. The Animal Compassion Foundation was dedicated to improving the quality of life of farm animals.

Accused of selling overpriced luxuries for finicky eaters, Whole Foods tried to expand its value offerings and narrow the pricing gap between the food it sold and the food that conventional grocers sold. The company recognized that there was a limit to how much it could expand its business if it just served wealthier individuals, and it engaged in an experiment in serving less advantaged people by setting up a store in Detroit, but it was uncertain how much revenue it could expect to obtain in poor, inner-city neighborhoods.

## Labor Relations

An area in which Whole Foods considered itself to be excelling was labor relations. It had been ranked many times as one of Fortune's 100 best companies to work for in America. It also touted the efforts it made in protecting the human rights of the workers in its supply chain. For instance, as far back as 2007, it had launched Whole Trade Guarantee, a purchasing initiative emphasizing the ethics and social responsibility of the products it imported from developing countries, based on criteria that included not only fair prices and environmentally sound practices but also higher wages and better labor conditions. In addition, Whole Foods introduced a Responsibly Grown rating system to assist customers in making well-informed buying choices with regard to worker welfare and other qualities of its flowers and produce. It also made a donation of 1% of the proceeds from the sale of Whole Trade certified products to the Whole Planet Foundation.

Whole Foods correctly pointed out that while the average CEO of a large company in the United States made more than 330 times what the average worker made, no one at Whole Foods, including the CEO, was allowed to earn a salary more than 19 times that of the average employee. However, what Whole Foods did not reveal was that the salary of top management was amply supplemented by bonuses and stock options that typically amounted to extra millions of dollars per year for most of its top executives while Whole Foods' lowest earners averaged barely above the minimum wage level of $13.15 an hour. This fact led some critics to characterize its business model as one of high prices and low wages.[61] Unlike Walmart, Whole Foods did provide most of its employees with health care and additional benefits, but the health insurance plan had high deductibles for general medical expenses and prescriptions. Only after an employee met the deductibles did the insurance cover 80% of the medical costs and prescriptions. Moreover, medications for mental illness were not covered. To compensate, employees did receive per-year personal wellness expenditures depending on years of service.

Whole Foods, in addition, had a very unique system for managing its employees. Called the soul of the company, employees were organized into thousands of self-managed and interlocking teams.[62] Every person, from entry-level positions all the way up to management, was hired on a temporary basis for 30 to 90 days until other team members voted them in as permanent employees. To achieve full-time status as a Whole Foods employee, the candidate had to receive a two-thirds positive vote from the other team members. Team members were encouraged to participate in the management of the stores. For instance, they helped decide what products to stock. They were asked in other ways to share their thoughts and give advice to management. Though team members were subjected to unrelenting financial pressure, the participative system on which the company relied generally yielded high morale. Each team reported its sales, costs, and profits daily, and these were publicly shared and compared with the results of the other teams. Since only the best-performing teams earned a share of the company profits, the competition among the work teams was fierce.

Other aspects of the work environment at Whole Foods were less favorable to its workers. The company had steadfastly opposed unions.[63] Union organizers had tried to unionize its stores in Berkeley in 1990 and in Austin in 1998, but the company opposed their efforts, and they were unsuccessful. The only store that successfully unionized was in Madison, Wisconsin, but the company then dismissed the store manager for allowing the unionization to happen. Though a 2004 ruling by the National Labor Relations Board upheld Whole Foods' actions, labor activists in Wisconsin accused the company of engaging in a campaign of union busting,

When truck drivers at the San Francisco–based distribution center voted to unionize in 2006, Whole Foods fired two of the drivers, altered its sick-leave policies, froze wage increases, and refused to provide information to the union to negotiate a contract. National Labor Relations Board investigators found that the company had harassed and disciplined employees to prevent them from unionizing. They concluded that Whole Foods had been engaged in retaliatory measures to discourage union activity. After an out-of-court settlement, Whole Foods had to reinstate the employees and reverse its policies.

The United Farm Workers (UFW) criticized Whole Foods for its refusal to support a campaign on behalf of strawberry field workers. In the late 1990s, the UFW had convinced several large supermarket chains to support improved wages and working conditions for strawberry pickers. Whole Foods instead held a National 5% Day, where 5% of that day's sales were donated to farmworkers' social services. When the UFW passed out literature at a store in Austin, the company called the police and had the people involved arrested. Embarrassed by the public outcry against its actions, Whole Foods promised to support a UFW grape boycott, but it then broke its promise and passed out literature to customers blasting the farmworkers.

When questioned, Mackey revealed himself to be very ambivalent about unions. He commented that he was not opposed to labor unions that had served important historical purposes.[64] He agreed that employees should have the right to unionize, but he felt that they should not be coerced to join unions or pay union dues against their will. They should have the legal right not to join unions.

In 2013, Whole Foods again ran afoul on labor issues. It suspended two workers in its Albuquerque store for speaking Spanish. It turned out that Whole Foods had a policy of speaking only English to customers and fellow workers, a policy that was against the law.

## The Environment and Energy

Whole Foods also touted how progressive it had been in matters of the environment and energy. It had taken many steps to make its energy sources more environmentally friendly. It purchased renewable energy credits from wind farms to offset 100% of the electricity used in its facilities in the United States and Canada, the largest wind energy credit purchase by a company in these countries.[65] The acquisition of these credits made Whole Foods the only Fortune 500 firm to purchase enough credits to offset *all* the electricity it used. The company estimated that this initiative was equivalent to taking about 60,000 cars off the road or planting 90,000 acres of trees. In 2007, the EPA applauded Whole Foods' actions in stimulating the development of renewable energy. In 2004, 2005, 2006, and 2008, the agency granted Whole Foods the status of Green Power Partner of the Year for its environmental contributions.

Many Whole Foods' stores served as collection points for the recycling of plastic bags. Like other co-ops and health food stores, it promoted the purchase of bulk food and other products in reusable packaging. To its customers, it offered Better Bags, made chiefly from recycled bottles. The company received the first Green Building award in Austin in 1998 for the expansion and renovation of its corporate headquarters. Because of the 42% waste reduction, EPA profiled the building as a trendsetter. In 2008, Whole Foods became the first U.S. supermarket chain to commit to the complete elimination of disposable plastic grocery bags. In 2013, the company started to build the first commercial-scale rooftop greenhouse in the United States above its Brooklyn store.

Yet, unlike many other companies, Whole Foods had not issued an environmental report with concrete goals. Instead, its report had vague statements about respecting the environment and reducing waste whenever possible. As a result of the absence of goals, there were no benchmarks for how well the company had implemented its values. Unlike Whole Foods, Walmart had very quantifiable energy and environmental goals. The three goals were (1) to be supplied 100% by renewable energy, (2) to sell products that sustained people and the environment, and (3) to create zero waste. While Foods did report carbon emissions to the Carbon Disclosure Project, but with a score of 61, it was not close to the leaders, who scored above 95.[66]

The words *global warming* and *climate change* were hardly found on its website, and the company had no explicit climate change policy, which was not accidental given the public statements that Mackey had made about the issue.[67] Mackey asserted that no scientific consensus existed regarding the causes of climate change and it would be a pity to allow hysteria about warming to result in higher taxes and increased regulation, which in turn would lower standards of living. He maintained that, historically, prosperity was correlated with warmer temperatures. Though he argued that global warming was perfectly natural, he claimed he was not a climate change sceptic.

Whole Foods also was criticized for the environmental messages it seemed to be sending with the signage in its stores.[68] Glossy pictures of local farmers standing near their crops were meant to educate shoppers about the advantages of organics. However, small, family farmers who grew their products locally made up a very small percentage of its sales. A banner in its stores provided reasons to buy organic by explaining that local farms relied on natural fertilizers like manure and compost rather than chemical ones and thereby avoided energy waste in the production of fertilizers. However, most of the organic foods that Whole Foods sold came from gigantic operations owned by big food conglomerates located thousands of miles from its stores, which resulted in wasting energy in transporting foods to the stores.

## Animal Rights

An area where Whole Foods stood out was in its activities on behalf of animal rights. For example, it educated customers about the killing of dolphins in the pursuit of tuna, and it worked with canneries to buy from fisheries that used methods that did not result in dolphin deaths. The company belonged to the Marine Stewardship Council, a global nonprofit that promoted sustainable fisheries. It began to sell seafood certified by the Marine Stewardship Council in 2000. In 2006, it chose to stop selling live lobsters and crabs; but in 2007, it made an exception for a Portland, Maine, supplier that met its standards.

Nonetheless, People for the Ethical Treatment of Animals had protested at Whole Foods' stores. They opposed the company's practice of purchasing duck liver from force-fed ducks, the tip of whose bills had been removed. Some of the activists criticized the company for selling any meat. In response, Whole Foods agreed to overhaul its procurement of meat. It ended the practice of selling traditionally raised veal, worked with ranchers on behalf of more humane methods, and educated them about the cruelty of animal testing of body care products.

In 2011, Whole Foods adopted a 5-Step Animal Welfare rating system the Global Animal Partnership promoted. This system provided transparency about the conditions of farm animals used in its products. Independent, third-party observers audited and certified farms' animal welfare practices. According to the quality and compassion standards the company implemented, it did not allow the pulling of feathers from live ducks, bill trimming, bill heat treatment, toe punching, slitting of feet webs, and toe removal. It prohibited ducks being treated with antibiotics or antimicrobials, cloned, or genetically modified, or not being allowed medical treatment.

Whole Foods also created the Animal Compassion Foundation. In 2014, it started a pilot program to sell rabbit meat in some of its stores. Because rabbits were the third most common mammal pet in the United States, the House Rabbit Society boycotted the firm. Protestors started a petition drive against the sale of rabbit meat and held national protests against the company's stores, despite the many policies for animal protection it had adopted.

Now that Amazon is Whole Foods' owner, what is it going to do about the grocer's approach to CSR? Is it an essential selling point that should continue to be emphasized, or a distraction that is incompatible with Amazon's strategy and culture? Should Amazon align the Whole Foods purchase with its strategy and values, or should it change its strategy and values to align them more with those of Whole Foods? Apply the weight-of-reasons framework to address these questions. As it considers its options and assesses their expected consequences, what principles should guide Amazon? Which stakeholders are most important to the company? Should conscious capitalism remain the vital foundation of Whole Foods?

## FURTHER READINGS

Arumgam, N. (2012). "We never said they're healthy": General Mills files to dismiss Fruit Snacks Lawsuit. *Forbes*. Retrieved from http://www.forbes.com/sites/nadiaarumugam/2012/03/29/we-never-said-theyre-healthy-general-mills-files-to-dismiss-fruit-snacks-lawsuit/

ASA Advertising Standards Authority. (2012). *ASA adjudication on Kellogg marketing and sales company*. Retrieved from http://www.asa.org.uk/Rulings/Adjudications/2012/3/Kellogg-Marketing-and-Sales-Company-(UK)-Ltd/SHP_ADJ_172001.aspx#.VEUqw_ldV8E

Breakfast cereal compared: Cereals from Post, Kellogg's & General Mills. (2013). *ACalorieCounter*. Retrieved from http://www.acaloriecounter.com/breakfast-cereal.php

Byrne, J. (2010). Nutri-grain legal challenge has no merit, says Kellogg. *Food Navigator-USA*. Retrieved from http://www.nutraingredients-usa.com/Regulation/Nutri-Grain-legal-challenge-has-no-merit-says-Kellogg

Carter, B. (2014). *Whole grains* (IBISWorld Industry Report 31123, Cereal Production in the US).

Cohen, D. A. (2007, February 21). *A desired epidemic: Obesity and the food industry*. Retrieved from https://www.rand.org/blog/2007/02/a-desired-epidemic-obesity-and-the-food-industry.html

Do you know what's in your protein bar? (2011). *The Oz Show*. Retrieved from http://www.doctoroz.com/blog/lisa-lynn/do-you-know-whats-your-protein-bar

Friedman, U. (2014). Two-thirds of obese people now live in developing countries. *The Atlantic*. Retrieved from http://www.theatlantic.com/international/archive/2014/05/two-thirds-of-the-worlds-obese-people-now-live-in-developing-countries/371834/

Gardner, G., & Halweil, B. (2000). *Underfed and overfed: The global epidemic of malnutrition* Washington, DC: Worldwatch Institute. Retrieved from http://www.worldwatch.org/nearly-two-billion-people-worldwide-now-overweight

Harris, J., Schwartz, M., Brownell, K., Sarda, V., & Dernbek. (2012). *Cereal facts 2012: Limited progress in the nutrition quality and marketing of children's cereals*. Retrieved from https://www.semanticscholar.org/paper/Cereal-FACTS-2012%3A-Limited-progress-in-the-quality-Harris-Schwartz/a0292657937ec8b4bad564dbf342eb5b1005095d

The Healthy Weight Commitment Foundation website: http://www.healthyweightcommit.org/

Horovitz, B. (2014). Cheerios drops genetically modified ingredients. *USA Today*. Retrieved from http://www.usatoday.com/story/money/business/2014/01/02/cheerios-gmos-cereals/4295739/

Hughlett, M. (2012). General Mills sued over whether Yoplait Greek Yogurt is yogurt. *StarTribune*. Retrieved from http://www.startribune.com/business/162301436.html

Kennedy, B. (2013). Kellogg pays for iffy mini-wheats claims. *msn money*. Retrieved from http://www.msn.com/en-us/money

Kitchen Stewardship. (2011). Cereal: One of the healthiest breakfast choices. Retrieved from http://www.kitchenstewardship.com/2011/10/03/cereal-one-of-the-healthiest-breakfast-choices/

Moss, M. (2014). *Salt, sugar, fat*. New York, NY: Random House.

Myers, W. (2013). 9 Smart protein-bar picks. *everyday Health*. Retrieved from http://www.everydayhealth.com/diet-and-nutrition-pictures/smart-protein-bar-picks.aspx

Nassauer, S. (2013). When the box says "Protein," shoppers say "I'll take it." *The Wall Street Journal*. Retrieved from http://online.wsj.com/news/articles/SB10001424127887324789504578384351639102798

Sha, A. (2010). Obesity. *Global Issues*. Retrieved from http://www.globalissues.org/article/558/obesity

Strom, S. (2014). Kellogg agrees to alter labeling on Kashi Line. *The New York Times*. Retrieved from http://www.nytimes.com/2014/05/09/business/kellogg-agrees-to-change-labeling-on-kashi-line.html?_r=0

Thomas, R., Pehrsson, P., Ahuja, J., Smieja, E., & Miller, K. (2013). Recent trends in ready-to-eat breakfast cereals in the U.S. *Procedia Food Science*. Retrieved from http://www.ars.usda.gov/SP2UserFiles/Place/80400525/Articles/Procedia FS2_20-26.pdf

Watson, E. (2014). The Bear Naked settlement against Kellogg's involved a $5 million payment. *Food Navigator-USA*. Retrieved from http://www.foodnavigator-usa.com/Regulation/Kashi-agrees-5m-all-natural-lawsuit-settlement-Bear-Naked-to-pay-325-000-to-settle-related-suit

Yale University Rudd Center for Food Policy & Obesity. (2014). Tracking how industry responds. Retrieved from http://www.yaleruddcenter.org/what_we_do.aspx?id=103

Zhu, C., Huang, R., & Cohen, M. (2012). Product reformulation and advertising abeyance: Using voluntary marketing initiatives to reduce childhood obesity. New York: New York University Stern School of Business. Retrieved from https://editorial express.com/cgi-bin/conference/download.cgi?db_name=IIOC2012&paper_id=496

# NOTES

1.  This case is partly based on material found in Marcus, A. A. (2015). *Innovations in sustainability: Fuel and food*. Cambridge, UK: Cambridge University Press.

2.  Material in this case has been adapted from Marcus, A. (2016). *The future of technology management and the business environment*. Old Tappan, NJ: Pearson. Retrieved from http://ptgmedia.pearson cmg.com/images/9780133996135/samplepages/9780133996135.pdf (pp. 59–61) and Marcus, A. A. (2019). *Strategies for managing uncertainty: Booms and busts in the energy industry*. Cambridge, UK: Cambridge University Press (pp. 162–167, 181–183).

3.  Material in this case has been adapted from Marcus (2016, pp. 55–59).

4.  Much of the material in this case comes from the transcripts from the *Frontline* documentaries on Facebook: https://www.pbs.org/wgbh/frontline/film/facebook-dilemma/transcript/. See also on the same topics Frenkel, S., Confessore, N., Kang, C., Rosenberg, M., & Nicas, J. (2018,

November 14). Delay, deny and deflect: How Facebook's leaders fought through crisis. *New York Times*. Retrieved from https://www.nytimes.com/2018/11/14/technology/facebook-data-russia-election-racism.html

5.  This case is an adaptation of material found in Marcus (2019, pp. 251–253, 264–265, 281–282, 360–363).

6.  Masterson, P. (2019, January 7). *The 10 biggest recalls in 2018*. Retrieved from https://www.cars.com/articles/the-10-biggest-recalls-in-2018-1420756943863/

7.  This case is an adaptation of one that originally appeared in Marcus (2015, pp. 203–204, 212–213, 215–216, 220–222, 226, 237–240).

8.  The authors of the report write, "Hunger afflicts at least 1.1 billion people, while another 1.1 billion consume more than they need, becoming overweight with harmful consequences. Meanwhile, virtually all of the hungry, many of the overweight, and others of normal weight are debilitated by a deficiency of essential vitamins and minerals" (p. 7). Gardner, G. T.,

& Halweil, B. (2000, March). *Underfed and overfed: The global epidemic of malnutrition* (Worldwatch Paper 150). Retrieved from http://www.worldwatch.org/node/840

9.  According to this report, overweight and obesity are defined using body mass index (BMI), a scale calibrated to reflect the health effects of weight gain. A healthy BMI ranges from 19 to 24; a BMI of 25 or above indicates overweight and brings increased risk of illnesses such as cardiovascular disease, diabetes, and cancer. A BMI above 30 signals obesity and even greater health risks.

10. Institute for Responsible Technology. (n.d.). *Health risks*. Retrieved from https://responsibletechnology.org/gmo-education/health-risks/

11. Google. (2004, April 29). Letter from the founders. *New York Times*. Retrieved from https://www.nytimes.com/2004/04/29/business/letter-from-the-founders.html

12. Valet, V. (2018, October 11). The world's most reputable companies for corporate responsibility for 2018. *Forbes*. Retrieved from https://www.forbes.com/sites/vickyvalet/2018/10/11/the-worlds-most-reputable-companies-for-corporate-responsibility-2018/#4cbd522c3371

13. Stoller, K. (2018, October 10). The world's best employers 2018: Alphabet leads as U.S. companies dominate list. *Forbes*. Retrieved from https://www.forbes.com/sites/kristinstoller/2018/10/10/the-worlds-best-employers-2018-alphabet-leads-as-u-s-companies-dominate-list/#5c8a2723382e; Valet, V. (Ed.). (2019, April 17). America's best large employers. *Forbes*. Retrieved from https://www.forbes.com/best-large-employers/#12adbf9efb3e. For other *Forbes* lists, see https://www.forbes.com/companies/google/?list=best-employers/#3dee3015d289

14. Warner, J., Ellmann, N., & Boesch, D. (2018, November 20). *The women's leadership gap: Women's leadership by the numbers*. Washington, DC: Center for American Progress. Retrieved from https://www.americanprogress.org/issues/women/reports/2018/11/20/461273/womens-leadership-gap-2/

15. Google. (n.d.-b). *Our $1 billion commitment to create more opportunity for everyone*. Retrieved from https://www.google.org/billion-commitment-to-create-more-opportunity/

16. Google. (2018a). *Environmental report 2018*. Retrieved from https://sustainability.google/reports/environmental-report-2018/; Google. (2010, July 20). *Reducing our carbon footprint with the direct purchase of renewable energy*. Retrieved from https://googleblog.blogspot.com/2010/07/reducing-our-carbon-footprint-with.html; NextEra Energy. (2010, July 20). *NextEra Energy Resources signs PPA with Google Energy to supply wind power*. Retrieved from https://www.nexteraenergyresources.com/news/contents/2010/072010.shtml; NextEra Energy. (n.d.). *NextEra Energy Resources signs PPA with Google Energy to supply wind power*. Retrieved from http://newsroom.nexteraenergy.com/news-releases?item=123429; Trabish. H. K. (2011, December 2). *Clean Power Finance channels 1 million into solar every day*. Boston, MA: Green Tech Media. Retrieved from. https://www.greentechmedia.com/articles/read/Clean-Power-Finance-Channels-1-Million-Into-Solar-Every-Day#gs.g2b9j6; BBC News. (2013, May 23). *Google acquires kite power generator*. Retrieved from https://www.bbc.com/news/technology-22636565; Hargreaves, S. (2011, June 14). *Google invests $280 million in SolarCity*. Retrieved from https://money.cnn.com/2011/06/14/technology/google_solarcity/index.htm

17. Google. (n.d.-a). *Environment projects: Once is never enough*. Retrieved from https://sustainability.google/projects/circular-economy/

18. Google. (2018b). *Transparency unleashed: How global fishing watch is transforming fishery management*. Retrieved from https://sustainability.google/projects/fishing-watch-impact/. See the GFW tool in Sullivan, B. (2016, September 15). *Mapping global fishing activity with machine learning*. Retrieved from https://blog.google/products/maps/mapping-global-fishing-activity-machine-learning/

19. Strand, G. G. (2008, March). Keyword: evil. Google's addiction to cheap electricity. *Harper's Magazine*. Retrieved from https://harpers.org/archive/2008/03/keyword/

20. Statista. (n.d.). *Worldwide desktop market share of leading search engines from January 2010 to April 2019*. Retrieved from https://www.statista.com/statistics/216573/worldwide-market-share-of-search-engines/

21. Finley, K. (2017, June 27). *Google's big EU fine isn't just about the money.* Retrieved from https://www.wired.com/story/google-big-eu-fine/

22. Google. (n.d.-c). *Ten things we know to be true.* Retrieved from https://www.google.com/about/philosophy.html

23. Mayer, D. (2016, February 9). Why Google was smart to drop its "Don't be evil" motto. *Fast Company.* Retrieved from https://www.fastcompany.com/3056389/why-google-was-smart-to-drop-its-dont-be-evil-motto

24. Jones, D. A., Willness, C. R., & Madey, S. (2014). Why are job seekers attracted by corporate social performance? Experimental and field tests of three signal-based mechanisms. *Academy of Management Journal, 57,* 383–404. Retrieved from https://journals.aom.org/doi/abs/10.5465/amj.2011.0848

25. Conger, K. (2018, June 1). *Google plans not to renew its contract for Project Maven, a controversial Pentagon drone AI imaging program.* Retrieved from https://gizmodo.com/google-plans-not-to-renew-its-contract-for-project-mave-1826488620

26. Wakabayashi, D., & Benner, K. (2018, October 25). How Google protected Andy Rubin. *New York Times.* Retrieved from https://www.nytimes.com/2018/10/25/technology/google-sexual-harassment-andy-rubin.html

27. U.S. Centers for Disease Control and Prevention. (n.d.). *Opioid overdose.* Retrieved from https://www.cdc.gov/drugoverdose/epidemic/index.html

28. Rashbaum, W. K., Rabin, R. C., & Hakim, D. (2019, April 11). Opioid sales reps swarmed New York at height of crisis. *New York Times.* Retrieved from https://www.nytimes.com/2019/04/11/health/opioids-sacklers-new-york-purdue.html

29. Fitzgerald, G. (1984). Dose-related kinetics of aspirin: Presystemic acetylation of platelet cyclooxygenase. *New England Journal of Medicine, 311,* 1206–1211. doi:10.1056/NEJM198411083111902

30. Mukherjee, D., Nissen, S. E., & Topol, E. J. (2001). Risk of cardiovascular events associated with selective COX-2 inhibitors. *JAMA Journal of the American Medical Association, 286*(8), 954–959.

31. Horton, R. (2004). Vioxx, the implosion of Merck, and aftershocks at the FDA. *The Lancet, 364*(9450), 1995–1996.

32. https://www.microsoft.com/en-us/legal/compliance/sbc/download

33. The material in this case has been adapted from Marcus (2019, pp. 324–339).

34. Smith, G., & Parloff, R. (2016, March 7). Hoaxwagen: How the massive diesel fraud incinerated VW's reputation—and will hobble the company for years. *Fortune.* Retrieved from https://fortune.com/longform/inside-volkswagen-emissions-scandal/

35. Walmart. (2014b, April 10). *Walmart and Wild Oats launch effort to drive down organic food prices.* Retrieved from https://corporate.walmart.com/newsroom/2014/04/10/walmart-and-wild-oats-launch-effort-to-drive-down-organic-food-prices

36. Kroll, A. (2012). Are Walmart's Chinese factories as bad as Apple's? *Mother Jones.* http://www.motherjones.com/environment/2012/03/walmart-china-sustainability-shadow-factories-greenwash

37. Walmart. (2014a). *Sustainability Index.* Retrieved from https://corporate.walmart.com/global-responsibility/environment-sustainability/sustainability-index

38. See the Sustainability Consortium website: http://www.sustainabilityconsortium.org/

39. Rabouin, D. (2018, May 5). *Here's why Warren Buffett is sticking with Wells Fargo.* New York, NY: Yahoo! Finance. Retrieved from https://finance.yahoo.com/news/heres-warren-buffett-sticking-wells-fargo-155814417.html

40. Roosevelt, P. (2019, August 30). King of the cross-sell. *Wall Street Journal.* Retrieved from https://www.wsj.com/articles/SB939439126362436146

41. Reckard, E. S. (2013, December 21). Wells Fargo pressure-cooker sales culture comes at a cost. *Los Angeles Times.* Retrieved from https://www.latimes.com/business/la-fi-wells-fargo-sale-pressure-20131222-story.html

42. Wattles, J., Geier, B., Egan, M., & Wiener-Bronner, D. (2018, April 24). *Wells Fargo's 20-month nightmare.* Retrieved from https://money.cnn.com/2018/04/24/news/companies/wells-fargo-timeline-shareholders/index.html

43. Pendergrass, P. (2016, October 14). How Wells Fargo's John Stumpf crashed himself. *Fortune.* Retrieved from http://fortune.com/2016/10/14/wells-fargo-john-stumpf-scandal/

44. Morgenson, G. (2017, August 31). Wells Fargo's testimony left some feeling shortchanged.

*New York Times.* Retrieved from https://www.nytimes .com/2017/08/31/business/wells-fargo-testimony.html

45.   Corkery, M. (2016, September 8). Wells Fargo fined $185 million for fraudulently opening accounts. *New York Times.* Retrieved from https://www.nytimes .com/2016/09/09/business/dealbook/wells-fargo -fined-for-years-of-harm-to-customers.html

46.   Merle, R. (2019, March 28). After years of apologies for customer abuses, Wells Fargo CEO Tim Sloan suddenly steps down. *Washington Post.* Retrieved from https://www.washingtonpost.com/ business/2019/03/28/wells-fargo-ceo-tim-sloan-step -down-immediately/?utm_term=.f09d69a4915b

47.   U.S. Department of Justice. (2018, August 1). *Wells Fargo agrees to pay $2.09 billion penalty for allegedly misrepresenting quality of loans used in residential mortgage-backed securities.* Retrieved from https://www.justice.gov/opa/pr/wells-fargo-agrees -pay-209-billion-penalty-allegedly-misrepresenting -quality-loans-used

48.   Merle, R. (2018, December 28). Wells Fargo reaches $575 million settlement for consumer abuses. *Washington Post.* Retrieved from https://www .washingtonpost.com/business/2018/12/28/wells -fargo-reaches-million-settlement-consumer -abuses/?utm_term=.248b7c252320

49.   This case has been adapted from material found in Marcus (2015, pp. 259–296).

50.   Mackey, J., & Sisodia, R. (2013). *Conscious capitalism.* Boston, MA: Harvard Business School. Retrieved from https://hbr.org/2013/01/cultivating-a-higher-conscious

51.   Ibid.

52.   Schiller, B. (2017, June 21). Now that Whole Foods belongs to Amazon, what happens to conscious capitalism? *Fast Company.* Retrieved from https:// www.fastcompany.com/40432785/now-that-whole -foods-belongs-to-amazon-what-happens-to -conscious-capitalism

53.   Ibid.

54.   Antenucci, A. (2014, August 29). Whole Foods sued for "understating" amount of sugar in yogurt. *New York Post.* Retrieved from http://nypost.com/ 2014/08/29/whole-foods-sued-for-understating -amount-of-sugar-in-yogurt/

55.   Paumgarten, N. (2010, January 4). Food Fighter: Does Whole Foods' CEO know what's best for you? *New Yorker.* Retrieved from https://www.newyorker .com/magazine/2010/01/04/food-fighter

56.   Dapen-Baron, M., & Nordhielm, C. (2010). *Whole Foods Market: What now.* Ann Arbor, MI: Ross School of Business.

57.   Marquis, C., Besharov, M., & Thomason, B. (2011). *Whole Foods: Balancing social mission and growth.* Boston, MA: Harvard Business School.

58.   See McKitterick, W. (2014). *Supermarkets and grocery stores in the US market size 2005–2025* (IBISWorld Industry Report 44511). Retrieved from https:// www.ibisworld.com/industry-statistics/market-size/ supermarkets-grocery-stores-united-states

59.   Mackey and Sisodia (2013).

60.   See the Whole Foods Website: http://www.wholefoods market.com/mission-values

61.   Bluejay, M. (2013). *Whole Foods Market: What's wrong with Whole Foods?* Retrieved from http:// michaelbluejay.com/misc/wholefoods.html

62.   Marquis et al. (2011).

63.   See Bluejay (2013).

64.   Cummins, R., & Murphy, D. (2013, January 31). Exposed: How Whole Foods and the biggest organic foods distributor are screwing workers. *AlterNet.* Retrieved from http://www.alternet.org/ food/exposed-how-whole-foods-and-biggest-organic -foods-distributor-are-screwing-workers?paging= off&current_page=1#bookmark

65.   Brady, P. (2009, September 15). *Energy credits fund new wind farm* [Blog]. Retrieved from http:// www.wholefoodsmarket.com/blog/whole-story/ energy-credits-fund-new-wind-farm

66.   Carbon Disclosure Project. (2014). Retrieved from https://www.cdp.net/en

67.   Franzen, C. (2013, January 18). *Whole Foods CEO John Mackey: Climate change "not necessarily bad"* [Blog]. Retrieved from http://talkingpoints memo.com/livewire/whole-foods-ceo-john-mackey -climate-change-not-necessarily-bad

68.   Pollan, M. (2006, June 14). *My letter to Whole Foods.* Retrieved from http://michaelpollan.com/ articles-archive/my-letter-to-whole-foods/

# Glossary

**Advocacy-based decision-making:** Team decision-making that involves conflict, and in which each participant seeks to persuade others that his or her way is the best

**Anthropocene:** The current geological period, in which human activity is the dominant force of change on the Earth's climate and environment

**Assumption of risk:** The defense in tort cases that the plaintiff was aware of and voluntarily assumed the risks associated with a product or service

**At-will employment:** The principle of U.S. labor law that employers may fire employees at their discretion—that is, that employees hold their jobs at the will of their employers

**Base of the pyramid:** An approach to business in which companies seek to earn profits by providing goods and services, and in some cases employment, economic empowerment, economic development, and other services, to the world's poorest people

**Both/and thinking:** The cognition that two seemingly irreconcilable objectives can be reconciled; the framing of a contradiction as a duality rather than a dualism

**Bounded rationality:** Limited cognitive capacity. Due to bounded rationality humans perceive and interpret some of the information available to their senses while filtering out other information

**Bribery:** The making of a corrupt payment to a foreign official for the purpose of obtaining or retaining business for or with, or directing business to, any person

**Business–NGO partnerships:** Collaborations between business and nongovernmental organizations (nonprofit organizations that address social and environmental issues)

**Cartel:** A group of seemingly independent companies that collude to set prices or restrict output for the purpose of increasing profits

**Chief ethics officer:** The employee with primary responsibility for ensuring ethical behavior by and within the organization

**Civil disobedience:** Activities in which individuals intentionally fail to comply with laws they believe are unethical as a form of protest against those laws

**Closing the circle:** Taking ownership of an ethical issue and taking all the steps necessary to effectively address it

**Coalition building:** Bringing individuals and groups together to work toward a common goal

**Code of conduct:** A set of rules, principles, standards, and policies regarding acceptable and unacceptable behavior by organizational members

**Cognitive biases:** Systematic errors that result in suboptimal decisions. Examples of cognitive biases include fundamental attribution error, confirmation bias, escalation of commitment, status quo bias, and stereotyping, among many more

**Cognitive dissonance:** The mental discomfort that one feels when evidence contradicts one's beliefs or expectations

**Cognitive diversity:** The state in which the members of a group have different perspectives and ways of thinking

**Collusion:** Illegal cooperation between companies

**Complexity theory:** The theory that explains the behavior of one element of a complex system and the system itself in terms of that element's interdependencies with other system elements

**Compliance-based ethics program:** An ethics program that sets out rules for behavior and punishes failure to comply with those rules

**Confirmation bias:** The cognitive bias in which one places too much emphasis on information that confirms one's existing beliefs, while ignoring or dismissing disconfirming information

**Conformity:** Compliance with the behaviors others expect one to perform

**Consequentialism:** The theory that the ethics of an action should be based on its consequences

**Constructive conflict:** Conflict in which participants have the intention of making the best decision for the team. Occurs when inquiry and advocacy are combined

**Contract theory (or social contract theory):** An approach to ethics that assesses the morality of an action based on whether it conforms to a set of social rules that preserve the basic rights and freedoms of all

**Contradiction:** A dynamic tension between opposite elements that together form a unity and logically presuppose each other for their very existence and meanings

**Contributory negligence:** The defense to a tort claim that the plaintiff's negligence contributed to his or her injury; an approach in tort law that apportions responsibility between the plaintiff and the defendant when both are found to have been negligent

**Corporate citizenship:** An approach to business in which corporations take a lead role in fulfilling the rights of a society's citizens

**Corporate governance:** The structures and processes used to direct and control a corporation

**Corporate social responsibility (CSR):** An approach to business characterized by exceeding legal compliance in order to make stakeholders and society better off

**Creating shared value:** An approach to business in which companies deploy their core resources and capabilities to create value for shareholders and society simultaneously

**Creative capitalism:** An approach to business in which companies, governments, and nongovernmental organizations work together to use capitalism to address grand challenges

**Cross-sector partnership:** Mechanism for cooperation between private sector, public sector, and nonprofit organizations to address an issue or problem

**Decision:** A specific commitment to action

**Decision process:** A set of actions that begins with the identification of a stimulus for action and ends with the specific commitment to action

**Deontology:** An ethical approach focusing on the means of actions; also known as the rights-based or Kantian approach

**Differentiation:** The strategy of having a distinct status and set of attributes that set the company's products and services apart from those of other firms

**Dilemma:** A particular type of unstructured decision in which one has a clear understanding of the problem but cannot decide between alternative courses of action, because all have undesirable aspects

**Discrimination:** The act of treating a person unfairly based on the social category one puts that person into

**Diversity:** The state of having variety (different elements)

**Double-loop learning:** Learning that occurs through questioning underlying goals and assumptions

**Dualism:** The division of a thing into two separate and opposed elements

**Duality:** The division of a thing into two interdependent and complementary elements

**Dual-process theory:** A theory that proposes that intuition and reasoning are separate and occur in different parts of the brain

**Embezzlement:** Theft of anyone's identity and core beliefs, and how it lives them out systematically through its activities and engagement with stakeholders

**Escalation of commitment:** The cognitive bias in which one continues following a course of action because of a commitment to that course, even though continuing to follow the course will lead to negative outcomes

**Ethical climate:** The atmosphere of an organization regarding how to address ethical issues

**Ethical decision:** A decision that the decision-maker perceives as involving questions of good and bad, right and wrong

**Ethical egoism:** The philosophy that self-interest is the basis of morality

**Ethical intuitions:** Intuitions to take actions that benefit others

**Ethical leadership:** The process of taking ethical actions to influence others to act ethically to achieve organizational goals

**Ethical organization:** An organization into which ethical values have been built into every element

**Ethical principles:** General propositions or guidelines that can be applied differently in different situations

**Ethical values:** The organization's values that explicitly pertain to ethics; the principles that govern behavior in addressing ethical issues

**Ethics assist line (or ethics hotline):** A mechanism that employees can use to seek advice on handling ethical issues and to report unethical behavior in the workplace

**Ethics of care:** An approach to ethical reasoning that emphasizes caring for those with whom we have interpersonal relationships

**Ethics program:** The policies and procedures for promoting and ensuring law-abiding and ethical behavior within an organization

**Ethos:** Persuasion based on the credibility of the speaker

**Exit:** Withdrawing from confronting an ethical dilemma

**Experimentation (or experimental learning):** Learning that occurs through hypothesis testing, in which the experimenter takes actions for which she or he has a hypothesis about the outcomes that will occur

**Extrinsic goods:** Goods that derive their value from what they can lead to—what they are "good for"

**Fast thinking:** Thinking that is automatic, effortless, and intuitive (also known as System 1 thinking)

**Federal Sentencing Guidelines for Organizations (FSGO):** Guidelines to ensure that sentences imposed for corporate crimes are consistent for all organizations, and to establish incentives for organizations to detect and prevent corporate crimes

**Feedback loops:** Behaviors of a system in which one action affects additional actions

**Fiduciary duty:** A duty of trust

**Foreign Corrupt Practices Act (FCPA):** A U.S. law that makes bribery illegal and requires companies to maintain adequate internal accounting systems and accurate records of transactions

**Foreseeability of harm:** The ability to reasonably anticipate or predict the negative consequences of an action (proving foreseeability is a requirement in tort cases)

**Framing:** The process of perceiving particular information from the environment and attaching specific meanings to it

**Fraud:** Illegal deception for the purpose of financial or other personal gain

**Fundamental attribution error:** The cognitive bias in which one attributes another person's behavior or performance to their internal characteristics while ignoring external factors

**Golden mean:** According to Aristotle, the desirable point that finds the middle between excess and deficiency of a virtue

**Grand challenges:** Complex global problems that affect the well-being of many people and can only be addressed through the coordinated efforts of many diverse stakeholders

**Groupthink:** A collective decision-making process characterized by a bias for conformity and consensus rather than creativity and critical thinking

**Heuristics:** Decision-making shortcuts or "rules of thumb," found in both fast and slow thinking

**Incremental decision-making process:** A decision-making process in which a major decision is made over time through a series of smaller decisions

**Industry-transforming innovations:** Innovations that produce products and services that disrupt or destroy existing industries

**Informed consent:** Permission to provide a service based on a customer or patient's acknowledgment that she or he is aware of and accepts the foreseeable consequences of receiving that service

**Inquiry-based decision-making:** Team-based decision-making that is collaborative and involves open exchange of viewpoints and the generation of new ideas

**Integrated theory:** A theory that sees fast and slow thinking as originating from a single system—fast thinking occurs first and is predominant, and slow thinking justifies the decisions of fast thinking

**Interdependence:** The mutual dependence of the parts of a system

**Interpersonal (or relationship-oriented) conflict:** Conflict that is personal, in which those involved view themselves as in conflict with one another

**Intrinsic goods:** Goods that have inherent value—that is, are "good" in and of themselves

**Just cause:** An exception to at-will employment, specifying that an employer must have a good reason for firing an employee

**Learning spiral:** A continuous learning process in which the organization moves toward ever-higher levels of knowledge

**Liability:** In tort cases, the responsibility of a defendant to reimburse the plaintiff for harm caused to him or her

**Logos:** Persuasion based on the use of logic

**Loyalty:** Support, devotion, faithfulness. Influences the decision to exit or use voice

**Managerial capitalism:** A form of capitalism in which directors and managers, rather than shareholders, control the company's decisions and direction

**Mechanistic organizations:** Organizations that operate precisely and efficiently. They are characterized by highly specialized and formalized work, centralized decision-making, and a tall hierarchy

**Mergers and acquisitions:** Types of transactions in which the ownership of businesses is combined

**Mission:** The organization's purpose; what it is and why it exists

**Money laundering:** The concealment of illegally obtained money, typically by transferring it through a seemingly legitimate transaction

**Moral imagination:** The ability to discover and evaluate new and unique ethical responses to ethical dilemmas

**Moral minimums:** Sets of minimum ethical standards that persons should follow in all circumstances; moral minimums are typically posed as injunctions against unethical behavior rather than as obligations to engage in ethical behavior

**Multisector partnerships:** Collaborations that include business, government, and nongovernmental organizations

**Negligence:** The failure to exercise appropriate care

**Obedience to authority:** Conformity with a request or demand from an authority figure

**Ombudsperson:** An employee who has been designated to hear anonymous or confidential claims of ethics violations, investigate these claims, decide how the claim should be handled, and implement appropriate changes

**Organic organizations:** Organizations that are able to adapt to their environments. They are characterized by low degrees of specialization and formalization, decentralized decision-making, and a flat hierarchy

**Organizational culture:** Shared assumptions and values regarding the appropriate ways to think and behave and the artifacts that express them

**Organizational learning:** The ability to recognize repeated patterns to affect change

**Organizational politics:** The activities through which organizational members acquire and use power.

**Organizational structure:** The arrangement of employees, groupings, tasks, and authority within an organization

**Paradox:** A statement made up of contradictory yet interrelated elements that seem logical in isolation but absurd and irrational when appearing simultaneously

**Pathos:** Persuasion based on an appeal to emotions

**Planetary boundaries:** A theoretical framework that identifies the earth systems processes that make human life possible, specifies the threshold levels at which human activity would exceed the capacities of these processes to continue to support human life, and assesses whether human activities are exceeding these thresholds

**Power:** The ability to carry out one's will despite resistance; the ability to get what you want

**Precautionary principle:** The principle that new technologies and practices that have uncertain consequences should not be undertaken

**Primary stakeholders:** Stakeholders with which the company has regular commercial interactions

**Principal–agent problem:** The problem that a director or a manager of a corporation does not fulfill his or her fiduciary duty to work on behalf of the shareholders

**Principal–agent relationship:** The fiduciary relationship between the board of directors and managers that oversee the company to act as agents of shareholders (principals)

**Privity of contract:** The legal doctrine that a contract may impose benefits and harms only on the parties to the contract and not on third parties

**Proximate cause:** In a tort case, an event that is deemed to have caused an injury

**Psychological safety:** The belief that an environment provides a safe place for interpersonal risk-taking

**Public–private partnerships:** Government–business collaborations

**Residual claimant:** The person who has the last claim on a company's net cash flow after the deduction of all other persons' claims

**Right to be heard:** The right of consumers to voice their concerns about products and services and to have those concerns resolved in a fair and timely manner

**Right to be informed:** The right of consumers to complete and truthful information about products and services, including their foreseeable consequences, so that they may make informed choices about whether to use or consume them

**Right to choose:** The right of consumers to choose from among a variety of options; the right to transact in a competitive rather than an anticompetitive marketplace

**Right to privacy:** The right to have one's personal information protected from public view

**Right to safe products and services:** The consumer right to products that present no foreseeable harm to health and life

**Secondary stakeholders:** Stakeholders that interact with the company less frequently than primary stakeholders, and often on a noncommercial basis

**Self-interest:** The motivation to take actions that benefit oneself

**Sensebreaking:** The disruption of sensemaking by an unusual event or contradictory evidence

**Sensemaking:** The process of identifying, interpreting, and acting on information from the external environment

**Servant leadership:** The leadership philosophy that emphasizes putting others first and helping them develop and perform at their best

**Shareholder:** A person who owns shares in a company. Typically has the right to elect the board of directors, receive dividends, participate in major decisions, and sue the company and its officers

**Shareholder capitalism:** A form of capitalism in which shareholders, rather than directors and managers, control the company's decisions and direction

**Shareholder theory:** The theory that the sole responsibility of business is to earn maximum returns for shareholders, within the boundaries of society's laws and customs

**Single-loop learning:** Learning that occurs through questioning actions

**Slow thinking:** Thinking that is controlled, deliberate, effortful, and involving reasoning

**Stakeholder:** An individual or organization that influences and is influenced by the company

**Stakeholder engagement:** The ongoing process of interacting and building relationships with stakeholders to resolve problems of mutual concern

**Stakeholder theory:** The theory that the responsibility of business is to create value for stakeholders, including shareholders

**Status quo bias:** The cognitive bias in which one prefers to maintain the current state of affairs even when a change of course should be considered

**Stereotype:** The cognitive bias in which one has a generalized belief about people of a particular social category

**Strict liability:** The legal doctrine that a person or organization can be found legally liable for the consequences of their actions even when they are not at fault

**Sustainable business:** An approach to business in which companies seek to have a positive impact on the economy, society, and the natural environment

**System:** A group of interdependent parts that is organized into a coherent, unified whole and exists for a specific purpose

**System processes:** The patterns of activities that recur over time within the system

**Systems structure:** The rules and arrangements that influence the activities that occur within the system

**Systems thinking:** Thinking to understand the nature of a system

**Task (or task-related) conflict:** Conflict in which there is disagreement about tasks and goals

**Tax evasion:** The illegal nonpayment or underpayment of taxes owed

**Team-based decision-making process:** A process in which members of a team work together to make decisions

**Teleology:** The theory that a thing can be explained in terms of its purpose or goal

**Tort law:** The area of law that imposes legal liability on those who cause harm to others and provides relief to those who are harmed (a tort is an act that causes harm)

**Trial-and-error learning:** Learning that occurs by trying different courses of action and observing the outcomes

**Triple-loop learning:** Learning that occurs through questioning underlying cultural assumptions and values and by being open to other cultural assumptions and values

**Trust:** The willingness to be vulnerable based on the belief that others' behaviors will have positive (or at least not negative) outcomes for you

**Truth to power:** To insist on an ethical and truthful response from those who hold authority

**Unstructured decision:** A decision for which there is no predetermined and explicit set of steps within the organization

**Utilitarianism:** An ethical approach focusing on the ends or consequences of actions; also known as teleology or consequentialism

**Utility:** Usefulness, value, benefit, pleasure

**Values:** The principles by which the organization will conduct itself as it seeks to achieve its vision

**Values statement:** A formal statement of the core beliefs, principles, and priorities that are shared within an organization

**Values-based ethics program:** An ethics program (also known as integrity-based program) that emphasizes living up to shared ethical values in addition to compliance with laws

**Virtue theory:** An approach to ethical reasoning focusing on qualities of ethical excellence, such as integrity and honesty

**Vision:** The organization's objective; the state it hopes to attain

**Voice:** Communicating one's grievance within the organization to address and change the situation

**Whistle-blower:** An organizational member who informs someone outside the organization of an organization's ethical behavior

**Whistle-blowing:** Calling attention to unethical behavior by informing someone outside the organization

# Index